From Green Industries to Green Jobs

From Green Industries
to Green Jobs

GALE
CENGAGE Learning®

Detroit • New York • San Francisco • New Haven, Conn • Waterville, Maine • London

GALE
CENGAGE Learning·

From Green Industries to Green Jobs

Project Editors: Miranda H. Ferrara,
Michele P. LaMeau

Production Technology Support: Luann Brennan,
Mike Weaver

Production Service: Kate Mannix, Graphic
World Inc.

Composition: Graphic World Inc.

Manufacturing: Rita Wimberley

Product Manager: Michele P. LaMeau

Publisher: David Forman

For product information and technology assistance, contact us at
Gale Customer Support, 1-800-877-4253.
For permission to use material from this text or product,
submit all requests online at **www.cengage.com/permissions.**
Further permissions questions can be emailed to
permissionrequest@cengage.com

Cover Images: Ecology Globe ©Ian O'Hanlon/Shutterstock.com, 2012;
Environmental Conservation ©Kabby/Shutterstock.com, 2012; Photo of Wind Power
Installation ©BESTWEB/Shutterstock.com, 2012; Two Electricians Installing Solar
Panels ©Lisa F. Young/Shutterstock.com, 2012; Approach Road Sign of Electric Car
Battery Recharge Station ©yaskii/Shutterstock.com, 2012.

While every effort has been made to ensure the reliability of the information
presented in this publication, Gale, Cengage Learning, does not guarantee the
accuracy of the data contained herein. Gale accepts no payment for listing; and
inclusion in the publication of any organization, agency, institution, publication,
service, or individual does not imply endorsement of the editors or publisher. Errors
brought to the attention of the publisher and verified to the satisfaction of the
publisher will be corrected in future editions.

EDITORIAL DATA PRIVACY POLICY: Does this product contain information about you
as an individual? If so, for more information about our editorial data privacy policies,
please see our Privacy Statement at www.gale.cengage.com.

Library of Congress Cataloging-in-Publication Data

From green industries to green jobs.
    p. cm.
  Includes bibliographical references and index.
  ISBN 978-1-4144-9623-8 (hardcover)
1. Environmentalists--Vocational guidance. 2. Environmental protection--Vocational
guidance. 3. Environmental engineers--Vocational guidance.

GE60.F76 2012
333.7023--dc23   2012005309

Gale
27500 Drake Rd.
Farmington Hills, MI 48331-3535

ISBN-13: 978-1-4144-9623-8   ISBN-10: 1-4144-9623-0

This title is also available as an e-book.
ISBN-13: 978-1-4144-9624-5; ISBN-10: 1-4144-9624-9
Contact your Gale, Cengage Learning, sales representative for ordering
information.

Printed in Mexico
1 2 3 4 5 6 7 16 15 14 13 12

Contents

Contents

Preface

From Green Industries to Green Jobs expands the career guidance provided by the U.S. Department of Labor's *Occupational Outlook Handbook (OOH)* by profiling 100 job titles that fall under the 12 unique Green Sectors identified by the National Center for O*NET Development. As such, this work focuses almost exclusively on the rise of jobs and occupations within the United States.

Many of tomorrow's fastest growing jobs in the United States are in so-called green industries and require new skills. What are these occupations? Which provide the greatest opportunity for the future? And how do you get trained for them? We hope that *From Green Industries to Green Jobs* helps answer these questions and more, while also providing sources for additional research and information. Each entry includes a complete occupational profile, including overviews of the green job, what jobs it is most similar to, what key skills are required to do the job, and what a day in the life of that job is like.

ARRANGEMENT

The 100 job profiles contained in *From Green Industries to Green Jobs* are organized alphabetically by Green Sector then numerically by standard occupational classification (SOC) codes.

The Green Sectors covered in this title include:

- Agriculture and Forestry
- Energy and Carbon Capture and Storage
- Energy Efficiency
- Energy Trading
- Environment Protection
- Governmental and Regulatory Administration
- Green Construction
- Manufacturing
- Recycling and Waste Reduction
- Renewable Energy Generation
- Research, Design, and Consulting Services
- Transportation

ENTRY FORMAT

Occupational essays are organized into eight primary sections describing different aspects of each job. Brief descriptions of each of these sections are provided in the following.

Nature of the Work. Each profile begins with an explanation of professional duties and responsibilities of the job. This section answers such questions as, "What do these professionals do all day? What equipment do they use on the job?" It also lists specializations available within the field and the effects technological advances may have on job performance.

Working Conditions. Although many occupations have regular working hours and pleasant surroundings, working conditions can vary. This section describes work hours, stress levels, the physical work environment, and safety conditions specific to a particular job title. It also informs users if a particular job requires irregular hours or frequent overtime, has a high rate of on-the-job injuries, or is performed in hazardous or unpleasant surroundings.

Employment. This section provides detailed information about employers for this profession, how many people in the United States and the world are employed, and where jobs are available.

Training, Other Qualifications, and Advancement. Preparation for most professional positions requires specialized vocational training, a college degree, and/or licensure or certification. This section describes what type of specific training is necessary, what courses should be taken, and if a degree (associate's, bachelor's, master's, or doctoral) is necessary. Testing, licensing, and certification data are provided, as well as details about continuing education requirements. This section also describes the advancement process, that is, what tasks are performed at the entry level and what advancement opportunities are available. In addition to formal preparation requirements this section also describes personal abilities and qualities that will help ensure success in the career.

Job Outlook. Many factors such as changing technology, government spending, and shifting demographics affect future employment in a specific field. This section identifies the growth rate for a specific occupation and which factors affect this growth. It also describes the competition for job openings and job security while employed.

Earnings. This section provides average wages and salaries for individuals in this occupation. National figures as well as entry-level wages, average wages, and wages for experienced workers are provided when available.

Related Occupations. This section lists occupations with similar functions or educational requirements for individuals with similar interests.

Sources of Additional Information. Associations, unions, and federal agencies are all excellent sources of career information. This section provides a list of organizations that have general career information or specific information regarding areas such as licensure or certification.

Further Reading. This section provides a list of the most useful sources or websites used to compile the entry.

AT A GLANCE FACT BOX

Each job profile also contains an **At a Glance Fact Box** that provides a concise summary of basic information from each entry, including:

- Standard occupational classification (SOC) reference number when available
- Preferred level of completed education
- Average salary
- Other useful information about the occupation, such as employment trends, training requirements, and industry outlook

SOURCES

Entries have been compiled by combining authoritative data from government sources, professional associations, original research, and publicly accessible sources both in print and on the Internet. These sources include general academic periodicals and books as well as websites and blogs.

FULLY INDEXED

From Green Industries to Green Jobs has been fully indexed to allow researchers to locate information by job title, SOC numbers, industry, and other avenues.

ACKNOWLEDGMENTS

Special thanks for the production of *From Green Industries to Green Jobs* go to Product Manager Michele LaMeau for leading this initiative. This book is the product of some innovative publishing work, as Michele applied techniques gleaned from our agile software development practice to the production of content, the result being high-quality production in record time. Thanks also to Miranda Ferrara, who served as hands-on mentor to Michele, David Forman, Mark Springer, Mike Huellmantel, and Keith Jones, each of whom played pivotal roles in making this book a reality, and to numerous others who shared their talents to create this volume.

SUGGESTIONS WELCOME

Comments on this title and suggestions on how to make subsequent and similar titles better are always welcome. Please write:

The Editor
From Green Industries to Green Jobs
Gale, Cengage Learning
27500 Drake Road
Farmington Hills, MI 48331-3535

Gale, Cengage Learning, does not endorse any of the occupations, organizations, or products mentioned in this title.

SECTOR OVERVIEW: AGRICULTURE AND FORESTRY

The agriculture and forestry industries are commonly grouped together to create this sector, and sometimes fishing-related industries are also included. However, this sector is largely dominated by agricultural businesses, such as farms, nurseries, and greenhouses, explains the U.S. Department of Labor's 2010–11 *Career Guide to Industries* (CGI). Because of this agricultural dominance, the sector's main subcategories are crop production and animal production. In addition, there are a range of careers devoted to supporting and supplementing agricultural work in a variety of ways, from farm managers and supervisors to agricultural inspectors and buyers to technicians and laborers.

This sector affects both the economy and people's daily lives because it produces food and many of the plants used for landscaping and other personal projects. Agricultural products are also one of the biggest commodities on the global market because foods are imported and exported all over the world. Because food production is essential to civilization and survival, agriculture remains one of the biggest employers in the United States and around the world.

However, as technology has become a greater presence in daily life, it has mechanized many aspects of both crop and animal farming, which reduces the number of human laborers required. Although the majority of farms remain relatively small, are often family owned, and are run by self-employed farmers, in some cases land is being purchased to create larger, corporate-owned farm conglomerates or agribusinesses. The CGI reports that less than 10 percent of farms in the United States are large enough to generate more than US$250,000 in sales each year, but this small group of farms produces 75 percent of the country's agricultural output.

Because of this trend, farmers, ranchers, and agricultural workers are listed by the U.S. Department of Labor's Bureau of Labor Statistics (BLS) as among the occupations with the largest projected decline during the decade between 2008 and 2018. However, this figure does not tell the whole story nor does the CGI's projection that employment in agriculture, forestry, and fishing will be largely stagnant in the coming years. In fact, some exciting changes and opportunities to restructure, as well as to apply technology in job-creating ways, are taking root.

AGRICULTURE AND FORESTRY GOES GREEN

Science and technology are transforming farming through everything from bioengineered crops that are resistant to pests or designed to require less water to automated animal vaccination and branding for animals, reports CGI. However, not every advance comes at the expense of jobs. Another factor is the greening of society.

As the consumers who purchase farmers' products grow increasingly interested in where these foods have come from and how they were produced, farms have begun adjusting their methods and practices accordingly. Green and sustainable approaches to farming that protect the long-term health of the environment, eschew chemicals in favor of natural fertilizers and pest control, and place a premium on animals' health and quality of life are increasingly popular, explains the Occupational Information Network's (O*NET) information on the Agriculture and Forestry Green Economy Sector. More than four million acres of crops and animal pasture were being farmed organically in 2005. Furthermore, sales of organic foods have quadrupled since 1997.

Growth in green farming, which is further encouraged by the 2008 Farm Bill that provides funding to farmers who want to convert to organic methods, has led to an increased demand for farming professionals with knowledge of organic farming and other sustainable, environment-protecting methods such as precision agriculture, which uses technology and precise mapping to limit waste and excess in planting, fertilizing, and watering of crops. In addition, support personnel trained to work with green and sustainable products are increasingly needed to support and facilitate this new green farming economy. These range from managers and supervisors to agricultural inspectors and buyers focused on organic foods, as well as precision agricultural technicians, which is an entirely new, emerging field.

The expanding environmentally conscious culture has also shown interest in locally grown produce and food products, which is providing a lifeline to many farmers who wish to retain their operations. Specialty farming, perhaps in conjunction with a local cooperative or to serve local restaurants and markets, is predicted to be where most of the new jobs in farming are generated in the coming years.

Movements such as Farming First have embraced the arrival of the green economy. They find the transition to sustainable development in agriculture to be essential not only for farmers' success but also for the environment's ability to meet the needs for food, animal feed, fuel, and a growing world population. To do this, the agriculture and forestry sector must minimize its impact on the environment and create sustainable methods and practices for farmers and others in the industry.

The array of venture capitalists who attended the Agriculture 2.0 Silicon Valley event in March 2010 also indicates the growing interest in green agriculture, reported Eric Wesoff of Greentech Media. There are opportunities for investors (and therefore growing green industry opportunities) in "water, nitrogen, phosphorous [sic], synthetic fertilizer, local foods, aquaculture, pests, and the move towards organics," Wesoff says.

At the conference, Tom Tomich of the UC Davis Agricultural Sustainability Institute reported that agriculture accounts for 4 percent of California's economy. "The idea of the dumb farmer is truly a myth," Tomich added. "Don't make that mistake …. Agricultural innovation responds to market forces." And those forces seem increasingly green.

THE AGRICULTURE AND FORESTY JOB MARKET

Traditionally farmers and others in the industry have primarily learned their trade through on-the-job experience, and 28 percent of those currently working in the sector do not have a high school diploma, reports the CGI. However, more of those interested in this field are seeking a college education in agricultural science, horticulture, botany, or another farming-related specialty. They may also seek training in business, marketing, and computers because these skills are a growing aspect of successful farming. In addition, knowledge of green farming practices and other new and emerging technologies and techniques can help those seeking to make a career in this sector.

Continuing education opportunities through county cooperative extension agencies, which can help connect universities, government research, and working farmers and ranchers, as well as through certifying organizations such as the American Society of Farm Managers and Rural Appraisers, are also essential for staying abreast of developments in the sector.

In terms of job location, as noted previously, agriculture and the resulting food supply are essential around the world, so employment in agriculture is widely available. In the United States, citrus crops are found in warmer southern and western states, whereas northern states focus on blueberries, apples, and potatoes, notes CGI. Grains, hogs, and cattle are raised throughout the Midwest, and many ranchers are found in the American Southwest and West. Poultry and dairy farms can be found throughout the country.

In addition, plants are grown in greenhouses in every state, and wholesale receipts for horticultural crops grown in greenhouses and nurseries grew 20 percent between 1998 and 2004, as reported in "Careers in the Green Industry," a 2005 article by Kevin McCarron. The National Gardening Association says spending on landscape installation and construction tripled between 1997 and 2002, from US$3.6 billion to US$11.2 billion. "All that growth means lots of jobs and variety for the people who decide what to grow and for the people who tend those plants," writes McCarron.

SOURCES OF ADDITIONAL INFORMATION

American Farmland Trust. http://www.farmland.org
American Society of Farm Managers and Rural Appraisers. http://www.asfmra.org
The International Farm Transition Network. http://www .farmtransition.org
The National Agricultural Library (AFSIC). http://www .nal.usda.gov
National Sustainable Agriculture Information Service (ATTRA). http://attra.ncat.org
U.S. Department of Agriculture, Cooperative State, Research, Education, and Extension Service. http:// www.csrees.usda.gov

FURTHER READING

Agriculture Business Week. *Archive for Going Green.* Accessed February 9, 2012. http://www .agribusinessweek.com/category/going-green/.

Bureau of Labor Statistics, U.S. Department of Labor. "Agriculture, Forestry, and Fishing." In *Career Guide to Industries, 2010–11 Edition.* Accessed December 15, 2011. http://www.bls.gov/oco/ cg/cgs001.htm.

Farming First. *Farming First's Guide to Green Economy Initiatives on Agriculture.* Accessed January 24, 2012. http://www.farmingfirst.org/green-economy.

McCarron, Kevin M. "Careers in the Green Industry: Jobs for People with Green Thumbs." In *Occupational Outlook Quarterly*, Spring 2005. Accessed December 15, 2011. http://www.bls.gov/ opub/ooq/2005/spring/art03.htm.

O*NET OnLine. *Agriculture and Forestry Green Economy Sector.* Accessed December 15, 2011. http://www .onetonline.org/find/green?n=1&g=Go.

Wesoff, Eric. "Green Agriculture—The Next Hot Investment Sector?" *Greentech Media*, March 25, 2010. Accessed February 9, 2012. http://www .greentechmedia.com/articles/read/Green-Agriculture-The-Next-Hot-Investment-Sector/.

FARMERS AND RANCHERS

NATURE OF THE WORK

Simply put, the farmer or rancher manages the operation of the farm, but a modern farm is complex. In addition to agricultural knowledge, farmers must have good business sense and be proficient in basic computer skills. A very large farm might have several specialized farmers focused on marketing, managing the crops or animals, or managing equipment, explains the U.S. Department of Labor's Bureau of Labor Statistics's (BLS) 2010–11 *Occupational Outlook Handbook* (*OOH*). In most cases, however, a farmer's work is diverse and requires everything from physical strength to agricultural knowledge to business acumen. Many farmers split their efforts between managing the business and contributing as hands-on workers.

Many farms are family owned and a 1997 University of Minnesota Extension study found that more than half of farming families value this lifestyle. Farm families "live, work, and play together," the study reports. The farmer and a few family members may run the farm alone or with a couple of hired workers, whereas other farms employ a staff of seasonal and full-time workers, notes the *OOH*.

More farmers are shifting toward a green, sustainable farming approach, which means they can produce food for the foreseeable future without damaging the ecosystem in the process, explained Andy Clark of the U.S. Department of Agriculture in a 2008 *USA Today* article by Judy Keen. This may mean implementing organic farming practices, which use natural, ecology-based processes and biodiverse growing selections based on what is best suited to local conditions to help crops and animals flourish rather than relying on chemical or other unnatural fertilizers and pest repellants that can do long-term damage to the environment, according to the International

AT A GLANCE FACT BOX

SOC: 11-9012.00
Preferred Education: Long-term on-the-job training, some postsecondary education
Average Salary: Varies
Other Information: Although employment in farming and ranching is predicted to decline slightly in the decade between 2008 and 2018, there are opportunities in the industry for those interested in smaller, specialty farming, including sustainable and organic methods

Federation of Organic Agriculture Movements (IFOAM) website.

Rather than spraying pesticides and fertilizers or irrigating their fields (unless it is with recycled water), green-focused farmers work to boost the level of organic matter in their soil and the health of their plants using compost and other naturally derived enrichments. They may also periodically grow crops, such as peas and beans that put nutrients back in the soil. Weeds, according to the IFOAM website, are controlled by mulching, hand-weeding, or crop rotation.

Even farmers who do not seek organic certification are choosing more sustainable, environmentally friendly methods for their farms. For example, the Kreidermacher farm in Minnesota has been in business since 1967 and uses biomass boilers to heat greenhouses, which reduces their use of petroleum. Ash produced by the boilers makes useful fertilizer and adding coconut fiber and rice hulls to the soil helps to retain water more effectively, Eric Kreidermacher, a member of the second generation to farm the land, explained in Keen's article.

On any crop-based farm, farmers must determine the right time for planting, fertilizing, and harvesting, as well as storing harvested goods until the best time to take them to market. Technology is increasingly present, as evidenced by the use of GPS systems on tractors and bioengineered seeds that may enhance efficiency and overall yield. For the green farmer this also means cutting the use of pesticides and irrigation, reports the U.S. Department of Labor's 2010–11 *Career Guide to Industries* (*CGI*).

The *OOH* notes that ranchers manage livestock, dairy, poultry, or other sorts of animal farms, so their focus is feeding and caring for their animals and maintaining a healthy living environment for them. On a dairy farm, cows must be milked at least twice a day. Ranchers may also oversee the breeding of their animals and be present, with or without veterinary assistance, when they give birth. Most ranchers also grow and harvest hay and other crops for their animals to eat, which they can do using natural, sustainable methods. Dave Petty, an Iowa farmer raising corn, soybeans, and cattle, has stopped tilling his fields at the end of the season because the remaining plant debris adds nutrients and moisture to the soil, he told *USA Today* in Keen's article.

Another big part of a rancher's work can be moving animals from different pastures to graze. Green-focused farmers will be especially careful to keep cattle from overgrazing any single particular part of their land. *CGI* reports that technology is also transforming ranchers' work as mechanized branding and vaccinating as well as GPS for locating herds saves valuable time.

The Occupational Information Network (O*Net) Summary Report on Farm and Ranch Managers notes that equipment used can include four-wheel-drive trucks; irrigation equipment; haymaking equipment and mowers; ladders, power saws, and other tools; animal feeders and insemination kits; milking equipment; and computer software for accounting, database management, scientific analysis and industrial control, e-mail, GPS, map creation, and payroll.

WORKING CONDITIONS

The work schedule on a farm is largely determined by Mother Nature. When crops are being planted and harvested, the workday begins when the sun comes up and often continues through sunset. At other times of the year, farmers may spend more time indoors as they manage their businesses via computer, plan for the next season, and market and sell their products. However, even in the slower seasons, farmers are outdoors making repairs to buildings and machinery.

Although some farming families in the University of Minnesota Extension study mentioned enjoying a spontaneous afternoon away from the farm on occasion, extended vacations are rarely possible.

On larger farms, managing farmers may spend a lot of time in meetings with various staff members, but in smaller operations, the farmer or rancher's work can be very physical, including lifting and carrying heavy loads. Work tends to be steady throughout the year on livestock farms or ranches, notes the *OOH*, as animals must be fed and cared for in all seasons.

Working on a farm or ranch can be dangerous, as the machinery could cause serious injury and any chemicals must be handled appropriately to protect workers, crops and animals, and the environment. Farmers and ranchers must remain alert on the job at all times. O*Net also reports that farm workers are exposed to the elements and insects while working outdoors and they may spend long periods of time standing or walking.

EMPLOYMENT

As of 2008, the *OOH* reports that almost 80 percent of the 1.2 million farmers and ranchers in the United States were self-employed. The remainder worked as seasonal or full-time agricultural managers. The United Nations' report "The Employment Imperative: Report on the World Social Situation 2007" states that, as of 2007, 45 percent of the world's labor force worked in agriculture, with the percentage being higher in developing countries where farming is less mechanized and modern. The decline in farming employment as farms grow more modern and efficient, as well as the trend of consolidation into larger operations, can be noted around the globe in both developing and developed countries.

The *OOH* notes that climate, topography, and soil quality dictate the best locations for farming and ranching and therefore also dictate the location of farming and ranching jobs. In the United States, California, Texas, Iowa, Nebraska, and Minnesota make the most money from agriculture, whereas Texas, Missouri, Iowa, Oklahoma, and Kentucky are the states with the greatest number of farms. However, a 2010 Earth Day report issued by the National Cattlemen's Beef Association noted that cattle are raised in every state in the United States.

TRAINING, OTHER QUALIFICATIONS, AND ADVANCEMENT

Traditionally, farmers learn the trade by growing up in a farming family, according to the *OOH*. As farming becomes more complex and new farmers enter farming from outside the profession, however, a two-year associate's degree or four-year bachelor's degree is another way to learn necessary skills. Even those who grow up in farming families often seek some sort of postsecondary education.

Future farmers and ranchers may earn degrees in business, with a focus on agriculture, agricultural economics, crop and fruit science, or animal science, among others. Agricultural colleges, which are part of all state university systems, offer technical courses on crops, growing and planting strategies, and plant diseases. Those interested in ranching and dairy farming can take courses in basic veterinary science and animal care. Classes on green and organic farming techniques and the impact of various pesticides are also increasingly available, as earth-friendly products are growing in popularity among consumers, driving more farmers toward green methods for their work.

Because farmers need at least basic computer and accounting skills as well as communication and management skills, coursework in these subjects may be helpful. Also important is knowledge on obtaining credit, relevant government programs, and safety regulations. Some degree of mechanical aptitude is also helpful, particularly for those on smaller operations who may be repairing machinery and buildings themselves.

In addition to formal education, those new to farming or ranching may begin their careers with on-the-job training as they work, sometimes long term, for experienced farmers. A few farms offer formal apprenticeships for those seeking practical training and there are government programs to help new farmers get started as well.

Although a license or certification is not required for farming and ranching, those in the field must stay up-to-date on advances and changes occurring in the industry. One way of doing so is by obtaining certification as an Accredited Farm Manager (AFM) from the American Society of Farm Managers and Rural Appraisers. This requires several years of experience, a college or graduate degree, and successful completion of tests "related to the business, financial, and legal aspects of farm and ranch management," explains the *OOH*.

Qualities that may help ensure success in farming or ranching include independence and strong decision-making skills, enjoyment of animals and the outdoors, an appreciation for building relationships and working with others in a noncompetitive environment, and comfort with a variety of tasks, from physical labor to managing people to business strategy.

JOB OUTLOOK

According to O*Net, employment for self-employed farmers is expected to decline moderately in the 10 years between 2008 and 2018, with a loss of 3 to 9 percent of jobs. This decline can be traced to increased productivity through technology, as well as consolidation of smaller farms into larger, corporate-owned agribusinesses.

However, there are opportunities in the industry for those interested in small-scale specialty farming, such as horticultural products including sod, ornamental plants and shrubs, Christmas trees, or fruits and vegetables grown in greenhouses. Organic food production, perhaps in conjunction with a community-supported cooperative, is another potential approach. In 2011 the United Nations declared that farmers around the world must embrace green methods to produce enough food for the population, reported Robert Evans of *Reuters News Service* on July 5.

EARNINGS

Income for farmers and ranchers varies from year to year based on their crop or animal yield as well as on fluctuations in market price and demand for their products. O*Net reported the 2010 median wages for farmers and ranchers to be US$29.21 per hour, or US$60,750 annually.

Additionally, it is important for self-employed farmers and ranchers to consider that they must provide their own life and health insurance. Some farmers receive government subsidies or other payments that supplement their farming income. A number of farmers who began farming at the turn of the 21st century or later have made farming a part-time career.

RELATED OCCUPATIONS

- Aquacultural managers
- Buyers and purchasing agents, farm products
- Range managers
- Farm and home management advisors
- First-line supervisors of aquacultural workers
- First-line supervisors of agricultural crop and horticultural workers
- First-line supervisors of animal husbandry and animal care workers
- Agricultural inspectors
- Farmworkers and laborers, crop
- Fishers and related fishing workers
- Horticultural specialty farmers

SOURCES OF ADDITIONAL INFORMATION

Alternative Farming System Information Center, NAL. http://www.nal.usda.gov

American Society of Farm Managers and Rural Appraisers. http://www.asfmra.org

ATTRA National Sustainable Agriculture Information Service. http://www.attra.ncat.org

The Beginning Farm Center. http://www.farmtransition .org/netwpart.html

Center for Rural Affairs. http://www.cfra.org/resources/
beginning_farmer
Family and Small Farm Program. http://www.csrees.usda
.gov/smallfarms.cfm
International Federation of Organic Agriculture
Movements. http://www.ifoam.org
National FFA Organization. http://www.ffa.org
U.S. Farmers & Ranchers Alliance. http://usfraonline.org

FURTHER READING

Bureau of Labor Statistics, U.S. Department of Labor.
"Agriculture, Forestry, and Fishing." In *Career Guide
to Industries, 2010–11 Edition.* Accessed December
15, 2011. http://www.bls.gov/oco/cg/cgs001.htm.
———. "Farmers, Ranchers, and Agricultural
Managers." In *Occupational Outlook Handbook,
2010–11 Edition.* Accessed December 5, 2011.
http://www.bls.gov/oco/ocos176.htm.
Department of Economic and Social Affairs, United
Nations. *The Employment Imperative: Report on the
World Social Situation 2007.* Accessed April 17,
2012. http://www.un.org/esa/socdev/rwss/
docs/2007/preface.pdf.

Evans, Robert. "New Green Farming Vital to End
Global Hunger: U.N." *Reuters*, July 5, 2011.
Accessed April 17, 2012. http://www.reuters
.com/article/2011/07/05/us-un-farms-
idUSTRE7641MT20110705.
Keen, Judy. "As Sustainable Farming Takes Root, Green
Thumbs Get Greener." *USA Today*, October 24, 2008.
Accessed January 24, 2012. http://www.usatoday.com/
news/nation/environment/2008-10-23-sustainable-
farms_N.htm.
Photius Coutsoukis and Information Technology
Associates. "Farmers." In *Occupational Information
Network*, revised August 11, 2006. Accessed
December 5, 2011. http://www.occupationalinfo
.org/onet/79999d.html.
O*NET OnLine. *Summary Report for: 11-9013.02—
Farm and Ranch Managers*, partially updated 2011.
Accessed December 5, 2011. http://www.onetonline
.org/link/summary/11-9013.02.
U.S. Department of Agriculture. *2007 Census of
Agriculture.* Accessed December 5, 2011. http://
www.agcensus.usda.gov/Publications/2007/Online_
Highlights/Fact_Sheets/index.asp.

PURCHASING AGENTS AND BUYERS, FARM PRODUCTS

——————◼——————

NATURE OF THE WORK

Purchasing agents and buyers of farm products are a vital link between agricultural producers and the grocery industry or other markets. Purchasing agents may focus on a specific product, such as milk, grain, Christmas trees, or tobacco, or buy a variety of products for the company or institution they serve. Some purchasing agents or buyers focus specifically on organic and sustainable products and an organic produce buyer is one example of a specialty buyer, notes "Careers in Organic Food Production," an article in the fall 2010 issue of *Occupational Outlook Quarterly* (*OOQ*). Whereas organic foods were once a niche market, sold mostly to health food stores, now nearly all conventional grocery stores stock at least a few organic choices.

Whatever their focus, like a buyer in any industry (retail merchandise, fashion, manufacturing), a farm product buyer's goal is to get the best deal for their employer, which means the best quality goods, delivered on time, for the least possible cost, notes the U.S. Department of Labor's 2010 to 2011 *Occupational Outlook Handbook* (*OOH*). To do this effectively, farm buyers and purchasing agents need a detailed knowledge of the crops or other goods they are purchasing and they must stay current with factors affecting supply and demand and carefully evaluate the suppliers (various types of farms and ranches) with which they choose to do business. This will involve on-site visits to various production or growing locations, as well as Internet research and attendance at trade shows and farming-industry conferences.

In 2012, Whole Foods Market grocery store's website described their global cheese buyer as both "an expert

---

AT A GLANCE FACT BOX

SOC: 13-1021.00
Preferred Education: High school diploma or equivalent, plus long-term on-the-job training
Average Salary: US$37,930 to US$67,440 annually
Other Information: Although most people currently working as purchasing agents or buyers of farm products have only a high school diploma, a college degree in agricultural/farm supplies retailing and wholesaling or agriculture-related coursework can help distinguish those seeking to enter the field. Specialized knowledge of organic foods can also be an important differentiating factor as this segment of the marketplace continues to grow.

---

at detecting international food trends" and someone knowledgeable enough to travel the world to locate cheeses that meet the stores' quality standards. The *Dictionary of Occupational Titles* index also notes that a grain buyer may collect product samples and send them to experts for quality analysis. In other cases, the buyer will be expected to be the expert, able to make a sound judgment about a product on his or her own.

Purchasing agents and buyers focused on organic foods need some added expertise to be sure they are getting a quality product that meets the qualifications desired by their employer, whether that is a grocery store, a wholesaler, or a company that makes organic processed foods, notes the *OOQ* article. Products may be labeled "100% Organic," "Organic," or "Made With Organic Ingredients," and their actual organic content varies accordingly, explains a 2007 article for GreenPromise.com. GreenPromise.com is a website registered in 2005 that provides green lifestyle buying guides, in-depth analysis, and a directory of green suppliers, among other resources.

Once the buyer or purchasing agent has identified a product and supplier, contract negotiations begin. The buyer calculates the product's market value and works with the seller to come to an agreement on price, amount, delivery date, and other terms. The transaction will likely occur via the Internet, notes the *OOH*. The buyer is then responsible for finding the most economical way to ship the product and for confirming that the shipment is correct in terms of content and quality when it arrives.

The purchasing agent also keeps records of all his or her transactions and may be in charge of directing workers as they unload and/or further process the goods that have been purchased, such as milling grain into flour or preparing Christmas trees for sale. Over time, a buyer or purchasing agent may cultivate relationships with trusted suppliers and advise them on ways to improve the quality or quantity of the products they produce, explains the Occupational Information Network (O*NET).

Equipment that buyers and purchasing agents use in their line of work include calculators, grain analyzers, and rulers, as well as a laptop computer with software for accounting, databases, e-mail, enterprise resource planning, and spreadsheets, reports O*NET.

WORKING CONDITIONS

Generally speaking, most buyers and purchasing agents work in comfortable offices, reports the *OOH*. However, those buying products from farms should expect to spend time in that setting, where dangerous machinery and potentially hazardous chemicals may be present. Some travel is involved with being a buyer, as it is important to examine suppliers and their products first-hand. This could even be international travel, depending on the type of product being purchased.

Stress may also be a considerable factor for purchasing agents and buyers of farm products. They face the challenge of finding reliable suppliers and securing agreeable contracts, as well as ensuring that products are delivered appropriately and on time, even in busy seasons or when crops did not yield as much as planned. Mother Nature injects an element of volatility into farming, possibly introducing floods or droughts, which have an impact on everyone who works in the industry.

EMPLOYMENT

Purchasing agents and buyers of farm products work for grocery stores, wholesalers, and producers of processed goods, and they may work for restaurants and other businesses as well, reports the *OOQ* article. Restaurants in particular may employ buyers who are knowledgeable about organic and sustainably grown foods, including those available from local farmers.

According to the *OOH*, about 42 percent of all types of purchasing managers, purchasing agents, and buyers work for wholesale trade or manufacturing businesses. Those who purchase farm products are largely employed by grocery-related industries. As of 2008, about 14,100 people in the United States were working as buyers or purchasing agents of farm products.

It is difficult to determine global employment numbers for this field, but some U.S.-based buyers may travel internationally in pursuit of cheese, seafood, and other imports. Others may focus on nearby suppliers in keeping with the growing consumer interest in organic and locally produced foods. Jobs are available throughout the country, but buyers interested in working with local farmers should seek employment in the most farm-rich parts of the country. The *OOH* notes that Texas, Missouri, Iowa, Oklahoma, and Kentucky are the states with the greatest numbers of farms.

TRAINING, OTHER QUALIFICATIONS, AND ADVANCEMENT

As of 2008, the U.S. Department of Labor's Bureau of Labor Statistics (BLS) reported that most people employed as buyers or purchasing agents for farm products had a high school diploma or the equivalent, but their most significant source of knowledge was long-term on-the-job training. Like so many careers in farming, much of what makes a good buyer is learned by practicing the trade. The *OOH* notes that many in this field begin as trainees or assistant buyers and that training periods may last from one to five years.

However, because farming is becoming a more complex and modernized industry, and because some technical knowledge of farming is essential to being an effective buyer, pursuing a college degree or other formal training can be helpful to those who want to succeed in this field. Specialized training is particularly important for agents and buyers working with organic food, notes the *OOQ* article. These agents and buyers may need continuing education to stay current in the field and advance in their careers.

The education website MyMajors.com suggests agricultural/farm supply retailing and wholesaling as a potential area of study, and coursework in crop or animal science may be helpful as well, depending on the buyer's area of product focus. Computer training related to the database, accounting, and spreadsheet programs that buyers and purchasing agents use is also helpful.

Although a license is not required to be a buyer or purchasing agent, the *OOH* notes that continuing education is essential for advancement in the field. Many professional societies offer seminars, and college courses in supply management may be helpful. Professional certifications are also suggested, particularly for those new to the field. The Institute for Supply Management offers the Certified Professional in Supply Management credential, and the American Purchasing Society offers certifications for purchasing professionals and purchasing managers. Each of these certifications requires work-related experience and education, as well as passing a written or oral exam.

O*NET notes that personal qualities of successful buyers include dependability and attention to detail. Buyers and purchasing agents should be confident and able to make informed decisions about the suppliers and products they encounter. Good communication and negotiating skills are also key to success in this field, as is the ability to remain calm and in control.

JOB OUTLOOK

The BLS's employment projections for the decade between 2008 and 2018 predict a small 2 percent decrease in the number of people employed as buyers of farm products due to increased productivity via the Internet and computer technology. The *OOH* also notes consolidation among farmers and others in the agricultural industry as a factor that may limit growth in this field, as well as the use of outsourced or offshore workers and services to complete buyers' tasks. O*NET estimates perhaps 3,100 job openings in this field during the decade between 2008 and 2018.

However, as organic and sustainably produced foods continue to become more mainstream, it seems likely that additional buyers and purchasers with expertise in this area will be needed.

EARNINGS

In 2010 O*NET reported the median wages for purchasing agents and buyers of farm products to be US$26.07 per hour and US$54,220 per year, whereas the *OOH* listed them as US$49,670 per year as of May 2008. There is quite a range for potential earnings in the field, as the middle 50 percent of those in the profession earned between US$37,930 and US$67,440 in 2008. The lowest 10 percent earned US$28,990 or less, and the top 10 percent brought in at least US$96,220.

RELATED OCCUPATIONS

- Nursery and greenhouse managers
- Wholesale and retail buyers, except farm products
- Farm and home management advisors

- Field-contact technician
- Field contractor
- Clean-rice broker
- Christmas-tree contractor
- Agronomy manager
- Cattle broker
- Chicken buyer
- Cotton agent
- Cream buyer
- Egg buyer
- Farm products shipper
- Feed and grain elevator manager
- Fish agent
- Grain buyer
- Hog trader
- Horse trader
- Import coordinator
- Livestock commission agent
- Produce buyer
- Tobacco buyer
- Walnuts field buyer
- Wheat buyer
- Wool buyer

SOURCES OF ADDITIONAL INFORMATION

American Purchasing Society. http://www .american-purchasing.com
ATTRA National Sustainable Agriculture Information Service. http://www.attra.ncat.org
Institute for Supply Management (ISM). http:// www.ism.ws
My Majors.Com Network. http://www.mymajors.com
National Institute of Governmental Purchasing (NIGP). http://www.nigp.org
Organic Trade Association. http://www.ota.com
U.S. Farmers & Ranchers Alliance. http://usfraonline.org

FURTHER READING

Bibler, Adam. "Careers in Organic Food Production." In *Occupational Outlook Quarterly* (Fall 2010). Accessed January 31, 2012. http://www.bls.gov/ opub/ooq/2010/fall/art01.pdf.
Bureau of Labor Statistics, U.S. Department of Labor. "Purchasing Managers, Buyers, and Purchasing Agents." In *Occupational Outlook Handbook, 2010–11 Edition.* Accessed December 15, 2011. http://www.bls.gov/oco/ocos023.htm.
O*NET OnLine. *Summary Report for 13-1021.00— Buyers and Purchasing Agents, Farm Products,* updated 2010. Accessed December 15, 2011. http:// www.onetonline.org/link/summary/13-1021.00.
Photius Coutsoukis and Information Technology Associates. "Purchasing Agents and Buyers, Farm

Products." *Occupational Information Network*, revised August 11, 2006. Accessed December 5, 2011. http://www.occupationalinfo.org/onet/21305a.html.

Thull, Kevin. "Buyer Beware: Not All Organic Food Is Created Equal," updated October 15, 2007. Accessed January 31, 2012. http://www.greenpromise.com/food-nutrition/organic/buyer-beware.php.

Whole Foods Market. *The Big Cheese: Cathy Strange, Whole Foods Market Global Cheese Buyer.* Accessed January 11, 2012. http://www.wholefoodsmarket.com/stores/departments/big-cheese.php.

PRECISION AGRICULTURE TECHNICIANS

NATURE OF THE WORK

The term *precision agriculture* means using technology such as global-positioning systems (GPS), geographic information systems (GIS), yield maps, and special sensors mounted on farm equipment to provide farmers with information about their land and crops, including soil composition, weeds, and terrain, so they can make better decisions and operate more efficiently, explains PrecisionAgWorks.com and scientists at Auburn University, according to a February 2011 release from the Alabama *States News Service*. When implemented effectively, precision agriculture enables farmers to save money and protect the environment.

Many green farming practices, organic certification, for example, are costly and may take farmers a long time to earn back their investment. Although precision agriculture requires some equipment and specialized knowledge, in many cases it almost immediately reduces the amount of chemicals and water needed and makes crop production more robust. Therefore, it brings a quick return on the farmer's investment of time and money.

John Fulton, an Auburn University biosystems engineering associate professor and precision agriculture specialist, told Alabama's *States News Service* in 2011 that about 60 percent of row-crop farmers in Alabama had adopted some precision agriculture methods in 2009. These farmers saved about US$10 million by reducing their use of fertilizer and pesticides. The fact that these reductions were also good for the environment helped explain why this approach was rapidly growing.

Precision agriculture technicians help interested farmers understand and use this new technology. They may also be in charge of much of the necessary data collection.

AT A GLANCE FACT BOX

SOC: 19-4099.02
Preferred Education: One- or two-year degree/certificate in precision agriculture
Average Salary: Unavailable because this is such a new job field
Other Information: Precision agriculture is a relatively new and rapidly growing field, thus employment is predicted to expand at least 20 percent by 2018. This field is appropriate for those with skills in math and science who are interested in farming and protecting the environment.

A precision agriculture technician's duties include developing and analyzing maps of farmland to determine where crops are flourishing and where they are not and collecting information about soil (how fertile is it? how moist? does it contain pests?) in a particular area. They then combine this and other information, using computer analysis, to determine an appropriate plan for planting, fertilizing, irrigating, and more explains the U.S. Occupational Information Network (O*NET) Summary Report for Precision Agriculture Technicians.

Rather than blanketing an entire farm with fertilizer, water, or pesticides, and possibly using multiple passes over the land, precision agriculture helps farmers determine which areas of their land need what. Using "variable rate" application methods, they can reduce waste by putting additives and water only where they are needed. After implementing precision agriculture techniques on 300 acres of cropland, Colorado farmers Robert Geisick and Larry Rothe learned they were watering too much and could cut back on irrigation. In some areas, they could reduce their use of fertilizer by 35 percent without affecting their grain yield, they told *Agricultural Research Magazine* in 2000. In Sudan, tractors with a GPS-based autosteering system have improved the speed and efficiency of planting each season and minimized erosion and soil damage by keeping wheels in specific "lanes," explained a January 2006 article in *ICT Update*.

According to *Farm and Ranch Guide*, continuing technological advances will further automate the data-gathering part of precision agriculture, Terry Griffin, associate professor and University of Arkansas Extension economist, reported at the January 2012 Precision Ag Summit. This means that implementing these techniques will require less time in data entry and give precision agriculture technicians more time for analysis and consultations with farmers.

Tools and technology used by precision agriculture technicians include complex controlling devices such as automatic land levelers and autosteering systems, yield-monitoring systems, moisture monitors and variable-rate sprayers, and laptop computers equipped with database and analytical software, map creation and spreadsheet software, and word processing programs, reports O*NET. Improvements in the field include the 2010 introduction of FieldRx, a web-based precision agriculture program that enables technicians to create detailed *prescriptions* for the water and additives needed on specific plots of land based on the crop being grown there.

WORKING CONDITIONS

Just as a career in precision agriculture calls for a unique set of skills, such as an interest in farming and the environment and talent in maps, mathematics, and science, it also features unusual working conditions. Precision agriculture technicians sometimes find themselves in the field gathering information about the crops and soil on a particular farm, but they also spend time indoors compiling the information they have gathered, creating informational maps, analyzing data, and working with computers.

Precision agriculture technicians also spend time working and communicating with other people. They demonstrate the site-specific techniques appropriate for a particular farm. They also develop relationships with the farmers for whom they work, whether on individual family farms or through an agricultural cooperative, as they consult with them to develop plans and strategies for maximum efficiency and highest crop yield year after year.

EMPLOYMENT

Because this is a new and rapidly growing field, precise employment numbers are difficult to determine. O*NET reported 65,000 people in the United States working as life, physical, and social science technicians in general during 2008. Precision agriculture technicians are a subset of that group.

However, experts agree that this career is on the rise, so whatever the number employed today, it is likely to increase in the United States and around the world. A study by the National Environmentally Sound Production Agriculture Laboratory (NESPAL) at the University of Georgia reported that precision agriculture is being adopted at varying rates across the globe, with the United States and European Union currently leading the way, according to a January 2010 story from *Delta Farm Press*. In addition, a great deal of precision agriculture research comes from Australian universities, and precision agriculture methods are being used in Africa.

Within the United States, Midwestern corn growers are currently the largest users of precision agriculture techniques, but use in California and the Southwest is rapidly growing, NESPAL has found. Any of these areas would be a good place to seek work as a precision agriculture technician. The *Delta Farm Press* also noted that farms that grow high-value crops and larger farms are the most likely to adopt precision agriculture methods.

An August 2011 U.S. Department of Agriculture (USDA) *Economic Information Bulletin* reported that younger farmers with more education are more likely to adopt precision agriculture techniques than their older counterparts or those without a college education. In addition, precision agriculture is an easier adaptation for farmers already using computers and technology as part of their work. This could indicate that the networking and job resources available at an institution of higher learning would be useful in finding farm work as a precision agriculture technician.

Finally, PathwaysToTechnology.org reports that precision agriculture technicians are employed by agribusiness consultants and farm chemical vendors. Governments are also employers.

TRAINING, OTHER QUALIFICATIONS, AND ADVANCEMENT

Those hiring precision agriculture technicians look for potential employees who have at least a one-year degree/certificate in the field. PathwaysToTechnology.org recommends a two-year degree/certificate in agricultural technology, precision agriculture, or a related field. A number of community and technical colleges offer certificates in precision agriculture. These require between 15 and 20 credit hours of coursework in precision agriculture methods including GIS and GPS, variable-rate technologies, yield monitoring, and remote sensing and crop scouting, as well as general agricultural and soil studies, irrigation training, and computer science and math skills.

In addition, chemical process technology, physical science technology, or general science technology are other possible areas of study. About 80 schools in the United States offer courses of study relevant to precision agriculture.

O*NET reports that 43 percent of current precision agriculture technicians have a bachelor's degree, 25 percent have an associate's degree, and 21 percent have some college but no degree completed.

On-the-job training is another important component of becoming a precision agriculture expert. Those starting out in the field do basic tasks while supervised by more experienced technicians or managers. As they gain experience, precision agriculture technicians may be given more complicated tasks and autonomy. Those with particularly good communication and leadership skills who stay current on the latest technology and developments in the field through continuing education are the most likely to advance to supervisor or coordinator positions or perhaps even to training other technicians or training farmers themselves.

Precision agriculture technicians need a unique set of skills and interests to thrive in this profession. They should be interested in farming and geography and enjoy being outdoors, but they also need technical skills and focus related to computers, mathematics, and precise data calculations, O*NET explains. Good communication and customer service skills are also important because precision agriculture technicians serve as consultants and advisors to the farmers with whom they work.

JOB OUTLOOK

Because of expanding public interest in green and sustainably produced products, particularly with regard to the food supply, as well as farmers' desire to save money and increase crop yield, precision agriculture is on the rise. In addition, as more farms seek to implement these methods, the advice and assistance precision agriculture technicians can provide will be invaluable.

An August 2011 USDA *Economic Information Bulletin* reported that yield monitoring, one of the core methods of precision agriculture, is now used on more than 40 percent of American grain crop fields. However, not many of these farmers have yet implemented the use of GPS-based maps or variable rate application machinery for fertilizers. This fact indicates the level of potential additional growth in the field.

O*NET lists this occupation as one with an especially bright future as it is a new and emerging career in a rapidly growing industry. Employment is predicted to grow by 20 percent or more during the decade between 2008 and 2018 according to the U.S. Department of Labor's Bureau of Labor Statistics (BLS) employment projections. There will be more than 100,000 job openings for precision agriculture technicians during that time period.

Speaking at the January 2012 Precision Ag Summit, Associate Professor and University of Arkansas Extension Economist Terry Griffin explained that years ago, farmers who had begun using tractors rather than horses to plow their fields were known as *mechanized farmers*, but years later, when tractors were used nearly everywhere, the word *mechanized* was dropped. *Farm and Ranch Guide* reported that Griffin predicts a point in the future where the distinction of *precision* farming will no longer be necessary. These methods will become part of everyone's agricultural way of life.

EARNINGS

Because this is a new job description, there are few statistics about what precision agriculture technicians earn. However, in 2010 the BLS reported that life, physical, and social science technicians (the general category of worker precision agriculture technicians fall under) earned an average of US$22.10 per hour and US$45,980 per year. O*NET reported earnings as slightly less, with a median hourly wage of US$20.84 and yearly salary of US$43,350.

In 2012, the state of Illinois reported precision agriculture technicians to be in demand and earning a median salary of US$48,980 per year, which IllinoisWorkNet.com notes as being above the national median.

RELATED OCCUPATIONS

Occupations that have similar functions, educational requirements, or are potential areas for advancement from a position as a precision agriculture technician include the following:

- Conservation scientists
- Engineering technicians
- Geographic information systems specialists
- Geospatial information scientists and technologists
- Surveying and mapping technicians
- Agronomist
- Agronomy consultant
- County extension agent
- Crop specialist
- Extension precision agriculture specialist
- GPS field data collector
- Nutrient management specialist
- Precision agriculture department manager

- Precision agriculture specialist
- Precision agronomist
- Precision crop manager
- Precision farming coordinator
- Research soil scientist

SOURCES OF ADDITIONAL INFORMATION

Farm Progress Companies, Inc. http://farmprogressdaily.com

The InfoAg Conference. http://www.infoag.org

International Society of Precision Agriculture (ISPA). http://www.ispag.org

Precision Ag Institute. http://www.precisionagworks.com

Precision Agriculture Research Association (PARA). http://www.montana.edu/para

FURTHER READING

Alabama Agricultural Experiment Station and College of Agriculture, Auburn University. "Alabama Farmers Reap Big Savings with Precision Ag." *Agricultural Communications and Marketing,* February 21, 2011. Accessed March 28, 2012. http://www.ag.auburn .edu/comm/news/2011/precisionag.php.

Hildebrant, Dale. "Large Crowd Learns about Precision Agriculture." *Farm and Ranch Guide,* January 26, 2012. Accessed January 29, 2012. http://www .farmandranchguide.com/news/regional/large-crowd-learns-about-precision-agriculture/article_bc86a066-4830-11e1-924a-001871e3ce6c.html.

Hollis, Paul. "Adopting Precision Agriculture." *Delta Farm Press,* January 15, 2010. Accessed March 9, 2012. http://deltafarmpress.com/management/adopting-precision-agriculture.

ICT Update. *Precision Farming.* Accessed March 9, 2012. http://ictupdate.cta.int/content/download/558/27276/file/30_EN.pdf.

IllinoisWorkNet. *Precision Agricultural Technicians.* Accessed March 9, 2012. http://www.illinoisworknet .com/vos_portal/residents/en/Prepare/Careers/career_listings.htm?occId=100531&occTyp=intro&occText=Precision+Agriculture+Technicians&isd=y.

O*NET OnLine. *Summary Report for: 19-4099.02—Precision Agriculture Technicians,* updated 2011. Accessed December 17, 2011. http://www .onetonline.org/link/summary/19-4099.02.

Pathways to Technology. *Precision Agriculture Technician.* Accessed April 24, 2012. http://pathwaystotechnology .org/jobs/jb_17.html.

Schimmelpfennig, Dave, and Robert Ebel. "On the Doorstep of the Information Age: Recent Adoption of Precision Agriculture." *USDA Economic Research Service Economic Information Bulletin,* Number 80, August 2011. Accessed January 29, 2012. http:// www.ers.usda.gov/Publications/EIB80/.

Stelljes, Kathryn Barry. "New Systems Research Targets Precision Agriculture's Effectiveness." *Agricultural Research Magazine* 48:10 (October 2000). Accessed December 17, 2011. http://nationalatlas.gov/articles/agriculture/a_precisionAg.html.

Thompson, Becky, compiler. *Educational and Training Opportunities in Sustainable Agriculture,* 19th ed. June 2009. Alternative Farming Systems Information Center, Information Research Services Branch, National Agricultural Library, Agricultural Research Service, U.S. Department of Agriculture. Accessed January 31, 2012. http://www.nal.usda.gov/afsic/pubs/edtr/EDTR2009.shtml.

FIRST-LINE SUPERVISORS/MANAGERS OF AGRICULTURAL CROP AND HORTICULTURAL WORKERS

NATURE OF THE WORK

First-line supervisors/managers at farms and horticultural businesses, which specialize in the bulk growing of fruits, vegetables, flowers, or ornamental plants, are expected to perform a variety of personnel and marketing tasks, as well as provide their workers with appropriate agricultural or horticultural guidance and expertise.

However, whether working on a farm or in a greenhouse, these supervisors/managers are first and foremost in charge of people. Although they may spend a small portion of their time (less than 20 percent) engaged in the same activities as their workers, the Occupational Information Network (O*NET) explains that the bulk of their efforts go toward hiring and training workers. They also must supervise their workers' efforts, including establishing goals and the means to meet them through production and marketing plans and schedules and keeping employee records for the owner of the farm, orchard, nursery, or greenhouse.

In addition, farming supervisors/managers can be valuable consultants and partners with the farmers for whom they work, and they may be an active part of many farmers' decisions to use green, environmentally friendly methods. In 2008, *Farm Industry News* reported that "basic crop management decisions," such as choosing not to till fields and working to maintain appropriate soil nitrogen levels, can have a huge impact on a farm's creation of global-warming gasses and can reduce them by at least 90 percent.

Instructing workers on how to farm according to the owner's wishes falls to the first-line supervisors/managers.

AT A GLANCE FACT BOX

SOC: 45-1011.07
Preferred Education: On-the-job training or apprenticeship, some postsecondary education
Average Salary: US$41,800 annually
Other Information: First-line supervisors/managers are employed by farms, nurseries, orchards, or greenhouses. Their diverse job requirements require them to be efficient managers of people, as well as skilled and detail-oriented farmers or horticulturalists who are knowledgeable about the latest advances and methods in farming.

They may assign duties related to soil preparation, planting, and irrigating using sustainable methods, as well as harvesting and crop storage. "Organic agriculture takes a proactive approach as opposed to treating problems after they emerge," notes the website for the International Federation of Organic Agriculture Movements (IFOAM). Therefore, managers on green farms must be proactive as well.

On a horticultural farm, which might be housed in a greenhouse, first-line supervisors/managers oversee plant production and assign work tasks related to cultivation, harvesting, packing products, or adjusting the greenhouse's environmental conditions, O*Net reports.

In either work environment, supervisors/managers must monitor workers for unsafe practices, as well as examine the plants for quality control and to determine if additional water, fertilization, or pest treatment is needed. In addition, a 2005 report by the United States Agency for International Development (USAID) noted that most horticultural crops require higher levels of fertilizers, water, and pest control than traditional farm crops. Therefore, careful use and management of chemicals or other treatments is particularly essential for horticultural endeavors to avoid negative environmental impact.

Because these supervisors/managers perform varied tasks, the equipment and tools they use can range from heavy farm machinery and trucks to irrigation and fertilizing equipment to harvesting and haymaking machinery to scheduling, accounting, and word-processing computer software, O*Net reports.

WORKING CONDITIONS

The agricultural work schedule is largely determined by the weather and seasons, reports the U.S. Department of Labor's 2010–11 *Occupational Outlook Handbook* (*OOH*). During planting and harvesting, supervisors/managers will have long days and little time off. During other portions of the year, the farm or greenhouse staff may work indoors and shift their focus to selling their crops or plants. Depending on the farm or greenhouse's area of specialty, the winter holidays or the landscaping season may be particularly busy for sales. Even in the slower months, management staff may be outdoors making repairs or improving buildings and machinery.

Agricultural work can be dangerous, as machinery can cause injury and any chemicals used must be handled appropriately for the health and safety of all. Because of their diverse and important responsibilities, supervisors/managers must remain alert and focused while on the job. Agricultural workers, including supervisors/managers, must withstand the elements and assorted outdoor pests, and they may also do considerable amounts of standing or walking, notes O*NET. The online resource Education-Portal.com adds that those working in greenhouses must be prepared for constant warm, humid conditions.

EMPLOYMENT

As of 2008, the *OOH* reports that 48,600 people are employed in the United States as first-line managers or supervisors of agricultural crop or horticultural workers. As mentioned previously, supervisors/managers are usually employed by larger farms, nurseries, orchards, or greenhouses, where they perform a variety of duties for the farmer or owner of the business.

Looking specifically at horticulture, a 2005 World Bank paper found the market for these specialty products to be growing steadily in the European Union. The report noted that developing countries have an opportunity to increase their trade revenue by exporting fruits, vegetables, and flowers. Horticultural expertise is needed to begin such endeavors, so there could be jobs around the world for those with the knowledge to create and manage these businesses.

A May 2010 U.S. Department of Labor's Bureau of Labor Statistics (BLS) report revealed that many supervisor/manager positions in the farming, fishing, and forestry industry are based in California and other states on the West Coast of the United States. California in particular is home to many fruit, vegetable, and other specialty growers. The University of Illinois Extension reports that as of 2002, Oregon, North Carolina, Michigan, Pennsylvania, Wisconsin, Washington, New York, and Virginia produced the most Christmas trees for the season, with Oregon in the lead at 6.5 million.

TRAINING, OTHER QUALIFICATIONS, AND ADVANCEMENT

The *OOH* reports that the most significant source of postsecondary education or training among first-line supervisors/managers is "work experience in a related occupation." There is no substitute for hands-on training and personally acquired horticultural or agricultural knowledge. Budding horticulturalists might get some experience by working part-time at a nursery then perhaps move on to intern or apprentice with a trained horticulturalist. There are also farm programs that offer apprenticeships for those beginning in farming, notes the *OOH*.

However, with technological advances, a growing emphasis on green and sustainable growing methods that preserve the environment, and an increasingly challenging business world for farmers, the agriculture and horticulture industries are growing more complex. According to a 2005 USAID report, "horticulture is perhaps the most knowledge intensive and dynamic agricultural system." Although historically most in the farming and horticulture industries have learned the trade through a family business, many now also earn an associate's or bachelor's degree, reports the *OOH*.

Future farming or horticultural supervisors and managers should perhaps pursue a degree in business with a focus on agriculture or horticulture, agricultural economics, or crop and fruit science. Most state universities include agricultural colleges, which offer technical courses on various crops, as well as growing and planting strategies, among other things. Some major universities also have departments of horticultural science.

Classes on green and organic farming techniques and the environmental impact of different approaches and farm-related chemicals are more available as demand for products grown sustainably, including horticultural specialty items, increases among consumers. Computer and accounting skills, along with communication and management skills, will help supervisors/managers with their jobs, so coursework in these subjects is also recommended.

No license or certification is needed for farming or horticulture, but those in the field need to stay current on the advances and changes in the industry. Certification as an Accredited Farm Manager (AFM) from the American Society of Farm Managers and Rural Appraisers may help with this. According to the *OOH,* to obtain this certification, on-the-job experience, a bachelor's degree, and a passing grade on exams related to the business side of farming are all needed. Horticultural specialists may earn an American Society for Horticultural Science Certified Horticulturist (ASHS-CH) certification by qualifying for and passing an examination, as well as completing continuing education credits, reports the ASHS website. The certification must be renewed every three years.

Qualities that may help ensure success as a supervisor/manager in crop farming or horticulture include strong decision-making skills, good organization and time management abilities, enjoyment of the outdoors and growing plants, clear communication and conflict-resolution skills, and comfort with a variety of tasks, from managing people to wielding a green thumb.

JOB OUTLOOK

The BLS predicts average growth (7 to 13 percent) and 16,300 job openings for this position during the 10 years between 2008 and 2018. Employment opportunities for self-employed farmers are expected to decline during this same period, and openings for agricultural managers are expected to rise by about 6 percent, which indicates the shifting nature of the industry. O*Net predicts that landowners will increasingly seek the services and knowledge of agricultural managers to run their farms.

The *OOH* reports that most industry growth will be in small-scale specialty farming, including organic food production and horticultural product offerings such as Christmas trees or flowers, fruits, and vegetables grown in greenhouses. A 2005 USAID report noted that "economic growth in horticultural products has far exceeded the growth of other agricultural commodities, and the demand for horticultural produce continues to accelerate in both domestic and international markets." Farms focused on growing sod, ornamental plants, and shrubs also have a bright outlook as the *OOH* predicts continued interest in home and business landscaping.

EARNINGS

In 2010, the BLS reported median wages for first-line supervisors and managers in crop farming and horticulture to be US$20.10 per hour and US$41,800 annually. On larger farms, salaried agricultural managers earned an average of US$775 per week in 2008, with the lowest paid 10 percent earning less than US$360 per week and the highest paid 10 percent earning more than US$1,700 per week.

RELATED OCCUPATIONS

- Agricultural and food scientists
- Agricultural inspectors
- Farm and home management advisors
- Purchasing managers, buyers, and purchasing agents
- Nursery and greenhouse managers
- Farm and ranch managers
- First-line supervisors of landscaping, lawn service, and groundskeeping workers
- Supervisors, field-crop farming
- Supervisors, tree-fruit and nut farming
- Supervisors, vegetable farming
- Supervisors, vine-fruit farming
- Supervisors, diversified crops
- Migrant leaders
- Field supervisors, seed production
- Harvest contractors
- Supervisors, insect and disease inspection
- Forest nursery supervisors
- Supervisors, Christmas-tree farm
- Supervisors, rose-grading

SOURCES OF ADDITIONAL INFORMATION

Alternative Farming System Information Center, NAL. http://www.nal.usda.gov
American Horticultural Society. http://www.ahs.org
American Management Association. http://www.amanet.org
American Society for Horticultural Science. http://www.ashs.org
ATTRA National Sustainable Agriculture Information Service. http://www.attra.ncat.org
Beginning Farmers: An Online Resource for Farmers, Researchers, and Policy Makers. http://www.beginningfarmers.org
Garden Centers of America. http://www.gardencentersofamerica.org
International Society for Horticultural Science. http://www.ishs.org
Mid-America Horticultural Trade Show. http://www.midam.org
National FFA Organization. http://www.ffa.org
Texas A&M University's Horticultural Business Information Network. http://hbin.tamu.edu

FURTHER READING

Bureau of Labor Statistics, U.S. Department of Labor. "Agriculture, Forestry, and Fishing." In *Career Guide to Industries, 2010–11 Edition*. Accessed December 15, 2011. http://www.bls.gov/oco/cg/cgs001.htm.

———. "Farmers, Ranchers, and Agricultural Managers." In *Occupational Outlook Handbook, 2010–11 Edition*. Accessed December 5, 2011. http://www.bls.gov/oco/ocos176.htm.

Global Horticulture Assessment Team. *Global Horticulture Assessment*. A report prepared for United States Agency for International Development (USAID), June 30, 2005 [California: UC-Davis, 2005]. Accessed December 27, 2011. http://pdf.usaid.gov/pdf_docs/pnadh769.pdf.

Hest, David. "Equation for Green Farming." *Farm Industry News*, May 1, 2008. Accessed January 24, 2012. http://farmindustrynews.com/fertilizer/equation-green-farming.

International Federation of Organic Agriculture Movements. *FAQ*. Last modified 2009. Accessed March 11, 2012. http://www.ifoam.org/sub/faq.html.

O*NET OnLine. *Summary Report for 45-1011.07—First-Line Supervisors of Agricultural Crop and Horticultural Workers*, updated 2010. Accessed December 15, 2011. http://www.onetonline.org/link/summary/45-1011.07.

Photius Coutsoukis and Information Technology Associates. "First-Line Supervisors and Manager/Supervisors— Agricultural Crop Workers." In *Occupational Information Network*, revised August 11, 2006. Accessed December 15, 2011. http://www.occupationalinfo.org/onet/72002a.html.

———. "First-Line Supervisors and Manager/Supervisors—Horticultural Workers." In *Occupational Information Network*, revised August 11, 2006. Accessed December 15, 2011. http://www.occupationalinfo.org/onet/72002e.html.

University of Illinois Extension. *Christmas Trees and More*. Accessed April 17, 2012. http://urbanext.illinois.edu/trees/facts.cfm

AGRICULTURAL INSPECTORS

NATURE OF THE WORK

Agricultural inspectors are charged with maintaining the safety, quality, and health of the public's food supply and agricultural resources, as well as the plants and animals from which these come. This means they ultimately have an impact on the safety and health of the general public.

Inspectors visit farms, food-processing plants, fishing and logging operations, and ports and borders to ensure compliance with all relevant laws and regulations explains the Occupational Information Network (O*NET) Online Summary Report on Agricultural Inspectors. Specifically, this can involve evaluating the cleanliness and presence of appropriate equipment and supplies as well as examining livestock and plants for signs of disease, chemical residue, or inadequate growth, according to the agricultural inspectors job description from O*NET.

Other duties may include weighing and measuring products such as eggs to certify their quality and grade and collecting samples from animals or plants for analysis. Agricultural inspectors must be prepared to act quickly and decisively in an emergency, such as the discovery of tainted products or an outbreak of illness, even if this means closing a plant or production facility.

Farms and facilities seeking, or seeking to maintain, organic certification have additional inspection standards related to those practices. These standards include growing fruits and vegetables without synthetic fertilizers and pesticides and raising animals without the use of growth hormones and antibiotics explains "Careers in Organic Food Production," an article in the fall 2010 issue of *Occupational Outlook Quarterly* (*OOQ*).

Organic farms and producers must follow an "organic production plan" that provides specific information about

AT A GLANCE FACT BOX
SOC: 45-2011.00
Preferred Education: Bachelor's degree and on-the-job training
Average Salary: US$41,670 annually
Other Information: The majority of agricultural inspectors are U.S. federal or state government employees. As organic farming and food production continues to move into the mainstream, there will be increasing work opportunities for specialized organic inspectors.

the crops and animals raised there, methods for fertilization and pest control, and production processes, notes the *OOQ* article. Agricultural inspectors review these plans and spend time examining the facilities and interviewing personnel about operating procedures to be sure everything matches the plan.

When the inspection is complete, the inspector's report goes to the agency that certifies the farm or production site as organic. According to the *OOQ* article, the report is considered when determining whether to grant or maintain organic-certified status.

A 2007 article by Cary Blake in *Western Farm Press* reports that agricultural inspectors who examine produce or other plant products entering Arizona are on the job five days a week, 16 hours a day at a point of entry near Yuma, Arizona. "Arizona Department of Agriculture inspectors are generally on the lookout for invasive pests and diseases such as the glassy-winged sharpshooter, citrus canker, gypsy moth, red imported fire ant, citrus greening, and mealybug," the article notes. Wood-boring pests have done extensive damage to tree populations in the eastern United States, the article continues. The inspectors work with a goal of keeping the environment in balance and preventing invasive pests from ruining local ecosystems.

In similar fashion, inspectors working with the U.S. Department of Agriculture's Animal and Plant Health Inspection Service (APHIS) must be ever vigilant in protecting the agricultural health of the United States against various pests and diseases, from the Asian long-horned beetle to foot-and-mouth disease, explains the agency's website.

Most agricultural inspectors focus on a particular product or agricultural area. Job titles of those in this profession can include grain inspector, plant protection specialist, apiary inspector, seed and fertilizer specialist, meat and poultry inspector, and plant pest inspector, among others, reports O*NET.

In addition, agricultural inspectors may be called upon to advise farmers and other growers and processors they visit on the latest developments in the industry as well as providing them with clearly written reports of their findings after inspection and any changes that must be made for compliance, reports the Dictionary of Occupational Titles (DOT). On occasion, agricultural inspectors may be asked to testify in legal proceedings. Inspectors who focus on organic-certified facilities must have specific expertise and knowledge of organic and sustainable practices. They are valuable as resources for the farmers and producers they visit (see "Training, Other Qualifications, and Advancement" for more details).

O*NET reports that tools and equipment used by agricultural inspectors include weight-testing kits, sorting and grading machines, and sample holders. They also use computers with Internet-browsing capability, image-processing software for photos, presentation software such as Microsoft PowerPoint, and spreadsheet and word-processing software.

WORKING CONDITIONS

Working as an agricultural inspector is by no means a 9-to-5 job, nor do these workers spend time in an office cubicle. Instead, their hours can be long and somewhat unpredictable and they work onsite where the agricultural products they are inspecting are produced or imported. Depending on the focus of his or her job, an agricultural inspector may travel to farms, meat-processing and other food-production plants, or ports and borders to inspect cargo being imported.

Job information on the Maryland Department of Agriculture website notes that some inspector jobs may require the ability to lift and carry as much as 100 pounds and other positions require a medical examination to be sure the worker is not color blind.

Finally, the O*NET Resource Center notes that working as an agricultural inspector can be stressful and challenging. Inspectors' findings have an important impact on both the U.S. public health and the financial standing of the businesses they are inspecting. When problems or violations are discovered, they may find themselves in uncomfortable or difficult situations where they must deal with angry or unhappy people.

EMPLOYMENT

The largest employer of agricultural inspectors in the United States is the federal government. As of 2011 the U.S. Department of Agriculture had more than 8,000 food inspectors on their payroll notes StateUniversity.com, a career-development website. APHIS also requires the use of inspectors for their efforts to protect the country's natural resources and agricultural health the agency's website explains.

Many state governments employ agricultural inspectors as well, and the U.S. Department of Labor's Bureau of Labor Statistics (BLS) reports that Idaho, Nebraska, and Iowa hire them in particularly large numbers compared with other states. ScienceBuddies.org, a science careers website, notes the California Department of Food and Agriculture and the Minnesota Department of Agriculture as other potential employers for agricultural inspectors.

The BLS reports put the overall number employed in this field in the United States somewhere between 16,600 and 17,000 in 2008. Worldwide employment is more difficult to pinpoint, but countries around the world have inspectors in place to protect public health and the food supply.

TRAINING, OTHER QUALIFICATIONS, AND ADVANCEMENT

The BLS reports that as of 2010 most of those working as agricultural inspectors have a bachelor's degree as well as some on-the-job training. Although there are potentially some positions available in this field that do not require a four-year degree, most do, and as competition for agricultural inspector positions intensifies, a college education can only be a benefit to a potential candidate.

In addition, as more farms and food producers shift to organic practices, agricultural inspectors who focus on organic inspections will be increasingly needed. For those jobs, formal training and certification is required, reports the *OOQ* article. The International Organic Inspectors

Association is the field's largest certifying body and offers training and accreditation for crop, livestock, or processing inspection. In many cases, working inspectors can pursue these certifications as ongoing training to stay current as they work and give themselves increased potential to find work in a growing part of their field.

For those just entering the profession, StateUniversity .com suggests earning a bachelor's degree in agricultural science or biology and finding opportunities to gain work experience in a related environment such as at a meat-processing plant or on a farm. Education-Portal.com adds that speaking both English and Spanish can be an asset for an agricultural inspector.

A detailed understanding of the laws that regulate agriculture is a key to success as an inspector, and this is where on-the-job training can be particularly helpful. Hands-on understanding of inspection procedures is also likely to be learned on the job in a training role.

A license is not required for every agricultural inspector, but the DOT notes that, in some cases, particularly when working with live animals, inspectors may be required to acquire a U.S. Department of Agriculture license for each of the commodities or animals they are inspecting.

Advancement within the field usually means moving to a supervisory position, reports StateUniversity.com. Promotions are based on individual job performance and the needs of the agency for which one works. Competition can be intense for these supervisory jobs.

Those most likely to do well with a career in agricultural inspection are particularly keen identifiers of problems and are able to recognize "when something is wrong or likely to go wrong," explains the O*NET Resource Center. Additional useful skills and abilities include being an excellent listener, communicator, and critical thinker, as well as having sound judgment and the ability to make decisions appropriately, reports O*NET. An enjoyment of science and scientific methods is also an asset, as is being detail-oriented and diplomatic and having the ability to offer constructive criticism and remain calm even when others are not, says ScienceBuddies.org.

JOB OUTLOOK

Based on information available in 2008, the BLS predicts a small increase in employment opportunities for agricultural inspectors, perhaps on the high end of average growth, which is 7 to 13 percent, between the years 2008 and 2018. Government sources estimate between 2,100 and 5,500 job openings in the field during that same time period.

However, a variety of variables could lead to an even more positive job outlook. The U.S. Department of Labor's 2010–2011 *Occupational Outlook Handbook* (*OOH*) notes

that a number of current government inspectors are expected to retire during the decade between 2008 and 2018, which would create advancement opportunities and new entry-level openings in the field. It also reports that passage of pending federal legislation, which calls for greater scrutiny of food products by the U.S. Food and Drug Administration, would result in an increased demand for agricultural inspectors to do this work. As of 2009, increased reports and incidences of foodborne illnesses, from bacterial contamination to mad cow disease, were also strengthening demand for agricultural inspectors' services.

As earth-friendly products and approaches continue to gain traction and market share, there may be increased demand and more opportunities for agricultural inspectors in green industries beyond organic farming and food production. A 2008 report titled *Job Opportunities for the Green Economy* notes that agricultural inspectors will be needed to monitor the burgeoning cellulosic biofuels industry and increasingly complex bioengineered food products and crops may also demand inspectors' attention. Staying current with continuing education is the best way for inspectors to be prepared for new opportunities in their field.

EARNINGS

In 2010 the median wages for agricultural inspectors were US$20.03 per hour and US$41,670 per year, O*NET reports. This is up slightly from the *OOH*'s reported annual median wage of US$41,170 in May 2008.

In addition, many inspectors who are employed by the U.S. federal government or a state government also receive benefits that usually include sick days, paid vacation, and health insurance, according to StateUniversity.com.

RELATED OCCUPATIONS
- Agricultural and food scientists
- Farmers and ranchers
- Purchasing agents and buyers, farm products
- Soil scientists
- Plant scientists
- Farm and home management advisors
- First-line supervisors/managers of aquacultural workers
- First-line supervisors/managers of agricultural crop and horticultural workers
- Fishers and related fishing workers

SOURCES OF ADDITIONAL INFORMATION

Ag World Support Systems. http://www.aginspections .com

Association of Fruit and Vegetable Inspection and Standardization Agencies. http://www.afvisa.org

International Organic Inspectors Association. http://
www.ioia.net

USAJOBS: the United States Government's official
employment information system. http://www
.usajobs.gov

USDA Animal and Plant Health Inspection Services.
http://www.aphis.usda.gov

USDA Food Safety and Inspection Services. http://www
.fsis.usda.gov

FURTHER READING

Bibler, Adam. "Careers in Organic Food Production." In
Occupational Outlook Quarterly, Fall 2010. Accessed
January 31, 2012. http://www.bls.gov/opub/ooq/
2010/fall/art01.pdf.

Blake, Cary. "Agricultural Inspections to Resume at
Ehrenberg, Arizona, Port of Entry." *Western Farm
Press*, July 21, 2007. Accessed January 18, 2012.
http://westernfarmpress.com/agricultural-inspections-
resume-ehrenberg-arizona-port-entry.

Bureau of Labor Statistics, U.S. Department of Labor.
"Agricultural Inspectors." In *Occupational Outlook
Handbook, 2010–11 Edition*. Accessed December 15,
2011. http://www.bls.gov/oco/ocos347.htm.

Education-Portal.com. *Agriculture Inspector: Job
Description and Requirements for Becoming an
Agriculture Inspector*. Accessed April 16, 2012. http://
education-portal.com/articles/Agriculture_Inspector_
Job_Description_and_Requirements_for_Becoming_
an_Agriculture_Inspector.html.

Maryland Department of Agriculture. *Agricultural
Inspector I*. Accessed April 16, 2012. http://www
.mda.state.md.us/jobclass/0737.php.

Net Industries. *Agricultural Inspector Job Description,
Career as an Agricultural Inspector, Salary,
Employment—Definition and Nature of the Work,
Education and Training Requirements, Getting the Job*.
StateUniversity.com. Accessed December 15, 2011.
http://careers.stateuniversity.com/pages/46/
Agricultural-Inspector.html.

O*NET OnLine. *Summary Report for: 45-2011.00—
Agricultural Inspectors*, updated 2010. Accessed
December 15, 2011. http://www.onetonline.org/
link/summary/45-2011.00.

Photius Coutsoukis and Information Technology
Associates. "Agricultural Inspectors." In the
Occupational Information Network, revised August 11,
2006. Accessed December 15, 2011. http://www
.occupationalinfo.org/onet/21911r.html.

Pollin, Robert, and Jeannette Wicks-Lim. *Job Opportunities
for the Green Economy: A State-by-State Picture of
Occupations that Gain from Green Investments*. A report
prepared by the Political Economy Research Institute
University of Massachusetts, Amherst, June 2008.
Accessed January 15, 2012. http://www.peri.umass
.edu/fileadmin/pdf/other_publication_types/Green_
Jobs_PERI.pdf.

Science Buddies.org. *Science Careers: Agricultural Inspector*.
Accessed April 16, 2012. http://www.sciencebuddies
.org/science-fair-projects/science-engineering-careers/
MicroBio_agriculturalinspector_c001.shtml.

SECTOR OVERVIEW: ENERGY AND CARBON CAPTURE AND STORAGE

The world's demand for energy is always on the rise. As populations grow, countries develop, and new technologies emerge, energy consumption rises concurrently, often outpacing the world's ability to produce it. As a result, older power-generating technologies such as coal and natural gas remain essential despite the emergence of newer, cleaner technologies such as solar or hydroelectric. Installation and development costs also inhibit switching to greener power-generating technologies. However, the fossil fuel-based energy technologies produce large amounts of pollution, most notably in their production of carbon dioxide (CO_2), which contributes to the greenhouse effect and global warming and ultimately to climate change. It has therefore become vital to find ways to reduce the environmental impact of existing energy-production techniques, creating new initiatives such as carbon capture and storage (CCS) programs (sometimes referred to as carbon capture and sequestration) and making existing careers such as power plant operator an important component of green energy.

CCS is a process by which CO_2 pollution created by power plants is separated, compressed, and stored to keep it from entering the atmosphere. This transforms energy production that has traditionally had a negative impact on the environment into an environmentally neutral process, ensuring that the world's energy needs can be met without harming the delicate balance required for climate stabilization. The International Energy Agency has concluded that the energy industry will need to be carbon neutral by 2050 to achieve this. Failure to do so would be environmentally disastrous.

CCS is, however, a difficult goal. The mix of technologies and professions is complex, and the funds required to get these systems into production and installed worldwide are prohibitive. Progress to date has been slow because of the large start-up costs that such systems require. As a result, CCS is still a nascent and quickly growing area in the job sector that requires cutting-edge technology and a large cast of contributors.

CCS systems consist of mechanisms designed to extract and compress the gas as well as transport infrastructure to remove the carbon dioxide from fossil fuel power plants or other installations to a permanent storage solution. The storage techniques vary from gaseous storage, liquid storage, and solid storage of CO_2, depending on whether the CO_2 will be repurposed or simply sequestered. The most common strategy for sequestering CO_2 is to compress it under tremendous pressure and inject it deep underground, trapping it and thus preventing it from entering the atmosphere and contributing to the greenhouse effect. This requires the contributions of engineers with experience in the construction of high-pressure pipeline systems, geologists, and other engineers to locate suitable areas for the gas to be injected and to monitor the sites once put into operation to make sure that the system installed can tolerate the pressures of the compressed gas. These installations also require traditional construction managers and workers to build the installations themselves.

Recognizing the economic and infrastructure challenges of creating these systems, governments have tried to encourage their adoption with direct action. In 2011, for example, the U.S. Department of Energy awarded $14 million to six integrated gasification combined cycle (IGCC) projects to improve the economics of developing power plants with CCS systems.

CCS has also augmented the role of the power plant operator. This career retains its traditional features, such as the supervision, maintenance, and operation of electricity-generating power plants. Power plant operators make sure that the power needs of the community are serviced properly, monitoring demand and adjusting output as needed to ensure power is supplied in a consistent manner. At the same time, they must inspect and adjust the equipment in their plants continually to ensure the plant's smooth operation.

Green initiatives such as CCS have added a new dimension to the role of the power plant operator. Operators working in fossil fuel plants must now be familiar with carbon capture technologies that are being installed in existing fossil fuel-based power plants or built into new plants. They will also need to be capable of interacting with the designers and installers of CCS systems such as IGCC to maintain the carbon capture profile of their plants. In addition to the traditional skill sets of electrical systems, boiler operation and maintenance, and basic mechanical knowledge, power plant operators will need to be familiar with the basic machinery and extraction components of a CCS system.

The role of the power plant operator in a nuclear facility will be less changed by CCS technologies because the disposal and handling of nuclear waste is generally handled separately from the operation of the plant itself.

These new developments in CCS technology and application have also created new licensing and educational opportunities and requirements for workers. Although power plant operators still largely learn their trade on the job, there are an increasing number of certifications that make finding a job and advancing in a career easier. Some programs offer two- or four-year degrees in this field, but these are not as valued as on-the-job training and experience. The professions involved in CCS design and installation, however, usually do require certifications and degrees because CCS systems are complex installations involving advanced disciplines such as engineering and geology.

Overall, CCS represents an incredible transformation of the fossil fuel-based energy field, with the potential to reduce or even eliminate the CO_2 pollution generated from energy production. A power plant operator career is a stable job field, offering steady opportunity despite the relatively static rate of new power plant construction. The development of CCS initiatives brings new job opportunities as systems are designed and installed and new training opportunities for existing careers as they evolve to match the new technological environment. The demand for energy will only increase as countries develop and technologies emerge. As a result this job sector is guaranteed to grow in all aspects: training and education requirements, job opportunities, and potential wages.

SOURCES OF ADDITIONAL INFORMATION

The Carbon Capture and Sequestration Technologies Program at MIT. http://sequestration.mit.edu
The Carbon Capture & Storage Association (CCSA). http://www.ccsassociation.org
International Energy Agency. http://www.iea.org
U.S. Department of Energy. http://energy.gov

FURTHER READING

Biello, David. "Carbon Capture and Storage: Absolute Necessity or Crazy Scheme?" *Scientific American,* March 6, 2009. Accessed April 9, 2012. http://www.scientificamerican.com/blog/post.cfm?id=carbon-capture-and-storage-absolute-2009-03-06.
———. "First Look at Carbon Capture and Storage in a West Virginia Coal-Fired Power Plant." *Scientific American,* November 6, 2009. Accessed April 9, 2012. http://www.scientificamerican.com/article.cfm?id=first-look-at-carbon-capture-and-storage.
Whiteman, Hilary and Ilana Hart. "Carbon Capture and Storage: How Does It Work?" *CNN.com.* Accessed April 9, 2012. http://edition.cnn.com/2008/TECH/science/07/29/carbon.capture/index.html.

POWER PLANT OPERATORS

NATURE OF THE WORK

Power plant operators supervise and control the electrical output of power plants and manage regular maintenance and inspection of the equipment. They work with power plant dispatchers to determine the level of power output needed and adjust reactors, generators, boilers, turbines, and auxiliary equipment to deliver the necessary voltage from the plant. They also regularly inspect the equipment in the plant and keep records of switching operations and load levels on generators, lines, and transformers. They are expected to make reports on any unusual activity in the plant, any maintenance or repairs performed during their shift, and any malfunctioning equipment they encounter.

Much of this work involves computer systems, especially logging in events and keeping records of load levels and load adjustments. The computer systems utilized in power plants are usually quite specific and unlike computer systems encountered at home or in academic or business settings, but a general comfort with computers and their software is required.

As green technologies such as solar, biomass, and wind become more economically viable and legally required, power plant operators must also be comfortable with advancing technologies and a rapidly changing field. Although traditional power plant technologies still dominate the electrical grid in the United States, a greater investment and reliance on green technologies in the future is assured. Worldwide, for example, the wind power market rose 6 percent in 2011, led by increasing use of this technology in China. Solar energy is being used increasingly in handheld personal electronics, offering a new inroad for solar energy to replace traditional batteries

and other power sources. And the United States has included incentives at both the federal and local levels to encourage development of biomass technologies and crops, most notably as part of the 2002 Farm Bill.

WORKING CONDITIONS

The bulk of the work is performed sitting or standing at a control station in the power plant. This work is not physically strenuous, but it does require a high level of concentration and attention. Power plant operators are expected to routinely conduct physical inspections of the plant. These rounds bring the operators into direct contact with dangerous conditions, exposing them to moving machinery and the threat of electric shock. If the operators work in a nuclear reactor power plant, they may be exposed to small amounts of radiation during the course of their work.

AT A GLANCE FACT BOX

SOC: 51-8013.00

Preferred Education: High school diploma or equivalency (nuclear power plant operators often have bachelor's degrees in engineering or the physical sciences, although this is rarely required)

Average Salary: US$47,850 to US$68,250 annually

Other Information: Approximately 40 percent of power plant operators belong to labor unions

---

Demand for electricity is present 24 hours a day, so most power plant operators work shifts of 8 to 12 hours in duration. Less desirable shifts are often rotated among operators to distribute them fairly. This can result in constantly shifting living and sleeping patterns.

Most power plant operator jobs exist in the utilities sector. However, some large private institutions such as hospitals maintain their own power plants and require trained staff to run them.

EMPLOYMENT

Throughout the United States, power plant operators held about 35,400 jobs (of which approximately 5,000 were in nuclear power plants) as of 2008. Job numbers tend to be very static because the number of operational power plants does not change often, but employment prospects are good because of the steady rate of retirement among older workers (due in part to layoffs and hiring freezes at utility companies in the 1990s). Although new power plants are being built, these are largely replacing older facilities that are being closed. The new plants will require fewer workers due to increased automation and efficiency, holding job openings static.

On the other hand, the increased requirements for clean energy mean that local governments and utilities are turning to alternative energy sources such as solar or biomass generators instead of traditional fossil fuel-based plants. Because the power yield of alternative plants is not as high as traditional fossil fuel plants, these installations need to be larger and more numerous to produce equivalent levels of electricity. Solar power, for example, requires large outdoor spaces in which to erect collection panels; wind farms require huge tracts of open, flat land to be efficient energy producers; and biomass installations can be extensive depending on the process and biomass source.

Alternatively, nuclear power is often touted as a cleaner energy source as it does not contribute to carbon emissions. Some governments, including the United States, have put funds into place to encourage a resurgence of investment in nuclear power for this reason, which could spur construction of new power plants. However, the high costs of building nuclear reactors, combined with community resistance to the perceived dangers of nuclear power, have made many utilities and companies rethink plans for a nuclear resurgence, which serves to inhibit new plants and the jobs they would offer.

TRAINING, OTHER QUALIFICATIONS, AND ADVANCEMENT

Most power plant operators do not have college degrees, although almost all do have high school or equivalency degrees. Most of the training and experience necessary for the job is gained through on-the-job training. Most power plant operators begin their career at a lower level working within a power plant environment to gain experience.

Experience in general mechanical maintenance is often a requirement, although specific maintenance techniques and equipment experience can be gained on the job. Experience with basic electrical work and techniques is also generally required.

Often a power plant American Society of Power Engineers (ASOPE) license is required. Sometimes local municipalities have local licensing requirements as well. ASOPE licensing includes an entry-level license program for people with minimal experience. As they gain experience they can sit for higher license levels. ASOPE licenses require a combination of minimum education/work experience requirements and a written test, for which the organization charges a fee (typically US$35–US$45).

In addition, any position that involves interacting with the national power grid, which includes all power plant operators, must be certified by the North American Electric Reliability Corporation (NERC). Four certification examinations are offered, depending on the specific position being considered.

Nuclear power plant operators are usually required to have some experience as power plant operators, typically around three years, before consideration. They are also required to be licensed by the Nuclear Regulatory Commission (NRC). The NRC's licensing is more demanding. After an initial application that lists the candidate's educational and work experience is received and reviewed, there is a mental and physical examination administered to ensure the candidate is physically and mentally capable of handling the demands of the position. If these are passed, there are written and on-site examinations that must be passed. It is important to note that licensing for nuclear power plant operators is specific to the plant the candidate will be working in and does not convey a general license to operate nuclear power facilities.

Good physical condition is helpful. Although the job is often sedentary, there are aspects that require lifting and operation of heavy equipment.

JOB OUTLOOK

The growth rate for power plant operator careers is fairly static. New power plant construction is largely offset by decommissioning of older power plants and more efficient power plants that require fewer staff members. However, the job field is predictable and the number of openings is fairly steady due to retirement of older workers.

In 2008 the U.S. Bureau of Labor Statistics estimated that there were 35,400 power plant operator jobs in the United States. Of these, about 5,000 were in nuclear facilities. No statistics are currently kept regarding how many of these positions are exclusively or partially involved with alternative energies; however, the Solar

Foundation estimates that in 2011 there were more than 100,000 total jobs associated with solar energy in the United States, a 6.8 percent growth over the previous year. While only a fraction of these jobs were power plant operator positions, solar energy clearly has the potential to increase job opportunities in the future.

Available positions for non-nuclear power plant operators are expected to decline by approximately 2 percent over the next decade, but employment of nuclear power plant operators is expected to grow by 19 percent as initiatives to prompt a nuclear resurgence domestically and internationally take effect.

The electrical grid is nationwide and made of many local points, so power plant operator jobs are available across the United States, with the number of available positions determined mainly by population size. Two-thirds of all power plant operator positions exist within the utilities sector.

EARNINGS

According to the U.S. Bureau of Labor Statistics, the median annual wage of power plant operators was US$58,470 in May 2008, with a spread from the lowest 10 percent (US$38,020) to the highest 10 percent (>US$80,390).

Washington offers the highest annual mean wage for power plant operators at US$77,400, as of May 2010, but it has a relatively low number of positions available, at 590. California is second in annual mean wage at US$73,670, but it offers many more employment opportunities, with 3,290 positions recorded in May 2010. Hawaii has the lowest annual mean wage at US$68,200.

RELATED OCCUPATIONS

- Stationary engineers and boiler operators
- Water/wastewater engineers

SOURCES OF ADDITIONAL INFORMATION

American Society of Power Engineers, Inc. http://www.asope.org

International Brotherhood of Electrical Workers. http://www.ibew.org

North American Electric Reliability Corporation. http://www.nerc.com

Nuclear Regulatory Commission. http://www.nrc.gov

World Association of Nuclear Operators. http://www.wano.org

FURTHER READING

Bureau of Labor Statistics, U.S. Department of Labor. "Power Plant Operators, Distributors, and Dispatchers." In *Occupational Outlook Handbook, 2010–11 Edition*, updated December 2009.

Accessed January 21, 2012. http://www.bls.gov/oco/ocos227.htm.

Employment Development Department, State of California. "Power Plant Operators." *California Occupational Guides,* 2005. Accessed March 28, 2012. http://www.calmis.ca.gov/file/occguide/power.pdf.

Get Into Energy. "Power Plant Operator." *GetIntoEnergy.com.* Accessed January 21, 2012. http://www.getintoenergy.com/careers_plant_operator.php.

GetSolar. *Solar Power Sees Growing Use in Gadgets,* August 18, 2011. Accessed April 9, 2012. http://www.getsolar.com/News/Solar-Energy-Facts/General/Solar-Power-Sees-Growing-Use-In-Gadgets-800574787.

Hamilton, James and U.S. Bureau of Labor Statistics. "Careers in Solar Power: June 2011—Report 2." *Green Jobs: Solar Power.* Accessed March 28, 2012. http://www.bls.gov/green/solar_power/solar_power.pdf.

Morales, A. "Wind Power Market Rose to 41 Gigawatts in 2001, Led by China." *Bloomberg Businessweek,* February 7, 2012. Accessed April 9, 2012. http://www.businessweek.com/news/2012-02-07/wind-power-market-rose-to-41-gigawatts-in-2011-led-by-china.html.

O'Grady, Eileen. "SCANA Studies Options, Nuclear Expansion Too Costly." *Reuters,* January 25, 2008. Accessed March 28, 2012. http://uk.reuters.com/article/2008/01/25/utilities-scana-nuclear-idUKN2556518620080125.

Smith, Deborah and Chris Thomas. "Investing Guru Warren Buffet Backs Away from Idaho Nuclear Power Plans." *Public News Service,* January 29, 2008. Accessed March 28, 2012. http://www.publicnewsservice.org/index.php?/content/article/19782/4209_1.

The Solar Foundation. *National Solar Jobs Census 2011,* October 17, 2011. Accessed March 28, 2012. http://thesolarfoundation.org/research/national-solar-jobs-census-2011.

Union of Concerned Scientists. *Growing Energy on the Farm: Biomass and Agriculture.* Accessed April 9, 2012. http://www.ucsusa.org/clean_energy/technology_and_impacts/impacts/growing-energy-on-the-farm.html.

———. *Nuclear Power: A Resurgence We Can't Afford,* updated August 2009. Accessed March 28, 2012. http://www.ucsusa.org/nuclear_power/nuclear_power_and_global_warming/nuclear-power-resurgence.html.

United States Nuclear Regulatory Commission. *Operator Licensing,* updated March 2011. Accessed March 28, 2012. http://www.nrc.gov/reactors/operatorlicensing.html.

SECTOR OVERVIEW: ENERGY EFFICIENCY

It is hard to exaggerate the importance of energy efficiency in the environmental movement. Energy efficiency refers to reducing the amount of fossil fuels emitted by energy consumption while maintaining the level of energy consumption. This is different from energy conservation, which means simply doing without the service. Energy efficiency reduces pollution in the form of greenhouse gases. It also reduces the energy costs to consumers.

As people have gained a deeper understanding of the importance of environmental awareness, phrases such as "living off the grid," "sustainable energy," and "solar farms" have become household terms. Consumers have moved toward energy efficiency by purchasing a compact fluorescent lightbulb or an Energy Star appliance or ensuring the attics and windows of buildings have proper insulation. Many simple actions such as using a revolving door in a building that has its heat or air conditioning on can help make a significant difference. Larger, more ambitious projects such as designing "smart" buildings and cars that do not rely on fossil fuels could also have a positive impact on the environment.

In the battle against climate change, energy efficiency is one of the best tools. According to the Lawrence Berkeley National Laboratory, it is the least expensive and the fastest approach to reducing greenhouse gases. Energy efficiency can also make a large difference in the economy by creating jobs and stimulating economic growth.

Careers in energy efficiency help bring about these changes. Many of the occupations in this sector are still emerging because of the green movement. Therefore, many jobs are obscure, but many long-standing careers have always been quietly green. Those that are not have begun the process of turning in this direction.

Some of these careers have a direct effect on energy efficiency. Insulators, for example, build constructions that ensure fewer carbon emissions by reducing the amount of heat or air conditioning lost from a building and thereby reducing the energy it takes to properly heat or cool the building. Insulators refer to themselves as environmentalists because their work dramatically increases energy efficiency. Likewise, weatherization installers and technicians fix drafty windows and ensure efficient heating and air conditioning. They may also conduct energy audits. Many businesses and homeowners are getting energy audits for their buildings. Energy auditors examine buildings for leaks in floors, windows, and insulation to recommend steps for greater energy efficiency.

Testing, adjusting, and balancing (TAB) technicians are important to maintaining air and water delivery systems. TAB technicians ensure that the air and water delivery systems operate efficiently, quietly, and safely throughout a building. Boilermakers would benefit with the enactment of a comprehensive energy bill. This would ensure that the industries that employ boilermakers, which are among the biggest producers of greenhouse gases, would have greener practices.

Heating and air conditioning mechanics, stationary engineers and boiler operators, and refrigeration mechanics also provide more energy-efficient means of cooling and heating homes and businesses, which may offer many employment opportunities. Maintenance technicians and repair workers fix and maintain motors, plumbing, electrical fixtures, and heating and cooling systems to use less energy. They also replace old systems with new equipment that uses less water and electricity. Fixing a leaky faucet or replacing incandescent light bulbs with compact fluorescent lamp (CFL) bulbs may sound like small changes, but small changes can make a huge difference.

Electrical power line installers and repairers make energy efficiency and infrastructure upgrades such as "smart grids," which are electrical grids that gather information about the use of energy in a system and then use that information to make the electrical system more efficient. Transportation, vehicle, equipment, and systems inspectors provide energy efficiency means for vehicles by ensuring that emission and safety standards are met.

Other careers such as general and operations managers and training and development specialists have jobs that do not directly impact the environment but that will require adjustment to meet environmental needs. Green measures including governmental policy and new technology are likely to cause significant change to these fields of work. New tasks, skills, knowledge, and credentials may be needed as the jobs incorporate green standards.

Electrical engineers, mechanical engineers, and energy engineers design the technology that we need for greater energy efficiency and sources of renewable energy, which will affect many other jobs in this sector. The field of energy engineering itself is emerging and specifically addresses alternatives to fossil fuel. The Massachusetts Institute of Technology (MIT), for example, has engineering students who produce creative ideas for the efficient use of energy and water. MIT implements many of these features on its campus. Engineers and architects are producing "smart buildings" with components such as natural ventilation and advanced daylighting systems, which use a combination of natural and electrical lights to illuminate a room and save energy. With regulations and financial incentives, more buildings with these features could make a significant dent in climate change.

In the early 2000s, MIT committed US$3 million to energy efficient changes. According to the Campus Energy Initiative, "These investments alone are estimated to save MIT over US$2.2 million annually in energy savings, providing additional strategic capital to reinvest in additional projects, while also reducing greenhouse gas emissions by over 22 million pounds annually."

Jobs in this sector vary in growth, but much of the growth depends on legislation. Lawmakers must pass bills that support making energy efficiency a priority if job growth is to be optimal. Contacting members of the U.S. Congress about support for such legislation would help bring about greater opportunities in the field.

In the Great Recession, which took place in the first decade of the 21st century, energy efficiency became one of the keys to employment opportunities. Various reports point to it as a job creator and a cost-effective tool for fighting poverty. The American Clean Energy Security Act (H.R. 2454) established a 10 percent energy efficiency resource standard and required one-third of the electric utility allowances to be used for energy efficiency. This could create more than 569,000 jobs in the United States by 2020 and more than 1 million jobs by 2030, according to an American Council for an Energy-Efficient Economy (ACEEE) study.

FURTHER READING

CareerOneStop.com. *New Green Occupations.* Accessed February 20, 2012. http://www.careeronestop.org/GreenCareers/WhatareGreenCareersNewGreenOccupations.aspx.

———. *What Are Green Careers?* Accessed February 20, 2012. http://careeronestop.org/GreenCareers/WhatareGreenCareers.aspx.

Cincinnati State Technical and Community College. *Electro-Mechanical Engineering Technology—Renewable Energy and Energy Efficiency Major (EMTR).* Accessed February 20, 2012. http://www.cincinnatistate.edu/real-world-academics/academic-divisions/center-for-innovative-technologies/programs-certificates-1/electrical-engineering-technologies-department#energy_efficiency_major.

Energy Efficiency Works. *Energy Efficiency Creates Jobs and Spurs Economic Development.* Accessed February 20, 2012. http://energyefficiencyworks.org/energy-efficiency-creates-jobs-and-spurs-economic-development.

International Brotherhood of Boilermakers. *Passing Comprehensive Energy Bill Ensures Future for Boilermakers.* Accessed February 20, 2012. http://www.boilermakers.org/resources/commentary/V48N4.

International Training Institute for the Sheet Metal and Air Conditioning Industry. *Careers—Testing, Adjusting, & Balancing.* Accessed February 20, 2012. http://www.sheetmetal-iti.org/careers/tab.shtml.

iseek.org. *Building Maintenance Workers.* Accessed February 20, 2012. http://www.iseek.org/careers/careerDetail?oc=100259&id=2.

Lawrence Berkeley National Laboratory. *What's Energy Efficiency? Why Is Energy Efficiency the Most Abundant, Cheapest Way to Reduce Greenhouse Gas (GHG) Emissions?* Accessed February 20, 2012. http://eetd.lbl.gov/ee/ee-4.html.

MIT Energy Initiative. *Building Efficiency Technologies.* Accessed February 20, 2012. http://web.mit .edu/mitei/research/innovations/efficiency .html.

————. *Campus Energy Projects.* Accessed February 20, 2012. http://web.mit.edu/mitei/campus/projects .html.

O*NET OnLine. *Green Occupation: 11-1021.00 General and Operations Managers.* Accessed February 20, 2012. http://www.onetonline.org/help/green/ 11-1021.00.

Whole Building Design Guide. *23 05 93: Testing, Adjusting, and Balancing for HVAC.* Accessed February 20, 2012. http://www.wbdg.org/design/230593.php.

TRAINING AND DEVELOPMENT SPECIALISTS

NATURE OF THE WORK

The role of a training and development specialist is to develop, deliver, monitor, and assess educational activities in an organization. *Training* activities are conducted to teach new employees (or newly promoted employees) how to do a particular job or perform a particular task, such as installing weather stripping or assembling a solar power system. *Development* activities help employees develop the skills and abilities necessary for progress along a career path or expand the range of functions the employees are qualified to perform. At the managerial and executive level, such development activities may involve learning general concepts such as team building and personnel development. In a larger sense, training and development also have a strong motivational component, for they provide workers with the skills and capabilities they need to be successful and boost their earning power. For simplicity's sake, the terms *trainer* and *training* will be used to encompass both training and development. In a green context, training activities are often conducted to help an organization's managers implement the principles of sustainability, and development activities are used to help streamline employees' energy efficiency, recycling habits, and other such environmental issues.

In some organizations, training is a human resources function, one carried out by a department or division whose specific function is to deliver training activities. In other organizations, the responsibility for training might be dispersed among the organization's departments and divisions, bringing it closer to the needs of particular groups of employees. Still other trainers find jobs in companies that specialize in providing training for other enterprises, usually

> ## AT A GLANCE FACT BOX
>
> **SOC:** 13-1151.00
> **Preferred Education:** Bachelor's degree
> **Average Salary:** US$57,280 annually
> **Other Information:** Environmental concerns will likely increase the need for training and development specialists to teach skills needed in the green economy

those that are too small to maintain an ongoing training department. In the 21st century, numerous companies have been formed whose sole service is to provide training designed to help other organizations go green.

A training and development specialist assesses training needs throughout an organization, often through surveys, focus groups, or consultation with managers, employees, and sometimes customers. Using the results of this needs assessment, the trainer develops training programs to meet those needs, then monitors and evaluates the programs to determine their effectiveness and to make adjustments if needed. Some of the programs a trainer develops are in written form, such as procedure manuals, instructional booklets, pamphlets, bulletin-board postings, and similar documents. Other programs are conducted in classroom settings and include simulations, role-playing, team exercises, videos, group discussions, and traditional lectures.

The government supports job training programs in which trainers are employed as case managers. Their job is to teach basic job skills to prepare clients to enter (or reenter) the workforce. In this capacity they assess training needs and guide their clients through necessary training.

In the context of a green economy, the training function is designed to help organizations provide products that conserve resources such as energy and water and that eliminate pollutants and greenhouse gases. In many cases, this training is focused on the construction industries, where architects and engineers need to learn how to implement the principles of sustainability into their designs and forms. Other training programs are designed to help organizations conduct their day-to-day operations in ways that conserve energy and water and eliminate waste. For example, a green trainer might help draft and implement policies that promote zero waste and conservation of water. This was an approach taken by the Deutsche Bank in Germany, which set a goal of a zero net emissions impact among all its facilities and established training functions to achieve that goal.

Some trainers might be involved in renewable energy training, energy auditing, Leadership in Energy and Environmental Design (LEED) certification (a certification program that enables building owners and operators to identify and implement measurable solutions for green building design, construction, and maintenance), and even eco-tourism. Green training can help people find jobs in industry sectors such as environmental engineering, alternative energy generation, and other types of "green-collar" jobs. Furthermore, as the U.S. economy continues to emphasize green jobs, green trainers can assist employees with job transitions, providing retraining and development programs that enable employees to learn new skills they can offer to employers in green industries.

WORKING CONDITIONS

The working conditions of trainers can vary considerably depending on the goals, size, and type of organization for which they work. Much depends on whether the emphasis is on knowledge or skills. Knowledge-based training is likely to be conducted almost exclusively in an office or classroom setting; it tends to resemble traditional schoolwork. In contrast, skills-based training is more likely to take place on-site: on a shop floor, in a studio, in a laboratory, at a construction site, or any location where an employee will exercise the skills the trainer is imparting. This type of skills-based training regularly involves hands-on demonstration and practice, requiring the trainer to travel to the site where training is needed.

Training programs are increasingly conducted via the Internet through avenues such as "webinars" and self-paced study courses. Accordingly, a trainer needs not only the people skills to interact with those being trained but also the computer skills necessary to deliver that training. E-learning and distance learning can also be a part of a company's green initiatives. Before the widespread use of the Internet, people had to travel to provide or receive training, usually at great expense to the organization. In the 21st century, this travel, with its attendant environmental impacts, can be reduced if not eliminated. E-learning also helps reduce the consumption of paper, along with the waste that paper materials often produce.

Trainers should be proficient in the use of a number of tools, including computers, LCD projectors, and overhead projectors, which have replaced the chalkboard in classroom situations. Some of the technological tools trainers routinely use include computer-based training software such as Adobe Captivate, Articulate Rapid E-Learning Studio, Halogen eLMS (that is, Learning Management System), and Qarbon ViewletBuilder Professional. Each of these programs is designed to help develop and deliver training programs. Trainers are also able to use document management software, graphics and photo-imaging software (e.g., Adobe Photoshop and Adobe Illustrator), and videoconferencing software (e.g., Cisco Systems WebEx and Microsoft NetMeeting).

EMPLOYMENT

According to the U.S. Department of Labor's Bureau of Labor Statistics (BLS), the number of training and development specialists in 2010 was about 203,870 (down from 216,600 in 2008, likely a result of the nation's steep recession). The states with the highest employment level were California, Texas, New York, Florida, and Pennsylvania. The states with the highest concentration of training and development specialists (relative to overall employment in the state) were Virginia, Georgia, Oklahoma, Nebraska, and Delaware. The metropolitan areas with the highest employment level were New York, New York; Atlanta, Georgia; Washington, DC; Houston, Texas; and Phoenix, Arizona. The metropolitan areas with the highest concentration of training and development specialists (relative to overall employment in the area) were Salem, Oregon; Columbia, South Carolina; Danbury, Connecticut; Trenton–Ewing, New Jersey; and Anniston–Oxford, Alabama.

TRAINING, OTHER QUALIFICATIONS, AND ADVANCEMENT

In one sense, trainers are not required to have any particular background or qualifications other than knowledge of how to do a job and the ability to explain how to do it to others. In the past, it was common for individuals with greater job experience to be called upon to train others, often by default. In recent years, however, training and development have become more specialized functions. Generally, organizations prefer trainers who have at least a bachelor's degree. Numerous colleges and universities offer degrees in organizational development, which provide a solid educational background for training and development. Other relevant degree programs include human resources, human resources administration, or industrial and labor relations. A degree in education, particularly with an emphasis on adult education, can also be an important credential.

In the context of a green economy, trainers themselves should gain green credentials, which they can then impart to others through the training function. Several organizations provide these green credentials. One, called Green Advantage, offers the Green Advantage (GA) Environmental Certification Exam. The Green Collar Association functions as a clearinghouse for green education and training courses from institutions as diverse as Yale University, The Earth Institute at Columbia University, Massachusetts Institute of Technology, the California Institute of Technology (Caltech), and the HVACRedu.net (for professionals in the heating, ventilation, air conditioning, and refrigeration industry). Sponsored by the U.S. Green Building Council, LEED provides training for employees in the building professions. Certification, combined with extensive on-the-job experience, can boost the career prospects of those who aspire to be training and development specialists.

A further boost can be provided by "Train-the-Trainer" certification. Several organizations, including PrepMasters, Langevin Learning Services, and the Training Clinic, provide courses designed to enhance training skills and abilities. Specialized courses in virtually any profession are also available. For example, the Forklift Certification organization offers a forklift safety training certification program that satisfies the safety requirements of the U.S. government's Occupational Safety and Health Administration.

JOB OUTLOOK

According to the American Society for Training and Development (ASTD), the green economy will continue to generate millions of new jobs and hundreds of billions of dollars in revenues. The ASTD cites the National Renewable Energy Lab, which claims that the chief barrier to the adoption of renewable energy and energy efficiency strategies is lack of skill and training. In 2007, President George W. Bush signed the Green Jobs Act. The purpose of the act is to train workers for green collar jobs.

The act authorized US$125 million per year to finance the Energy Efficiency and Renewable Energy Worker Training Program, a program designed for veterans, at-risk younger people, displaced workers, and families living in poverty.

The job outlook for training and development specialists is bright. The BLS projects that the number of training and development specialists will grow to 267,100 by 2018. This increase of 23 percent over 2008 is much faster than the average rate of growth for all occupations. This job growth is driven in part by the United States' conversion to a green economy, which will demand an increase in the number of professionals who can provide training in new industries and promote green practices in existing industries.

EARNINGS

According to the BLS, the average annual salary for a training and development specialist in 2010 was US$57,280. Starting salaries for trainers with a bachelor's degree were about US$45,000 per year. Those in the 10th percentile earned US$31,110; those in the 90th percentile earned US$89,490. The middle half earned between US$40,640 and US$71,170 per year. Salaries, however, can vary depending on the industry sector. Average salaries for trainers in computer systems design and related services were US$61,110; for those in hospitals, US$56,540; for those in insurance companies, US$55,190; and for those involved in the management of companies, US$54,800. Local government trainers earned US$52,080, whereas those in state government earned US$48,480.

The top-paying states for training and development specialists were the District of Columbia, Washington, New Jersey, California, and Connecticut. The lowest-paying states were Montana, North and South Dakota, Oklahoma, Arkansas, and Mississippi.

RELATED OCCUPATIONS

- Training and development managers
- Management analysts
- Instructional coordinators
- Recreation workers
- First-line supervisors of office and administrative support workers

SOURCES OF ADDITIONAL INFORMATION

Green Advantage Environmental Certification. http:// greenadvantage.org
Green Collar Association. http://www.greencollar.org
Green for All. http://greenforall.org

FURTHER READING

Bhatia, Palak, Times of India Group. *Green Training Is a Concept That Is Fast Catching Up in the Professional World Today.* Last updated November 15, 2011. Accessed February 16, 2012. http://www.itsmyascent .com/web/itsmyascent/hr-zone/-/asset_publisher/ 4htH/content/helping-companies-go-green.

Bureau of Labor Statistics, U.S. Department of Labor. "Human Resources, Training, and Labor Relations Managers and Specialists." In *Occupational Outlook Handbook 2010–11 Edition.* Accessed February 16, 2012. http://www.bls.gov/oco/ocos021.htm.

———. "Training and Development Specialists." Accessed February 16, 2012. http://www.bls.gov/ oes/current/oes131151.htm.

Deutsche Bank. *Banking on Green—Passion for Sustainability.* Accessed April 5, 2012. http://www .banking-on-green.com/index_e.htm.

European Centre for the Development of Vocational Training. *Future Skill Needs for the Green Economy: Skill Needs for Green Jobs and Sustainable Development.* Dictus Publishing: Thessaloniki, Greece, 2011. Available at http://www.cedefop .europa.eu/EN/Files/5501_en.pdf.

Fien, John, Rupert Maclean, and Man-Gon Park, eds. *Work, Learning and Sustainable Development: Opportunities and Challenges (Technical and Vocational Education and Training: Issues, Concerns and Prospects).* New York: Springer, 2010.

Green Advantage. *Green Advantage Environmental Certification.* Accessed February 16, 2012. http:// www.greenadvantage.org.

Green Collar Association. *Featured Educational Institutions.* Accessed February 16, 2012. http:// www.greencollar.org/environmental_education.php.

Green for All. *The Green Jobs Act.* Accessed February 16, 2012. http://www.greenforall.org/what-we-do/ working-with-washington/the-green-jobs-act.

Mills, Stacy. "ASTD Creates Training Resources to Meet 'Green' Trend." *ASTD*, October 9, 2009. Accessed April 3, 2012. http://www1.astd.org/Blog/post/ASTD-Creates-Training-Resources-to-Meet-Green-Trend.aspx.

O*NET OnLine. *Training and Development Specialists.* Accessed February 16, 2012. http://www.onetonline .org/link/summary/13-1151.00.

Warren, Michael. *Principles of Green Learning for Corporate Training and Development.* Accessed February 16, 2012. http://www.bestthinking.com.

INSULATION WORKERS, FLOOR, CEILING, AND WALL

NATURE OF THE WORK

Proper insulation reduces energy consumption by maintaining climate control in a building while keeping out cold in winter and heat in summer. Floor, ceiling, and wall insulation workers apply insulation in attics and exterior walls. An insulation worker blows in loose-fill insulation while a helper feeds a machine with fiberglass, cellulose, or rock-wool insulation. Meanwhile, another worker uses a compressor hose to blow the insulation into the space being filled. For covering walls or other flat surfaces, insulation workers may use a hose to spray foam insulation onto a wire mesh that provides a rough surface that adds strength to the finished surface and allows the foam to cling to it. This may be followed by a drywall installation or an application of a final coat of plaster for a finished appearance. Insulation workers staple fiberglass or rock-wool batts to exterior walls and ceilings in new construction or on major renovations before the drywall, paneling, or plaster walls are put into place.

The environmental aspect of insulation is significant. Most insulators understand that people are more conscious of energy consumption in the 21st century and that proper insulation can reduce up to 95 percent of heat losses and gains. Most (85 percent) of the energy consumed in the United States comes from fossil fuels, which may soon be too rare and valuable to spend. The by-products of these combustion fuels are carbon dioxide and water vapor, which are greenhouse gases and hence contribute to climate change. Proper insulation helps alleviate these problems.

Not only is insulation a cost-effective way of preserving natural resources, but mechanical engineer

Christopher P. Crall considers it one of the best sustainable technologies available, giving it the label "greener than trees." He calculates that "one would need to plant roughly 46 trees to achieve the same CO_2 reductions achievable by insulating one foot of 350°F pipe."

In addition, insulators may use recycled materials and materials that are produced locally to be easier on the environment.

WORKING CONDITIONS

Insulation workers may work with hazardous materials and the job can be dangerous. In general, the work is indoors in residential and industrial settings. Insulators spend most of the workday on their feet, standing, bending, or kneeling. They often work in confined spaces or on ladders. Coordination rather than strength is a requirement in the profession. Workers in industrial settings often insulate pipes and vessels at high temperatures, making burns a possibility. In addition, the work can irritate the eyes, skin, and respiratory system because of the release of minute particles from insulation materials, especially when they are blown.

There is a high rate of injuries and illnesses in this profession and therefore workers must follow strict safety guidelines. They need protection from insulating irritants. Safety requirements include working in well-ventilated areas; wearing protective suits, masks, and respirators; and taking decontamination showers if necessary. Because insulation is usually applied after buildings are enclosed, weather conditions are less relevant to the work environment than to the work environment of some other construction workers.

According to one professional, "Construction jobs are a little stressful, mostly because of schedules and deadlines and the pressure of completing the job in the correct time. Most construction work is done during the day, during the week though it is much earlier than normal office jobs. I would say the average day starts at 6:00 AM to 7:00 AM and will end 8 hours later, Monday through Friday."

Overtime pay is dictated by the government for hourly workers and also by union labor agreements. There could be instances, however, in which workers are not paid overtime.

The nature of the work environment varies. Construction workers in general enjoy and take great pride in their work. However, there are times during the construction process when they may experience uncomfortable temperatures and conditions.

EMPLOYMENT

About 92 percent of insulation workers were employed in the construction industry, with 50 percent working for drywall and insulation contractors. In 2008 28,000 floor, ceiling, and wall insulators were employed, with a faster-than-average projected growth rate of 14 to 19 percent by 2018.

In an interview, a professional insulator reported that "Building construction hasn't taken off as much as we would like in the last year so employment is still down a little compared to five or so years ago. I am hopeful that work is on the horizon and we will help get those unemployed in the industry back to work."

TRAINING, OTHER QUALIFICATIONS, AND ADVANCEMENT

The U.S. Environmental Protection Agency (EPA) offers mandatory certification for insulation workers who work with asbestos. Insulation contractor organizations have developed voluntary certification programs to help workers demonstrate and prove their skills and knowledge of residential and industrial insulation. To determine if and how insulation can benefit industrial customers, the National Insulation Association offers a certification in performing an energy appraisal.

Workers who demonstrate their skill may advance to supervisor, shop superintendent, or insulation contract estimator. Alternatively, they may set up their own insulation business. Advancement opportunities depend on the employer and the amount of work available. In general, if the employee performs at a high level and is dependable, he or she will advance to a position of more responsibility and therefore more money.

For those who aspire to advance in the field, being bilingual in Spanish and English is a huge plus. Spanish-speaking workers make up a large part of the construction workforce in many areas of the United States and the ability to communicate instructions in both languages puts workers at a significant advantage.

Educational requirements are minimal. Although not all workers have graduated from high school, employers prefer to hire high school graduates. Prospective workers who have taken high school courses in blueprint reading, shop mathematics, science, pattern layout, woodworking, and general construction are also at an advantage in the profession.

Experienced insulation workers provide instruction and supervision to most new workers. Trainees begin with simple jobs, including carrying insulation or holding material while it is being fastened into place. It can take up to four years to complete on-the-job training. Typically, learning to install insulation in residential buildings requires less training than in commercial and industrial buildings. As workers' experience increases and they require less supervision, their pay increases.

During all phases of insulation, trainees in formal apprenticeship programs receive in-depth instruction. Contractors who install and maintain mechanical industrial insulation generally provide apprenticeships. A joint committee of local insulation contractors and the local union of the International Association of Heat and Frost Insulators and Allied Workers may also provide apprenticeship programs. Programs usually include four or five years of on-the-job training with classroom instruction. To demonstrate their knowledge of the trade, apprentices must pass practical and written tests.

Personal attributes that are helpful in the job include initiative, dependability, attention to detail, cooperation, persistence to overcome obstacles, achievement and effort, adaptability and flexibility, integrity, self-control, and innovation. Physical abilities are of great importance to this work, including manual dexterity, trunk strength, and stamina.

JOB OUTLOOK

There is an excellent outlook for job opportunities for insulation workers. Not only are there opportunities created by a growing demand for insulation workers, but job openings will arise from the need to replace workers who retire or otherwise leave the labor force. However, many insulation workers leave the occupation each year due to the irritating nature of many insulation materials, combined with the fact that the working conditions are often difficult.

The growth rate is good considering the impact of the new international Energy Conservation Code requirements for additional insulation in buildings. Naturally, the growth rate is directly related to the economy.

Considering the current state of new and rehabilitation work, the competition is strong for the few positions available. Job security depends entirely on the employer and on the employee's performance. In insulation work as in all construction jobs, an employee must go where the work is.

Union workers get health benefits as part of the union agreement under which they are working. In an open shop (non-union), health benefits depend entirely on the employer's ability to provide them.

EARNINGS

The average salary for insulation workers is a median hourly wage of US$17.37, or average annual salary of US$36,120. The pay scale for union workers again depends on the union agreement. Open-shop workers are usually paid what the market will bear. All federal government work is covered by the Davis-Bacon Act. The contracting officer for the federal agency procuring construction work will issue a wage rate determination for all craft workers. This states the minimum compensation they are entitled to receive for the project they issue for bidding. The wages will vary depending on the region of the country where the work is being performed. The wage rate determination is a matter of public record. Consult the U.S. Department of Labor for details.

RELATED OCCUPATIONS

- Carpenters
- Carpet, floor, and tile installers and finishers
- Drywall and ceiling tile installers, tapers, plasterers, and stucco masons
- Roofers
- Sheet metal workers

SOURCES OF ADDITIONAL INFORMATION

National Insulation Association. http://www.insulation .org/index.cfm

Insulation Outlook magazine. http://www.insulation.org

International Association of Heat and Frost Insulators and Allied Workers. http://www.insulators.org

North American Insulation Manufacturers' Association. http://www.naima.org

FURTHER READING

Bureau of Labor Statistics, U.S. Department of Labor. "47-2131 Insulation Workers, Floor, Ceiling, and Wall." In *Occupational Employment Statistics: Occupational Employment and Wages, May 2010.* Accessed March 19, 2012. http://www.bls.gov/oes/ current/oes472131.htm.

———. "Insulation Workers." In *Occupational Outlook Handbook, 2010–11 Edition.* Accessed March 19, 2012. http://www.bls.gov/oco/ocos208.htm.

Careers.Org. *Occupation Profile for Insulation Workers, Floor, Ceiling and Wall.* Accessed March 19, 2012. http://occupations.careers.org/47-2131.00/ insulation-workers-floor-ceiling-and-wall.

Cavey, Brian. Personal e-mail interview, January 24, 2012.

Crall, Christopher P. "Insulation: Greener than Trees!" *Insulation Outlook,* January 2009. Accessed March 19, 2012. http://www.insulation.org/articles/article .cfm?id=IO090101.

National Mechanical Insulation Committee. *Mechanical Insulation Design Guide—Materials and Systems,* updated August 16, 2011. Accessed March 19, 2012. http://www.wbdg.org/design/midg_materials.php.

Occupational Safety and Health Administration. *Green Jobs Hazards: Weather Insulating/Sealing.* Accessed March 19, 2012. http://www.osha.gov/dep/ greenjobs/weather_spf.html.

O*Net OnLine. *Summary Report for Insulation Workers, Floor, Ceiling, and Wall.* Accessed March 19, 2012. http://www.onetonline.org/link/summary/ 47-2131.00.

Smith, Don. Personal interview by e-mail, February 7, 2012.

SECTOR OVERVIEW: ENERGY TRADING

INDUSTRIES IN THE ENERGY TRADING SECTOR

Although the Global Industry Classification Standard used by Morgan Stanley defines the energy system as comprising companies primarily working with oil, gas, coal, and consumable fuels, it is made up of many sub-industries with specific functions in the world energy market.

The energy industry is a complex market made up of a variety of activities and products associated with petroleum and gas, electricity, coal, nuclear fission, water, wind, solar, and firewood. The petroleum industry includes oil companies, petroleum refiners, fuel transport, and end-user sales at gas stations. The gas industry includes natural gas extraction, gas manufacture, and natural gas distribution. The electrical power industry includes electricity generation, electric power distribution, and electricity sales. The coal industry includes coal mining, refining, and power-generating operations. The nuclear power industry uses nuclear fission to generate electricity and heat. The renewable energy industry creates alternative and sustainable energy and technologies, including hydroelectric power, wind power, and solar power generation. The traditional energy industry collects and distributes firewood for cooking and heating.

Natural gas and electricity are major commodities in the energy market, along with coal, nuclear power, hydroelectric power, solar power, wind energy, and oil. Deregulation of the energy industry has resulted in more active trading and has turned it into a major financial market. Energy trading involves both physical and financial trades and delivery and receipt of energy products as well as cash transfer. Further analysis of the energy industry and energy trading reveals market division into spot markets and the forward market, reflecting both the local and futures aspects of this vast industry. The energy trading industry's primary activities are buying and selling common and alternative energy as a commodity, but it encompasses many specialized professions such as carbon credit traders, carbon trading analysts, energy brokers, investment underwriters, and securities and commodities traders.

HOW THE ENERGY TRADING INDUSTRY IS GOING GREEN

Along with conventional gas, oil, and electricity, renewable energy is a large part of the energy trading industry. The industry is going green in many ways, encouraging innovations in renewable resources while saving money and the environment. The Obama administration has supported and encouraged many different green energy initiatives. The U.S. Department of Energy offers millions of grant and investment dollars through a wide variety of incentive programs for green energy, including grants for advanced hydropower technologies, grants for offshore wind power, investments in carbon capture technologies, and smart grid workforce training programs.

Pumped storage hydropower is the largest capacity form of grid energy storage available as of 2011, storing energy in the form of water to be used during high electrical demands and accessed by pumping. In 2011 U.S. Department of Energy grants were awarded for pumped storage hydropower plants in Illinois and

California, a 51-mile hydroelectric power project in Oregon, a small hydropower research and development project in Colorado, and a low-head hydropower unit in Texas.

Green energy technologies include development of wind power technologies without the traditional challenges of unsightly equipment, noise, and capacity of existing wind turbines. In 2011 U.S. Department of Energy grants were awarded to many organizations in the southern and eastern United States for wind power projects. Pennsylvania State University is developing a computer model cyber wind facility to generate wind turbine farm data. ABB, Inc., in North Carolina is identifying offshore wind development sites and studying wind energy collection and delivery. The BioDiversity Research Institute in Maine is studying marine animals at risk in offshore wind power operations.

In 2011 U.S. Department of Energy grants were also awarded for carbon capture technology projects to study and implement ways to prevent carbon dioxide from being released into the atmosphere. Throughout the United States, organizations such as the University of North Carolina, Georgia Tech Research Corporation, and GE Global Research in Niskayuna, New York, are studying and developing sorbents, solvents, and membranes to capture and contain harmful carbons and prevent their release into the air and atmosphere.

The U.S. Department of Energy and the American Recovery and Reinvestment Act of 2009 provided $100 million dollars for 52 smart grid training programs to train 30,000 U.S. workers in smart grid technologies. Smart grid training prepares people to be part of a workforce, including technicians, engineers, and managers for the electric power sector, modernizing electrical power systems and sustainable carbon management. Community colleges and state universities as well as energy companies such as General Electric and Mississippi Power, received smart grid workforce training funds.

DEVELOPMENTS RELATED TO USING NEW GREENER ENERGY TECHNOLOGIES

Green technology developments in energy production are supported by entities such as the Office of Fossil Energy, the U.S. Energy Information Administration, and the Office of Nuclear Energy.

Innovative, clean coal-based technologies will benefit U.S. energy security while reducing the environmental impact of carbon-producing energy processes. For instance, CPS Energy of San Antonio, Texas, plans to purchase power from the Texas Clean Energy Project, which is developing clean coal production with integrated gasification combined cycle, which produces just 10 percent of the emissions of traditional coal plants.

The Obama administration's Green Button Initiative provides plans to give consumers access to their electrical energy usage data so they can reduce consumption, save energy, and understand their options for green improvements such as residential solar power.

Lead-free solder technology involves solder from tin, silver, and copper patented by Ames Laboratory for use in electronics and the military, reducing environmental toxins and pollutants. This alternative solder is not only clean and green, but it provides stronger solder seals than traditional lead solder.

Small modular nuclear reactors, which can be flexible to locations and population needs and are safer designs than large permanent nuclear reactors, are rapidly being designed in 2012. They will provide savings in cost and energy production as well as safer, cleaner energy.

SOURCES OF ADDITIONAL INFORMATION

U.S. Department of Energy. http://energy.gov

FURTHER READING

Asplund, Richard W. *Profiting from Clean Energy: A Complete Guide to Trading Green in Solar, Wind, Ethanol, Fuel Cell, Carbon Credit Industries, and More.* Hoboken, New Jersey: John Wiley & Sons, Inc., 2008.

British Petroleum. *Statistical Review of World Energy 2011.* Accessed March 8, 2012. http://www.bp.com/sectionbodycopy.do?categoryId=7500&contentId=7068481.

Edwards, Davis W. *Energy Trading and Investing: Trading, Risk Management and Structuring Deals in the Energy Market.* New York: McGraw-Hill, 2009.

Global Association of Risk Professionals. *Foundations of Energy Risk Management: An Overview of the Energy Sector and Its Physical and Financial Markets.* Hoboken, New Jersey: John Wiley & Sons, Inc., 2008.

Morgan Stanley Capital International. *Standard & Poor's Global Industry Classification Standard.* Accessed March 8, 2012. http://www.mscibarra.com/resources/pdfs/MK-GICS-DIR-3-02.pdf.

Murray, Barrie. *Power Markets and Economics: Energy Costs, Trading, Emissions.* Oxford, UK: John Wiley & Sons, Ltd., 2009.

Newel, Peter, Max Boykoff, and Emily Boyd. *The New Carbon Economy: Constitution, Governance and Contestation.* Oxford, UK: Wiley-Blackwell, 2012.

Shively, Bob, and John Ferrare. *Understanding Today's Electricity Business.* Laporte, Colorado: Enerdynamics LLC, 2009.

———. *Understanding Today's Natural Gas Business.* Laporte, Colorado: Enerdynamics LLC, 2010.

Spurga, Ronald C. *Commodity Fundamentals.* Hoboken, New Jersey: John Wiley & Sons, Inc., 2006.

U.S. Department of Energy. *News & Blog.* Accessed March 8, 2012. http://energy.gov/news-blog.

CARBON CREDIT TRADERS

NATURE OF THE WORK

With the 21st century reality of pollution damage and regulatory and legislative controls comes the responsibility and legal requirement to reduce and eliminate carbon emissions. Carbon credits, the government regulated rights to emit a specified amount of carbon dioxide into the environment, are treated as a commodity in the world energy market and are regulated similar to securities. Commodities agents experienced in the financial markets and the regulation of carbon emissions handle the trading and selling of carbon credits. Carbon credit traders provide advisory services to companies and corporations regarding the value of carbon credits and how to obtain and use them. They also work directly with exchanges trading in carbon allowances, such as the Chicago Climate Exchange, European Climate Exchange, NASDAQ OMX Commodities Europe, and the European Energy Exchange.

Although carbon markets are important, they are unstable. Despite this instability, they remain key to the solutions to climate change threats. Carbon trading is a vital, challenging, and lucrative career. A carbon trader sells carbon credits from companies with excess credits to companies who have exceeded legal limits for emissions and need to buy rights to emit excess. When a company or corporation wishes to buy or sell carbon credits, carbon credit traders relay the order through the appropriate exchange, negotiating prices, making sales, and handling all aspects of the transactions. Traders must know the current and prospective future market values, existing and pending legislation and regulations, and the trading processes in the exchanges.

AT A GLANCE FACT BOX

Preferred Education: Bachelor's degree in business, finance, accounting, or economics

Average Salary: US$95,000 annually

Other Information: Traders with advanced education and industry certification will have increased opportunities for advancement. Some organizations, such as the Chicago Climate Exchange in Illinois, require traders to register with their organization to participate in carbon credit trading. As of 2012, there are six exchanges worldwide that trade in carbon allowances: the European Climate Exchange in London, England; the Chicago Climate Exchange; NASDAQ OMX Commodities Europe in Oslo, Norway; Powernext in Paris, France; Commodity Exchange Bratislava in Slovakia; and the European Energy Exchange in Leipzig, Germany.

Carbon credit traders' jobs have developed and evolved in the securities and exchange industry from similar financial industry careers such as stockbrokers and traders. They are green industry sector jobs involved in reducing pollution through financial incentives. Carbon credit trader positions have been in existence since 1990 with the U.S. Clean Air Act, which prompted the Acid Rain Program (a U.S. Environmental Protection Agency program meant to reduce the emissions of sulfur dioxide and nitrogen oxides, which are the main causes of acid rain); 1997 with the Kyoto Protocol in Japan; and 2001 with the Marrakesh Accords in Morocco.

Carbon credit traders are part of the complex financial and green industries. New and significant pollution reduction technologies, such as carbon-capturing sorbents, solvents, and films, affect the current and future value of carbon credits. Companies that produce carbon emissions and the carbon credit traders with which they work must be knowledgeable in cap and trade policies and systems, carbon finance, carbon leakage, carbon offset, carbon projects, voluntary emissions reductions, and energy speculation. All of which are considered areas of expertise in the Energy Trading Green Sector.

Carbon credits are assets whose existence and value fluctuate depending on evolving legislation and regulation. Successful handling of carbon credits involves risk but has the potential for great monetary reward. Careers in carbon credit trading have a global scope with opportunities to handle trades in different areas of the world depending on clientele and location. With the market for carbon credits and trading emission rights more than doubling each year, the sophistication required of those in the energy trading industry must keep pace. Knowing the markets, keeping up with evolving legislations and governing bodies, and managing the inherent risk in commodities requires knowledgeable, experienced traders.

WORKING CONDITIONS

The typical working conditions of carbon credit traders are comfortable offices and busy, stressful work environments. Traders spend their work hours in offices, exchange floors, customer meetings, and other corporate settings. Carbon credit traders work 40 to 50 hours per week. They use computers, mobile phones, and other communications devices, and they consult with financial and carbon industry experts. They follow the financial and environmental industries by watching environmental trends, energy markets, and economic developments. Career advancement requires advanced education and training requiring ongoing learning in the form of industry certifications, conferences, and degrees such as MBAs.

EMPLOYMENT

As of 2008, the U.S. Department of Labor's Bureau of Labor Statistics (BLS) reported there were more than 300,000 securities, commodities, and financial services sales agents in the United States, including carbon credit traders. About half of these financial industry employees work in stock exchanges and banking operations in or near major metropolitan areas. The worldwide credit trading market was estimated to be a US$30 billion industry

in 2008 with speculations of growth to US$1 trillion by 2018 and accompanying job growth for those in energy trading positions.

Reviews of energy trends and usage in 2010 showed strong growth. The future demand for energy will fuel the need for controlling carbon emissions and carbon credit trading. Growth of all securities and commodities employment is expected to increase 9 percent between 2010 and 2018. Established carbon credit traders with advanced training and knowledge of market conditions will have the best employment prospects.

Occupations related to carbon credit trading include financial analysts, insurance sales, financial advisors, and real estate brokers. Similar training, knowledge, and skill sets are used in these careers. Knowledge of and experience with global finance and business management are foundations of the advancement of a carbon credit trader.

TRAINING, OTHER QUALIFICATIONS, AND ADVANCEMENT

A bachelor's degree in business, finance, accounting, or economics is the minimum level of education required for carbon credit traders. Sales experience in areas such as real estate, insurance, and other financial vehicles is strongly preferred. An MBA or professional certification is the norm, as well as advanced training through industry conferences and seminars such as the Carbon Expo and the Wall Street Green Trading Summit. Traders in the financial services sectors must obtain securities licensure.

There are many colleges and universities, such as the University of Houston's Bauer College of Business and Harvard Business School, that offer green industry coursework as part of undergraduate and graduate degrees. Many trading firms seek new college graduates with solid internship experience to learn on the job and through industry educational services. Financial industry experience is a vital component in this career path. Carbon credit trading education and training takes between five and 10 years, depending on the degree programs sought.

JOB OUTLOOK

The BLS reported that, as of 2010, competition was high for securities, commodities, and financial services, including carbon credit trading. Business professionals with finance education and experience who are interested in the carbon markets have good opportunities for lucrative careers. The states with the highest concentrations of jobs in commodities are New York, California, Texas, Illinois, and Florida. The top-paying states for commodities jobs include Connecticut; New York; Washington, DC; Maine; and Arkansas. Top-paying cities for commodities jobs include Bridgeport, Connecticut; San Francisco, California; and New York, New York.

EARNINGS

In 2010 the average annual wage for securities and commodities professionals was US$95,000, with top wages reaching six figures. Industries paying the highest wages for securities and commodities careers include securities and commodity contracts intermediation and brokerage, depository credit intermediation, and management of companies and industries.

The five states with the highest annual wages in securities and commodities in 2010 were Connecticut (US$168,000), California (US$140,000), New York (US$128,000), North Carolina (US$128,000), and Arkansas (US$127,000). The states with the lowest annual wages (less than US$75,000) include Nevada, Michigan, Ohio, Kentucky, and Kansas.

RELATED OCCUPATIONS

Jobs related to carbon trading analysts include accountants and auditors, actuaries, budget analysts, financial managers, insurance sales agents, insurance underwriters, personal financial advisors, and securities, commodities, and financial services sales agents. Financial professionals similar to carbon trading analysts also work to promote the financial industries and professional accreditation in such organizations as the Financial Industry Regulatory Authority, the American Academy of Financial Management, and the Certified Financial Analyst Institute.

SOURCES OF ADDITIONAL INFORMATION

Bayon, Ricardo, Amanda Hawn, and Katherine Hamilton. *Voluntary Carbon Market: An International Business Guide to What They Are and How They Work.* UK and USA: Earthscan, 2009.

Burger, Marcus. *Managing Energy Risk: An Integrated View on Power and Other Energy Markets.* West Sussex, England: John Wiley & Sons Ltd., 2007.

Chorafas, Dimitri N. *Energy, Environment, Natural Resources and Business.* Surrey, England: Gower Publishing Limited, 2011.

Freestone, David, and Charlotte Streck. *Legal Aspects of Carbon Trading: Kyoto, Copenhagen and Beyond.* New York: Oxford University Press, Inc., 2009.

John, Klaus D., and Dirk Rubbelke. *Sustainable Energy.* Abingdon, Oxon, and New York, New York: Routledge, 2011.

Labatt, Sonia, and Rodney R. White. *Carbon Finance: The Financial Implications of Climate Change.* Hoboken, New Jersey: John Wiley & Sons, Inc., 2007.

Newell, Peter, Max Boykoff, and Emily Boyd. *The New Carbon Economy: Constitution, Governance and Contestation.* West Sussex, UK: John Wiley & Sons Ltd, 2012.

FURTHER READING

Asplund, Richard W. *Profiting from Clean Energy.* Hoboken, New Jersey: John Wiley & Sons, 2008.

BP. *Energy Outlook 2030.* Accessed April 16, 2012. http://www.bp.com/sectiongenericarticle800.do?categoryId=9037134&contentId=7068677.

Bureau of Labor Statistics, U.S. Department of Labor. "41-3031 Securities, Commodities, and Financial Services Sales Agents." In *Occupational Employment Statistics: Occupational Employment and Wages, May 2010.* Accessed April 16, 2012. http://www.bls.gov/oes/current/oes413031.htm.

———. "Securities, Commodities, and Financial Services Sales Agents." In *Occupational Outlook Handbook, 2010–2011 Edition.* Accessed April 16, 2012. http://www.bls.gov/oco/ocos122.htm#oes_links.

Environmental Protection Agency. *Acid Rain Program.* Accessed April 16, 2012. http://www.epa.gov/airmarkets/progsregs/arp/index.html.

Green Careers Guide. *Carbon Trader.* Accessed April 16, 2012. http://www.greencareersguide.com/Carbon-Trader.html.

United Nations Framework Convention on Climate Change. *Kyoto Protocol.* Accessed April 16, 2012. http://unfccc.int/kyoto_protocol/items/3145.php.

CARBON TRADING ANALYSTS

NATURE OF THE WORK

The carbon market is a complex financial system based on reducing carbon emissions through trading carbon credits, which are permits to emit a specific amount of carbon dioxide. Carbon credits are an alternative to taxing or regulating credit emissions and create financial incentives for pollution control rather than penalties. Jobs held by carbon trading analysts are career positions in the financial industry, specifically the carbon trading industry, and are part of a larger green industry working toward clean energy solutions in a global economy. Carbon trading is a large commodity market with many opportunities for financial gain. Whereas carbon traders buy and sell credits for clients, carbon trading analysts study current and developing carbon markets and emissions legislation and programs and report on activities, trends, and advances in the carbon industry. Analysts in academic settings may focus more on carbon policies and government programs, whereas analysts in private industry positions may focus more exclusively on predicting the impact of pricing on carbon trading programs and legislation. For example, David Victor and Michael Wara, two leading Stanford University carbon trade analysts, have authored working papers and articles about the successes and failures of carbon markets.

Carbon trading analysts often work in academia or private companies, or as public commodities brokers. They work in business, government, and academic office settings, studying and reporting on complex financial aspects of carbon emissions controls. They work with other professionals such as investment consultants and bankers, securities and commodities brokers, and portfolio management professionals in the securities and commodities industry. Carbon trading is

AT A GLANCE FACT BOX

Preferred Education: Bachelor's degree in an area such as finance, computer science, or mathematics
Average Salary: US$70,000 to US$86,000 annually
Other Information: The carbon market is viewed as the best way to control and reduce pollution. Carbon trading analysts must stay informed of new zero-emissions technologies such as carbon capture and storage in the green trading sector. Pending legislation and regulations regarding carbon emissions create opportunities for carbon trading analysts.

intertwined with the green industry and the financial industry, and has the potential for serious growth by the year 2020 according to industry predictions. Several countries, including the United States, are either considering or in the process of implementing cap and trade programs that will substantially increase carbon credit trading. Carbon market analysts closely follow global developments and predict and estimate volumes and prices in carbon credits based on clean energy industry trends and activities.

As part of the clean energy markets and green industry in the financial sector, carbon trading analysts:

- Study trends and pending legislation and research and develop analytical tools for carbon trading pricing models, market dynamics measurements, and trading systems performance

- Confer with carbon market experts and specialists about trading strategies, market developments, and industry trends and indicators
- Analyze strengths and weaknesses of carbon credit programs
- Predict trends in growth and prices for carbon trading based on current and historical data and emerging governmental policies
- Report on carbon market indicators such as securities trading, risk management, and carbon market regulation

WORKING CONDITIONS

Typical working conditions of carbon trading analysts are physically comfortable and mentally challenging. Analysts work in office environments with other business and industry professionals, use computers, and consult with professionals and experts in industries such as clean energy markets, carbon trading, financial markets, and academic research. An analyst's work involves compiling and comprehending data, which involves much reading and writing. They may publish research papers, newspaper, magazine, and trade journal articles, and books. Hours for carbon trading analysts are long, normally 50 hours per week, because of the intense data-based and research-based nature of their work. Their work may also include travel for conference and association attendance and training or business meeting attendance in other countries.

EMPLOYMENT

As of 2008, there were more than 250,000 financial analysts in the United States, a number that includes carbon trading analysts. Many work in major financial centers or large academic settings. Others work in government and private industry. Graduates with degrees in science, technology, finance, mathematics, and computer science and who have finance and carbon market experience have an advantage in competition for carbon trading analyst jobs.

TRAINING, OTHER QUALIFICATIONS, AND ADVANCEMENT

Financial analysts in the carbon market and clean energy industry must have a bachelor's degree, and advanced positions require a master's degree. Most companies require a degree in finance, business, statistics, or economics. Advanced degrees are usually preferred and having knowledge of or experience in advanced finance-related areas such as bond valuation and risk management are advantageous. Knowledge of and experience in political

science, globalization, and clean energy trends worldwide are areas of specialization valuable to carbon trading analysts.

Because credit trading analysts study and report on areas involving securities, different licenses may be required and can be obtained from the Financial Industry Regulatory Authority. Special licensure is normally employer-sponsored and specific to a company's business needs, not required before hire. Financial analysts work with advanced data tools including spreadsheets, statistical packages, mathematical software, and sophisticated numerical modeling programs. Carbon trading markets often include foreign markets and analysts with international expertise will have opportunities to work with companies that maintain global positions. Advanced training in and knowledge of foreign markets, cultures, and governmental developments in emissions control is helpful.

There are special financial analyst certifications for carbon trading analysts. The Chartered Financial Analyst designation is sponsored by the CFA Institute and requires a four-year degree, four years of related work experience, and specialized study to pass three rigorous exams in advanced areas such as financial markets and instruments, asset valuation, and securities analysis.

Carbon trading analysts also benefit from industry association memberships for education, industry knowledge, and introduction to industry experts. The International Emissions Trading Association (IETA) has working groups that share knowledge and discussion of issues including emerging trading markets, U.S. market oversight, carbon capture and storage, and voluntary markets. IETA also hosts business roundtables, industry briefings by experts, and conferences and organizes carbon market trade fairs and forums. The Climate Markets & Investment Association (CMIA), an international trade association for those involved in finance and investments in emissions reduction, provides advocacy, facilitates industry knowledge, and educates members on carbon market issues.

Advancement as a carbon trading analyst involves moving into areas of specialized knowledge and experience, publishing relevant and accurate papers and books, or leading large teams of effective carbon market analysts.

JOB OUTLOOK

The U.S. Department of Labor's Bureau of Labor Statistics (BLS) reports that employment of financial analysts is expected to grow much faster than average, with tough competition for new graduates. Although financial analyst jobs are expected to increase by 20 percent between 2008 and 2018, carbon trading analyst jobs are affected by market and government policy changes and may not grow as fast as traditional financial analyst positions. Strong educational preparation with an advanced degree in finance or business along with specialization in international finance or clean energy markets is recommended.

States that lead the nation in the employment of financial analysts are Delaware, Massachusetts, New York, and Connecticut, along with Washington, DC. The metropolitan areas with the highest employment of analysts are New York, New York; Boston, Massachusetts; Chicago, Illinois; Los Angeles, California; and Washington, DC. The metropolitan areas with the highest concentration of analysts relative to the total number of jobs in the area include Bridgeport–Stamford–Norwalk, Connecticut; Boston–Cambridge–Quincy, Massachusetts; New York, New York; Wilmington, Delaware; and San Francisco, California.

EARNINGS

As of May 2010, the mean hourly wage for financial analysts was US$41.36, and the mean annual wage was US$86,040. Top wages reached more than US$140,000 annually. Top paying states for financial analysts in 2010 were New York (US$108,790), Connecticut (US$100,560), California (US$99,580), Oregon (US$94,040), along with the District of Columbia (US$93,470). Top paying cities included Bridgeport, Connecticut; San Francisco, California; New York, New York; Naples, Florida; and Los Angeles, California.

RELATED OCCUPATIONS

Jobs related to carbon trading analysts include accountants and auditors, actuaries, budget analysts, financial managers, insurance sales agents, insurance underwriters, personal financial advisors, and securities, commodities, and financial services sales agents. Financial professionals similar to carbon trading analysts also work to promote the financial industries and professional accreditation in such organizations as the Financial Industry Regulatory Authority, the American Academy of Financial Management, and the Certified Financial Analyst Institute.

SOURCES OF ADDITIONAL INFORMATION

International Emissions Trading Association. http://www
.ieta.org

FURTHER READING

Asplund, Richard W. *Profiting from Clean Energy.* Hoboken, New Jersey: John Wiley & Sons, 2008.

Bayon, Ricardo, Amanda Hawn, and Katherine Hamilton. *Voluntary Carbon Market: An International Business Guide to What They Are and How They Work.* UK and USA: Earthscan, 2009.

Brohe, Arnaud, Nick Eyre, and Nicholas Howarth. *Carbon Markets: An International Business Guide.* UK and USA: Earthscan, 2009.

Bureau of Labor Statistics, U.S. Department of Labor. "Financial Analysts." In *Occupational Outlook Handbook, 2010-11 Edition.* Accessed February 16, 2012. http://www.bls.gov/oco/ocos301.htm.

———. "13-2051 Financial Analysts." In *Occupational Employment Statistics, Occupational Employment and Wages, May 2010.* Accessed February 16, 2012. http://www.bls.gov/oes/current/oes132051.htm.

Cassio, Jim, and Alice Rush. *Green Careers.* Gabriola Island, British Columbia, Canada: New Society Publishers, 2009.

cbsalary.com. *Carbon Trading Analyst Salary.* Accessed February 16, 2012. http://www.cbsalary.com/salary-calculator/chart/Carbon+Trading+Analyst?usd=1&uas=&kw=VP%2C+International+Equity+Sales+Trading&ujt=&jn=&tid=230744&ns=1.

Chorafas, Dimitri N. *Energy, Environment, Natural Resources and Business.* Surrey, England: Gower Publishing Limited, 2011.

GlassDoor.com. *Trading Analyst Salaries.* Accessed February 16, 2012. http://www.glassdoor.com/Salaries/trading-analyst-salary-SRCH_KO0,15.htm.

Hashmi, Dr. M.A. *A Complete Guide to the Global Carbon Market.* Shreveport, Louisiana: Max Energy, 2009.

Newell, Peter, Max Boykoff, and Emily Boyd. *The New Carbon Economy: Constitution, Governance and Contestation.* West Sussex, UK: John Wiley & Sons, 2012.

The New York Times Energy & Environment. "Carbon Trading May Be Ready for Its Next Act." Accessed February 16, 2012. http://www.nytimes.com/2011/11/14/business/energy-environment/carbon-trading-may-be-ready-for-its-next-act.html.

O*NET OnLine. *Summary Report for: 13-1161.00—Market Research Analysts and Marketing Specialists.* Accessed February 16, 2012. http://www.onetonline.org/link/summary/13-1161.00.

———. *Summary Report for: 13-2099.01—Financial Quantitative Analysts.* Accessed March 21, 2012. http://www.onetonline.org/link/summary/13-2099.01.

INVESTMENT UNDERWRITERS

NATURE OF THE WORK

The energy trading sector has taken many traditional careers and given them a new focus and future. Investment underwriters are included in this group. A career as an investment underwriter requires a solid foundation and education in business or finance and interest and experience in the financial markets. Investment underwriters in the energy markets study energy legislation, energy commodities such as carbon credits and energy futures, and new and emerging energy technologies to advise clients on energy markets and commodities for investments and manage the risk of energy sales. They perform due diligence, negotiate financial deals, and analyze market trends to underwrite investments.

The U.S. Department of Labor's Bureau of Labor Statistics (BLS) categorizes investment underwriters as financial specialists. They are financial professionals who advise clients in the financial industry. Investment underwriters work with clients in energy markets and alternative energy sources, verifying and underwriting transactions in the sales and purchase of energy. They analyze energy trends, prices, regulations, and technologies to advise clients on where the best energy investments are.

Investment underwriters are financial professionals who work with other professionals such as accountants, lawyers, brokers, and business executives. The work they perform in the energy trading sector is very similar to that of investment underwriters in other areas of the overall financial industry, but it requires special niche knowledge and experience in energy. Often, that knowledge and experience must keep pace with rapid changes in the developing energy commodities industry. The most important commodities in the energy markets are natural

gas and electricity, but a wide range of additional energy commodities includes gasoline, oil, pollution, carbon emissions, and alternative fuels such as solar and wind power. Trends in energy that affect the financial markets include costs and sources of fossil fuels, national and international pollution legislation and regulation, and new technologies such as thin-film solar panels, concentrated photovoltaics, and wind energy storage. Energy industry investments provide corporate opportunity to create stewardship profitably and investment underwriters facilitate those investments.

Working closely with energy brokers, investment underwriters manage the risk of buying and selling energy commodities such as gas, electricity, carbon credits, solar, and wind power. They work with sophisticated financial analysis software and market data to study the markets, stay current with changes in regulation and energy technologies, and analyze current and historical energy prices. Investment underwriters meet with clients and energy brokers to facilitate deals and sales and provide investment consulting advice.

The following are some common tasks that investment underwriters in the energy sector perform:

1. Underwrite purchases and sales of energy products such as electricity and carbon credits
2. Research energy companies, supply and demand, and energy pricing as part of due diligence for clients
3. Advise clients about energy trends, legislation, credit risks, and regulations
4. Analyze the energy industry, energy prices, and energy markets
5. Report on risks and opportunities of energy investments

WORKING CONDITIONS

Working conditions for investment underwriters in the energy trading sector are typical of those in the financial industry. They work in comfortable office environments, meeting with clients and other professionals, use computers and financial analysis programs, attend industry events, and seek continuing education in their field. Because energy investing is a specialized part of the financial industry and transactions can be very large and involve risk that must be managed, investment underwriting in energy can be stressful.

Investment underwriters work for investment banks, securities and commodities traders, government offices, and private investment companies. They work in tandem with the investment brokers who buy and sell commodities, researching and underwriting the transactions before contracts are signed and deals are finalized. The financial industry overall is a conservative industry. Working apparel for investment underwriters is business attire: formal business suits for both men and women.

Investment underwriters need to have business savvy, including negotiating skills, financial analysis skills and expertise, and a good understanding of business and corporate dealings. They benefit from additional training and education in the financial industry, the energy markets, and global energy regulation and deregulation. This education can be advanced degrees such as master's degrees, professional industry certifications, and legal licensures. Because energy deregulation has turned energy into a financial commodity, those working in the financial aspects of the energy sector have seen career opportunities develop with changes and developments in the energy industry.

EMPLOYMENT

There were just over 300,000 investment underwriter job numbers as of 2008, which is similar to that for financial brokers, the financial professionals they work with. More than half of financial professionals such as investment underwriters work for investment banks and government entities and related firms. Others work for private employers. About 15 percent of financial professionals are self-employed. Graduates need degrees in business, finance, and accounting to compete for jobs in the most prestigious firms.

TRAINING, OTHER QUALIFICATIONS, AND ADVANCEMENT

Investment underwriters need a bachelor's degree in finance, business, accounting, economics, or statistics and benefit from a master's degree and professional certification for advanced positions. Membership in and certification from energy organizations and associations is also beneficial to underwriting careers. Energy associations that benefit investment underwriters include the American Public Power Association, the Illinois Energy Professionals Association, and the Certified Energy Professionals. Underwriters in the energy sector must have knowledge and experience in risk management and energy markets, and employers provide ongoing training in securities analysis, public speaking, leadership, and financial software programs. Industry conferences offer additional training.

Investment underwriters may function as securities dealers in stocks and bonds, which requires a federal license as a registered securities agent. Such licenses include the Series 7, general securities representative, and Series 66, investment advisor, earned through examination by the Financial Industry Regulatory Authority along with a work experience requirement. Certifications for underwriters include the Certified Risk Professional (CRP) through the Banking Administration Institute (BAI) and the Chartered Financial Analyst (CFA) certification through the CFA Institute, requiring a four-year degree and related work experience.

JOB OUTLOOK

The job outlook for investment underwriters is similar to that for securities, commodities, and financial services sales agents. According to the BLS, the number of financial specialists jobs, including investment underwriters, is projected to grow about as fast as the average for all jobs, with a 9 percent growth between 2008 and 2018. Competition for financial jobs is tough, and applicants with solid education and experience have an advantage in the job market. States with the highest employment of investment underwriters include Florida, New Jersey, New York, Michigan, and North Carolina. Cities with the highest employment of underwriters include White Plains, New York; Los Angeles, California; and Chicago, Illinois.

EARNINGS

The BLS reports that as of May 2010, the mean hourly wage for financial specialists such as investment underwriters was US$32.17, and the mean annual wage was US$60,980. Top earners earned US$50.01 per hour or US$104,010 annually. The five states with the highest annual mean wage in 2010 were Connecticut (US$82,230), Virginia (US$72,380), Illinois (US$72,070), and Colorado (US$71,540), along with Washington, DC (US$89,540).

RELATED OCCUPATIONS

Like investment underwriters, the following jobs require business savvy and an understanding of financial markets:

- Accountants and auditors
- Actuaries
- Budget analysts
- Cost estimators
- Credit analysts
- Financial managers
- Loan officers

SOURCES OF ADDITIONAL INFORMATION

American Public Power Association. http://www
.publicpower.org
Association for Financial Professionals. http://www
.afponline.org
CFA Institute. https://www.cfainstitute.org
Illinois Energy Professionals Association. http://www
.ilepa.org
The Institute of Management Accountants. http://www
.imanet.org

National Association of Insurance and Financial
Advisors. http://www.naifa.org

FURTHER READING

Bureau of Labor Statistics, U.S. Department of Labor. "13-2099 Financial Specialists, All Others." In *Occupational Employment Statistics: Occupational Employment and Wages, May 2010*. Accessed March 9, 2012. http://www.bls.gov/oes/current/oes132099.htm.
———. "Securities, Commodities, and Financial Sales Agents." In *Occupational Outlook Handbook, 2010–11 Edition*. Accessed March 26, 2012. http://www.bls.gov/oco/ocos122.htm.
Edwards, Davis W. *Energy Trading and Investing: Trading, Risk Management and Structuring Deals in the Energy Market*. New York: McGraw-Hill, 2010.
Fiorenzani, Stefano, Samuele Ravelli, and Enrico Edoli. *The Handbook of Energy Trading*. West Sussex, England: John Wiley & Sons, 2012.
Fleuriet, Michel. *Investment Banking Explained: An Insider's Guide to the Industry*. New York: McGraw-Hill, 2008.
Lott, Tom. *Vault Career Guide to Investment Banking*. New York: Vault, Inc., 2007.
O*NET OnLine. *Green Occupation: 13-2099.03—Investment Underwriters*. Accessed March 9, 2012. http://www.onetonline.org/help/green/13-2099.03.
———. *Summary Report for: 13-2099.03—Investment Underwriters*. Accessed March 9, 2012. http://www.onetonline.org/link/summary/13-2099.03.
Vault.com. *Job Survey: Underwriter*. Accessed March 26, 2012. http://www.vault.com/survey/occupational/CNA-Financial-Corp.-12002.html.

ENERGY BROKERS

NATURE OF THE WORK

A career as an energy broker requires an interest in facts, numbers, and statistics, an ability to work with people and be persuasive, and a degree in business or finance. Energy broker careers have developed with the energy and green industries after the start of energy deregulation in the late 1990s. Energy brokers buy and sell energy for customers to help them save money by getting the best rates on the energy they use. They are professionals in the financial and energy industries, with a combination of sales, consultation, and research responsibilities.

The U.S. Department of Labor's Bureau of Labor Statistics (BLS) categorizes energy brokers under securities, commodities, and financial services sales agents. They are part of the group of financial professionals who buy, sell, and advise clients on the value of securities and commodities. Energy brokers deal in energy markets and alternative energy sources, arranging transactions in the purchase of energy, forecasting energy supply and demand, and negotiating prices and contracts for energy sales. They analyze customer bills and utility rate structures to advise clients on how to get the best deals on electric and gas utilities.

Energy brokers consult on a wide variety of energy sources, including electricity, gas, and alternative energy sources such as solar and wind power. They meet with clients and with energy company representatives, buy and sell energy in securities and commodities exchanges, and monitor contracts to ensure they are implemented properly. Their work is mentally challenging and can be stressful. Pay is based on commissions and bonuses and competition for customers can be intense. Some brokers perform a range of measurement tasks, including monitoring air velocity and temperature and analyzing heating systems.

AT A GLANCE FACT BOX

SOC: 41-3099.01
Preferred Education: Bachelor's degree
Preferred Specialty: Business, finance, accounting, or economics
Average Salary: US$50,000 to US$95,000 annually
Other Information: Alternative titles for energy brokers include account executive in energy sales, energy consultant, energy engineer, energy manager, and energy sales consultant

Some common tasks energy brokers perform are the following:

- Purchase and sell energy and energy derivatives
- Negotiate prices and contracts for energy sales
- Forecast energy supply and demand and price energy based on markets and developing legislation
- Analyze customer bills and usage and compare utility rate structures
- Make cold calls to prospect for new customers

WORKING CONDITIONS

Typical working conditions for energy brokers are very busy corporate office and meeting environments and trading floors of busy securities exchanges. They work in private industry and government and spend a significant amount of time meeting with clients and attending industry events.

Energy brokers spend a lot of time prospecting for new customers, including cold calling for business and networking. Working in the financial industry, they wear business apparel and work 45 to 55 hours per week.

Energy brokers work with telephones, computers, data, and specialized software including customer relationship management and financial analysis software. Some use testing equipment such as air velocity and temperature monitors, catalytic combustion analyzers, heat tracing equipment, infrared imagers, and multimeters. They must have a solid understanding of financial and energy markets, economics, and business. They work with financial industry professionals including corporate clients, bankers, and securities and commodities traders. They must keep current on energy trends, market conditions, legislation, rates, and rate structures.

Energy brokers need to be results oriented, have a desire for accomplishment and achievement, and be able to work independently, accept responsibility, and maintain autonomy. An energy broker's work style includes analytical thinking, integrity, attention to detail, dependability, initiative, cooperation, adaptability, persistence, innovation, and extra effort. Those who pursue careers as energy brokers should be interested in working with ideas, searching for facts, figuring out problems, and using logic to address work-related issues. They need above-average mathematical and analytical abilities.

EMPLOYMENT

As of 2010, there were more than 277,000 securities, commodities, and financial services sales agents in the United States, including energy brokers. Most jobs are in major financial centers and in the finance and insurance sectors. Energy brokers work in government and private industry. Graduates with degrees in business, finance, accounting, and economics and who have energy market experience have an advantage in competition for energy broker jobs. Personal qualifications to be an energy broker include excellent interpersonal and communication skills, the ability to work in a team, ambition, and the ability to analyze and understand numbers. Sales experience is very valuable to energy broker careers.

TRAINING, OTHER QUALIFICATIONS, AND ADVANCEMENT

Energy brokers must have at least a bachelor's degree in finance, business, economics, or statistics. Advanced positions require a master's degree and professional certification. Brokers benefit from membership in and certification from organizations such as the Illinois Energy Professionals Association, the American Public Power Association, the Association of Energy Engineers, the Texas Electricity Professionals Association, and the Certified Electricity Professionals. Knowledge and experience in advanced

finance areas such as energy trading and risk management are advantageous to energy brokers. Employers of energy brokers provide intensive training in areas of securities analysis, effective speaking, and sales techniques. They also sponsor attendance at industry conference and training seminars.

Energy brokers may buy and sell energy futures and securities and may require licensure from the Financial Industry Regulatory Authority (FINRA). Most states also require brokers to pass the Uniform Securities Agents State Law Examination. Energy brokers work with advanced data tools and software that requires specialized training. Advanced training in and knowledge of energy trends and legislation are specialty areas for energy brokers. Financial analyst certifications benefit energy brokers working in exchanges buying and selling energy derivatives. The Chartered Financial Analyst designation, sponsored by the CFA Institute, requires a four-year degree and four years of related work experience, and the applicant must pass three rigorous exams in advanced areas such as financial markets and instruments, asset valuation, and securities analysis.

JOB OUTLOOK

The BLS reports that employment of securities, commodities, and financial services sales agents, including energy brokers, is expected to have an average growth. Employment in this area is expected to grow 9 percent between 2008 and 2018, although there will be more job applicants than openings. Advances in office automation and financial and analytical technology will affect the numbers of workers in the financial industry, including energy brokers.

Competition for energy broker jobs may be less intense for new graduates in smaller firms than in larger firms and exchanges. Graduates with degrees from prestigious schools and with advanced degrees and certifications, such as master's degrees in business administration and CFA designations have improved job prospects. Employment in the financial and securities and commodities industries can be volatile and dependent on market conditions and the state of the economy.

The top-paying U.S. states for energy brokers include Connecticut, New York, Maine, and Arkansas, along with Washington, DC. States with the highest employment for energy brokers include New York, Illinois, Texas, Massachusetts, Connecticut, and Arizona. The top-paying cities for energy brokers include Stamford, Connecticut; San Francisco, California; New York, New York; Durham, North Carolina; and Santa Fe, New Mexico.

EARNINGS

As of May 2010 the mean hourly wage for securities, commodities, and financial services sales agents, including energy brokers, was US$45.73, and the mean annual wage was US$95,130. Top wages reached US$124,000 annually. Top-paying states for financial analysts in 2010 were New York (US$108,790), Connecticut (US$100,560), California (US$99,580), Oregon (US$94,040), along with Washington, DC (US$93,470). Top-paying cities included Bridgeport, Connecticut; San Francisco, California; New York, New York; Naples, Florida; and Los Angeles, California.

RELATED OCCUPATIONS

Occupations related to that of energy brokers include:

- Financial analysts
- Insurance sales agents
- Loan officers
- Personal financial advisors
- Real estate brokers and sales agents

SOURCES OF ADDITIONAL INFORMATION

American Public Power Association. http://www.publicpower.org

American Solar Energy Society. http://www.ases.org

American Wind Energy Association. http://www.awea.org

Association of Energy Engineers. http://www.aeecenter.org

Center for Energy Workforce Development. http://www.cewd.org

Illinois Energy Professionals Association (ILEPA). http://www.ilepa.org

The London Energy Broker's Association (LEBA). http://www.leba.org

Solar Electric Power Association. http://www.solarelectricpower.org

Solar Energy Industries Association. http://www.seia.org

Wholesale Market Brokers' Association (WMBA). http://www.wmba.org.uk

FURTHER READING

Asplund, Richard W. *Profiting from Clean Energy.* Hoboken, NJ: John Wiley & Sons, Inc., 2008.

Bureau of Labor Statistics, U.S. Department of Labor. "Securities, Commodities, and Financial Sales Agents." In *Occupational Outlook Handbook, 2010–11 Edition.* Accessed March 9, 2012. http://www.bls.gov/oco/ocos122.htm.

———. "41-3031 Securities, Commodities, and Financial Services Sales Agents." In *Occupational Employment Statistics, Occupational Employment and Wages, May 2010.* Accessed March 9, 2012. http://www.bls.gov/oes/current/oes413031.htm.

Cassio, Jim, and Alice Rush. *Green Careers: Choosing Work for a Sustainable Future.* Gabriola Island, BC, Canada: New Society Publishers, 2009.

cbsalary.com. *Energy Broker Salary.* Accessed March 9, 2012. http://www.cbsalary.com/salary-calculator/chart/Energy+Broker?usd=1&uas=&kw=Energy+Broker&ujt=Energy+Broker&jn=&tid=230752&ns=1.

Chorafas, Dimitri N. *Energy, Environment, Natural Resources and Business.* Surrey, England: Gower Publishing Limited, 2011.

GlassDoor.com. *Energy Broker Salaries.* Accessed March 9, 2012. http://www.glassdoor.com/Salaries/energy-broker-salary-SRCH_KE0,13.htm.

Mcnamee, Gregory. *Careers in Renewable Energy: Get a Green Energy Job.* Masonville, CO: PixyJack Press LLC, 2008.

O*NET OnLine. *Summary Report for: 41-3099.01— Energy Brokers.* Accessed March 9, 2012. http://www.onetonline.org/link/summary/41-3099.01.

———. *Summary Report for: 17-2199.03—Energy Engineers.* Accessed March 9, 2012. http://www.onetonline.org/link/summary/17-2199.03.

Peterson's Green Careers in Energy. Lawrenceville, NJ: Peterson's, 2010.

SECURITIES AND COMMODITIES TRADERS

NATURE OF THE WORK

Securities and commodities traders make money by speculating on financial instruments such as stocks, bonds, and commodities. They buy and sell securities and study the financial markets, relying on their knowledge of the financial industry and the markets in which they trade, as well as good timing and decision-making. The markets in the green energy sector that securities and commodities traders study include carbon credits, solar energy, and wind power.

Securities and commodities traders work at stock exchanges buying and selling, in offices analyzing target companies and investment opportunities, and with clients, traders, and managers arranging trading deals and strategies. They work with professionals from investment banking and brokerage firms. Traders issue, purchase, and sell financial instruments such as stocks, bonds, derivatives, and mutual funds. They also offer advisory services or consulting. Securities and commodities traders lead a fast-paced, stressful career life working in the financial industry. Trading in the energy sector involves buying and selling carbon credits, initial public offerings of new companies developing green energy technologies, and stocks and bonds in energies such as natural gas, electricity, and solar. It also involves consulting services to companies and investors on how to obtain and use carbon credits.

Traders in the energy sector must know the energy markets and keep up with historical, current, and developing energy pricing, trends, technologies, and regulation. They are educated financial professionals working with other financial professionals in business and exchange environments. They work directly with exchanges trading in

AT A GLANCE FACT BOX

SOC: 41-3031.03

Preferred Education: Bachelor's degree in business, finance, accounting, or economics

Average Salary: US$95,000 annually

Other Information: Securities and commodities traders in the energy sector benefit from advanced education and industry certification. They must register with securities and commodities exchanges such as the Chicago Climate Exchange to participate in carbon credit trading. Six exchanges trading in carbon allowances in 2012 include the European Climate Exchange, the Chicago Climate Exchange, NASDAQ OMX Commodities Europe, PowerNext, Commodity Exchange Bratislava, and the European Energy Exchange.

carbon allowances, such as the Chicago Climate Exchange, the European Climate Exchange, NASDAQ OMX Commodities Europe, and the European Energy Exchange.

Energy markets are important in the financial industry but they can also be unstable. There is an element of speculation in trading that professionals seek to balance with risk management. A large part of the energy trading sector dealing with the green economy is carbon trading. Carbon traders buy and sell carbon credits for companies with excess credits or companies that need more credits to account for their emissions. Carbon traders relay buy and sell orders through exchanges, negotiate prices, and handle all parts of the transactions. They must know the carbon credit niche of the energy industry, current and future pollution legislation, and the trading processes of the exchanges.

Securities and commodities traders who deal in the energy sector have traded carbon credits since 1997 with the Kyoto Protocol in Japan, 2001 with the Marrakesh Accords in Morocco, and 1990 with the 1990 Clean Air Act that prompted the Acid Rain Program (a U.S. Environmental Protection Agency initiative that aimed to decrease the amounts of sulfur dioxide and nitrogen oxides released into the atmosphere) in the United States. They are key players in the financial and green industries. Carbon-capturing sorbents, solvents, and films are new and significant pollution reduction technologies that affect the current and future value of carbon credits. Traders working with carbon emissions must be knowledgeable in cap and trade, carbon finance, carbon leakage, carbon offset, carbon projects, voluntary emissions reductions, and energy speculation, all areas of expertise in the green industry.

Careers in securities and commodities trading can be global in scope, especially in the energy sector, with opportunities for profit from global markets. Carbon credits and emission rights are growing each year, and traders must stay current with markets, evolving legislation and governing bodies, and risk management.

WORKING CONDITIONS

Typical working conditions of securities and commodities traders are comfortable offices and busy, stressful work environments. Traders spend their work hours in offices, exchange floors, customer meetings, and other business and corporate settings, with ongoing training from industry associations and conferences. Traders work 40 to 50 hours per week, using computers, mobile phones, and other communications devices. They also frequently consult with financial industry experts. Traders working in the energy trading sector follow the financial and environmental industries, studying energy markets, environmental trends, and economics developments. Securities and commodities trading careers require advanced education and training, as well as ongoing learning in the form of industry certifications, licensures, and conferences.

EMPLOYMENT

The U.S. Department of Labor's Bureau of Labor Statistics (BLS) reported there were more than 300,000 securities, commodities, and financial services sales agents in the United States in 2008. These financial industry employees work in stock exchanges and banking operations in or near major metropolitan areas, especially New York City.

The world-wide credit trading market was estimated to be US$30 billion in 2008, with speculations of growth to US$1 trillion by 2018. This would lead to accompanying job growth for those in energy trading positions. Reviews of energy trends and usage in 2010 showed strong growth. The future demand for energy will fuel the future need for controlling carbon emissions as well as carbon credit trading. Growth of all securities and commodities employment is expected to grow 9 percent between 2010 and 2018. Established carbon credit traders with advanced training and knowledge of market conditions will have the best employment prospects.

TRAINING, OTHER QUALIFICATIONS, AND ADVANCEMENT

A bachelor's degree in finance, business, accounting, or economics is required for securities and commodities traders. Sales experience in such areas as insurance, real estate, and other financial vehicles is strongly preferred by employers and beneficial on the job. A master's of business administration or professional certification is also helpful, and advanced training through industry conferences and seminars such as the Carbon Expo and the Wall Street Green Trading Summit is necessary for carbon trading preparation. To sell securities, traders in the financial services sectors must obtain securities licensure. New college graduates with valuable experience and a competitive advantage through internships have an advantage in the job market.

The typical preparation for a career in securities and commodities trading includes a four-year degree, with internships almost required for a competitive advantage, and an advanced degree plus industry training. Colleges and universities that offer green industry coursework as part of undergraduate and graduate degrees include the University of Houston's Bauer College of Business and Harvard Business School. Financial industry experience in banking, insurance, financial sales and marketing, or accounting is essential to a career as a trader.

JOB OUTLOOK

The BLS reports as of 2010 that competition for securities, commodities, and financial services careers is high, and this includes carbon credit trading. Business professionals with finance education and experience interested in the carbon markets have good opportunities for lucrative careers. The states with the highest concentrations of jobs in commodities are New York, California, Texas, Illinois, and Florida. The top paying states for commodities jobs include Connecticut, New York, Maine, and Arkansas as well as Washington, DC. Top paying cities for commodities jobs include Bridgeport, Connecticut; San Francisco, California; and New York, New York.

EARNINGS

According to the BLS the average annual wage for securities and commodities professionals was US$95,000 in 2010, with top wages even higher. Industries paying the highest wages for securities and commodities careers are securities and commodity contracts intermediation and brokerage, depository credit intermediation, and management of companies and industries.

The five states with the highest 2010 securities and commodities annual wages were Connecticut (US$168,000), California (US$140,000), New York (US$128,000), North Carolina (US$128,000), and Arkansas (US$127,000). States with the lowest annual wages include Nevada, Michigan, Ohio, Kentucky, and Kansas.

RELATED OCCUPATIONS

Jobs related to securities and commodities traders include financial analysts, insurance sales agents, loan officers, personal finance advisors, and real estate brokers and sales agents. Experienced finance professionals work to promote the industry in various organizations such as the American Academy of Financial Management and the Securities Industry and Financial Markets Association.

SOURCES OF ADDITIONAL INFORMATION

Burger, Marcus. *Managing Energy Risk: An Integrated View on Power and Other Energy Markets.* West Sussex, England: John Wiley & Sons Ltd., 2007.

Chorafas, Dimitri N. *Energy, Environment, Natural Resources and Business.* Surrey, England: Gower Publishing Limited, 2011.

Freestone, David and Charlotte Streck. *Legal Aspects of Carbon Trading: Kyoto, Copenhagen and beyond.* New York: Oxford University Press, Inc., 2009.

John, Klaus D. and Dirk Rubbelke. *Sustainable Energy.* Abingdon, Oxon and New York, New York: Routledge, 2011.

Labatt, Sonia and Rodney R. White. *Carbon Finance: The Financial Implications of Climate Change.* Hoboken, New Jersey: John Wiley & Sons, Inc., 2007.

Newell, Peter, Max Boykoff, and Emily Boyd. *The New Carbon Economy: Constitution, Governance and Contestation.* West Sussex, UK: John Wiley & Sons Ltd., 2012.

FURTHER READING

Asplund, Richard W. *Profiting from Clean Energy.* Hoboken, New Jersey: John Wiley & Sons, Inc., 2008.

Brandt, Peter L. *Diary of a Professional Commodity Trader: Lessons from 21 Weeks of Real Trading.* Hoboken, New Jersey: John Wiley & Sons, Inc., 2011.

British Petroleum. *Energy Outlook 2030.* Accessed March 19, 2012. http://www.bp.com/sectiongenericarticle800.do?categoryId=9037134&contentId=7068677.

Bureau of Labor Statistics, U.S. Department of Labor. "41-3031 Securities, Commodities, and Financial Services Sales Agents." In *Occupational Employment Statistics: Occupational Employment and Wages, May 2010.* Accessed March 19, 2012. http://www.bls.gov/oes/current/oes413031.htm.

———. "Securities, Commodities, and Financial Services Sales Agents." In *Occupational Outlook Handbook, 2010–11 Edition.* Accessed March 19, 2012. http://www.bls.gov/oco/ocos122.htm.

———" Securities, Commodities, and Other Investments." In *Career Guide to Industries, 2010–11 Edition.* Accessed March 19, 2012. http://www.bls.gov/oco/cg/cgs029.htm.

Green Careers Guide. *Carbon Trader.* Accessed March 19, 2012. http://www.greencareersguide.com/Carbon-Trader.html.

O*NET OnLine. *Summary Report for: 41-3031.03—Securities and Commodities Traders.* Accessed March 19, 2012. http://www.onetonline.org/link/summary/41-3031.03.

United Nations. "Kyoto Protocol." *Framework Convention on Climate Change.* Accessed March 19, 2012. http://unfccc.int/kyoto_protocol/items/3145.php.

SECTOR OVERVIEW: ENVIRONMENT PROTECTION

The environment protection sector comprises jobs that help reduce the negative impact of human actions on the environment, restore damaged ecosystems, and build sustainable ways of life for the future. In the middle of the 20th century, environment protection jobs were seldom found. In the 2010s, however, this green sector is one of the fastest-growing job markets, with more than 100 environment protection jobs in existence ranging from air-quality control specialists, natural science managers, and landscape architects to environmental engineers, soil and plant specialists, reporters and correspondents, and fish and game wardens.

The rise in environmental awareness during the latter part of the 20th century has created jobs in the field of environment protection. The United States and the world began to realize the importance of human impact on the environment and the need to take steps to protect the environment for future generations. People also began to explore the idea that they could save money, and maybe even make money, by serving as a steward for the environment.

As a result of the environmental movement, advocates and legislators worked together to create laws and regulations to protect the environment and people's health. These regulations called for policy makers, lobbyists, attorneys, managers, and conservationists to make and enforce new policies. Scientists, engineers, and other specialists were hired to study, develop, and carry out solutions to problems such as oil spills, air pollution, landfills, and contaminated ground water.

As technological advances were developed to combat ongoing environmental problems, new jobs surfaced. By the beginning of the 21st century, more than US$400 billion was spent annually worldwide on environmental protection, supporting hundreds of thousands of jobs.

Some of the most popular careers are in environmental sciences, environmental law, environmental business, conservation, environmental engineering, environmental communications, environmental lobbying, and the social sciences.

Environmental protection jobs generally fall into nine categories:

- Management
- Architecture and engineering
- Life, physical, and social services
- Education, training, and library
- Arts, design, entertainment, sports, and media
- Protective service
- Farming, fishing, and forestry
- Construction and extraction
- Installation, maintenance, and repair

MANAGEMENT POSITIONS

Environment protection management positions include those in the field of construction, engineering, natural sciences, water resources, and redevelopment. For example, a construction manager may be charged with helping to provide and sustain clean water resources at locations around the world. The manager might use his or her skills in civil and mechanical engineering to ensure that projects meet objectives by carefully planning, staffing, and scheduling construction projects as well as performing budget management and quality control, and ensuring safety protocols are followed.

ARCHITECTURE AND ENGINEERING

This category of jobs includes landscape architects, water/wastewater engineers, environmental engineers, and environmental engineering technicians.

Engineers work with scientists, planners, hazardous waste technicians, and experts in law and business to solve problems and help protect the environment. For example, they might inspect facilities or programs to be sure they are operating effectively and complying with environmental regulations. They might design systems, processes, or equipment for control, management, or remediation of water, air, and soil quality. They may also advise corporations or government agencies of procedures that should be followed when cleaning up contaminated sites.

Landscape architects design gardens, public parks and playgrounds, residential areas, college campuses, shopping centers, golf courses, and parkways so that they not only serve a function but also are beautiful and fit in with their natural environment.

LIFE, PHYSICAL, AND SOCIAL SERVICES

This category of environment protection jobs includes many occupations from soil and plant scientists, zoologists, and wildlife biologists to industrial ecologists, hydrologists, and environmental economists.

Soil and plant scientists study all aspects of crops and other farming plants, trees, and shrubs including their growth in soils and the control of pests. They also study the makeup of soils and their effects on plant or crop growth. These scientists may also classify and map soils and investigate the effects of alternative practices on soil and crop productivity.

Zoologists study the origins, behavior, diseases, genetics, and life processes of animals and wildlife. They may specialize in wildlife research and management and collect and study data to determine the effects of the environment on the present and potential use of land and water habitats.

Hydrologists research the distribution, circulation, and physical properties of underground and surface waters. They also study precipitation, its rate of infiltration into the soil, its movement through the earth, and its return to the ocean and atmosphere. Environmental economists study the economics of environmental protection and use of the natural environment. They evaluate and quantify the benefits, costs, incentives, and impacts of alternative options using economic principles and statistical techniques. Industrial ecologists use the principles and processes of natural ecosystems to develop models for industrial systems. They use what we know about the physical and social sciences to increase the effective use of natural resources in the production and use of goods and services.

EDUCATION, TRAINING, AND LIBRARY

Farm and home management advisors fall under this category. These professionals advise, teach, and help individuals and families who are involved in agriculture, agricultural-related processes, or home economics activities. They may demonstrate procedures and apply research findings to solve problems, and they may instruct and train professionals in product development, sales, and the use of machinery and equipment. Agricultural agents, farm and feed management advisors, home economists, and extension service advisors are all considered farm and home management advisors.

Farm and feed management advisors consult with farmers and livestock producers to help them with crop and animal production techniques. They may, for example, help farmers with their financial planning by helping them balance their income statements.

Home economists organize and conduct consumer education services or research programs for equipment, food, textile, or utility companies. They also advise individuals and families on home management practices, such as budget planning, meal preparation, and energy conservation. They may work in government, private industry, or colleges and universities to research family relations or child development, develop new products for the home, or uncover facts on nutrition.

Extension service advisors may prepare literature for educational and informational purposes; collect and evaluate data to determine community program needs; organize, advise, and participate in community activities and organizations such as county and state fair events; conduct classes on subjects such as nutrition, home management, or farming techniques; or maintain records of services provided and the effects of such services.

ARTS, DESIGN, ENTERTAINMENT, SPORTS, AND MEDIA

Reporters, correspondents, and public relations specialists fall under this category. Reporters and correspondents often inform the public and others of environment protection problems and accomplishments. In many cases, their ability to bring problems to light leads to solutions to those problems.

Public relations specialists may work for corporations or government agencies. Their task is also to inform the public about environment protection accomplishments and solutions. They are often called upon to communicate with the public about solutions to problems, such as oil spills, to alleviate damage to their company.

PROTECTIVE SERVICE

The jobs of fish and game wardens fall under this category of environment protection jobs. The people in these positions are typically assigned a certain area to protect from fish and game law violations. They also investigate reports of damage to crops or property by wildlife.

FARMING, FISHING, AND FORESTRY

The occupations of first-line supervisors/managers of logging workers and forest and conservation workers comprise this category. Supervisors and managers oversee and coordinate the activities of logging workers.

Forest and conservation workers perform the manual labor necessary to develop, maintain, or protect forests, forested areas, woodlands, wetlands, and rangelands. They may raise and transport seedlings; control insects, pests, and diseases that can harm plants; and build structures that control water, erosion, and leaching of soil.

CONSTRUCTION AND EXTRACTION

This category of environment protection jobs includes hazardous material removal workers. These workers identify, remove, pack, transport, and dispose of materials that can be hazardous to the environment and humans, including asbestos, lead-based paint, and used oil, fuel, transmission fluid, radioactive materials, or contaminated soil. Special training and certification is needed to work in this field.

INSTALLATION, MAINTENANCE, AND REPAIR

General maintenance and repair workers fall into this category. These workers use their skills to keep machines, mechanical equipment, and/or the structure of a building or other establishment in repair. To keep the items they work on in good repair, the workers often use the combined skills of two or more maintenance occupations or craft occupations. People in this profession may be involved in pipe fitting; boiler making; insulating; welding; machining; carpentry; repairing electrical or mechanical equipment; installing, aligning, and balancing new equipment; and repairing buildings, floors, or stairs.

FURTHER READING

O*NET OnLine. *O*NET Code Connector*. Accessed December 28, 2011. http://www.onetcodeconnector .org.

PollutionIssues.com. *Careers in Environmental Protection*. Accessed December 28, 2011. http://www .pollutionissues.com/Br-Co/Careers-in-Environmental-Protection.html#ixzz1hNi4KgHX.

NATURAL SCIENCES MANAGERS

NATURE OF THE WORK

As worldwide attention turns to protecting natural resources and creating an overall "greener" economy, the demand for natural sciences managers is on the rise. This is rarely an entry-level position; most natural sciences managers begin their careers as a scientist in one of many disciplines and then advance to a management position after several years. What these scientists-turned-managers typically have in common is a focus on the environment, whether it's remediating damaged lands, improving air quality, or studying how people, plants, or animals can best adapt to climate change.

The key word in this job title is *manager*. Regardless of scientific discipline, natural sciences managers oversee other scientists, technicians, and field and support staff. Because they are rarely top executives, much of their time is spent achieving goals set by others and reporting progress and results to their superiors. In addition, these managers are often contacts for clients and environmental regulators. Thus they have regular contact with many people and must be able to explain proposals, findings, and progress so that they are easily understood by all.

What natural sciences managers are called depends on the industry. Natural sciences managers overseeing a team of oceanographers and biologists could be called coastal management planners or water team leaders. Those working in the mining industry may hold the title mineral and aggregate resources planner. Other general titles are research and development director, environmental manager, laboratory manager, or project manager.

These general titles may still hold clues to the type of work the natural sciences manager is engaged in. For

example, Brenda Winkler of Minnesota-based Bay West is a professional geologist who oversees cleanup of abandoned hazardous waste sites that fall under the U.S. Environmental Protection Agency's Superfund environmental cleanup program, radar stations at U.S. Air Force bases, decommissioned U.S. Army munitions plants, and other sites. Her roles in writing proposals, inspecting sites, and reporting on the progress and results of her team's work are reflected in her job title, project manager. Other groups led by a natural sciences manager may be involved in research; thus, the manager may be referred to as a research and development director. This research can vary widely depending on the team members and the industry in which they are working. The manager may conduct the research himself or herself or may have a more advisory and supervisory role.

Regardless of job title, a natural sciences manager is often the project designer, setting schedules, goals, and deadlines. In addition, this person may be the trainer when a project requires team members to learn new technologies. Like managers in most industries, the natural sciences manager is also an administrator, often involved in setting or maintaining a budget and recruiting, hiring, evaluating, and, if necessary, firing employees.

New technologies have a great effect on the tasks performed by a natural sciences manager. For example, real-time soil and water sampling results are becoming more common, allowing quicker turnaround and eliminating the need for managers to send samples to a lab. Yet in some ways technology is outpacing the regulations to which managers must adhere. Bay West's Winkler notes that on-site sampling is sometimes only allowed as a preliminary technique whose results must be supported by lab tests. "When we take a sample, we have to do so much quality assurance and quality control to make sure it can stand up in a court of law," she said. Such requirements may make it difficult to use new technologies to their fullest when the need for strong evidence prevails: "If we have someone we can identify as responsible for certain [for contamination or other damage], they have to pay for it," Winkler said.

WORKING CONDITIONS

Because of their supervisory role, natural sciences managers mainly work in offices. They face fewer of the physical demands placed on scientists who work in the field. Instead, mental and emotional demands are intensified. These managers are often in charge of finding and allocating funding. They may be primary decision makers or arbitrators. And they may work long hours when a deadline looms or while traveling.

Despite being office-based, many managers still spend job time outdoors. For those managing projects, site walks are often necessary before a proposal is made, before project startup, during the work, and after project completion. Job sites can be dangerous, particularly when the team is involved in repairing damage to soil, sediment, groundwater, and natural water sources. The natural sciences manager may be needed to help write and implement the safety plan for a particular site and project.

For remediation and other projects, these plans may need to comply with federal Hazardous Waste Operations and Emergency Response guidelines, and all team members, including the manager, may need to complete initial 40-hour training and annual 8-hour refresher courses. Exposure to pollutants, gases, dust, and odors is possible in some jobs. The same is true of hazardous conditions (such as exposure to high voltages, combustibles, explosives, and chemicals). When proper precautions are taken, injuries are uncommon and rarely serious.

EMPLOYMENT

As of May 2010, nearly 46,000 natural sciences managers were employed in the United States, according to the U.S. Department of Labor. Jobs are concentrated in California and New England, with a fair number in Alaska and other northwestern states. Many positions are based in metropolitan areas, but the managers may travel to more remote sites.

Most natural sciences managers are employed by companies specializing in research and development. There are also many federal and state government jobs. Pharmaceutical and medical companies, as well as architectural and engineering firms, may hire people for or advance them to this managerial position. Increasingly, opportunities for natural sciences managers working on environmental protection and remediation are appearing overseas.

TRAINING, OTHER QUALIFICATIONS, AND ADVANCEMENT

Natural sciences managers generally have years of work experience before their first management job. Learn More Indiana, a website developed in partnership with several state departments and commissions, reports that nearly 68 percent of natural sciences managers have spent at least four years in their field and upward of 36 percent have more than ten years of work experience.

Although people with good management skills may advance to this position with just a bachelor's degree, a master's degree is more common. Natural sciences managers are still primarily scientists and must be experts in their discipline and capable of running a project and a team. Licenses or certifications mostly relate to the scientist's discipline rather than his or her managerial role, and holding a certification such as professional geologist or professional engineer can be beneficial. Certifications are state specific, and managers of projects in different parts of the country may need to acquire multiple licenses.

A new trend, the professional science master's degree (PSM), is affecting entry into natural sciences manager jobs. As it relates to natural sciences, this degree prepares students to work in research or project management. The ScienceMasters website, which promotes the degree, counted 246 programs in a range of disciplines as of January 2012. This number is expected to grow rapidly in the coming years, because "industry needs employees who not only understand the technical nature of their projects, but the business and legal aspects as well, and are able to communicate their mission to broad audiences. Students in this unique program learn just that," wrote Lois A. Dimpfel, a former IBM executive, for the ScienceMasters website.

For example, the University of Maryland University College now offers a Master of Science in Environmental Management. In addition to giving students a well-rounded education in waste management, pollution control, watershed planning, and similar areas, it trains them to "develop a team and manage an environmental project/program for an organization or government agency," according to the university's website. Students can take this training further by adding a Master of Business Administration through a dual-degree program; University College requires students to complete only three additional courses if they first earn the environmental management degree.

In a similar vein, Southern Illinois University–Edwardsville offers an Environmental Science Management program that culminates in a PSM. It emphasizes internship and business courses, combining them with environmental science courses. It helps students find internships at local companies and features an advisory board that includes consulting firms and utility companies, as well as the National Corn to Ethanol Research Pilot Plant and biotech giant Monsanto.

Once they reach the management level, natural sciences managers looking to advance their careers may simply run projects with bigger budgets or may move into a nontechnical management or executive position. Some return to school to study business management or computer technology; others earn a professional project manager certification within their state.

Like most managers, the best natural sciences manager is a "people person." But in dealing with natural sciences, mistakes are not easily correctable and can have serious consequences, so accuracy and exactitude are also important traits. Because they oversee teams, managers should be open to innovations from others. Perseverance is also important. "The entry-level [scientist] positions don't pay much, but if you go in and show you're willing to work, you can move up rapidly," said Bay West's Winkler. "It can be a sacrifice. But it's important to just get your foot in the door."

JOB OUTLOOK

Growth is expected in natural sciences management through 2018. Openings are expected to increase 15 percent nationwide and up to 21 percent in states such as California, according to the CareerOneStop website sponsored by the U.S. Department of Labor. However, traditional employers such as the federal government have long been sending jobs related to site remediation and pollution control to state agencies, which often hire private companies that offer environmental and industrial services and may reduce the number of managers and scientists employed directly. Although growth within government agencies could be stunted in coming years, opportunities are anticipated with private companies, particularly in environmental sciences, remediation, and protection.

EARNINGS

The mean annual wage for natural sciences managers is US$130,320 as of May 2010, according to the U.S. Department of Labor. Those earning US$155,490 or more often work in medical and pharmaceutical manufacturing rather than scientific or environmental fields. Only 10 percent of employees earn less than US$67,290, with state government employees most likely to fall in this lower wage bracket. Once scientists break into management, they may find salaries enhanced by valuable benefits such as stock options and bonuses.

RELATED OCCUPATIONS

The work done by natural sciences managers is similar to that done by people in managerial and executive positions in other fields, particularly engineering. These managers may come from one of many occupations, including the following:

- Atmospheric and space scientists
- Chemists
- Environmental scientists and specialists
- Geoscientists
- Hydrologists
- Materials scientists

SOURCES OF ADDITIONAL INFORMATION

Association of Environmental & Engineering Geologists. http://www.aegweb.org
Association for Women Geoscientists. http://www.awg.org
National Ground Water Association. http://www.ngwa.org

FURTHER READING

Bureau of Labor Statistics, U.S. Department of Labor. "11-9121 Natural Sciences Managers." In *Occupational Employment Statistics: Occupational Employment and Wages, May 2010,* updated May 17, 2011. Accessed April 10, 2012. http://www.bls.gov/oes/current/oes119121.htm.
———. "Engineering and Natural Sciences Managers." In *Occupational Outlook Handbook, 2010–11 Edition.* Accessed January 4, 2012. http://www.bls.gov/oco/pdf/ocos009.pdf.
CareerOneStop. "*Occupation Profile: Natural Sciences Managers.*" Accessed January 24, 2012. http://www.careerinfonet.org/occ_rep.asp?nodeid=2&optstatus=000110111&next=occ_rep&jobfam=11&soccode=119121&stfips=&level=&id=1&ES=Y&EST=Natural+Sciences+Managers.
Learn More Indiana. *Career Profiles: Natural Sciences Managers.* Accessed January 24, 2012. http://

www.learnmoreindiana.org/careers/exploring/Pages/
CareerProfiles.aspx?VID=7&SOC=11912100&
LID=0&RFP=1&RBP=615.

Pappano, Laura. "The Master's as the New Bachelor's."
New York Times, July 22, 2011. Accessed April 10,
2012. http://www.nytimes.com/2011/07/24/
education/edlife/edl-24masters-t.html?
pagewanted=all.

ScienceMasters. *Professional Science Master's: Employer
Testimonials.* Accessed January 24, 2012. http://
www.sciencemasters.com/Default.aspx?tabid=67.

Southern Illinois University–Edwardsville. *Professional
Science Master's in Environmental Science Management.*
Accessed January 24, 2012. http://www.siue.edu/
artsandsciences/environment/psm.shtml.

University of Maryland University College. *Programs:
MBA/Master of Science in Environmental
Management.* Accessed January 24, 2012. http://
www.umuc.edu/grad/gradprograms/mba-additional
.cfm#CP_JUMP_28279.

Winkler, Brenda (professional geologist and project manager,
Bay West) in discussion with the author, January 2012.

SOIL AND PLANT SCIENTISTS

NATURE OF THE WORK

Agricultural practices have wide-reaching effects on the health of the soil, ecosystems, and people who eat the food produced on farmland. Increasing crop yields, making plants resistant to diseases and insects, adding or changing nutrients in foods, and other practices related to soil and plant science can stress and strain the environment. Everyone from manufacturers of widely used commercial pesticides to shoppers in local grocery stores has become more conscious of the need to develop and use environmentally safe products and methods for managing weeds, pests, and diseases. As this trend continues, the expertise of both plant and soil scientists is crucial to ensure agricultural sustainability.

In the broadest sense, plant scientists study plants to improve crop productivity and soil scientists study soil composition and its role in plant growth. There are many specialized jobs within these broad job categories. For example, agronomists and crop scientists study not only productivity but also ways to enhance nutritional value and desirable seed characteristics. Crop-research scientists and plant breeders use crop management and genetic engineering to obtain ideal qualities in crops such as higher yield, adaptability to certain climates or soil types, and pest and disease resistance. Horticulturists also study plant breeding and how to best store, process, and transport plants and their yields. Plant pathologists may focus on weed control, disease resistance, or pest control for plants.

In soil science, soil fertility experts address soil management and productivity. People with soil science degrees may also have job titles such as conservation planner, soil and water quality specialist, watershed technician, or

---

AT A GLANCE FACT BOX

SOC: 19-1013.00
Preferred Education: Bachelor's degree
Average Salary: US$34,400 to US$101,700 annually
Other Information: Crops are produced on about one-fifth of the U.S. land area and this proportion is decreasing. However, 15 percent more job opportunities for soil and plant scientists are expected through 2018.

---

wetland specialist. In related fields, entomologists study insects and how they relate to plant life, and apiculturists focus such studies on bees. Soil and plant scientists who work to protect natural resources are generally classified separately as soil or plant conservationists.

Although scientists have long studied plants and soil, green technologies have led to new roles, skills, and knowledge in these positions. Some even refer to the plant science industry as "the Green Industry." Scientists are increasingly being called on to add their expertise to the manufacture of green fuels, the installation of green or "living" roofs, and the creation of urban green spaces. Biotechnology and nanotechnology are also becoming important components of plant and soil studies, and bioengineering and genetic modification of crops and food animals are fiercely debated topics that offer many areas of study. As worldwide populations grow and the amount of land being farmed continues to decrease, pressure to use such techniques will only increase.

In some ways, the daily working lives of plant and soil scientists are similar as both are likely to conduct experiments and research, consult with other scientists on best practices, and make recommendations to other professionals or the public. They may use similar tools in the lab and field, and most rely heavily on analytical, database, and mapping software. Although a limited number of plant and soil scientists teach at a university or other school, those working for private companies or government agencies may lead seminars or workshops.

However similar the jobs seem at first glance, the actual work done by plant scientists can vary greatly from that done by soil scientists. Plant scientists may develop plant varieties that produce more food, withstand more diseases, and adapt to more soils and climates. Some focus on controlling and eliminating weeds. Those overseeing projects may present findings on how to balance environmental health with increased crop output.

Many soil scientists work for the U.S. government, classifying and mapping soils. These scientists may then advise private businesses or individuals on the best land and soil practices. Those in research and development may conduct soil surveys and study how fertilizing, tilling, and crop-rotation affect the ground in which crops are grown. Soil scientists may also work with engineers to solve soil problems at construction sites, with foresters to improve soil management, or with farmers to implement or improve composting and other waste management practices.

WORKING CONDITIONS

Technologies related to soil and plants increasingly place scientists in lab settings. Their research is generally classified as *basic* when studying how plants grow or *applied* when finding ways to improve that growth. In addition to lab-based jobs, soil and plant scientists work at agricultural research stations, farms, or other outdoor and sometimes remote locations. Supervisors may mainly work in an office. Although work hours vary based on job site and employer, most soil and plant scientists have a consistent schedule. Those who spend time outdoors may find that hours and working conditions vary seasonally due to weather and harvest schedules.

Although caution in labs and other settings is always necessary to ensure personal safety, fieldwork has the highest likelihood of on-the-job injuries for soil and plant scientists. Soil scientists in particular must be observant and careful to avoid injury. John Simon of Simon & Associates, a soils and environmental consulting firm in Virginia, wrote in a 2010 issue of the journal *Crops & Soils*

that taking soil samples can mean working with and around large and potentially dangerous equipment, such as backhoes and hydraulic push probes. The areas in which samples are taken can also present hazards such as buried utility lines, unstable ground prone to cave-ins, or chemical contamination. Both plant and soil scientists could experience back strain and other minor injuries or allergic reaction to plants or insects while in the field.

EMPLOYMENT

About 12,100 people are employed as soil and plant scientists nationwide as of May 2010, according to the U.S. Department of Labor. Most are involved in scientific research or product development or are employed by higher-education institutions. Others work for the federal government, product wholesalers, and management and consulting firms. Companies and agencies in Iowa and California employ the most soil and plant scientists, followed by those in North Carolina, Minnesota, and Illinois.

Job types in these fields may vary widely by location. For example, the University of Wyoming website notes that many of its soil science graduates are employed by mining companies, a key industry in the state. It encourages students interested in working as county soil scientists or for consulting or reclamation companies to broaden their job search to surrounding states where more opportunities in these areas are available.

Opportunities are also available internationally for soil and plant scientists, particularly those interested in conducting research or helping to implement agricultural practices in developing countries. Some scientists leave the United States to share their expertise with those in countries struggling to farm sustainably or to produce enough food for their population. The U.S. Department of Agriculture also offers students the opportunity to learn about international agricultural trade and work with the U.S. Foreign Agricultural Service through its International Agricultural Internship Program.

TRAINING, OTHER QUALIFICATIONS, AND ADVANCEMENT

Every state has at least one college that offers an agricultural science degree for undergraduates, which is usually the minimum requirement for a job in product development or applied research. Some schools classify soil and plant science under agricultural science; others have a combined Plant and Soil Science Department or offer separate courses of study. Some employers consider candidates with a degree in biology, chemistry, physics, or certain engineering specialties for plant or soil science jobs. At this level, a broad course of study can lead to more employment opportunities than those found with a specialized course of study. In addition to life and physical science courses, many soil and plant scientists study business practices and management, math, statistics, and computers.

With the expansion of green technologies and increased interest in environmentally safe agricultural practices, many universities have adapted their degree programs so that their students are best prepared for careers in soil and plant science. For example, the University of Vermont emphasizes that its Department of Plant and Soil Science trains students in sustainability by titling its majors "Sustainable Landscape Horticulture" and "Ecological Agriculture." "If we solve the problems with soil-plant systems, then environmental problems decrease," notes the department's mission statement on the University of Vermont website.

Many schools also offer advanced programs, giving students the opportunity to earn the master's degree needed for a research position at a university. Soil chemistry, soil physics, and other soil sciences, as well as agricultural and horticultural plant breeding, agronomy, biochemistry, entomology, and range science and management, are among the common courses at higher education levels. Students split time among the classroom, field, and lab for many of these courses.

Fieldwork can be particularly important plant and soil science training and students are often encouraged to undertake work study or summer internships before graduation. Some schools, such as the University of Vermont, run their own farm and offer summer courses for students in areas including soil studies; nutrient, pest, and disease management; and organic farming.

Plant scientists rarely need licensing, but some states require licensing for soil scientists. The soil scientist may need to work under a licensed scientist and pass an exam, but requirements vary by state. Certifications are available for both soil and plant scientists by societies tied to the Agronomic Science Foundation and may help boost a candidate's resume.

Good plant and soil scientists are observant, analytical, and creative thinkers. Those who excel in their jobs typically enjoy working outdoors and solving problems. Processing information is a daily task, so the computer proficient have more job opportunities.

JOB OUTLOOK

Although sustainable agriculture practices and green technology are not expected to dramatically increase soil and plant science job openings, the U.S. Department of Labor expects employment growth. By 2018, it anticipates 2,200 more people will be employed as plant and soil scientists than were employed in 2008.

Food will always be in demand so this job market fluctuates less than those of other industries. Companies developing crop-related technologies and practices may be less stable, and their employees may shift positions or employers more frequently, either by their own choice or by necessity, than people working for U.S. government agencies or universities.

EARNINGS

On average, soil and plant scientists earn around US$62,600 each year, according to the U.S. Department of Labor. The highest paid earn around US$101,700 annually, with many plant scientists who work with pesticide or fertilizer manufacturers earning top dollar. U.S. government scientists averaged about US$79,100 in 2009. For the same year, the National Association of Colleges and Employers said graduates with a plant sciences bachelor's degree earned US$33,456 annually.

RELATED OCCUPATIONS

Many agricultural jobs relate to soil and plant science as well as a range of other positions such as:

- Agricultural inspectors, managers, and technicians
- Chemists
- Farmers and ranchers
- Materials scientists
- Soil and water conservationists
- Zoologists and wildlife biologists

SOURCES OF ADDITIONAL INFORMATION

Agronomic Science Foundation. https://www.a-s-f.org/
American Society of Agronomy. https://www
   .agronomy.org
Crop Science Society of America. https://www.crops.org
International Agricultural Internship Program. http://
   www.fas.usda.gov
International Union of Soil Sciences. http://www.iuss.org
Natural Resources Conservation Service. http://www
   .nrcs.usda.gov
Soil Science Society of America. https://www.soils.org

FURTHER READING

Bureau of Labor Statistics, U.S. Department of Labor. "19-1013 Soil and Plant Scientists." In *Occupational Employment Statistics: Occupational Employment and Wages, May 2010,* last modified May 17, 2011. Accessed March 26, 2012. http://www.bls.gov/oes/current/oes191013.htm.
———. "Agricultural and Food Scientists." In *Occupational Outlook Handbook, 2010–11 Edition.* Accessed January 16, 2012. http://www.bls.gov/oco/ocos046.htm.

O*NET OnLine. "Summary Report for: 19-1013.00—Soil and Plant Scientists." Accessed January 16, 2012. http://www.onetonline.org/link/summary/19-1013.00.

Simon, John. "Safety Protocols for Soil Sampling." *Crops & Soils*, March–April 2010. Accessed January 17, 2012. https://www.certifiedcropadviser.org/files/certifications/certified/education/self-study/exam-pdfs/243.pdf.

University of Vermont. "Plant and Soil Science." Acessed January 17, 2012. http://www.uvm.edu/~pss/.

University of Wyoming. "Ecosystem Science & Management: Soil Science." Accessed January 17, 2012. http://www.uwyo.edu/esm/undergraduate-programs/esm-minors/what-is-a-soil-scientist.html.

U.S. Environmental Protection Agency. "Ag 101: Land Use Overview." Accessed January 17, 2012. http://www.epa.gov/agriculture/ag101/landuse.html.

ZOOLOGISTS AND WILDLIFE BIOLOGISTS

NATURE OF THE WORK

Zoology is the study of animals, and wildlife biology focuses that study on undomesticated mammals, birds, and fish. Much of the work done by zoologists and wildlife biologists is considered an applied science; that is, the goal of studies and other work is to solve a problem, rather than simply to generate information. Many zoology and wildlife biology problems today relate to how animals and their habitats are colliding with people and their expanding reach into areas once considered remote. One emphasis is on the use of land and water resources by both people and wildlife. Another is on how to use animal husbandry and conservation techniques to expand managed species populations, such as those in zoos and wildlife parks. Other areas of focus include hunting regulations for big game, handling of predators of livestock, and preventing the spread of diseases from wild to domesticated animals and vice versa.

As they advance in their careers, wildlife biologists often specialize in a particular animal, habitat, or type of interaction and may be referred to as fisheries biologists, fish health biologists, wildlife managers, or conservation resources management biologists. Zoologists also are generally classified according to the species they study. Distinct titles such as batrachologist (amphibians), entomologist (insects), ichthyologist (fish), and primatologist (primates) are sometimes used. Marine biology is a related specialty, albeit one with small employment numbers.

Fieldwork is common for zoologists and particularly for wildlife biologists. They are generally part of a team of technicians, researchers, laboratory assistants, and other scientists. Much of their fieldwork relates to studying and managing wildlife. They may count species populations, study how industry is affecting a particular population, or

AT A GLANCE FACT BOX

SOC: 19-1023.00
Preferred Education: Master's degree
Average Salary: US$35,700 to US$93,500 annually
Other Information: Federal and state agencies, such as the U.S. Fish and Wildlife Service and state departments of natural resources, employ nearly 11,000 wildlife biologists and zoologists

learn about the habits, genetics, and survival or decline of a species. Fieldwork may entail the use of specialized tools such as traps, tagging equipment, and global positioning system devices. They often collect specimens that are then taken into a laboratory for further study.

When not in the field, these scientists spend time compiling and analyzing their findings. They must also dedicate time to securing funding for their projects, generally through grants. Some even work primarily as grant writers for their team or organization. Others work as consultants for government agencies that set environmental regulations or for lawmakers dealing with potential wildlife legislation. Still other consultants work with private businesses designing land development, transportation, mining, or utility projects to assist them in attaining the necessary permits and compliance documentation.

Sometimes wildlife biologists are working on the same issue from different angles. A current topic is the delisting of the gray wolf, a species that has been protected by the U.S. Endangered Species Act for 40 years, but whose management is being turned over to state and in some cases tribal control in several Northern Rocky Mountain and Great Lakes states. Wolf numbers have been rising nationwide, according to Secretary of the Interior Ken Salazar in a December 2011 press release about Michigan, Minnesota, and Wisconsin, which were most recently affected by the delisting.

However, although some wildlife biologists and other animal scientists worked to ensure population growth and delisting of the species, other wildlife biologists see the management plans in some states as a threat. Some of these biologists work for environmental groups that have fought the delistings, such as the Western Watersheds Project, or worked to place scientific safeguards on state wolf management plans, such as Defenders of Wildlife.

WORKING CONDITIONS

Although many biologists work in laboratories, those who work with animals tend to do a large amount of research outdoors, often in remote wildlife habitats. Zoologists are more likely to work in controlled environments than are wildlife biologists, although the line between the two is often blurred.

The work can be quite physical for those in the field, and people working on long-term study projects may find themselves living in the field for an extended period. Depending on the species under study and the information being sought, the primary work time may be at night, in poor weather, at high altitudes, or in other harsh conditions. However, standard attire, gear, and precautions for the given environment are usually all that are needed to ensure personal safety. Those working with wildlife may need to take additional precautions because of the unpredictability of their study subjects or other animals in the area.

Laboratory work occasionally has its own set of hazards, particularly in working with animal-produced venoms and toxins.

Stresses related to these jobs are generally related to the financial end of the work, where grants are needed, rather than to the research. Deadlines to apply for grants and to release study results may result in long hours in the office.

EMPLOYMENT

About 17,400 people were employed as zoologists or wildlife biologists in 2010, according to the U.S. Department of Labor's Bureau of Labor Statistics (BLS). More than two-thirds of the jobs were with government organizations, usually state or federal. The U.S. Fish and Wildlife Service in particular employs large numbers of wildlife biologists and fishery biologists, which it lists as two of its

"mission critical" positions, and notes that biologists are a key part of a workforce that forms "the front line of conservation on National Wildlife Refuge System lands." Other zoologists and wildlife biologists are employed by companies that specialize in management, consulting, or research and development. These scientists can also be found working with museums, historical sites, and social advocacy organizations. California, Washington, Florida, and Oregon are home to the largest numbers of zoologists and wildlife biologists; Alaska is also a popular location for this type of work.

TRAINING, OTHER QUALIFICATIONS, AND ADVANCEMENT

Although the Fall 2006 *Occupational Outlook Quarterly* reports that most zoologists and wildlife biologists hold a bachelor's degree, employers are increasingly seeking candidates with master's degrees. "Call it credential inflation," wrote Laura Pappano in a 2011 *New York Times* article, going on to note that more than twice as many master's degrees had been awarded in 2009 than were awarded two decades earlier. Some schools may not offer a specialization in zoology or wildlife biology until the graduate level, so the appropriate bachelor's degree may be in biological science. Scientists may even need to earn a doctoral degree before they are able to undertake their own studies. Certifications are available for wildlife biologists, such as those through the Wildlife Society, but are not necessary for employment in the field.

Because much of the work of zoologists and wildlife biologists relates to the environments in which various species live, environmental courses are often recommended, as are courses in hydrology, botany, geography, and statistics. Those who wish to work with species protected by or likely to be protected by state or federal laws should study current regulations. Grant writing can be another helpful course.

Many people in these fields start out as research assistants, technicians, or field biologists. They may progress to running a team or even doing their own study as a project manager or a senior or principal scientist. Some may advance to become natural sciences managers, take on another administrative position, or return to a university to teach. Some zoologists become zoo directors. Some wildlife biologists become conservationists or range managers.

Patience is a key trait for zoologists and wildlife biologists because much of their time may be spent waiting for the events or conditions they are trying to observe to occur. Studies of this type are often lengthy, so these scientists must be self-disciplined. They should also be able to explain their project clearly to others, particularly those who might supply funding or set regulations. Fieldwork requires good health and physical strength.

JOB OUTLOOK

According to *Occupational Outlook Quarterly,* 5,900 job openings are anticipated for college graduates as zoologists or wildlife biologists through the decade ending in 2020. Overall, the BLS expects employment for these two careers to grow by 3 to 9 percent through 2020. However, U.S. federal funding is a key factor in the employment outlook for zoologists and wildlife biologists. For example, increasing costs in operating refuges and rising salaries have led to position reductions or early retirement, including many biologists and refuge managers, within the National Wildlife Refuge System in recent years. "According to a workforce planning report completed in October 2009, 19 percent of the Refuge System's employees plan to retire by 2014—and that was before a federal pay freeze was announced," Greg Siekaniec, deputy director for policy of the U.S. Fish and Wildlife Service, wrote on the system's website. Still, such turnover can lead to greater opportunities for new graduates.

On the research side, the BLS reported that in biological sciences about one in four grant proposals is approved. However, increases in the early 2000s through some federal funding sources had since tapered off, and continued concerns about the U.S. national debt were likely to affect funding and perhaps job opportunities in the wildlife biology and zoology fields.

EARNINGS

On average, zoologists and wildlife biologists earn US$61,660 annually, according to May 2010 figures from the BLS. However, the salary can vary widely, from less than US$35,660 to more than US$93,450 per year, depending on the type of work being done. Those working at museums or historical sites or for social advocacy organizations tend to earn salaries near the lower end of the wage bracket, closely followed by state and local government employees. In contrast, those who work for scientific research and development services and those employed by the U.S. government tend to earn salaries in the upper tier of the wage bracket. This is reflected by the top-paying locations for this occupation: Washington, DC, and Maryland. Massachusetts, Hawaii, and Connecticut are also noted for their high wages in this field. The National Association of Colleges and Employers found that biological scientists with an undergraduate degree earned US$44,700 on average upon taking a research and development position in 2011.

RELATED OCCUPATIONS

Many other unrelated jobs that are less focused on animals are options for people with interests similar to those of zoologists and wildlife biologists, including the following:

- Agricultural technicians
- Forester and conservation technicians
- Environmental engineers
- Environmental science and protection technicians
- Environmental scientists and specialists
- Natural sciences managers

SOURCES OF ADDITIONAL INFORMATION

American Institute of Biological Sciences. http://www .aibs.org
Federation of American Societies for Experimental Biology. http://www.faseb.org
The Wildlife Society. http://joomla.wildlife.org
Zoological Association of America. http://www.zaoa.org

FURTHER READING

Bureau of Labor Statistics, U.S. Department of Labor. "19-1023 Zoologists and Wildlife Biologists." In *Occupational Employment Statistics: Occupational Employment and Wages, May 2010,* last modified May 17, 2011. Accessed March 9, 2012. http:// www.bls.gov/oes/current/oes191023.htm.
———. "Biological Scientists." In *Occupational Outlook Handbook, 2010–11 Edition.* Accessed February 2, 2012. http://www.bls.gov/oco/ocos047.htm.
Crosby, Olivia, and Roger Moncarz. "The 2004–14 Job Outlook for College Graduates." In *Occupational Outlook Quarterly,* Fall 2006. Accessed March 9, 2012. http://www.bls.gov/opub/ooq/2006/fall/art03.pdf.
National Association of Colleges and Employers (NACE). *Salary Survey: January 2012.* Accessed January 11, 2012. http://www.naceweb.org/uploadedFiles/ NACEWeb/Research/Salary_Survey/Reports/ SS_January_report4web.pdf.
O*Net OnLine. *Summary Report for: 19-1023.00— Zoologists and Wildlife Biologists.* Accessed February 1, 2012. http://www.onetonline.org/link/summary/ 19-1023.00.
Pappano, Laura. "The Master's as the New Bachelor's," *New York Times,* July 22, 2011. Accessed March 9, 2012. http://www.nytimes.com/2011/07/24/ education/edlife/edl-24masters-t.html?pagewanted=all.
Siekaniec, Greg. "Chief's Corner: Tomorrow Is Yours to Change." National Wildlife Refuge System, U.S. Fish & Wildlife Service, *Refuge Update,* March/April 2011. Accessed March 9, 2012. http://www.fws.gov/refuges/ RefugeUpdate/MarchApril_2011/chiefscorner.html.
U.S. Department of the Interior. *Salazar Announces Recovery of Gray Wolves in the Western Great Lakes, Removal from Threatened and Endangered Species List.* Accessed March 9, 2012. http://www.fws.gov/ midwest/News/release.cfm?rid=490.
U.S. Fish & Wildlife Service. "Southwest Region: FY 2004–2009." In *National Wildlife Refuge System Workforce Plan.* Accessed February 3, 2012. http:// www.fws.gov/southwest/refuges/docs/R2% 20Workforce%20Plan.pdf.

ATMOSPHERIC AND SPACE SCIENTISTS

—■—

NATURE OF THE WORK

Atmospheric and space scientists take data collected by radar, satellites, and air, ground, and ocean stations. The scientists then analyze the data and turn them into forecasts and reports, many of which are released directly to the public. New technologies are enabling researchers to learn more about our planet and its place in the universe. As they do so, their data play a larger role in protecting our environment.

Although "weatherman" may be the first job that comes to mind when people think of atmospheric science, predicting whether the sun will shine tomorrow is only a tiny part of the work done in this field. These scientists address broad issues such as global warming and ozone depletion, and their knowledge is invaluable in solving problems related to growing food, controlling pollution, and managing water resources. They work closely with oceanographers, environmental scientists, hydrologists, and even computer scientists to learn how the atmosphere interacts with Earth's features and how to model and simulate atmospheric changes. These scientists are similar to historians as they use past records of precipitation and temperature to predict future trends in weather both locally and globally.

In this field specialties are distinguished by the type of work undertaken. The field has long been divided among operation meteorologists, who make short-term weather predictions, and climatologists, who study long-term patterns. Micrometeorologists do similar work on the smallest scale, studying changes within as little as one square mile and one day. The field also includes physical meteorologists, who study physical and chemical properties of the atmosphere.

AT A GLANCE FACT BOX

SOC: 19-2021.00
Preferred Education: Bachelor's degree
Preferred Specialty: Meteorology or atmospheric science
Average Salary: US$45,000 to US$132,100 annually
Other Information: The U.S. government is the single largest employer of atmospheric and space scientists. Most government employees work at National Weather Service stations in the United States. However, private consulting firms are expected to hire the most employees in coming years.

The "space scientist" part of this job title could be used by astronomers. It also could be applied to those studying space travel and exploration or research performed on the International Space Station, where jobs are few and are nearly impossible to attain. As it relates to the atmosphere, space scientists study space weather, examining how events outside of Earth's atmosphere and solar–weather relationships affect Earth's environment, climate, and health. In September 2011 scientists with the National Oceanic and Atmospheric Administration (NOAA) began running a new forecasting model that predicts when space weather events will affect Earth. Although such predictions mainly interest airline and satellite operators, power companies, and corporations relying on global positioning systems, there is enough general interest in such new technologies that NOAA makes its models available to the public online.

In recent years, other areas of specialty have been added to the field of atmospheric and space science. One is environmental meteorology. These experts focus on air quality and how it affects other natural resources such as water. They may report their findings in environmental impact statements and offer ways to reduce or otherwise address air pollution. Others specialize in agricultural meteorology, looking at how drought and airborne pests and pollutants affect crop and soil quality. They also investigate the effects of deforestation and urbanization on the planet's atmosphere. Bioclimatologists take long-term climate study a step further to learn about its effects on both the health and the activities of people, animals, and plants.

Atmospheric and space scientists are experts in data collection and analysis. Satellite meteorology in particular is increasingly important as the technology improves. There are thousands of artificial satellites orbiting Earth, many providing the data scientists need to make their forecasts. NOAA, in partnership with the National Aeronautics and Space Administration (NASA) and the U.S. Air Force, operates many of these satellites. It is currently preparing its next generation of satellites and plans to launch the system in 2015. This system is expected to make it easier for scientists to monitor extreme weather events and give more accurate predictions, thanks to anticipated improvements in resolution and speed of delivery of satellite images. NOAA also partners with agencies in other countries to operate satellites with global orbits, allowing forecasters to extend weather predictions up to 10 days. These polar satellites also provide data used for environmental monitoring and research of, for example, sea temperature changes, volcanic activity, and forest coverage.

In addition to satellites, a variety of weather analysis–specific software has been designed to assist scientists in their predictions. However, these scientists still use standard spreadsheet, word processing, and image software in their work. They also use tools that vary from a simple thermometer or rain gauge to complex Doppler radar equipment.

Everyone in this field spends time examining and creating maps, photographs, and charts showing weather conditions. Graphics that can be understood by untrained individuals are often produced by complex computer programs that the scientists must be proficient in running. Those studying specific phenomena may present their results to specialized groups that deal with agriculture, environmental health, fire prevention, or transportation. Others present their weather forecasts over the television, radio, or Internet to a wide audience.

WORKING CONDITIONS

The primary office of an atmospheric or space scientist is a weather observation station. Although some "stations" are unmanned devices, such as a collection of sensors on a weather buoy in an ocean, many are buildings filled with equipment and offices staffed by meteorology experts. Station locations vary widely, from airports or military bases to crowded cities or sparsely populated rural areas; some, called weather ships, are even afloat. But not all meteorologists are in such stations. Some work outdoors. Others are in television or radio station studios. And increasingly, private consulting firms hire these scientists to work in their offices or directly in the field.

Regardless of location, most scientists who predict short-term weather patterns work irregular hours. Weather stations operate continuously, and despite today's automated technology, staff members must handle unexpected changes in atmospheric conditions, even during nights, weekends, and holidays. When blizzards, hurricanes, or tornados occur, these scientists may work extremely long shifts. Such schedules, and the events that prompt them, can be stressful. Those in the field may directly face some of this extreme weather and the hazards that accompany them.

EMPLOYMENT

More than 8,600 atmospheric and space scientists, including weather analysts and forecasters, were employed in the United States as of May 2010 according to the U.S. Department of Labor. The majority work for the federal government. NOAA spreads most of these scientists across the country in weather stations run by the National Weather Service, although some NOAA meteorologists are in research centers. Other federal agencies employ these scientists as well, including the Defense Department.

Some atmospheric and space scientists work in the private sector for scientific organizations, universities, and research and development groups. Radio and television broadcasters employ many of them, usually in weather departments and often on air or camera. Most workers in this field live in Colorado, followed by Texas, California, Maryland, and Massachusetts.

TRAINING, OTHER QUALIFICATIONS, AND ADVANCEMENT

Most atmospheric and space scientists begin their careers with a bachelor's degree, although those planning to specialize or undertake research go on to earn a master's or even a doctoral degree. The U.S. government, as the largest employer of these scientists, sets the education standards most employers expect of new hires: meteorology/atmospheric science, advanced math, and physics courses, as well as physical science courses such as chemistry, oceanography, hydrology, statistics, and computer science. Students may take these courses yet earn their degree in a related field, such as geoscience, math, physics, oceanography, or engineering.

Because many new graduates in this field enter the job market with similar qualifications, a second bachelor's or a master's degree can make a job candidate stand out and offer a wider range of jobs, locations, and pay. Courses or secondary degrees in broadcasting, journalism, government affairs, or business and economics are good choices for work at a television station, environmental agency, or consulting firm. The American Meteorological Society sees global change research as its own field of study, and interested students should combine atmospheric science courses with courses in basic sciences, ecology, oceanography, and geophysics.

A geoscience background is increasingly important to atmospheric research. The National Center for Atmospheric Research employs many people in its Advanced Study Program. Many of these employees have bachelor's degrees in more general sciences, such as engineering or mathematics, but advanced degrees in environmental sciences and geosciences. This assists in research on, for example, how a decline in sea ice will affect the climate system or how warming global temperatures will affect different areas.

New graduates headed for jobs with the National Weather Service should expect to start as interns and move through several offices as they learn about regional weather systems. Meteorologists interested in becoming consultants or radio or television forecasters may seek certification from the American Meteorological Society.

JOB OUTLOOK

The latest trend in atmospheric and space science is a shift from government to private employers. The U.S. Department of Labor expects a 15 percent job growth through 2018, with the most openings created by consulting firms and other private businesses. This shift reflects technological advances that make weather predictions more accurate and the technology itself more accessible. Anyone whose business is affected by weather, such as farmers, construction managers, and insurance and utility companies, wants access to the most precise, up-to-date, and targeted weather information possible and increasingly turns to private consulting firms for such data.

For the same reasons that job openings are expected to increase, the number of students graduating in the field is on the rise, adding competition for positions. The Department of Labor soon expects more graduates with degrees related to atmospheric science than there are jobs available. Those with broad skills, internship or other work experience, and additional degrees will be best positioned to take advantage of job opportunities with private companies.

EARNINGS

Atmospheric and space scientists earn US$88,010 per year on average, according to the Labor Department's May 2010 statistics. Those working for the U.S. government had an average salary of US$93,661 in March 2009, and the National Weather Service's starting salary as of July 2010 was about US$25,600 to US$31,700, plus locality pay, per year, depending on education and experience. The highest-paid 10 percent of these scientists earn more than US$132,130 annually.

RELATED OCCUPATIONS

Occupations that have similar functions or educational requirements or are potential goals for advancement by an atmospheric or space scientist include the following:

- Chemists
- Engineers
- Environmental scientists and specialists
- Geoscientists
- Hydrologists
- Materials scientists
- Natural sciences managers

SOURCES OF ADDITIONAL INFORMATION

American Meteorological Society. http://www.ametsoc.org
National Center for Atmospheric Research. http://ncar.ucar.edu
National Oceanic and Atmospheric Administration. http://www.careers.noaa.gov

FURTHER READING

American Meteorological Society. "Challenges of Our Changing Atmosphere: Careers in Atmospheric Research and Applied Meteorology." Accessed January 19, 2012. http://www.ametsoc.org/pubs/careers.html.
Bureau of Labor Statistics, U.S. Department of Labor. "19-2021 Atmospheric and Space Scientists." In *Occupational Employment Statistics: Occupational Employment and Wages, May 2010.* Last modified May 17, 2011. Accessed February 24, 2012. http://www.bls.gov/oes/current/oes192021.htm.
———. "Atmospheric Scientists." In *Occupational Outlook Handbook, 2010–11 Edition.* Accessed January 17, 2012. http://www.bls.gov/oco/ocos051.htm.
National Center for Atmospheric Research. "Advanced Study Program." Accessed January 19, 2012. http://www.asp.ucar.edu/.

National Oceanic and Atmospheric Administration. "Operational Environmental Satellites." Accessed January 19, 2012. http://www.nesdis.noaa.gov/pdf/GOESPOESsatellites-2011.pdf.

———. "Space Weather Prediction Model Improves NOAA's Forecast Skill." Last modified October 19, 2011. Accessed February 24, 2012. http://www.noaanews.noaa.gov/stories2011/20111019_spaceweather.html.

National Weather Service. "Frequently Asked Questions (FAQ): Employment in Meteorology." Accessed January 19, 2012. http://www.srh.noaa.gov/oun/?n=faq-employment.

University Corporation for Atmospheric Research. "Discovering the Atmospheric Sciences: A Channel for Prospective Students." Accessed January 19, 2012. http://www.ucar.edu/student_recruiting.

ENVIRONMENTAL SCIENTISTS AND SPECIALISTS, INCLUDING HEALTH

NATURE OF THE WORK

Environmental scientists and specialists help set regulations to preserve and clean the environment and, whether working for government agencies or for private companies, help ensure that these regulations are followed. As they advance in their field, they may focus on waste disposal; decontamination of hazardous sites; construction and development risks; food safety; health hazards; or clean air, water, or soil.

Because environmental protection is the primary focus of environmental scientists and specialists, environmental science is a green career by default. Thus greener technologies are expected to increase employment opportunities for these workers in the future but not greatly change the scope or requirements for these jobs.

Many people with this career conduct or are otherwise involved in research studies. The scientist, specialist, and entire research team pool knowledge from a range of scientific and engineering disciplines in the course of their work. When starting a project, they decide which data collection method best applies to the study and then develop their research model. They then monitor environmental impacts, working as a team with other scientists, as well as engineers and technicians. Once the problem has been identified and data have been collected, the team devises ways to reduce or eliminate the negative effects on the environment, wildlife, and people.

Environmental scientists and specialists usually spend their time gathering and compiling data; creating models, graphs, and charts, usually using a variety of computer

AT A GLANCE FACT BOX

SOC: 19-2041.00
Preferred Education: Master's degree
Average Salary: US$37,900 to US$108,000 annually
Other Information: Job availability for environmental scientists and specialists is expected to increase 28 percent by 2018, faster than the average rate for all occupations. Private consulting firms, state governments, and local governments are expected to have the most job openings, with 26,000 openings for college graduates projected through 2014.

programs and software; and analyzing measurements and observations, such as soil or water samples, pollution emissions, or meteorological, mineralogical, or atmospheric information. This research is often used to write risk assessments, technical proposals, positions standards, and grant proposals. The researchers then present their findings to managers, regulators, and sometimes the public.

This field is already considered a specialization of physical and life sciences. Geosciences and hydrology are considered separate fields from environmental science. The environmental science field can be further specialized in environmental biology or chemistry, environmental ecology and conservation, ecological modeling, or fisheries science. Distinct titles may be given based on the scientist's or specialist's focus, such as air pollution analyst, soils analyst, or water quality analyst. Although the subfields vary in their specific activities, a growing focus on interconnection of life processes means many areas of study and research overlap. As a result, some universities, such as North Carolina State University, have updated their B.S. in Environmental Science degree programs so that they are more interdisciplinary.

In the information age, many companies and government agencies seek people with good information technology and information management skills. Experienced workers in this field may have little familiarity with geographic information systems, computer modeling, and digital mapping, making training with these technologies a big selling point for people entering the field.

In addition to the software mentioned above, environmental scientists and specialists often find themselves using analytical and compliance programs designed specifically for scientific use, as well as more consumer-focused software, such as database, graphics, and photo software. Fieldwork tools are often specialized for jobs in this sector and relate to taking samples of air, soil, or water; analyzing and testing these samples; or detecting radiation.

WORKING CONDITIONS

Regular fieldwork is typical for many entry-level positions as environmental scientists and specialists learn about their area of focus. With advancement, they may spend more time in an office or laboratory. In the field, weather can be extremely variable, depending on the area being studied, and good physical shape can make many tasks easier and more enjoyable. Scientists and specialists can experience long working hours and stress when they seek funding, meet report deadlines, and travel to meet with prospective clients. Fieldwork may result in long days or unusually long hours if the area of study calls for an atypical schedule.

Depending on the project's focus, environmental scientists and specialists may work in areas that have pollutants and other contaminants or work in hazardous conditions. Appropriate safety gear is typically part of their field or laboratory equipment. Some jobs put these workers at risk of health hazards ranging from bee stings to disease or infection, so appropriate precautions and thorough understanding of associated risks are crucial. Managers may also find themselves responsible for the health and safety of their technicians or others on the team. The rate of on-the-job injuries remains low, however, because people in these careers and the companies or organizations they work for usually ensure their safety in the field or laboratory.

EMPLOYMENT

Nearly 81,700 individuals in the United States hold jobs as environmental scientists or specialists, including health, according to the U.S. Department of Labor. Most work for state governments or consulting services; others are employed by architectural firms, engineering companies, and local or federal government offices. Some are self-employed. Most people in this field work in California, Texas, and Florida, with somewhat smaller numbers in Washington State, Virginia, and other parts of the country.

The private consulting firms that employ environmental scientists and specialists are generally either enormous, employing more than 15,000 workers total, or small enough to have a staff of less than a dozen. The size of the firm can often affect the scope of work for an environmental scientist or specialist. Dr. Charles A. Andrews, president of consulting firm S.S. Papadopulos and Associates, Incorporated, notes that some smaller firms conduct high-quality research and thus may be preferable to large companies. However, he emphasizes that prospective employees should always do their research before accepting a job with a company of any size, because the type and quality of environmental investigations can vary widely.

TRAINING, OTHER QUALIFICATIONS, AND ADVANCEMENT

Although most employers prefer to see a master's degree when reviewing resumes for environmental scientists and specialists, a bachelor's degree in any life or physical science discipline may suffice at the entry level. As the field grows, more job experience and education are becoming necessary to find solid positions, particularly in the private sector. Robert Lamonica, president of the consulting firm Leggette, Brashears & Graham, Incorporated, noted that private companies "are placing a premium on entry-level candidates who have master's degrees, although candidates with bachelor's degrees and several years of good experience are also desirable."

Depending on the desired focus, study of data analysis, physical geography, geochemistry, environmental regulations, business, marketing, advanced mathematics, statistics, and economics can be helpful and open the new environmental scientist or specialist to wide-ranging job opportunities. Research and work experience in an environmental science discipline is often required. For example, North Carolina State University advises environmental science majors to work as an intern, at a summer job, or in another work experience setting in a relevant area before graduation.

Although there are no standard testing requirements for initial jobs in this field, government agencies often give applicants a qualifications assessment to evaluate education, training, and experience. Licensing and certification are generally not required for environmental scientists or specialists, but requirements may vary by state and by position, particularly with employment by a government body. For example, Virginia requires wastewater specialists to hold certifications in nutrient management planning, erosion and sediment control, and stormwater inspection. Thus, it is best to contact the hiring organization or company before applying to determine whether a license or certification is required or helpful in attaining a job. Certifications, such as those offered by the National Registry of Environmental Professionals, can also be tools in the search for a higher-level job or more specialized position.

Environmental research and study of environmental regulations and laws are often primary tasks for entry-level positions. Many environmental scientists and specialists hold their first jobs as field analysts or laboratory research assistants or technicians. As they become more familiar with their field, they may advance to more managerial roles. Those who want to teach or conduct research at a university may go on to earn a PhD. North Carolina State University notes that positions as researchers or directors of government agencies also require advanced degrees.

People who like to solve problems, both concrete and abstract, often make the best environmental scientists and specialists. Strong communication skills, both oral and written, are needed for this career, as are computer skills. The abilities to be observant, describe complex processes, and think critically could be considered prerequisites for a job as an environmental scientist or specialist.

JOB OUTLOOK

In the United States, 44 percent of environmental scientists and specialists are employed by government agencies, according to the U.S. Department of Labor. As the population continues to grow worldwide and place greater strain on environmental resources, the need for environmental scientists and specialists is expected to increase. The U.S. Department of Labor predicts that the numbers of all jobs in this field will grow more quickly than the average rate for all occupations, anticipating a 28 percent increase by 2018. Private consulting firms are expected to do most of this hiring, followed by state and local governments. Despite these predictions, economic recession and lack of new construction may result in some layoffs, particularly in the private sector.

Environmental scientists and specialists can ensure that their jobs are secure and that they are competitive in their field by staying up-to-date on the increasingly complex environmental laws and learning to solve the remediation and engineering problems that are becoming the

purview of environmental consulting firms. Furthering knowledge of current and new technology can also keep employees secure in their positions and open doors to advancement.

EARNINGS

The mean annual salary in environmental science in May 2010 was US$67,810, according to the U.S. Department of Labor. North Carolina State University, citing industry data, found that starting salaries for those with an environmental science degree range from US$30,000 to US$40,000 per year. The U.S. Department of Labor puts the top 10 percent of workers at a US$107,990 annual wage.

RELATED OCCUPATIONS

The following occupations are among those that involve tasks or educational requirements similar to those of environmental scientists and specialists. In addition, some people in this field may advance to the position of natural sciences manager.

- Atmospheric and space scientists
- Chemists
- Engineering technicians
- Engineers
- Geoscientists
- Hydrologists
- Materials scientists
- Science technicians
- Soil and water conservationists

SOURCES OF ADDITIONAL INFORMATION

National Association of Environmental Professionals. http://www.naep.org

National Environmental Health Association. http://www.neha.org/index.shtml

National Registry of Environmental Professionals. http://www.nrep.org

FURTHER READING

American Geosciences Institute. *Guide to Geoscience Careers and Employers.* Accessed March 9, 2012. http://guide.agiweb.org/employer/index.html.

Andrews, Charles A. *Environmental Consulting Firms: A Profile.* Alexandria, VA: American Geosciences Institute. Accessed January 9, 2012. http://guide.agiweb.org/employer/Essay.html?Author=andrews&Category=ECF.

Bureau of Labor Statistics, U.S. Department of Labor. "19-2041: Environmental Scientists and Specialists, Including Health." In *Occupational Employment Statistics: Occupational Employment and Wages,*

May 2010. Accessed January 4, 2012. http://www .bls.gov/oes/current/oes192041.htm.

———. "Environmental Scientists and Specialists, Including Health." In *Occupational Outlook Handbook, 2010–11 Edition.* Accessed January 9, 2012. http://www.bls.gov/oco/ocos311.htm.

CareerOneStop. "Environmental Scientists and Specialists, Including Health." In *Occupational Profile.* Accessed January 11, 2011. http://www .careerinfonet.org/occ_rep.asp?nodeid=2&optstatus= 000110111&next=occ_rep&jobfam=19&soccode= 192041&stfips=&level=&id=1&ES=Y&EST= environmental+scientist.

Crosby, Olivia, and Roger Moncarz. "The 2004–14 Job Outlook for College Graduates." *Occupational*

Outlook Quarterly, Fall 2006. Accessed January 12, 2011. http://www.bls.gov/opub/ooq/2006/fall/ art03.pdf.

Lamonica, Robert. "Jobs in the Core Fields: Environmental." *Geotimes,* February 2001. Accessed January 12, 2012. http://www.geotimes.org/feb01/ jobscorefields.html.

North Carolina State University. "Environmental Science." *Majors & Careers.* Accessed January 9, 2012. http://www.ncsu.edu/majors-careers/do_ with_major_in/showmajor.php?id=30.

Virginia.gov. "Career Guide for Environmental Scientist/ Specialist." *Virginia Jobs.* Accessed January 12, 2011. http://jobs.virginia.gov/careerguides/ EnvironmentalScientist.pdf.

HYDROLOGISTS

◼

NATURE OF THE WORK

Hydrologists play roles in a range of activities related to natural resources. Some may work on environmental protection or cleanup; others may work as consultants or researchers for private companies addressing water supply usage, hydropower, irrigation, or inland navigation. As water resources become more precious, human energy needs skyrocket, and as risk of contamination grows in the coming years, demand for the knowledge and expertise of hydrologists is likely to increase. Population growth, particularly in coastal regions, is also expected to open new and expanded opportunities for hydrologists.

A career in hydrology often begins with an undergraduate course of study in geosciences, environmental science, or engineering. Hydrologists work with both underground and surface water; many specialize in one type. They may also study precipitation, the effect of soil on water infiltration, and the cycling of water through the earth, ocean, and atmosphere. These areas of study have them working closely with geoscientists, soil scientists, and atmospheric scientists, often in a team or collaborative setting. Water conservationists and hydrologists may do similar work, particularly if they are focused on ensuring safe, clean water for households, businesses, and communities. Oceanography is considered a subspecialty of hydrology. To excel in this field, knowledge of geosciences, biology, and chemistry is important. Biological oceanographers or marine biologists often enter their careers through emphasis on biology-related fields of study, rather than hydrology.

Technological advances have improved results from hydrological studies, but they have also burdened hydrologists with the need to learn to use new techniques and

---

AT A GLANCE FACT BOX

SOC: 19-2043.00
Preferred Education: Master's degree
Average Salary: US$48,300 to US$112,500
Other Information: Hydrologists usually specialize in surface water or groundwater. Either focus can take them to distant, remote locations. The field varies widely, from multimillion-dollar projects related to hydroelectric dams to household wells and drainage.

---

instruments in their research. Hydrologists are almost constantly building on their initial degrees and education so that they can apply the latest hardware, software, and research techniques to their work.

Work can vary widely, depending on the location and interests of the hydrologist. Those in coastal areas may become more involved in hazard assessment related to new construction, floods, landslides, hurricanes, and rising sea levels. Those in higher elevations may study shrinking glaciers, melting permafrost, and other effects of climate on ice and snow. Others may focus on groundwater pollution, water conservation, and storm water management.

Although some hydrologists work on long-term, large-scale water conservation and climate change–related projects, people in this field are increasingly working with city and county governments on ways to manage and protect local water resources most efficiently. For example, Philadelphia, Pennsylvania, is investing US$1.6 billion over the next 20 to 25 years to improve its storm water management. After years of constructing roadways, buildings, and other surfaces, the city has been inundated by storm water that runs off as a waste product, becomes contaminated, and overflows into creeks and other natural waterways. Philadelphia is now working to treat storm water as a resource and plans to create a green storm water infrastructure network to manage it. Green, or "living," roofs, rain gardens, and soil-water-plant systems are all part of the plan to push Philadelphia toward urban sustainability.

One level of the Philadelphia project involves hydrologic and hydraulic monitoring, in which hydrologists and others use long-term records of stream and sewer system flow in the area to assess the current impact on waterways near the city and to predict how to best reduce the risk of contamination and improve the sewer system. With the implementation of the "Green City, Clean Water" project, such data will also be used to evaluate the effectiveness of storm water management and water restoration efforts. "The impact of small-scale green infrastructure projects that affect only a few city blocks or a few acres of impervious cover will generally be easier to detect within a small sewer catchment rather than at [U.S. Geological Survey] stream gauging stations with relatively very large drainage areas," notes the Philadelphia Water Department website. Projects such as these put hydrologists to work in their local area and draw on their experience to develop new ways of managing and preserving water.

More generally, the work of a hydrologist typically starts with observing and collecting data in the field. The hydrologist then analyzes this data and models the water conditions observed. These models are used to forecast potential flooding, droughts, and other events. Some models may be used to advise engineers on transportation, wastewater treatment, and hydropower construction projects or make recommendations on how to allocate water resources or how to prevent waterborne diseases. Those with a focus on environmental protection may use their models and results to help prevent water contamination or minimize erosion or sedimentation.

Those who advance to management positions are often more involved in setting and implementing public policies on drilling, codes, pollution, and erosion. They may have to present findings to government officials, in courts or hearings, or publicly. They may supervise a staff of research assistants and technicians, or they may play a lead role in a team of engineers, environmental scientists, and others working on climate assessments or conservation recommendations. Some hydrologists spend a lot of time writing reports and assessments. They may also investigate and write recommendations on how to handle complaints and conflicts related to public water sources. Others spend more time supervising the actual construction and maintenance of flood control systems, hydroelectric dams, and other water-related infrastructure.

Hydrologists employ a range of computer-based technologies in their work, including water-specific analytical software; computer-aided design (CAD) software; and database, graphics, photo, and mapping programs. In the field, specialized tools such as water, pressure, and sediment logging instruments, gauges, analyzers, and samplers may be used. Such equipment may be used to measure stream flows, lake levels, or water volume changes. Hydrologists are usually responsible for installing and maintaining their own monitoring equipment, which may be too specialized to be handed to an outside contractor.

WORKING CONDITIONS

Hydrologists spend a lot of time doing fieldwork, frequently at remote sites that require them to pay attention to their surroundings for abrupt changes in weather, wildlife activity, and other natural occurrences. Oceanographers may undertake long trips on research vessels. Those studying streams and landlocked bodies of water may need to travel by helicopter, four-wheel drive vehicles, and even foot to reach and survey their study sites. Such fieldwork can entail long, irregular hours and even days or weeks away from home and families. Some travel may be international.

However, some hydrologists may spend most of their time in offices or laboratories, particularly those who are reviewing and making recommendations on site plans and permits, advising contractors on code and well drilling requirements, or administering programs and creating regulations for hydroelectric power plants, waste treatment facilities, or wells.

Any work hazards and injuries are generally related to the variable climate, weather, and terrain in which hydrologists work while in the field. Hydrologists working at contaminated or polluted sites may require protective gear and safety equipment and can face additional risks. Appropriate precautions generally ensure the safety of the hydrologist in any of these situations.

EMPLOYMENT

Of the more than 6,900 hydrologists in the country, most work for the federal government or for architecture firms, engineering firms, or consulting companies, according to the U.S. Department of Labor. Many also work for state and local governments. California is a primary location for work in hydrology, as are Colorado, Florida, Washington, and Texas. Far more people in the

United States are employed as geoscientists than in the more specialized field of hydrology.

TRAINING, OTHER QUALIFICATIONS, AND ADVANCEMENT

Although some employers accept hydrologists as entry-level technicians or research assistant positions with only a bachelor's degree, 42 percent of people in this career also hold master's degrees, according to the Occupational Information Network (O*NET). With either degree, from their initial work as technicians or assistants, hydrologists can advance to lead projects or manage programs. Those interested in running research projects or teaching at a college or university often must obtain a PhD. However, those with an advanced degree may find competition fierce for these research and teaching jobs.

Hydrology is rarely offered as a degree choice at universities; rather, students graduate with a hydrology or water studies concentration and a degree in environmental science, geosciences, or engineering. Courses in other life and physical sciences, chemistry, advanced mathematics, and natural resource conservation and management are usually advised, as well as modeling, data analysis, and other computer-related courses. Work experience before graduation may be highly desired or required by some companies and government agencies.

Hydrologists may need a license in some states to work on public and private projects. State licensing boards usually review the applicant's education, prior work experience, and scores on a licensing exam, although requirements vary by state. Where licensing is not required, voluntary certifications may be recommended, such as those from the American Institute of Hydrology for surface water hydrology, groundwater hydrology, or water quality, as well as hydrologic technician.

Those interested in a career in hydrology may find that employers pay close attention to their computer training and skills. Digital mapping, global positioning systems, and geographic information systems have become essential tools in this field. Those who wish to work internationally or travel as part of their careers may find they need to be proficient in a second language.

JOB OUTLOOK

The U.S. Department of Labor's projected growth rate in the hydrology field is faster than the national average for the next six years, reflecting increasing efforts worldwide to protect the environment and enhance human usage of natural resources. Jobs are also expected to open up as currently employed scientists retire.

Despite this growth, federal and state governments, which now employ more than 40 percent of hydrologists, are likely to reduce their job openings for budget reasons, according to the U.S. Department of Labor. Many government agencies are also contracting more frequently with private consulting firms, where most of the new job opportunities are expected to appear.

EARNINGS

Hydrologists earn US$79,280 on average and as much as US$112,490 per year, according to the U.S. Department of Labor's May 2010 statistics. Entry-level positions can come with a much lower salary. For example, the U.S. Geological Survey hires entry-level hydrologists with a bachelor's degree and work experience or with some work toward a graduate degree at annual starting salaries of about US$31,310 or US$38,790, respectively, based on 2011 pay schedules.

RELATED OCCUPATIONS

Occupations that have similar functions or educational requirements or have potential areas for advancement from a position as a hydrologist include the following:

- Atmospheric and space scientists
- Chemists
- Environmental scientists and specialists
- Geoscientists
- Materials scientists
- Natural sciences managers

SOURCES OF ADDITIONAL INFORMATION

American Institute of Hydrology. http://www .aihydrology.org

U.S. Geological Survey. http://www.usgs.gov

FURTHER READING

American Institute of Hydrology. *Membership Categories.* Accessed January 12, 2012. http://www.aihydrology .org/membership_categories.html.

Bureau of Labor Statistics, U.S. Department of Labor. "Geoscientists and Hydrologists." In *Occupational OutlookHandbook, 2010–11 Edition.* Accessed January 12, 2012. http://www.bls.gov/oco/ocos 312.htm.

———. "Hydrologists." In *Occupational Employment Statistics: Occupational Employment and Wages, May 2010.* Accessed January 4, 2012. http://www .bls.gov/oes/current/oes192043.htm.

CareerOneStop. "Hydrologists." *Occupational Profile.* Accessed January 12, 2012. http:// www.careerinfonet.org/occ_rep.asp?nodeid=2& optstatus=000110111&next=occ_rep&jobfam= 19&soccode=192043&stfips=&level=&id=1&ES= Y&EST=hydrologist.

Ledesma Groll, Tiffany, and Glen Abrams. "Green City, Clean Waters." *Construction Today,* Spring 2010. Accessed January 12, 2012. http://gbca.com/news/construction-today/pdf/GBCA-CT-GREEN-CITY.pdf.

O*NET OnLine. *Summary Report for: 19-2043.00—Hydrologists.* Accessed January 12, 2011. http://www.onetonline.org/link/summary/19-2043.00.

Philadelphia Water Department. "Hydrologic and Hydraulic Monitoring." *Green City, Clean Waters.* Accessed January 12, 2012. http://www.phillywatersheds.org/what_were_doing/waterways_assessment/hydrology.

U.S. Geological Survey. *What Is Hydrology and What Do Hydrologists Do?* Accessed January 12, 2012. http://ga.water.usgs.gov/edu/hydrology.html.

FARM AND HOME MANAGEMENT ADVISORS

NATURE OF THE WORK

Not long ago, farm and home management was a dying skill in the Western world. People had moved from environments in which they produced their own food, clothing, and other necessities to ones in which they purchased such items ready-made. Recently, however, that trend has begun to shift, with renewed interest in how the food we eat is grown, how the clothes we wear are made, and how our consumer patterns affect our world. That is not to say that all city dwellers and suburbia residents are going to give up their apartments and houses to move to rural farms, although some have. However, urban homesteading, vertical gardening, and other practices that allow people to supplement their modern lifestyles with traditional farm and home management techniques are becoming more popular each year.

As of January 2012, Amazon.com carried more than 11,000 books on green living, more than 1,800 books in its canning and preserving section, and dozens of books with *urban homestead* in the title. This is not an archival collection because many of the books were published in the last three or four years. In addition, many are in e-book form, reflecting current interest in green home management practices.

Many of the authors of these books had to turn to experienced sources for their work. Because of this, there is a need for agricultural extension educators, home economists, feed and farm management advisors, farm business management consultants, and so on. These people have a wealth of knowledge about longstanding practices and recent innovations in running a farm, ranch, or home. As the job titles indicate, this advisory field is vast. The full *farm and home management advisor* title applies

---

AT A GLANCE FACT BOX

SOC: 25-9021.00
Preferred Education: Bachelor's degree
Average Salary: US$23,300 to US$74,200 annually
Other Information: About 17 percent of U.S. citizens live in rural communities, and less than 2 percent earn a living as farmers. Farm and home management advisors, however, work as extension agents in about 3,000 U.S. counties.

---

mainly to people who work with individual homeowners and small-scale farmers, often working under the title *extension agent*. Extension agents are trained in a science and provide agriculture-related advice or are focused on home management and programs such as those related to nutrition and childcare, among others.

Cooperative extension services grew out of the establishment of land-grant universities, which receive federal funding for programs in agriculture and other technical disciplines. In 1914, extension programs formally began to link these colleges and the U.S. Department of Agriculture, improving farm management and production over the years. In 2012 there were more than 100 land-grant schools nationwide, mainly public schools such as Texas A&M University but also privately funded universities such as Cornell University. The extension program now has about 2,900 offices and covers four areas of interest: agriculture, family and consumer services, natural resources, and community and economic, leadership, and youth development.

Extension agents are responsible for programs in all of these areas. They shape the programs by studying issues and trends in their field. They also run the programs, preparing budgets, meeting with local governments and organizations, and supervising and training other extension workers and volunteers. These advisors must keep up-to-date on research in their field so that they can teach others through demonstrations, workshops, and articles. For example, those who are experts in animal husbandry may write about farm-breeding techniques, design housing facilities for livestock, or recommend how to turn animal waste into a resource. An agent with a bachelor's degree in dietetics may teach people how exercise and diet can help prevent chronic disease or grocery shopping techniques that are good for wallets and waistlines.

As computer technology extends into rural communities, farm and home management advisors are increasingly using the Internet to share their knowledge. County cooperative extension services run websites for their local area, publishing articles whose regional slant is beneficial to local residents. In addition, the extension system has launched eXtension .org, a site that provides information organized into nearly 50 resource areas. Extension associates and other advisors answer questions, record and webcast demonstrations, and even supply online training programs.

Technology has also changed the techniques used by homeowners and farmers, and much of the work of extension agents and other advisors involves training people to use these new tools. Crop-share lease, manure, and machinery rental rates are all numbers that can be crunched using online calculators. Specialized computer programs let farmers determine how much they should pay for farmland or project the cost of operating a piece of farming machinery. Some of the machinery itself is increasingly computerized, and farmers are relying on tools such as global positioning systems to speed planting and harvesting processes. Biofuels and bioenergy technologies are also changing the shape of farming, as are genetically engineered crops and an increased focus on organic products that affect insecticide use and irrigation practices. Today's extension agents are often asked for advice on how to best use these tools and technologies.

The extension system is not the only advisory group specializing in home and farm management. Some states run independent agencies or have local branches of the National FFA Organization that advise on farm management techniques. The Rodale Institute and other nonprofit organizations also offer farmer training programs, organic gardening workshops, and other outreach efforts. For commercial operations, *farm management advisors* are contracted to improve production and thus profits. They may specialize in particular aspects of farm management

such as irrigation, animal husbandry, or plant pathology. Some are business advisors, and others help farmers negotiate leases and contracts and prepare for necessary inspections. Finally, the *home management advisor* title is sometimes used with social services programs.

WORKING CONDITIONS

Farm and home management advisors spend a lot of time in the field, whether it is standing in a cornfield talking to farmers or visiting a home to advise on care of an elderly parent. On-site demonstrations, field trips, and community events are generally part of the job. These activities may require the advisor to work evenings or weekends or undertake physical labor. Such activities may put advisors outdoors in poor weather or in close contact with livestock, but injuries are rare with appropriate precautions.

When not in the field, these advisors are often found at a desk, reviewing the latest research online, talking with other experts, or preparing articles or brochures. Stress levels are generally low in this field, and office work usually fits a 9-to-5 schedule.

EMPLOYMENT

The U.S. Department of Labor's Bureau of Labor Statistics (BLS) estimates that about 10,700 people are employed as farm and home management advisors. Most work with universities and other schools, but local and state governments also use such advisors. Cooperative extension offices are linked to both groups. Some farm and home management advisors work independently or with a private firm as consultants for farmers and ranchers, targeting their services to a farm's specific needs.

In the United States, Pennsylvania, Florida, Indiana, North Carolina, and Kansas are all popular locations for farm and home management advisors. However, opportunities exist in many other locations. Some advisors work in developing countries to help people improve local farm and home management. The extension system has programs in American Samoa, Guam, and other U.S. territories, as well as throughout the United States.

TRAINING, OTHER QUALIFICATIONS, AND ADVANCEMENT

A bachelor's degree is the minimum requirement for people who want to professionally advise others on farm and home management practices. However, just as job titles vary widely in the field, so do specific educational requirements. The Virginia Cooperative Extension says that for an agent faculty position, the prospective employee must hold a degree, preferably a master's degree, in a relevant discipline. Agents within the agricultural and natural resources section can specialize in horticulture, animal science, or crop and soil science. In contrast, those who wish to work with family and consumer programs might major in nutrition, family/human development, or financial management. Agronomy, range science, environmental chemistry, sociology, home economics, educational administration, and biomathematics are all examples of the topics studied academically by current state extension service directors and administrators.

In the extension system and with many other farm and home advisory groups, advisors start out in an assistant or associate position before moving up to an advisor or agent position. District, director, and administrator positions are all possible areas for advancement. Many people in these upper positions hold a doctoral degree in their field. Any testing, licensing, or certification requirements are related to the advisor's specialty rather than to the advisory position itself.

Good farm and home management advisors are organized and self-disciplined. They are curious and enjoy learning about a range of topics. They are also social and like to share their knowledge with others. Those who can break complex, technical information into written or oral presentations that are easily understood by the general public do best in this job.

JOB OUTLOOK

The BLS predicts that there will be little or no change in the number of job opportunities for farm and home management advisors in the next few years. Only a small percentage of people in the United States are employed as farmers, and the ratio of urban to rural residences is rising.

The number of local extension offices has been dropping in recent years. Instead, many are combining into regional offices. Despite this, the extension system is being used by a wider variety of people than in the past and has extended its reach to more urban and suburban areas in recent years. Burgeoning interest in organic products, green technologies, and sustainable practices is leading to increased demand for the knowledge of experts on a range of farm and home management issues. Those who become experts in the latest trends and practices are likely to be in demand.

EARNINGS

On average, farm and home management advisors were earning US$47,640 per year as of May 2010 according to the BLS. The highest-paid advisors earn more than US$74,170 per year. Less than 10 percent earn less than US$23,290 annually. According to the North Carolina State University Cooperative Extension website, the starting salary in 2009 for an extension agent with a bachelor's degree was US$32,807, with a master's degree was US$38,124, and with a PhD was US$41,315.

RELATED OCCUPATIONS

Farm and home management advisors are typically experts in a particular discipline and may have worked in another job related to that specialty before taking on an advisory role. The following are a few of the other occupations related to the farm and home management advisor job:

- Agricultural inspectors
- Agricultural technicians
- Environmental economists
- First-line supervisors/managers of agricultural crop and horticultural workers
- Purchasing agents and buyers, farm products
- Soil and plant scientists
- Soil and water conservationists
- Zoologists and wildlife biologists

SOURCES OF ADDITIONAL INFORMATION

International Farm Management Association. http://www.ifmaonline.org//index.php

National Center for Appropriate Technology Sustainable Agriculture Project. https://attra.ncat.org

National FFA Organization. http://www.ffa.org

National Institute of Food and Agriculture. http://www.csrees.usda.gov

FURTHER READING

Bureau of Labor Statistics, U.S. Department of Labor. "Agriculture, Forestry, and Fishing." In *Career Guide to Industries, 2010–11 Edition.* Accessed January 30, 2012. http://www.bls.gov/oco/cg/cgs001.htm.

———. "25-9021 Farm and Home Management Advisors." In *Occupational Employment Statistics: Occupational Employment and Wages, May 2010,* last modified May 17, 2011. Accessed March 9, 2012. http://www.bls.gov/oes/current/oes259021.htm.

NC State University Cooperative Extension. *Employment Opportunities in Cooperative Extension: Application Procedures/FAQ.* Accessed February 3, 2012. http://www.ces.ncsu.edu/Bar/jobs/.

O*NET OnLine. *Summary Report for: 25-9021.00— Farm and Home Management Advisors.* Accessed January 30, 2012. http://www.onetonline.org/link/summary/25-9021.00.

U.S. Department of Agriculture, National Institute of Food and Agriculture. *Directory: State Extension Service Directors/Administrators.* Accessed February 3, 2012. http://www.nifa.usda.gov/qlinks/pdfs/state_directory.pdf.

———. *Partnerships: About Us—Extension.* Accessed February 3, 2012. http://www.csrees.usda.gov/qlinks/extension.html.

Virginia Cooperative Extension. *Extension Agent Job Descriptions.* Accessed February 3, 2012. http://www.ext.vt.edu/agentjobdescriptions.html.

REPORTERS AND CORRESPONDENTS

—■—

NATURE OF THE WORK

Reporters and correspondents have long followed the latest political, economic, and social trends and analyzed and reported on their implications for people and the planet. Innovations in green technology and economic activities that relate to our use of the world's natural resources have led to a new "beat": environmental reporting.

This development can be exemplified by the *Huffington Post,* an Internet-only newspaper. In June 2008, the *Huffington Post* launched HuffPost Green, a section devoted to all things green. *Sustainable investing, eco-friendly,* and *clean technology* were becoming common terms on the web and in print, and people interested in environmental news soon found their way to the section. Three years later the *Huffington Post* passed the *New York Times* in monthly unique user visits, combining direct traffic to its site and traffic through AOLNews.com. In November 2011, the Natural Resources Defense Council, an environmental action organization, honored the media company's president and editor-in-chief, Arianna Huffington, because she "prioritized environmental news and green solutions."

By launching HuffPost Green, the *Huffington Post* became one of many publications to treat articles on environmental topics somewhat differently from those in a standard news section. Newspapers and other news media have long had science sections and dedicated science journalists, and one of the myriad topics they cover is environmental research. In contrast, environmental journalists tend to cover a broader range of environmental issues, from pollution to legislation, and a narrower range of scientific research. In either case, what makes these people good at their jobs are their skills as journalists.

AT A GLANCE FACT BOX

SOC: 27-3022.00
Preferred Education: Bachelor's degree
Average Salary: US$20,000 to US$75,200 annually
Other Information: About 45,100 Americans hold jobs as reporters and correspondents working in print, broadcast, and online news media. Some of these specialize in writing about the environment or science or cover those topics as part of their work in other areas.

"There's pretty much nothing different from being an environmental journalist and being a standard journalist—it's just your subject is the environment," said Katie Zemtseff, an environmental reporter at the *Seattle Daily Journal of Commerce.* Zemtseff writes about the environment as it relates to the built environment, such as sustainable development, wastewater treatment and disposal, and the environmental effects of public projects, for the trade publication. "With any subject you're reporting on, you have to have the ability to take something complex and make it clear," she said. Because environmental journalists often deal with scientific and technical topics, "you might need to be a little stronger in this [ability] as an environmental journalist," she added.

In general, a reporter gathers information, analyzes its content, and then writes an article that is published or broadcast. Some topics are assigned by editors or other managers; others are pitched to supervisors by the reporter based on research and tips. Reporters may work with photographers or videographers to enhance a story visually. In small organizations, they may play all three roles. Correspondents do similar work outside a publication's main geographic location and many times from another country.

Technology has changed the world of newsgathering. Reporters and correspondents may now need to be familiar with a range of software and hardware. Those who are presenting their reports remotely may do so through a mobile broadcast unit. Those who are based in an office may do initial research online from their desks. Some technological changes are beneficial to reporters and correspondents, such as the increased ease of finding and contacting people via the Internet. However, in many ways technology has added to the workload, as journalists may find themselves managing a blog, Facebook page, Twitter account, and YouTube playlist related to their work, as well as fulfilling their traditional duties.

WORKING CONDITIONS

Working as a reporter can be stressful. News does not happen within a 9-to-5 weekday window and working long hours and weekends can be the norm. Newscasters and those regularly covering events may work irregular hours. Most reporters are juggling several articles at once and must be able to prioritize their workload and manage their time effectively to avoid additional stress. These priorities and deadlines change constantly as events occur, and journalists must be able to quickly grasp the important points and present them in print or before a camera with little preparation. Correspondents, particularly those in war zones and remote areas, face other stresses related to the physical surroundings in which they work. However, most reporters spend their time writing about dangers and hazards rather than experiencing them firsthand.

Newsrooms tend to be noisy places with few private offices and many distractions. Those who work for a broadcasting company must be comfortable in front of a camera and lights. Furthermore, as more news organizations expand online, reporters who once only saw their byline and perhaps their photo at the top of a story are being increasingly asked to step in front of the camera to present their work for a webcast.

EMPLOYMENT

As of May 2010, about 45,100 Americans were working as reporters and correspondents. The U.S. Department of Labor's Bureau of Labor Statistics (BLS) found that most of these are employed by publishers of media such as newspapers, magazines, and books. About 10,600 people in this field work for radio and television broadcasters, with another 400 or so working for cable and subscription radio and television companies. The BLS found nearly 2,400 reporters and correspondents at companies publishing and broadcasting exclusively online, and these employees were among the highest paid in their field. New York has long been the principal location for publishing and broadcasting companies. California, Texas, Illinois, and Ohio also have a large number of people working in these industries.

TRAINING, OTHER QUALIFICATIONS, AND ADVANCEMENT

Most reporters and correspondents earn a bachelor's degree in journalism or mass communications. Some universities place their journalism majors in the English department, whereas others offer the degree through a communications department. In either case, a broad liberal arts education is important because reporters and correspondents cover a large range of topics. Other majors may be satisfactory for journalists who have either student newspaper or internship experience and want to specialize in a certain subject area such as politics and the environment. For many employers, practical experience, rather than the type of degree, is the most important factor in choosing a new staff member. Some students work toward a minor or dual degrees in journalism and biology, environmental science, or a related major to fulfill both requirements.

"Pretty much all reporters come from all walks of life and are either trained in writing or fell into writing," said the *Seattle Daily Journal of Commerce*'s Zemtseff, who moved into her position as environmental reporter after a more general reporting internship with the paper. Initially, "you take whatever job you can, wherever that happens. Later on as you develop you can negotiate and move into another field," such as general communications or public involvement. "If you have some experience, you can do anything," she said.

Many journalists work their first few years at a small newspaper or broadcasting station. Many soon move to a larger metropolitan publication or broadcaster that offers only internships or freelance work to inexperienced reporters and seeks a well-rounded portfolio of clips or other published work from potential employees. As reporters advance in their field, they often specialize in an area of expertise, such as green technologies, scientific discoveries, or environmental issues. Some start as correspondents, whereas others graduate to this role after working locally. Those who garner a following through their work may be asked to write a regular news column or blog or to moderate a community forum. Those who want to continue working as reporters and correspondents often stay in the industry rather than returning to school for graduate and postgraduate work. However, some enter these programs directly from their undergraduate studies to hone their skills before entering the field, and others return to school so that they can teach, research, or advance to management positions.

Good reporters listen well, think critically, and write clearly. They must be adept at managing their time and be self-disciplined about meeting deadlines. As computer-based and online technologies develop, reporters increasingly need to be tech savvy and able to adapt to different forms of presenting news, including using graphics, podcasts, blogs, and live online feeds. A good reporter or correspondent has high regard for facts and ensures that any information presented publicly is accurate and has been verified. Commentators, critics, and analysts may have room in their work for slant and opinions, but reporters are generally required to present an objective view of every story.

JOB OUTLOOK

Opportunities in the news industry are expected to decline in coming years. The BLS estimates a drop in jobs of 8 percent through 2018 from 2008 numbers. A worldwide decline in newspaper readership, consolidation of publishing and broadcasting companies into wide-reaching media groups, and loss of advertising revenue are all factors affecting this decline. Online and mobile news operations are becoming key players in the industry, and new technologies and continued demand for news are likely to add to their value.

Zemtseff said that in the five years she has been the environmental reporter for the *Seattle Daily Journal of Commerce*, there has been a shift in awareness about green issues and the way they are handled in the media. As more people become interested in environmental issues, articles that once only appeared in science sections and specialty publications are more frequently finding their way onto the front pages of newspapers and onto nightly news broadcasts. "It's becoming such a big part of daily life, and people's awareness has just changed drastically," she said. "I'm not sure whether [the environmental reporter job] will be as prevalent in the future. It could just be absorbed by other beats …. Or it could remain its own beat." Because few environmental issues occur in isolation, Zemtseff noted that there could be benefits to environmental reporting becoming more integrated with broader traditional news categories of politics, business, or technology.

EARNINGS

A survey by the National Association of Colleges and Employers found that the 2011 entry-level salary for reporters and correspondents was US$24,500 annually. Once established in their career, reporters and correspondents earn US$43,708 per year on average, according to the BLS's May 2010 numbers, with those in the top wage bracket earning more than US$75,230 per year.

RELATED OCCUPATIONS

The abilities to write and communicate orally are the key skills that link reporters and analysts to many other occupations, such as the following:

- Atmospheric and space scientists
- Public relations specialists
- Sales representatives

SOURCES OF ADDITIONAL INFORMATION

Council for the Advancement of Science Writing. http://casw.org

Dow Jones News Fund. https://www.newsfund.org

National Association of Broadcasters. http://www.nab.org

National Association of Science Writers. http://www.nasw.org

Society of Environmental Journalists. http://www.sej.org

FURTHER READING

Bureau of Labor Statistics, U.S. Department of Labor. "27-3022 Reporters and Correspondents." In *Occupational Employment Statistics: Occupational Employment and Wages, May 2010,* last modified May 17, 2011. Accessed March 9, 2012. http://www.bls.gov/oes/current/oes273022.htm.

———. "News Analysts, Reporters, and Correspondents." In *Occupational Outlook Handbook, 2010–11 Edition.* Accessed January 24, 2012. http://www.bls.gov/oco/ocos088.htm.

Huffington, Arianna. "Announcing HuffPost Green: Our New Eco-News and Opinion Section." *Huffington Post,* June 4, 2008. Accessed March 9, 2012. http://www.huffingtonpost.com/ariannahuffington/announcing-huffpost-green_b_105033.html.

National Association of Colleges and Employers (NACE). *Salary Survey: January 2012.* Accessed January 11, 2012. http://www.naceweb.org/uploadedFiles/NACEWeb/Research/Salary_Survey/Reports/SS_January_report4web.pdf.

"Wendy Schmidt, Eric Schmidt and Arianna Huffington Honored by NRDC." *Huffington Post,* November 14, 2011. Accessed April 10, 2012. http://www.huffingtonpost.com/2011/11/14/schmidt-arianna-huffington-nrdc_n_1087202.html.

Yarow, Jay. "Chart of the Day: *Huffington Post* Traffic Zooms Past *The New York Times*." *Business Insider,* June 9, 2011. Accessed April 10, 2012. http://www.businessinsider.com/chart-of-the-day-huffpo-nyt-unique-visitors-2011-6.

Zemtseff, Katie (environmental reporter, the *Seattle Daily Journal of Commerce*) in discussion with the author, January 2012.

PUBLIC RELATIONS SPECIALISTS

NATURE OF THE WORK

Public relations specialists are hired to ensure that an organization, a company, or a client is viewed in a positive light. Their success in doing so can greatly affect whether the company gains and maintains customers, sees profits rise, or even continues to do business. Showing that the company cares about and addresses environmental issues can help create and maintain this favorable image. Thus, companies often turn to specialists in the public relations field to plan, coordinate, and place their environmental efforts, big or small, in the public eye.

The trend for promoting all things green has become so widespread in recent years that it has generated a new term: *greenwashing*, making an environmental-responsibility claim that is at best tenuous and at worse false. As people become more conscious about the sustainability of things they use, companies have been increasingly churning out products and services that claim to save the environment, protect natural resources, or lighten landfill loads. In 2010 the U.S. Federal Trade Commission (FTC) released proposed guidelines to limit greenwashing and other "unqualified" eco-friendly claims. Although those guidelines have not been finalized and are voluntary, the *New York Times* reports that the FTC has been filing more complaints about purported environmental benefits of services and products.

Although such complaints are often leveled against manufacturers rather than their promotional representatives, public relations specialists are directly affected by the growth in and potential regulation of environmental marketing. They must learn about and be able to explain all aspects of the product, service, or project they are promoting. "Ensuring that the thing in question really is

green before you start talking about it should go a long way toward preventing greenwash problems," notes the *From Greenwash to Great* handbook from OgilvyEarth, the sustainability-focused marketing arm of public relations giant Ogilvy & Mather. The company is one of many proactively attempting to find ways to inform the public about environmental efforts by clients without overreaching in their claims. The handbook goes on to explain how to conscientiously promote a company or product in today's green-focused world.

Not all public relations efforts are directly related to business. Nonprofit groups, interest groups, government agencies, and even political campaigns hire public relations specialists to help them garner support for a project or goal. Such specialists are often the go-betweens for these groups and the media, rather than directly interacting with the public, leading to the titles of media specialist and communications specialist for some jobs. Those who work with government agencies may be referred to as public affairs or public involvement specialists. Press secretaries work for agencies ranging from a city mayor's office to the White House in the U.S capital.

In any of these roles, public relations specialists may focus on environmental issues. They may work for a conservation group to generate public response to environmental conflicts. They may help a solar technology company develop a marketing campaign for its products or garner media attention for the latest advances in the field and their client's role in them. They may work on a team with legislative and regulatory experts to help a manufacturer navigate laws and advocate its interests in environmental regulations, such as those aimed to reduce emissions.

Some people interested in bringing public input into projects that affect their communities and local environment have shifted into another realm, that of public involvement. The field grew out of federal and state requirements put into place in the 1970s and 1980s that emphasized the need for public input while planning and deciding how to implement large-scale public works projects. Whereas the public relations field tends to seek public approval at the start of a project, those in public involvement are more interested in public input on how to address an issue. Most public involvement companies have a highly diverse staff, including biologists, chemists, land use experts, and political scientists. In addition, many have a payroll with multiple positions for those trained in communications in general and public relations in particular.

People who work in public involvement and relations are often busy all day, every day, juggling many tasks and keeping in contact with a range of people and organizations to continue to promote their clients' products and services. In addition to many phone conversations and e-mail exchanges, public relations specialists often write press releases announcing their clients' plans and successes. They may be in charge of organizing, preparing materials for, and hosting events, as well as promoting them. In today's technology environment, they may also manage social networking pages or Twitter about such events for their clients.

WORKING CONDITIONS

Public relations specialists are constantly on the move, and people who cannot handle stress, short deadlines, long hours, and shifting schedules rarely do well in the field. Overtime is often a part of the job, sometimes regularly and sometimes only when a special event or project is occurring. Travel and evening engagements to participate in community meetings or entertain clients are also common. However, safety or unpleasant working environments are rarely issues in this field.

Even when they are not officially at work, many people in the public relations field are on call in case news breaks

that needs an immediate response to ensure the company or organization remains in good standing. Therefore, they generally enjoy working in a high-profile, fast-paced environment and are comfortable mixing work with daily life via smartphones, e-mail, and other technology.

EMPLOYMENT

The public relations field is large, with nearly 225,600 people working in it as of May 2010 according to the U.S. Department of Labor's Bureau of Labor Statistics (BLS). A large number are employed by organizations focused on promoting a professional, political, or social group. However, most people in the field work for advertising or public relations companies, which are then hired by another company to provide all public relations services to enhance the work of the company's in-house staff. Nearly 17,000 public relations specialists are employed by colleges and universities to promote the school. Those teaching communications courses at such institutions are not included in this number. Local government agencies and private businesses may contract out for public relations services, but many large organizations have an in-house staff.

Most people in this field are currently in large cities, especially in California, New York, and Texas, but opportunities increasingly exist in other areas with public relations firms that cater to a local clientele. As global interconnectivity continues to expand, international jobs or United States-based jobs with international clients are expanding as well, particularly for those who speak a second language.

TRAINING, OTHER QUALIFICATIONS, AND ADVANCEMENT

Many people entering the public relations field earn a communications-related degree, often in journalism, mass communications, marketing, or public relations specifically. Journalists with work experience may find their writing, reporting, and deadline-oriented abilities coveted by public relations firms. Others earn a bachelor's degree in a different discipline, such as environmental studies or a science, and hone their communications skills through an internship or other work experience so that they can promote a company or organization in their area of expertise. However, regardless of their degree's focus, anyone interested in pursuing a career in public relations is advised to undertake an internship while still in school. It not only provides work experience but also gives connections for job opportunities after graduation.

This area of study is usually under a communications department and for good reason: the job is all about providing information concisely and clearly. In addition to excellent speaking and writing skills, public relations specialists must be competent organizers, researchers, decision makers, problem solvers, and motivators. People who are social, confident, innovative, and assertive yet flexible excel in this job.

Early in this career, a public relations specialist may be one of several members of a team working on a project and may be given tasks related to learning about the company or the topic it addresses by following news reports, gathering background materials, answering phone calls and emails, and compiling information into internal reports. Later, specialists may move to larger or higher-profile projects, be put in charge of a team, or even head a public relations department or move to an executive position from which they oversee efforts to enhance and maintain an organization's public image. Experts in this field often find success in opening their own consulting firm or public relations office and working independently.

Experienced public relations specialists may seek certification through an industry organization such as the Public Relations Society of America or the International Association of Business Communicators. Although not necessary, such certifications can lead to more or better positions in the field.

JOB OUTLOOK

Job opportunities for public relations specialists are expected to grow quickly in the coming years. A large number of openings is expected: up to 24 percent more by 2018 than there were in 2008, according to the BLS. The *Occupational Outlook Quarterly* anticipates that 70,000 public relations jobs will be open to college graduates through 2014. Competition is still likely to be stiff for jobs for *Fortune 500* companies and national organizations, particularly at the entry level. However, global businesses are providing more opportunities in other countries and within the United States, making second-language skills a significant asset. Job security related to these large groups can be fairly volatile, reflecting a reliance on clients to keep work flowing and budgets high.

EARNINGS

The National Association of Colleges and Employers' January 2012 salary survey found that on average, public relations specialists earn US$35,800 annually in their first job. The mean annual wage for established workers in this field is US$59,150, according to May 2010 statistics published by the BLS. Top-paying jobs can have annual salaries of US$95,200 or more.

Public relations specialists who work for advertisers are generally known to make more than those who work for other organizations. However, despite the large numbers of public relations specialists at advertising firms and those promoting various organizations and colleges and universities, the top-paying employers for public relations experts are the U.S. government and the U.S. Postal Service, which the BLS reports as paying, on average, annual salaries of about US$85,500. People who promote computer-related companies or car manufacturers are nearly as highly paid.

RELATED OCCUPATIONS

Public relations specialists must be good communicators, making their role similar to that of other jobs, such as the following:

- Green marketers
- Marketing managers
- Reporters and correspondents
- Wholesale and manufacturing sales representatives
- Wholesale and retail buyers, except farm products

SOURCES OF ADDITIONAL INFORMATION

International Association of Business Communicators. http://www.iabc.com
International Association for Public Participation. http://www.iap2.org
Public Relations Society of America. http://www.prsa.org

FURTHER READING

Bureau of Labor Statistics, U.S. Department of Labor. "27-3031 Public Relations Specialists." In *Occupational Employment Statistics: Occupational Employment and Wages, May 2010,* last modified May 17, 2011. Accessed March 20, 2012. http://www.bls.gov/oes/current/oes273031.htm.
———. "Advertising and Public Relations Services." In *Career Guide to Industries, 2010–11 Edition.* Accessed January 30, 2012. http://www.bls.gov/oco/cg/cgs030.htm.
———. "Public Relations Specialists." *In Occupational Outlook Handbook, 2010–11 Edition.* Accessed January 24, 2012. http://www.bls.gov/oco/ocos086.htm.
Crosby, Olivia, and Roger Moncarz. "The 2004–14 Job Outlook for College Graduates." In *Occupational Outlook Quarterly,* Fall 2006. Accessed March 20, 2012. http://www.bls.gov/opub/ooq/2006/fall/art03.pdf.
National Association of Colleges and Employers (NACE). *Salary Survey: January 2012.* Accessed January 11, 2012. http://www.naceweb.org/uploadedFiles/NACEWeb/Research/Salary_Survey/Reports/SS_January_report4web.pdf.
Nelson, Gabriel, and Amanda Peterka (Greenwire). "FTC Proposes Crackdown on 'Greenwashing.'" *New York*

Times, October 6, 2010. Accessed March 20, 2012. http://www.nytimes.com/gwire/2010/10/06/ 06greenwire-ftc-proposes-crackdown-on-greenwashing-42606.html?pagewanted=all.

OgilvyEarth. *From Greenwash to Great: A Practical Guide to Great Green Marketing (without the Greenwash).*

Accessed January 30, 2012. http://www.ogilvyearth .com/wp-content/uploads/2011/05/Greenwash_ Digital.pdf.

O*NET OnLine. *Summary Report for: 27-3031.00—Public Relations Specialists.* Accessed January 25, 2012. http:// www.onetonline.org/link/summary/27-3031.00.

FISH AND GAME WARDENS

NATURE OF THE WORK

Fish and game wardens are the police officers of the natural world, watching over public use of waterways and wild lands. They are often thought of as law enforcement officers for hunting, fishing, and boating regulations, but their daily tasks are usually divided among public safety, wildlife protection, and community stewardship activities. They are key players on search-and-rescue teams, and they respond to accidents, natural disasters, and other complaints. Fish and game wardens have a long history in these roles. In California, wardens were the first peace officers, working nearly 50 years before the establishment of the state's highway patrol.

The duties of fish and game wardens can vary depending on the level of government at which they are employed. The U.S. Fish and Wildlife Service employs refuge officers who work closely with other national wildlife refuge staff and enforce federal laws that affect natural resources. However, most wardens are trained and employed by states. Local wardens are often trained by the state but assigned to a county or region. Wardens at all government levels usually enforce federal fish and wildlife laws as well as state-specific ones, not only within their jurisdiction but also in surrounding areas.

A jurisdiction can be extensive and in coastal states may include vast ocean areas where state or federal laws are enforced. Those in states bordering Mexico or Canada, such as Texas and California, may be considered terrestrial wardens and be heavily involved in homeland security and patrolling the international border in their area. Those who patrol major waterways and oceans may be designated marine wardens and are heavily involved in fisheries enforcement.

Although many game warden duties relate to law enforcement, those laws are often in place to ensure protection of natural resources, and wardens are sometimes referred to as conservation, wildlife, or refuge officers.

AT A GLANCE FACT BOX

SOC: 33-3031.00
Preferred Education: Associate's degree or two years of college
Average Salary: US$55,650 annually
Other Information: Fish and game wardens often oversee huge areas of rural and rugged land, each warden covering about 3,500 square miles in states such as Nevada

They are involved not only in reporting or apprehending violators but also in addressing the violations and how they affect the environment. In California, if a hazardous spill occurs anywhere off of state highways or in the ocean within 200 miles of the California coast, wardens are the primary responders. The top warden on the scene of such an accident may be the incident commander, supervising not only other wardens but also responders from the U.S. Coast Guard and other agencies.

Poaching has become a key issue for some agencies. Many wildlife departments operate hotlines or websites through which citizens can report poaching and other violations. Arkansas is taking the technology further with an anonymous text messaging system for reporting such crimes and plans to add an iPhone application. California has a special unit in its Department of Fish and Game that targets commercial poaching operations, particularly of abalone, sturgeon, and bear. Its members have training in investigative techniques and their efforts have resulted in more than US$1 million in fines and 100 accumulative years of prison and jail terms in recent years according to the California Fish and Game Wardens Association.

As with the reporting system for poaching in Arkansas, technology is continually changing the fieldwork of fish and game wardens. The tools they use to monitor activities and enforce regulations have long included maps and cameras, but today's global positioning system devices, digital video cameras, and advanced night-vision and high-powered optics have considerably enhanced their arsenal. Mobile applications for smartphones that access state and federal enforcement records allow them to check everything from criminal records to boat, vehicle, and firearm registration, a capability particularly useful for wardens checking permits and licenses while in the field.

Not all time is spent outdoors patrolling public lands and enforcing regulations. Wardens are also administrators, and they log desk hours investigating issues related to licenses and permits and preparing reports and testimony for hearings. They act as investigators at a scene rather than bringing in outside investigators as in other law enforcement branches, and they may work with lab technicians and scientists to learn from their evidence. They may also work with other government agencies to create environmental regulations, such as those related to timber harvest in forested areas or commercial activity near water sources. They are often the public face of the department, presenting programs and information to other officials, landowners, and resource users.

WORKING CONDITIONS

Although they may not be enforcing laws in areas with large violent crime rates, fish and game wardens are nevertheless law enforcement officers and must be physically and mentally prepared to face such dangers should any occur. They often work alone in remote areas, where it is difficult to bring in or sometimes even contact backup officers, and encounters with armed hunters and other civilians are increasingly common. They also face potential dangers from wildlife encounters and foul weather. The U.S. Department of Labor, however, reports this occupation had the lowest number of job fatalities of all law enforcement officers from 2003 to 2010.

Because of the potential physical and emotional stresses of the job, applicants are usually required to see both a physician and a psychologist before their game warden training begins. This is not only out of concern for the warden's safety; game wardens are sworn peace officers who carry firearms and back up other law enforcement agencies, so it is in the public interest that they undergo rigorous training and exams. Many departments require them to pass a physical fitness test because much of their patrol time is on foot and may be through rugged terrain.

As with most law enforcement positions, fish and game wardens rarely work a standard schedule. Texas is among the states that give time off rather than additional pay for overtime hours. In California, most wardens work from home offices and are nearly always on call. Many of their busiest days are those when other people do not work, particularly weekends and holidays. Although many public areas bear signs indicating closure after dark, often the only way to keep people out is with patrols.

EMPLOYMENT

U.S. fish and game wardens are employed exclusively by government agencies, with the majority working for state governments. There are about 7,200 people working as fish and game wardens in the United States according to the Department of Labor. Georgia and Florida have the largest employment base, followed by Texas, Tennessee, and Louisiana. In many states, new hires have little say in where they work within the state. According to the Texas Parks and Wildlife Department, "Assignments will be made where vacancies exist statewide and shall be made in the best interest of the department."

TRAINING, OTHER QUALIFICATIONS, AND ADVANCEMENT

Although many states accept people with associate's degrees into their game warden training programs, some prefer a bachelor's degree. Work as a conservation or refuge officer with the federal government usually requires a four-year degree. Common majors are related to biological science, natural resources, forestry, or law enforcement. Some universities offer degrees in fish and wildlife management that are ideally suited for people seeking this career.

Education rarely ends there for wardens. Most states have a training academy, where cadets spend three to 12 months training for the role. The courses teach cadets about the policies they will be upholding and the tactics they can use to do so. They undergo physical training, including that necessary for water rescue and personal defense, and they study first aid techniques. Upon graduating, they generally must pass the licensing exam for peace officers before they can begin work.

Once commissioned, fish and game wardens can move up through several levels of authority and pay based primarily on experience and performance. In some states, wardens can advance to become lieutenants who specialize in a specific area or program, captains who supervise other officers, and chiefs who run a department. With experience, there are also opportunities for other law enforcement roles, including investigative and administrate positions.

Good fish and game wardens have a personal connection with the environment and enjoy outdoor recreation.

They must be comfortable not only with meeting new people but also with working alone. All of the traits valued in law enforcement such as responsibility, respectability, honesty, and integrity are important for fish and game wardens as well.

JOB OUTLOOK

The U.S. Department of Labor expects population increases throughout the country to spur growth for police services in general. However, some states are struggling to fill game warden positions, citing lower salaries and fewer benefits in comparison with other law enforcement agencies. In Nevada, only 31 game wardens patrol the 110,000-plus square miles of the state, each covering an average area of 3,567 square miles. In California, the monthly starting salary for a highway patrol officer is US$5,537 to US$6,732, compared with US$3,581 to US$4,698 for a fish and game warden. Organizations such as the California Fish and Game Wardens Association are seeking to narrow that pay gap and change other benefit differences.

In most government agencies, budget cuts are the biggest threat to job security. However, staff reductions for law enforcement occupations are usually made by discontinuing a position when someone retires, and trained wardens are often in demand at other agencies if they lose a job for budget reasons.

EARNINGS

Fish and game wardens earn an annual mean salary of US$55,650 according to the U.S. Department of Labor. The Department's May 2010 figures indicated that the lowest paid workers in this occupation earn less than US$31,130 per year; the highest paid have annual incomes of US$81,250 or more. State government wages tend to be the highest, followed by federal and then local governments. Those working in urban areas generally earn more than those in rural ones, although in some states, rural areas offer more job opportunities.

In most states, people accepted for the game warden training program earn entrance pay during their months in the course. After completing all requirements and receiving a commission as game warden, pay is generally based on years of experience and job performance, possibly with additional monthly stipends for continuing education or other certifications. In Texas, the entry-level salary for commissioned game wardens was around US$39,000 in 2009.

RELATED OCCUPATIONS

In their law enforcement role, fish and game wardens have duties similar to those of many other law enforcement officials, as well as paramedics and firefighters. On the environmental and conservation side, the following occupations share some functions:

- Agricultural inspectors
- Forest and conservation workers
- Soil and water conservationists

SOURCES OF ADDITIONAL INFORMATION

California Fish and Game Wardens Association. http://www.californiafishandgamewardens.com

Federal Wildlife Officers Association. http://www.fwoa.org

National Oceanic and Atmospheric Administration's National Marine Fisheries Service. http://www.nmfs.noaa.gov

National Wildlife Refuge Officers Association. http://www.nwroa.org

North American Wildlife Enforcement Officers Association. http://naweoa.org

FURTHER READING

AmmoLand.com. "Arkansas Game & Fish Commission Offers New System to Turn in Poachers," January 25, 2012. Accessed March 2, 2012. http://www.ammoland.com/2012/01/25/arkansas-game-fish-commission-offers-new-system-to-turn-in-poachers/.

Bureau of Labor Statistics, U.S. Department of Labor. "33-3031 Fish and Game Wardens." In *Occupational Employment Statistics: Occupational Employment and Wages, May 2010,* last modified May 17, 2011. Accessed February 7, 2012. http://www.bls.gov/oes/current/oes333031.htm.

———. "All Worker Profile, 2003–2010." In *Census of Fatal Occupational Injuries.* Accessed February 6, 2012. http://www.bls.gov/iif/oshwc/cfoi/all_worker.pdf.

———. "Police and Detectives." In *Occupational Outlook Handbook, 2010–11 Edition.* Accessed February 5, 2012. http://www.bls.gov/oco/ocos160.htm.

California Department of Fish and Game. *Fish and Game Warden Career: Compensation.* Accessed February 6, 2012. http://www.dfg.ca.gov/enforcement/career/compensation.aspx.

California Fish & Game Wardens Association. *Special Operations Unit.* Accessed February 7, 2012. http://www.californiafishandgamewardens.com/specops.htm.

Nevada Department of Wildlife. *Become a Nevada Game Warden.* Accessed February 6, 2012. http://ndow.org/about/jobs/warden_recruit_brochure.pdf.

Texas Parks and Wildlife Department. *Game Warden: Career Opportunities.* Accessed February 5, 2012. http://www.tpwd.state.tx.us/warden/career_opportunities/.

SECTOR OVERVIEW: GOVERNMENTAL AND REGULATORY ADMINISTRATION

A governmental or regulatory administration management career in the United States may involve working for a public or private organization to help shape public policy, enforce safety rules and laws, create new buildings or neighborhoods, or oversee operations on construction jobs, environmental assessment or protection efforts, or other types of projects. In addition to U.S. federal organizations, city departments, and other local agencies, nonprofit organizations and private organizations also employ building inspectors, urban planners, project engineers, compliance managers, financial analysts, and other types of governmental and regulatory managerial professionals.

THE GOVERNMENT AND REGULATORY INDUSTRY GOES GREEN

In recent years, the popularity of *green practices*, which can range from recycling materials to improving water quality, has led to an increase in governmental and regulatory careers that involve creating, evaluating, and enforcing sustainable living practices and policies.

Since 1970, when the government created the U.S. Environmental Protection Agency (EPA), public interest in protecting the environment has grown. Green building, for example, which involves using environmentally conscious practices during construction and designing buildings to be energy efficient, is expected to grow from 6 billion square feet in 2010 to 53 billion square feet by 2020, according to the 2010 "Green Building Certification Programs" report from market research and consulting firm Pike Research.

Approximately 2.7 million Americans are employed in some aspect of the green economy according to the 2011 "Sizing the Clean Economy: A National and Regional Green Jobs Assessment" report from the Brookings Institution, a nonprofit public policy organization based in Washington, DC.

The U.S. Green Building Council, a Washington, DC-based nonprofit that promotes green building and design, estimates that the green construction-related workforce will reach 3.3 million between 2009 and 2013. From 2000 to 2008, the industry had just 1 million workers.

The rapidly growing government and regulatory management sector of the job market includes several new and emerging green industry-related occupations, according to O*NET.

Some occupations have a clear tie-in with the growing emphasis on green living. Environmental engineers, for example, handle toxic materials control, air pollution, and public health. Similarly, soil and water conservationists help landowner and management officials stop erosion and protect their property, and sustainability specialists work with green building practices.

In its 2009 "Greening of the World of Work: Implications for O*NET-SOC and New and Emerging Occupations" report, O*NET defined more than 15 governmental or regulatory administration management occupations as *green increased demand,* industries that are expected to experience an increase in employment, *green enhanced skills occupations,* or *green new and emerging occupations.*

Enhanced skills occupations involve industries in which green economy technology and practices have changed specific job tasks, skill sets, and general know-how. New and emerging occupations involve new fields and positions that have been created as a result of the green economy.

TYPES OF GOVERNMENTAL AND REGULATORY ADMINISTRATION JOBS

Although many industries, organizations, and other agencies employ governmental and regulatory administration officials, the specific positions vary and can include the following:

- Chief sustainability officers, regulatory affairs managers, and compliance managers
- Regulatory affairs specialists, energy auditors, sustainability specialists, and financial analysts
- Environmental engineers and nuclear engineers
- Soil and water conservationists, urban and regional planners, transportation planners, and other types of life, physical, and social services jobs
- Arbitrators, mediators, and conciliators
- Agricultural inspectors
- Construction and building inspectors and other types of construction and extraction positions
- Inspectors, testers, sorters, samplers, or weighers
- Transportation, equipment, and systems inspectors

BECOMING A GOVERNMENTAL OR REGULATORY MANAGER

Because of their specialized nature, some green industry administrator positions, such as building code inspector, nuclear waste management engineer, or fuel testing/verification technician, require specific knowledge and experience. The skills workers need to properly perform these positions range from a thorough understanding of how law and government works to additional education and training.

Several schools offer government- and/or regulatory-related programs. According to a Fall 2010 survey from the National Association of Schools of Public Affairs and Administration (NASPAA), an organization of 275 institutions that offer programs in public affairs, public policy, public administration, and nonprofit management, students can choose from 136 master of public administration programs and at least 20 public policy master-level programs.

Fifty-seven schools offer city, community, and regional planning undergraduate and graduate programs, and 248 offer a public administration bachelor's degree program according to the College Board, a nonprofit organization that promotes higher education advocacy and research.

OTHER TRAINING

Some green governmental or regulatory administrator positions require a formal, collegiate education. Building-based urban planners, engineers, and architects typically have a bachelor's degree, according to the U.S. Department of Labor's Bureau of Labor Statistics (BLS). Financial analysts also often have a four-year degree.

Further education and degrees are common in some governmental and regulatory fields. Thirty percent of regulatory affairs managers, for example, also had a master's degree, and 6 percent had also obtained a doctoral or other professional degree. However, vocational school training, in-office experience, or an associate's degree may be more common for some governmental or regulatory administrator positions, such as the energy auditor occupation.

Additional jobs, including those that involve installing energy-efficient appliances, may instead require detailed training and instruction. Installation experts can become certified through programs run by groups such as the North American Board of Certified Energy Practitioners, a volunteer board of renewable energy stakeholder representatives from the solar industry, renewable energy organizations, state policymakers, educational institutions, and other groups.

THE MANAGEMENT JOB MARKET

Many sustainable government and regulatory positions require workers to complete higher education programs. Therefore, the additional expense and time spent earning a degree may pay off when individuals begin looking for a job, as several regulatory and government-related jobs are expected to grow in the next few years.

Conservation is expected to continue to be a growing green field. From 2003 to 2010, 121,000 new conservation jobs were created according to the Brookings Institution study. Waste management was also a booming field, hiring 119,000 new workers between 2003 and 2010. In North Carolina alone, recycling jobs rose 5 percent.

Certain transportation jobs, which are considered green because of the reduction in release of nitrous oxides when items are sent via train rather than truck, are also forecast to grow. In one month in 2011, seven railroad companies added a total of nearly 1,200 jobs, according to the Brookings Institution.

SOURCES OF ADDITIONAL INFORMATION

The College Board. https://bigfuture.collegeboard.org
Occupational Outlook Handbook. http://www.bls.gov/oco
U.S. Environmental Protection Agency (EPA). http://www.epa.gov
U.S. Green Building Council. http://www.usgbc.org

FURTHER READING

Brookings Institution. *Sizing the Clean Economy: A National and Regional Green Jobs Assessment.* Accessed March 20, 2012. http://www.brookings.edu/reports/2011/0713_clean_economy.aspx.

NASPAA. *2009–10 Roster of Accredited Programs.* Accessed March 20, 2012. http://www.naspaa.org/accreditation/document/OfficialRosterAccreditedPrograms09-10_9.1.pdf.

O*NET OnLine. *Greening of the World of Work: Implications for O*NET-SOC and New and Emerging Occupations.* Accessed March 20, 2012. http://www.onetcenter.org/dl_files/Green.pdf.

PikeResearch. *Green Building Certification Programs.* Accessed March 20, 2012. http://www.pikeresearch.com//research/green-building-certification-programs.

CHIEF SUSTAINABILITY OFFICERS

NATURE OF THE WORK

In its 2009 "Greening of the World of Work: Implications for O*NET-SOC and New and Emerging Occupations" report, O*NET singled out the chief sustainability officer role as a regulatory position that showed growth potential. The chief sustainability officer's position typically involves communicating and coordinating sustainability challenges and solutions with the company management, shareholders, or customers. Chief sustainability officers may also create or oversee a sustainability strategy designed for the entire corporation.

In some cases, chief sustainability officers may also be responsible for following guidelines set by other organizations. If applicable governmental or environmental regulations exist, sustainability officers may need to ensure a company's or organization's programs are compliant with those regulations.

The Growing Role of the Chief Sustainability Officer

The chief sustainability officer role is one of the governmental and regulatory positions that has experienced growth in recent years and, in many ways, is still a new and emerging field.

The *New York Times* reported in March 2009 that a growing number of companies, including software company SAP and medical materials provider PGI, were adding chief sustainability officers to oversee organization-wide corporate environmental programs. Many report directly to the company president.

Some of the industry growth is undoubtedly related to the increased focus in the United States on green products

---

AT A GLANCE FACT BOX

SOC: 11-1011.03
Preferred Education: Bachelor's or master's degree in business administration or similar field
Average Salary: US$165,080 annually
Other Information: The first known chief sustainability officer position was created in 2004

---

and services. O*NET has denoted the chief sustainability officer role as a Bright Outlook occupation. This is a job that O*NET has projected will grow quickly, feature numerous job openings, or could be considered a new and emerging profession.

Other growing fields O*NET has identified include the following:

- Air quality control specialists, who perform emissions control research and provide facilities with permits
- Greenhouse gas emissions permitting consultants, who collect and analyze data and help plan gas emission reduction measures
- Sustainability specialists, professionals who address organizational environmental issues, including green building procedures and waste management

Corporate America Goes Green Green products and services have grown in popularity in the United States and appear to still be on the rise. According to a 2011 Gallup survey of 31,000 consumers in 26 countries, commissioned by the wind turbine manufacturer Vestas Wind Systems A/S, 50 percent of consumers say they will pay more for products from green companies that use renewable energy.

Green building projects also appear to be on the rise. Construction of green homes is expected to grow to become 29 to 38 percent of the residential building market by 2016, increasing from US$17 billion to between US$87 and US$114 billion, according to McGraw-Hill Construction's *Green Home Builders and Remodelers Study*.

There is a good reason for this trend. Homeowners who go green may profit from their investment. Solar panels, a green home element, helped increase home values in California, according to a 2011 Lawrence Berkeley National Laboratory study that examined home sales over a more than 8-year period.

As green items and production procedures become more popular, companies have begun to place a larger emphasis on ensuring that their processes are environmentally friendly. In 2004, chemical and product producer DuPont was the first company to appoint a chief sustainability officer, Linda Fisher, according to consulting and recruiting company Weinreb Group's "CSO Back Story: How Chief Executive Officers Reached the C-Suite" 2011 report. (Her title in March 2012, according to the DuPont website, is Vice President–DuPont Safety, Health & Environment and Chief Sustainability Officer.)

There are approximately 29 chief sustainability officers who currently work for publicly traded U.S. companies, according to the Weinreb Group's report.

Being a Chief Sustainability Officer Chief sustainability officers regularly perform many tasks that help companies make their operations and/or the products and services they produce greener. Chief sustainability officers may create or enact plans to deal with environmentally related issues such as recycling, energy use, reducing waste or pollution, green construction, or education of employees about green practices. Their role may also involve overseeing and assessing how effective sustainability programs are by creating methodologies or other techniques to gauge the success or failure of various green efforts.

A chief sustainability officer's job may also include working with the media. Sustainability officers may need to spearhead marketing promotions for certain green efforts or promote environmental practices and programs to television, Internet, or print media outlets.

Part of the job often involves research as well. Chief sustainability officers are frequently responsible for discovering information about environmental issues, solutions, and technological advances that might be of interest to their company's shareholders.

Tools of the Trade Chief sustainability officers use a number of technological and other tools to perform their work. These tools can range from common office supplies, such as calculators and photocopiers, to enterprise resource planning software.

WORKING CONDITIONS

As top organizational executives, chief sustainability officers often work in office environments and have the aid of a support staff, according to the U.S. Department of Labor's Bureau of Labor Statistics (BLS). However, the job can involve a considerable time investment. Top executives frequently work more than 40 hours per week, logging in extra time on weekends and evenings.

Travel is typically part of the chief executive officer role and may also be part of the chief sustainability officer position. Attending association conferences and meeting with other company officials or external organizations are reasons for travel.

As with many top executive positions, which often involve considerable pressure, chief sustainability officers may feel pressure to meet certain environmental goals or quickly implement intensive programs to produce immediate results. However, if their role is fairly new within an organization, long-term goals and objectives may change or may still be determined.

EMPLOYMENT

As of 2008 there were currently 400,000 chief sustainability officers in the United States. From 2008 to 2018, O*NET predicts there will be 112,500 job openings in the chief sustainability officer industry.

The manufacturing industry was one of the top chief sustainability officer employers as of 2008. A large number of chief sustainability officers were also self-employed.

TRAINING, OTHER QUALIFICATIONS, AND ADVANCEMENT

Business-specific degrees are not necessarily a requirement to become a chief sustainability officer. According to the Weinreb Group's "CSO Back Story: How Chief Executive Officers Reached the C-Suite" 2011 report, just 4 of the 29 chief sustainability officers held master's of business administration degrees. However, according to the BLS, many top corporate executives have a bachelor's or a master's degree in business administration, liberal arts, or another area.

Experience at a company or organization may help a professional become a chief sustainability officer. The majority of chief sustainability officers were internally promoted to the position and had been with the company for 16 years on average, according to the Weinreb Group's report.

Some management associations, such as the American Management Association, offer courses and programs on sustainability. Certain colleges are also showing an interest in sustainability management. Schools including the University at Buffalo in New York, Alfred State College, and the State University of New York have created chief sustainability officer positions. A separate organization, the Association for the Advancement of Sustainability in Higher Education, works to promote sustainable efforts and best practices among college and university administrations.

Although formal education requirements may vary, writing skills may be an important part of the chief sustainability officer job. A chief sustainability officer may need to create presentations, reports, or formal proposals to present to company employees, governmental officials, public interest groups, or product or service suppliers.

Chief sustainability officers may also be responsible for assessing proposals that organizations submit to see whether the plans are possible to enact, if they will work with other preexisting green programs, and if they will work with any budgetary constraints.

JOB OUTLOOK

The projected growth for the chief sustainability officer field from 2008 to 2018 is not necessarily robust. In fact, the BLS estimates that there will be little to no change in the chief sustainability officer job market.

Despite calling the chief sustainability officer role a Bright Outlook occupation, which, in some cases, can indicate anticipated job growth in an industry, O*NET anticipates little to no change in the chief sustainability officer industry employment levels, projecting a 2 percent to negative 2 percent growth. O*NET's classification is likely due to the field's status as a new and emerging profession and the anticipated availability of job openings.

However, with a BLS-projected 112,500 job openings, the chief sustainability officer position should remain a valid career option for the governmental/regulatory industry.

EARNINGS

On average, chief sustainability officers earn US$165,080 per year or US$79.37 per hour, according to O*NET.

RELATED OCCUPATIONS

Management occupations with similar job responsibilities include the following:

- Administrative services managers
- Advertising, marketing, public relations, and sales managers
- Computer and information systems managers
- Financial managers

SOURCES OF ADDITIONAL INFORMATION

American Management Association (AMA). http://www .amanet.org
Association for the Advancement of Sustainability in Higher Education (AASHE). http://www.aashe.org

FURTHER READING

Bureau of Labor Statistics, U.S. Department of Labor. "Measuring Green Jobs," *Green Jobs.* Accessed March 16, 2012. http://www.bls.gov/green/home.htm.

Chen, Allen. "A Bright Spot for Solar: Berkeley Lab Study Finds that Photovoltaic Systems Boost the Sales Price of California Homes." *Berkeley Lab,* April 21, 2011. Accessed March 19, 2012. http://newscenter.lbl.gov/news-releases/2011/04/21/bright-spot-for-solar/.

Galbraith, Kate. "Companies Add Chief Sustainability Officers." *The New York Times,* March 2, 2009. Accessed March 19, 2012. http://green.blogs .nytimes.com/2009/03/02/companies-add-chief-sustainability-officers/.

McGraw-Hill Construction. *Green Homes Builders and Remodelers Study.* Accessed March 12, 2012. http://www.construction.com/about-us/press/green-homes-market-expected-to-increase-five-fold-by-2016.

O*Net OnLine. *Greening of the World of Work: Implications for O*NET-SOC and New and Emerging Occupations.* Accessed March 16, 2012. http://www .onetcenter.org/dl_files/Green.pdf.

———. *Summary Report for: 11-1111.03—Chief Sustainability Officer.* Accessed March 16. 2012. http://www.onetonline.org/link/summary/11-1011.03.

Vestas. *Global Consumer Wind Study 2011.* Accessed March 16, 2012. http://www.vestas.com/Files/Filer/EN/Press_releases/BloombergVestas_june_2011/Global_Consumer_Wind_Study_2011.pdf.

Weinreb Group. *CSO Back Story: How Chief Executive Officers Reached the C-Suite.* Accessed March 16, 2012. http://weinrebgroup.com/wp-content/uploads/2011/09/CSO-Back-Story-by-Weinreb-Group.pdf.

REGULATORY AFFAIRS MANAGERS

—■—

NATURE OF THE WORK

The regulatory affairs manager position involves establishing, overseeing, or coordinating a company's internal procedures to make sure they are in-line with predetermined standards and regulations according to O*NET, a U.S. job database being developed by the U.S. Department of Labor/Employment and Training Administration (USDOL/ETA). Unlike specific governmental affairs specialist positions that were established to primarily address issues outside of an organization, the regulatory affairs/compliance manager role tends to focus more on internal processes and conditions.

However, regulatory affairs managers may also oversee the process of obtaining a government agency's approval for the company's products or they may also be responsible for creating regulatory compliance practices.

The Green Economy and the Regulatory Affairs Manager Position Although price can be a deciding factor in many consumers' purchasing decisions, consumers across the world plan to buy more environmentally friendly or green products according to a 2011 study involving more than 9,000 people in eight countries.

The ImagePower Global Green Brands Survey, from communications agency Cohn & Wolfe, management consultant Esty Environmental Partners (EEP), brand consulting firm Landor Associates, and research-based consultancy Penn Schoen Berland, a unit of the WPP Group, found that consumers planned to buy green everyday products, as well as big-ticket purchases such as cars and technology items. More than 60 percent of consumers

---

AT A GLANCE FACT BOX

SOC: 11-9199.01

Preferred Education: Most regulatory affairs manager positions require a four-year bachelor's degree

Average Salary: US$96,450 annually

Other Information: On-the-job training and experience are highly recommended

---

said they wanted to purchase items from environmentally responsible companies.

Thus, as green living becomes more popular and as consumers express a desire to buy more green products, more companies are making a conscious effort to reduce any negative impact their production processes might have on the environment and therefore will green these processes as well as their products. Sustainable corporate responsibility is not a new trend. A 2007 Forbes article noted that large and small U.S. companies had already begun to consider and correct any potentially harmful environmental effect. (The article noted McDonald's, which paid attention to its suppliers' sustainability efforts; Office Depot, which created a system to better showcase the green goods it sold; and Gap, Adidas, and H&M as early corporate pioneers.)

The rise of corporate ecological responsibility has given way to a number of new positions such as the chief sustainability officer role and new responsibilities for managers, including regulatory affairs managers. At companies that have embraced green principles, the regulatory affairs manager's role may have switched from primarily ensuring that products and procedures are compliant and protecting public safety to instituting and overseeing new practices to make production more environmentally friendly.

The green economy has introduced new technologies that require approval, implementation, and perhaps future updates as new regulations are released. These technologies will help increase demand for regulatory affairs managers in the coming years according to the Hawaii Green Jobs Initiative website from the Hawaii Department of Labor and Industrial Relations.

The Regulatory Affairs Manager Role A regulatory affairs manager typically performs a variety of tasks that are both green-related and administrative. Regulatory affairs managers may be in charge of filling out and submitting applications to regulatory agencies or writing internal reports or other items. A regulatory affairs specialist may be responsible for performing more basic office duties, such as labeling materials or keeping files on the various stages of approval a specific product has gone through. However, a regulatory affairs manager is more likely to be in charge of reviewing all materials before they are sent to a regulatory agency to make sure they are accurate, complete, and sent on time.

Regulatory affairs managers may also be asked to advise new project teams or entire departments within a company on the development process, assessment, creation, or promotion of various green or other products.

Regulatory Skills Logical thinking plays a part in the regulatory affairs manager role; they are often asked to design policies and suggest steps to either establish regulatory compliance or maintain a current level of compliance. Regulatory affairs officials also need to be able to interpret recent changes to regulations or requirements to ensure the company's policies and procedures are compliant, which is particularly important in regard to new and emerging green production procedures and technologies.

Solid coordination skills are also key. Regulatory affairs managers often need to oversee the various steps involved in preparing documents or other items required for regulatory approval. If an external agency requests a response involving specific products, the regulatory affairs manager may also need to handle the question.

Product issues and complaints involving regulatory entities that require specific documentation may also fall under the regulatory affairs manager role; regulatory affairs managers may also need to manage the process of producing audits, product recalls, or inspections. If an external agency requests additional information, a company's regulatory affairs manager will often be responsible for supplying it.

WORKING CONDITIONS

The regulatory affairs manager's day may be composed of meetings because the manager is often required to advise project teams, communicate with government sources, or meet with other organizations. Regulatory affairs managers must also perform a considerable amount of research and reading. As the company source for ensuring that operations and products are compliant with current rules and regulations, regulatory affairs managers must stay up-to-date on preexisting and potential standards and other regulations.

As with similar occupations, regulatory affairs managers may also need to supervise or train other workers. Regulatory affairs specialists use a variety of instruments and tools to perform their jobs, ranging from scanners and computers to analytical software that helps them manage documents and create spreadsheets.

EMPLOYMENT

As of 2008, 898,000 regulatory affairs managers worked in the industry. The government was one of the top sectors employing regulatory affairs managers. Many of the other regulatory affairs managers were self-employed.

TRAINING, OTHER QUALIFICATIONS, AND ADVANCEMENT

Roughly 64 percent of regulatory affairs managers had a bachelor's degree. Thirty percent had also earned a master's degree, and 6 percent had a doctoral or other professional degree.

According to the Regulatory Affairs Professionals Society (RAPS), an international organization for regulators who work with health care products, most regulatory professionals have a bachelor's degree; more than half also hold an advanced degree, most frequently in either a scientific or technical field. Some universities and colleges offer undergraduate and graduate regulatory affairs programs; however, work experience remains an important job qualification according to RAPS.

RAPS also offers Regulatory Affairs Certification (RAC), a certification program that, according to the organization, has qualified more than 5,000 specialists, as well as ongoing educational programs on the regulatory requirements for various industries.

JOB OUTLOOK

Several regulatory and government-related jobs are expected to grow in the next few years, including the regulatory affairs management occupation. Regulatory affairs management positions are projected to see an increase of 7 to 13 percent during the 10-year period from 2008 to 2018. The regulatory affairs management industry is forecasted to see 297,500 job openings during the same time period.

However, the regulatory affairs manager occupation is not expected to experience as robust growth as other related roles in the field. For example, the regulatory affairs specialist, a related non-management position in the field, is expected to see a much faster than overage growth rate of more than 20 percent.

Nonetheless, as more companies place a greater emphasis on reducing the waste and pollution they produce during manufacturing and other green efforts, the regulatory affairs manager occupation may see additional growth. Some regions are already beginning to note an increase. According to Colorado State University's Regulatory Affairs Certificate program description, regulatory affairs management is a "rapidly growing field." According to CSU, the number of Colorado-based regulatory affairs managers is forecast to increase 17 percent to more than 22,000 industry members by 2016. The University of California, Irvine, also offers a regulatory affairs manager specialized study program via its extension program.

EARNINGS

On average, regulatory affairs managers earn US$96,450 a year or US$46.37 per hour.

RELATED OCCUPATIONS

Positions that involve similar job tasks and roles to the regulatory affairs manager position include sales managers, database administrators, accountants, teachers, chemists, environmental engineers, and criminal investigators.

SOURCES OF ADDITIONAL INFORMATION

Regulatory Affairs Professionals Society. http://www.raps.org

REGULATORYAFFAIRSMGRS. 830 Punchbowl Street, Room 304, Honolulu, HI 96813, 808-586-9013.

FURTHER READING

Bureau of Labor Statistics, U.S. Department of Labor. *Green Jobs.* Accessed March 1, 2012. http://www.bls.gov/green/home.htm.

Colorado State University. *Regulatory Affairs Certificate Program.* Accessed March 1, 2012. http://www.online.colostate.edu/certificates/regulatory-affairs.dot.

Hawaii Department of Labor and Industrial Relations. *Hawaii Green Jobs Initiative.* Accessed March 1, 2012. https://greenjobshawaii.hirenethawaii.com/default.asp?pg=C-.

O*NET OnLine. *Summary Report for: 11-9199.01— Regulatory Affairs Managers.* Accessed March 1, 2012. http://www.onetonline.org/link/summary/11-9199.01#WagesEmployment.

Phenicie, Carolyn. "Corporate America Goes Green." *Forbes.com,* October 3, 2007. Accessed March 1, 2012. http://www.forbes.com/2007/10/03/green-companies-environment-oped-cx_cph_1003green.html.

University of California, Irvine. *Regulatory Affairs Management Program.* Accessed March 1, 2012. http://unex.uci.edu/certificates/life_sciences/regulatory/.

WPP. "Consumer Interest in Green Products Expands Across Categories." *WPP,* June 8, 2011. Accessed March 1, 2012. http://www.wpp.com/wpp/press/press/default.htm?guid=%7B29de2868-995d-479a-9976-392a622fc7db%7D.

COMPLIANCE MANAGERS

NATURE OF THE WORK

A compliance manager ensures that all components of a company or business act in accordance with ethical and other regulatory requirements on the federal, state, and local level, according to the Occupational Information Network (O*NET), a U.S. job database being developed by the U.S. Department of Labor Employment and Training Administration. Because of the additional regulations and requirements that federal and local governments may require to ensure a company's or organization's production processes are ecologically safe and leave the least possible negative impact on the environment, compliance managers' responsibilities, along with the general demand for compliance managers, have changed in the early part of the 21st century.

O*NET has designated the compliance manager position as one that is green because it is changing worker skill requirements quickly due to sustainable economy-related technologies and activities. It is also considered a "bright outlook" occupation, which means it is expected to grow rapidly and will feature numerous job openings. As an emerging green occupation, the compliance manager field should experience increased demand. The U.S. Department of Labor's Bureau of Labor Statistics (BLS) estimates that the compliance officer industry grew 0.5 percent from 2011 to 2012.

What a Compliance Manager Does Compliance managers are in charge of developing or instituting methods to make a company or organization's processes compliant with local, state, or federal regulations. They may also be responsible for confirming that set regulation

---

AT A GLANCE FACT BOX

SOC: 11-9199.02
Preferred Education: Bachelor's degree
Average Salary: US$96,450 annually
Other Information: Additional certification, workplace training, and experience may be helpful for advancement

---

policies have been recorded and properly implemented. Compliance managers generally examine, assess, and determine if procedures or processes at a company are compatible with compliance requirements for permits, licenses, and other types of certification and approval.

As part of their work, compliance managers may be asked to create risk management plans after determining what compliance or procedural risks exist. If any compliance issues arise, compliance managers will likely be the ones to investigate breaches or misconduct. From time to time, compliance managers review processes to ensure that proper steps are being taken and that predetermined plans are being followed.

Communication also plays a part in the compliance manager's role. In some cases, compliance managers may need to create or convey new ways to assess, communicate, or confirm that compliance requirements are being met and share them with other parts of the organization. Writing skills are important because compliance managers sometimes need to establish procedures and policies in writing. They may also spearhead the completion of compliance reports that need to be filed with regulatory agencies. If compliance matters necessitate further investigation, the compliance manager is often the one responsible for determining if future checks and confirmations are needed.

WORKING CONDITIONS

Compliance managers often work indoors. Typical tasks they perform include writing reports, filling out and submitting applications, and researching regulations. They use many different types of technology and office aids to complete their work. Common tools can range from fax machines, computers, and photocopiers to spreadsheet creation programs and specialized compliance software.

Compliance managers who work for small businesses may perform slightly different tasks than managers who work for large corporations. To represent their interests, small business compliance managers are able to participate in the development of certain regulations through the Regulatory Flexibility Act (RFA), which was amended by the Small Business Regulatory Enforcement Fairness Act (SBREFA). The RFA helps small businesses express concerns and share needs before certain environmentally related regulations are enacted as they may be more adversely affected by such regulations than larger companies with more money and resources at their disposal. Recently published compliance guides involve topics such as emission standards for air pollutants from industrial, commercial, and institutional boilers; lead-based paint use; and renewable fuel program changes.

The U.S. Environmental Protection Agency (EPA), which tracks environmentally related federal and state enforcement and compliance activities using several databases, says that it also frequently takes small businesses' needs into consideration when making rules that could significantly affect small businesses. Compliance is key according to the EPA because it "helps organizations or individuals meet their obligations under environmental laws and regulations." In the 2011 fiscal year, US$19 billion was spent on compliance efforts and environmental improvement programs. The EPA also offers a compliance and enforcement database for roughly 800,000 regulated facilities throughout the United States called Enforcement & Compliance History Online (ECHO), which showcases five years' worth of facility inspections, enforcements, violations, and other information.

EMPLOYMENT

As of 2008, approximately 898,000 managers were employed in the industry, according to O*NET estimates. The government was one of the top managerial employers.

According to the BLS, 53,840 compliance officers, or 2.65 percent of the industry, worked for the U.S. federal executive branch. U.S. state and local governments ranked a close second, employing 29,040 and 26,670 compliance officers respectively.

California has the highest compliance officer employment level, with 23,800 compliance officers working in the state. Texas, with 20,070 compliance managers working in the state, ranked a close second. New York, Florida, and New Jersey were the third, fourth, and fifth states, respectively, with the highest employment level for the compliance manager occupation. Many other compliance managers are self-employed.

TRAINING, OTHER QUALIFICATIONS, AND ADVANCEMENT

A bachelor's degree is generally required for entry-level employment. Significant on-the-job experience and training, however, are the largest sources of post-secondary education in the field. Compliance managers also need to carefully follow changes to the industry and new green production trends because their job involves not only being informed about recent regulatory environment and other changes but also being able to ascertain how any recent changes could affect policies and procedures at their companies.

As environmental compliance needs have increased to meet companies' growing demand for qualified professionals, several universities and colleges have begun offering environmentally focused compliance programs. The University of California Irvine Extension's program launched a four-part Webinar certification series in 2012 on current sustainability trends. The third session, "Being in Compliance with Sustainability Reporting," deals specifically with the environment and compliance management. Completion of all four sessions, which were created for working professionals who are responsible for sustainable programs, results in credit approved by the Green Building Certification Institute (GBCI).

The National Registry of Environmental Professionals (NREP) plans to offer a computerized exam in 2013 for a Certified Environmental and Safety Compliance Officer (CESCO) certification. According to the NREP, the program was created to "fill the urgent need by government and the public for skilled and knowledgeable individuals to work protecting individuals and facilities in construction, government, utilities, business and industry."

JOB OUTLOOK

The BLS has forecast 14 percent growth between 2008 and 2018 for management, business, and financial occupations, a category that includes compliance officers and management analysts who offer ideas to enhance government operations. Between 2008 and 2018, O*NET estimates that there will be 297,500 job openings in the field and forecasts that the industry will grow between 7 percent and 13 percent. This faster than average growth rate is in part because of the growing green economy and the increased demand for compliance managers who can oversee sustainable production processes to ensure that they are compliant.

EARNINGS

Compliance managers earn, on average, US$96,450 per year or US$46.37 per hour. BLS estimates are somewhat lower, placing the average compliance officer salary at US$62,140. However, the BLS lists the high salary for this industry at US$94,880 and the lower end of the pay scale at US$34,540.

Washington, DC, was the top-paying area, offering compliance officers an average annual mean wage of US$82,190 as of 2010. Massachusetts ranked second with an average annual salary of US$74,250. The third top-paying state for compliance professionals was Connecticut, where compliance officers made, on average, US$72,050 a year.

RELATED OCCUPATIONS

Jobs similar to the compliance manager position include environmental compliance inspectors, construction and building inspectors, and financial examiners.

Like the compliance manager role, the chief sustainability officer occupation, energy audit position, and environmental certification specialist role have also been denoted as new and emerging occupations. The green economy will create an additional need for workers in those industries and require workers with specialized, green process-friendly skill sets.

SOURCES OF ADDITIONAL INFORMATION

California Occupational Guides. http://www.calmis.ca.gov

International Association of Risk and Compliance Professionals (IARCP). http://www .risk-compliance-association.com

The National Registry of Environmental Professionals (NREP). http://www.nrep.org

FURTHER READING

Bureau of Labor Statistics, U.S. Department of Labor. *Measuring Green Jobs*. Accessed March 1, 2012. http://www.bls.gov/green/home.htm.

———. *Occupational Employment Statistics: 13-1041 Compliance Officers*. Last updated May 17, 2011. Accessed March 1, 2012. http://www.bls.gov/oes/current/oes131041.htm#(3).

National Registry of Environmental Professionals. *Environmental Certifications Offered*. Accessed March 1, 2012. http://www.nrep.org/environmental-certifications.php.

O*NET OnLine. *Summary Report for: 11-9199.02— Compliance Managers*. Accessed March 1, 2012. http://www.onetonline.org/link/summary/11-9199.02.

The University of California, Irvine Extension. "Current Trends in Sustainability." Course catalog for Spring semester 2012. Accessed March 1, 2012. http://unex.uci.edu/courses/sectiondetail.aspx?year=2012&term=SPRING&sid=00079.

U.S. Environmental Protection Agency. *Compliance*. Accessed March 22, 2012. http://www.epa.gov/lawsregs/compliance.

REGULATORY AFFAIRS SPECIALISTS

NATURE OF THE WORK

Regulatory affairs specialists plan, lead, or organize production at an organization to ensure that the process is compliant with regulations and standard operating procedures, according to O*NET. The regulatory affairs specialist position has been identified by O*NET as a Green New and Emerging occupation, one that is likely to change as technology advances and green practices such as recycling, sustainable building, and resource conservation increase in popularity, resulting in new jobs in the regulatory affairs industry. The skills and experience regulatory affairs specialists will be required to have may change because of the growing green economy. Entirely new positions or roles in the field may also be created.

A large portion of the regulatory affairs specialist industry growth will be the result of the green economy's expansion and subsequent new regulations implemented to produce more environmentally conscious products according to iSeek, a career, education, and job resource website from the Minnesota Department of Employment and Economic Development and the Minnesota Department of Education.

What Regulatory Affairs Specialists Do General regulatory affairs specialist job tasks can include coordinating and recording internal processes, such as inspections, audits, and registrations, or renewals. Regulatory affairs specialists also are sometimes in charge of gathering and completing materials that are sent to regulatory agencies.

In addition to a four-year bachelor's degree, regulatory affairs specialists may also need or benefit from

---

AT A GLANCE FACT BOX

SOC: 13-1041.07
Preferred Education: Bachelor's degree
Average Salary: US$28.23 per hour or US$58,720 annually
Other Information: Additional workplace training and experience may be helpful

---

on-the-job training and experience. Most have degrees in science, particularly in the life sciences, clinical science, and/or engineering, according to the Regulatory Affairs Professionals Society (RAPS).

Because various industries employ regulatory affairs specialists, who are sometimes also referred to as compliance specialists, there are many ways a professional can specialize and carve out a niche in the industry. For example, some regulatory specialists may focus on the approval process surrounding new drugs, working and making contacts within the medical industry. A position that involves drug approval would also potentially involve working with government agencies such as the U.S. Food and Drug Administration.

Specific tasks often performed by regulatory affairs specialists include offering a technical review of data to ensure that regulatory-related submissions are complete and correct, assessing whether regulations or changes to any preexisting rules have been properly expressed throughout the company via its policies and actions, and maintaining internal files to gain approval of products that the company makes.

Regulatory affairs specialists use a number of different tools to complete their work. Although some specific skills are necessary to perform this work, including critical thinking skills, the ability to communicate and work with groups, and experience instructing others on subjects such as company procedures, the growth of technology in the past few decades has helped make the regulatory affairs specialists job more efficient and effective.

In addition to the typical office equipment such as computers and fax machines, regulatory specialists may also use various types of software that help them track and assess work, such as analytical software, statistical software, document management software, and database user interface software. As the green economy advances and grows, regulatory affairs specialists are likely to use new tools to conduct their work. They may also need to learn and work with new regulations and compliance requirements that have been created to ensure that products and their production have less of an impact on the environment.

WORKING CONDITIONS

The working environment that regulatory affairs specialists operate in each day can vary. In some cases, regulatory specialists may need to meet in person with individuals who work for the government or other organizations, which will require them to work outside of the office.

When in the office, regulatory affairs specialists do not necessarily spend the entire workday at their desks working on the computer. They may need to schedule or attend internal meetings, possibly to educate different sections of the company on following regulations. In some cases, they may need to observe certain departments or processes to gather data about the company's overall efficiency or compliance with certain standards.

Because being a regulatory affairs specialist may involve overseeing projects and recommending ways to improve operations, it can be a challenging position. Company divisions and employees do not always respond well to change. Therefore, people who become regulatory affairs specialists need to be able to accept criticism and remain calm during high-stress situations.

However, regulatory affairs specialists should feel safe, both physically and professionally, while they are at work. Unlike some more dangerous jobs, the regulatory affairs specialist position is one that generally involves good working conditions and provides a considerable amount of job security.

EMPLOYMENT

As of 2008, 260,000 regulatory affairs industry employees worked in the industry in the United States. Many companies employ regulatory affairs specialists. Any company that needs to gain government approval for products or enact safety regulations, such as medical equipment product manufacturers and companies that produce pharmaceuticals, could potentially have a regulatory affairs specialist.

Regulatory affairs specialists work to ensure that the production process and the items created are made in accordance with the applicable company, city, federal, and other requirements. Therefore, as more companies place a greater emphasis on being green, more specialists will be needed to handle the additional compliance to rules and regulations. Thus, if green products and environmentally conscious production methods continue to grow, the regulatory affairs industry should see a number of additional jobs open up.

TRAINING, OTHER QUALIFICATIONS, AND ADVANCEMENT

Approximately 78 percent of regulatory affairs specialists had a four-year bachelor's degree, according to O*NET. An additional 16 percent also had their master's degree, and just 3 percent had some college experience but no degree.

While obtaining experience, some individuals who are new to the regulatory affairs field may begin by gathering data or other tasks that do not involve as much responsibility as other tasks, such as managing an international project. Familiarity with procedures and approval processes can help a regulatory affairs specialist work effectively.

A solid understanding of how the U.S. government works, including government regulations and requirements and laws, is also an important qualification along with strong critical thinking and analysis abilities. The position often involves assessing procedures or deciding on the best way to obtain approval from an external agency. Some regulatory affairs specialists also serve as project managers, overseeing the process of product approval or implementing a new company-wide policy.

Professionals can opt to join RAPS, an international organization for regulatory specialists whose jobs involve working to guarantee the safety and availability of healthcare products. RAPS offers a certification program for professionals to obtain Regulatory Affairs Certification (RAC). More than 5,000 specialists have earned the qualification.

The organization also offers online education courses and sponsors several conferences and events around the United States each year. Its continuing education programs are offered in subjects such as regulatory requirements for medical devices and pharmaceutical products and biomedical business and legal management essentials.

Individuals can be certified in four categories: U.S. regulations, European Union regulations, Canadian regulations, or the General Scope certification. The latter helps strengthen professionals' overall practice skills and includes information on global standards.

JOB OUTLOOK

According to RAPS, on a global level, the largest number of regulatory-related professionals currently work in the industry sector. However, academic institutions, research organizations, and other sectors also employ regulatory affairs specialists. This trend may increase in the coming years as the green economy increases and more specialists are needed to ensure that any newly enacted, green-related regulations are being followed.

The growing popularity of green manufacturing methods and green products is one reason some organizations have projected that the regulatory affairs specialist field will grow in the next few years. O*NET has projected that between 2008 and 2018, the industry will swell by more than 20 percent, a rate that was designated as being "much faster than average," with an anticipated 108,500 job openings available during the same time. The growth is expected to be industry-wide and regional. Some regions and states also anticipate a heightened need for regulatory affairs specialists. Minnesota, for example, expects the field to grow by more than 28 percent through 2019.

CNNMoney.com/PayScale.com gave the industry a B in job security and future growth when it listed it as one the top careers to work in on its "Best Jobs in America 2009" list. CNNMoney.com/PayScale.com ranked the field's growth potential as even higher than O*NET's forecast. According to the "Best Jobs in America 2009" regulatory affairs specialist listing, the field should grow by 25 percent by 2018.

O*NET has labeled regulatory affairs specialists as a Bright Outlook occupation. Their work can help the company protect local resources and become generally greener, and can also help organizations spend less. Because regulatory affairs specialists are responsible for coordinating and tracking and potentially improving internal regulatory processes, they may be able to decrease the effect of their company's production process on the environment, reduce waste, or make the company greener in other ways, while also saving it money.

Companies may be hiring more regulatory affairs specialists in part because going green has become increasingly popular in recent years. Greening operations is not just a trendy choice. It can have a big effect on the bottom line. Companies can take advantage of environmentally related grants, for example, a North Carolina winery was able to trim US$7,000 a year in natural gas and electricity costs after undergoing solar energy-related renovations paid for by a grant from the North Carolina Green Business Fund, the *Morganton News Herald* reported in December 2011. Under the Waste Reduction Awards Program of the Department of Resources Recycling and Recovery (CalRecycle), the award winners, a mix of small businesses and large corporations in California, reportedly prevented more than 2.3 million tons of material from going into landfills and saved more than US$200 million in the process.

EARNINGS

A CNNMoney.com/PayScale.com career profile, part of its "Best Jobs in America 2009" compilation, lists US$103,000 as the high salary for the regulatory affairs specialists industry. The average salary was US$72,800, according to CNNMoney.com/PayScale.com. According to O*NET, the current average pay is a bit lower: US$28.23 per hour or approximately US$58,720 per year.

RELATED OCCUPATIONS

Similar jobs/titles include regulatory affairs managers and compliance officers. Occupations that are similar also require the employee to perform tasks such as coordinating, supervising, training, and managing processes or people. These requirements are found in roles such as database administrators, sales managers, accountants, and environmental engineers.

SOURCES OF ADDITIONAL INFORMATION

Regulatory Affairs Professionals Society (RAPS). http://www.raps.org

FURTHER READING

Bureau of Labor Statistics, U.S. Department of Labor. "Measuring Green Jobs." *Green Jobs.* Accessed March 2, 2012. http://www.bls.gov/green/home.htm.

California Department of Resources Recycling and Recovery (CalRecycle). *CalRecycle Announces 2011 Waste Reduction Award Winners: California Organizations Recognized for Green Business Practices.* Accessed March 16, 2012. http://www.calrecycle.ca.gov/newsroom/2011/12Dec/22.htm.

CNNMoney.com/PayScale.com. *Best Jobs in America 2009.* Accessed March 1, 2012. http://money.cnn.com/magazines/moneymag/bestjobs/2009/snapshots/87.html.

iSeek. *Regulatory Affairs Specialist*. Accessed March 1, 2012. http://www.iseek.org/careers/careerDetail?id=1&oc=100533#outlook.

Moorman, Alexandria. "Grant Helps Dream Take Root." *Morganton News Herald,* June 21, 2011. Accessed March 16, 2012. http://www2.morganton.com/news/2011/jun/21/grant-helps-dream-take-root-ar-1140332/.

O*NET OnLine. *Summary Report for: 13-1041.07—Regulatory Affairs Specialists*. http://www.onetonline.org/link/summary/13-1041.07.

ENERGY AUDITORS

NATURE OF THE WORK

Energy auditors conduct thorough reviews of buildings, building systems, or process systems energy usage. In some situations they may also perform investment grade audits of entire structures or systems, according to the Occupational Information Network (O*NET).

O*NET identified energy auditors as a new and emerging occupation. Due to the growing focus on environmental awareness and protection, O*NET has selected certain fields, such as the energy auditor industry, as those that are "sufficient to create the need for unique work and worker requirements" resulting in "the generation of a new occupation relative to the O*NET taxonomy." The industry is expected to grow by as much as 13 percent between 2008 and 2018.

Energy auditors use a number of tools in their day-to-day work. Air velocity and temperature monitors help them assess energy usage and conditions. Leak-testing equipment, including smoke generators and blower doors, are also items energy auditors may use.

In addition to other tools, such as digital multimeters and two-way radios, energy auditors sometimes use technology, such as scientific or analytical software that helps them diagnose and chart energy usage, and database user interface and query software. Additionally, energy auditors often use the same types of technology many office workers use, including Microsoft Excel, which can be used to create spreadsheets, Internet browser software, and e-mail.

Energy auditors are also expected to inspect equipment or buildings, to assess data based on their findings, and to record pertinent information. A basic knowledge of local or industry-specific standards, regulations, and

---

AT A GLANCE FACT BOX

SOC: 13-1199.01

Preferred Education: Vocational school training, in-office experience, or an associate's degree. Formal education may not be required, but workers most likely need a year or two of training to become energy auditors.

Average Salary: US$62,450 annually

Other Information: The *Dictionary of Occupational Titles* refers to the position as an "energy-conservation representative"

---

laws is also important, as companies and organizations need to remain compliant.

Assessment is an important step in the energy auditing process; however, analyzing the data that have been collected is also important. Energy auditors may also offer suggestions to reduce energy use and provide a projection of the costs that will be saved if the suggested techniques are used.

WORKING CONDITIONS

Energy auditors who focus on identifying ways to improve energy usage in residential areas may spend time inspecting homes or parts of multi-unit complexes. Such work can include physical tasks, such as inspecting furnace settings and usage, reviewing the home's heating and energy cost history, and examining different areas of the home, including its attic, basement, crawlspaces, and other areas, noting wasteful conditions and potential ways to improve them.

Poor wall, floor, ceiling, or attic insulation, uninsulated pipes, and windows that leak are all conditions that may result in a loss of energy in homes. An energy auditor may suggest homeowners reduce their hot water or overall home temperature, weather strip their windows, or perform other tasks to increase their home's energy efficiency. An auditor may also be able to offer information about energy-related loans to help pay for home improvements.

Energy auditors may also work on larger-scale projects, such as inspecting a building or monitoring and assessing energy usage at a company or part of a company. Although such a job would undoubtedly involve more time and effort than examining a single-family home, many of the tools and skills used would be the same. Examination skills, for example, would play a part in a large building or company energy audit as would meticulously recording and assessing all findings. However, the work may be of a different nature, involving procedures such as inspecting the mechanical systems in a building or performing tests to ascertain the energy consumption of various systems.

Similarly, the recommendations for reducing energy usage may be different in larger structures. Energy auditors may tie their energy usage suggestions to increasing production and efficiency and decreasing cost in a company or building energy audit. As such, previous experience working on similar types of energy audits may help an energy auditor properly assess and enhance the energy usage at a large-scale facility.

In either situation, communication skills play a part. Energy auditors need to be able to explain and clearly convey suggestions for energy improvement to the clients, whether those clients are large companies, organizations, or individual homeowners.

EMPLOYMENT

As of 2008, there were approximately 1,091,000 professionals working in the United States as energy auditors according to O*NET. Similar job titles can include energy rater, energy consultant, building performance consultant, home energy rater, and home performance consultant.

As evidenced by the more than 20 international chapters in the Association of Energy Engineers (AEE), an industry association with more than 15,000 members in 84 countries, energy auditors are not exclusive to the United States. In fact, the AEE has chapters worldwide in countries including Armenia, Canada, Hong Kong, Hungary, and Mexico.

Organizations like the AEE can help industry members network and find new jobs. Websites, such as EnergyVortex.com, also list open green-focused energy auditor and other jobs.

TRAINING, OTHER QUALIFICATIONS, AND ADVANCEMENT

According to O*NET, moderate preparation is needed to become an energy auditor. Most energy auditor positions are preceded by vocational school training, in-office experience, or an associate's degree. Typically, although formal education may not be required, workers need a year or two of training to become an energy auditor.

Thirty-eight percent of energy auditors had some college experience but no degree, 33 percent had a high school diploma or equivalent degree, and roughly 25 percent had an associate's degree according to O*NET.

Other skills that energy auditors need include knowledge of building materials, tools, and methods; mathematical know-how (including algebra, geometry, and statistics) to compute current energy usage and potential reductions and resulting savings; and familiarity with computers and other electronic equipment. An understanding of electronics and design can also be useful when assessing energy usage.

A specialty registered apprenticeship program exists for energy auditors who work with existing homes, according to the U.S. Department of Labor. The apprenticeships, which offer on-the-job training and national industry certification, help place applicants with companies to learn more about energy auditing. The program is run by employer, employer association, and labor management organization sponsors.

However, there is an overall shortage of established energy efficiency training programs according to a recent study conducted by the U.S. Department of Energy's Lawrence Berkeley National Laboratory. According to the report, the energy auditor industry and job demand within it have grown partially because the federal government, as well as some state governments, have increased their budgets for energy efficiency programs due to the American Recovery Reinvestment Act funding.

The AEE offers energy certification programs, including a Certified Energy Auditor (CEA). Applicants must possess certain educational or training prerequisites and take an exam to be certified. Once certified, professionals are required to garner continuing education credits by taking specific courses that have been approved by the AEE. Continuing education courses can also help energy auditors keep current with recent industry trends, new tools that may help them perform their job, and updated or changed regulations that could affect the way they work.

Energy auditors may also offer training and education. In some instances, auditors may inform customers about how energy efficiency works and advise them on how to cut expenses by reducing household appliance use or engaging other techniques. The process requires decision-making abilities as energy auditors need the ability to develop plans for energy reduction. Stellar customer service and interpersonal skills and experience are advantageous because energy auditors need to convey their findings and solutions to their clients.

JOB OUTLOOK

According to the AEE, a combination of increasing energy costs and organizations exhibiting energy inefficiency have helped demand for experienced, qualified energy auditors grow. In 2008, the industry had 1,091,100 employees and 368,300 new jobs are expected to open up by 2018, an anticipated growth of 7 to 13 percent.

As of 2008, educational services and the U.S. government were the top industries employing energy auditors in the United States.

EARNINGS

Energy auditors, on average, are paid more than the median household income, which is US$50,221, according to U.S. Census data. Auditors' 2010 median annual salary, according to O*NET, was US$62,450, or US$30.02 per hour.

RELATED OCCUPATIONS

- Energy auditor and analysts (existing homes)
- Energy engineers
- Electrician
- Agricultural technician

SOURCES OF ADDITIONAL INFORMATION

Association of Energy Engineers. https://www.aeecenter .org

EnergyVortex. http://www.energyvortex.com

Renewable Energy and Energy Efficiency Partnership. http://www.reeep.org

FURTHER READING

Association of Energy Engineers. *Certifications.* Accessed March 23, 2012. https://www.aeecenter.org/i4a/ pages/index.cfm?pageID=3330.

Bureau of Labor Statistics, U.S. Department of Labor. *Career Guide to Industries, 2010–11 Edition.* Accessed March 23, 2012. http://www.bls.gov/oco/cg.

Information Technology Associates. *Energy-Conservation Representative.* Accessed March 23, 2012. http://www.occupationalinfo.org/95/ 959367018.html.

O*NET OnLine. *Summary Report for: 13-1199.01— Energy Auditors.* Accessed March 23, 2012. http:// www.onetonline.org/link/summary/13-1199.01.

SUSTAINABILITY SPECIALISTS

NATURE OF THE WORK

Although sustainability specialists could potentially work in any industry, according to O*NET they most often are employed in the scientific, managerial, and technical consulting fields. Sustainability specialists are sometimes also called institutional sustainability program specialists, sustainability coordinators, or corporate sustainability managers.

Sustainability specialists deal with sustainability issues that can range from green building procedures to waste stream management and help companies and organizations reduce their impact on the environment. A sustainability specialist typically works with management to develop a sustainability program for the entire organization.

Creating a sustainability plan can involve establishing reduction or conservation objectives or programs, which may sometimes involve working with other sustainability professionals. A sustainability specialist's work may also require tracking waste production, energy or natural resource use, and recycling.

After researching a company's various sustainability indicators, a specialist may then determine what sustainability programs would work best in terms of cost effectiveness, adaptation, and potential overall success within an organization. The resources that are needed to implement the sustainability plan will also be a component of the sustainability analyst's suggested course of action.

Once a plan has been determined, part of a sustainability specialist's role is to educate the organization on what green building or waste stream management options are available and which options could help the organization become more environmentally friendly. A sustainability

specialist would probably present this information to the leaders in an organization.

If a plan is agreed on, the next phase of a sustainability specialist's role is to establish methods to convey the sustainability plan to the necessary sections of an organization, which may involve creating a website or other marketing piece that illustrates the new sustainability initiatives. In some cases, sustainability goals may be conveyed through a presentation or written report.

Once a new sustainability program has been implemented, a sustainability specialist may be called on to provide ongoing support to ensure that the program runs smoothly. Sustainability specialists, in some cases, may also assist in securing funding for the programs they suggest by submitting grant applications, rebate forms, or other items.

Sustainability specialists use the same tools as many other professionals, such as e-mail, fax machines, spreadsheet software, graphics software, and analytical or scientific software.

WORKING CONDITIONS

Big-picture thinking and planning is often a huge part of a sustainability specialist's job and day-to-day work.

Sustainability specialists are information gatherers and analysts and often also serve as environmental best practice resources for organizations and members of the community. The alterations that sustainability specialists suggest often involve water resources, waste management, construction practices, and heating, ventilation, and air conditioning systems, according to iSeek, a career, education, and job resource site sponsored by Minnesota's Department of Education, Department of Employment and Economic Development, and several other state departments.

The recommendations sustainability specialists make often involve processes or equipment that their audience may not be familiar with. Therefore, they may be called on to explain how sustainable practices and tools work and what benefits they can offer.

Because information sharing comprises such a large part of the sustainability specialist position, meetings that are in-person or via phone are common. A sustainability specialist should be comfortable speaking in front of others and giving presentations. Sustainability specialists also need to stay current on recent industry and technology changes that relate to the environment and conservation and have a thorough understanding of environmental regulations and compliance standards.

An additional potential job benefit of the sustainable specialist field is the chance for professionals to make positive environmental changes in large organizations and to feel like their job makes them proponents for change.

EMPLOYMENT

Although the U.S. Department of Labor's Bureau of Labor Statistics' (BLS) research includes environmental scientists and specialists in this category as well, it says that about 37 percent of environmental scientists were employed by local and state governments as of 2008, and 21 percent worked in scientific, management, and technical consulting services.

About five years after the nonprofit International Society of Sustainability Professionals (ISSP) association was started, the organization already had more than 600 members. The group's membership comprises sustainability consultants, coordinators, and other sustainability professionals.

Although most are from North America, the organization also has an international component. According to ISSP statistics, 45 percent of its members work in the industry as consultants. An additional 12 percent work in the manufacturing industry, and 14 percent work in the service industry.

TRAINING, OTHER QUALIFICATIONS, AND ADVANCEMENT

For most private sector and governmental environmental specialist jobs, a bachelor's degree is adequate. However, a master's degree is often preferred, according to the BLS. Unless the specialist is doing some kind of college-level teaching or a research-only job, a doctoral degree is usually not required.

For an entry-level position, a bachelor's degree in an earth science will suffice. A master's in environmental science is considered to be an advantage by many companies because it provides an interdisciplinary approach to the natural sciences.

A bachelor's degree in environmental science provides a background in chemistry, biology, and geometry. Courses on hazardous waste management, environmental legislation, and hydrology are good undergraduate classes to take if a student hopes to someday work for an environmental consulting firm or for the government.

Environmentally related experience or research can also help increase marketability. Business, economic, or finance courses can help increase the specialist's skill set.

A certificate program is offered by the ISSP. This program helps professionals in the field prepare for positions such as sustainability director, sustainability coordinator, sustainability consultant, or climate officer.

JOB OUTLOOK

O*NET calls the sustainability specialist field a Bright Outlook industry that contains numerous job openings and strong prospects for the future. Forecasting a 7 to 13 percent growth in the field from 2008 to 2018, O*NET also has predicted that in the same 10-year time period, the industry will have 368,300 job openings. As of 2008, 1,091,000 professionals work within the sustainability specialist field.

Some regions and states have echoed O*NET's positive outlook for the industry. According to the Employment Development Department of California, the sustainability specialist occupation, which it refers to as *sustainability program coordinator*, is expected to become a larger part of California's job market, despite being fairly new. Although this position is likely to be affected by the recently challenged economy, demand for sustainability program coordinators is expected to increase.

EARNINGS

Sustainability specialists, on average, make approximately US$62,450 per year or US$30.02 an hour as of 2010 according to O*NET. The most recent BLS figures indicate that the lowest 10 percent of environmental science specialists made between US$45,340 and US$78,980. The top earners in the field were paid more than US$102,610. The starting salary for a sustainability specialist with a bachelor's degree in environmental science in 2009 was US$39,160 a year, according to the National Association of Colleges and Employers.

RELATED OCCUPATIONS

Other occupations that deal with preserving or researching the environment are:

- Atmospheric scientists
- Biological scientists
- Chemists and materials scientists
- Conservation scientists and foresters
- Engineering technicians
- Engineers
- Epidemiologists
- Geoscientists and hydrologists
- Physicists and astronomers
- Science technicians
- Surveyors, cartographers, and surveying and mapping technicians

SOURCES OF ADDITIONAL INFORMATION

The International Society of Sustainability Professionals (ISSP). http://www.sustainabilityprofessionals.org/

FURTHER READING

Bullet staff. "Sustainability Major Paying-Off in Post-Graduate Search." *The Bullet,* January 25, 2012. Accessed March 19, 2012. http://umwbullet .com/2012/01/25/sustainability-major-paying-off-in-post-graduate-job-search/.

Bureau of Labor Statistics, U.S. Department of Labor. "Environmental Scientist and Specialist." In *Occupational Outlook Handbook, 2010–11 Edition.* Accessed March 19, 2012. http://www.bls.gov/oco/ocos311.htm.

Employment Development Department. *California Occupational Guides: Sustainability Program Coordinators in California.* Accessed March 19, 2012. http://www.calmis.ca.gov/file/occguide/Sustainability-Program-Coordinators-Green.pdf.

iSeek. "Sustainability Specialists." *Green Careers.* Accessed March 19, 2012. http://www.iseek.org/industry/green/careers/greenDetail?soc=131199&onet=13-1199.05.

O*NET OnLine. *Summary Report for: 13-1199.05—Sustainability Specialists.* Accessed March 19, 2012. http://www.onetonline.org/link/summary/13-1199.05.

FINANCIAL ANALYSTS

NATURE OF THE WORK

Financial analysts carry out quantitative analyses of information that affect public or private institutions' investment programs. Job titles for this industry include securities analyst, investment analyst, equity research analyst, credit products officer, operational risk analyst, planning analyst, research analyst, and real estate analyst.

Green Growth in the Financial Analyst Industry Green living, which ranges from consumers requesting products that are environmentally safe and create little waste to manufacturers retooling production methods to eliminate waste and reduce emissions to builders using high-efficiency, low-impact materials, has become increasingly popular in recent years. Despite the economic recession since 2008, consumers purchased more green products in 2008 than in 2007, according to a survey of 9,000 consumers in America, Europe, China, and Japan conducted by global business strategy consulting firm Boston Consulting Group.

This study found that in the United States, one in six consumers said they systematically shopped for green items in 2008. Environmental concern seemed to be a key factor, because 61 percent said they felt the environment was in "a very bad state."

Partially because of this green economic growth, the financial analyst industry is likely to change, according to O*NET. Financial analysts may have several specific tasks, which will require additional skills and knowledge of various green topics that relate to green practices in the future. Analysts may be asked to locate investments that have the potential to be both financially and environmentally

---

AT A GLANCE FACT BOX

SOC: 13-2051.00
Preferred Education: Bachelor's degree
Average Salary: US$74,350 annually
Other Information: The finance and insurance field and organizations that dealt with the management of companies and enterprises were the top industries that employed financial analysts as of 2008

---

profitable, such as investments involving increasing or protecting a clean water supply, or to assess the financial aspects of green construction projects.

To properly determine what the environmental and financial benefits of new types of green technology might be, financial analysts will need to understand how the technology works and its potential benefits and risks. Financial assessments of new procedures and technology are particularly important in projects that need funding. Therefore, financial analysts may be asked to provide information to venture capital firms and for government grants that are earmarked for green projects before either entity will sign on to support the work.

Financial analysts, in some cases, may also be required to assess the potential financial success of alternative energy sources or fuel production methods, including factors such as anticipated revenue and implementation cost.

Environmental factors such as climate change may also play a part in a financial analyst's work because of a need to predict the cost of a sudden climate alteration or other issue.

Types of Financial Analysts Financial analysts frequently fall into two categories, according to the U.S. Department of Labor's Bureau of Labor Statistics (BLS). The first is buy-side analysts, who help create investment plans for institutional investors such as hedge funds, mutual funds, well-funded nonprofit organizations, and insurance companies with large reserves to invest. The second is sell-side analysts, who assist banks and other securities dealers to sell investments such as bonds and stocks.

The financial analyst position can involve a number of different job-related tasks. Financial analysts may be asked to review financial information and provide predictions for economic or business (green-related or otherwise) and overall industry conditions. The information analysts provide helps companies and other organizations make informed investment decisions.

To assess information, analysts may need to create charts and graphs, illustrate reports, and use computer spreadsheets. Their work may involve tracking changes and developments in certain fields, such as business, industrial technology, and the financial industry.

Part of the analyzing may also involve closely following corporate and industry-wide developments as well as developments in the overall economy and new developments in environmental procedures and technologies, using information from investment banking companies, respected trade publications, government agencies, and other official sources. Analysts use that information to assess upcoming trends and factors that could affect price and investment risk and other factors that might make investment plans stronger or weaker. Observing patterns and recent events helps financial analysts suggest favorable investments to companies, investment firms, or the general public, including recommendations about what time would be best to make the suggested investments. Financial analysts may also help decide the prices for certain securities when offered publically.

Common financial analysis tools include some typical office equipment items, such as desktop, notebook, and personal computers; personal digital assistants (PDAs); and calculators. Search and/or information retrieval software to access U.S. economic data and investment personalization platforms may prove helpful. Spreadsheet software that allows analysts to record and examine large amounts of data is also useful. Not surprisingly, financial analysis software is often used, including software that offers the ability to download data into Excel spreadsheets, apply technical analysis indicators, analyze financial derivatives, and more.

WORKING CONDITIONS

A financial analyst's day could involve gathering financial information, reviewing data (possibly with the help of a software program), transcribing and updating data, or other tasks. Often, meetings and calls take up much of an analyst's day.

For a financial analyst, reviewing data involves much more than simply reading a few charts. Research needs to be broken down into different sectors in some cases. In others, analysts need to try to identify why certain patterns are emerging. For investments in rapidly evolving fields, such as green technology, financial analysts may need to keep current on recent trends and developments to predict what future financial trends will be.

The position often also has an instructional/public speaking component. Financial analysts may also be required to present their findings or recommendations to coworkers, supervisors, or other individuals in person, via phone, or through e-mail.

O*NET has labeled the financial analyst role as one that can be stressful, often requiring a personality type that can accept criticism and deal effectively with demanding situations. The BLS also described the role as deadline-oriented, often involving frequent travel and long hours, with research often occurring outside of the average workday because of the hectic schedule.

EMPLOYMENT

Organizations are using financial analysts to monitor foreign markets as investments become more and more globally varied. Generally, foreign market-focused financial analysts center their work around a single country or region. It is considered an advantage if analysts speak any native languages, understand the local culture, or are otherwise familiar with their market territory.

New York, New York, is a major financial analyst hub. Many analysts are employed by financial institutions that are based there. Some financial analysts work in the government or have a private industry job. According to the BLS, roughly 47 percent were in the insurance and finance sectors, which include banks, insurance carriers, and commodity brokers.

In regard to the green economy, financial analysts typically work in four major sectors, according to O*NET: the energy efficiency sector, governmental and regulatory administration sector, green construction sector, and the research, design, and consulting services sector. Financial analysts who work in the energy efficiency industry may analyze projects that involve increasing energy efficiency. Those who are employed in the governmental and regulatory administration field handle analysis of green topics such as pollution reduction, public policy, and environmental conservation. Analysts who focus on green construction will work with sustainable design- and green building-related projects and activities, which may involve commercial or residential buildings. The research, design, and consulting services sector often involves what O*NET calls *indirectly green occupations,* including energy research or consulting.

TRAINING, OTHER QUALIFICATIONS, AND ADVANCEMENT

O*NET has designated the financial analyst industry as one that requires "considerable preparation," noting that in most cases, a 4-year bachelor's degree is required. The degree may be in a variety of fields, including finance, accounting, statistics, business, or economics.

In fact, 84 percent of financial analysts hold a bachelor's degree. An additional 16 percent also have a master's degree. For many financial analyst positions, professionals must have a master's degree in finance or a master's of business administration degree, according to the BLS.

Several organizations offer financial analysts specific training to learn more about green investing. Northern California's U.S. Green Building Council chapter, for example, presented a three-part workshop series in 2011 called "The Competitive Edge: Financial Tools for Green Building Investments."

Financial analysts may also opt to specialize in equity, bond, commodity, portfolio management, or another particular investment area. Analysts may also need to have professional licenses and certifications to either be considered for the position or to properly perform the work involved.

To qualify for the CFA Institute-sponsored Chartered Financial Analyst (CFA) title, financial analysts need to have a bachelor's degree, have four years of work experience, and take three tests, which cover subject areas such as financial markets, accounting, asset valuation, and corporate finance. The exams can require hundreds of hours of studying.

However, according to the BLS, licenses and certifications are generally pursued after a financial analyst is hired by an organization because they require employer sponsorship. If a financial analyst who has significant experience in the industry moves to a new company, the analyst has to renew licenses at that time. Certifications in the industry are becoming more common and are often suggested by employers.

In addition to a degree, it often takes a significant amount of task-specific knowledge or on-the-job experience to become a financial analyst. Knowing about options pricing, risk management, and organizational budgeting also can be helpful.

Critical thinking, reading comprehension, and math skills play a role in being a financial analyst. Analysts' work also requires them to possess complex problem-solving skills,

which help them brainstorm and evaluate solutions. Decision-making abilities are also key because in some instances, analysts will need to determine which action or plan will be the most cost-effective and successful option. Because financial analysts often need to present oral or written reports on their findings, economic activity, or company- or corporation-specific results and plans, speaking and interpersonal communication skills are also important.

JOB OUTLOOK

With an estimated 251,000 financial analysts in the field as of 2008, 95,200 job openings are expected to become available in the time period between 2008 and 2018, according to O*NET.

The BLS projected a faster-than-average growth rate at 20 percent or higher for the same 10-year time period. The BLS attributes the anticipated increase to the growing global diversification and complex nature of investments, noting that companies will probably want to hire more financial analysts to assess and suggest investment options as the amount of mutual and hedge funds, and assets invested in the funds, rises.

As green living grows in popularity, more investors may also start looking for green investment opportunities. In 2009, citing Morningstar data, *The Wall Street Journal* reported that approximately three dozen green-centric portfolios existed, many of which involved companies that dealt with clean energy or other environmental efforts. *The Wall Street Journal* also noted that additional funds encourage environmentally conscious investing by monitoring holdings for specific green factors.

Despite the upcoming growth, the BLS also advises financial analysts to expect strong competition in the field, especially for workers who are new to it. The anticipated number of workers who would like to enter the industry is high, possibly because of the favorable pay rate, and "keen competition is anticipated for these highly paid positions." To stand out, the BLS recommends that financial analysts pursue certifications and graduate degrees to ensure that their academic background and work experience are centered on finance.

EARNINGS

As of 2010, financial analysts, on average, made approximately US$74,350 per year or US$35.75 per hour, according to O*NET. In general, financial analysts "earn high wages," according to the BLS. The BLS estimated the average financial analyst's salary as slightly less, US$73,150 in 2008. The lowest 10 percent of workers in the field earned less than US$43,440, and the top 10 percent made more than US$141,070 a year. A large part of a financial analyst's compensation may involve a hefty annual performance-based bonus.

RELATED OCCUPATIONS

Related occupations include accountants, auditors, personal financial advisors, actuaries, economists, and auditors. These jobs often require workers to coordinate tasks, supervise others, and possibly train workers.

The career advancement trajectory for a financial analyst may involve taking on bigger projects and eventually overseeing financial analyst teams. Analysts may also become fund or portfolio managers, advising companies or funds on investing.

SOURCES OF ADDITIONAL INFORMATION

American Academy of Financial Management. http://www.aafm.us

CFA Institute. http://www.cfainstitute.org

FURTHER READING

The Boston Consulting Group. "Shoppers Are Defying the Financial Crisis and Buying Green Products, Says The Boston Consulting Group." Press release, January 20, 2009. Accessed March 22, 2012. http://www.bcg.com/media/PressReleaseDetails.aspx?id=tcm:12-8055.

Bureau of Labor Statistics, U.S. Department of Labor. "Financial Analysts." *Occupational Outlook Handbook, 2010–11 Edition.* Accessed March 22, 2012. http://www.bls.gov/oco/ocos301.htm.

O*NET OnLine. *Summary Report for: 13-2051.00— Financial Analysts.* Accessed March 22, 2012. http://www.onetonline.org/link/summary/13-2051.00.

Prior, Anna. "The Price of Green." *The Wall Street Journal,* October 5, 2009. Accessed March 20, 2012. http://online.wsj.com/article/SB100014240529702045185045744186831559719 54.html.

U.S. Green Building Council, Northern California Chapter. *The Competitive Edge: Financial Tools for Green Building Investments.* Accessed March 22, 2012. http://www.usgbc-ncc.org/index.php?option=com_content&task=view&id=497&Itemid=326.

ENVIRONMENTAL ENGINEERS

NATURE OF THE WORK

The U.S. Department of Labor's Bureau of Labor Statistics (BLS) defines the engineering profession as an occupation in which professionals use scientific and mathematic principles to create economical solutions for technical issues.

Similarly, environmental engineers work to avoid, control, or correct environmental risks by performing research and then creating and executing a plan for action. Environmental engineers use engineering principles to deal with pollution control, waste treatment, and other issues, according to the Occupational Information Network (O*NET), a job database from the U.S. Department of Labor/Employment and Training Administration (USDOL/ETA).

The work of an environmental engineer covers such areas as toxic material control, water quality issues, air pollution, public health, and land management, according to the American Academy of Environmental Engineers (AAEE), an organization that caters to environmental engineer professionals. Subspecialties within those categories offer environmental engineers the opportunity to focus on specific environmental topics.

Environmental engineers are sometimes known by a variety of titles, including environmental analysts, hazardous substances engineers, regulatory environmental compliance managers, and environmental remediation specialists. Their work may involve partnering with hazardous waste technicians, environmental scientists, law and business officials, and other engineers to handle emerging environmental issues, or assessing how compliant

---

AT A GLANCE FACT BOX

SOC: 17-2081.00
Preferred Education: Bachelor's degree
Average Salary: US$78,740 annually
Other Information: The top industries that employ environmental engineers include the scientific and technical services industries and the U.S. government

---

certain industrial or municipal facilities or pre-existing programs are with current environmental rules.

The results of the compliance assessments may lead to writing a report to these facilities that suggests ways to make a building or program more environmentally friendly. Environmental engineers also are able to design environmentally friendly soil, water, or air management systems. They also examine and update permits, strategies, or internal procedures to make them more compliant.

In some cases, environmental engineers may also be responsible for tracking how environmental programs are advancing. If a negative incident has occurred, an organization may employ an environmental engineer to help correct contaminated sites according to O*NET. Environmental engineers may also be called on to educate employees about challenges facing the environment.

Environmental engineers use a number of technical tools in their work. O*NET notes that air velocity and temperature monitors, mass spectrometers (which can measure the mass and relative concentration of atoms and molecules), flowmeters (which measure the mass and volumetric flow rate of a gas or liquid), spectrophotometers (which measure the reflective properties of a material), and photometers (which measure light intensity) are some of the items environmental engineers use to gauge conditions and effects.

Various software programs are also available to help environmental engineers work, including computer-aided design, or CAD software; scientific and analytical software; and software that helps environmental engineers determine compliance levels.

WORKING CONDITIONS

Because environmental engineers' work involves local and global environmental concerns, their daily work can range from performing research to analyzing data to creating municipal water supply systems. Broad environmental issues such as acid rain, ozone depletion, and global warming are examples of the topics environmental engineers may encounter during research or project implementation.

Within different organizations, the role of an environmental engineer can vary greatly. Environmental engineers can assist clients in clean-up efforts, risk prevention, regulation compliance, and many similar topics. In whichever area an environmental engineer decides to specialize, job satisfaction is likely to be high. According to the AAEE, the environmental engineer occupation "provides a comfortable salary, job security, and considerable personal satisfaction."

EMPLOYMENT

In the general engineering field, environmental engineers are the eighth largest engineering specialty. Approximately 54,300 engineers work as environmental engineers according to recent BLS data. By comparison, of the 1.6 million engineers employed in the United States, the largest specialty section, civil engineers, was comprised of 278,400 engineers. Industries with the highest levels of employment in environmental engineering include the architectural, engineering, and related services field (14,270); management, scientific, and technical consulting services (9,990); and state (7,160) and local (3,960) government. Approximately 30 percent of engineers work in the professional, scientific, and technical services industries.

The states with the highest levels of employment are California, which employs 6,080 environmental engineers; Florida, which employs 3,100; New York, which employs 3,070; and Texas, which employs 2,940 environmental engineers.

TRAINING, OTHER QUALIFICATIONS, AND ADVANCEMENT

Ninety percent of professionals working in the field have a bachelor's degree and 10 percent have a master's degree, according to O*NET data. Workplace and vocational training and previous job experience can also be considered benefits in the job marketplace.

Environmental engineers need a Bachelor of Science in engineering, preferably one in environmental, civil, mechanical, or chemical engineering, according to the AAEE, which also notes that an increasing number of employers prefer job candidates who also have a master's degree.

In addition to a degree and an educational background in the hard sciences, technology, engineering, and mathematics (STEM) subjects, O*NET notes that environmental engineers typically need to have a knowledge of engineering science procedures, design techniques and principles, construction and building, and strategic business planning.

Several soft skills, such as critical thinking skills, problem solving and decision making skills, and operations analysis skills, which allow environmental engineers to determine product requirements that affect what they design, are also important.

The AAEE also offers industry professionals the opportunity to become a Board Certified Environmental Engineer (BCEE) or a Board Certified Environmental Engineering Member (BCEEM). To become certified, environmental engineers have to pass a written and oral examination. The AAEE certification program, which also involves a review by an AAEE admission panel, is accredited by the Council of Engineering and Scientific Specialty Boards.

Students can also join the AAEE. Prospective environmental engineers who are currently in school and working toward a degree in an environmental engineering program can become a part of the organization without paying a fee.

JOB OUTLOOK

The demand for environmental engineers has historically outweighed the supply of job seekers according to the AAEE. Although the BLS estimates that in general, engineer employment will not show above-normal growth in the next 10 years, it noted that job opportunities should be positive and that different specialties within the engineering field will show growth patterns.

The environmental engineering field should see growth that's significantly faster than average; the industry is expected to see an increase of 20 percent or higher according to O*NET. Due to companies' increased focus on correcting environmental issues and being compliant with environmental regulations, the BLS projected that the environmental engineering field would grow 31 percent over the same time period. Population growth, combined with companies becoming more focused on preventing environmental issues instead of correcting mishaps after they've occurred, should increase the need for environmental engineers' services in the coming decade, which should have a positive effect on the job market.

Currently, O*NET data indicate that 54,000 employees work in the field. Between 2008 and 2018, the environmental engineering industry is forecasted to have 27,900 openings.

EARNINGS

In the late 1990s, salaries for environmental engineers with a bachelor's degree ranged from US$36,000 to US$42,000, according to the AAEE; some were as high as US$48,000. A master's degree during that time meant an environmental engineer could earn US$40,000 to US$45,000; professionals could earn US$42,000 to US$50,000 with a Ph.D.

As the field has grown, salaries have followed suit. Today, the average annual salary for an environmental engineer is US$78,740, with an average hourly rate of US$37.86 according to O*NET.

Utah is the U.S. state in which environmental engineers make the highest salary at US$110,650 annually; Alabama ranks second, with environmental engineers taking home an average annual salary of US$100,540, the BLS says.

Similar to many industries, environmental engineers frequently see fast, large salary increases in the beginning of their career; as they progress, salary increases often decrease in frequency and size according to the AAEE. However, moving into a management role may allow for significant increases in the latter part of an environmental engineer's career.

RELATED OCCUPATIONS

Occupations that are similar to an environmental engineer include roles where a professional coordinates, manages, or trains other employees—such as an environmental engineer or chemist. Careers that involve natural science and mathematics, including agricultural scientists, geoscientists, and atmospheric scientists, are also similar.

SOURCES OF ADDITIONAL INFORMATION

The American Academy of Environmental Engineers. http://www.aaee.net

FURTHER READING

Bureau of Labor Statistics, U.S. Department of Labor. "Engineers." In *Occupational Outlook Handbook, 2010–11 edition.* Accessed January 25, 2012. http://www.bls.gov/oco/ocos027.htm.

———. "17-2081.00 Environmental Engineers." In *Occupational Employment Statistics: Occupational Employment and Wages, May 2010.* Last modified May 17, 2011. Accessed January 25, 2012. http://www.bls.gov/oes/current/oes172081.htm#ind.

O*NET OnLine. *Summary Report for: 17-2081.00— Environmental Engineers.* Accessed January 16, 2012. http://www.onetonline.org/link/summary/17-2081.00.

NUCLEAR ENGINEERS

NATURE OF THE WORK

Nuclear engineers are sometimes also referred to as nuclear reactor engineers, nuclear licensing engineers, nuclear design engineers, system engineers, or criticality safety engineers. In general, nuclear engineers create or assist in the creation of power by creating, advancing, overseeing, and operating nuclear power plants. Their work may also involve other aspects of handling nuclear fuel, including fuel production and waste disposal; they may also be involved with fusion energy. Specialties within the field include determining medical uses for radioactive materials and working with nuclear power that is used for the National Aeronautics and Space Administration (NASA) or the U.S. Navy.

AT A GLANCE FACT BOX

SOC: 17-2161.00
Preferred Education: Most entry-level engineering positions require a bachelor's degree in engineering
Average Salary: US$99,920 annually
Other Information: Nuclear engineers who work for defense contractors may need to also obtain security clearance

Nuclear Energy and the Environment Nuclear energy can be used to produce electricity. However, nuclear energy does not produce greenhouse gases or air pollutants, which have been linked to smog and acid rain, because nuclear power is created by making heat through fission, not fossil fuel burning. This is why it is often considered a clean form of energy according to the Nuclear Energy Institute (NEI).

According to the U.S. Environmental Protection Agency (EPA), burning oil, coal, gas, and other fossil fuels contributes to 41 percent of carbon dioxide emissions, more than any other source. To reduce overall carbon dioxide emissions, the EPA suggested reducing the total energy consumption in the United States and increasing the amount of electricity that is generated from renewable or low carbon fuel sources. Although nuclear energy can be considered a low carbon fuel source due to its lack of greenhouse gas production, the EPA noted that creating nuclear power requires extraction and long-term storage of radioactive waste, which can cause other concerns.

To protect public safety, plants that produce nuclear power act in compliance with the Clean Air Act of 1970, legislation established to increase air quality in the United States. The nuclear energy industry has also set standards to protect the people of the United States and the environment. Current safety measures include proper fuel disposal, water quality protection, and ensuring areas surrounding nuclear power plants are safe for plants and wildlife. All U.S. facilities that produce nuclear power have instituted programs that are monitored by the U.S. Nuclear Regulatory Commission and state regulators to assess and maintain environmental quality.

The increased focus on safety and regulation has helped garner interest in nuclear power as an energy source. Before the Clean Air Act of 1970, oil was used to produce 12 percent of the electricity in the United States; nuclear energy created only 1 percent. As of 2012 nuclear power is responsible for 20 percent of U.S. electricity, and oil is used to create less than 1 percent. The United States currently houses 104 nuclear plants in 31 states according to a March 15, 2011, *Wall Street Journal* article.

Nuclear energy use is likely to increase in the future. As president of the United States, Barack Obama has expressed a strong desire to turn the United States into a low-carbon economy and has expressed strong support for nuclear energy. In his 2011 State of the Union address, Obama suggested that by 2035 the nation should be generating 80 percent of its electricity from clean energy sources, including nuclear energy production, wind, solar, and other types of energy.

However, although the typical production of nuclear energy can be considered safe, accidents can cause large-scale environmental issues such as the March 11, 2011, meltdown of three reactors at a nuclear power plant in Japan. An earthquake and tsunami disabled the power and emergency generators, which led to a number of explosions at the Fukushima Daiichi nuclear power station and the release of radioactive gases. Tap water in Tokyo, which was 170 miles away from the plant, was found to contain radioactive materials, according to the *New York Times*. The accident caused more than 80,000 people to evacuate; 22,000 had died as a result as of July 2011. Within a month of the accident, Japan changed its disaster ranking from a 5 to a 7, which essentially, according to the *New York Times*, equated the disaster with the 1986 Chernobyl crisis.

The Chernobyl accident occurred on April 26, 1986, in Chernobyl, Ukraine, and resulted in large amounts of radioactive materials being released into the environment. Twenty-eight workers died within four months, and it is possible that 4,000 deaths may someday occur as the result of the accident, according to the U.S. Nuclear Regulatory Commission (NRC).

Engineers and Nuclear Safety In addition to working on general nuclear plant processes, the nuclear engineer position involves researching various aspects of specific nuclear engineering projects or solving issues concerning improper waste disposal or nuclear energy use. Nuclear engineers work to correct nuclear energy-related issues by using nuclear science principles and other training they have received, according to the Occupational Information Network (O*NET), a U.S. job database created by the U.S. Department of Labor's Employment and Training Administration (USDOL/ETA).

In some instances, nuclear engineers may need to create equipment such as traditional shielding devices or reactor cores or be in charge of ensuring that nuclear plants run smoothly and operate according to safety regulations. This could involve establishing nuclear plant operation procedures or safe systems for waste or fuel disposal. To properly monitor nuclear facilities, nuclear engineers may need to investigate operations and proactively single out any procedures that breach predetermined safety requirements and that could cause issues in the future.

If construction projects involve nuclear energy, nuclear engineers could be asked to work with building contractors, nuclear facility review boards, and other parties to assist in creating a cost estimate and overall proposal.

Testing can also be a large component of a nuclear engineer's job. They may be asked to test nuclear material usage or disposal techniques, conduct experiments to assess how nuclear fuel and machinery behaves in certain conditions, and determine methods of increasing productivity using nuclear fuel. Nuclear engineers also need to follow updates to nuclear fuel usage and technology through research, technical journals, and other sources.

When nuclear accidents or issues occur, nuclear engineers often take on a prominent role. Nuclear engineers may be called upon to suggest solutions and gather information about what happened to establish new preemptive measures.

Nuclear engineers often use a number of software programs to perform their work, including computer-aided design (CAD) software, scientific and analytical software, and basic spreadsheet and presentation software, which can help engineers illustrate and convey their power-related suggestions and best practice measures. Engineers may also use nuclear power-specific tools, such as nuclear reactor control rod systems, nuclear power logging instruments, and, for safety, facial shields.

WORKING CONDITIONS

Being a nuclear engineer involves computer work; software can help engineers track and assess data and make projections that will help them determine the most effective safety and usage systems. Nuclear engineers potentially handle project or employee management, administrative, and other tasks on a given workday according to the *California Occupational Guide,* produced by the Employment Development Department (EDD) of California. Nuclear engineers may also prepare budgets or help educate others about nuclear power.

Unless they handle facility construction, which requires a mobile worksite office, nuclear engineers typically work in research laboratories, universities, industrial plants, or private offices. Travel to job sites or facilities may also be required.

Safety issues are, of course, a central concern in the nuclear engineer field. Engineers who work with reactor fuels, radioisotopic materials, and other types of fissionable matter need to take additional precautions such as donning protective clothing and film badges, thermoluminescent dosimeters, and other devices that measure radiation exposure. Nuclear engineers' workspaces should be clean, brightly lit, and well ventilated.

If offices and employees pay careful attention to safety measures, the workplace can be kept secure. However, even with a stringent focus on safety, nuclear engineering work can be stressful because of the urgent pressure to correct defective nuclear equipment to minimize a radioactive material leak.

EMPLOYMENT

Although the largest specialty section of the 1.6 million engineers employed in the United States is civil engineers, with 278,400 who work in the field, nuclear engineers are the 13th largest engineering specialty in the engineering industry.

Recent U.S. Department of Labor's Bureau of Labor Statistics (BLS) data suggest that approximately 16,900 engineers are employed as nuclear engineers. Thirty percent of engineers worked in the professional, scientific, and technical services industries; 36 percent worked in the manufacturing industry.

TRAINING, OTHER QUALIFICATIONS, AND ADVANCEMENT

Most entry-level engineering jobs require a bachelor's degree in engineering, although college graduates who have a natural science or mathematics degree may be able to fill some engineering positions. Employers may want a nuclear engineer to have an educational background in the traditional science, technology, engineering, and mathematics (STEM) courses.

Because many engineers have crossover training in other specialized sectors of engineering, they may be able to switch fairly easily to work in another related engineering discipline. Some nuclear engineers also possess additional degrees. Thirty-six percent of industry members have a master's degree in addition to a bachelor's degree; 14 percent possess a doctoral or professional degree.

The U.S. federal government also has an additional job requirement: Engineers the government employs must be U.S. citizens. Some, including nuclear engineers and engineers working for defense contractors, are also required to possess additional security clearance.

Nuclear engineers may also opt to join the American Nuclear Society (ANS), a nonprofit, international organization founded in 1954 that is composed of approximately 11,000 engineers, scientists, administrators, and educators who represent more than 1,600 corporations, educational institutions, and government agencies.

JOB OUTLOOK

Accidents such as Chernobyl and Fukushima and the subsequent environmental fallout did not seem to fuel interest in the nuclear engineering occupation. However, the future looks bright for members of the industry.

Despite a 30-year decline in the nuclear energy industry several years ago, due in part to an older workforce that was approaching retirement, the nuclear engineering sector began seeing an increased demand for workers according to a 2008 *US News & World Report* article. The article said the ANS estimated that 700 nuclear engineers would be required to fully meet the anticipated demand and to replace retiring industry members.

Because the amount of nuclear engineering graduates entering the workforce is relatively low (240, according to the article), nuclear engineers will likely find strong employment conditions and a high number of job openings.

O*NET data indicate that 17,000 employees work in the field. Between 2008 and 2018, the nuclear engineering industry is predicted to have 5,400 openings. A 7 to 13 percent growth rate is forecast for the industry. Most of the growth is expected to occur in research and development and engineering services with additional expansion in defense-related areas, waste management, and medical technology.

The utilities industry, which employs 42 percent of nuclear engineers, is the top nuclear engineer employment sector; the professional, scientific, and technical services field is the second largest source of jobs, employing 34 percent of nuclear engineers; and the government is third, with 13 percent.

EARNINGS

Compared with other bachelor degree recipients, engineers have some of the highest starting salaries. Nuclear engineers ranked fourth among the various types of engineers according to 2009 data from the National Association of Colleges and Employers, which said that at the time, nuclear engineers earned an average annual salary of US$61,610.

The average annual salary for a nuclear engineer in 2010 was US$99,920, with an average hourly rate of US$48.04. Regionally, nuclear engineers in Washington, DC, make the highest salary of US$142,930; nuclear engineers in Idaho, who make US$123,860 a year, hold the second spot, and Wisconsin nuclear engineers, who make US$122,100, rank third, according to the BLS.

RELATED OCCUPATIONS

Positions that are similar to the nuclear engineer profession include architectural and engineering managers, civil engineers, mechanical engineers, and electric engineering technicians.

Careers that involve project coordination, staff management, and work-related knowledge and experience also have tasks similar to those involved in the nuclear engineer role.

SOURCES OF ADDITIONAL INFORMATION

American Nuclear Society. http://www.new.ans.org
Nuclear Energy Institute. http://www.nei.org

FURTHER READING

Bureau of Labor Statistics, U.S. Department of Labor. "Engineers." In *Occupational Outlook Handbook, 2010–11 Edition,* last updated December 17, 2009. Accessed March 2, 2012. http://www.bls.gov/oco/ocos027.htm.

———. "17-2081 Environmental Engineers." In *Occupational Employment Statistics: Occupational Employment and Wages, May 2010,* last updated May 17, 2011. Accessed March 2, 2012. http://www.bls.gov/oes/current/oes172081.htm#ind.

California Employment Development Department. *Transportation Inspectors.* Accessed March 2, 2012. http://www.calmis.ca.gov/file/logistics/log-trans-inspectors.pdf.

Favole, Jared, and Tennille Tracy. "Obama Stands by Nuclear Power." *The Wall Street Journal,* March 15, 2011. Accessed March 2, 2012. http://online.wsj.com/article/SB100014240527487033639045762009973216100488.html.

Go, Alison. "The New Hot Job: Nuclear Engineering." *U.S. News & World Report,* August 14, 2008. Accessed March 2, 2012. http://www.usnews.com/education/articles/2008/08/14/the-new-hot-job-nuclear-engineering.

The New York Times. "Nuclear Energy." *The New York Times,* February 16, 2012. Accessed March 2, 2012. http://topics.nytimes.com/top/news/business/energy-environment/atomic-energy/index.html.

Obama, Barack. *Remarks by the President in the State of the Union Address, 2011.* Accessed March 2, 2012. http://www.whitehouse.gov/the-press-office/2011/01/25/remarks-president-state-union-address.

O*NET OnLine. *Summary Report for: 17-2161.00—Nuclear Engineers.* Accessed March 2, 2012. http://www.onetonline.org/link/summary/17-2161.00.

United States Nuclear Regulatory Commission. *Backgrounder on Chernobyl Nuclear Power Plant Accident.* Last updated February 4, 2011. Accessed March 2, 2012. http://www.nrc.gov/reading-rm/doc-collections/fact-sheets/chernobyl-bg.html.

SOIL AND WATER CONSERVATIONISTS

———————■———————

NATURE OF THE WORK

Like foresters, conservation scientists, who pay close attention to environmental concerns, oversee the growth and use of natural resources in forests and other land areas that provide minerals, water sources, and other products to support both animals and humans. Specifically, conservation scientists aid ranchers, farmers, and other land management officials to prevent land erosion and make their property a better growing environment, according to the U.S. Department of Labor's Bureau of Labor Statistics (BLS). Conservation scientists may work on public land. Others consult with private landowners about how to manage their land to keep it a healthy and productive space.

Frequently, conservation scientists focus on pest control, conservation of native species, and economic issues related to land use, soil conservation, or other particular areas. Their work may involve coordinating efforts with the federal or local government or individual landowners. An increasing amount of conservation scientists also work with government officials and landowners to decide ways land can be used for leisure purposes.

Soil Conservationists Soil conservationists, who help landowners by examining the source of any soil erosion and create solutions to stop it, are one of the two most common types of conservation scientists. Soil conservationists are sometimes called land reclamation specialists, land resource specialists, erosion control specialists, environmental analysts, resource conservation specialists, or land managers.

In some instances, soil conservationists perform yearly or more frequent checks to ensure that land maintenance

---

AT A GLANCE FACT BOX

SOC: 19-1031.01
Preferred Education: Most jobs require a bachelor's degree; research and teaching positions usually require a graduate degree
Average Salary: US$58,720 annually
Other Information: About 68 percent of conservation scientists and foresters work for U.S. federal, state, or local governments

---

programs are effective and remain compliant with local government regulations. If they find any issues, soil conservationists are able to suggest techniques to manage nutrients and slow erosion, according to O*NET.

Water Conservationists Water conservationists focus on protecting water supply sources, improving water quality, and averting groundwater contamination. In their day-to-day work, water conservationists may work directly with government officials or private landowners.

Tools of the Trade Several devices help conservation scientists test and assess current conditions. These include clinometers, which measure tree height; increment borers and bark gauges, which measure tree growth; and diameter tapes, which measure tree diameter.

Soil and water conservationists may also use geographic information system (GIS) data and aerial photographs to survey large areas of nature and assess how land is being used. Global positioning systems (GPS) are also often used. Both soil and water conservationists often log environmentally related data into online tools that help identify patterns and suggest solutions.

Conservationists may also be responsible for assessing or recommending certain GIS applications that will help control groundwater and air quality, environmental risk factors, and water issues. Once they have analyzed the data, conservationists design and help implement plans to conserve water and soil.

When creating a conservation program, land conservationists take many factors into account. For example, they may examine and estimate how moving from low-precision irrigation technologies to high-precision technologies, which may include computer-monitored systems, will improve land productivity.

The type of wetland that is present will affect what recommendations the conservationist makes. To identify the wetland, conservationists may gather or analyze biodata. In addition, they may at some point be asked to deal with concerns about wetland jurisdiction.

In some cases, soil and water conservationists may be asked to serve as the middleman to work out conflicts between landowners, government officials, or other organizations.

WORKING CONDITIONS

Although some soil and water conservationists work indoors in laboratories or offices, many perform a significant amount of fieldwork, conducting research outdoors. Individuals who are new to the profession and conservationists who work as independent contractors frequently spend most of their workday outdoors, often alone.

Because many soil and water conservationist positions involve at least some degree of fieldwork, conservationists should be comfortable working outdoors and performing physical tasks such as walking long distances. They should also be ready to move to a new location if needed for work.

Weather and the distance that must be traveled can make the work more difficult. In addition, soil and water conservationists may need to work overtime when natural disasters such as forest fires occur because they may be needed to help thwart soil erosion. Hurricanes, floods, and mud slides can also create extra work for conservationists.

EMPLOYMENT

Soil conservationists may start out working in a single conservation area or district and then progress to working with a larger area, either on the state level or national level. In the later part of their career, after receiving an advanced degree, many soil and water conservationists may take on a management role or work directly on policy issues.

In 2008, conservation scientists and foresters comprised roughly 29,800 jobs in the United States, according to the BLS. Of these, 74 percent worked in the U.S. government. The U.S. Department of Agriculture's Natural Resource Conservation Service employs most soil conservationists. Some universities also employ conservation scientists, but overall, they work in nearly every county in the United States.

As evidenced by the Soil and Water Conservation Society (SWCS), a nonprofit scientific and educational organization, conservationist jobs are not exclusive to the United States. The membership of SWCS comprises more than 5,000 members worldwide.

TRAINING, OTHER QUALIFICATIONS, AND ADVANCEMENT

To work as a conservation scientist, individuals commonly have a bachelor's degree in environmental science, natural resource management, agricultural science, or rangeland management. To hold a research or teaching position, conservationists typically need a master's degree or doctoral degree.

Conservationist programs often include life science classes such as forest sciences and biology, natural resources and conservation, and natural resources management and policy as part of their focus on science, technology, engineering, and mathematics (also known as the STEM disciplines). Field experience is often a component of soil and water conservationists' study. Students must either work in a work-study job with a private or federal or state industry or attend a session in the field. Students also often work in the summer in forest environments or land conservation programs.

However, many schools do not offer a soil conservation degree. Thus, many conservationists hold a degree in agronomy, general agriculture, environmental studies, hydrology, crop or soil science, or a related field such as forestry or range management.

According to O*NET, 67 percent of conservationists have a bachelor's degree, 14 percent have an associate's degree, and 10 percent of professionals who work in the industry have some college experience but no degree.

A special apprenticeship program exists for soil conservation technicians according to the U.S. Department of Labor. The apprenticeships, which offer on-the-job training and national industry certification, place applicants with companies to learn more about conservation. The program is run by employer, employer association, and labor management organization sponsors.

JOB OUTLOOK

Conservationists with a bachelor's degree, strong communication skills, and technical knowledge stand the best chance of finding work when they enter the job market. Future conservationists who are still in school should encounter a robust job market when they graduate. As more conservationists retire, the number of openings in the field is expected to grow, according to the BLS, which estimates employment in the field should expand at an average rate in the next few years.

As of 2008 18,000 soil and water conservationists work in the industry, according to O*NET data. The BLS predicts that employment in the conservation industry will increase by 12 percent from 2008 to 2018. Strong growth is expected particularly in federal, state, and local governments, in part because preventing and controlling wildfires has become increasingly important to many government agencies. Other factors, including an increased focus on maintaining the food supply and food safety, should help spur more job opportunities in the soil and water conservation fields.

Environmental concerns will also play a part in job growth. As conservation efforts gain funding and support, more forest management and land resource conservation experts will be needed. In addition, private sector companies that work with land development will probably require conservationist assistance to manage soil and water systems and meet ecological requirements.

EARNINGS

As of May 2008, the average salary for conservation scientists was US$58,720 according to the BLS. O*NET estimates place the annual soil and water conservationist salary close to BLS figures at US$59,310. The highest paid conservation scientists made US$86,910, according to the BLS; mid-range salaries ranged from US$45,320 to US$73,280, and the lowest 10 percent of salaries were approximately US$35,190. Soil conservationists who worked for the federal government earned an average of US$69,483.

Government jobs also offered some additional perks. Conservation scientists who held local, state, or federal jobs obtained better benefits on average than conservationists who worked for smaller firms. Private firms also offered more lucrative health, pension, and vacation benefits.

RELATED OCCUPATIONS

Occupations that are similar to the soil and water conservationist profession include the following:

- Biologists
- Environmental scientists and specialists
- Foresters
- Landscape architects
- Soil and plant scientists

In some instances, soil conservationists may transition into becoming a farm management advisor, land appraiser, or work in other similar fields.

SOURCES OF ADDITIONAL INFORMATION

Soil and Water Conservation Society. http://www.swcs.org

FURTHER READING

Bureau of Labor Statistics, U.S. Department of Labor. "Conservation Scientists and Foresters." In *Occupational Outlook Handbook, 2010–11 Edition.* Accessed March 20, 2012. http://www.bls.gov/oco/ocos048.htm.

O*NET OnLine. *Summary Report for: 19-1031.01—Soil and Water Conservationists.* Accessed March 20, 2012. http://www.onetonline.org/link/summary/19-1031.01.

U.S. Department of Labor. *State Apprenticeship Information.* Accessed March 20, 2012. http://www.doleta.gov/OA/sainformation.cfm.

URBAN AND REGIONAL PLANNERS

NATURE OF THE WORK

Urban and regional planners help structure short- and long-term use and growth plans for local communities and regions according to the U.S. Department of Labor's Bureau of Labor Statistics (BLS). They are sometimes called city planners, but urban and regional planners may work in cities, in suburbs, or in very sparsely populated areas. They typically recommend private property zoning regulations and locations for roads and other structures. They may also need to estimate population growth patterns to determine how land and resources will best work for residential and commercial use.

Planners' paths may cross with those of a number of different professionals in related fields, including civic leaders, landowners, and the general public. They may also be asked to help resolve disputes that arise between community leaders, citizens, and other parties.

Because of the increased focus on environmental protection and preservation in recent years, urban and regional planners' work often involves taking green building or living methods into account when designing projects and new structures. They may need to directly assist with environmental conservation efforts to prevent pollution, preserve forests, and place landfills, as well as influence locations of schools and placement of other types of infrastructure.

Community planning work involves investigating land use and creating reports on the location of current structures and natural elements, the population breakdown, the amount of local industry, and economic trends. Recommendations that urban and regional planners supply are often paired with cost estimates for the structural additions or changes.

AT A GLANCE FACT BOX

SOC: 19-3051.00
Preferred Education: Master's degree
Average Salary: US$59,810 annually
Other Information: Roughly 66 percent of urban and regional planners work for local U.S. governments

---

As part of their work with community development, urban planners are sometimes involved with creating economically or ecologically related legislation, which may help enhance a given area's business prospects, create public housing, or establish public recreation areas. A knowledge of local building and zoning codes can be helpful.

In some cases, planners may be called on to determine new methods of public transportation as an area's population grows.

Computers help urban and regional planners log and compare information used to create improvement suggestions and programs. Software, databases, and other tools help them estimate future growth and plan-related expenses. Geographic information systems have become increasingly popular tools that planners use to create maps, compare them with population patterns, and create development plans.

Urban and regional planners may also use analytical or scientific software or computer-aided design software to estimate and create new items or areas, according to O*NET.

WORKING CONDITIONS

Travel is often a part of the urban and regional planner occupation. Site visits to development areas may be necessary to examine geographical and other components. Planners who handle site inspections can potentially spend most of their daytime hours working remotely on assignment.

Weekend and evening hours are common in the profession. Because hearings and meetings that could affect development plans often occur at night or during weekends, urban and regional planners may need to work outside of the standard 9 to 5 hours to meet committees or the general public.

Urgent deadlines and intense project schedules can cause the workday to be stressful. Working with concerned (or just curious) citizen groups and other organizations may also add time and extra effort to community development projects.

EMPLOYMENT

Many urban and regional planners work mainly in one or more specific areas, such as urban design, community expansion, or transportation planning. They typically move on to projects with more responsibility that can involve designing a large, new development or creating a plan's budget once they have worked in the field for several years. Planners who work in the public sector also can become community planning directors, dealing directly with officials and managing employees.

As of 2008, there were roughly 38,400 urban and regional planning jobs in the United States, according to BLS data. Industries that employ planners include engineering, architecture, and technical consulting.

TRAINING, OTHER QUALIFICATIONS, AND ADVANCEMENT

Some colleges offer an urban planning bachelor's degree (according to the BLS, 15 U.S. schools offered an accredited bachelor's program as of 2009). However, although some graduates can attain entry-level urban or regional planning jobs, it can be difficult for them to advance in the field without a higher degree.

A master's degree from a qualified program (as of 2009, 67 schools offered an accredited master's degree) offers urban and regional planners the best preparation for a variety of roles in the field and is also required for most entry-level federal, state, and local government jobs. Approximately 48 percent of professionals in the field have a bachelor's degree, and 52 percent also have a master's degree according to O*NET.

Classes in computer science and statistics are also suggested because urban and regional planning work frequently involves statistical research and computer models. Urban planning students will learn how to plan for land use, handle community development issues, and incorporate environmental change into their suggestions for the community. Preprofessional experience is often recommended. Graduate students may attend workshops, obtain internships with certified planners, and get local government experience before entering the workforce.

Most planners do not need to be licensed to work in the field. As of 2009, New Jersey was the only state that required urban and regional planners to obtain a license according to the BLS. New Jersey planners need to take an overall urban/regional planning test and a test that focuses on specific state laws. Planners can also become registered in other states in different ways.

Although Michigan does not require planners to be licensed, if they want to refer to themselves as *community planners*, the state requires them to register, a process that involves having a certain amount of professional experience and taking a national- and state-based examination.

Urban and regional planners have to possess the ability to visualize areas and designs spatially and remain flexible enough to work with different perspectives. Communication is also key. Planners often need to express ideas and suggestions verbally and may also need to express their ideas in written proposals.

Urban and regional planners also can join a number of professional organizations to help advance their career, including the American Planning Association, composed of planners, citizens, and elected officials; the Planning Accreditation Board; and the American Institute of Certified Planners, which certifies professionals who pass an examination and meet certain career-based qualifications.

JOB OUTLOOK

The urban and regional planner industry should experience a faster-than-average expansion in the coming years according to the BLS, which anticipates that the majority of new positions will be in wealthy, quickly growing areas. Population growth is expected to be a large factor in overall planning industry growth. Some planners will probably be called upon to create new sewage systems, road infrastructure, public buildings, and other features of entirely new neighborhoods.

The market is forecast to grow 19 percent from 2008 to 2018. An increased need for state and local government-provided transportation, housing, and other public services is expected to fuel job growth in the industry. Other organizations that handle development and historic preservation efforts could also create new planning jobs.

The private sector, including scientific and technical services and professional industries, should have the biggest job growth. Urban and regional planners can expect to help engineers and architects work with builders to tackle development aspects such as environmental issues and building security.

Obtaining a master's degree offers the best chance of finding job placement in the field during the 2008 to 2018 growth period.

EARNINGS

Urban and regional planners earned, on average, approximately US$59,810 as of 2008, according to the BLS. The average annual urban and regional planner salary according to O*NET data was, as of 2008, slightly higher at US$63,040 annually or US$30.31 per hour.

According to BLS data, the lowest 10 percent of salaries in the field were less than US$37,960 per year. The highest paid 10 percent of urban and regional planners earned US$91,520. The mid-range salary for an urban or regional planner was between US$47,050 and US$75,630.

The agricultural and engineering industry, which offered a median salary of US$63,770, scientific research community, and scientific management and technical consulting services industry employed the largest numbers of urban and regional planners. Professionals employed in the scientific research and management and technical consulting services industries made an average salary of between US$59,160 and US$60,750. Urban and regional planners employed by local governments made approximately US$58,260 per year, and planners who worked for colleges and other professional schools earned an average of US$57,520.

RELATED OCCUPATIONS

Similar occupations include the following:

- Actuaries
- Civil engineers
- Environmental engineers
- Geographers
- Landscape architects
- Surveyors

SOURCES OF ADDITIONAL INFORMATION

American Institute of Certified Planners (AICP). http://www.planning.org/aicp

American Planning Association (APA). http://www.planning.org

Planning Accreditation Board (PAB). http://www.planningaccreditationboard.org

FURTHER READING

Bureau of Labor Statistics, U.S. Department of Labor. "Urban and Regional Planners." In *Occupational Outlook Handbook, 2010–11 Edition.* Accessed March 20, 2012. http://www.bls.gov/oco/ocos057.htm.

O*NET OnLine. *Summary Report for: 19-3051.00— Urban and Regional Planners.* Accessed March 20, 2012. http://www.onetonline.org/link/summary/19-3051.00.

———. "Urban and Regional Planners." In *Occupational Information Network.* Accessed March 20, 2012. http://www.occupationalinfo.org/onet/27105.html.

TRANSPORTATION PLANNERS

NATURE OF THE WORK

Transportation planners typically design and present new transportation systems or ways to improve current transportation systems according to the Occupational Information Network (O*NET), a U.S. job database being developed by the U.S. Department of Labor/ Employment and Training Administration (USDOL/ETA). Because their work may involve planning transportation systems for new communities, planners often work to establish transportation methods that will have minimal impact on the environment and will preserve natural resources.

According to the U.S. Department of Transportation Federal Highway Administration (FHWA), transportation planners need to contemplate how projects will impact both humans and the environment, which can involve considering how to protect wetlands, local wildlife, and other environmental concerns. The FHWA has two offices that focus on environmental issues. It uses the National Environmental Policy Act (NEPA) to help assess how each project it reviews will affect the environment.

Green Transportation Planning Economic Sectors The systems and suggestions transportation planners devise may be for local communities or larger, regional areas, so it is not surprising that the governmental and regulatory administration sector provides a large portion of the environmentally related transportation planning jobs. Transportation planners who work in governmental and regulatory administration positions may be involved in efforts to reduce pollution, shape public policy, or enforce current regulations.

AT A GLANCE FACT BOX

SOC: 19-3099.01
Preferred Education: Most transportation planning positions require a master's degree
Average Salary: US$74,520 annually
Other Information: Transportation planning can be considered a specialization within the overall urban and regional planning field

---

Other sectors of the economy that provide transportation planning jobs include research, design, and consulting services, which may offer jobs that are indirectly tied to the growing green economy, such as consulting positions and the transportation sector. Planners who work in the transportation sector often work to prevent negative environmental effects from trains, trucks, and other methods of transit. No matter what sector transportation planners work in, with today's increasing emphasis on green practices and sustainability, environmental concerns are likely to factor into the projects on which they work.

Transportation planners who work on mass transit systems also help the environment by reducing auto use. The U.S. Environmental Protection Agency (EPA) has identified automobiles as a major contributor to greenhouse gas emissions. In 1990 greenhouse gas emissions were 24.8 percent; in 2003, the transportation sector contributed 27 percent of all U.S. greenhouse gas emissions, according to the EPA, which also noted that transportation greenhouse gas emissions grew by a larger amount than any other economic sector during that timeframe.

Job Tasks Planners may need to determine what the transportation priorities for a region or community should be using estimates about future land use, traffic, population growth, and economic trends. Transportation planners aim to reduce a project's effect on the environment and potentially offer a positive green effect on the community. The industry's dedication to preserving the environment was cemented with the passing of the NEPA of 1969, which created a framework for federal agencies to undertake environmental planning projects.

To incorporate an awareness of the effect humans have on the environment into plans, transportation planners may need to examine issues that relate to an area's long-term needs, land use regulations, and the potential impact a new transportation system could have on a community.

Transportation planners sometimes work in teams. Creating new local or national transportation plans may require planners to work directly with other industry professionals, such as engineers, to examine, assess, and resolve more difficult planning situations.

Although transportation projects involve construction, particularly in the early stages, planners often need to complete paperwork. When the transportation project involves green elements or sustainability goals, transportation planners may need to create environmental assessments or impact statements. Transportation planners may also be called upon to present their recommendations at public hearings. In some cases, they may meet with public groups to assess their opinion about upcoming projects and plans. A transportation planner's suggestions and ideas may be showcased in either a report or through a verbal presentation.

Planning Tools Data from geographic information systems (GIS), traffic modeling software, or other sources may be part of the information transportation planners review and assess. Planners often have to estimate what improvements or changes to an area's transportation system will cost and what materials and manpower the project will require. Transportation planners may also review transportation system plans to ensure they are compliant with local laws and requirements. In some cases, transportation planners may be asked to brainstorm ideas for pedestrian areas, bus facilities, or parking structures.

Transportation planners use a number of tools to complete their work such as computers, digital image printers, computer-aided design (CAD) software, map creation software, database user interface software, and analytical and scientific software.

WORKING CONDITIONS

A transportation planner's job involves research, using computers and software to analyze information, communicating their findings with the local government or general public, problem solving, and developing solutions.

Transportation planning can be considered a specialization in the overall urban and regional planner field according to the U.S. Department of Labor's Bureau of Labor Statistics (BLS). Other areas that professionals within the urban and regional planner occupation may focus on include urban design, code enforcement, and community development. As such, some transportation planners may also perform general urban and regional planning tasks such as investigating land use, which is particularly important when factoring environmental concerns into a transportation plan; considering population demographics; and performing site inspections to determine short- and long-term plans for local communities and regions.

Transportation planning work, particularly work involving large projects such as developing a transportation system for a new community, can involve a significant amount of responsibility and as a result can be stressful. Transportation planners should be able to react calmly to challenges, maintain self-control, and keep their anger in check. Serving as a project leader and remaining flexible can also help a transportation planner work effectively.

The transportation planning occupation is a job that offers a strong feeling of personal accomplishment because workers are able to fully utilize their skill set. Transportation planners are also able to perform creative work and make independent decisions. The job offers a fair amount of job security and positive working conditions.

Transportation planners typically work a standard 40-hour workweek, although some overtime may be required. They also receive industry-standard benefits, such as health insurance and paid vacation. They mostly work out of offices, although visits to worksites may be necessary. Transportation planning requires much collaboration with other professionals, so transportation planners must be comfortable working with others.

EMPLOYMENT

As of 2008, approximately 33,000 transportation planners were working in the field (by comparison, there were roughly 38,400 overall urban and regional planning jobs in the United States as of 2008). The top industries that employed transportation planners included government and the professional, scientific, and technical services industries, according to O*NET data.

TRAINING, OTHER QUALIFICATIONS, AND ADVANCEMENT

Students at most college-level planning departments should be able to customize their coursework to specialize in transportation planning. Urban and regional planning students can specialize in other areas, including urban redevelopment, city-based design, and economic preparation. Planning students may also focus on natural resources planning, which involves helping communities find the best ways to use available land to protect and use natural resources such as rivers and other bodies of water.

Approximately 65 percent of transportation planners working in the field have a bachelor's degree. An additional 35 percent have a master's degree.

O*NET also notes that the transportation planning field frequently requires a background in transportation and highway engineering, which is considered to be one of the science, technology, engineering, and mathematics (STEM) educational disciplines.

Basic Skills Transportation planners should have a basic knowledge of several processes, structures, and the environment they are working in. Perhaps most notably, transportation planners need to thoroughly understand how transportation works, including how people and items are transported via ground, water, and air, as well as understand the geography of the area they work in. Familiarity with an area's natural resources and land structures can also help transportation planners accurately incorporate environmental resources and concerns into their suggestions and transit plans.

An understanding of local laws, codes, and other legal matters can be helpful. A skill set involving mathematics, management and administration experience, engineering, and electronics is a plus. Transportation planners will also benefit from inductive reasoning skills, which provide the ability to link pieces of information to come to a conclusion, the ability to recognize or predict problems, and deductive reasoning skills.

Certification and Professional Associations Some transportation planners may become certified as Professional Transportation Planners (PTP) through a program offered by the Transportation Professional Certification Board (TPCB) for transportation planners with previous education and experience. The TPCB administered 49 exams in 2010, with more than 79 percent of test takers passing the exam, according to TPCB data.

Some professionals may also join the Institute of Transportation Engineers (ITE), an international educational and scientific association for transportation professionals that promotes ground transportation research, planning, design, policy development, and management. The association, which was founded in 1930, is composed of transportation planners, consultants, engineers, educators, and researchers and has nearly 17,000 members according to ite.org. ITE also offers transportation planning professionals additional industry resources, such as an online guide to designing transportation systems for communities and tips on planning functional pedestrian facilities.

JOB OUTLOOK

The transportation planner industry should experience a faster than average expansion in the coming years. O*NET estimates that 23,800 job openings, which is not far off from O*NET's estimate of jobs that are currently available in the field (33,000), will become available in the transportation planning industry in the 10-year period between 2008 and 2018. O*NET has, in fact, labeled the transportation planner occupation as a "bright outlook" occupation, which refers to certain industries that have been denoted as "expected to grow rapidly in the next several years" due to the increasing popularity of green practices and products. O*NET also says the transportation planner field "will have large numbers of job openings."

In fact, the transportation planning industry is expected to grow by 20 percent or more from 2008 to 2018. The BLS has forecast an increased need during the same time period for urban and regional planners to create entirely new communities due to population growth. The need for transportation planners is likely to grow because of that growth as well because road infrastructure will be a key element of many new communities. (The urban and regional planning industry is expected to grow 19 percent from 2008 to 2018, according to BLS data.)

Urban and regional planners will be called upon to help engineers and architects confer with builders to correct and create various aspects of development such as building security and environmental issues. Indeed, green occupations are likely to increase as the demand for ecologically friendly technology and structures grows. Jobs are anticipated to be available in industries that work with public and private organizations on conservation, preventing pollution, and regulation enforcement. Additional opportunities that involve determining policies and increasing efficiency or reducing the environmental impact of different types of transportation, such as mass transit, are also expected to be available.

As an emphasis on green living and green building increases, more transportation planners may be utilized to help make current transportation systems more environmentally friendly or to create entirely new transportation systems that will reduce auto use and emissions and improve air quality.

EARNINGS

Transportation planners make, on average, approximately US$74,520 per year or US$35.88 per hour as of 2010.

RELATED OCCUPATIONS

Similar occupations include civil engineers, landscape architects, geographers, actuaries, surveyors, and environmental engineers. Jobs that are similar to transportation planning involve organizing, supervising, or overseeing other workers.

SOURCES OF ADDITIONAL INFORMATION

Environmental Protection Agency. http://www.epa.gov
Federal Highway Administration. http://fhwa.dot.gov
Institute of Transportation Engineers. http://www.ite.org
Transportation Professional Certification Board. http://www.tpcb.org

FURTHER READING

Bureau of Labor Statistics, U.S. Department of Labor. *Occupational Outlook Handbook, 2010–11 Edition.* Accessed February 16, 2012. http://www.bls.gov/oco/ocos057.htm.

Bureau of Labor Statistics, U.S. Department of Labor. *Urban and Regional Planners.* Accessed February 16, 2012. http://www.bls.gov/oco/pdf/ocos057.pdf.

Federal Highway Administration. *Environmental Review Toolkit.* Accessed February 16, 2012. http://environment.fhwa.dot.gov/index.asp.

Gayle, Steven. *What Is the Value of the Professional Transportation Planner Certification?* Transportation Professional Certification Board: Washington, DC, 2012. Accessed February 16, 2012. http://www.tpcb.org/ptp/comparison.asp.

O*NET OnLine. *Green Occupation: 19-3099.01— Transportation Planners.* Accessed February 16, 2012. http://www.onetonline.org/help/green/19-3099.01.

———. *Summary Report for: 19-3099.01— Transportation Planners.* Accessed February 16, 2012. http://www.onetonline.org/link/summary/19-3099.01.

ARBITRATORS, MEDIATORS, AND CONCILIATORS

NATURE OF THE WORK

Arbitrators, mediators, and conciliators aid negotiation and conflict resolution through discussion and also work to resolve conflicts outside of the court system by getting all involved parties to agree, according to the U.S. Department of Labor's Bureau of Labor Statistics (BLS). Although their goal to resolve a disagreement is similar to that of a traditional court proceeding, members of the arbitration, mediation, and conciliation industry frequently focus on different methods to achieve a final outcome.

Alternative dispute resolution, a series of confidential processes that can help resolve disputes outside of court in a more casual setting, is one technique arbitrators, mediators, and conciliators often use. If the involved parties cannot come to a resolution during the dispute process, the items discussed during the process cannot be used in court at a later date.

Members of the arbitration field may have a number of titles, including arbitrator, mediator, commissioner, alternative dispute resolution (ADR) coordinator, alternative dispute resolution mediator, or community relations representative, according to O*NET. Regardless of their title, arbitrators, mediators, and conciliators handle much more than simply negotiating divorce proceedings and property disputes. As in many fields, the arbitration, mediation, and conciliation industry has seen growth as a result of the increased emphasis in the United States on green, environmentally friendly processes, technologies, and products. Arbitrators, mediators, and conciliators who focus on green-related negotiations and conflicts typically specialize in the reconciliation and determination of conflicts that involve environmental concerns, such as urban planning or natural resource protection.

According to the nonprofit Dispute Resolution Board Foundation, dispute resolution methods have been used in regional planning endeavors by state highway departments and have been approved for use on California and Florida highway projects.

The Green Economy and the Legal Industry A number of legal occupations may grow as a result of the green economy, including attorneys, paralegals, legal assistants, and arbitrators, mediators, and conciliators. The growth will be due in part to the need for arbitrators, mediators, and conciliators to possess new skills because of an increased focus on green practices and regulations in legal battles and disputes. This is likely the reason that O*NET has denoted the field as a Green Enhanced Skills occupation, which will require industry members to possess additional knowledge to properly work on green-related disputes and issues.

Arbitration, Mediation, and Conciliation Work Typically, arbitrators, mediators, and conciliators meet with disputing parties to identify what issues exist, why they exist, and what each party is hoping the resolution will include. Members of the arbitration and mediation field may be asked to oversee negotiations or be involved in the decision-making process.

Professionals in the arbitration and conciliation field often use mediation techniques to get disputants to communicate and see each other's side. Hearings may be needed to assess what the source of the disagreement is. Arbitrators, mediators, and conciliators decide what course of action to recommend by comparing aspects of what parties are disagreeing about to rules, laws, or potential liability.

Their work may involve some simple administrative tasks such as setting up times for everyone to meet. Arbitration and mediation work can also involve writing agreements for the disagreeing parties to sign and preparing written opinions or recaps of case decisions. Public speaking may also play a role. In some cases, arbitrators, mediators, and conciliators may be asked to give presentations about what mediation and arbitration involve to schools or community groups.

Arbitration Arbitrators are typically businesspeople or attorneys who specialize in a specific industry according to the BLS. Compulsory arbitration, one of the two main types of arbitration, involves parties presenting their conflict to one or more impartial arbitrators for a final decision. The involved parties can reject what the arbitrator decides and may opt to have a court trial. In the second main type of arbitration, voluntary arbitration, parties that disagree select one or more arbitrators and share their issues, and the arbitrators then offer a final, binding decision.

Mediation As unbiased parties who help people settle their disputes outside of court, mediators can offer ideas and recommendations, but the disputing parties are ultimately responsible for deciding the final course of action. In many cases, mediators are used when the opposing parties hope to salvage a relationship after the conflict.

If the opposing parties cannot come to a conclusion during the private, confidential proceedings, they can decide to resolve the matter another way. Although the division of mediation-related costs is often determined before mediation begins, in many cases, mediators work as volunteers to resolve disputes or they may be court staff members. Mediation may be the most reasonable method of resolving a dispute because courts frequently

ask non-volunteer mediators to either offer their services at a low cost or allow the parties to split the expense.

Conciliation Like mediation, conciliation, also called *facilitation*, involves a neutral party helping disagreeing parties settle a matter that is under debate. Before the conciliation process begins, the involved parties must agree on whether or not they will obey what the conciliator suggests.

Tools of the Trade In addition to computers, scanners, fax machines, and other basic office equipment, arbitrators, mediators, and conciliators sometimes use common types of software to conduct research and solve problems. Popular software options in the arbitration and mediation field include e-mail, office suite software, word processing software, Internet browser software, and spreadsheet software.

Green Enough? Green occupations are positioned to evolve and change and potentially grow in the future because of the increased popularity of green technologies and practices. Because the growing green economy is likely to require arbitrators, mediators, and conciliators to have a specialized set of skills to work on disputes that involve green practices, products, or sustainable production, O*NET has labeled the arbitration, mediation, and conciliation industry as a green occupation.

However, that classification has come under criticism from at least one source, Iowa Senator Charles Grassley (R), who has questioned several federal agencies' stimulus spending. In 2010, according to a press release from Grassley's campaign, Grassley said the U.S. Department of Labor was directing green job-related stimulus funding from the Green Jobs Act of 2007 meant for energy conservation efforts to a kind of work that was "not what most people would think of as green jobs."

Grassley has expressed concern about the energy efficiency and renewable energy worker retraining efforts paid for through the Green Jobs Act of 2007 as well as the Department of Labor's distribution of stimulus dollars meant to support green jobs in industries that O*NET has identified as being green industries, including the arbitration, mediation, and conciliation field. "I'm a strong supporter of green jobs, and taxpayers deserve an honest reporting of how their money is being spent—this kind of work is not what most people would think of as green jobs," Grassley said in a press release. "It's a matter of responsible stewardship of tax dollars. Since February 2009, the Department of Labor has given out US$490 million in stimulus dollars for 'green jobs training,' and the department tells me that it's still working to define green jobs."

The O*NET profile, updated in 2011, still lists these positions as green jobs.

WORKING CONDITIONS

Arbitrators, mediators, and conciliators should have strong negotiation skills, listening skills, critical thinking abilities, and judgment and decision-making skills, according to O*NET. Arbitration and mediation field members should also have a certain level of social perceptiveness, noting people's reactions to statements and suggestions and comprehending what has prompted that reaction.

During any given workday, arbitrators, mediators, and conciliators may be asked to negotiate and resolve conflicts with others, solve problems for other parties seeking their help, interpret and explain information to different people, and gauge how important certain things are to the people they are dealing with.

According to the BLS, because the meetings are private, arbitrators, mediators, and conciliators frequently work in offices or meeting rooms and may work off-site at predetermined places where negotiation proceedings are scheduled. Some also work from home. However, no matter what their work environment is, arbitration and mediation professionals typically work a 35- to 40-hour work week, unless extra time is required during contract negotiations.

EMPLOYMENT

According to O*NET, arbitrators, mediators, and conciliators often work in two major green economy sectors. One sector is governmental and regulatory administration, which includes private and public organizations that may focus on regulation enforcement, reducing pollution, or dealing with public policies. The other sector is the research, design, and consulting services industry, which involves jobs that are indirectly related to the green economy such as research or energy consulting work.

Approximately 6,920 professionals work in the arbitration and mediation field, according to the BLS. The professional, scientific, and technical services industry has the highest levels of employment in the arbitrator and mediator industry, with approximately 1,330 professionals.

State and local government are the second largest source of arbitrator and mediator jobs. State governments employ approximately 1,280 arbitrators and mediators while local governments employ 1,190.

California is the state that offers the highest employment level. Approximately 1,010 jobs are available in the state. New York, which employs 640 arbitrators and mediators, offers the second highest employment level. Florida (550 jobs), Texas (420 jobs), and Massachusetts (320 jobs) rank third, fourth, and fifth respectively.

Use of arbitrators, mediators, and conciliators has become more popular due in part to acceptance and encouragement in industries such as architecture and construction. In 2007 the American Institute of Architects (AIA) released a new edition of several key contract documents, which included information about potentially using a third-party "initial decision maker" and optional binding dispute resolution proceedings.

At about the same time, in 2007 to 2008, the AIA's Committee on Architecture for Education published information, available on the AIA website, indicating that the industry had "reached a tipping point," noting that "sustainability now appears to be on everyone's radar." Green design has helped spur some building projects in recent years, such as school construction, according to the AIA, a trend fueled in part by global warming fears and state-funded green construction programs.

The American Arbitration Association (AAA), a not-for-profit, public service organization with 30 offices in the United States, Mexico, and Singapore, that is dedicated to resolving disputes through the use of arbitration, mediation, conciliation, negotiation, democratic elections, and other voluntary procedures, also offers information about construction industry arbitration and mediation procedures to members of the construction, financial, and real estate industries. The AAA, which serves as a general advocate for the arbitration industry and also provides a forum for dispute hearings and impartial experts for cases, notes that construction-related disagreements are often resolved through arbitration.

In 2010, 143,349 cases were filed with the association in commercial, construction, labor, employment, insurance, international, and claims program dispute matters. The organization also says that alternative dispute resolution services have been used in several energy sectors, including the renewable, alternative, and sustainability energy sector.

TRAINING, OTHER QUALIFICATIONS, AND ADVANCEMENT

According to the BLS, training requirements in the arbitration and mediation field can vary. Some mediators may receive training through independent programs, such as volunteering at a community center that offers mediation, national membership associations, and postsecondary schools. Specific training is often required to work in state- or court-funded mediation programs.

However, most mediators finish a 40-hour basic course and a 20-hour advanced training program. Many also have a law degree or may possess a public policy master's degree or other advanced degree.

According to O*NET, 46 percent of professionals in the arbitration, mediation, and conciliation industry have a bachelor's degree. Twenty-two percent have some college education but no degree, and 15 percent have a master's degree.

Industry professionals can also opt to obtain additional training through organizations such as the AAA, which provides administrative services, including assisting in the appointment of mediators and arbitrators, scheduling hearings, and providing information on dispute resolution options in the United States and globally through its International Centre for Dispute Resolution.

The AAA also offers training courses through its American Arbitration Association University. The AAA's online education portal also includes back issues of its *Dispute Resolution Journal* publication, which includes green industry articles such as the one published in the May/October 2010 issue entitled "Green Building: Trend or Megatrend?"

JOB OUTLOOK

The job market for arbitrators, mediators, and conciliators is expected to see faster than average growth in the 10-year period between 2008 and 2018 according to O*NET, which forecasts a 14 to 19 percent growth rate for the industry. O*NET anticipates that there will be 3,200 job openings from 2008 to 2018 in the arbitration, mediation, and conciliation field. This is not bad, considering that *Money* magazine and Salary.com estimated that there were just 5,150 total jobs in the field in 2004 in their joint "Best Jobs in America" list.

The industry may expand due in part to the expense and time delays that official litigation often involves. Arbitration, mediation, and other forms of preventing litigation can help the parties involved in a dispute save money and resolve issues more quickly, according to the BLS. The field should also grow because all jurisdictions now offer some sort of a dispute resolution program. Some areas require parties who are dealing with certain issues, such as child custody, to confer with a mediator.

Although there is no guarantee that the increasingly popular emphasis on green living will help add jobs to the field, it is likely to add new job requirements. Arbitrators, mediators, and conciliators working on disputes that involve topics such as green building should be familiar with the materials, procedures, and desired outcomes involved with green building.

EARNINGS

The median annual salary of arbitrators, mediators, and conciliators is US$66,460, or US$31.95 per hour, according to the BLS. O*NET estimates the average salary to be lower, at US$55,800, or US$26.83 per hour.

The industries offering the highest pay to arbitrators and mediators include the federal government, which, according to the BLS, offers an annual median wage of US$119,670. The legal service industry ranks second, paying an average annual wage of US$100,110.

Salary can vary greatly from state to state. In California, the state that offers the highest employment level for arbitrators and mediators, the average annual salary is US$105,800. Virginia, the state with the highest arbitrator and mediator salary rate, pays professionals in the industry an average annual salary of US$136,660.

RELATED OCCUPATIONS

Occupations similar to arbitrators, mediators, and conciliators include:

- Insurance adjusters, examiners, and investigators
- Lawyers
- Licensing examiners and inspectors
- Political scientists
- Title examiners, abstractors, and searchers

SOURCES OF ADDITIONAL INFORMATION

American Arbitration Association. http://www.adr.org

FURTHER READING

Bureau of Labor Statistics, U.S. Department of Labor. "23-1022.00 Arbitrators, Mediators, and Conciliators." In *Occupational Employment Statistics: Occupational Employment and Wages, May 2010.* Accessed April 5, 2012. http://www.bls.gov/oes/current/oes231022.htm.

———. "23-1022.00 Arbitrators, Mediators, and Conciliators." In *Standard Occupational Classification.* Accessed March 20, 2012. http://www.bls.gov/soc/2000/soc_g1c2.htm.

CNNMoney. "Arbitrators, Mediators, and Conciliators." *Best Jobs in America.* Accessed March 20, 2012. http://money.cnn.com/magazines/moneymag/bestjobs/2006/snapshots/108.html.

The Dispute Resolution Board Foundation. *Introduction to the DRB Database.* Accessed April 5, 2012. http://www.drb.org/database_intro.htm.

Grassley, Chuck. "Grassley works to stop squandering of tax dollars for green jobs." Press release, September 24, 2010. Accessed March 20, 2012. http://www.iowapolitics.com/index.iml?Article=212000.

Harness, Suzanne H., and Kenneth W. Cobleigh. *2007 AIA Contract Documents®: Key Issues of Interest to Owners.* Accessed March 20, 2012. http://info.aia.org/SGNActionToolKit/2010/procurement/Contract%20Documents/Articles/2007%20AIA%20Contract%20Documents%20Key%20Issues%20of%20Interest%20To%20Owners.pdf.

O*NET OnLine. *Summary Report for: 21-1022.00—Arbitrators, Mediators, and Conciliators.* Accessed March 20, 2012. http://www.onetonline.org/link/summary/23-1022.00.

CONSTRUCTION AND BUILDING INSPECTORS

NATURE OF THE WORK

Construction and building inspectors examine structures such as bridges, buildings, highways, and sewers to ensure the structures were built, renovated, or fixed in accordance with applicable zoning rules and construction codes. Certain building regulations, which include local building ordinances and national codes published by the International Code Council (ICC), govern construction in the United States to ensure that the structures are safe for public use. Therefore, construction and building inspectors should be familiar with national and local requirements.

Building regulations have been in effect for thousands of years according to the ICC, a nonprofit organization that has worked to develop a single set of comprehensive and coordinated national model construction codes since its founding in 1994. Building codes date back to the Babylonian Empire in 2200 BCE and have been in use in the United States since the 1700s.

Construction and building inspectors typically inspect construction projects throughout the building process to ensure that construction is in line with local and national requirements. If an inspector discovers during a visit that the plans or codes are not being followed, the first step is often to inform the person in charge on the worksite. However, if the violation continues, a government inspector can create a *stop-work* order.

Permit issues may also be an inspector's responsibility. If building is occurring and the necessary permits are not in place, inspectors, particularly those who work for municipalities, will instruct violators to let them inspect the building site and encourage the builders to arrange for the necessary permits.

AT A GLANCE FACT BOX

SOC: 47-4011.00
Preferred Education: A high school diploma is considered a basic requirement; however, an increasing number of entry-level construction and building inspectors have a bachelor's degree
Average Salary: US$54,320 annually
Other Information: Construction and building inspectors who work in regions prone to natural disasters may need to be aware of extra design and procedural regulations that make the structures safer during traumatic events

---

Plan Examiners Plan examiners assess building plans before construction. They ensure that the plans work with the building site, including testing soil conditions and construction footing placement as well as ensuring that the finished product will fall within building code guidelines.

Since the 1990s, green building has become more prevalent and has developed into a larger, more organized industry, which now includes local U.S. city-sponsored green building programs and national green building guidelines, according to the U.S. Environmental Protection Agency (EPA). Thus, the plan examiner role is likely to involve increased attention to green building practices.

Building Inspectors Building inspectors are generally concerned with the overall safety of a building and its level of construction quality according to the U.S. Department of Labor's Bureau of Labor Statistics (BLS), and may focus on one area, such as reinforced concrete buildings. Inspectors should be familiar with numerous aspects of construction, ranging from the storage of materials to scheduling, billing procedures, and change orders, according to the Association of Construction Inspectors (ACI). Examining alarms, smoke control methods, sprinklers, and other fire safety aids, as well as risk factors such as proximity to other buildings, are also typical building inspector tasks.

Inspection Aids Although there are several different types of inspectors, many use similar tools in their day-to-day tasks. Metering devices, tape measures, and other handheld tools that help gauge distances, length, and other elements are commonly used. Some tools are items found in most offices. Inspectors may use calculators, accounting and compliance software, and spreadsheet software.

Inspectors often use computers to record findings during site visits and general project information such as permit records, which reduces the paperwork they need to carry and allows them to immediately fax or e-mail code violations and other findings.

Construction and Building Inspectors and the Environment The building and construction inspector industry has been identified by O*NET as a Green Enhanced Skills occupation. This is an occupation that is likely to be affected by the expected growth in green technology and activity, requiring new, unique inspection skills that are related to green building.

To encourage green building, many cities and regions have implemented green building initiatives. San Francisco, for example, offers priority in permit processing via coordination with the city's planning department, Department of Building Inspection, and Department of Public Works to projects that commit to achieving Gold Leadership in Energy and Environmental Design certification, through the national program developed by the U.S. Green Building Council in 2000.

To determine whether green construction methods and materials have been correctly used, building inspectors assess a structure's energy efficiency, sustainable material use, and general environmental health factor, according to the International Association of Certified Home Inspectors (InterNACHI), which offers a free online course in green building. If, for example, an inspector found a short-cycling furnace or other item that could prompt large energy consumption during an inspection, it might merit mentioning because it would require home appliance service. A checklist offered by InterNACHI includes suggested green inspection items such as looking for exterior lighting controlled by motion sensors, composite recycled materials used in construction, and other items, which are each awarded a point ranking during the inspection process.

WORKING CONDITIONS

Although in some cases, construction and building inspectors may work in groups with other, specialized inspectors on large projects, typically, they work individually on projects, according to the BLS.

Construction inspectors may be asked to create a field report or recap of what they have observed on a single day at the construction site. They may also write a thorough inspection report about their experiences at a site over several days, which requires significant time to review project-related documents, visit the site, and become very involved in what tasks are occurring, according to the ACI.

Construction and building inspectors usually work alone during the day as they travel to and from building sites and log and review findings, according to the BLS. They often work a 40-hour work week unless a busy building period in a project requires overtime. Self-employed, nongovernment inspectors, however, may work nontraditional night and weekend hours.

Construction and building inspection work is generally considered to be a safe job. However, accidents are possible, particularly at sites where safety regulations are not being followed. In 2002, a building inspector in Virginia's Chesterfield County was injured when he fell nine feet from the second floor of a home he was inspecting after stumbling over a hole in the floor that had not been protected with cones, taping, or a guardrail, according to *Virginia Lawyers Weekly*. The publication also noted that Occupational Safety and Health Administration (OSHA) regulations require that safety precautions be taken to identify such structures.

To increase safety, inspectors wear standard construction site safety gear such as hardhats.

EMPLOYMENT

In 2008 the economy supported approximately 106,400 building and construction inspector jobs according to the BLS. Forty-four percent of the jobs involved working for municipal or county building departments.

Smaller jurisdictions may only employ a few general inspectors, but in larger areas, an inspection department may include several different positions, including inspectors who focus on certain types of building, such as electrical inspectors or elevator inspectors. The inspector who won the Building Association of Texas 2011 Code Professional of the Year award, for example, oversaw 50 residential and commercial building inspectors and was responsible for the administration and implementation of the residential and commercial building codes for all construction in Austin, Texas.

Engineering and architecture firms employed an additional 27 percent of construction and building inspectors who work as contractors or on a per-inspection fee, many of whom were home inspectors hired by property buyers. State governments and various other service industries provided the majority of other inspector jobs. A small number (8 percent) were self-employed.

TRAINING, OTHER QUALIFICATIONS, AND ADVANCEMENT

According to the BLS, although many states require a license or certification to work as a building and construction inspector, training requirements can differ based on the job or area. If a state or jurisdiction requires certification or licensure, it will likely involve a combination of education, experience, and an examination. Inspectors are often required to take educational classes throughout their career and renew their license or certification. Ongoing education is particularly important for construction and building inspectors because they need to stay updated on new building practices and codes.

Inspectors may also be required by their state to be certified by the ICC or another industry association as a Certified Building Official (CBO) or other title. All fifty states and Washington, DC, have implemented the ICC's suggested codes at the state or jurisdictional level. Even if it is not required, the BLS suggests that being certified by an industry association or other source may help an inspector's chances in the job market.

While industry experience is helpful, a high school diploma is often considered the only basic requirement for inspecting work. A building inspection technology associate degree or certification program is available at many community colleges, which may be why an increased number of entry-level construction and building inspectors have a college degree. For inspectors who work in construction, it is important to have a strong background in the materials, procedures, and other requirements involved in building and repairing different types of structures, according to O*NET.

JOB OUTLOOK

The inspector industry is forecast to have faster than average growth in the coming years. Construction and building inspector jobs are expected to increase by 17 percent between 2008 and 2018, according to the BLS.

Many industry organizations, including the ICC, support green building and offer guidelines to ensure that industry members use sustainable building methods without compromising safety. (The ICC is an active legislative advocate for green building and has established the International Energy Conservation Code and the International Green Construction Code Public Version 2.0.)

The building industry's growing focus on green design and construction will also help spur the construction and building inspection field. Industry analysts also expect that several other factors will help create additional positions in the industry. For example, inspector jobs for the government and positions at companies that handle engineering and architectural services are expected to grow because of an increased focus on public safety and a higher quality of construction.

The nature of the construction and building inspector job may change as the industry grows. Building information modeling and other new technology should make reviewing plans faster and easier, freeing up time and money to focus on inspections.

Although new opportunities are expected, construction and building inspectors may face new competition as their industry grows. The BLS also notes that the field's growth might be affected by increased interest in the industry from other workers, such as construction workers who are hoping to move into less physically taxing jobs with higher salaries. Certification and job experience may become required qualifications to obtain a position in the construction and building inspecting industry.

As of 2010, 106,400 construction and building inspectors were employed in the industry. By 2018, 124,200 inspectors are expected to work in the field, a 17 percent increase, according to the BLS. O*NET notes that the additional required knowledge and field specializations for occupations such as the construction and building inspection position may spur an increase in jobs in the field.

EARNINGS

Construction and building inspectors earned, on average, US$54,320 per year or US$26.11 per hour, as of May 2010. The mid-range of construction and building inspectors earned US$52,360 according to BLS data.

Local governments, one of the largest employment sources for construction and building inspectors, paid a mean annual wage of US$54,730 or US$26.31 per hour. Inspectors who worked in architectural, engineering, and other similar industries earned, on average, US$52,770 per year.

RELATED OCCUPATIONS

Similar occupations include the following:

- Fire inspectors
- Freight and cargo inspectors
- Industrial safety engineers
- Real estate appraisers and assessors

SOURCES OF ADDITIONAL INFORMATION

Association of Construction Inspectors. http://www.aci-assoc.org

International Association of Certified Home Inspectors (InterNACHI). http://www.nachi.org/green.htm

International Code Council. http://www.iccsafe.org

FURTHER READING

Arzola, Sylvia. "City's Chief Building Inspector Awarded 'Code Professional of the Year.'" October 21, 2011. Accessed March 19, 2012. http://www.ci.austin.tx.us/news/cnews.cfm?nwsid=4167.

Bureau of Labor Statistics, U.S. Department of Labor. "47-4011: Construction and Building Inspectors." In *Occupational Employment Statistics: Occupational Employment and Wages, May 2010.* Accessed March 19, 2012. http://www.bls.gov/oes/current/oes474011.htm.

———. "Construction and Building Inspectors." In *Occupational Outlook Handbook, 2010–11 Edition.* Accessed March 19, 2012. http://www.bls.gov/oco/ocos004.htm.

Environmental Protection Agency (EPA). *Green Building History in the U.S.* Accessed March 19, 2012. http://www.epa.gov/greenbuilding/pubs/about.htm#4.

O*NET OnLine. *Summary Report for: 47-4010.00—Construction and Building Inspectors.* Accessed March 19, 2012. http://www.onetonline.org/link/summary/47-4011.00.

Seattle New Building Energy Efficiency Policy Analysis. *Case Study: City of San Francisco Green Priority Permitting Program.* Accessed March 19, 2012. http://www.seattle.gov/environment/documents/GBTF_SanFran_Green_Permit_Case_Study.pdf.

Virginia Lawyers Weekly. "Fall at Construction Site Mediated." *Virginia Lawyers Weekly,* May 9, 2005. Accessed March 19, 2012. http://valawyersweekly.com/2005/05/09/fall-at-construction-site-mediated/.

INSPECTORS, TESTERS, SORTERS, SAMPLERS, AND WEIGHERS

■

NATURE OF THE WORK

Careful monitoring of the production process can help ensure a product that a company creates is the correct size and weight and fulfills all other contract stipulations.

In many cases, a quality assurance inspector, also sometimes referred to as a quality control inspector, is brought in to assess various aspects of the production process. Other related job titles are sorter, sampler, tester, and weigher. The quality control inspection industry has been flagged by the U.S. Occupational Information Network (O*NET) as a green industry, which is forecast to increase in size and scope as the emphasis on environmentally friendly production processes becomes more popular.

Within the manufacturing industry, green practices are gaining acceptance. The U.S. Department of Commerce defines green manufacturing as "the creation of manufactured products that use processes that minimize negative environmental impacts, conserve energy and natural resources, are safe for employees, communities, and consumers and are economically sound." However, the term *green manufacturing* can also refer to the sustainable production methods used to create products or, as the United Nations defined it in its 1987 "Report of the World Commission on Environment and Development," a process that "meets the needs of the present without compromising the ability of future generations to meet their own needs."

A number of organizations, both public policy organizations and private companies, are embracing the green manufacturing trend. The National Council for Advanced Manufacturing, a Washington, DC–based policy and

AT A GLANCE FACT BOX

SOC: 51-9061.00
Preferred Education: High school diploma or GED
Average Salary: US$35,550 annually
Other Information: Inspectors, testers, sorters, samplers, and weighers should be skilled at math and communication, have good vision, and possess strong hand-eye coordination

program organization founded in 1989, has said one of its central goals is to help U.S. manufacturing become more sustainable by helping its members find out how to create sustainable manufacturing business opportunities, close supply chain loops, and generally become more efficient.

Using nearly US$1 million in federal funds it received from the U.S. Department of Energy in 2009, Western Michigan University's Manufacturing Research Center began the Green Manufacturing Initiative to encourage professional and government organizations, industry members, and universities to share sustainable manufacturing research to create green manufacturing programs.

In addition, some states have placed an increased emphasis on green production of goods. For example, Oregon has a Green Jobs Council that published a study in 2010 examining green product-related employment trends in the state.

Some quality control professionals test items before they progress to production. Others handle the final confirmation that a product was created correctly according to the U.S. Department of Labor's Bureau of Labor Statistics (BLS). This may involve calibrating instruments that gauge weight, size, or other aspects of a product; repairing products; setting up test equipment; and sharing their findings.

Inspectors Quality control inspectors examine, test, organize, try, or weigh non-agricultural raw materials and manufacturer parts or products for imperfections, wear, and production problems. Depending on the item an inspector is reviewing, the specific tasks and safety checks may differ. Quality control inspectors use a combination of their senses—feel, sight, sound, smell, and taste—to determine whether or not a product has flaws.

Sorters Sorters specifically divide goods by different qualifications such as color, material, length, and size. Like other types of quality control specialists, sorters may also be required to record data.

Testers To assess what a product's overall lifetime will be, what parts will wear out first, and how the product can be made stronger, testers repetitively test sample products under different conditions.

Weighers Weighers gauge the weight of different amounts of materials used in an item's production.

Samplers Samplers examine a production sample for errors or imperfections.

Items That Assist Quality Control Inspectors Quality control inspectors use a variety of instruments. These include calibrated resistance measuring equipment, such as digital resistance meters, resistivity meters, and resistance meters; gauges or inspection fixtures; and integrated circuit testers, such as logic test systems and manufacturing defect analyzers.

Quality control inspectors use micrometers, alignment gauges, and other hand-held measurement devices. They also frequently use electronic inspection equipment, such as coordinate-measuring machines, which help them measure dimensional accuracy. Later they may assess the results using specialized software. Voltmeters, which measure a circuit's voltage; ammeters, which measure electrical current; and ohmmeters, which measure electrical resistance, may be used to test electrical devices.

WORKING CONDITIONS

A quality control inspector may review one product during an entire shift or examine a number of products during a workday. Completion of the task could involve working at night or on the weekend and logging in overtime to ensure production occurs. Typical quality inspection tasks include obtaining and documenting information, observing processes, assessing quality levels, checking for compliance with predetermined regulations or standards, and conveying relevant findings and problems to coworkers and supervisors.

A quality control inspector's work environment is contingent on what type of workplace and industry the inspector works in. In large manufacturing organizations, for example, an inspector may be surrounded with dirt and noise. Another quality control inspector may conduct tests in a tidy environment. In some sectors, inspectors' jobs may involve heavy lifting and very little sitting. However, manufacturing inspectors typically have fairly stationary jobs.

EMPLOYMENT

In 2008 approximately 464,700 inspecting, testing, sorting, sampling, and weighing jobs existed in the United States according to BLS data. Roughly 69 percent of professionals worked in manufacturing establishments that produced motor vehicle parts, semiconductor and other electronic components, plastics, aerospace products, and other items. Inspection professionals also worked in wholesale trade; employment services; and professional, scientific, and technical services.

TRAINING, OTHER QUALIFICATIONS, AND ADVANCEMENT

Training requirements differ depending on what tasks each job involves. However, in many cases, employers prefer that a quality control inspector gain real-life experience while working rather than attending a postsecondary training program. A high school diploma typically is adequate preparation to work in the industry.

Some professionals choose to become certified by the American Society for Quality (ASQ), which offers 15 types of quality control certifications. The ASQ is a professional standards-based association established in 1946 that currently has more than 85,000 members worldwide. Its certification program includes a combination of job experience requirements and an exam.

Learning about computer-aided design in high school or after graduation can also help improve a candidate's chances in the U.S. job market.

JOB OUTLOOK

Employment opportunities in the quality control inspector industry are expected to slowly decrease, according to the

BLS. Two contributing factors are an increase in automated inspection methods and the increased role other production workers are taking on in the inspection process.

Many companies are placing a stronger emphasis on quality and greater product output. However, because many companies are replacing inspectors with automated equipment, the BLS forecasts that employment of testers, sorters, and other quality control inspectors will decrease by 4 percent between 2008 and 2018. Another industry trend, manufacturers relocating overseas, may also contribute to the industry-wide decline.

O*NET anticipates that the quality inspection industry will experience a slow to moderate decline of 3 to 9 percent from 2008 to 2018, with a projected 77,900 openings being available in the field.

However, the industry still has an opportunity for growth according to ASQ's December 2008 Quarterly Quality Report. This report indicates that quality improvement has failed to meet customer expectations in most industries and implies that companies could achieve better results by increasing quality systems and procedures. Human inspectors will still be needed in certain industries, particularly ones that require product examinations that involve smell, texture, appearance, and taste.

EARNINGS

Inspectors, testers, sorters, samplers, and weighers earned, on average, US$35,550 per year, or US$17.09 per hour, as of May 2010, according to BLS data. The employment services and aerospace product and parts manufacturing industries, two of the industries with the highest levels of quality control professional employment, paid, on average, US$29,230 and US$47,720, respectively. The mid-range salary for quality control inspector professionals was US$33,030.

RELATED OCCUPATIONS

Occupations that are related to quality control inspecting due to similar job tasks and other factors include the following:

- Computer-controlled machine tool operators
- Aircraft structure, surfaces, rigging, and systems assemblers
- Machinists
- Metal and plastic model makers

SOURCES OF ADDITIONAL INFORMATION

American Society for Quality. http://asq.org

National Council for Advanced Manufacturing. http://nacfam.org

FURTHER READING

Bureau of Labor Statistics, U.S. Department of Labor. "51-9061 Inspectors, Testers, Sorters, Samplers, and Weighers." In *Occupational Employment Statistics: Occupational Employment and Wages, May 2010.* Accessed March 8, 2012. http://www.bls.gov/oes/current/oes519061.htm.

———. "Inspectors, Testers, Sorters, Samplers, and Weighers." In *Occupational Outlook Handbook, 2010–11 Edition.* Accessed March 8, 2012. http://www.bls.gov/oco/ocos220.htm#nature.

International Trade Administration. *How Does Commerce Define Sustainable Manufacturing?* Accessed March 8, 2012. http://trade.gov/competitiveness/sustainablemanufacturing/how_doc_defines_SM.asp.

O*NET OnLine. *Summary Report for: 51-9061.00— Inspectors, Testers, Sorters, Samplers, and Weighers.* Accessed March 8, 2012. http://www.onetonline.org/link/summary/51-9061.00.

Oregon Environmental Council. *About Us.* Accessed March 8, 2012. http://www.oeconline.org/about-us.

United Nations. "Report of the World Commission on Environment and Development." 96th plenary meeting, December 11, 1987, United Nations Department of Economic and Social Affairs. Accessed March 8, 2012. http://www.un.org/documents/ga/res/42/ares42-187.htm.

Western Michigan University Manufacturing Research Center. *Green Manufacturing Initiative.* Accessed March 8, 2012. http://www.wmich.edu/mfe/mrc/greenmanufacturing/.

TRANSPORTATION VEHICLE, EQUIPMENT AND SYSTEMS INSPECTORS, EXCEPT AVIATION

NATURE OF THE WORK

According to the Federal Motor Carrier Safety Administration, 247,421,120 motor vehicles were registered in the United States as of 2005. However, that number includes only trucks, buses, hazardous material transport carriers, and other similar vehicles. Transportation inspectors are needed to inspect those vehicles, but they may also include rail transport officials such as freight inspectors or car inspectors and other officials who inspect other types of vehicles, according to the U.S. Department of Labor's Bureau of Labor Statistics (BLS).

With the exception of inspectors who work in the aviation industry, transportation vehicle, equipment, and systems inspectors are known by a number of titles, including chief mechanical officer and rail technician according to O*NET, the Occupational Information Network, a U.S. job database being developed by the U.S. Department of Labor/Employment and Training Administration (USDOL/ETA). Transportation inspectors may also be known as smog check technicians, diesel engine inspectors, smog technicians, transit vehicle inspectors, or emission inspection technicians. Transportation inspectors are professionals who examine equipment or goods to ensure they will operate safely when transporting people or goods.

Greening of the Industry The transportation vehicle, equipment, and systems inspectors industry has been denoted as a green industry, or one that will experience increased employment opportunities and demand and

---

AT A GLANCE FACT BOX

SOC: 53-6051.07

Preferred Education: Previous experience in a similar field is the most common source of postsecondary training or education

Average Salary: US$57,640 annually

Other Information: O*NET ranks this position as an occupation that requires medium preparation such as training in vocational schools, on-the-job training, or an associate's degree

---

possibly require additional skills due to the growing popularity of environmentally friendly trends. Groups such as the Intergovernmental Panel on Climate Change (IPCC) are actively campaigning for major changes in the way citizens use and create methods of transportation.

Burning fuel when driving can significantly increase the amount of carbon dioxide in the atmosphere, according to the U.S. Environmental Protection Agency (EPA). An increase in the amount of carbon dioxide, due in part to vehicle emissions, contributes to changing our climate's balance according to the IPCC, which also says the annual carbon dioxide concentration growth rate was larger from 1995 to 2005 than it had been for more than 30 years prior. As Americans seek ways to reduce automobile-related fossil fuel consumption, the public transportation sector, including the transportation inspector industry, is likely to experience growth.

A transportation inspector's green-related work may involve determining the emissions levels of a vehicle or vehicles, examining the tests used to determine emissions levels, and determining what appropriate amounts of emissions are, factoring in the vehicle's age. Inspectors may also be asked to make physical alterations to parts of a vehicle such as the fuel system or engine.

Mass Transit's Green Options An inspector's work, as a result of additional federal and local goals to reduce air pollution and global warming, may include inspecting mass transit methods and systems, which offer a more environmentally friendly option than individual automobiles.

According to train company Amtrak, its train service is 20 percent more energy efficient than commercial airlines and 30 percent more efficient than cars. The train company has also replaced diesel-powered round-trip trains with electric trains and increased electric service in some areas, much of which is generated from non-fossil fuel sources.

Inspectors who work with mass transit may determine what service and schedule changes are needed, identify potential hazards along the route, or work to find out what causes delays and therefore wastes fuel, according to California Employment Development Department's (EDD) transportation inspector occupation guide.

Inspecting Higher-Efficiency Automobiles Inspectors should also be familiar with the various components of alternative fuel vehicles such as electric and hybrid cars. In recent years, organizations have launched a number of public efforts to reduce transportation-related waste and quell environmental concerns. According to the Sierra Club, an environmental advocacy organization founded in 1892, transportation contributes to roughly one-third of all U.S. carbon dioxide emissions. Automakers have responded by creating greener cars. The Sierra Club endorses the use of vehicles powered by sustainable low carbon fuels and electricity. These vehicles use mechanisms that, 30 years ago, transportation inspectors most likely would not have been required to check, assuming they even had a system to assess the instruments' quality. Inspectors who are entering the workforce now need to possess a thorough understanding of how high-efficiency vehicles work.

As green technology advances and becomes more complex, transportation inspectors will undoubtedly need to become familiar with how new environmentally friendly technologies and systems work and stay up-to-date on new developments. In addition to the introduction of hybrid, battery electric, and other alternative fuel vehicles in recent years, research facilities such as the U.S. Department of Energy's Argonne National Laboratory are currently developing new technologies for more efficient diesel engines, better heavy-duty vehicle energy use, and software to help develop vehicle technology. Changes such as these will require new safety and performance checks that inspectors will need to be comfortable performing.

Inspection Work Specifics In general, transportation inspectors examine transportation equipment, systems, or vehicles to make sure they are made and can be used in accordance with accepted safety standards and regulations. When green components are involved and inspectors are working with a vehicle designed with environmental impact in mind, they also often complete a number of additional tasks.

Transportation inspectors may conduct emissions inspections by attaching on-board diagnostic (OBD) scanner cables to determine which emissions the vehicle will be releasing into the air and to see how it compares with current emission standards. Inspectors may also visually check how much smoke diesel or gas-run vehicles release. If a vehicle doesn't have any OBD equipment, transportation inspectors may need to do a low-pressure fuel evaluative test (LPFET) to see if the vehicle is discharging any harmful emissions. Some inspectors also opt to use handheld controllers and inspection devices that examine the components of a vehicle remotely.

Because motor vehicles involve potentially hazardous and difficult-to-transport materials such as gasoline and oil, transportation inspectors may also need to create or assess the ways that vehicle-related materials are packaged or shipped to ensure the process is safe. If a vehicle is judged to be a high-risk commercial motor vehicle, transportation inspectors may need to assess data from a thermal imaging unit (TIU) or other system and schedule additional checks in the future.

Some safety checks involve the overall condition of the vehicle. Inspectors may investigate to find out if a vehicle's parts are damaged, supervise part replacement or vehicle repair, assess how systems are running by monitoring meters and gauges during vehicle operation, and confirm that regular maintenance is being performed. Transportation inspectors look for equipment damage and potential malfunctions and check for evidence of wear and tear.

In some cases, transportation inspectors serve as watchdogs. Inspectors who work with transportation vehicles, equipment, and systems may inspect repairs that were made to vehicles or equipment to ensure the issues were corrected, hand out notifications, and recommend courses of action when issues are found, and they may also investigate safety violation complaints.

To perform their work, transportation inspectors use items such as automotive exhaust emission analyzers, scanners, and bar code readers, as well as scientific and analytical software and database user interface software.

WORKING CONDITIONS

Inspecting transportation vehicles and equipment can involve a number of tasks. In addition to their inspection duties, transit vehicle inspectors' general responsibilities include maneuvering equipment such as forklifts, boats, or other types of vehicles and recording and sharing their findings.

Transportation inspection is not necessarily relaxing, calm work. Because mistakes can cost not only millions of dollars in damaged products but also lives, the position can be stressful. There is also the chance that inspectors may disagree with company owners over the best course of action.

Somewhat strenuous physical work may also be required. Transportation inspectors often need to use their entire body during the course of their workday, lifting items, climbing onto platforms, bending down, and performing other physical tasks. However, transportation inspectors can help avoid injury by wearing hardhats, thick boots, gloves, and other protective gear.

EMPLOYMENT

Transportation inspectors work in the transportation sector to produce new transit systems and programs but their work frequently has a green connotation as well. Transportation inspectors often help make transportation more efficient and may work to lessen any impact they might have on the environment. Inspectors also work in the energy efficiency sector, which generally involves tasks such as building smart grids, and in governmental and regulatory administration, where transportation inspectors are often involved with public and private entities to help decrease pollution, enforce regulations, and protect natural resources.

In 2008, employment in the transportation vehicle, equipment, and systems inspectors industry was roughly 26,900 according to the BLS. California had the highest employment level in the transportation inspector industry, providing jobs for 2,590 professionals, who earned an average annual salary of US$59,520. Texas ranked second, employing 2,430 transportation inspectors and offering jobs with an annual mean wage of US$60,310.

The top industries that offered transportation vehicle, equipment, and systems inspectors employment as of 2008 were the U.S. government and the transportation and warehousing industry.

TRAINING, OTHER QUALIFICATIONS, AND ADVANCEMENT

To learn about the green aspects of vehicle inspection, industry members can take individual courses from organizations such as the West Virginia University-based National Alternative Fuels Training Consortium (NAFTC), which offers courses on understanding the difference between battery-electric and hybrid-electric vehicles, hydrogen fuel–cell engines and similar technology, and other topics.

Other organizations, such as the U.S. Department of Energy's Federal Energy Management Program, offer online courses on green topics such as how to manage a federal fleet through best practices that reduce greenhouse gas emissions and petroleum consumption and increase alternative fuel use.

To enter the field, a higher education degree may not be necessary. Approximately 52 percent of professionals in the industry had some college experience but did not have a college degree; 32 percent had a high school diploma or an equivalent degree, and 10 percent had an associate's degree. Previous experience in a similar field was the most significant source of postsecondary training or education in the transportation inspector field.

A background in the science, technology, engineering, and math (STEM) educational disciplines may be helpful in the transportation inspection industry to become an automotive engineering technology/technician. A bachelor's degree and work experience may qualify a transportation inspector to work in a specific industry such as a boat inspector who has an engineering degree and worked for the U.S. Coast Guard.

Communication skills also play a part in the transportation inspector's job. Inspectors may be called upon to write a report on their findings or the resulting actions that their findings inspired. These reports might also examine carrier operating rules, testing programs, or employee qualifications and recommend a waiver of federal standards on certain requests.

JOB OUTLOOK

The BLS forecasts that the transportation vehicle, equipment, and systems inspectors industry will experience a faster than average growth from 2008 to 2018. However, the increase in the industry isn't necessarily because of the green economy. Transportation inspectors will need additional skills to test for environmental effects and examine high-efficiency vehicles, which is why O*NET denoted the job as a green-enhanced skills occupation. However,

O*NET also noted that the impact of the green economy may or may not result in an increased demand for workers in the transportation inspector field.

The transportation vehicle, equipment, and systems inspectors field should see a speedy growth of 14 percent to 19 percent in the 10-year period between 2008 to 2018, with a projected 11,300 job openings in the field. This growth rate may instead be based on an increased need for safety. Widely publicized accidents and mishaps in recent years have helped to fuel the increased emphasis on safety in the transportation industry. After a tour bus accident in Virginia resulted in four deaths and a similar accident in New York resulted in 15 deaths, in June 2011 Federal Motor Carrier Safety Administration (FMCSA) administrator Anne Ferro issued a request for an increase in random tour bus safety inspections and funding for more safety inspectors according to the United Transportation Union (UTU).

In 2008, the Railway Safety Improvement Act, which requires the installation of automatic braking capabilities on certain train tracks by late December 2015, was passed in the wake of a train collision in Chatsworth, California, that resulted in 25 deaths and 135 injuries, according to a January 2012 MSNBC blog post.

As transportation accidents receive more media coverage, the public's desire for more frequent and stringent safety checks may cause an increased demand for additional transportation inspectors to perform the work.

EARNINGS

As of 2010, transportation vehicle, equipment, and systems inspectors earned a median annual salary of US$57,640. The hourly wage for the position was US$27.71.

Transportation inspectors who worked in the federal executive branch earned as much as US$100,920 according to the BLS; inspectors employed in the automotive repair and maintenance industry earned an average of US$32,880.

RELATED OCCUPATIONS

Locomotive engineers, rail yard engineers, subway and streetcar operators, ship engineers, and traffic technicians are all occupations considered to be similar to transportation vehicle, equipment, and systems inspectors.

SOURCES OF ADDITIONAL INFORMATION

Argonne National Laboratory. http://www.anl.gov

Federal Energy Management Program. http://www.eere.energy.gov/femp

Intergovernmental Panel on Climate Change. http://www.ipcc.ch

National Alternative Fuels Training Consortium. http://www.naftc.wvu.edu

The U.S. Department of Transportation Federal Motor Carrier Safety Administration. http://www.fmcsa.dot.gov

U.S. Environmental Protection Agency. http://www.epa.gov

FURTHER READING

Amtrak. *Defining Energy Efficiency.* Accessed March 2, 2012. http://www.amtrak.com/servlet/Satellite?c=WSArticlePage&cid=1153323727125&pagename=WhistleStop%2FWSArticlePage%2FBlank_Template.

Bureau of Labor Statistics, U.S. Department of Labor. "53–6051 Transportation Inspectors." In *Occupational Employment Statistics: Occupational Employment and Wages, May 2010.* Last updated May 17, 2011. Accessed March 2, 2012. http://www.bls.gov/oes/current/oes536051.htm.

California Employment Development Department. *Transportation Inspectors.* Accessed March 2, 2012. http://www.calmis.ca.gov/file/logistics/log-trans-inspectors.pdf

O*NET Online. "Summary report for transportation vehicle, equipment, and systems inspectors, except aviation," http://www.onetonline.org/link/summary/53-6051.07.

Sharrock, Justine, Laurie Udesky, and Stuart Silverstein. "Railroad Companies Fight Safety Rules, with Help from GOP and Obama." Open Channel on MSNBC.com, January 19, 2012. Accessed March 2, 2012. http://openchannel.msnbc.msn.com/_news/2012/01/18/10186068-railroad-companies-fight-safety-rules-with-help-from-gop-and-obama.

Sierra Club. *Green Transportation Solutions: Clean Cars.* Accessed March 2, 2012. http://www.utu.org/worksite/safety.htm.

United Transportation Union. *Safety.* Accessed March 2, 2012. http://www.sierraclub.org/transportation/cleancars/default.aspx.

SECTOR OVERVIEW:
GREEN CONSTRUCTION

—■—

A century ago, society tended to exert effort to conquer the natural environment for the benefit of people. In the 21st century, however, recognition is growing that resources are finite, the world is more crowded, and the natural environment needs to be protected, not vanquished. To that end, a wide range of construction professionals, including architects, engineers, urban planners, and construction managers, along with people in the construction trades, electricians, plumbers, carpenters, roofers, masons, and many others, are adopting the principles of green construction. That is, these professionals are using construction techniques and materials that limit the environmental impact of a building.

According to figures from a 2004 EPA survey, nonresidential buildings consume many resources. They account for 39 percent of the nation's total energy use and 68 percent of total electricity use. Buildings also account for 12 percent of total water use, 38 percent of total carbon dioxide emissions, and 60 percent of nonindustrial waste generated from construction and demolition.

These figures, however, are declining, and they are likely to decline dramatically as green construction grows and spreads. According to a report issued by McGraw-Hill Construction, the value of green nonresidential construction increased by a factor of 14 from 2005 to 2010 and will likely triple, to as much as US$145 billion, between 2010 and 2015. Furthermore, the U.S. Green Building Council estimates that the green construction industry employed one million workers between 2000 and 2008 and that by 2013 the number will rise to 3.3 million. Not counted in these figures are the legions of men and women employed by suppliers of green building products.

This explosive growth has been the result not only of the environmental movement but also of cost savings that green construction has introduced. Many executives point to the cost savings, particularly the lower energy costs, of green buildings. To achieve these savings, many construction firms seek certification from the U.S. Green Building Council's Leadership in Energy and Environmental Design program, which sets standards to rate buildings according to their sustainability.

WHAT IS GREEN CONSTRUCTION?

Green construction tends to focus on five major categories of activity. The first of these is location. Urban planners are finding ways to site buildings that reduce the need for the public to drive to them, thus reducing carbon emissions from petroleum fuels in vehicles. Architects and builders are making use of existing structures, retrofitting them for new purposes in an environmentally friendly way. Brownfields, or abandoned facilities that might present environmental hazards, are being reclaimed for use as sites for varied building projects. Many of these brownfields, because of their age, are located in places close to urban centers, making them ideal sites for facilities that reduce the need for people to drive.

A second category is energy efficiency. Architects and engineers are using principles such as daylighting to reduce the need for artificial light. In cold weather climates they are positioning buildings in ways that allow the sun to be a major source of heat for the building. Buildings are being equipped with energy-saving appliances, particularly those that have earned the ENERGY STAR designation established by the U.S. Environmental

Protection Agency and the U.S. Department of Energy. Some buildings are able to achieve a net energy consumption of zero and may even produce more energy than they consume through the use of photovoltaic solar panels, wind turbines, and other renewable energy technologies.

A third category is water conservation. To conserve potable, or drinkable, water, green buildings make use of graywater, or water from showers, washing machines, and the like. They are also making use of rainwater. The result is that plumbers may be required to install separate storage tanks and pipes to separate potable water from nonpotable water. Further water-efficient appliances and fixtures, such as aerated faucets, reduce water consumption. Landscape architects pay particular attention to reducing the need for water in a building's surroundings.

Indoor air quality is a fourth category of green construction. Many building materials, including carpets, insulation, and paints, emit pollutants that can build up inside a building, posing health hazards to occupants. Heating, ventilation, and air conditioning professionals, painters, insulation contractors, and others can mitigate these dangers.

A final category is referred to as "on-site practices." This refers to the use of renewable and recyclable resources, such as the wood used for flooring. The recycling of building materials, including scrap, plays an important role in green construction. Concrete removed from an existing site, for example, can be reused as road base at another site.

JOBS IN GREEN CONSTRUCTION

Jobs in green construction encompass every activity from conception to finished structure. Green construction projects begin with urban planners, who develop short- and long-term plans for land use, growth, and development in a community. They continue with architects who design green buildings, landscape architects who design the building's surroundings, and civil, mechanical, and electrical engineers who develop the processes that convert concept into reality. These professionals, on average, can earn annual wages in excess of US$60,000 and in some cases in excess of US$80,000.

When a project is under way, green construction is in the hands of construction workers, including managers (who can earn an average of US$85,000 per year) and laborers (whose average earnings are approximately US$31,000). Various specialty trades take part as well. These include carpenters; electricians; heating, ventilation,

and air conditioning installers; plumbers; insulation installers; painters; glaziers; and roofers. People working in these trades can earn an average wage between US$31,000 and US$51,000 per year.

In sum, green construction provides jobs for people with a wide range of skills and education. As green construction becomes more widespread, it will likely boost job prospects.

SOURCES OF ADDITIONAL INFORMATION

Associated Builders and Contractors, Inc. http://www.abc.org

Green Building Certification Institute. http://www.gbci.org

National Center for Construction Education and Research. http://www.nccer.org

U.S. Environmental Protection Agency. http://epa.gov

U.S. General Services Administration. http://www.gsa.gov

U.S. Green Building Council. http://www.usgbc.org

FURTHER READING

Associated Builders and Contractors. *Green Contractor Certification.* Accessed March 19, 2012. http://www.greenconstructionatwork.com/Tools_Resources/Green_Contractor_Certification.aspx.

Environmental Protection Agency. *Sustainable Design and Green Building Toolkit for Local Governments.* Washington, DC: U.S. Environmental Protection Agency, 2010.

General Services Administration. *The New Sustainable Frontier: Principles of Sustainable Development.* Washington, DC: U.S. General Services Administration, 2009.

International Living Building Institute. *Living Building Challenge.* Accessed March 19, 2012. https://ilbi.org/lbc.

Liming, Drew. *Careers in Green Construction.* June 2011, Bureau of Labor Statistics. Accessed March 19, 2012. http://www.bls.gov/green/construction/construction.pdf.

McGraw-Hill Construction. *Green Outlook 2011: Green Trends Driving Growth.* Accessed March 19, 2012. http://aiacc.org/wp-content/uploads/2011/06/greenoutlook2011.pdf.

National Institute of Building Sciences. *Sustainable.* Accessed March 19, 2012. http://www.wbdg.org/design/sustainable.php.

Schlager, Neil, and Jayne Weisblatt, eds. *Alternative Energy.* 3 vols. Detroit, MI: Thomson Gale, 2006.

CONSTRUCTION MANAGERS

NATURE OF THE WORK

A construction manager coordinates a construction project, whether it is a small home or a building in a hospital complex. The manager may plan the overall project schedule, set and maintain its budget, and hire and supervise subcontractors. On large projects, the manager may perform these tasks for a specific stage, such as site preparation. Depending on the tasks undertaken, the project's size, and how involved a construction manager is in the hands-on work, this person may be referred to as a construction superintendent or supervisor, a project engineer or manager, or a general contractor; alternatively, a construction manager may oversee other workers with these titles.

Regardless of the title, in the construction industry the concern of job seekers is not so much what the job entails as where to find the work. A construction manager needs a project to manage, and many have found it difficult to maintain positions in recent years. But as construction companies scale back their workforce, those with varied skills and specialized training, particularly in green construction practices, are finding and keeping jobs.

"Some skeptics are saying that economically things are challenged so nobody wants to do green building. But I haven't seen that to be the case," said Yancy Wright, director of Sellen Sustainability in Seattle, a wholly owned subsidiary of one of Washington State's largest general contractors, Sellen Construction. Numbers released at the Greenbuild conference in Toronto in October 2011 back up that statement: 35 percent of design and construction jobs are reportedly green, and McGraw-Hill Construction expects that share to increase 10 percent by 2014.

As its name indicates, the Sellen consulting firm focuses on sustainable building, not only for the construction

---

AT A GLANCE FACT BOX

SOC: 11-9021.00
Preferred Education: Work experience or a bachelor's degree
Average Salary: US\$50,240 to US\$150,250
Other Information: Construction managers trained in green building practices are in demand. McGraw-Hill Construction reports 35 percent of design and construction jobs in 2011 are reportedly green, which should increase to 45 percent by 2014.

---

company's clients but throughout the industry, providing training to various tradespeople and contractors. Sellen Sustainability teaches best management practices to workers at all levels. The courses enhance classroom discussions on climate change and global warming with green jobsite tours led by site managers so that the students can apply what they have learned to their own jobsites. Wright said the goals are to make the unemployed more marketable and to help the employed advance in the field. "It's not creating a new workforce; it's integrating sustainable thinking into our existing workforce," he said.

Although more readily accepted in some urban environments, such thoughts are not the sole purview of large firms in large cities. Everyone on a jobsite must be aware of environmentally sensitive areas of the site, practices that ensure an energy-efficient structure, and waste reduction efforts. Throughout the country, construction managers are training themselves and/or employees in green practices.

"I keep sending my guys to training so they understand the why of what we're doing, and that really helps them figure out the hows," said Len Ford, president and owner of Ford Construction in Kalispell, Montana, for nearly 25 years.

"The first quarter of this business is really conserving energy with a better envelope," he said, adding that collecting and generating energy does not have nearly the return of energy conservation. "I think probably 80 percent of our home building improvement effort ought to focus on energy. Maybe 15 percent goes into improving water consumption. And maybe 5 percent of what we talk about is where the lumber's coming from."

Early involvement in a project by the construction manager is crucial in green construction. Green projects often must be approached holistically, integrating changes in various trades, and these changes need to be made in the design stage and then overseen by the construction manager throughout the project. For example, heating and cooling are primary ongoing costs of a dwelling, second only to property taxes. Therefore, using more energy-efficient siding and windows requires changes in ventilation to ensure little moisture and high air quality. These changes in turn affect the work of roofers, insulators, plumbers, and many other subcontractors on the project, and a construction manager must keep this in mind and guide the subcontractors to effectively accomplish the construction's goals.

WORKING CONDITIONS

Most construction managers are either based out of a permanent company office or a field office for a particular project but spend much of their time on the jobsite. Some projects, typically residential, may involve a 40-hour workweek with occasional overtime. Large commercial projects with multiple managers may require workers around the clock. Regardless, most construction managers are, at least unofficially, on call at all times and may need to alter their schedule if materials are delayed or weather prevents progress.

Managers must take care while on jobsites because they often move among groups of workers and may not be fully aware of their surroundings. The construction industry has a high rate of fatalities, more than any other industry in 2010, and supervisors of construction and extraction workers average a higher number of injuries than all trade workers except construction laborers.

EMPLOYMENT

As of May 2010, there were more than 191,400 construction managers in the United States according to the U.S. Department of Labor. Texas and California hold the most jobs, followed by Florida and New York.

Most construction managers are self-employed, hired by contractors on a project-by-project basis. They mainly work in nonresidential construction, often employed by large construction companies or trade subcontractors such as electrical contractors. Some of the others manage primarily residential projects. Those who run their own construction business may use on-site superintendents to oversee individual projects. These superintendents may also be full-time managers or may split their time between managing and building.

TRAINING, OTHER QUALIFICATIONS, AND ADVANCEMENT

Construction managers often have years of experience in the industry. They may have worked in a range of positions on jobsites, learning about subcontractor jobs firsthand. Although some earn the job strictly through work experience, many prospective managers now attain a degree. Although business management and engineering were once the closest degrees to the construction management job, many universities now offer specialized programs in construction management, science, or technology.

These degrees are mainly beyond the undergraduate level. As master's degrees become more common among today's job applicants in all fields, some universities offer construction-focused coursework at this higher level. One such school is the University of Texas at El Paso. Its civil engineering department began offering a master of science in construction management in 2011, adding to a certificate program in construction management they had been offering for three years. Open to students who hold an undergraduate degree in a field such as engineering, architecture, or business, the program focuses on management skills, estimating costs and schedules, and law and safety issues. Electives relate to finance or engineering, such as environmental or wastewater engineering. The program has an internship requirement, and like most master's programs tends to place students with large construction or construction management companies that are likely to offer permanent positions upon graduation. The program is already popular; the university estimated enrollment of 30 students in the program's first semester and 80 students are anticipated by 2014.

Another increasingly important form of education for construction managers, particularly those working on green projects, is certification. As the green construction industry has grown, organizations have created standards that certify buildings according to their level of sustainability. They also offer accreditation to the professionals who construct them. The U.S.

Green Building Council's Leadership in Energy and Environmental Design (LEED) program offers green associate and accredited professional certifications to construction managers and other professionals in the industry. The National Center for Construction Education and Research also offers continuing education in sustainable construction management. Although such certifications are not necessary, they attest to a construction manager's knowledge of and commitment to sustainable building practices. They can also aid advancement to larger, greener projects and companies.

Construction managers are multitaskers, particularly those who manage and produce. Schedules for many projects are fast, particularly when delays make deadlines tight. Decisions often must be quick and clear, and managers need to prioritize problems and come up with solutions on demand. They must work and communicate well with a range of clients, employers, suppliers, and subcontractors to ensure a smooth flow of materials and work. Spanish speakers are increasingly in demand in many parts of the country.

JOB OUTLOOK

The downturn in the U.S. economy and particularly the real estate industry in recent years has drained the construction industry. States such as Nevada, Arizona, Florida, and California saw large construction job losses from May 2004 to May 2010 according to the Department of Labor. Wyoming and North Dakota, however, saw construction employment boosts and wage increases beginning in May 2006, primarily caused by an oil boom. First-line supervisors had the largest absolute increase in jobs in these states.

However, such job growth brings environmental concerns. Much of the speedy construction on housing for workers in oil and natural gas fields runs counter to green building practices, and some people are worried about the larger environmental impacts of developing such fields and their effects on air and water quality. If the industry recovers as predicted and the need for construction managers nationwide rises, those focused on green development may find more opportunity in green construction hubs such as the Pacific Northwest.

In all regions, renovation rather than new construction is a likely area for potential job growth. Construction managers experienced in remodels and upgrades will likely be in increasing demand if they also bring knowledge of ways to improve the energy efficiency of older structures for today's world.

"The existing stock of housing and commercial buildings that are out there all need help and are in the built environment now," said Ford Construction's owner. "Considering the economy we have now and for the near-term future, there's a lot more gains to be made by renovating for energy efficiency than building new."

EARNINGS

Construction managers who act as first-line supervisors are among the highest-paid employees in the industry, earning US$94,240 on average with a range of less than US$50,240 to more than US$150,250 annually, according to the U.S. Department of Labor. The 2011 entry-level salary for construction science and management majors was US$50,670 per year, reported the National Association of Colleges and Employers. Specialists in non-residential construction, such as hotels and lodges, computer facilities, landfills, and oil and gas extraction, tend to be among the highest-paid. Those working on either coast in any specialization also tend to make more than construction managers in the interior United States.

RELATED OCCUPATIONS

Many construction managers come from a background in a construction trade, such as carpenter or electrician. Other jobs offer relevant skills:

- Architects
- Construction and building inspectors
- Engineering managers
- Engineers
- Landscape architects
- Natural sciences managers

SOURCES OF ADDITIONAL INFORMATION

American Council for Construction Education. http://www.acce-hq.org
American Institute of Constructors. http://www.aicnet.org
Construction Management Association of America. http://www.cmaanet.org
National Center for Construction Education and Research. http://www.nccer.org
U.S. Green Building Council. http://www.usgbc.org

FURTHER READING

Bureau of Labor Statistics, U.S. Department of Labor. "11-9021 Construction Managers." In *Occupational Employment Statistics: Occupational Employment and Wages, May 2010,* last modified May 17, 2011. Accessed February 16, 2012. http://www.bls.gov/oes/current/oes119021.htm.
———. "All Worker Profile, 2003–2010." In *Census of Fatal Occupational Injuries.* Accessed February 6, 2012. http://www.bls.gov/iif/oshwc/cfoi/all_worker.pdf.
College of Engineering, University of Texas at El Paso. *New Master's Program in Construction Management.*

Accessed February 9, 2012. http://engineering.utep
.edu/news022111.htm.

Ford, Len (president and owner, Ford Construction) in
discussion with the author, February 2012.

National Association of Colleges and Employers. *Salary
Survey: January 2012.* Bethlehem, PA: NACE, 2011.
Accessed January 11, 2012. http://www.naceweb
.org/uploadedFiles/NACEWeb/Research/Salary_
Survey/Reports/SS_January_report4web.pdf.

PR Newswire. "Greenbuild: Growing Green Building
Market Supports 661,000 Green Jobs in the U.S."
October 4, 2011. Accessed February 16, 2012. http://
www.prnewswire.com/news-releases/green
build-growing-green-building-market-supports-
661000-green-jobs-in-the-us—a-third-of-the-design-
and-construction-workforce—according-to-new-
mcgraw-hill-construction-study-131093378.html.

U.S. Green Building Council. *LEED Professional
Credentials.* Accessed February 6, 2012. http://www
.usgbc.org/DisplayPage.aspx?CMSPageID=1815.

Wright, Yancy (director, Sellen Sustainability) in
discussion with the author, February 2012.

ARCHITECTS, EXCEPT LANDSCAPE AND NAVAL

NATURE OF THE WORK

People need constructed spaces where they can live, work, eat, play, worship, govern, and take part in numerous other activities. Thus, they rely on architects to design spaces and environments where these activities can take place, such as homes, apartment buildings, churches, governmental buildings, airports, office buildings, hospitals, schools, gymnasiums and athletic stadiums, or libraries. Architects design virtually any type of constructed space, ranging from small single-family dwellings to office complexes and even entire communities. Using the principles of both art and science, architects first determine which buildings and structures are needed and what characteristics those buildings and structures must have. They then transform their findings into concepts for designs, reflected in plans, drawings, specifications, and scale models. These designs are used by others in the construction of the project.

Architects also spend part of their time drafting letters and other documents necessary to the project: contracts, project manuals, schedules, and the like. They consult with building owners and other professionals on how to make best use of constructed space. A green architect, for example, might consult with a mechanical engineer to determine the most effective way to reduce the amount of energy a building uses. Architects are often involved in site selection, they prepare environmental impact studies and land-use studies, and, in common with all architects, they develop cost projections, obtain construction bids, negotiate with contractors, and supervise the work of contractors to ensure that they are meeting specifications for the project.

AT A GLANCE FACT BOX

SOC: 17-1011.00
Preferred Education: Bachelor's degree
Average Salary: US$78,530 annually
Other Information: All states require architects to be licensed by completing a degree in architecture, completing an internship under the supervision of a licensed architect, and passing the Architect Registration Examination

The jobs held by green architects in many respects are little different from those in the profession as a whole, and in fact, in the 21st century, the distinction between architects in general and green architects in particular has been rapidly disappearing. No longer would an architect simply site a building anywhere; see the building as a collection of steel, wood, glass, and other materials; and rely on the burning of fossil fuels to heat, cool, ventilate, and light the building. Rather, architects in the 21st century are placing much more emphasis on a building as a system that interacts with its natural environment in ways that reduce its environmental impact. By paying attention to that environment, architects can design buildings that initially might be more expensive but over time are cheaper because they consume fewer resources. Therefore, green architects, working with other professionals such as engineers, urban planners, landscape designers, interior designers, manufacturers, and construction companies, focus on developing and using innovative technologies and renewable resources to create buildings and structures that use energy efficiently and have minimal impact on their environment.

Here are just a few examples of the steps that green architects are taking to reduce the environmental footprint of the buildings they design. Much of this activity focuses on commercial buildings, which consume 66 percent of the electricity used in the United States and are responsible for 35 percent of all U.S. carbon emissions.

1. Using solar energy for heating and lighting. One way architects do this is by incorporating greenhouses, atriums, and solar buffer spaces to provide some of a building's heating needs. Solar photovoltaic features and solar water heating can be designed right into the skin of a building.
2. Reducing glare and overheating with controllable shading.
3. Using wind pressure and solar radiation to power ventilation systems. Natural ventilation systems can help reduce "sick-building syndrome" caused by the buildup of interior pollutants and toxins. It is often pointed out that the improved health of workers in the building, reflected by fewer sick days and greater productivity and efficiency, can pay for the additional cost of a green ventilation system.
4. Using thermal mass and shading to control internal temperatures.
5. In private homes, many architects are incorporating stone and other materials that have high thermal mass, air spaces, insulated glazing, and vents. These kinds of walls store heat from the sun and channel it into living spaces.

WORKING CONDITIONS

Typically, the working conditions of architects are comfortable. Architects spend most of their time in offices, where they meet with clients and potential clients, use computers and drafting equipment to prepare designs and three-dimensional models, and consult with contractors, engineers, and other professionals who might be involved in a project. Often, however, the architect has to visit construction sites to ensure that projects are being constructed according to specifications. Hours for many architects are quite long, exceeding 50 hours per week, because of the deadline-driven nature of architectural projects.

EMPLOYMENT

As of 2008, there were about 141,000 architects in the United States. Sixty-eight percent of these architects worked for architectural, engineering, and related firms.

Others worked for construction firms and government agencies responsible for government housing, construction of government buildings, or community planning. About 21 percent of architects are self-employed. Graduates with degrees in architecture face competition for jobs in the most prestigious firms.

TRAINING, OTHER QUALIFICATIONS, AND ADVANCEMENT

The designation *architect* is legally restricted to individuals licensed by each state in the United States. State governments use guidelines established by the National Council of Architectural Registration Boards (NCARB) to license architects. To become an architect, a person has to satisfy three major requirements: education, training, and licensure.

Most states require prospective architects to complete a degree program at one of the nation's 123 schools recognized by the National Architectural Accrediting Board (NAAB); a few states accept degrees from nonaccredited programs. Typically, architectural graduates follow one of two routes. The first is a Bachelor of Architecture degree, which generally takes five years to complete and includes coursework in architectural history and theory, computer-aided design, mathematics, engineering, construction methods, physical sciences, and other disciplines. A key portion of the architect's education is the design studio, at which the student can put theory into practice by creating drawings or three-dimensional models of structures.

The other route is for an aspiring architect with a degree in another discipline to complete a master's degree in architecture, a process that can take from one to five years, depending on the nature of the student's background. A student with a degree in a discipline such as engineering would likely be able to complete the master's degree in architecture more quickly than would a student whose undergraduate degree is in biology. Also, it should be noted that some schools offer degrees called a Bachelor of Science in Architecture, a Bachelor of Science in Architectural Studies, or a Bachelor of Art in Architectural Studies. These are pre-professional degrees that are not recognized by the NAAB, although completion of one of these degrees can shorten the time needed to complete a master's degree. Most schools of architecture are recognizing the current emphasis on green architecture and are including courses that incorporate this topic. Some schools, however, place more emphasis on green architecture and sustainability than do others. Examples include the San Francisco Institute of Architecture and the Arizona State University School of Sustainability.

The second major requirement is training, usually in the form of a three-year internship under the supervision of a licensed architect, although a portion of that requirement can be met by internship work performed while still in school. All states adhere to the training standards created by the Intern Development Program of the American Institute of Architects and the NCARB.

The third major requirement is passing a licensure examination called the Architect Registration Examination. The examination consists of seven parts, called *divisions*: programming, planning, and practice; site planning and design; building design and construction systems; schematic design; structural systems; building systems; and construction documents and services. To become a licensed architect, a person has to pass all seven parts of the exam (which can be taken in any order) within a period of time specified by each state.

Numerous initiatives and programs enable architects to design buildings that achieve the goals of the green movement. The U.S. Green Building Council (USGBC), for instance, states that it "is committed to a prosperous and sustainable future through cost-efficient and energy-saving green buildings. Our community of leaders is working to make green buildings available to everyone within a generation." To that end, the USGBC offers a certification program in green architecture. The program is called *LEED*, meaning Leadership in Energy and Environmental Design. LEED enables building owners and operators to identify and implement measurable solutions for green building design, construction, and maintenance, including such matters as sustainable site development, energy efficiency, water savings, indoor air quality, and the use (and reuse) of sustainable building materials. The USGBC offers a number of resources, including publications and certification exams, to foster its goal of green buildings.

Another initiative is called Net Zero. Under the terms of this initiative, architects and allied professionals design buildings that use solar energy, thermal mass, super insulation, heat recovery systems, wind turbines, air tightness, orientation (e.g., to the sun or prevailing winds), and other characteristics to achieve a net energy use of zero and a net carbon emission footprint of zero. The International Living Building Institute sponsors the Living Building Challenge, an educational and certification program that addresses seven performance areas in the design and construction of buildings: water, energy, site, health, materials, equity, and beauty. Finally, the American Institute of Architects (AIA) sponsors an initiative called the 2030 Commitment. The AIA's goal is to persuade member firms to take a lead role in reducing greenhouse gas creation and energy consumption in the buildings they design and operate. The long-term goal is that by the year 2030, these practices will be standard and all newly constructed buildings will be climate neutral, that is, operating without emitting greenhouse gases. All of these organizations provide training and resource materials that contribute to the architect's continuing education and to the goals of the green movement.

JOB OUTLOOK

According to the U.S. Department of Labor's Bureau of Labor Statistics, the number of architects is projected to grow to 164,200 by 2018, a 16 percent increase from 2008. The five states that lead the nation in the employment of architects are California, New York, Texas, Florida, and Illinois. The metropolitan areas with the highest employment of architects are New York City, Chicago, Boston, Washington, DC, and Los Angeles. The metropolitan areas with the highest concentration of architects relative to the total number of jobs in the area include Boulder, Colorado; the Charleston, South Carolina, region; the Boston metropolitan area; Billings, Montana; and the San Francisco, California, region.

EARNINGS

As of May 2010, the mean hourly wage for architects was US$37.75. The mean annual wage, based on a work year of 2,080 hours, was US$78,530. An architect in the 10th percentile earned US$20.61 per hour, or US$42,860 annually. An architect in the 90th percentile earned US$57.45 per hour, or US$119,500 annually.

The five states with the highest annual mean wage in 2010 were California, Vermont, Nevada, Alaska, and Connecticut. The states with the lowest annual mean wage included Montana, North Dakota, Kansas, Oklahoma, Mississippi, and Maine.

RELATED OCCUPATIONS

Architects are involved with both the design and the construction of buildings and other structures. Commercial and industrial designers, graphic designers, and interior designers all have jobs that have a similar design component to architects. In the construction component, construction managers, engineers, landscape architects, and urban and regional planners have similar responsibilities.

SOURCES OF ADDITIONAL INFORMATION

Byrne, Elizabeth Douthitt. *Finding Information on Green Building Materials.* Berkeley, CA: Environmental Design Library, UC Berkeley, 2011.

Frej, Anne B. *Green Office Buildings: A Practical Guide to Development.* Washington, DC: Urban Land Institute, 2005.

Hawken, Paul, Amory Lovins, and L. Hunter Lovins. *Natural Capitalism: Creating the Next Industrial Revolution.* Boston: Back Bay Books, 2008.

Kibert, Charles J. *Sustainable Construction: Green Building Design and Delivery.* New York: Wiley, 2005.

Roodman, David Malin, and Nicholas Lenssen. *A Building Revolution: How Ecology and Health Concerns are Transforming Construction.* Washington, DC: Worldwatch Institute, 1995.

U.S. Environmental Protection Agency. *Sustainable Design and Green Building Toolkit for Local Governments.* Washington, DC: Author, 2010.

U.S. General Services Administration. *The New Sustainable Frontier: Principles of Sustainable Development.* Washington, DC: Author, 2009.

U.S. National Science and Technology Council. *Federal Research and Development Agenda for Net-Zero Energy, High Performance Green Buildings.* Washington, DC: Author, 2008.

FURTHER READING

American Institute of Architects. *2030 Commitment.* Accessed January 25, 2012. http://www.aiachicago.org/2030.asp.

Association of Collegiate Schools of Architecture. *Online Guide to Architecture Schools.* Accessed February 27, 2012. http://www.acsa-arch.org/schools/guide-to-architecture-schools.

Bureau of Labor Statistics, U.S. Department of Labor. "Architects, Except Landscape and Naval." In *Occupational Outlook Handbook, 2010–11.* Accessed February 27, 2012. http://www.bls.gov/oco/ocos038.htm.

_____. "17-1011 Architects, Except Landscape and Naval." In *Occupational Employment and Wages, May 2010.* Accessed February 27, 2012. http://www.bls.gov/oes/current/oes171011.htm.

Education-Portal.com. *What Degrees Do You Need to Be an Architect?* Accessed January 25, 2012. http://education-portal.com/what_degrees_do_you_need_to_be_an_architect.html.

International Living Building Institute. *Living Building Challenge.* Accessed January 25, 2012. https://ilbi.org/lbc.

National Architectural Accrediting Board. *NAAB-Accredited Architecture Programs in the United States.* Accessed January 25, 2012. http://www.naab.org/architecture_programs/.

PayScale.com. *Salary for Architect,* 2011. Accessed February 24, 2012. http://www.payscale.com/research/US/Job=Architect_%28but_not_Landscape_or_Naval%29/Salary.

Schlager, Neil, and Jayne Weisblatt, eds. *Alternative Energy* (3 vols). Detroit, MI: Thomson Gale, 2006.

U.S. Green Building Council. *Welcome to the USGBC.* Accessed February 27, 2012. http://www.usgbc.org/Default.aspx.

LANDSCAPE ARCHITECTS

—■—

NATURE OF THE WORK

Architects and landscape architects often work hand in hand. Whereas architects design structures, landscape architects design the environment in which structures are placed. The public wants attractive, functional, and environmentally friendly surroundings, so they turn to landscape architects to design public spaces such as gardens, parks, greenbelts, walkways, and golf courses, as well as the grounds surrounding office complexes, shopping centers, residential developments, and schools and colleges. Landscape architects make decisions about the placement of features such as sidewalks and driveways, parking areas, fences, culverts, drainage features, water features and fountains, gardens, lawns, trees and shrubs, and monuments and decorative features, all in harmony with the surrounding environment. Landscape architects also restore natural spaces that have been disturbed by human activity. Thus, they often play a major role in the restoration of wetlands, stream corridors (that is, watershed ecosystems along bodies of water), landfills, and mined and forested areas.

In the 21st century, *landscape architect* and *green landscape architect* are virtually synonymous terms, for by its very nature, landscape architecture seeks to preserve and enhance the natural environment. A green approach to landscape architecture will ensure, for example, that drainage systems improve or even provide new habitats for plants and animals. Landscaping can reduce energy consumption by providing shade for buildings. Windbreaks, which again reduce energy consumption, can be created by fencing, trees, and shrubbery, as well as by siting buildings in ways that take advantage of natural landforms. Landscape architects frequently design *green roofs*, roofs covered with some

type of vegetation, to reduce the building's consumption of energy for heating and cooling. The principles of green landscape architecture have enabled the areas surrounding nuclear power plants to become wildlife preserves and wetlands because these plants discharge water. These areas provide habitat for fish and endangered species of birds such as bald eagles, red-cockaded woodpeckers, peregrine falcons, and osprey, and also for non-endangered species such as wild turkeys, sea lions, bluebirds, kestrels, wood ducks, and pheasant. Furthermore, a modern landscape architect will strive to minimize the use of water, particularly in arid and semiarid regions, by using the principles of xeriscaping, a word formed from the Greek word *xeros*, meaning "dry," and *landscaping*. Thus, in designing grounds, a landscape architect will make decisions about soil amendment and appropriate plant selection and about ways to conserve water through irrigation systems, mulching, the use of stone and gravel, and the use of alternative turfs (such as native grasses, which often need far less water than typical lawn grasses).

A landscape architect's initial task is to examine and plan the site, usually in collaboration with architects, engineers, surveyors, hydrologists, environmental scientists, and other relevant professionals. They begin by examining what is already there: the slope of the land, the soil and vegetation, the climate, and natural drainage, as well as existing buildings, roads, sidewalks, and the like. The next step is to prepare a preliminary design that meets the needs of the client but that also conforms to local, state, and federal regulations, such as those intended to protect wetlands or areas of historical significance. To help clients visualize the project, landscape architects use computer-aided design and video simulations. Further, landscape architects, particularly those who work on large projects, are familiar with the use of geographic information systems that capture, store, manipulate, and manage data about geography. These systems have been described as the merger of cartography (map-making), database technology, and statistical analysis.

Once they have completed plans for a project, including sketches, models, cost estimates, and written reports, they submit them to the client for approval, making any modifications the client wants. They also submit their plans to appropriate regulatory agencies for approval and possible amendment. Once the project is agreed upon, the landscape architect prepares materials lists and schedules for construction and hires firms to do the actual work. When the project is under way, landscape architects monitor the progress of installation, construction, and planting.

Many landscape architects are generalists, allowing them to work on all types of projects. Others specialize in certain types of projects, such as street and highway beautification, shopping centers, playgrounds, or residential developments. Other landscape architects specialize in remediation and restoration of the environment, land-use planning, environmental impact assessment, or landscape planning for the government. Many landscape architects are becoming more involved with preservation of historical sites, including battlefields, cemeteries, structures with historical value or significance, and heritage sites.

A landscape architect has to be familiar with a wide range of tools, including digital cameras, camcorders, aerial photographs and maps, computers and computer software (especially computer-aided design software), scanners, blueprints, and drafting, recording, surveying, and construction equipment.

WORKING CONDITIONS

Working conditions for landscape architects are generally comfortable. Landscape architects spend considerable time in offices preparing designs, drawings, reports, models, cost estimates, and construction schedules. Time will also be spent in meetings with other professionals, including architects, landscape engineers, hydrologists, environmental scientists, and foresters. In addition, the landscape architect will devote time to meeting with clients and potential clients to learn about their needs and preferences for projects. Depending on the nature of the project, the landscape architect will spend some time in the field overseeing projects and ensuring that they are being completed according to specifications. In some cases, the landscape architect might spend more time on-site than in the office.

Although many landscape architects work a traditional 40-hour work week, many work considerably longer hours, particularly because of the deadline-driven nature of the work. In addition, seasonal weather can play a major role in the landscape architect's schedule. Particularly in areas with four-season climates, most landscape projects have to be started and completed during the spring, summer, and fall, before winter weather sets in. In these circumstances, the landscape architect might be required to work long hours.

EMPLOYMENT

In 2008 the number of landscape architects was about 26,700 in the United States. Just over half were employed in architectural, engineering, and related services. About 6 percent worked for U.S. state and local governments and about 21 percent were self-employed. The states with the highest numbers of landscape architects were California, Florida, Texas, Washington, and New York. The metropolitan areas with the highest employment of landscape architects were those surrounding Seattle, Washington; Atlanta, Georgia; Washington, DC; Boston, Massachusetts; and New York, New York. The states with the highest concentration of landscape architects relative to the total number of jobs in that state were Washington, Maryland, Wyoming, Delaware, and Colorado.

TRAINING, OTHER QUALIFICATIONS, AND ADVANCEMENT

Nearly every U.S. state imposes licensing requirements on landscape architects. Usually those requirements include a degree in landscape architecture from an accredited institution, work experience, and a passing score on the Landscape Architect Registration Examination (LARE). It should be noted that only licensed professionals are allowed to call themselves *landscape architects*. Many people are employed in landscaping businesses, but landscape architects must be distinguished from landscapers who perform labor such as lawn mowing, tree and shrub trimming, and construction of retaining walls and walkways. Put simply, landscapers are not licensed.

The Landscape Architecture Accreditation Board of the American Society of Landscape Architects grants accreditation to degree programs in landscape architecture. As of 2012, 68 U.S. colleges offered either bachelor's or master's degree programs in landscape architecture that were either fully accredited or were "candidacy" schools, meaning that they were on their way to full accreditation. The two undergraduate degrees offered are the Bachelor of Landscape Architecture and the Bachelor of Science in Landscape Architecture. Usually, these programs take four to five years to complete. A person with an undergraduate degree in a field other than landscape architecture can complete the education requirement by earning a Master of Landscape Architecture degree; this degree generally takes about three years to complete, although students with an undergraduate degree in landscape architecture can complete the master's degree in less time. These programs typically include course work in subjects such as surveying, landscape design and construction, landscape ecology, site design, and others. An important component is the design studio, where students learn to use computer-aided design, geographic information systems, video simulation, and model building to design projects. Students who take part in internship programs can boost their chances for employment after graduation.

Most states require landscape architects to be licensed by passing the Landscape Architect Registration Examination (LARE), which is sponsored by the Council of Landscape Architectural Registration Boards. This test consists of two portions: a graphic portion and a multiple choice portion. To take the examination, applicants need a degree and one to four years of work experience under the supervision of a licensed landscape architect. States with no accredited landscape architecture degree program allow applicants to take the LARE if they have sufficient supervised work experience. Thirteen U.S. states require a state examination in addition to the LARE. A state examination focuses on matters unique to that state, including climate conditions, soil, flora, and environmental regulations.

Most states require some form of continuing education. In the United States and Canada, continuing education is provided through the Landscape Architecture Continuing Education System (LACES). This is an online tool that provides landscape architects access to some 130 approved continuing education providers. Examples of courses offered are business practices, campus planning and design, green roofs, historic preservation, site planning, sustainable development and design, and numerous others. In time, landscape architects can advance to become project managers, with responsibility for scheduling, budgeting, and overseeing the project. Those who work in a landscape architecture firm can eventually become a partner with an equity stake in the firm.

JOB OUTLOOK

According to the U.S. Department of Labor's Bureau of Labor Statistics (BLS), employment prospects for landscape architects are very good and will grow faster than the average for all occupations. The BLS expects employment in the profession to increase 20 percent by 2018 (compared with 2008). Driving much of this job growth is the demand for landscape architects who can design environmentally sustainable projects, for example, projects that can reduce energy demands for heating and cooling, manage rainwater runoff in a way that avoids pollution, or conserve water resources.

The job prospects of landscape architects are closely tied to the state of the economy. During a recession, organizations often curtail building and development projects, reducing the demand for the services of landscape architects.

New graduates generally face stiff competition for jobs in the most prestigious landscape architectural firms. Many firms prefer to hire graduates with internship experience. Those with strong technical skills, strong communication skills, and knowledge of environmental codes and regulations are likely to find more employment opportunities.

EARNINGS

As of May 2008, the median annual wage for a landscape architect was US$58,960. The 50 percent in the middle earned annual wages between US$45,840 and US$77,610. The bottom 10 percent earned less than US$36,520, whereas the top 10 percent earned in excess of US$97,370.

The top-paying states were California (US$86,340), Massachusetts (US$80,590), Connecticut (US$79,610), Idaho (US$79,290), and Nevada (US$74,950). The states with the lowest pay included North Dakota, Iowa, Oklahoma, Arkansas, Mississippi, and Kentucky. The top-paying metropolitan regions were those surrounding San Jose, California (US$116,790); Santa Barbara, California (US$96,620); Bridgeport, Connecticut (US$96,510); San Diego, California (US$93,330); and San Luis Obispo, California (US$87,840). Occupying sixth place was Toledo, Ohio (US$86,100).

RELATED OCCUPATIONS

Other jobs that require similar proficiency in construction and design include:

- Architects
- Construction managers
- Urban and regional planners
- Surveyors, cartographers, photogrammetrists, and surveying and mapping technicians
- Engineers

SOURCES OF ADDITIONAL INFORMATION

Ahern, Jack, Elizabeth Leduc, and Mary Lee York. *Biodiversity Planning and Design: Sustainable Practices.* Washington, DC: Island Press, 2006

Alliance for Historic Landscape Preservation. http://www.ahlp.org

American Society of Landscape Architects. http://www.asla.org

Canadian Society of Landscape Architecture. http://www.csla.ca

Council of Educators in Landscape Architecture. http://www.thecela.org

Council of Landscape Architectural Registration Boards. http://www.clarb.org

Landscape Architecture Foundation. http://lafoundation.org

National Association of GIS-Centric Solutions. http://www.nagcs.org

U.S. Department of the Interior, Office of Surface Mining Reclamation and Enforcement. http://www.osmre.gov

FURTHER READING

Bureau of Labor Statistics, U.S. Department of Labor. "Landscape Architects." In *Occupational Outlook Handbook, 2010–11 Edition.* Accessed March 21. 2012. http://www.bls.gov/oco/ocos039.htm.

———. "17-1012 Landscape Architects." In *Occupational Employment Statistics: Occupational Employment and Wages, May 2010.* Accessed March 21, 2012. http://www.bls.gov/oes/current/oes171012.htm.

PayScale.com. *Salary for Landscape Architect Jobs,* 2011. Accessed March 23, 2012. http://www.payscale.com/research/US/Job=Landscape_Architect/Salary.

Schlager, Neil, and Jayne Weisblatt, eds. *Alternative Energy* (3 vols). Detroit, MI: Thomson Gale, 2006.

U.S. Environmental Protection Agency. "Restoration Techniques: The USDA Natural Resources Conservation Service Watershed Technology Electronic Catalog (WTEC)." *Watershed Academy Web.* Accessed March 23, 2012. http://www.epa.gov/owow/watershed/wacademy/acad2000/restor.html.

CIVIL ENGINEERS

NATURE OF THE WORK

Civil engineer is an umbrella designation for professionals with a wide range of interests. In general, civil engineers plan, design, and supervise the building of infrastructure: roads, bridges, harbors, channels, dams, power plants, irrigation projects, mines, subdivisions, pipelines, airports, wastewater treatment facilities, and the like. Some specialize in a specific field, such as land development, construction, structural design (which deals with the way the load-bearing parts of a structure's physical framework support each other in sharing the load), hydraulic design (which ensures that structures such as culverts and bridges can handle flooding and remain traversable), soil mechanics (which examines the mechanical, or load-bearing, properties of soils, which can vary according to the soil's air, water, and mineral content), wastewater treatment, or solid waste management. Civil engineers sometimes work with other specialists to deal with such problems as soil or groundwater contamination, conservation, or energy development.

A civil engineer might be called upon to carry out a wide range of specific tasks. One might be to compute load and grade requirements, water flow rates, or material stress factors to determine design specifications for a project. Another might be to test soils and other materials to determine whether structural foundations and building materials (asphalt, steel, concrete, and the like) are strong enough for the project. Yet another task might be to analyze drawings, maps, survey reports, blueprints, aerial photographs, and other geological and topographical data to assist in planning a project.

Civil engineering is undergoing sweeping changes as a result of the green movement. Many civil engineers, for

example, are focusing on green construction techniques to create energy-efficient buildings. Others are focusing on retrofitting existing residential and commercial buildings to consume fewer resources and emit fewer pollutants. Still others specialize in green energy production, which involves designing facilities that generate solar, wind, geothermal, and biomass power. Some civil engineers provide technological solutions that improve the efficiency and cleanliness of energy from traditional nonrenewable resources such as coal, gas, and oil.

Civil engineers perform a number of tasks that are central to a green economy. These might include analyzing manufacturing processes and byproducts to find engineering solutions that will lessen the output of carbon dioxide and other pollutants, studying traffic patterns and environmental conditions with the goal of reducing the project's impact on the environment, designing energy efficient and environmentally sound structures, designing and engineering systems to efficiently dispose of biological, chemical, and toxic wastes, finding and implementing engineering solutions to reclaim contaminated sites or clean up industrial accidents, ensuring that engineering activities comply with environmental health and safety regulations, identifying risks and developing risk-management strategies for engineering projects, and preparing such documents as environmental impact statements.

Typically, civil engineers conceptualize and design the major features of a project. They then direct the process of creating plans, writing specifications, and preparing budgets and cost estimates. They also prepare property deeds, property descriptions, and right-of-way maps (i.e., boundary surveys of parcels of land that need to be acquired for such features as roadways or drainage facilities). Civil engineers often go out into the field to survey property, investigate sites, or supervise and inspect construction. They often sample and test construction materials or soil, either in the field or in a laboratory. Civil engineers who specialize in structural work make detailed calculations to ensure that design features are consistent with structural requirements. They want to ensure, for example, that a truss of given dimensions is able to support the load it is designed to carry. In the field, civil engineers inspect projects to ensure that they conform to plans and specifications; they may also examine existing structures to determine whether they need to be repaired or replaced.

Civil engineers, with a focus on transportation, design streets and highways or alter existing roadways to improve the flow of traffic. These engineers survey the land, make preliminary plans, prepare reports on the project's environmental impact, and select, inspect, and test the materials used in the project. Some civil engineers specialize further by focusing on traffic signs, "impact devices" (i.e., guard rails and the like), or pedestrian traffic. Some study a community's population growth and business and industrial trends to provide information and recommendations about future transportation needs.

WORKING CONDITIONS

Working conditions for civil engineers can vary depending on the engineer's specialty and the particular project. Civil engineers often spend considerable time in offices meeting with clients and potential clients to determine their needs and preferences. They also spend time in the office preparing plans, specifications, cost estimates, environmental impact studies, deeds, maps, and other documents needed for the project. Further, civil engineers meet with other related professionals, such as architects, landscape architects, hydrologists, and contractors to coordinate their activities.

Many projects, however, require civil engineers to spend time in the field. Civil engineers have to carry out such tasks as surveying land, taking soil samples, examining construction materials, and monitoring construction to ensure that the project conforms to specifications. Sometimes civil engineers have to travel to remote areas, and sometimes they have to temporarily relocate to oversee an extensive project.

Civil engineers have to be proficient in the use of numerous tools, including electronic distance meters and Rhodes arcs (devices used in topographical surveys), traffic counters, levels, measuring and surveying rods, various kinds of scales, speed sensors, measuring devices, and drafting equipment. Technological tools include various analytical and scientific software programs (e.g., Trimble Geomatics Office, a surveying tool, or HEC-1, a hydrology software tool designed by the U.S. Army Corps of Engineers), computer-aided design software such as Autodesk AutoCAD, graphics and photo-imaging software, map creation software (ESRI ArcView or graphic information system software), project management software (Microsoft Project, the Gordian Group's PROGEN Online software), and routine office technology such as e-mail, word processing, and spreadsheets.

EMPLOYMENT

According to the U.S. Department of Labor's Bureau of Labor Statistics (BLS), just under 250,000 civil engineers were employed in May 2010. The states with the highest employment level were California, Texas, Florida, New York, and Pennsylvania. The metropolitan areas with the largest number of civil engineers included the regions surrounding Houston, Texas; Los Angeles, California; New York City; Washington, DC; and Seattle, Washington. The states with the highest concentration of civil engineers relative to the total number of jobs in the state were Alaska, Washington, Colorado, Hawaii, and Wyoming. The metropolitan areas with the highest concentration of civil engineers relative to the total number of jobs in the area were the Kennewick–Pasco–Richland area of Washington State; the College Station–Bryan area of Texas; Carson City, Nevada; Olympia, Washington; and Yuba City, California.

TRAINING, OTHER QUALIFICATIONS, AND ADVANCEMENT

Not all persons who perform civil engineering tasks are licensed engineers. Licensing, however, entitles the license holder to certain benefits, such as the ability to certify designs and plans with a seal (similar to the process of notarizing a document), bidding for government contracts, becoming a principal of a firm, offering engineering services to the public, and performing consulting services.

Some career counselors would say that preparation for a career as a licensed civil engineer begins in high school with advanced courses in calculus, physics, and chemistry. The first step toward licensure is a bachelor's degree from one of the 521 schools or colleges of engineering accredited by the Accreditation Board for Engineering and Technology; in addition, 37 schools offer fully accredited master's degree programs in engineering. It should be noted that many schools offer degrees in both civil engineering and engineering technology; the former is more theoretical and conceptual, whereas the latter is more practical and focuses on application and implementation.

The next step is to pass the FE, or Fundamentals of Engineering, Exam, administered by the National Council of Examiners for Engineering and Surveying (NCEES). This eight-hour exam consists of two parts. The morning session is the same for all engineering examinees. For the afternoon session, the examinee is required to select a particular type of engineering, one of which is civil engineering. About 79 percent of civil engineering examinees pass the FE Exam on the first try.

The third step is to acquire work experience. State requirements vary, but in general the applicant has to have at least one and up to four years of experience working under the supervision of a licensed civil engineer.

Work experience leads to the final step, which is to pass the PE, or Professional Engineer, Exam. All PE Exams focus on a particular engineering discipline. Civil engineers can choose among five sub-specialties: construction, structural, transportation, water resources and environmental, and geotechnical (which has to do with such matters as soil composition and stability, foundations, retaining walls, and the like). Unlike the FE Exam, the PE Exam is open book, meaning that the examinee can bring printed resources to the exam and consult them. Currently, about 65 percent of first-time test takers pass the civil engineering PE Exam.

Most states require licensed civil engineers to complete continuing education courses. Many such courses are offered through the American Society of Civil Engineers in the form of seminars, on-site training, Webinars, and online or DVD courses. Whereas some states require a certain number of continuing education hours annually, most require a certain number, 24 to 30 is common, over a two-year period.

One issue civil engineers have to contend with is licensure in more than one state. This issue applies not just to civil engineers who practice in border cities but also to civil engineers who might be required to travel to distant sites to design or implement projects. In most instances, *comity licensure* allows a civil engineer licensed in one state to gain licensure in other states. The NCEES offers a service that enables applicants to store and transmit professional records in seeking licensure in another state.

JOB OUTLOOK

According to the BLS, the job outlook for civil engineers, particularly those with "green" credentials, is bright. The BLS projects that job opportunities for civil engineers will grow much faster than average; the projected number of new job openings through 2018 is 114,600, an increase of nearly 50 percent.

The job prospects of civil engineers are closely tied to the economy. During a recession, the government and private organizations often curtail building and development projects, reducing the demand for civil engineering services. That said, what will drive the growth of the civil engineering profession in the future is the nation's need to upgrade its infrastructure, which was given a "D" grade by the American Society of Civil Engineers in 2009. Furthermore, President Barack Obama declared December 2011 Critical Infrastructure Protection Month, drawing attention to the need to upgrade the nation's infrastructure.

EARNINGS

According to the BLS, the mean annual wage for a civil engineer in 2010 was US$82,280, or an hourly wage of US$39.56. The median figure was US$77,560, or US$37.29 per hour. The middle half had earnings ranging from US$61,590 to US$97,990. The bottom 10 percent earned an average of US$50,560; the top 10 percent earned an average of US$119,320. The top paying states were California, Louisiana, Alaska, Texas, and New Jersey. The lowest paying states were Montana, Wyoming, North Dakota, South Dakota, and West Virginia. The top paying metropolitan areas were the regions surrounding Lafayette, Louisiana; Salinas, California; Riverside–San Bernardino, California; San Jose–Santa Clara, California; and Houston, Texas.

RELATED OCCUPATIONS

Jobs that have similar duties to civil engineers include:

- Landscape architects
- Aerospace engineers
- Industrial safety and health engineers
- Marine architects
- Materials engineers
- Mining and geological engineers
- Petroleum engineers
- Electrical drafters
- Mechanical drafters
- Civil engineering technicians

SOURCES OF ADDITIONAL INFORMATION

Accreditation Board for Engineering and Technology. http://www.abet.org

American Society of Civil Engineers. http://www.asce.org

Hansen, Karen, and Kent Zenobia. *Civil Engineer's Handbook of Professional Practice*. Reston, VA: ASCE Press, 2011.

FURTHER READING

American Society of Civil Engineers. "The Role of the Civil Engineer in Sustainable Development." *Policy Statement 418*, 2010. Accessed February 24, 2012. http://www.asce.org/Content.aspx?id=8475.

———. *2009 Report Card for America's Infrastructure*. Accessed January 25, 2012. http://www.asce.org/reportcard.

Bureau of Labor Statistics, U.S. Department of Labor. "Civil Engineer." In *Occupational Employment Statistics: Occupational Employment and Wages, May 2010*. Accessed February 23, 2012. http://www.bls.gov/oes/current/oes172051.htm#ind.

Employment Development Department, Labor Market Information. "Civil Engineers." *California Occupational Guide (39)*, 1998. Accessed February 24, 2012. http://www.calmis.ca.gov/file/occguide-archive/engcivil.htm.

Na'amani, Loai. "Civil Engineering and Novel Technology: Where Do They Meet?" Paper presented in the 1st FEA SC Seminar Series (Technical Session VI), July 7, 2002, published in the *1st FEA SC Proceedings*. Accessed March 26, 2012. http://www.loai-naamani.com/Academics/CEandIT.htm.

National Council of Examiners for Engineering and Surveying. *Welcome to NCEES*. Accessed February 23, 2012. http://www.ncees.org.

O*NET OnLine. *Green Occupation: 17-2051.00—Civil Engineers*. Accessed February 24, 2012. http://www.onetonline.org/help/green/17-2051.00.

———. *Summary Report for: 17-2051.00—Civil Engineers*. Accessed February 24, 2012. http://www.onetonline.org/link/summary/ 17-2051.00.

Perks, Alan, et al. "'Entrusted to Our Care': Guidelines for Sustainable Development." *Canadian Society for Civil Engineering, 2007*. Accessed March 26, 2012. http://www.csce.ca/docs/CSCE-SD%20Guidelines_22Jan07.pdf.

Quimby, T. Bart. *A Beginner's Guide to Structural Engineering*, 2011. Accessed March 26, 2012. http://www.bgstructural-engineering.com.

ELECTRICAL ENGINEERS

NATURE OF THE WORK

Electrical engineering encompasses anything having to do with electricity, electrical components, or electrical systems. However, this description fails to capture the wide diversity of specific tasks that electrical engineers are qualified to perform. Generally, electrical engineers design, develop, test, and supervise the manufacture of electrical equipment: motors, machinery controls, lighting equipment, wiring, radar and navigation systems, communications systems, power generation systems, and the electrical systems used in motor vehicles and aircraft.

Like any engineer, the electrical engineer frequently consults with commercial, industrial, or governmental customers and potential customers about their needs for products or projects. They design electrical instruments, facilities, equipment, components, end products, and systems and then implement their designs. They are adept at using computer-assisted engineering and design software. They perform detailed mathematical calculations to create standards and specifications for products and systems. They direct and coordinate such activities as manufacturing, construction, installation, maintenance, and testing to make sure that products or systems comply with specifications, codes, safety standards, and the needs of customers, a process that often involves observation of a completed installation in operation. They also provide necessary support and documentation.

On a more theoretical level, electrical engineers plan and implement research methods and procedures so that they can apply the principles of electrical theory to engineering projects. For example, electrical engineers plan the layout of power generating plants, along with distribution lines and substations. They help with the development of

AT A GLANCE FACT BOX

SOC: 17-2071.00
Preferred Education: Bachelor's degree
Average Salary: US$87,770 annually
Other Information: Starting salaries for electrical engineers are among the highest for all college graduates

capital project programs for new equipment or major repairs to old equipment. They gather data about commercial and residential development and population trends to determine the adequacy and efficiency of existing electrical systems in communities.

More day-to-day tasks include preparing specifications for materials and equipment that need to be purchased, supervising project team members, examining and testing vendors' products, and overseeing production of products to ensure that they are delivered on time and according to specifications. Electrical engineers also create technical drawings, specifications for electrical systems, and in some cases topographical maps (for use in such applications as power grid systems). Along these lines, they often carry out field surveys, relying on maps, graphs, diagrams, and other data to spot and correct power system problems. They investigate customer complaints when electrical products do not perform as promised. They develop budgets and estimate costs for labor, materials, and construction or manufacture.

Electrical engineering is undergoing important changes as a result of the green economy. Many electrical engineers, for example, are trying to increase energy efficiency by constructing "smart grids," a design concept in energy grids with goals including greater security, efficiency, safety, economy, reliability, and environmental friendliness. Other electrical engineers focus on green construction and retrofitting existing structures to make them more energy efficient and to reduce emission of carbon and other greenhouse gases. An example might be a building that uses electrical systems and components that minimize the need for electric lighting by taking natural lighting into consideration. Still others take an interest in the generation of renewable energy: solar, wind, geothermal, and biomass. Others strive to make the delivery of energy produced by traditional nonrenewable sources (coal, gas, oil) more environmentally friendly. The terms *electrical engineering* and *electronics engineering* are sometimes used interchangeably. Strictly speaking, the two fields are different. Electrical engineers have traditionally focused their attention on generating and supplying power, so they might specialize in power system engineering or electrical equipment manufacturing. Electronics engineers work on applications of electricity to control systems or signal processing. They design, develop, test, and supervise the manufacture of a wide range of technologies, from music players to global positioning systems to aviation electronics to signal processing. Although some electrical engineers work in computer-related areas, those who focus entirely on computer hardware are generally called computer hardware engineers.

WORKING CONDITIONS

Working conditions for electrical engineers can vary widely depending on the nature of the engineer's specialty and the particular project. Electrical engineers often spend considerable time in offices meeting with clients and potential clients to determine the clients' needs and preferences. They also spend time in offices, laboratories, or industrial plants doing calculations and preparing specifications, budgets, cost estimates, environmental impact studies, and other documents needed for the project. Furthermore, electrical engineers often meet with related professionals, including architects, contractors, and various other types of engineers, whether civil, aerospace, computer hardware, electronics, industrial, materials, mining, nuclear, or petroleum, to coordinate their activities on a project.

Electrical engineers also spend time in the field, monitoring projects to ensure that they conform to specifications and troubleshooting when they do not. Many electrical engineers have to travel to distant work sites both in the United States and abroad, and they sometimes have to relocate temporarily to oversee an extensive project.

Electrical engineers have to be proficient in the use of a wide variety of tools depending on their area of specialization. These might include laboratory evaporators (vacuum system/thermal evaporators, electron beam evaporators, filament evaporators, metal evaporation systems), semiconductor process systems (molecular beam epitaxy systems, wafer steppers, wire bonders, wet chemical clean benches), signal generators (programmable function generators, synthesized continuous wave generators, vector signal generators), spectrometers (auger electron spectrometers, secondary ion mass spectrometers, X-ray photoemission spectrometers), and numerous others. Electrical engineers also need to be proficient in the use of such analytical and scientific software as Hewlett-Packard's Semiconductor Parameter Analyzer, Synopsys PrimeTime, and the Tektronix EZ-TEST. Electrical engineers also know how to use computer-aided design software such as Autodesk AutoCAD software, integrated development environment software such as Eclipse IDE, and numerous other software packages and platforms.

EMPLOYMENT

In 2008, the most recent year for which accurate data is available, 157,800 electrical engineers were employed in the United States, according to the U.S. Department of Labor's Bureau of Labor Statistics (BLS). The states with the highest employment level were California, Texas, New York, Massachusetts, and Florida. The metropolitan areas with the largest number of electrical engineers included the regions surrounding Los Angeles, California; Boston, Massachusetts; San Jose–Santa Clara, California; Dallas, Texas; and Washington, DC. The states with the highest concentration of electrical engineers (relative to the total number of jobs in the state) were Alaska, Massachusetts, Idaho, Alabama, and Delaware. The metropolitan areas with the highest concentration of electrical engineers (relative to the total number of jobs in the area) were the regions surrounding Binghamton, New York; Kokomo, Indiana; Huntsville, Alabama; Palm Bay–Melbourne–Titusville, Florida; and Lowell, Massachusetts.

TRAINING, OTHER QUALIFICATIONS, AND ADVANCEMENT

Not all persons who perform electrical engineering tasks are licensed engineers. Licensing, however, allows the license holder to certify designs and plans with a seal (analogous to notarizing a document), submit bids for government contracts, be a principal of a firm, provide consulting services, and perhaps most importantly, offer engineering services to the public.

Preparation for a career as a licensed electrical engineer can begin as early as high school with advanced courses in such subjects as algebra, geometry, calculus, trigonometry, physics, and chemistry. The first step toward licensure is a bachelor's degree. Typically, electrical engineers earn a bachelor's of science in electrical engineering from one of the more than 500 schools or colleges of engineering accredited by the Accreditation Board for Engineering and Technology. Students who want to earn a master's degree can do so at one of 37 schools that offer fully accredited master's degree programs in engineering. Students investigating colleges and universities should examine the programs carefully. Some programs are designed to emphasize industrial practices and thus prepare students for jobs in industry; others are more theoretical and designed to prepare students for graduate study. Although a graduate degree is often necessary for research positions, entry-level electrical engineers normally need just a bachelor's degree.

The next step is to pass the Fundamentals of Engineering (FE) exam. This eight-hour exam, administered by the National Council of Examiners for Engineering and Surveying (NCEES), consists of two parts. The first part, which tests basic engineering concepts, is the same for all engineering examinees. For the second part, the examinee is required to select a particular type of engineering, one of which is electrical engineering. About 67 percent of electrical engineering examinees pass the FE exam on the first try, which is the lowest percentage among the major engineering disciplines.

The next step is to acquire work experience. Applicants generally have to have at least one and as many as four years of experience working under the supervision of a licensed engineer, although state requirements regarding work experience vary.

Work experience leads to the final step, which is to pass the Professional Engineering (PE) exam. All PE exams focus on a particular engineering discipline. Electrical engineers can choose among three subspecialties: computer, electrical and electronics, and power. In contrast to the FE exam, the PE exam is open book, so the examinee can bring certain kinds of printed resources to the exam and consult them. About 61 percent of first-time test takers pass the electrical engineering PE exams.

Licensed electrical engineers in most states are required to complete continuing education courses. Many such courses are offered through the Institute of Electrical and Electronics Engineers. Sometimes states impose an annual requirement, but more commonly the requirement is to complete a certain number of continuing education hours, usually 24 to 30, over a two-year period.

Electrical engineers often have to be licensed in more than one state. This is a common need for electrical engineers who practice in border cities, but it also becomes an issue for those who travel to distant sites to design or implement projects. *Comity licensure* enables an electrical engineer licensed in one state to obtain a license in other states. The NCEES helps with this process by offering a service that applicants can use to store and transmit professional records in seeking and maintaining licensure in other states.

Many electrical engineers work for the U.S. government, particularly the U.S. Department of Defense. These engineers need to be able to pass background checks to gain security clearances.

JOB OUTLOOK

According to the BLS, the job outlook for electrical engineers is not very positive. The number of electrical engineers is expected to grow to about 160,500 by the year 2018, an increase over 2008 of just 2,700 jobs, or about 2 percent. During this period, demand for electrical devices, including electric power generators, wireless phone transmitters, high-density batteries, and navigation systems, should remain strong, providing employment opportunities for electrical engineers. Dampening the job outlook for recent college graduates, however, are international competition and the availability of engineering services performed in other countries, usually at lower cost. Defense cutbacks could also reduce the demand for electrical engineers. According to the BLS, electrical engineers who can provide engineering expertise and design services to manufacturers should have the best job prospects.

EARNINGS

According to the BLS, the mean annual wage for an electrical engineer in 2010 was US$87,770, or an hourly wage of US$42.20. The median figure was US$84,540, or US$40.65 per hour. The middle half had earnings ranging from US$66,880 to US$105,860. The bottom 10 percent earned an average of US$54,030; the top 10 percent earned an average of US$128,610. The top-paying states were Massachusetts (with a mean annual wage of US$103,350), Alaska (US$102,120), California (US$99,120), and Maine (US$95,940), as well as Washington, DC (US$98,670). The lowest paying states were Montana, Wyoming, North Dakota, South Dakota, and Mississippi. The top paying metropolitan areas were the regions surrounding Sherman–Denison, Texas (US$123,650); Sacramento, California (US$120,670); Wilmington, North Carolina (US$116,010); Beaumont–Port Arthur, Texas (US$112,930); and Santa Barbara, California (US$112,720).

RELATED OCCUPATIONS
- Aerospace engineers
- Electrical and electronic engineering technicians
- Electrical and electronics installers and repairers
- Electricians
- Electro-mechanical technicians

SOURCES OF ADDITIONAL INFORMATION

Accreditation Board for Engineering and Technology. http://www.abet.org

Institute of Electrical and Electronics Engineers. http://www.ieee.org

Junior Engineering Technical Society. http://www.tsaweb.org

National Council of Examiners for Engineering and Surveying. http://www.ncees.org

FURTHER READING

Braun, David. "Teaching Sustainability Analysis in Electrical Engineering Lab Courses." *IEEE Transactions on Education,* 53, no. 2 (May 2010), pp. 243–247. Accessed March 2, 2012. http://digitalcommons.calpoly.edu.

Bureau of Labor Statistics, U.S. Department of Labor. *Occupational Employment and Wages, May 2010.* *17-2071 Electrical Engineers.* Last updated May 17, 2011. Accessed March 2, 2012. http://www.bls.gov/oes/current/oes172071.htm.

———. *Engineers.* Accessed March 2, 2012. http://www.bls.gov/oco/pdf/ocos027.pdf.

CareerPlanner.com. *Electrical Engineer.* Accessed March 2, 2012. http://job-descriptions.careerplanner.com/Electrical-Engineers.cfm.

iSeek Green. *Electrical Engineer Interview.* Accessed March 2, 2012. http://www.iseek.org/industry/green/careers/electrical-engineer.html.

Miller, Joe. "What Is the Smart Grid?" *SmartGridNews.com,* April 17, 2009. Accessed March 2, 2012. http://www.smartgridnews.com/artman/publish/commentary/What_Is_the_Smart_Grid-567.html.

O*Net OnLine. *Green Occupation: 17-2071.00—Electrical Engineers.* Accessed March 2, 2012. http://www.onetonline.org/help/green/17-2071.00.

———. *Summary Report for: 17-2071.00—Electrical Engineers.* Accessed March 2, 2012. http://www.onetonline.org/link/summary/17-2071.00.

University of Lille. *Electrical Engineering and Sustainable Development: Contribute to the Challenges of Our Society.* Accessed March 2, 2012. http://master-ase.univ-lille1.fr/uploads/E2D2/presentation.pdf.

MECHANICAL ENGINEERS

NATURE OF THE WORK

Mechanical engineering is the branch of engineering that deals with objects and systems in motion, from particles to machines to systems. Because a large number of manufactured objects require motion to operate, mechanical engineering is one of the most diverse disciplines in engineering. Mechanical engineers design, test, and produce a wide range of objects, from small component parts (for example, the nozzle of a printer or the thermostat on a heater) to large systems (for example, a helicopter or a machine tool).

The chief job of a mechanical engineer is to bridge the gap between an idea for a product and the marketplace in which it will be sold and used. Mechanical engineers, then, need a broad range of skills and abilities. In particular, they need to understand the nature of the forces that manufactured objects in motion are subjected to, such as heat, cold, and other stressors. They then have to determine the best way to make the product so that it performs reliably.

Mechanical engineers play a major role in a wide spectrum of industries. In the automotive industry, they design and manufacture every system and subsystem, including the chassis, the engine, the transmission, and the vehicle's sensors. In the aerospace industry, they design aircraft, engines, and control systems. In biotechnology, they design such objects as implants, prosthetic devices, and fluidic systems (that is, systems that use the principles of fluid dynamics to perform analog or digital operations, similar to those that might be performed by electronics). In the computer and electronics industries, mechanical engineers have a hand in such products as disk drives, printers, semiconductors, and cooling systems. In energy conversion, mechanical engineers design gas and wind turbines, fuel cells, and solar energy systems. They also

AT A GLANCE FACT BOX

SOC: 17-2141.00
Preferred Education: Bachelor's degree
Average Salary: US$82,480 annually
Other Information: Licensed mechanical engineers must complete a bachelor's degree in engineering, have work experience under the supervision of a licensed engineer, and pass a licensing exam

develop systems for environmental control such as heating and air conditioning systems, refrigeration, and compressors. For manufacturers, mechanical engineers develop machine tools, prototypes, and processes for microfabrication (such as for computer chips). At the smallest level, mechanical engineers develop and implement microelectromechanical systems, or MEMS. These are very small devices (one to 100 micrometers) driven by electricity and used in a wide variety of applications, from computers to printers to the accelerometer that deploys a car's airbag.

Those wishing to become mechanical engineers have to study a wide range of subjects. A partial list includes mathematics (including statistics), materials, solid and fluid mechanics, thermodynamics, heat transfer, instrumentation, design, and manufacturing. More specialized subjects include biomechanics, cartilage and tissue engineering, energy conversion, laser-assisted manufacturing, combustion, MEMS, fracture mechanics, nanotechnology, micropower generation (that is, small-scale generation of power that frees a home, business, or community from a larger power grid), tribology (that is, friction, lubrication, and wear, from the Greek word *tribo,* meaning "I rub"), and vibrations (engineering schools offer courses in vibration or noise and vibration). The broad nature of mechanical engineering opens career opportunities in a wide range of industries.

Mechanical engineering is changing as a result of the green economy. More mechanical engineers are finding employment in industry sectors that promote greater energy efficiency, particularly by designing *smart grids* that deliver power in a safer, cheaper, more reliable, and more environmentally friendly manner. Others are finding positions related to green construction, using engineering technologies to construct or retrofit commercial and residential buildings according to the principles of sustainability. Still others are interested in industries that provide renewable energy, including solar, wind, geothermal, and biomass energy. Alternatively, many turn their attention to making traditional, nonrenewable forms of energy, such as gas, oil, and coal, cleaner and more efficient. In the transportation sector, mechanical engineers study and try to reduce the environmental impact of transportation systems such as cars, mass transit, trucking, and freight rail. More specifically, a mechanical engineer in the green economy might apply the principles of mechanical engineering to robotics, biomedical engineering, or waste management; use combustion analyzers or pressure gauges to calculate energy losses for buildings; design heating and cooling systems that boost energy efficiency; direct the installation of equipment that makes use of renewable energy sources; or evaluate product designs and prototypes for their environmental impact.

WORKING CONDITIONS

Mechanical engineers spend considerable time in offices meeting with clients and potential clients to determine their needs and preferences. They also spend time doing calculations and preparing plans, specifications, cost estimates, environmental impact studies, and other documents needed for the project. Furthermore, depending on the nature of the project, mechanical engineers meet with other related professionals, including industrial engineers, materials engineers, computer hardware engineers, biomedical engineers, and others to coordinate their activities.

Working conditions for mechanical engineers vary widely because these professionals work in so many different fields. A mechanical engineer might spend considerable time in laboratories and testing facilities, using such tools as flow meters (for example, laser Doppler anemometers, digital particle image velocimeters, and pitot tubes), vibration isolators, semiconductor process systems (for example, etchers, lithography equipment, and wafer dicing saws), optical laser scanners, and signal generators. Because they often have to oversee manufacturing processes, mechanical engineers are likely to spend most of their time in manufacturing facilities.

Technological tools commonly used by mechanical engineers include analytical and scientific software such as MAYA Nastran (a heat transference measurement tool) and ReliaSoft Weibull++6 (a tool for analyzing data pertaining to a product's or component's lifetime reliability), computer-aided design software such as Autodesk AutoCAD, computer-aided manufacturing software, and development environment software (for example, National Instruments' LabVIEW, a programming environment that enables mechanical engineers to develop measurement and testing control systems).

Mechanical engineers typically work a 40-hour workweek, but the deadline-driven nature of the engineering profession dictates that they may work longer hours.

EMPLOYMENT

According to the U.S. Department of Labor's Bureau of Labor Statistics (BLS), 234,400 mechanical engineers were employed in the United States in May 2010. The U.S. states with the highest employment level were Michigan, California, Texas, Ohio, and Pennsylvania. The metropolitan areas with the largest number of mechanical engineers included the regions surrounding Warren–Troy–Farmington Hills, Michigan; Houston, Texas; Los Angeles, California; Chicago, Illinois; and New York, New York. The states with the highest concentration of mechanical engineers relative to the total number of jobs in the state were Michigan, Connecticut, South Carolina, Indiana, and Utah. The metropolitan areas with the highest concentration of mechanical engineers relative to the total number of jobs in the area were Warren–Troy–Farmington Hills, Michigan; Niles–Benton Harbor, Michigan; Greenville, South Carolina; Kalamazoo, Michigan; and Huntsville, Alabama.

TRAINING, OTHER QUALIFICATIONS, AND ADVANCEMENT

A mechanical engineer does not necessarily need to be a licensed engineer, but licensing not only confers prestige but also allows the license holder to certify designs and plans with a seal (similar to the process of notarizing a document), become a principal in a firm, submit bids for government contracts, offer consulting services, and offer engineering services to the public.

High school students can begin their preparation for a career as a licensed mechanical engineer by taking advanced courses in subjects such as algebra, geometry, calculus, physics, biology, and chemistry. The student who wants to become a mechanical engineer will then earn a bachelor's degree from one of the 521 schools or colleges of engineering accredited by the Accreditation Board for Engineering and Technology. A student who would like to earn a master's degree can do so from any one of 37 master's degree programs in engineering that are fully accredited.

After completing the degree, the aspiring mechanical engineer will take the Fundamentals of Engineering (FE) exam. This exam, which is administered by the National Council of Examiners for Engineering and Surveying (NCEES), consists of two parts. The first part, which tests basic engineering concepts, is the same for all engineering examinees. The second part has the examinee select a particular type of engineering such as mechanical engineering. About 79 percent of mechanical engineering examinees pass the FE exam on the first try.

The third step is to acquire experience in the workplace. State requirements vary, but the applicant generally is required to have between one to four years of experience working under the supervision of a licensed mechanical engineer.

This work experience leads to the final step, which is to pass the Professional Engineering (PE) exam. Unlike the FE exam, the PE exam focuses entirely on one particular engineering discipline. Mechanical engineers can choose among three subspecialties: heating, ventilation, and air conditioning (HVAC) and refrigeration; mechanical systems and materials; and thermal and fluids systems. The PE exam is open book, thus allowing the examinee to bring printed resources to the exam. Currently, about 73 percent of first-time test takers pass the mechanical engineering PE exams.

Mechanical engineers have to complete continuing education courses in most states. Many such courses are offered through the American Society of Civil Engineers in the form of seminars, on-site training, webinars, and online or DVD courses. Some states require a certain number of continuing education hours annually. Most, however, require a certain number of continuing education hours, commonly 24 to 30, over a two-year period.

Career paths for mechanical engineers are highly flexible and variable because of the breadth of the profession. Mechanical engineers can work in traditional industries such as power generation, automobile manufacturing, shipbuilding, and aviation or they can work in cutting-edge technologies such as nanotechnology, bioengineering, and green construction.

JOB OUTLOOK

According to the BLS, the job outlook for mechanical engineers, particularly those with "green" credentials, is mixed. On the one hand, job opportunities for mechanical engineers are projected to grow slower than average for all occupations. Nevertheless, by the year 2018 the number

of mechanical engineers is projected to increase above 2008 levels by 6 percent to about 253,100. The effects of emerging technologies in such fields as biotechnology, materials science, and nanotechnology will create some new job opportunities. Additionally, people with degrees in mechanical engineering will be able to apply their knowledge and skills in other sectors.

EARNINGS

According to the BLS, the mean annual wage for a mechanical engineer in 2010 was US$82,480, or an hourly wage of US$39.65. The median figure was US$78,160, or US$37.58 per hour. The middle half had earnings ranging from US$62,360 to US$98,150. The bottom 10 percent earned an average of US$50,550; the top 10 percent earned an average of US$119,480. The average starting salary for a new mechanical engineer in 2009 was US$58,766.

The top-paying states were Alaska (US$99,400), Washington, DC (US$96,310), Virginia (US$94,530), Colorado (US$92,010), and California (US$90,860). The lowest-paying states were Montana, North Dakota, South Dakota, Nebraska, Arkansas, and Mississippi. The top-paying metropolitan areas were the regions surrounding Idaho Falls, Idaho (US$126,320); Bloomington–Normal, Illinois (US$116,760); Washington, DC (US$112,780); San Jose–Santa Clara, California (US$104,380); and Santa Barbara, California (US$103,230).

RELATED OCCUPATIONS

Jobs with a similar emphasis on science and mathematics include:

- Agricultural and food scientists
- Architects
- Atmospheric, biological, and environmental scientists
- Chemists and materials scientists
- Computer scientists
- Engineering technicians

SOURCES OF ADDITIONAL INFORMATION

Accreditation Board for Engineering and Technology. http://www.abet.org/index.aspx

American Society of Heating, Refrigerating and Air-Conditioning Engineers. http://www.ashrae.org

American Society of Mechanical Engineers. http://www.asme.org

National Council of Examiners for Engineering and Surveying. http://www.ncees.org

National Society of Professional Engineers. http://www.nspe.org/index.html

Society of Automotive Engineers. http://www.sae.org

FURTHER READING

Brown, Alan S. "Sustainability: ASME's Third Annual Survey Finds That Engineers Are Still Trying to Understand How Sustainability Fits into Their Workflow." *MEMagazine,* November 2011. Accessed March 1, 2012. http://memagazine.asme.org/Articles/2011/November/Sustainability.cfm.

Bureau of Labor Statistics, U.S. Department of Labor. *Engineers.* Accessed March 1, 2012. http://www.bls.gov/oco/pdf/ocos027.pdf.

———. "17-2141 Mechanical Engineers." In *Occupational Employment Statistics: Occupational Employment and Wages, May 2010.* Last updated May 17, 2011. Accessed March 1, 2012. http://www.bls.gov/oes/current/oes172141.htm.

Ciocci, Richard C. "Characterizing Sustainable Mechanical Engineering." *Technology Interface,* Spring 2006. Accessed April 10, 2012. http://engr.nmsu.edu/~etti/Spring06/11_Ciocci-Accepted/index.cgi.

Department of Mechanical Engineering. *Trends in Mechanical Engineering Careers.* New York: Stony Brook University. Accessed March 1, 2012. http://me.eng.sunysb.edu/index.php?option=com_content&view=article&id=60%3Atrends-in-mechanical-engineering-careers-&catid=66&Itemid=83.

Department of Mechanical Engineering. *What Is Mechanical Engineering?* New York: Columbia University. Accessed March 1, 2012. http://me.columbia.edu/pages/dptoverview/whatisme/index.html.

O*NET OnLine. *Green Occupation: 17-2141.00—Mechanical Engineers.* Accessed March 1, 2012. http://www.onetonline.org/help/green/17-2141.00.

———. *Summary Report for: 17-2141.00—Mechanical Engineers.* Accessed March 1, 2012. http://www.onetonline.org/link/summary/17-2141.00.

Sloan Career Cornerstone Center. *Mechanical Engineering.* Accessed March 1, 2012. http://www.careercornerstone.org/mecheng/mecheng.htm.

ENERGY ENGINEERS

NATURE OF THE WORK

Energy engineer is an umbrella term for professionals who work in a wide variety of settings. A person whose title is energy engineer may very well have been trained as an electrical, mechanical, petroleum, or nuclear engineer or possibly even as an architect. As the term suggests, energy engineers play key roles in the production, transmission, or use of energy in homes and businesses. The sources of that energy, though, are many and varied, and in the context of a green economy, they include solar and biomass facilities, wind farms, nuclear power plants, and even emerging technologies such as wave and tidal power. Further, at the consumption end, energy engineers play leading roles in green building techniques, green architecture, and the provision of energy-efficient heating, ventilation, and air conditioning systems (HVAC). HVAC engineering is a subdiscipline of mechanical engineering. In the 21st century, even conventional or traditional energy engineers, particularly those in the petroleum industry, are likely to be paying closer attention to the principles of green energy use to ensure that the facilities they provide to their constituencies, clients, the public, or government operate in ways that are as cost-effective, energy-efficient, and clean as possible.

Energy engineers perform a host of tasks, depending on the context in which they work. They evaluate energy efficiency and strategies for renewable energy in community settings, commercial and government buildings, warehouses, wastewater treatment facilities, manufacturing facilities, schools and college campuses, and even prisons. With a strong background in mathematics and statistics, they quantify the performance of energy systems, the life-cycle costs of an energy system, and emission reduction, usually using engineering software specifically designed for

---

> ## AT A GLANCE FACT BOX
>
> **SOC:** 17-2199.03
> **Preferred Education:** Bachelor's degree in engineering
> **Average Salary:** US$90,270 annually
> **Other Information:** Energy engineers often enter the field with architectural, electrical, mechanical, nuclear, petroleum, or other engineering backgrounds

---

the purpose. Energy engineers write both preliminary and detailed energy audit reports. They identify, quantify, and maximize opportunities for energy savings, both during the design stages for new buildings and during the process of retrofitting existing buildings. They often act as consultants for construction or renovation clients who are seeking a Leadership in Energy and Environmental Design (LEED) certification from the U.S. Green Building Council (USGBC) for their project. LEED allows the operators and owners of buildings to identify and implement measurable solutions for green building design, construction, and maintenance. Included are matters such as sustainable site development, water savings, indoor air quality, the use (and reuse) of sustainable building materials, and energy efficiency. The USGBC offers a number of resources, including publications and certification exams, to foster the construction of green buildings.

Energy engineers are often required to conduct on-site observations and field inspections to collect data used in energy conservation analyses or to direct the work of contractors to ensure that they implement energy management projects as designed and do so in conformity with local, state, and federal laws. In this regard, they often have to inspect or monitor energy systems, including HVAC or daylighting (windows or other openings such as skylights that maximize natural light in a building) systems, to measure their potential energy savings. They might be called on to conduct research or gather data about alternative or renewable energy systems and technologies and to make recommendations to clients about energy system selection, climate-control systems, energy modeling, methods for logging data, energy management control systems, lighting systems, daylighting design, sustainable design, and energy auditing. In accomplishing these goals, energy engineers often consult with architects, mechanical engineers, and electrical engineers, reviewing their plans and specifications to evaluate them from the point of view of energy efficiency.

WORKING CONDITIONS

Energy engineers are likely to spend a considerable portion of their time working indoors in offices, performing calculations, preparing energy audits, reviewing the plans and specifications of other professionals such as architects, electrical engineers, and mechanical engineers, and completing similar tasks. In this regard, energy engineers coordinate with these other professionals to determine the feasibility of a project and to coordinate plans and specifications. They also typically spend a great deal of time meeting with clients to understand their needs and preferences for a project as well as to make recommendations. In addition, depending on the context, energy engineers might have to work outdoors, when they visit construction sites to ensure that installations are being made in accordance with plans and specifications and to adjust plans based on problems that arise.

Energy engineering requires exactness and accuracy, for mistakes can delay construction projects, often at great cost. Any type of engineering job is likely to be deadline driven, so although energy engineers typically work a standard 40-hour work week, they often have to work longer hours to meet an impending deadline. A career as an energy engineer could involve travel to distant locations, even overseas, and the energy engineer could be asked to relocate temporarily for the duration of a complex project.

Energy engineers make use of a range of tools and technologies, most of which are designed to help the engineer implement the principles of green building design and sustainability. Examples of tools include air velocity and temperature monitors, catalytic combustion analyzers (useful, for example, in developing techniques for reducing soot from diesel exhausts), infrared imagers, heat tracing

equipment (which monitors and maintains temperatures in pipelines, storage tanks and vessels, and pipeline equipment), and multimeters (devices that measure electric current, voltage, and usually resistance). Technologies used by energy engineers include various types of analytical and scientific software. These might include the Architectural Energy Corporation's ENFORMA Building Diagnostics software, which provides automated diagnostics for a building's HVAC system; Autodesk's Ecotect software, a sustainable building design tool that measures energy metrics such as thermal performance, solar radiation, daylighting, and shadows and reflections (from the sun); or EnergySoft's EnergyPro software, used to model energy systems and performance. In addition, energy engineers are expected to be conversant with routine office technologies such as computer-aided design software, spreadsheet software, and word-processing software.

EMPLOYMENT

In 2008 engineers held about 1.6 million jobs in the United States. Among these were about 157,800 electrical engineers, 54,300 environmental engineers, 21,900 petroleum engineers, and 16,900 nuclear engineers. The U.S. Department of Labor's Bureau of Labor Statistics (BLS) provides a classification called *Other Engineers* that undoubtedly includes numerous professionals who work in the field of energy engineering; in 2008 there were approximately 183,200 such engineers.

TRAINING, OTHER QUALIFICATIONS, AND ADVANCEMENT

The first step in becoming an energy engineer is to earn at least a bachelor's degree in engineering from one of the 521 schools or colleges of engineering accredited by the Accreditation Board for Engineering and Technology. As noted earlier, many professionals enter the field of energy engineering with degrees in fields such as electrical, mechanical, or petroleum engineering and even with degrees in architecture. Some colleges of engineering offer degrees specifically in energy engineering or in closely allied fields. Examples include degrees in renewable energy engineering, energy resources engineering, and environmental resources engineering. At some schools, energy engineering is folded into larger departments, so that the potential student might attend, for example, a School (or Department) of Energy and Mineral Engineering. As an example of specialization in the field, Australia's University of New South Wales offers degrees in its School of Photovoltaic and Renewable Energy Engineering. In either case, the student interested in energy engineering will take core courses in the statics of engineering, chemistry, mechanical engineering, engineering graphics, engineering dynamics, hydrology, mathematics and statistics, and structural design.

The next step is to pass the Fundamentals of Engineering Exam (FE Exam), which is administered by the National Council of Examiners for Engineering and Surveying (NCEES). This eight-hour exam consists of two parts. The first part is the same for all engineering examinees and covers basic engineering concepts. For the second part, the examinee is required to select a particular type of engineering, such as mechanical, electrical, or civil engineering. Those interested in a career in energy engineering with a green orientation might be interested in the exam in environmental engineering.

The third step is to acquire work experience. State requirements vary, but generally the applicant has to have at least one and as many as four years of experience working under the supervision of a licensed engineer. This work experience leads to the final step, which is to pass the Principles and Practice of Engineering Exam (PE Exam), also administered by the NCEES. The professional who sits for this exam is required to select an area of specialization. Those interested in a career in energy engineering might choose to take the PE Exam in architectural, environmental, nuclear, petroleum, or mechanical: HVAC and refrigeration engineering. After passing the PE Exam, the engineer is fully licensed, a requirement before engineering services can be offered to the public.

Energy engineers can advance in their careers through certification, and green energy engineers can find a wide range of certification programs to enhance their credentials. The Association of Energy Engineers (AEE) offers a number of certification programs that enable a professional with experience to become, for example, a Certified Energy Manager, a Certified Energy Auditor, or a Renewable Energy Professional. The Academy of HVAC Engineering offers advanced continuing education programs for those who are interested in the field, as does the Society of Petroleum Engineers.

Typically, a beginning engineer works under the supervision of more experienced engineers. Large companies may offer beginning engineers formal classroom training. As engineers acquire experience and knowledge, they are likely to be assigned more difficult projects and given greater independence, allowing them to create designs, solve problems, and make decisions. They may also supervise a staff or a team of engineers and technicians. Engineering credentials can also be useful in sales. A person with a background in energy engineering is equipped to explain to potential customers the benefits, uses, and technical specifications of a product that has implications for energy production, transmission, or usage.

JOB OUTLOOK

Again, *energy engineer* encompasses engineering professionals from a range of specialties. For those who come to the field as electrical engineers, the job outlook is not very encouraging. According to the BLS, the number of electrical engineers is expected to grow to about 160,500 by the year 2018, an increase of just 2 percent compared with the number in 2008. Other fields are more promising. The number of environmental engineers is expected to grow rapidly, as much as 31 percent, far above the average for all occupations, as the public, government, and industry gain greater awareness of the benefits of green energy production and use. The number of nuclear engineers is expected to grow by about 11 percent, which is about average for all engineer occupations. The number of petroleum engineers is also expected to grow rapidly by about 18 percent.

EARNINGS

According to the BLS, the average annual salary for energy engineers in the United States is about US$90,270 (US$43.40 per hour). Starting salaries for those with a bachelor's degree cluster around US$60,000: US$61,610 for nuclear engineers, US$60,125 for electrical engineers, and US$58,766 for mechanical engineers. The highest starting salaries go to petroleum engineers, who can expect to make salaries of US$83,121.

RELATED OCCUPATIONS

- Architects
- Construction and building inspectors
- Construction managers
- Heating, air conditioning, and refrigeration mechanics and installers
- Mechanical engineers

SOURCES OF ADDITIONAL INFORMATION

The Academy of HVAC Engineering. http://www.hvac-academy.com

Accreditation Board for Engineering and Technology. http://www.abet.org/index.aspx

American Nuclear Society. http://www.ans.org

American Society for Engineering Education. http://www.asee.org

Association of Energy Engineers. http://www.aeecenter.org

National Council of Examiners for Engineering and Surveying. http://www.ncees.org

National Society of Professional Engineers. http://www.nspe.org

Society of Petroleum Engineers. http://www.spe.org

FURTHER READING

Bureau of Labor Statistics, U.S. Department of Labor. "Engineers." In *Occupational Outlook Handbook, 2010–11 Edition.* Accessed March 23, 2012. http://www.bls.gov/oco/ocos027.htm.

———. *Engineers.* Accessed March 23, 2012. http://www.bls.gov/oco/pdf/ocos027.pdf.

———. "17-2199: Engineers, All Other." In *Occupational Employment and Wages, May 2010.* Accessed March 23, 2012. http://www.bls.gov/oes/current/oes172199.htm.

Capehart, Barney L., Wayne C. Turner, and William J. Kennedy. *Guide to Energy Management,* 7th ed. Lilburn, GA: Fairmont Press, 2011.

Education-Portal.com. *Become an Energy Engineer: Education and Career Information.* Accessed March 23, 2012. http://education-portal.com/articles/Become_an_Energy_Engineer_Education_and_Career_Information.html.

Illinois workNet Center. *Energy Engineers.* Accessed March 23, 2012. http://www.illinoisworknet.com.

"KMB Design Group Completes 100th Solar Project." *PR Newswire,* May 5, 2011. Accessed January 24, 2012. http://www.prnewswire.com/news-releases/kmb-design-group-completes-100th-solar-project-121307349.html.

O*NET OnLine. *Green Occupation: 17-2199.03— Energy Engineers.* Accessed March 23, 2012. http://www.onetonline.org/help/green/17-2199.03.

ARCHITECTURAL DRAFTERS

— ■ —

NATURE OF THE WORK

Broadly speaking, the chief duty of an architectural drafter is to prepare detailed drawings of architectural designs and building plans using specifications an architect provides. Many architectural drafters work for architects who take a green focus on their work, designing buildings in ways that conserve resources of energy and water and that use sustainable materials.

More specifically, an architectural drafter gathers and assembles data necessary to complete an architectural design, often visiting job sites to take necessary measurements. Architectural drafters draw both rough and detailed plans for foundations, structures, and buildings and base the plans on preliminary concepts, sketches, engineering calculations, specification sheets, and similar data, all with a view to create green projects. They also create freehand drawings and the lettering that accompanies drawings.

They analyze the technical side of an architect's design concept and then calculate such factors as weight, volume, and stress to ensure that the design concept is something that can be built. Additionally, architectural drafters use computer-aided design and drafting (CADD) equipment to lay out and plan the arrangements of structures as well as to produce designs, working drawings, charts, and other types of records. Because of this computer expertise, architectural drafters are sometimes referred to as CADD operators.

In a more administrative capacity, architectural drafters supervise, coordinate, and inspect the work of draftspersons, technicians, and technologists on construction projects. (An architectural technologist is a professional who provides building design and construction services, concentrating on the technology of construction.) An architectural drafter often serves as the architect's representative at construction sites, ensuring the builder complies with design specifications and, under the architect's supervision, advises the builder on design corrections. In this way, the architectural drafter helps ensure that the green goals of the project are being met.

Architectural drafters might check the dimensions of materials that are to be used in constructing a building and assign numbers to lists of materials to enable everyone involved to keep track of them and to ensure that the project is being constructed with minimum waste. They are also likely to determine the instructions and procedures that should be followed, basing them on design specifications and the amount of materials required. Under an architect's supervision, they prepare such documents as cost estimates, contracts, bids, and technical reports for projects.

AT A GLANCE FACT BOX

SOC: 17-3011.01
Preferred Education: Associate's degree
Average Salary: US$48,740 annually
Other Information: Employers generally prefer to hire applicants with at least two years of training at a technical institute, community college, or four-year college or university

---

They also examine building codes, laws, space and site requirements, and other materials to determine how these requirements might affect architectural design. Many of these requirements have a bearing on the sustainability and green characteristics of the project.

Architectural drafters prepare drawings of interior designs and landscaping for presentation to the client. These landscape designs are likely to emphasize conservation of resources. They then reproduce drawings, either on copy machines or by tracing them using transparent paper and drafting instruments. They also create landscape, architectural, and display models. Finally, architectural drafters can be called on to coordinate the structural, mechanical, and electrical designs of a project and determine the best method of presenting them in graphic illustrations of building plans.

Any and all of these activities can take place in a green economic environment. For example, an architectural drafter might work in an architectural firm that designs new green buildings or that retrofits existing buildings to make them more environmentally friendly. An architectural drafter, then, might also be required to perform such tasks as calculating the heat loss and gain of buildings and structures to determine the required specifications for energy-efficient layout and equipment.

WORKING CONDITIONS

Drafters are likely to spend most of their time in offices preparing designs, plans, specifications, reports, and other documents needed for a project. Although the office environment is likely to be comfortable, drafters spend considerable time doing detailed work at the computer, subjecting themselves to eyestrain and back, hand, and wrist discomfort. Occasionally a drafter may have to go into the field to, for example, examine and inventory building materials or troubleshoot projects on behalf of the architect.

Architectural drafters make use of a variety of tools. Chief among them are traditional drafting equipment, including compasses; triangular scales; French curves (templates that enable drafters to draw curves of varying radii); architects' scales (specialized rulers with multiple units of length); scanners (for example, three-dimensional laser digitizers, sonic digitizers); and tablet computers, also called graphics tablets, digitizing tablets, graphics pads, drawing tablets, or pen tablets (which enable the drafter to create drawings digitally).

Technological tools used by architectural drafters include computer-aided design and drafting equipment (for example, various Autodesk Alias products, Autodesk AutoCAD, or Bentley Systems MicroStation). Drafters are conversant with the use of graphics and photo-imaging software such as Adobe Systems After Effects, Corel PaintShop Pro, and Softimage 3D Extreme. Furthermore, drafters know how to use optical character readers and scanning software, pattern design software (such as AutoCAD 100 Plus Hatch Pattern Library), and spreadsheet software such as Microsoft Excel.

EMPLOYMENT

According to the U.S. Department of Labor's Bureau of Labor Statistics (BLS), 118,400 architectural and civil drafters were employed in May 2010 (the BLS combines the two specialties because they are so closely related). The states with the highest employment levels were California, Texas, Florida, New York, and Pennsylvania. The metropolitan areas with the largest number of architectural and civil drafters included the regions surrounding Los Angeles, California; New York, New York; Houston, Texas; Chicago, Illinois; and Boston, Massachusetts. The states with the highest concentration of architectural and civil drafters relative to the total number of jobs in the state were Montana, Utah, Wyoming, Hawaii, and Florida. The metropolitan areas with the highest concentration of architectural and civil drafters relative to the total number of jobs in the area were Kennewick–Pasco–Richland, Washington; Cheyenne, Wyoming; Pensacola, Florida; Fargo, North Dakota; and Orlando, Florida.

TRAINING, OTHER QUALIFICATIONS, AND ADVANCEMENT

In general, architectural drafters are not required to have any particular credentials to gain employment. However, employers strongly prefer to hire applicants who have at least two years of training in drafting at a technical institute, community college, or four-year college; usually, this education results in either a certificate or an associate's degree. Employers seek job applicants who have well-developed skills in drafting and mechanical drawing; who know drafting standards, science, mathematics, and engineering technology; and whose background in CADD techniques is solid.

A person interested in a drafting career might begin preparation in high school with courses in mathematics, science, and, if such courses are available, computer technology, computer graphics, design, and drafting. The American Design Drafting Association, which certifies drafting programs, has certified a number of such programs in high schools; a person who completes such a program at the high school level is designated as an "apprentice drafter."

The next step is to enroll in a drafting program at a technical institute, community college, or four-year college or university (although few four-year institutions offer drafting programs). An aspiring drafter who wants to remain in his or her community might contact potential employers to inquire about the type of school from which they prefer to hire. In all cases, the aspiring drafter should contact schools to inquire about the employment record of their graduates and the kinds of instructional facilities they provide.

Technical institutes typically offer rigorous technical training and less general education in comparison with community colleges. Compared with technical institutes, community colleges are more likely to offer courses in drafting theory.

Many graduates of two-year drafting programs continue their education at four-year colleges and universities, often taking classes in subjects such as mathematics and even completing degrees in engineering or architecture. This additional course work at a four-year institution may boost the job prospects of an architectural drafter. It should also be noted that the U.S. Armed Forces provide technical training in drafting that can be applied to civilian jobs, although additional training might be necessary.

Architectural drafters do not have to be licensed or certified. However, the American Design Drafting Association has created a certification program that demonstrates to potential employers that the applicant has knowledge and understanding of recognized practices in the drafting profession.

Those who wish to obtain certification are required to pass the Drafter Certification Test, which tests applicants on basic drafting concepts such as working drawings, geometric construction, and the standards and terminology of architecture. Applicants can take the "AD" exam to become an architectural certified apprentice drafter or the "CD" exam to become an architectural certified drafter. Any person can take the exams, regardless of education or credentials.

Typically an entry-level drafter, or junior drafter, does routine work under close supervision. After junior drafters have gained experience, they may become intermediate drafters, working on more difficult assignments with less supervision. These drafters might have to exercise more judgment, and they might have to perform calculations when they prepare or modify drawings. In time, a drafter may become a senior drafter, supervisor, or designer, working on the most difficult projects with minimal supervision. In many cases, employers pay for the continuing education of drafters.

Whatever career path a drafter takes, certain skills and aptitudes are crucial. Mechanical ability and visual aptitude are crucial. Drafters must draw well, with accuracy and attention to detail. Artistic ability can also be helpful, particularly in specialized fields. Knowledge of construction methods and manufacturing techniques can be equally helpful. Potential drafters should have good interpersonal skills as they will interact with architects, engineers, surveyors, other professionals, and sometimes customers. Knowledge of the principles of green construction, green landscape architecture, and sustainability will be helpful for practitioners in this field as well.

JOB OUTLOOK

According to the BLS, job growth for drafters in general is expected to be slower than average until the year 2018. However, by 2018 architectural and civil drafters will enjoy average job growth of about 9 percent over 2008 figures.

Driving this job growth will be increases in the U.S. population and the need for the United States to upgrade its infrastructure. Dampening job growth is the ability of firms to outsource drafting work overseas, often at lower cost. The best job prospects will be enjoyed by those with at least two years of postsecondary education in a drafting program and strong technical skills, particularly in the use of computer-aided design and drafting equipment.

Three additional factors affect the job prospects of drafters. One is the condition of the economy. During recessions, the construction and manufacturing industries slow, meaning that drafters might be laid off and firms will not likely hire new drafters. The second is the increasing tendency of companies to hire drafters on a temporary or contract basis, often using temporary employment services. The third is the condition of local industry. Because the demand for drafters is closely tied to the needs of local industry, drafters with a particular specialty might enjoy better or worse job prospects given the nature of the industrial base in their community.

EARNINGS

According to the BLS, the mean annual wage for architectural and civil drafters in 2010 was US$48,740, or an hourly wage of US$23.43. The median figure was US$46,430, or US$22.32 per hour. The middle half had earnings ranging from US$37,070 to US$58,660. Those in the bottom 10 percentile earned an average of US$29,990; those in the top 10 percentile earned an average of US$72,150.

The top paying U.S. states were Connecticut (US$55,320), Maryland (US$54,950), California (US$54,900), and Arizona (US$54,050) as well as Washington, DC (US$54,730). The lowest paying states were North Dakota, South Dakota, Nebraska, Alabama, Kentucky, and West Virginia. The top paying metropolitan areas were the regions surrounding Kennewick–Pasco–Richland, Washington (US$66,460); Oakland, California (US$64,970); Springfield, Illinois (US$64,670); San Jose–Santa Clara, California (US$63,670); and Oxnard–Thousand Oaks–Ventura, California (US$63,650).

RELATED OCCUPATIONS

Other fields that have similar duties to architectural drafters include:

- Architects
- Commercial and industrial designers
- Engineering technicians
- Surveyors
- Cartographers
- Surveying and mapping technicians
- Photogrammetrists

SOURCES OF ADDITIONAL INFORMATION

Accrediting Commission of Career Schools and Colleges. http://www.accsc.org

American Design Drafting Association. http://www.adda.org

College Board, *Architectural Drafting.* http://www.collegeboard.com/csearch/majors_careers/profiles/majors/15.1303.html

Jefferis, Alan, and David Madsen. *Architectural Drafting and Design,* 3rd ed. Clifton Park, New York: Delmar Cengage Learning, 1995.

FURTHER READING

American Design Drafting Association. *Professional Certification Program.* Accessed March 2, 2012. http://www.adda.org/content/view/25/39.

Bureau of Labor Statistics, U.S. Department of Labor. "Drafters." In *Occupational Outlook Handbook, 2010–11 Edition,* last updated December 17, 2009. Accessed March 2, 2012. http://www.bls.gov/oco/ocos111.htm.

———. *Occupational Employment and Wages, May 2010: 17-3011 Architectural and Civil Drafters.* Last updated May 17, 2011. Accessed March 2, 2012. http://www.bls.gov/oes/current/oes173011.htm.

CareerPlanner.com. *Architectural Drafter.* Accessed March 2, 2012. http://job-descriptions.careerplanner.com/Architectural-Drafters.cfm.

Halpin, JoBeth. *Architectural Drafting Fundamentals.* Triton College, River Grove, Illinois. Accessed March 2, 2012. http://academics.triton.edu/faculty/jhalpin/ARC109/lectue_week_two.html.

O*NET OnLine. *Green Occupation: 17-3011.01—Architectural Drafters.* Accessed March 2, 2012. http://www.onetonline.org/help/green/17-3011.01.

———. *Summary Report for: 17-3011.01—Architectural Drafters.* Accessed March 2, 2012. http://www.onetonline.org/link/summary/17-3011.01.

University of Minnesota. *Interior Design Student Handbook: Part 2: Basic Drafting Standards and Symbols.* Accessed March 2, 2012. http://www.iar.unicamp.br/lab/luz/ld/Arquitetural/livros/interior%20design%20student%20handbook.pdf.

CONSTRUCTION CARPENTERS

NATURE OF THE WORK

Although the typical image of a carpenter is a person who works with wood, that definition encompasses only a small part of the many jobs and materials carpenters are responsible for during a project. Carpenters work with wood, drywall, fiberglass, plastic, and concrete. They connect materials with nails, screws, glue, and other fasteners. Carpenters also are responsible for sawing, sanding, drilling, and other such tasks to complete a project.

Carpenters work from the tile on the first floor all the way up to the roofline. They perform not only the labor but also the quality control that ensures surfaces are level and walls are plumb. There are few aspects of a construction project in which they are not involved. Depending on the size and scale of a project, a particular carpenter may focus on one stage of construction or one part of a building. But on many smaller buildings, the carpenter is integral to the entire project and may frame walls; build stairs; hang doors; and install windows, cabinets, and trim. The carpenter may also take on tasks often handled by other specialists, such as insulation, masonry, roofing, drywall, and siding.

Many carpenters are generalists, working on projects such as building a new home, remodeling a kitchen, and constructing offices for small businesses. Some carpenters specialize in finish work, dealing with floors, trim, and railings. Others make cabinets or handcraft doors and other wood features of a home. Still others construct concrete forms or scaffolding for large construction firms or work on expansive industrial or public work projects.

Carpenters can be the most influential workers on a jobsite when it comes to reducing waste, recycling, and improving energy efficiency. They are also crucial in implementing building practices that conserve energy and materials and improve the overall quality of a structure.

AT A GLANCE FACT BOX

SOC: 47-2031.01
Preferred Education: High school diploma or GED
Average Salary: US$24,650 to US$71,660 annually
Other Information: Optimum value engineering, which is a framing technique that lowers the amount of lumber and other materials used in construction, can save building owners more than 12 percent of direct construction costs and even more in operating costs, increasing demand for carpenters familiar with advanced framing practices

Many of these practices must be planned into the design of a project because they can change the footprint, structural support for the roof, and other factors that cannot be adjusted on the fly. Carpenters must be able to read blueprints and understand the overall goals of the designs to ensure proper implementation.

One technique used by carpenters to help conserve energy is to create a double-wall system, placing one stud wall inside another and leaving a gap between the two that is filled with insulation. The walls are offset to ensure thermal consistency. Such construction, however, must be drawn into the design because it makes the walls thicker and affects floor space.

Although double-wall systems increase the insulative value of a building, some green builders are eschewing the practice because it can use up to 25 percent more wood than traditional construction. They are using another technique that cuts down on lumber while increasing energy efficiency. This technique is called *advanced framing* or *optimum value engineering*. It increases stud spacing when framing walls, floors, and rafters and thereby creates more space for insulation. Other practices that are part of this technique focus on modular design, reducing wall heights, and using a single rather than double top plate to conserve materials.

Many of these practices either go unnoticed by occupants or are encouraged by them because they can save hundreds of dollars in lumber costs and hours of labor time when done by experienced carpenters and contractors. A focus on greener construction materials and technologies can even be instigated by clients, whose personal health issues, environmental awareness, or operating expense concerns drive them to request changes in building practices. In smaller communities, the availability of green materials is often driven by client demand, and that demand lowers material costs and increases the number of carpenters and other workers skilled in using them.

Such material changes are particularly important as forests shrink and large-diameter trees become valued for more than basic construction. Engineered wood, which is made from tree species that have smaller diameters and grow more quickly, appears throughout modern buildings. This product is popular in flooring but can also be used to replace dimensional lumber in walls. Recycled wood and composite products are incorporated into decks, doors, and window frames, putting waste wood and plastics to use. Carpenters initially may need to learn how to use these and other materials to their best effect, but once learned such knowledge can be invaluable for future projects.

WORKING CONDITIONS

Carpentry is a physical job. Carpenters may spend several days on ladders working over their heads, other days shifting heavy materials and structures into place, and other days on their knees installing flooring or trim. They may work a fairly set schedule as they check off the tasks that constitute a months-long construction project, they may juggle multiple projects, or they may work overtime to meet a deadline. They work in all types of weather and temperatures, ideally scheduling interior jobs for winter months in cold climates and exterior tasks in spring and fall in hot ones. But many factors can lead them to frame a building in January and work in a hot attic space in August.

Typical carpentry tools and materials can have sharp edges and rough surfaces, and carpenters have a high rate of nonfatal injuries, mainly through equipment use on the jobsite according to the U.S. Department of Labor. They experience the second-highest number of job fatalities of any construction trade, with falls causing 43 percent of fatalities. The rate of fatal injuries in this occupation has been declining, however, with less than half as many fatalities in 2010 as in each of the years from 2004 to 2007.

EMPLOYMENT

More than 620,000 people in the United States work as construction carpenters, making this one of the largest construction industry occupations according to U.S. Department of Labor statistics. Nearly half of all residential construction workers are carpenters, but many work in nonresidential construction as well. Some carpenters specialize in finishing or structural work. Despite the downturn in the U.S. economy, as of May 2010 California was home to the most carpenters, followed by New York, Pennsylvania, Texas, and Florida. Workers in Hawaii and Alaska are among the highest paid. Most carpenters are employed by construction companies, but about one-third are considered independent subcontractors. As such, they must pay self-employment tax and carry their own liability insurance, depending on the state in which they are working.

TRAINING, OTHER QUALIFICATIONS, AND ADVANCEMENT

When learning the carpentry trade, many workers sign on as helpers to experienced carpenters, picking up techniques and best practices on the job. Some start working as carpenters while in high school or community college and supplement that work with classes in English and Spanish, geometry, physics, mechanical drawing, and other construction-related disciplines during the school year. On the job, carpenters learn to follow blueprints and select, lay out, cut, and assemble materials. They also learn techniques for installing windows, doors, trim, and fixtures in new and existing structures. Most importantly, they learn how their work affects the work done by the many other tradespeople involved in a construction project.

For those who want more formal training, apprenticeships are an option. Apprenticeship programs generally last four years and train apprentices in all aspects of carpentry, from framing and concrete formwork to reading blueprints and using layout instruments. In addition to class work, some of which may be counted toward an associate's degree, the apprentices work alongside experienced carpenters on construction projects so that when they complete the program they are prepared for a position in the field.

Some programs offer green construction–specific classes. For example, a program through the Carpenters International Training Fund teaches everything from using salvaged, recycled, and energy-efficient materials to implementing environmentally friendly construction practices. The Energy & Environmental Building Alliance also runs a "Houses That Work" training program that travels throughout the United States and Canada. The local sessions adapt green building practices to the climate in which the carpenter and other attendees work. The workshops focus on a range of practices that affect the work of carpenters, including ventilation, indoor air quality, air sealing, siding and window replacement, and green remodeling techniques.

Such formal training leads to certifications, which, although not necessary for a carpentry job, can help show the carpenter's knowledge and lead to contracts and advancement. Many carpenters use this advancement to become supervisors and then general contractors, using their whole-site knowledge of building to lead projects. Others focus more on their woodworking skills to specialize in cabinetry or furniture building. Some work for large construction firms as construction managers, whereas others start their own business in residential or commercial construction.

To advance to many of these positions, carpenters need to be comfortable communicating with clients, suppliers, and other construction workers. They need to be able to estimate materials, timeframes, and project costs and then ensure these estimates are adhered to as the work is completed. Physical strength and stamina are always important.

JOB OUTLOOK

National and local economies significantly affect the growth rate of the construction industry. States that are hit particularly hard by a downturn or upswing in the real estate market also tend to see the largest decreases or increases in employment for construction workers. From May 2004 to May 2010, the states with the greatest percentage of construction job losses, including construction carpenters and carpenter helpers, were Nevada, Arizona, Florida, and California, according to the U.S. Department of Labor. Interestingly, these were also among some of the states with the highest increase in mean wages for construction workers.

Looking ahead, many agencies are optimistic about a resurgence in construction jobs in their state. The *Occupational Outlook Quarterly* predicts average growth through 2018, particularly for those who complete an apprenticeship. The California Economic Development Department expects 25,700 new carpenter jobs within the state by 2016. The desire for energy-efficient homes and workspaces should fuel remodels throughout the country, and carpenters experienced with green building techniques are in increasing demand for new construction.

EARNINGS

Carpenters generally earn an hourly wage; US$21.10 is the national mean wage reported by the U.S. Department of Labor, or US$43,890 per year. On the low end of the scale, some workers may have an annual wage of no more than US$24,650. Those mainly in nonresidential construction tend to earn nearly 18 percent more than those on residential projects as of May 2010. A few make more than US$71,660 per year, but these people are rarely working in residential or nonresidential construction. Rather, they are employed by utility, motion picture, and oil companies, among other specialties.

RELATED OCCUPATIONS

Carpenters often take on tasks done by other construction workers, such as the following:

- Cement masons and concrete finishers
- Construction equipment operators
- Electricians
- Plumbers
- Pipefitters and steamfitters
- Rough carpenters

SOURCES OF ADDITIONAL INFORMATION

Carpenters International Training Fund. https://www.carpenters.org

Energy & Environmental Building Alliance. http://www.eeba.org

Partnership for Advancing Technology in Housing. http://www.pathnet.org

United Brotherhood of Carpenters and Joiners of America. http://www.carpenters.org

FURTHER READING

Bureau of Labor Statistics, U.S. Department of Labor. "The 2008–18 Job Outlook in Brief." In *Occupational Outlook Quarterly,* Spring 2010. Accessed February 16, 2012. http://www.bls.gov/opub/ooq/2010/spring/home.htm.

———. "47-2031 Carpenters." In *Occupational Employment Statistics: Occupational Employment and Wages, May 2010,* last modified May 17, 2011. Accessed February 16, 2012. http://www.bls.gov/oes/current/oes472031.htm.

———. "Carpenters." In *Occupational Outlook Handbook, 2010–11 Edition.* Accessed February 16, 2012. http://www.bls.gov/oco/ocos202.htm.

Carpenters Training Committee for Northern California. *FAQ's Apprenticeship.* Accessed February 7, 2012. http://www.ctcnc.org/Home.aspx/Page/7#faq.

College of Design, Construction, and Planning, University of Florida. *Optimum Value Engineering,* copyright 2008. Accessed February 16, 2012. http://web.dcp.ufl.edu/stroh/ValueEngineering.pdf.

Energy & Environmental Building Alliance. *About Houses That Work*. Accessed February 16, 2012. http://www.eeba.org/housesthatwork/about.htm.

Environmental Defense Fund. *California Green Jobs Guidebook*. Accessed January 16, 2012. http:// www.edf.org/climate/california-green-jobs-guidebook.

National Association of Home Builders Research Center. *ToolBase TechSpecs: Advanced Framing Techniques*. Accessed February 16, 2012. http://www.toolbase .org/pdf/techinv/oveadvancedframingtechniques_ techspec.pdf.

CEMENT MASONS AND CONCRETE FINISHERS

NATURE OF THE WORK

Cement masons and concrete finishers work with the same material: concrete. Cement is the powdery binding material; adding gravel, sand, and water creates concrete. Concrete is the most widely used construction material and is found throughout a construction project. Structural beams, retaining wall panels, floors, and walkways all can be made of concrete. It is also used to build everything from dams to roads to lighthouses.

Cement masons and concrete finishers work on all of these projects, but some jobs have distinct titles, particularly when creating outdoor surfaces. Segmental pavers install pavement, usually made of concrete or brick, for everything from patios to parking lots. Terrazzo workers and finishers do the same work as cement masons initially but then add more material to create attractive surfaces of colorful aggregate chips. Step finishers specialize in the final stages of concrete stairways.

Concrete's popularity stems from its availability and low cost. Although the core materials used to make concrete are abundant and the product itself can be recycled for other uses, such as into the gravel base of roadways, the Portland cement ingredient is not "green." Concrete is costly in terms of the energy used and the carbon dioxide released in Portland cement production. "In other words, we should use as much concrete, but with as little Portland cement as possible," wrote Columbia University Professor Christian Meyer in a paper presented at the 2005 International Conference on Construction Materials. Some manufacturers add industrial byproducts to the mix, such as fly ash or condensed silica fume, instead of cement powder, and some contractors and cement masons

AT A GLANCE FACT BOX

SOC: 47-2051.00
Preferred Education: High school diploma or GED
Average Salary: US$23,100 to US$63,400 annually
Other Information: Cement masons are increasingly hired to work on buildings created from insulated concrete forms, which can save up to 20 percent in heating and cooling costs over wood-framed structures

use recycled concrete debris, glass, or carpeting in concrete mixes for construction projects.

The use of concrete in a construction site is also evolving as the industry emphasizes greener practices. Insulated concrete forms (ICFs), which are typically interlocking concrete walls enclosed in insulative panels, can replace exterior walls and help achieve the airtight envelope desirable in green structures. Recent research from the Massachusetts Institute of Technology (MIT) found ICF homes save up to 20 percent in operational costs compared with traditional wood-framed homes. MIT researchers also reported that using concrete instead of steel in commercial buildings can help reduce annual energy costs by 5 to 6 percent, a rate expected to increase if radiant floor systems and other energy-efficient features are also installed.

Pervious concrete is another innovation arising from sustainable building practices. This highly porous concrete allows water to pass through it, reducing the runoff common with traditional concrete surfaces. Storm water can reach the water table, and the surface is less prone to the ice and standing water that typically build up after snow and rain. Such porous surfaces use a special concrete mix or permeable pavers made of clay or other materials. This practice is proving cost effective for large-scale projects. For example, New Albany, Ohio, replaced a street with permeable pavers instead of conventional asphalt when city planners determined that installing and maintaining either system would cost nearly the same.

Cement masons usually do the bulk of the concrete work in residential or nonresidential construction. They first work as designers, laying out the forms to hold wet concrete in place until it sets. On large projects, they next become supervisors, overseeing the chute man pouring concrete from a mixing truck and construction laborers spreading the material, or take on these tasks themselves for smaller projects. Then they level and smooth the surface and edges of the concrete to prevent chipping.

Cement masons may also do finishing work, or concrete finishers may step in. Concrete finishers set joints into the concrete to prevent cracks in unwanted places, resmooth and wash the surface, and create the desired texture, color, or other finish.

Although the general process is the same regardless of the structure being created, every pour is different because of numerous natural factors. Concrete setup time is affected by temperature, wind, and moisture. This is where the expertise of a cement mason shows most clearly. The difference between concrete work done by a knowledgeable mason and that done by an inexperienced one can be visible to even the untrained eye and in some cases can be the difference between whether a structure stands or falls.

The knowledge of how to create the best results in the given environmental conditions must be accompanied by an understanding of how the tools of the trade can aid that goal. The toolbox of a cement mason contains many traditional implements that have long been used to work with concrete: straightedges, bull floats, edgers, groovers, and trowels. New technologies, however, are coming into play. For example, Blastcrete Equipment makes a skid steer attachment that can pump concrete, grout, and other materials using a hydraulic system. The tool's rubber delivery line that can pump material up to 50 vertical feet is particularly useful for ICFs and other forms. Powerful, next-generation pump trucks, hydraulic cutters, and electromagnetic concrete testing equipment are among the tools recently released on the market that can save masons and contractors time and money on the job site.

WORKING CONDITIONS

Cement masons and concrete finishers are typically contract workers, so they may spend a few days on one project and the rest on another to fill out a work week. Although prep days can be relatively leisurely, pour days can be long and intense because the concrete must be finished before it fully sets. Both jobs require the worker to be in good physical shape and spend much time bending and kneeling.

Although concrete is increasingly used for interior surfaces such as floors and countertops, most masons and finishers work with this material outdoors. Schedules may shift because of wet weather or extreme temperatures. The job is messy and sturdy boots, kneepads, gloves, and clothing are required. There are, however, few hazards beyond those common for labor-intensive work. People in these jobs have a relatively low rate of fatalities, with just four fatal injuries in the United States in 2010 and none the prior year according to the U.S. Department of Labor. Most injuries in this field result from falling concrete blocks or are equipment-related.

EMPLOYMENT

As of May 2010, nearly 141,000 people in the United States were working as cement masons or concrete finishers according to the U.S. Department of Labor. Many are masonry contractors for commercial and residential construction, but some undertake public works projects, such as highways and bridges, and others are involved in manufacturing cement and concrete products. Many masons work in Texas and California. Places such as Hawaii, California, and Florida, where earthquakes and hurricanes are concerns for built environments, are increasingly hiring cement masons for ICF work on construction projects.

TRAINING, OTHER QUALIFICATIONS, AND ADVANCEMENT

Cement and concrete workers often start their construction careers as laborers, learning on the job how to work with concrete. They may then enter an apprenticeship program to formalize their training. On-site training and course work for such programs usually include learning how to place and level concrete, work with sealants, and deal with defects and repairs. In west Texas and New Mexico, a registered cement mason apprentice must be supervised on-site for 4,000 hours and spend classroom time at a community college or union-run school.

Specialized courses teach experienced cement masons and concrete finishers to work with the latest materials in green construction. The National Association of Home Builders and the Insulating Concrete Form Association both offer courses in ICF installation, and many manufacturers offer training to cement masons and other contractors who work with their products. Seminars are also available for installation of permeable pavers and pervious concrete. Certifications in such specializations or in more general skills are not necessary but can help concrete workers advance in the industry.

Those who have worked as masons or finishers may shift to operating concrete trucks or working as operating engineers and running other construction equipment. Some advance to become supervisors, construction managers, or building inspectors. Others, particularly those interested in green building, may leave the workforce temporarily to earn a bachelor's degree in a construction, architecture, or science discipline. Increasingly, hands-on opportunities for students to work on green building projects are being offered at universities such as North Carolina State. Its landscape architecture students have been designing and installing common areas on campus that manage stormwater runoff. The students plan and research the projects and then lay permeable pavers, plant rain gardens, and install other features.

For both entry-level and experienced concrete workers, reliability and teamwork skills are necessary. Physical strength is required for many tasks, and those good with numbers and at visualizing the intended results of their efforts often do well.

JOB OUTLOOK

Although job growth has been slow or in decline throughout the construction industry in recent years, some occupations not associated with building construction have not declined. From 2006 to 2010, highway maintenance workers saw the greatest employment increase among all construction occupations, a gain that helped masonry workers who specialize in transportation projects. The U.S. Department of Labor expects growth in jobs for cement masons and concrete finishers to be around average in the coming years and emphasizes that entry-level prospects are good in these jobs.

As construction on green buildings increases, those familiar with sustainable practices are increasingly in demand. Concrete workers experienced with ICF construction and pervious concrete installation may find their schedules filled by contractors and landscape architects working on sustainable projects.

EARNINGS

Cement masons and concrete finishers earn an average hourly wage of US$18.89 nationwide, or a mean annual wage of US$39,290 according to the most recent U.S. Department of Labor figures. For 10 percent of workers in this field, the annual wage is less than US$23,130. On the high end, workers may make more than US$63,400

each year. Hospital construction, mining projects, or public works projects are among those paying the most money to masons. The highest-paid masonry workers tend to live Alaska or Hawaii or in states with a high cost of living, such as New York, Illinois, or California.

RELATED OCCUPATIONS

Cement masons and concrete finishers may advance to become construction managers or inspectors. Other construction workers may use the same skills, such as the following:

• Insulation workers
• Operating engineers and other construction equipment operators
• Pipe fitters and steamfitters
• Rough carpenters

SOURCES OF ADDITIONAL INFORMATION

Insulating Concrete Form Association. http://www.forms.org

Mason Contractors Association of America. http://www.masoncontractors.org

National Association of Home Builders. http://www.nahb.org

National Concrete Masonry Association. http://www.ncma.org

FURTHER READING

Bureau of Labor Statistics, U.S. Department of Labor. "47-2051 Cement Masons and Concrete Finishers." In *Occupational Employment Statistics: Occupational Employment and Wages, May 2010,* last modified May 17, 2011. Accessed February 16, 2012. http://www.bls.gov/oes/current/oes472051.htm.

———. "All Worker Profile, 2003–2010." In *Census of Fatal Occupational Injuries.* Accessed February 6, 2012. http://www.bls.gov/iif/oshwc/cfoi/all_worker.pdf.

———. "Cement Masons, Concrete Finishers, Segmental Pavers, and Terrazzo Workers." In *Occupational Outlook Handbook, 2010–11 Edition.* Accessed February 13, 2012. http://www. bls.gov/oco/ocos204.htm.

Mason Contractors Association of America. "Permeable Pavers in Action: Using Permeable Pavers Goes Beyond Cost," November 16, 2011. Accessed February 20, 2012. http://www.masoncontractors.org/2011/11/16/permeable-pavers-in-action.

Meyer, Christian. "Concrete as a Green Building Material," invited lecture, in *Proceedings of the Third*

International Conference on Construction Materials, ConMat '05, Vancouver, British Columbia, August 22–25, 2005. Accessed February 20, 2012. http://www.civil.columbia.edu/meyer/publications/publications/87%20Concrete%20as%20a%20Green%20Building%20Material.pdf.

New Mexico Building & Construction Trades Council. *Operative Plasterers' and Cement Masons' International Local #254.* Accessed February 7, 2012. http://nmbctc.org/partners/pcm254.html.

Ochsendorf, John. "Life Cycle Assessment (LCA) of Buildings," Interim Report. Cambridge, Massachusetts: Concrete Sustainability Hub, Massachusetts Institute of Technology, December 2010. Accessed February 20, 2012. http://web.mit.edu/cshub/news/pdf/BuildingsLCAsummaryDec2010.pdf.

Ryals, James. "Students Build Landscape Legacy." *North Carolina State University,* September 15, 2011. Accessed February 20, 2012. http://www.ncsu.edu/features/2011/09/students-build-landscape-legacy.

CONSTRUCTION LABORERS

NATURE OF THE WORK

Construction laborers have one of the most diverse jobs on a construction site. Most are hired to assist contractors and subcontractors in different trades, meaning every jobsite and every person they work under can greatly affect their daily tasks. Just as they require little specialized training to begin a career in overall construction, construction laborers require little specialized training in green building because others usually determine the materials and practices to be used.

However, specialized training can be helpful and sometimes even crucial for advancement. Experienced laborers who can build on their jobsite training and who understand the entire process in which they are participating may find that their skills are desired even in a poor job market. Without specialized training, entry-level laborers are valued if they can adapt quickly to using unfamiliar materials and can follow green procedures such as reducing waste and recycling materials on the jobsite.

When it comes to green construction, the qualities that make a good laborer include the ability to follow directions, to work in a team or independently on a task, and to willingly learn to do things in new ways. Once a structure is enclosed and roofing, drywall, and other surface materials are in place, there are few opportunities to go back and fix earlier issues. This is particularly true with green buildings, which usually feature an airtight envelope that requires attention to detail when constructing to avoid the air loss common in other structures. Green construction employers prize laborers who ensure such details are not overlooked.

AT A GLANCE FACT BOX

SOC: 47-2061.00
Preferred Education: High school diploma or GED
Average Salary: Varies
Other Information: Construction laborer jobs can be competitive, particularly in certain regions with a large available labor force. Those who learn green building practices or trade-specific skills are most likely to find ongoing work.

Because their daily tasks are varied, work for construction laborers can range further afield from the standard commercial versus residential categories of many other workers in the construction industry. They may still be prepping a site, cleaning tools, or helping to break ground or raise a roof, but the final form of the project could be a house, a border patrol station, a wind farm, or a fitness facility.

Although most construction laborers are generalists, various job titles exist for their role. Some work with specific subcontractors and are referred to as helpers for carpenters, form builders, or plumbers, for example. Through their work, construction laborers may develop specialized skills that can prepare them for a journeyman job in a specific trade. Those certified as hazardous materials removal workers are considered a specialized subcategory of the construction laborer field.

WORKING CONDITIONS

Construction laborers often have the lowest stress levels on a jobsite, primarily because they are making fewer decisions and working more on tasks and goals assigned by managers or supervisors. Most work a set schedule, but when deadlines are tight or delays push a project off pace, they may need to work longer days or weeks. Almost all of their work is done on a jobsite, much of it outside of an office building and in a variety of weather. Construction laborers move into the built spaces as work requires, but until insulation, doorways, and windows are installed, they are working in an empty shell with few comforts. Dust, noise, and hazards such as uneven surfaces are all part of the job.

Construction laborers should be in good physical condition to avoid injury during lifting, carrying, or other tasks. Regardless of physical stamina and condition, however, injuries are still part of the job in the construction industry and for laborers in particular. The construction industry had more fatal injuries than any other in 2010, although the rate was down nearly 40 percent from 2006 according to the U.S. Department of Labor. Within that industry, construction laborers receive more fatal injuries than any other group. Most deaths are related to falling or being hit by construction equipment. The rate of nonfatal injuries from using tools on a site is also high. Those who follow safety protocols and remain aware of their surroundings while working are most likely to avoid injury.

EMPLOYMENT

More than 770,000 people in the United States work as construction laborers according to May 2010 statistics from the U.S. Department of Labor. It is the largest construction occupation in the United States. These laborers are hired for a range of projects, but most spend their time working on commercial buildings, followed by homes. Others work on highway, bridge, utility, or other heavy or civil engineering projects. Texas and California have the highest employment levels for construction laborers. Texas workers in general earn less than the mean national wage in the field. Many other construction laborers are found in New York, Illinois, and Florida.

TRAINING, OTHER QUALIFICATIONS, AND ADVANCEMENT

Construction laborers usually enter the workforce from high school, sometimes for the duration of their career in the construction industry and sometimes on their way to developing more specialized skills in a specific construction trade. Most of their construction skills are learned on the job, although a background that includes geometry, physics, welding, and vocational courses is helpful.

In addition to worksite training, courses and certifications are available to construction workers through sources such as the Laborers' International Union of North America (LIUNA) Training and Education Fund. The organization offers both general and green construction programs for the construction laborer and others looking to expand their work skills in the construction industry. Safety is a key component of the general course, with separate modules for preventing heat stress, back injury, and hearing damage. Safety when operating tools ranging from portable saws to sandblasters, as well as maintenance of these tools, is also emphasized.

The green construction program through LIUNA teaches some of the reasons environmentally friendly practices are used and how they affect the current and future work of construction laborers. It also teaches laborers about green rating systems, procedures, and energy sources that they may encounter on the job. Although no state mandates that workers at any level learn how to implement green building practices, such knowledge is increasingly in demand in the workforce.

As they learn more about their jobs, construction laborers may advance to lead a team of other workers or specialize in a particular aspect of a building project, particularly for large nonresidential buildings. Those who enjoy a leadership role may advance to become construction managers, particularly if they are willing to further their formal education. Those who prefer to work in a specific trade may decide to undertake an apprenticeship so that they can be licensed as an electrician, plumber, or other tradesperson. Some laborers with an interest in machines and mechanics focus on operating light equipment early in their careers so that they can advance to operating heavy equipment and work as operating engineers over time.

Whether starting in their career or preparing to advance it, construction workers must be versatile and able to switch tasks as needed throughout the course of their day. Those with the ability to listen closely to directions and then perform the required tasks without direct supervision are the most likely to succeed and advance in their jobs.

JOB OUTLOOK

Construction laborers have been hit particularly hard by economic woes in the latter part of the first decade of the 21st century. As budgets get tighter and fewer construction projects are available, contractors are often forced to work with smaller crews. Although those looking for rock-bottom savings may stack their team with construction laborers, many contractors and construction managers pass the tasks of those workers to skilled laborers who can integrate the tasks into their daily work without greatly lengthening the overall project schedule.

"The superintendents are putting their bags back on now. They are producing as well as managing, which is how we did it for years," said Len Ford, owner and president of Ford Construction in Montana, the fifth-highest state in terms of concentration of construction jobs, according to the U.S. Department of Labor. "In many ways, I think we all like it that way. When you're hands-on, it's really easy to make sure the outcomes are what you want them to be."

The U.S. Department of Labor found that from May 2006 to May 2010, helpers for various skilled construction workers constituted four of the seven construction jobs that had the largest percentage decrease in employment, sometimes more than 50 percent. For comparison, overall construction employment decreased by 25 percent during the same period. Some of the states that employ the most construction laborers, such as Florida and California, were among the hardest hit.

However, more recent estimates show that the industry may be turning around. The Associated General Contractors of America reported 21,000 new jobs were added in the construction industry in January 2012 and that, combined with job increases in the prior month, construction employment was at a two-year high. Although still far below its April 2006 peak and potentially more affected by an unseasonably mild winter in some regions than by sustained growth, association officials said the increase was "heartening" and that they found many contractors were expecting the market to rebound in 2013 or 2014.

In addition, the U.S. Department of Labor marks construction laborer jobs as one of the few in the field likely to see faster than average growth through 2018, mainly because of additional government spending on infrastructure. Laborers with expansive skill sets and experience in specialized areas and practices, including those related to green building, are likely to be in the greatest demand.

EARNINGS

Construction laborers are some of the lowest-paid workers in the construction industry, with a mean hourly wage of US$16.15, or US$33,590 per year, according to U.S. Department of Labor statistics. Some laborers make US$18,570 or less each year, but those in the highest-paid positions or who can find work year-round earn more than US$57,520 annually. In general, nonresidential construction pays slightly better than residential construction for laborers. Those earning better-than-average wages tend to work in specialized industries, such as natural gas, electrical, and coal mining and distribution. Hospitals also tend to be a source of well-paid projects for construction

laborers. Hawaii is the top-paying state for these workers, and wages in New Jersey, Alaska, New York, and Massachusetts are also high.

RELATED OCCUPATIONS

Construction laborers do physically demanding work, making their jobs similar to the following positions in other fields:

- Forest and conservation workers
- Freight, stock, and material movers
- Logging workers
- Structural metal fabricators and fitters

SOURCES OF ADDITIONAL INFORMATION

Laborers' International Union of North America Training and Education Fund. http://www .liunatraining.org

National Center for Construction Education and Research. http://www.nccer.org

FURTHER READING

Associated General Contractors of America. *The 2012 Construction Hiring and Business Outlook,* February 3, 2012. Accessed March 2, 2012. http://www.agc.org/ galleries/news/2012_Construction_Hiring_ and_Business_Outlook_%20Report.pdf.

Bureau of Labor Statistics, U.S. Department of Labor. "47-2061 Construction Laborers." In *Occupational Employment Statistics: Occupational Employment and Wages, May 2010,* last modified May 17, 2011. Accessed March 2, 2012. http://www.bls.gov/oes/ current/oes472061.htm.

———. "All Worker Profile, 2003–2010." In *Census of Fatal Occupational Injuries.* Accessed February 6, 2012. http://www.bls.gov/iif/oshwc/cfoi/all_worker .pdf.

———. *Census of Fatal Occupational Injuries Summary, 2010.* Accessed February 6, 2012. http://www.bls .gov/news.release/cfoi.nr0.htm.

Ford, Len (president and owner, Ford Construction) in discussion with the author, February 2012.

Laborers' International Union of North America Training and Education Fund. *Construction Course: General Construction.* Accessed February 6, 2012. http://www.liunatraining.org/education/curriculum/ construction/general.cfm.

Liming, Drew. *Careers in Green Construction.* Bureau of Labor Statistics, U.S. Department of Labor, June 2011. Accessed March 2, 2012. http://www.bls.gov/ green/construction/construction.pdf.

OPERATING ENGINEERS AND OTHER CONSTRUCTION EQUIPMENT OPERATORS

NATURE OF THE WORK

Construction equipment operators and operating engineers do the heavy lifting on a jobsite using a range of machinery. Stacks of steel beams, piles of earth, and other weighty objects need to be moved regularly on construction sites. Other equipment is used to dig trenches, backfill holes, and grade surfaces. The machines themselves are heavy and just moving them through the landscape can have devastating effects. Green building often involves not only using green materials and practices but also protecting the environment surrounding the structure, and equipment engineers and operators play an important role in ensuring such protection.

The generic name for the numerous categories of construction machines, "heavy equipment," speaks volumes about the damage that can be caused if they are not operated with care. Some jobsites border wetlands, animal habitats, and other environments that owners and builders are trying to preserve. Others require operators to follow strict protocols to avoid runoff into lakes and rivers or damage to easily eroded banks or shorelines.

In coming years, energy production is expected to increase in the United States, increasing opportunities for equipment operators, according to the U.S. Department of Labor. Although pipeline construction has made headlines recently, greener energy options also need people to operate construction equipment. Both smart power grid and wind farm construction are on the list of projects that rely on operating engineers and other construction equipment operators.

Operator jobs are often referred to by the type of machine being run. Paving or asphalt spreader operators are driving or running controls for equipment related to

---

AT A GLANCE FACT BOX

SOC: 47-2073.00
Preferred Education: Associate's degree or vocational certification
Average Salary: US$26,500 to US$71,300 annually
Other Information: More opportunities for construction equipment operators and operating engineers are expected through 2018, particularly in jobs related to energy production such as building wind farms and smart grids

---

road construction. Pile-driver operators drive steel or wood beams into the ground for building foundations or bridges. Crane operators lift heavy components such as I-beams or wind turbine blades from trucks and into place. Those referred to as general operating engineers or construction equipment operators often use a range of machines such as booms, excavators, hoists, loaders, and more. Pneumatic equipment on the jobsite may also be their responsibility. They may move trucks and trailers around and to a site, either for their own equipment or for other operators.

Drive and *lift* refer more to the actions of machines than of operators. Most construction equipment has a variety of valves, wheels, pedals, and other controls that operators use to make the machine perform. Computerized systems, joystick-style controls, and other technologies have become common.

Operating machinery is only one part of this job, however. Most engineers and operators are responsible for the equipment they use, and they must ensure it works when needed. The hydraulic systems and inboard computers on construction machines are complex, so operators are rarely responsible for making large repairs. Maintenance and minor repairs remain part of the job, however, particularly for those who own an operating company or their own equipment.

WORKING CONDITIONS

Few equipment operators and engineers have need for an office, although they may own or have access to a garage for maintenance work. Work conditions are rarely described as pleasant; machinery operation can be a dirty, noisy, and bone-rattling job. High winds, heavy rainfall, and freezing temperatures are not suitable conditions for certain types of equipment and the heavy loads they are shifting. Such conditions can push back a construction schedule and require equipment operators to work long hours or weekends to get the project back on track. Remote jobsites can also require workers to spend long days at work or even move nearby for the project's duration. Some large projects run around the clock, with equipment operators and others working after dark under light towers.

In an industry known for having a number of injuries and fatalities, construction equipment operators have a relatively high rate of injury. Protective gear is necessary for equipment operators, and great care must be taken to ensure the operators' and other workers' safety when machines are running. The Occupational Safety and Health Administration (OSHA) sets standards for powered industrial truck operation that employers must use to develop safety training plans. They must certify that employees are trained and operators must undergo reevaluation every three years.

EMPLOYMENT

Equipment operators comprise a large portion of construction workers, nearly 335,000 in May 2010 according to the U.S. Department of Labor. Most of these subcontractors are hired by contractors for a specific project. Many are employed, directly or indirectly, by local governments, operating everything from city street cleaners to snowplows. Others operate equipment for government-funded construction projects, such as streets and bridges, or for private quarrying and mining operations. Large numbers are based out of Texas, California, and Pennsylvania, although equipment operators in California tend to earn far more than those in either Pennsylvania or Texas.

TRAINING, OTHER QUALIFICATIONS, AND ADVANCEMENT

Most people who learn to operate construction equipment do so on the job, running a specific piece of equipment and learning how the machine can be useful to the project. Some may start as construction laborers who operate lighter equipment to prove their ability to work safely with heavy equipment. Others have experience driving large vehicles or operating industrial machines before they join a construction team.

In addition to on-the-job training, formal programs are offered for equipment operators. The Laborers' International Union of North America Training and Education Fund is one such organization. Its safe operation and maintenance course for rough terrain forklift work is designed for construction laborers and meets OSHA requirements, according to the organization's website. The International Union of Operating Engineers also offers training in the form of apprenticeships that typically last three years. Such hands-on training is often viewed as more valuable than training through classroom studies and simulated machine usage, which is done at some vocational schools. In either case, formal training is rarely tied to general education, although many contractors require their equipment operators to have a high school diploma or equivalent. Mechanical training or experience may give an entry-level operator an edge over other job applicants.

Equipment operators often advance to larger roles and more specific tasks or to a supervisory position as they build up work experience. They may choose to specialize in a type of construction or work for a large company or government agency running a particular piece of machinery. Some focus on maintaining and repairing equipment whereas others choose to move into a construction trade or field related to operating machinery. Still others start their own equipment business or train other operating engineers and equipment operators.

Although there are no general licensing requirements for operating heavy equipment or for working on green building projects, some specific equipment such as cranes typically require the operator to be certified in their use. In addition, many construction equipment operators must move their machines to and from the jobsite and need a state commercial driver's license (CDL) to do so. The Associated Training Services Network noted in December 2011 that employers are increasingly seeking heavy equipment operators with a CDL.

Although many equipment operators spend their time behind the controls of a large machine rather than doing the manual lifting of construction laborers, it is still important to be in good physical shape when taking on this role. Good vision, hand-eye coordination, and balance are also important, as is comfort with heights or small spaces. People who excel in this job are generally mechanically inclined and enjoy finding out how things work.

JOB OUTLOOK

Construction occupations have seen cutbacks in recent years because of a struggling U.S. economy. Although every other U.S. state saw a drop in construction employment numbers from May 2004 to May 2010, oil field development spurred employment growth in the industry in North Dakota and Wyoming. Operating engineers and other construction equipment operators comprised one of the groups affected by this growth in Wyoming, which saw an overall construction employment increase of more than 10 percent and a wage increase of more than 18 percent. The U.S. State Department estimates that if the Keystone XL Pipeline project through the central United States goes ahead, 6,000 construction jobs would be created, although other sources have pegged that number at 13,000 to 20,000 jobs in construction and manufacturing.

Green jobs are opening up in other areas of the United States as well. For example, in southern Wyoming, landowners are working to create wind associations and have set aside 2 million acres for wind farms, according to an article in *The Christian Science Monitor.* Such farms need local equipment operators to build access roads and operate cranes that lift turbine components into place. In addition, the Associated Training Services Network reported many overseas opportunities for heavy equipment operators such as jobs building infrastructure in developing countries. In addition, U.S. military installations often need operating engineers. Such work may require additional training and often places operators in remote or even hostile areas, so it should not be undertaken lightly.

EARNINGS

Construction equipment operators earn an average hourly wage of US$21.55, or US$44,830 annually, according to the U.S. Department of Labor. Pile-driver operators, a small subgroup of about 4,200 workers as of May 2010, tend to make more than the overall equipment operator average, around US$25.00 per hour. The overall equipment operator wage bracket ranges from less than US$26,460 to more than US$71,310 per year. Although hourly wages are relatively high compared with those for other construction jobs, weather tends to have a greater effect on the work performed by construction equipment operators, resulting in fewer worked days per year than in other construction trades.

Those earning the highest wages tend to work directly for large private companies, including hospitals, power companies, and those operating oil pipelines. High wages are common in Hawaii, California, New York, and Alaska. The greater Bay Area of San Francisco, San Mateo, and Redwood City in California, which had the highest mean wage for construction workers in May 2010, saw equipment operators earning at least 55 percent more than the national average. However, construction employment numbers in that area were below the U.S. average.

RELATED OCCUPATIONS

People who operate construction equipment typically use skills found in jobs that work with other machinery, including the following:

- Bus and truck mechanics and diesel engine specialists
- Heavy and tractor-trailer truck drivers
- Industrial machinery mechanics
- Industrial truck and tractor operators
- Rail-track laying and maintenance equipment operators

SOURCES OF ADDITIONAL INFORMATION

Associated Training Services Network. http://www.heavyequipmentschool.com
International Union of Operating Engineers. http://www.iuoe.org
Laborers' International Union of North America Training and Education Fund. http://www.liunatraining.org
National Center for Construction Education and Research. http://www.nccer.org
Pile Driving Contractors Association. http://www.piledrivers.org

FURTHER READING

Associated Training Services Network. *Posts Tagged "Commercial Drivers License."* Accessed February 10, 2012. http://www.heavyequipmentschool.com/?tag=commercial-drivers-license.
Banerjee, Neela, and Christi Parsons. "Obama Administration to Deny Keystone XL Oil Pipeline Permit." *Los Angeles Times,* January 18, 2012. Accessed February 6, 2012. http://articles.latimes.com/2012/jan/18/news/la-pn-obama-administration-to-reject-keystone-xl-pipeline-20120118.
Bureau of Labor Statistics, U.S. Department of Labor. "47-2073 Operating Engineers and Other Construction Equipment Operators." In *Occupational Employment Statistics: Occupational Employment and Wages, May 2010,* last modified May 17, 2011. Accessed February 16, 2012. http://www.bls.gov/oes/current/oes472073.htm.
———. "Construction Equipment Operators." In *Occupational Outlook Handbook, 2010-11 Edition.* Accessed February 10, 2012. http://www.bls.gov/oco/ocos255.htm.
FreeOSHAInfo.com. *Frequently Asked Questions about Powered Industrial Truck Operator Training.* Accessed February 10, 2012. http://www.freeoshainfo.com/

pubpages/Files/Forklift%20%20PIT/FAQAbout
ForkliftTraining.pdf.

Handy, Stephen G. "Why We Need the Keystone XL
Pipeline." *Standard-Examiner,* January 24, 2012.
Accessed February 16, 2012. http://www.standard
.net/stories/2012/01/24/why-we-need-keystone-
xl-pipeline.

Laborers' International Union of North America
Training and Education Fund. *Construction Course:*

*Rough Terrain Forklift: Safe Operation and
Maintenance.* Accessed February 6, 2012. http://
www.liunatraining.org/education/curriculum/
construction/roughTerrain_SafeOperation.cfm.

Vance, Erik. "Wind Power: Clean Energy, Dirty
Business?" *Christian Science Monitor,* January 26,
2012. Accessed March 28, 2012. http://www
.csmonitor.com/Environment/2012/0126/
Wind-power-Clean-energy-dirty-business.

ELECTRICIANS

NATURE OF THE WORK

The work done by electricians is "wired" to energy-efficient construction. They install and maintain the energy systems of buildings, which can run from a variety of green technologies such as solar panels on a residential home to smart grids at power plants. Electricians must be knowledgeable about these technologies and about changes in building codes, practices, and usage that affect how energy is brought into and consumed in homes, offices, and other spaces.

The United States used 20 percent of the world's energy in 2008, which was more than any other country in the world according to statistics from the U.S. Department of Energy. Buildings accounted for almost 40 percent of the U.S. share, more than industry or transportation. Sustainable building practices that emphasize energy efficiency can affect these numbers, but a building is only as efficient as its occupants. Consider a post-occupancy audit of a green office building in Portland, Oregon. Although the structure met expectations set during initial construction, solar panel energy savings were mostly wiped out by a coffee kiosk, walk-in freezer, and other features added later according to an October 2011 article in *Oregon Business* magazine. Thermostats set at higher-than-average temperatures also cut into energy savings.

"The real frontier for driving energy use down is in operations and behavior of occupants," Tom White of consulting firm Green Building Services told the magazine. He noted that such behaviors and operations of electrical devices such as computers, cell phones, and other devices plugged into a building's energy system can influence up to one-quarter of a building's energy use. At

AT A GLANCE FACT BOX

SOC: 47-2111.00
Preferred Education: Associate's degree or vocational certification
Average Salary: US$29,400 to US$80,890 annually
Other Information: The United States accounts for 20 percent of the world's energy consumption and more than one-third of this consumption relates to buildings, whose energy systems are installed by electricians

some large corporations such as Microsoft, this plug load can account for nearly as much energy as a building's base load.

Electricians are fundamental to this focus on changing occupant behaviors because their work can give building owners more control over how occupants use spaces. They can install programmable thermostats, timers, smart power strips, and occupancy and motion sensors that adjust temperatures, shut down devices, and turn off lights when a room is empty or an appliance is not in use. They can also install submeter systems, which measure and analyze energy consumption to pinpoint inefficiencies. Such metering technology and even more technologically advanced "smart" buildings can lead to significant savings in both energy and operating costs. For example, a case study of the Microsoft campus in Redmond, Washington, used automated fault detection to find a leaking chilled water valve that would have cost nearly US$11,300 in annual wasted energy. A San Jose, California, school that installed submetering technology and software learned its gym's air conditioners ran all night. Changing this practice led to a 250 percent return on investment.

It may be some time before such installations make up the bulk of the workload for electricians, but all of the skills and knowledge they use today will remain useful. Electricians use drawings and related information to determine where circuits, outlets, and other equipment should be placed and where malfunctioning equipment is located. They then assemble and install an electrical conduit, pull wires through it, splice and tape the wires, and connect them to controls and fixtures. Their work is mainly invisible to a building's occupants once the job is finished, hidden by walls, ceilings, and floors, but without it nothing would run.

Although many materials used by electricians are small and inexpensive, the volume of materials needed in a building adds up. Copper wiring in particular is expensive, so electricians work to minimize waste when installing wire. Their primary focus, however, is not on materials conservation but on safety. Improperly installed wiring can be at a minimum hazardous and at worst disastrous. Electricians must be up-to-date on current building codes and test all of their installations and repairs to ensure the equipment and system are not faulty.

Electricians work on all types of buildings but may specialize in residential or nonresidential structures or in construction or maintenance. They also work on automated and robotic factory systems, transportation networks, wind turbines, and a range of other complex systems. Some install and repair electrical power lines. Others connect solar panels to a building's energy system and are trained as solar photovoltaic installers.

WORKING CONDITIONS

The working environment of electricians varies widely. On one project they may be outdoors, on another indoors. The next project may put them high in the air, the following one in a subbasement. On some days they may be in all of these locations. Most have set hours, but they may also work weekends or evenings when meeting a construction project deadline or making emergency repairs. Those employed by energy-generating companies may be on one shift of a 24-hour schedule.

Stress in this line of work tends to be rare, but hazards are not. Electricians must be careful to avoid injuries from live wires. Shocks, burns, cuts, falls, and other injuries can occur if safety procedures are not followed. According to the U.S. Department of Labor, electricians have the third-highest rate of fatalities of all construction trades, mainly resulting from electrocution.

EMPLOYMENT

"Electrician" is considered the largest high-paying construction occupation. More than half a million people were employed as electricians in the United States as of May 2010 reported the U.S. Department of Labor. The vast majority work as electrical contractors, but a few are employed by local governments, electrical power companies, ship builders, or mining companies. California and Texas tend to have the most jobs for electricians, followed by New York, Florida, and Illinois. But with the economic downturn in the United States that began in 2008, only the oil-boom states of North Dakota and Wyoming had an increase in construction employment from May 2006 to May 2010. Electricians were found to have contributed to this increase in Wyoming in particular.

Green job opportunities are on the horizon for electricians. Across the country, electricians and other electrical workers are installing solar farms for football stadiums and other energy-draining facilities, electric vehicle charging stations for the newest generation of cars, and wind turbines to generate energy. In the future, a multibillion U.S. dollar investment in smart-grid technology is expected to create thousands of new jobs in Illinois.

TRAINING, OTHER QUALIFICATIONS, AND ADVANCEMENT

Many electricians begin their careers and undergo initial training at the same time through a paid apprenticeship program such as the joint program of the National Electrical Contractors Association and International Brotherhood of Electrical Workers. This program offers four specialty areas (outside lineman, installer technician, inside wireman, and residential wireman) and lasts three to five years, depending on the specialty. Programs are run through training centers throughout the country and give apprentices the option of earning 17 to 60 semester credit hours, depending on the program. Because many electricians enter a program directly from high school, such credits can be helpful in future efforts toward a degree and advancement in the field.

Internship programs combine classroom work with on-the-job training, during which apprentices are paid a portion of a professional electrician wage. While in the classroom, trainees study math, mechanical drawing, electrical theory, building codes, and safety practices. On the job, they learn how to install circuit panels, cables, conduit, and switches and then test their installations.

Most states require electricians to be licensed. Licensing requirements usually call for several years of work experience, a passing score on an exam, and proven knowledge of electrical codes, although requirements vary by state. Master electrician licenses, which some states require for electrical contractors, are typically only issued after the electrician has earned an electrical engineering degree or worked in the trade for seven years. Those working for government agencies and on public works projects may need to obtain a special license. Regardless of the type of license or certification they hold, electricians must continue to learn about updates to electrical codes throughout their careers.

The first level of advancement for licensed electricians is usually to supervisor. Some become project managers, construction managers, or site superintendents for construction projects. Others work as inspectors focused on electrical systems or broaden their knowledge to become building inspectors or energy performance testers. Some obtain an electrical contractor's license and start their own business.

Electrical work is physical, although not usually too strenuous. Good eyesight, hand–eye coordination, and dexterity are important, as is the ability to work in cramped spaces and at heights. Supervisors, managers, or business owners need skills in estimating costs, setting budgets and schedules, and working with a range of other people. Those who speak both English and Spanish have an advantage in such leadership opportunities.

JOB OUTLOOK

Although the construction industry as a whole has struggled recently, population growth and the need for electrical system upgrades are expected to keep job growth steady for electricians in coming years. Energy from natural sources such as the wind, sun, or ground are influencing and changing the systems installed and maintained by electricians, so learning about these energy sources and the ways they affect electrical installations is important. Those with skills related to welding, plumbing, electronics, and computers will also be in higher demand as more buildings install integrated energy systems. Much of an electrician's future work will involve upgrading existing buildings to meet new codes and standards, particularly until the United States' economy and housing market rebound.

EARNINGS

Electricians generally earn a mean hourly wage of US$24.91 or mean annual wage of US$51,810 according to the Department of Labor. As of May 2010, the bottom 10 percent of electricians earned less than US$29,400 (the top 10 percent made more than US$80,090 annually). Those at the low end of the bracket are typically apprentices on their first jobs receiving US$9 to US$14 per hour, but those wages rise steadily throughout the apprenticeship and generally jump upon completion of the program.

Those working in the natural gas industry tend to be among the highest paid in their field, particularly in Alaska. Electricians for companies that generate, transmit, or distribute power are also highly paid, as are those employed by local government agencies. Illinois, Hawaii, New York, and New Jersey are also among the top-paying states for electricians, with the greater Chicago, Illinois area; Honolulu, Hawaii; New York, New York; and Newark, New Jersey, among the highest-paying metropolitan areas.

RELATED OCCUPATIONS

Other jobs use skills and knowledge required for electrical work, such as the following:

- Electrical and electronic equipment assemblers
- Electrical and electronics repairers
- Electrical, electronics, and electromechanical engineering technicians
- Electrical, electronics, and electromechanical engineering technologists
- Electrical powerline installers and repairers
- Heating and air conditioning mechanics and installers
- Refrigeration mechanics and installers
- Solar photovoltaic installers
- Solar energy installation managers
- Solar thermal installers and technicians

SOURCES OF ADDITIONAL INFORMATION

Home Builders Institute. http://www.hbi.org

Independent Electrical Contractors, Inc. http://www.ieci.org

International Brotherhood of Electrical Workers. http://www.ibew.org

National Electrical Contractors Association. http://www.necanet.org

National Joint Apprenticeship and Training Committee. http://www.njatc.org

FURTHER READING

Accenture. *Energy-Smart Buildings: Demonstrating How Information Technology Can Cut Energy Use and Costs of Real Estate Portfolios.* October 6, 2011. Accessed February 16, 2012. http://www.greenbiz.com/sites/default/files/energy-smart-buildings-whitepaper.pdf.

Baker, Linda. "Are Green Buildings Really Saving Energy?" *Oregon Business,* October 2011. Accessed February 16, 2012. http://www.oregonbusiness.com/articles/104-october-2011/5928-are-green-buildings-really-saving-energy.

Bureau of Labor Statistics, U.S. Department of Labor. "47-2111 Electricians." In *Occupational Employment Statistics: Occupational Employment and Wages, May 2010,* last modified May 17, 2011. Accessed February 16, 2012. http://www.bls.gov/oes/current/oes472111.htm.

———. "Electricians." *In Occupational Outlook Handbook, 2010-11 Edition.* Accessed February 17, 2012. http://www.bls.gov/oco/ocos206.htm.

———. *Safety and Health: Dangerous Jobs.* Accessed February 7, 2012. http://www.bls.gov/iif/oshwc/cfar0020.pdf.

National Joint Apprenticeship and Training Committee. *Apprenticeship Training.* Accessed February 7, 2012. http://www.njatc.org/training/apprenticeship/index.aspx.

Sinai, Nick. "Smart Buildings = Better Buildings." The White House Office of Science and Technology Policy, November 4, 2011. Accessed February 16, 2012. http://www.whitehouse.gov/blog/2011/11/04/smart-buildings-better-buildings.

U.S. Department of Energy. "Buildings Sector." In *2010 Buildings Energy Date Book,* last modified March 2011. Accessed February 16, 2012. http://buildingsdatabook.eren.doe.gov/Chapter Intro1.aspx.

PIPE FITTERS AND STEAMFITTERS

NATURE OF THE WORK

Pipes find their way into many parts of a structure. They bring water or natural gas in and drain gray water and waste out. They can also be used to irrigate the surrounding landscape or channel water away from the foundation. Different types of pipes are used for each purpose, and pipes are made from a variety of materials that work best with their intended use.

Just like there are many types of pipes, there are many jobs related to working with them. Pipe fitters and steamfitters are among the more specialized occupations within a group that also includes plumbers, sprinkler fitters, and pipe layers. Unlike plumbers, who often work alone on residential or commercial buildings, pipe fitters usually work in teams. They work with large pipes on large projects such as piping systems for oil refineries, municipal water and sewer systems, or natural gas pipelines. Steamfitters generally work with pipes that are used to move high-pressure gases or liquids for refrigeration or ventilation systems. Some may specialize in heating, ventilation, and air conditioning (HVAC) systems and work as HVAC mechanics and installers. These jobs are seeing strong growth because of the need for mechanical ventilation systems in energy-efficient, sustainable buildings. Regardless of the job title, basic training for most jobs related to plumbing, pipe fitting, and steam fitting is usually similar.

Pipe fitters and steamfitters are experts in the materials they use. They are involved in all aspects of pipe system construction from laying out the system using blueprints and computer models to assembling and installing the network of pipes, supports and hangers, pumps, timers, controls, and other equipment that make the system

work. They may use a variety of scheduling and drafting software to plan and design their projects. These computer-based tools help to ensure that the system works within the framework of a building so that it doesn't intrude with structural walls, interfere with other building components such as electrical systems, or decrease the insulation and airtight qualities of the building. In addition to working as installers, pipe fitters and steamfitters maintain and repair piping systems.

Green construction and green energy generation have increased the need for pipe fitters and steamfitters in many industries. For example, some cities and counties require a licensed steamfitter to install geothermal boilers and heating systems for residential and commercial buildings. Biomass boilers and stoves are often installed by pipe fitters who are trained to work with such equipment. Both pipe fitters and steamfitters are becoming involved in the construction and operation of geothermal, ethanol, and biomass power plants as cleaner energy sources are sought worldwide. Such plants have large and complex piping systems. The typical ethanol plant can require up to 95,000 linear feet, or nearly 18 miles, of piping that is welded, threaded, flanged, or coupled together by steamfitters and pipe fitters according to a 2008 article in *Ethanol Producer Magazine*.

WORKING CONDITIONS

Pipe fitters and steamfitters tend to work in industrial settings, unlike the more residential or commercial projects typically undertaken by plumbers. When working on construction projects, they may have a set schedule but may work long hours to ensure their portion of the project is completed according to the overall construction timeline. However, construction jobs tend to be temporary and people in these fields often find additional work in the repair and maintenance of piping systems. When focused on repair work, pipe fitters and steamfitters may work regular hours as they test and monitor piping systems but may be on call at night or on weekends in case of emergencies.

Depending on the setting, pipe fitters and steamfitters may work many feet off the ground, and the contents of pipes can be highly toxic, flammable, or explosive. These conditions can lead to deadly accidents, as can incidents related to jobsite vehicles or equipment, such as manlifts, devices that have an endless belt that moves in one direction only with steps or handholds used to move people from one floor to another. Although injury and fatality rates for these workers are lower than those in many other construction trades, since 2008 they have been about three times higher than those for pipelayers, who typically work with pipes that are not in use and thus have less contact with their contents, according to the U.S. Department of Labor.

EMPLOYMENT

The U.S. Department of Labor's Bureau of Labor Statistics (BLS) reports employment numbers for pipe fitters and steamfitters combined with those for plumbers. It estimates nearly 359,000 people hold one of these three positions. This trio of jobs, therefore, is the fifth largest construction occupation in the United States. The top five U.S. states that have the most jobs for people who work with piping are California, Texas, New York, Florida, and Illinois. Pipe fitters and steamfitters tend to work on utility system construction and may also be hired for natural gas, shipbuilding, or water and sewage projects. One of the main construction areas for pipe fitters is related to pipes for natural gas, where they typically make up 6 percent of the construction workforce on a pipeline project according to a report by the Argonne National Laboratory.

TRAINING, OTHER QUALIFICATIONS, AND ADVANCEMENT

A high school diploma is required by most apprenticeship programs and contractors who train and employ people who work with piping systems. Some pipe fitters and steamfitters choose to earn an associate's degree or graduate from a vocational program before entering the field, although this is not required by most employers. Courses related to construction and welding, drafting, business, chemistry and physics, and math can all give useful background knowledge to workers in this trade.

Rather than college or vocational programs, some pipe fitters and steamfitters choose to move directly into a state-approved apprenticeship after graduation from high school. Such programs are typically run by a local union branch and onsite training with local companies often leads directly to a job. In California, the U.S. state with the highest rate of employment in this field, an apprentice industrial plumber pipe fitter earns 35 percent of the journeyman's wage during the five years spent completing the program, according to the state's Department of Industrial Relations. The U.S. military also offers training in these trades through programs that are viewed highly by civilian contractors and companies.

Apprentices typically learn basic skills applicable to all types of jobs that involve working with piping systems before training to work in industrial settings as pipe fitters and steamfitters. Some apprenticeship programs are being revamped to train these tradespeople in skills that relate to sustainable building and green construction projects not only in the United States but in other countries as well. In Wisconsin, the apprenticeship curriculum for steamfitters is being revised to include courses on green technologies and energy management systems. In Ontario, Canada, a course on biofuels and biomaterials is being created as part of the steamfitters' apprenticeship program in that province.

Many states require pipe fitters and steamfitters to be licensed before they can work independently in the field. Work experience and an exam are typical prerequisites for licensing, although the requirements vary. Some states require special licenses for pipe fitters who work on gas lines.

Those who complete apprenticeship programs with a focus on green construction may find themselves well-placed for future advancement. Steamfitter and pipe fitter apprentices who go on to work on biomass projects may find job opportunities with biofuel and ethanol production companies, working to install, develop, or even manage the latest biofuel systems. They may also work as managers or inspectors for green building projects.

Although some pipe fitters work alone, most work as part of a crew to move and install pipes that are too large for one person to handle. The ability to work both independently and on a team is important in this job, and people who can speak both English and Spanish are in demand for teams in some areas, particularly in supervisory roles. Pipe fitters and steamfitters must also be cautious and able to follow site safety plans and avoid injuries and burns on the job. They should also be comfortable working in small, cramped spaces and at high elevations at times.

JOB OUTLOOK

Job growth for pipe fitters and steamfitters is expected to be greater than the national average in the coming years. California anticipates 6,900 new job openings for pipe fitters and plumbers by 2016. This growth is likely to be aided by a move toward sustainable electricity generation in the state, particularly from geothermal energy. Geothermal power plants produce about 4.5 percent of California's electricity according to a June 2009 report, but the state has plans to build two new geothermal facilities in coming years.

In small markets, pipe fitters and steamfitters who are also trained to weld pipes and install insulation may find more job opportunities in new construction. In larger markets, government infrastructure projects are expected to help the job outlook for pipe fitters and steamfitters as a growing U.S. population leads to the development of new power, water, and wastewater treatment plants.

EARNINGS

As a group, pipe fitters, steamfitters, and plumbers earn an average of US$24.21 hourly or US$50,360 annually as reported in the U.S. Department of Labor's May 2010 data. The lowest-paid workers in this group earn less than US$27,580 annually; the highest-paid tradespeople earn more than US$79,920 per year. Those who work on mining projects or with foundries or vehicle manufacturers are among the individuals earning the most in this trade, as are pipe fitters who work on natural gas pipeline projects in Alaska. Independent contractors may initially appear to earn higher wages than those directly employed by a company, but they must take any state-required insurance, such as liability insurance, and self-employment taxes out of those reported earnings.

RELATED OCCUPATIONS

When employment numbers and wages are reported, pipe fitters and steamfitters are often grouped with plumbers, sprinkler fitters, and pipelayers. In addition, they may work with or as HVAC installers or mechanics. They can advance to become construction managers, construction and building inspectors, or production managers for bio-fuel, biomass, geothermal, or hydroelectric energy. Their jobs are closely related to those that deal with the installation and repair of mechanical systems, such as the following:

- Aircraft structure, surfaces, rigging, and systems assemblers
- Boilermakers
- Electricians
- Refrigeration mechanics and installers
- Sheet metal workers
- Stationary engineers and boiler operators
- Structural iron and steel workers
- Welders, cutters, and welder fitters

SOURCES OF ADDITIONAL INFORMATION

Home Builders Institute. http://www.hbi.org

Mechanical Contractors Association of America. http://www.mcaa.org

National Association of Home Builders. http://www.nahb.org

National Center for Construction Education and Research. http://www.nccer.org

Plumbing-Heating-Cooling Contractors Association. http://www.phccweb.org

United Association of Journeymen and Apprentices of the Plumbing and Pipefitting Industry. http://www.ua.org

FURTHER READING

Bureau of Labor Statistics, U.S. Department of Labor. "47-2152 Plumbers, Pipefitters, and Steamfitters." In *Occupational Employment Statistics: Occupational Employment and Wages, May 2010,* last modified May 17, 2011. Accessed March 7, 2012. http://www.bls.gov/oes/current/oes472152.htm.

———. "Plumbers, Pipelayers, Pipefitters, and Steamfitters." In *Occupational Outlook Handbook, 2010–11 Edition.* Accessed February 13, 2012. http://www.bls.gov/oco/ocos211.htm.

Division of Apprenticeship Standards, California Department of Industrial Relations. *Apprenticeship Programs Information Guide.* Accessed February 7, 2012. http://www.dir.ca.gov/databases/das/descOfAppr.html.

Environmental Defense Fund. *California Green Jobs Guidebook.* Accessed January 16, 2012. http://www.edf.org/climate/california-green-jobs-guidebook.

Folga, S. M. "Natural Gas and Pipeline Technology Overview." *Argonne National Laboratory,* November 2007. Accessed March 7, 2012. http://corridoreis.anl.gov/documents/docs/technical/APT_61034_EVS_TM_08_5.pdf.

Nipissing University. "Biomass Network Group Receives Trillium Funding." July 7, 2010. Accessed March 7, 2012. http://www.nipissingu.ca/about-us/newsroom/Pages/Biomass-Network-Group-Receives-Trillium-Funding.aspx.

Sobolik, Jessica. "Connecting the Pipes." *Ethanol Producer Magazine,* July 08, 2008. Accessed March 7, 2012. http://www.ethanolproducer.com/articles/4458/connecting-the-pipes.

State Building and Construction Trades Council of California. "PLAs on Three New Power Plants to Bring Thousands of Building Trades Jobs," November 3, 2011. Accessed March 7, 2012. http://www.sbctc.org/doc.asp?id=297.

PLUMBERS

NATURE OF THE WORK

In the late 1990s film *Wag the Dog*, Dustin Hoffman's character says that producing movies is like being a plumber: "Do your job right and nobody should notice." Faucets that flow with hot and cold water, toilets that flush with the press of a lever, dishwashers and washing machines that start with the touch of a button: These actions and more happen in homes with little thought because a plumber has done his or her job right.

Plumbers work with pipes, valves, and fittings, assembling them in a network that laces almost entirely unseen through a building to supply water to and remove waste from it. Although their work is similar to that of pipefitters, steamfitters, and pipelayers, who tend to work in industrial settings, plumbers mainly work in nonresidential and commercial buildings. In industrial settings, they focus on restrooms, lunchrooms, and other areas used by the building's personnel rather than piping related to the industry itself. They follow detailed blueprints when working on new construction but often must puzzle through piping layouts in existing buildings to make repairs. Their knowledge of how systems work, the building codes that affect the type of materials that are used and where they are located in a structure, and how piping systems interact with or avoid other components of a building makes them valuable resources on a job site for construction or renovation and to architects and others designing piping systems.

Plumbers today are enhancing this knowledge with experience designing and installing gray water systems, information about water-efficient appliances on the market, and training in energy-saving and sustainable

AT A GLANCE FACT BOX

SOC: 47-2152.02
Preferred Education: Associate's degree or vocational schooling
Average Salary: US$27,600 to US$79,900 annually
Other Information: Most plumbers work for companies such as plumbing contractors that employ fewer than 20 people and often have no more than four employees

practices. Some conservation advocates argue that such training should be mandatory.

"America needs to save water, and the plumbing industry needs to be part of the solution," said Megan Lehtonen, director of Green *Plumbers* USA, in an interview published in the *Utne Reader*. "The water we have is the water we're going to have, and Americans use on average twice as much as people in other [developed] countries. We can do better." Lehtonen added that plumbers should be representatives of this change, using their skills and knowledge to encourage home and building owners to take steps that conserve water and energy.

Some changes are simple, such as swapping out older fixtures for low-flow toilets and aerating faucets. Others require plumbers to install separate systems for potable and nonpotable water. The latter, which may be rainwater or gray water from washing machines, showers, and sinks, can be run through a system of pipes to a storage tank and then be used to water landscaping, fill ponds, bathe pets, and flush toilets. This system must be kept separate from those used to supply drinking and cooking water and to remove blackwater flushed from toilets or drained from garbage disposals.

Those who work in a variety of structures are generally referred to as journeyman plumbers. Others may specialize in residential, pump, irrigation, or backflow systems. Some plumbers are also certified to install piping for natural gas lines, heating and cooling systems, or medical gas.

Plumbers ideally start a project by studying drawings that show where new plumbing should be placed or where existing plumbing can be found and then finding these areas within the structure. They may use saws and other tools to cut into walls for access to piping areas. They then cut, thread, bend, and otherwise manipulate pipes so that they can be connected as required by their purpose and the space. They seal joints, check for leaks, and connect the system to exterior water or sewer lines and appliances, faucets, and drains.

Pipes can be made from many materials, such as plastic, copper, or other metals, and plumbers must know the best places to use certain materials and how to best connect certain pipes. Water and waste moving through such connections is usually under pressure, which can wear on the network over time, making repairs inevitable. Much plumbing work involves fixing issues ranging from leaky faucets and clogged drains to burst pipes and nonresponsive pumps. Even during a construction industry slump, good plumbers rarely find themselves short of work.

WORKING CONDITIONS

Plumbers mainly work on residential and commercial buildings, rather than in industrial settings where pipe fitters and steamfitters are found. They often work unusual hours because of the need to fit into an opening in a construction schedule or to answer a nighttime call about a burst water pipe. They may move heavy pipes, although less frequently than their industrial-based counterparts, and they often work in cramped, dark, wet, or cold spaces. Although their jobs present challenges, stress is usually low unless they face a work shortage and related financial strain. Injuries tend to be lower than in other construction jobs although these workers must use care to avoid on-the-job falls, burns, and cuts.

EMPLOYMENT

Plumbing, pipefitting, and steamfitting together form one of the largest construction occupations in the United States. The U.S. Department of Labor's Bureau of Labor Statistics (BLS) estimates nearly 359,000 people are in these positions throughout the United States. Most plumbers are independent contractors, although some own a plumbing services company or are employed by a large nonresidential construction firm. Although building complexes such as hospitals, universities, or corporate campuses may employ in-house plumbers, many have chosen to contract out such services.

As with other jobs in the construction industry, California, Texas, New York, Florida, and Illinois are among the states with the most people in plumbing-related occupations. Plumbers are in high demand as of 2012 in North Dakota and Montana, where the expansion of oil fields in the Williston Basin has triggered a construction boom in housing for oil workers and their families. Such construction often overlooks energy efficiency and sustainability, but plumbers with knowledge of such practices may find opportunities to recommend energy-efficient appliances and practices to contractors and owners.

TRAINING, OTHER QUALIFICATIONS, AND ADVANCEMENT

Apprenticeships are the primary form of training for plumbers. Because most states require plumbers to be licensed, a formal or informal apprenticeship with a sponsoring organization or an experienced plumber is the best way to get into this trade. Formal programs generally last five years for plumbers, during which time the apprentice works alongside a master plumber for an entry-level wage, usually half that of an experienced plumber. After several years of work experience, apprentices and trainees can take a licensing exam to be certified as master plumbers. They may need separate training and exams before they can work on gas lines.

Applicants for plumbing jobs must be at least 18 years old, and many apprenticeship programs require, at minimum, a high school diploma or equivalent. Although no specific coursework is required for people who want to become plumbers, those who have studied math, physics, computers, drafting, and construction techniques at a high school or community college are better placed for a career in this field. Native English speakers who learn to speak Spanish may advance faster to supervisory positions.

Although certifications are not necessary for licensed plumbers, they can help them learn about sustainable construction and find more work. Programs such as those through Green *Plumbers* USA provide environmental training and licensing for plumbing tradespeople. The Green *Plumbers* curriculum was prompted by severe drought in Australia and was adopted in the United States in 2008. More than 3,000 plumbers were certified in the U.S. program's first two years. Participants are taught to provide water-use audits, tankless water heaters, high-efficiency showerheads and toilets, solar hot water systems, and other features to home and building owners. They can also learn about sustainable urban irrigation practices, pump technologies, and natural treatment techniques for wastewater.

Early in their careers, plumbers may work on basic water supply and waste removal systems in homes or buildings. As they become more experienced, they may move into working with specific green technologies such as installing and repairing heat pumps, biomass boilers, solar thermal systems, and rainwater harvesters. Many start their own plumbing contractor companies, initially working independently but later supervising a team of plumbers and doing less of the actual work themselves. Others may advance to become construction managers or inspectors. Those seeking new challenges in their field may train to become water systems designers or installers for energy-efficient systems in residential and commercial buildings or return to school to become water/wastewater engineers.

Many plumbers work directly with customers, particularly when repairing existing piping, so good customer service skills are important. Those who like to solve puzzles, can think conceptually, and can combine mechanical, mathematical, and construction skills to install and repair systems do well in this job. Bookkeeping, scheduling, and management skills are desirable for plumbers looking to start their own contractor businesses.

JOB OUTLOOK

As building codes are updated to reflect new levels of energy efficiency and the technologies that can achieve them, plumbers who are experienced welders and can install efficient water systems are likely to see growth. The BLS expects faster than average growth in this job through 2018, noting that "increasing emphasis on water conservation should require retrofitting to conserve water, leading to employment growth for plumbers."

Money can be a huge driver in job security and competition in the plumbing trade. Many state and local agencies, as well as the federal government, offer incentive programs to home and building owners who install energy- and water-saving plumbing systems. Such systems and the devices connected to them can also generate hefty savings in operating costs. Plumbers who can design and install such systems in new construction or retrofitted structures are likely to be in the highest demand in their local communities.

EARNINGS

Plumbers and those in related occupations earn, on average, US$24.21 per hour or US$50,360 per year according to May 2010 statistics from the BLS. Most earn between US$27,580 and US$79,920 annually. Pipe fitters and steamfitters tend to make more than plumbers, although

wages can vary widely depending on the types of construction the plumber is involved in and the cost of living in which the plumber is working. Although wages may be higher for those who are independent contractors, those workers need to pay their own self-employment taxes and carry contractors insurance with liability and property coverage as required by the state in which they work.

RELATED OCCUPATIONS

Plumbers do work similar to that of pipe fitters, steamfitters, pipelayers, and sprinkler fitters. They also share skills with other construction workers who should have some knowledge of plumbing systems and those who repair other types of mechanical systems, such as the following:

- Construction carpenters
- Electricians
- Heating and air conditioning mechanics and installers
- Refrigeration mechanics and installers
- Welders, cutters, and welder fitters

SOURCES OF ADDITIONAL INFORMATION

Green *Plumbers* USA. http://www.greenplumbersusa.com
Plumbing-Heating-Cooling Contractors Association. http://www.phccweb.org
United Association of Journeymen and Apprentices of the Plumbing and Pipefitting Industry. http://www.ua.org

FURTHER READING

Bureau of Labor Statistics, U.S. Department of Labor. "47-2152 Plumbers, Pipefitters, and Steamfitters." In *Occupational Employment Statistics: Occupational Employment and Wages, May 2010,* last modified May 17, 2011. Accessed March 7, 2012. http://www.bls.gov/oes/current/oes472152.htm.
———. "Plumbers, Pipelayers, Pipefitters, and Steamfitters." In *Occupational Outlook Handbook, 2010–11 Edition.* Accessed February 13, 2012. http://www.bls.gov/oco/ocos211.htm.
Division of Apprenticeship Standards, California Department of Industrial Relations. *Apprenticeship Programs Information Guide.* Accessed February 7, 2012. http://www.dir.ca.gov/databases/das/descOfAppr.html.
Gelt, Joe. "Home Use of Graywater, Rainwater Conserves Water—and May Save Money." *University of Arizona, Water Resources Research Center.* Accessed February 14, 2012. http://ag.arizona.edu/azwater/arroyo/071rain.html.
Kellner, Jessica. "Power to the Green Plumbers: Green *Plumbers* USA Director Megan Lehtonen on

Inciting a Wastewater Revolution." *Utne Reader,* January–February 2010. Accessed March 7, 2012. http://www.utne.com/Environment/Power-to-the-Green-Plumbers.aspx.

Liming, Drew. "Careers in Green Construction." *Bureau of Labor Statistics, U.S. Department of Labor,* June 2011.

Accessed March 7, 2012. http://www.bls.gov/green/construction/construction.pdf.

Washington State Department of Labor & Industries. *Facts about State Certification for Plumbers*, April 2010. Accessed March 7, 2012. http://www.lni.wa.gov/IPUB/627-022-000.pdf.

ROOFERS

NATURE OF THE WORK

Roofs are the first line of defense against moisture, keeping every layer of a structure below them dry. A poorly designed or installed roof can lead to water damage, rot, and other problems, allowing water to leak in from outside the building or vapor to build up on the inside of the roofing system. Because they take the brunt of weather for a building, roofs must be replaced or repaired far more frequently than most parts of a well-built structure. This ensures a solid job market for those who install and repair roofs. However, that market is shrinking for roofers who only focus on traditional practices and materials because more experienced workers in other construction trades take on this work during lean times and roofers with knowledge of storm water mitigation, energy-efficient materials, and sustainable building techniques grab an ever-larger portion of roofing work.

The outer layer of a modern roof can be made of many types of materials from metal or asphalt to clay tiles or vegetation. Some of these outer layers require different installation techniques, and roofers are usually familiar with several methods that relate to the most common roofing materials used in their area. Underneath, roofers have added layers on the roof's structural support and decking. These various layers act as water barriers, vapor barriers, and insulation for the building's top surface. Flashing is also installed and other techniques are used to make joints watertight and to direct water away from the structure.

Although when properly installed the multiple layers of a roof aid in the durability and airtightness of a building, both prime goals of green construction, some of these

traditional materials and practices are not green in either their content or their effects. Cutting corners on insulation in a roofing system can reduce energy efficiency. The traditional materials used for a roof's outer layer can absorb ultraviolet rays and release this solar energy as heat, changing the microclimate of an urban area until it is measurably warmer than the surrounding landscape that has not yet been as fully developed. These materials also must be replaced regularly, and many times the old shingles and other components end up in landfills rather than recycling centers. These bulky materials can fill multiple truckloads, leaving a large carbon footprint as they are transported to and from the construction site.

These concerns have led manufacturers to experiment with new materials and roofers to explore new practices. Postindustrial rubber and plastic shingles, liquid waterproofing, spray foam insulation, and reflective coatings are just a few of the recent innovations in roofing materials. Increasingly, other elements such as trees, grasses, and solar panels are being installed directly on roofs. These developments bring recycling, water management, longevity, and other environmental tenets into the roofing industry.

Many of these materials and techniques require changes to the daily tasks of roofers. Some products, such as liquid applied membranes, require specialized tools and training to ensure they are installed correctly. Green roofing systems need extra layers or materials among traditional ones that are often novel to roofers. Some designs require roofers to work alongside contractors with whom they rarely had contact in the past, including electricians and landscapers, and schedules may shift to accommodate this extra work on a building's highest surface. Some roofers may even undertake electrical and other training so that they can install solar panels, sensors, and other components along with roofing materials.

WORKING CONDITIONS

Although less technically complex than some other construction jobs, roofing is a physically demanding profession. Roofers work outdoors, high above the ground, and on sloped, steeply angled surfaces. Although they rarely work in cold or rainy weather because of the dangers associated with slick icy or wet surfaces, they often work on hot summer days in direct sunlight when temperatures can be significantly higher on a dark roof surface than the ground. Even on job sites where roofing products are lifted by a crane or other machinery to the top of the building, roofers must move heavy materials while working up on the roof. Some days are mainly spent climbing up and down ladders and scaffolds; others keep the roofer constantly bending and kneeling as materials are secured in place.

Depending on the region, roofers may work seasonally, spending long hours and weekends on job sites in warm months so that they can earn enough money to get through winter when work is scarce. They may also work overtime when summer squalls are anticipated or to make up for delays that developed elsewhere in the construction schedule.

Roofers are some of the most likely construction workers to be injured or killed by falls, the cause of 75 percent of fatal injuries according to the U.S. Department of Labor. Although the fatality rate is lower than in some other construction trade jobs, an average of 68 job-related deaths occurred each year since 2002. Following proper safety procedures and using safety equipment such as rope and harness systems can prevent most roofing accidents.

EMPLOYMENT

Nearly 100,000 people work as roofers in the United States, according to the U.S. Department of Labor's statistics from May 2010. Most roofers are independent roofing contractors or work for them, although some are self-employed and a few work full time for residential and nonresidential construction companies. Many work in states known for their large construction industries, such as California, Florida, and New York.

Some European countries are particularly advanced in their green roof ambitions. Denmark and Switzerland require all new flat roofs in Copenhagen, Basel, Zurich, and Luzern to be vegetated. Other European countries are increasingly calling for green or living roofs in urban areas to reduce the heat island effect, in which temperatures are measurably higher in built-up areas than in nearby rural areas.

But the United States is also calling for many of these practices in increasing numbers. New York, New York, and Annapolis, Maryland, are among those offering tax credits for buildings that bear green roofs and many other local governments are emphasizing green building and sustainable roofing in their public construction projects. Some have instituted programs that encompass eco-roofs as well as storm water management, invasive plant eradication, and environmental protection, such as Portland, Oregon's "Grey to Green" initiative.

TRAINING, OTHER QUALIFICATIONS, AND ADVANCEMENT

Most roofers begin working while in or after graduating high school, learning the trade from more experienced roofers on the job. Apprenticeships and other formal training can get a roofer into better paid positions faster, and most of these require a high school diploma or general education development certificate. Apprenticeships typically last three years, during which time apprentices spend most of their logged hours in paid training on job sites and the rest in classrooms learning about the math, safety, and techniques and tools used in the trade. These apprenticeships are often regulated by a state agency, and in most states those who finish the program receive a certificate of completion. Roofers typically do not need licenses, but those who also work as electricians must be licensed in that trade as required by the state in which they work.

Entry-level work in the roofing trade, whether coupled with formal or informal training, typically consists of carrying materials and equipment, setting up scaffolds and rigging, and performing other labor-intensive tasks. Workers soon begin measuring, cutting, and installing flashing, shingles, and other materials. As they advance, they may learn to install less common roofing materials, work more independently, and develop sustainable roofing techniques. They may become supervisors or estimators, team up with landscape architects to design vegetative roofing systems, or start their own roofing business. Some expand into the electrician trade or work with solar products and become solar photovoltaic installers, solar thermal technicians, or solar energy installation managers.

Roofers must be extremely comfortable with heights and have good balance, physical strength, and flexibility. Knowledge of math, metalworking, and mechanical drawing can be useful, as can experience as a construction laborer on other parts of job sites. Much of a roofer's work involves repairing or replacing roofs, and a roofer should be able to spot problems with the old roofing system and resolve them as they work. Although they often work solo or in pairs, teamwork can be important on large projects and green building sites.

JOB OUTLOOK

Despite several years of job shortages and a slowdown in the construction industry from 2007 to 2009, the outlook for construction jobs in general and roofing jobs in particular is hopeful. Roofers who can install energy-efficient roof ventilation systems, skylights, and other features will increasingly be in demand according to the Economic Development Department in California. The department predicts California will have 4,000 new roofing jobs by 2016. Nationwide, however, expectations are for slower growth as other construction workers can handle roofing jobs, meaning experienced roofers who branch into other construction trades or those who have experience working on green roofs and energy-efficient projects will see the most demand.

Versatile roofers are also more likely to stay in the roofing occupation longer. Traditionally, the roofing field has had high turnover rates because of the strenuous nature of the work and the common view that it is a temporary job. Expansion of the tasks and green technologies that affect roofing, however, are giving new challenges to workers in this field, which could mean greater retention in employment numbers.

EARNINGS

Roofers, who are generally paid by the hour or project rather than salaried, earn US$18.21 per hour or US$37,880 per year on average according to the U.S. Department of Labor. Those at the lowest end of the pay scale earn less than US$22,030 each year, but the highest-paid roofers can earn more than US$60,610 annually. Some of the highest-paid roofers work through the U.S. government on federal buildings and military installations or through local school districts on elementary and secondary school buildings. Hawaii, Connecticut, and Minnesota are home to some of the highest-paid workers in this field. Workers who are members of the United Union of Roofers, Waterproofers, and Allied Workers usually see better wages and benefits than nonunion roofers. Most entry-level jobs are held by apprentices, who typically earn about half the wage of an experienced roofer in their first year of the program.

RELATED OCCUPATIONS

Roofers use some of the same materials and skills as other construction workers, such as the following:

- Cement masons and concrete finishers
- Construction carpenters
- Construction laborers
- Insulation workers
- Rough carpenters
- Sheet metal workers

SOURCES OF ADDITIONAL INFORMATION

Green Roofs for Healthy Cities. http://www .greenroofs.org

Living Architecture Academy. http://grhc .sclivelearningcenter.com

National Roofing Contractors Association. http://www .nrca.net

United Union of Roofers, Waterproofers, and Allied Workers. http://www.unionroofers.com

FURTHER READING

Bureau of Labor Statistics, U.S. Department of Labor. "47-2181 Roofers." In *Occupational Employment Statistics: Occupational Employment and Wages, May 2010,* last modified May 17, 2011. Accessed February 29, 2012. http://www.bls.gov/oes/current/ oes472181.htm.
———. "Roofers." In *Occupational Outlook Handbook, 2010-11 Edition.* Accessed February 14, 2012. http://www.bls.gov/oco/ocos212.htm.
———. *Safety and Health: Dangerous Jobs.* Accessed February 7, 2012. http://www.bls.gov/iif/oshwc/ cfar0020.pdf.
Environmental Defense Fund. *California Green Jobs Guidebook.* Accessed January 16, 2012. http:// www.edf.org/climate/california-green-jobs- guidebook.
Greenroofs.com. *Industry Support.* Accessed February 14, 2012. http://www.greenroofs.com/Greenroofs101/ industry_support.htm#US.
Liming, Drew. *Careers in Green Construction.* U.S. Bureau of Labor Statistics, June 2011. Accessed

February 29, 2012. http://www.bls.gov/green/
construction/construction.pdf.

U.S. Environmental Protection Agency. *Heat Island Effect*. Accessed February 14, 2012. http://www
.epa.gov/hiri/.

West, Richard. "Web Exclusive: How Green is Green?" *Roofing Contractor,* September 1, 2009. Accessed February 29, 2012. http://www
.roofingcontractor.com/articles/web-exclusive-
how-green-is-green.

HEATING AND AIR CONDITIONING
MECHANICS AND INSTALLERS

NATURE OF THE WORK

Heating and cooling form the greatest operating costs of a home or office. They are also among the most important features of a building, affecting the appeal and comfort of a living area or workspace far more than a view or a plush carpet ever could. The heating, ventilation, and air conditioning (HVAC) systems that regulate temperature, humidity, and air flow are crucial, as are the HVAC technicians who install, repair, and maintain these systems.

HVAC systems use motors, fans, pumps, and other features to mechanically ventilate a building. Installing these systems requires the installer to have the skills of an electrician, pipe fitter or plumber, and sheet metal worker. The installer follows blueprints for a project to create a network of fuel and water pipes and pumps, air ducts and vents, electrical wiring, thermostats and electronic controls, and other components that control the air quality and thus the health of the occupants of a home or office. The HVAC installer may later maintain this network and make repairs as needed, or a different HVAC mechanic may step in to ensure the system runs properly and does not become a source of mold and other harmful airborne contaminants. HVAC technicians may also be responsible for maintaining and repairing elevators, refrigeration equipment, and other mechanical systems in a commercial building. They are also salespeople, selling the service contracts that set a schedule of regular maintenance for an HVAC system. In less populated regions, they may also insulate pipes and other parts of a building in new construction.

The more energy efficient a building is, the more important HVAC systems become. In many ways, green construction is all about airtight construction. One of the

---

AT A GLANCE FACT BOX

SOC: 49-9021.01
Preferred Education: Associate's degree or vocational certification
Average Salary: US$26,500 to US$67,000 annually
Other Information: By 2018, many residential HVAC systems will need to be replaced, ensuring a new round of contracts for HVAC mechanics and installers

---

first goals of a green building project is to conserve energy. Builders put in layers of insulation, install multipane windows, and seal gaps behind outlets, vents, and pipes that let air through in older homes. The tighter building envelope significantly affects the energy efficiency of such structures. Green buildings use an average of 30 percent less energy than conventional ones according to Capital-E and the U.S. Green Building Council, which developed the Leadership in Energy and Environmental Design (LEED) rating system for green construction.

Increasing energy efficiency reduces the passive ventilation that keeps air moving in and out of traditional structures. As a result, green buildings need mechanical ventilation to achieve a similar effect. Even people who are less concerned about green construction are drawn to the conservation factors achieved with airtight construction, such as conservation of resources and money.

"Everybody is becoming more concerned with conservation. It really affects everybody, not just the green movement," said John McCrorie of McCrorie Heating & Cooling in Montana, which has the fifth-largest concentration of construction jobs in the country according to the U.S. Department of Labor. "In the past, when homes were not real tight, they were over ventilated, and overventilated homes are heating and cooling more than what is necessary."

The capacity and complexity of HVAC systems are on the rise. As green buildings make greater use of HVAC systems, careful installation and maintenance also become increasingly important because of the risk of mold contamination from the relative humidity increase experienced with green construction. This is particularly important in the humid southeastern United States.

Changes in pump systems are affecting the work of HVAC technicians as well. Tax credits that are available from the U.S. government and local utility companies through 2016 have sparked interest in geothermal and air-source heat pumps. "Such credits can reduce the installation costs of such systems by 30 percent," said McCrorie, "making a device that is costly to install initially but less expensive to run over time all the more attractive. These systems tap into the earth or use outside air to heat and cool a structure."

"Air source and geothermal are the same concepts; it's just a matter of where you transfer the heat from," said McCrorie. "It's much more of a precision installation, especially when you're transferring heat from the ground. Everything's got to be right on." But he added that such precision and technological advances are some of the best things about HVAC work. "I enjoy every day because every day is different. It's challenging…, especially for mechanically minded people who want to know how stuff works and ways to improve on things every time they do a job or motion."

WORKING CONDITIONS

HVAC technicians focus on either installation or maintenance of systems. The former often have more varied schedules, with long workdays when they are wrapping up their part of a new construction project and less intense ones when bidding on projects, ordering supplies, and doing other preparatory tasks. Mechanics usually have less fluctuation in schedules, although they may be on call in case a system fails. Service contracts ensure steady work as they require a regular return to buildings to test and adjust equipment. Mechanics often repair heating systems in the summer and air-conditioners in the winter. Those who work on heat pumps, which both heat and cool a space, service these units at any time of the year.

Whether installing or repairing an HVAC system, technicians may work outdoors or indoors in uncomfortable conditions in which the climate is not yet under control. They often must work in high, cramped spaces. Rates of injury are fairly low in the HVAC field, but they can occur, particularly from falls or exposure to harmful substances such as refrigerants. Electrical shock, frostbite, burns, and other injuries are also possible if appropriate precautions are not taken.

EMPLOYMENT

In the United States, more than 224,000 people install and repair HVAC systems according to the U.S. Department of Labor. About half of these people work for heating, air conditioning, and plumbing contractors. Many of the rest are self-employed subcontractors who work on individual projects, but some hold permanent positions with a construction company. Texas, Florida, California, New York, and Pennsylvania are among the states with the highest levels of employment for HVAC technicians.

These workers are employed across a range of industries, as most buildings are climate controlled in some way. Factories, stores, schools, apartment complexes, and private homes are just a few of the structures that need the services of HVAC mechanics and installers.

TRAINING, OTHER QUALIFICATIONS, AND ADVANCEMENT

HVAC systems have become more common and more complicated in recent years, making appropriate training ever more important. Some HVAC technicians learn on the job, starting their careers as construction laborers or helpers of electricians, plumbers, or pipe fitters before working as an assistant to an HVAC expert. Many, however, enter an apprenticeship or technical school program directly after graduating high school. In such programs, they learn the basics of the job, essential safety practices, and building codes and regulations that must be followed. Most of these programs run three to five years, encompassing classroom-based instruction and hands-on on-site training. A state agency generally sets the education standards, length, and pay rates for an apprentice and then awards a certification upon completion of the program. The programs themselves are often run by a labor union or community college. Once HVAC mechanics and installers gain some work experience, they must pass an exam to obtain the license required by most states. They also must be certified to work with refrigerants, which requires a written exam approved by the U.S. Environmental Protection Agency.

The learning does not stop there. Green practices and products are changing the construction industry and experienced HVAC technicians are continually adding to their knowledge base to ensure they are at the top of their field. Organizations such as the National Center for Construction Education and Research offer courses designed to teach HVAC workers about energy efficiency, LEED ratings, and sustainable building practices.

Those with years of HVAC experience as subcontractors may become business owners, hiring other mechanics and installers to do the field work while they focus on writing proposals and winning contracts. They may also advance to a supervisor, service manager, sales, or test and balance specialist position. As energy efficiency becomes a primary goal in new construction and remodeling projects, energy management is a developing trend in the industry. For example, an energy field auditor, who checks HVAC equipment, ducts, lighting, windows, and other energy-efficiency features of a commercial or industrial building and then recommends improvements, may come from a background as an HVAC technician.

In many ways, HVAC work is a service job, requiring good people and communication skills. Heavy objects often must be lifted or shifted, so being in good physical condition is also important. In addition, an understanding of math and physics, an ability to read blueprints, and a familiarity with computers are all useful.

JOB OUTLOOK

Although construction jobs have suffered greatly since 2008 because the U.S. economic slump has limited new construction, a need for greater efficiency of buildings has made HVAC systems increasingly important for both residential and commercial projects. For example, the California Economic Development Department pegs HVAC installation and servicing as one of the fastest-growing sectors in the energy-efficiency industry. It estimates that by 2016 there will be 2,500 new job openings for HVAC and refrigeration mechanics and installers in the state. This growth projection should be reflected nationwide because existing buildings and homes need to be upgraded for energy efficiency. Those with experience in the latest energy-efficient designs and computer-controlled systems are likely to be in the greatest demand.

EARNINGS

The mean annual wage for HVAC mechanics and installers is US$44,860, or US$21.57 per hour, with a range of about US$26,490 to about US$66,930 according to the U.S. Department of Labor. By far, most of these people work as subcontractors and are brought in by construction companies for a specific project. Some HVAC suppliers, however, run full-service companies that sell, install, and maintain their equipment. Those who make the highest wages are generally employed in an industry outside general construction, such as vehicle manufacturing or power generation. Highly paid HVAC contractors are also found in Alaska and Hawaii, as well as Washington, DC, and many metropolitan areas of California.

RELATED OCCUPATIONS

HVAC mechanics and installers work with many of the materials used in other jobs, such as the following:

- Boilermakers
- Electricians
- General maintenance and repair workers
- Pipe fitters and steamfitters
- Plumbers
- Refrigeration mechanics and installers
- Sheet metal workers

SOURCES OF ADDITIONAL INFORMATION

Air-Conditioning, Heating, and Refrigeration Institute. http://www.ahrinet.org
HVAC Excellence. http://www.hvacexcellence.org
International Ground Source Heat Pump Association. http://www.igshpa.okstate.edu
Mechanical Contractors Association of America, Mechanical Service Contractors of America. http://www.mcaa.org
National Occupational Competency Testing Institute. http://www.nocti.org
Plumbing-Heating-Cooling Contractors. http://www.phccweb.org

FURTHER READING

Bureau of Labor Statistics, U.S. Department of Labor. "49-9021 Heating, Air Conditioning, and Refrigeration Mechanics and Installers." In *Occupational Employment Statistics: Occupational Employment and Wages, May 2010,* last modified May 17, 2011. Accessed February 16, 2012. http://www.bls.gov/oes/current/oes499021.htm.
———. "Heating, Air Conditioning, and Refrigeration Mechanics and Installers." In *Occupational Outlook Handbook, 2010–11 Edition.* Accessed February 14, 2012. http://www.bls.gov/oco/ocos192.htm.
Environmental Defense Fund. *California Green Jobs Guidebook.* Accessed January 16, 2012. http://www.edf.org/climate/california-green-jobs-guidebook.
Kats, Greg. *The Costs and Financial Benefits of Green Buildings: A Report to California's Sustainable Building Task Force,* October 2003. Accessed January 16, 2012. http://www.usgbc.org/Docs/News/News477.pdf.

Liming, Drew. *Careers in Green Construction*. Bureau of Labor Statistics, U.S. Department of Labor, June 2011. Accessed February 16, 2012. http://www.bls.gov/green/construction/construction.pdf.

McCrorie, John (owner, McCrorie Heating & Cooling) in discussion with the author, February 2012.

Odom, J. David, Richard Scott, and George H. DuBose. *The Hidden Risks of Green Buildings: Why Building Problems Are Likely in Hot, Humid Climates,* August 2009. Accessed February 16, 2012. http://www.rci-online.org/interface/2009-08-odom-scott-dubose.pdf.

O*NET OnLine. *Summary Report for: 49-9021.01—Heating and Air Conditioning Mechanics and Installers*. Accessed January 31, 2012. http://www.onetonline.org/link/summary/49-9021.01.

SECTOR OVERVIEW: MANUFACTURING

———— ■ ————

Manufacturing is a process that uses raw materials to create products for sale to consumers. These products can range from aircraft carriers to microwave ovens; the scope of products that can result from manufactured processes is endless. Manufacturing processes have evolved over the years because of technological advances, consumer needs, and environmental changes. In the 21st century, it is difficult to imagine a world in which production was not conducted on a mass scale. However, it is important to put this into perspective. Mass manufacturing is the result of the Industrial Revolution, which occurred between 1750 and 1860. It began in the United Kingdom and spread across Europe and North America. The Industrial Revolution completely overhauled the process of manual labor by introducing machinery to do the work humans had done before. This made it much simpler to produce goods that before had needed much physical labor to produce.

THE INDUSTRIAL REVOLUTION

Prior to the Industrial Revolution, everything individuals used in their daily lives was the direct result of human and animal labor. After the Industrial Revolution, however, machines began to replace human labor. Steam and other forms of power began replacing human and animal efforts in production, and the factory system was introduced, leaving traditional manufacturing behind. Every year during this time machines were upgraded, increasing productivity and boosting commerce. People were fascinated with such change and encouraged it, and the environmental impact of the Industrial Revolution was not considered until some 200 years later. Unfortunately, the Industrial Revolution caused several environmental issues such as unsustainable population growth and a dependency on the earth's limited resources for the manufacturing process.

The beginning of the 21st century introduced an unprecedented world population of seven billion people. This is a growth of 400 percent in a single century. To put this growth into perspective, at the beginning of the Industrial Revolution the world population was around 700 million. Such human growth is inevitably tied into an increased use of resources both man-made and natural, and it stresses the need for resources exponentially. Coal and fossil fuels were used to support manufacturing and were thought of as inexhaustible resources until geophysicists brought to light their limitations and the impact these fuels were having on the environment. Even so, it took years for government and political leaders to heed warnings on limited natural resources. The 20th and 21st centuries introduced such great demand on these fuels that it has been hard to ease such reliance. Geophysicists, politicians, and others have slowly begun to realize the manufacturing industry could not continue this way indefinitely.

A SHIFT TO SUSTAINABLE MANUFACTURING

In recent decades there has been a shift in philosophy when it comes to manufacturing. Manufacturers originally followed a completely consumer approach with no consideration of environmental impact, but by the dawn of the 21st century, many consider the ecological effects of manufacturing when designing and producing goods. According to the U.S. Department of Commerce, *sustainable manufacturing* is "the creation of manufactured products that use processes that minimize negative environmental impacts, conserve energy and natural resources, are safe for employees, communities, and consumers and are economically sound." The United Nations defines *sustainable manufacturing* as manufacturing that "meets the needs of the present without compromising the ability of future generations to meet their own needs." In essence, sustainable manufacturing is a shift from creating a product solely for immediate use toward a process that considers the product's cost on the environment from inception to mass production.

Sustainable manufacturing is not only geared toward creating green products, but also toward implementing a process that minimizes the risks to businesses that are involved in sustainable manufacturing, thereby encouraging them to use it. The U.S. Department of Commerce has laid out steps for sustainable manufacturing to maximize production efficiency (reducing production costs and emissions) while simultaneously using raw materials that are reusable after the product's demise. In the U.S. Department of Commerce's start-up guide to sustainable manufacturing it details seven steps to environmental excellence that provide information for businesses to help meet the changing demands of consumers and compliance laws. Three categories sum up this process: *prepare, measure, improve.*

The process begins by having a clear vision and setting goals for the intended company, choosing indicators and understanding the data at hand. This includes creating a team within the business to review the impact on the environment it has and to set goals accordingly. During this phase milestones should be set and assessed as progress is made. The second step includes measuring raw materials used during the production process and how this impacts the environment. The facility itself is closely assessed at this stage as well. Energy consumption, air and water quality, and greenhouse gas emissions are carefully examined. The third step is improvement; in this phase all information collected is carefully diagnosed and solutions are suggested. Suggestions should aim to improve the efficiency of the manufacturing process and facility and the sustainability of the product manufactured.

Businesses of all sizes are increasingly paying attention to this new form of green manufacturing. There are several reasons why sustainable manufacturing is important. Investors are increasingly looking for businesses that are acting in an environmentally healthy manner. Globally, the market for low-carbon products is estimated to be valued over US$5 trillion and continues to grow yearly, according to the U.S. Department of Commerce's "Seven Steps to Environmental Excellence." This demand represents both a growing customer base and new compliance laws being implemented by governments for environmentally sound practices. Penalties

for avoiding such practices may include loss of revenue from customers and governmental fines. On the other hand, adopting such practices helps businesses save money, build a solid reputation, attract green investors, and encourage innovation.

SUSTAINABLE MANUFACTURING AND JOB CREATION

According to the Sustainable Manufacturing & Growth Initiative the manufacturing sector has seen the loss of 6 million jobs in the past decade. Although these are large losses, manufacturing continues to be a vital player in the U.S. economy, adding US$160 billion into research and development yearly. Because of the growing trend in sustainable manufacturing and the green industry, there is also a growing demand for trained professionals in this emerging field. Positions in this field include but are not limited to:

- Management positions such as division manager, plant manager, assistant plant manager, vice president of manufacturing
- Design positions such as design and industrial engineering, manufacturing engineering, research
- Project and production positions such as safety manager, safety coordinator, project engineer, project manager, production worker, quality control manager, production engineering manager
- Distribution positions such as distribution manager, shipping and receiving manager, shipping and receiving clerk, logistics engineer
- Materials positions such as materials manager, handler, distributor, purchasing manager, buyer
- Facilities positions such as logistics specialist, facilities manager, technician, machinist

FURTHER READING

Hackett, Lewis. "Industrial Revolution." *History World International*, 1992. Accessed February 28, 2012. http://history-world.org/Industrial%20Intro.htm.

Keybridge Research LLC. *Sustainable Manufacturing & Growth Initiative*. Industrial Energy Consumers of America, July 23, 2010. Accessed February 29, 2012. http://www.ieca-us.com/documents/IECAEconomicImpactStudySFPVFinal.pdf.

International Trade Administration. "How Does Commerce Define Sustainable Manufacturing?" U.S. Department of Commerce. Accessed February 28, 2012. http://trade.gov/competitiveness/sustainablemanufacturing/how_doc_defines_SM.asp.

McLamb, Eric. "The Ecological Impact of the Industrial Revolution." *Ecology Global Network*, September 18,

2011. Accessed February 28, 2012. http://www
.ecology.com/2011/09/18/ecological-impact-
industrial-revolution/.

National Council for Advanced Manufacturing.
Sustainable Manufacturing. Accessed April 3,
2012. http://www.nacfam.org/PolicyInitiatives/
SustainableManufacturing/tabid/64/
Default.aspx.

OECD. "Seven Steps to Environmental Excellence."
OECD Sustainable Manufacturing Tool Kit, 2011.
Accessed February 28, 2012. http://www.oecd.org/
dataoecd/55/60/48704993.pdf.

LOGISTICS ENGINEERS

NATURE OF THE WORK

Logistics engineers rely heavily on strong managerial and mathematical skills. *Logistics* is defined as a scientific technique used to evaluate, oversee, and control inventory. A logistics engineer is responsible for production, sales, management, and staff to maintain capital and monetary flow and gains. These engineers track a company's production progress from start to finish, ensuring the highest levels of efficiency, quality, and safety. Logistics engineers are constantly experimenting with new methods to increase efficiency in production while maintaining product quality. This involves keeping up with the development of new green technologies that boost transportation time, costs, and fuel consumption.

These engineers study the procurement process. Based on these studies, logistics engineers offer suggestions on staffing, facilities, maintenance, or any area that deals with the efficiency and production of a product from start to finish. In addition to evaluating the current system of production, logistics engineers are responsible for forecasting change in production circumstances. Changing circumstances include, but are not limited to: changes in carbon emissions standards legislation, changes in other environmental standards, rising or falling fuel costs, and new transportation technologies, which have to be evaluated for their potential to maximize transportation efficiency, such as time and fuel costs.

Because these engineers are part of supply chain management and, according to *The Logistics Engineering Handbook*, are responsible for "the movement, storage, processing and inventory of finished goods," it is their proactive involvement that impacts energy use during manufacturing, storing, and transportation of goods.

AT A GLANCE FACT BOX

SOC: 13-1081.01
Preferred Education: Master's degree
Average Salary: US$49,700 to US$112,830 annually
Other Information: Logistics engineering is considered a growing "green" industry with potential growth of 7 to 13 percent by 2018, according to the U.S. Department of Labor's Bureau of Labor Statistics (BLS)

For instance, these engineers will decide on the technology, supplies, and type of transportation used for producing, storing, and delivering products. In essence, they are the individuals responsible for securing the production, storage, and transportation facilities that will ensure the use of innovative, green technologies throughout the process.

Green Responsibilities Not only are logistics engineers responsible for tracking production efficiency from start to finish, but they are also responsible for the reverse logistics process and its evaluation. This means they track recycling trends, or the reuse of and disposal of a consumed product. Environmental reviews are conducted for the storage buildings and distribution processes, as well as the transportation involved in the distribution process, to detect and treat inefficiencies in each step of the transportation/

storage process. Logistics engineers have green responsibilities for documenting the carbon waste related to the transportation of goods, and they can offer solutions to minimize the carbon waste from transportation. This helps create sustainable transportation by convincing companies to save money while making choices that have fewer negative effects on the environment.

WORKING CONDITIONS

Logistics engineers work approximately 40 or more hours per week. The time commitment for each project varies. Because facility efficiency is the responsibility of such engineers, they are often required to travel to off-site facilities to inspect them. This may require long-distance travel. Such engineers are the adhesive that keeps the production intact, on time, and efficient. This means that any deficiency in the process is often their responsibility to sort through and adjust. Because of this responsibility, this can be a high-stress managerial position.

EMPLOYMENT

According to *Green Careers in Energy*, more than half of supply chain managers, a field that includes logistics engineers, are self-employed contractors. Eleven percent work for government agencies, and the 32 percent remaining work for companies that deal with the transportation of goods (i.e., manufacturers, retail chains, and companies contracted for the transportation of goods). According to the U.S. Department of Labor's Bureau of Labor Statistics (BLS), in 2010 about 202,990 people were employed in this field. The states with the highest level of employment for this industry are Michigan, California, Texas, Pennsylvania, and Ohio.

TRAINING, OTHER QUALIFICATIONS, AND ADVANCEMENT

An undergraduate degree is a minimal requirement for this field. Undergraduate degrees in fields such as logistics, engineering, and transportation are preferred by employers. Although an undergraduate degree is a minimum requirement for entry into this occupation, many employers prefer advanced degrees/certifications to complement undergraduate studies. Certification in Transportation and Logistics (CTL) is available for logistics engineers. To qualify for this certification, an undergraduate degree is necessary, as well as three years of field activity. Certification is appealing to employers and aids in the advancement process.

Other certification programs are available through:

- The Association for Operations Management (http://www.apics.org)
- The Institute for Supply Management (http://www.ism.ws)

- The International Society of Logistics (http://www.sole.org)
- The Supply Chain Council (http://supply-chain.org)
- The Council for Supply Chain Management Professionals (http://cscmp.org)

Senior managers supervise entry-level engineers, and middle management positions generally are available after four years of experience. Seniority typically comes after 11 years of experience. Senior positions in the industry include the Head Logistics Department and the Director of Logistics Engineers positions in various companies. Advancement possibilities vary from one company to another.

JOB OUTLOOK

This career is considered to be among the new and emerging careers. The increased potential lies in the ability of such engineers to reduce the negative impact sourcing goods has on the environment. The attention given to the use of green technology is expanding, especially in the transportation industry, an area where logistics engineers are primarily concerned.

In addition to increased attention, clean fuels are also receiving research funds. By the end of 2011, there was a total of US$450 million in newly invested funds in the natural gas vehicle sector. This boosts America's Natural Gas Highway initiative, which is focused on creating more natural gas fueling opportunities across U. S. highways for trucking companies to use. In addition to creating the infrastructure to support natural gas fueling, the funds are also to be used for development, construction, and support management, which includes logistics engineers to facilitate maximum efficiency.

EARNINGS

About 10 percent of entry-level logistics engineers earn US$23.89 per hour (US$49,700 annually). Twenty-five percent earn US$29.50 per hour (US$61,360 annually), and the median wage for a logistics engineer is US$36.59 per hour (US$76,100 annually). Experienced engineers earn US$44.74 (US$93,070 annually). The highest earners in this field make US$54.23 per hour (US$112,830 annually).

RELATED OCCUPATIONS

- Logistics manager
- Industrial engineer
- Statistical research specialist
- Quality assurance engineer
- Supply chain analyst
- Inventory analyst

- Sourcing manager
- Director of operations
- Vendor manager
- Purchasing manager
- Transportation manager

SOURCES OF ADDITIONAL INFORMATION

The Association for Operations Management. http://www.apics.org

The Council for Supply Chain Management Professionals. http://www.cscmp.org

The Institute for Supply Management. http://www.ism.ws

The International Society of Logistics. http://www.sole.org

The Supply Chain Council. http://www.supply-chain.org

FURTHER READING

Berman, Jeff. "Clean Energy Receives $150 Million Investment, brings 2011 total to $450 Million." *Logistics Management*. Accessed January 18, 2012. http://www.logisticsmgmt.com/article/clean_energy_receives_150_million_investment_brings_2011_total_to_450_milli.

Bureau of Labor Statistics, U.S. Department of Labor. "17-2112 Industrial Engineers." In *Occupational Employment and Wages, May 2009*. Accessed January 17, 2012. http://www.bls.gov/oes/2009/may/oes172112.htm.

Cover, Ben, John I. Jones, and Audrey Watson. *Science, Technology, Engineering, and Mathematics (STEM) Occupations: A Visual Essay*. Accessed January 17, 2012. http://www.bls.gov/opub/mlr/2011/05/art1full.pdf.

Jobs Online. Logistics Engineers Job Description. Accessed January 17, 2012. http://www.jobsonline.net/business-financial-operations-logisticsengineers-n27216202.

Peterson's. *Green Careers in Energy: The Indispensable Guide for Students and Career Changers*. Lawrenceville, NJ: Author, pp. 142–145, 2010.

Taylor, G. Don, ed. *Logistics Engineering Handbook*. Boca Raton, FL: Taylor & Francis Group, LLC, pp. 11-4, 11-13, 2008.

BIOCHEMICAL ENGINEERS

NATURE OF THE WORK

Biochemical engineers work closely with those in the field of chemical engineering. They deal extensively with biological materials and translate these materials into substances that help enhance the quality of life standards of the population they serve. The skills needed in this field include expertise in biology, chemistry, and engineering, which is what makes them a *biochemical engineer*. Many biochemical engineers conduct research in such areas as complex fermentation processes to aid in better storage of materials and the preservation of foods. They also research complex health issues, such as the course and processes of diseases such as cancer to develop better treatments and, when possible, cures. These engineers study and develop systems that deal directly with the chemical interactions of humans, the environment, animals, microorganisms, and other biological materials.

There are varied areas influenced by biochemical engineering, ranging from human and veterinary medicine and dentistry to the food science industry. For instance, in the food science industry biochemists research and develop strategies to create inexpensive sources of nutrients to help extend the shelf life of food and boost food production on a mass scale. These professionals take laboratory processes and apply them to large-scale manufacturing systems intended for commercial success. The application of this may involve enhancing already existing products or creating new ones.

The biochemical field includes the following sciences: biophysical chemistry, molecular biology, immunochemistry, neurochemistry, and bioinorganic and bioorganic chemistry. Jobs in this field vary depending on which specialization the biochemical engineer chooses, such as

AT A GLANCE FACT BOX

SOC: 17-2199.01
Preferred Education: Bachelor's degree in biochemical engineering or a related field for entry level positions. Advanced degrees are recommended for advancement.
Average Salary: US$74,950 to US$112,630 annually
Other Information: This industry is expected to grow at an 11 percent rate through 2018. Employment opportunities range from private research firms to institutions of higher education.

developmental biochemistry, clinical chemistry, pharmaceutical chemistry, enzyme chemistry, protein chemistry, or steroid chemistry. However, regardless of specialization, all biochemists will work in a research laboratory at some point in their career. In these laboratories biochemical engineers test new theories or develop new products and processes within the biochemistry field. Biochemical engineers are usually aided by laboratory technicians or research assistants. Tasks conducted on a daily basis in this field include experiments dealing with chemicals, the filtering of liquids, distilling ingredients, and testing various processes on microorganisms. Tools used in the laboratory for such processes include test tubes, flasks, beakers, electron microscopes, centrifuges, and spectrophotometers (which measure the reflective properties of materials by wavelength). Because all procedures and experiments are sensitive to even the slightest change, it is essential that biochemical engineers are extremely accurate and use technological advances such as computerized data in their research. The findings of such experiments are often presented to the scientific community in trade journals.

Green Energy and Chemical Engineers Bioscientists and biochemists within the green engineering field concur on the need for production of energy and materials from "green" feed stocks such as biomass and microorganisms (e.g., cyanobacteria, copepods, and prokaryotes) to reduce energy waste, greenhouse gas emissions, and water consumption. The aim of such processes is to allow consumption rates of energy to balance the earth's restoration systems, creating a sustainable consumption/restoration process. To reach such goals, biochemical engineers must discover ways to use fossil fuels to their maximum efficiency and to increase both the use and efficiency of renewable energy. Although individuals can contribute to this by carefully controlling heating and air conditioning settings in the home and using energy efficient appliances, engineers working behind the scenes can push change forward by creating major upgrades in the efficiency of systems in use currently and offering new products and processes that are in themselves green.

WORKING CONDITIONS

Biochemical engineers may work alone or as part of an extended team. Depending on the level of education and experience, such engineers may have research assistants to help complete routine daily tasks. Depending on their position and experience, they may work under supervision or may be the supervising director of such a team. Such engineers usually work in laboratories that are well-lit, well-ventilated, and well-equipped. Schedules tend to be regular and include a 40-hour work week. However, overtime is required when necessary to meet a deadline or complete a project.

EMPLOYMENT

According to the U.S. Department of Labor's Bureau of Labor Statistics (BLS) this is a top-rated industry for employment. Industries with the most employment in this field include basic chemical manufacturing; resin and synthetic rubber, artificial synthetic fibers and filaments manufacturing; pesticide, fertilizer, and other agricultural chemical manufacturing; petroleum and coal products manufacturing; as well as other chemical product and preparation manufacturing areas. Top paying industries, according to the BLS, include management, scientific, and technical consulting services. U.S. states with the

highest rates of employment in this field are Texas, California, Ohio, New Jersey, and Illinois.

TRAINING, OTHER QUALIFICATIONS, AND ADVANCEMENT

To gain employment as a biochemical engineer, a prospective applicant must have a bachelor's degree in biochemical engineering or a related field. As in other engineering fields, a bachelor's degree will provide opportunity for an entry-level position. Advanced degrees such as a master's or doctoral degree will help expand opportunities and advancement within the field. Depending on place of employment and specialty within biochemical engineering, entry level duties will vary. Some examples of typical entry-level biochemical engineering duties include troubleshooting production defects, creating Standard Operating Principles (SOPs) for equipment, running tests to help establish new products, modifying existing formulas and process settings to increase efficiency and capacity, working on wastewater treatment projects, and working on improving the quality of existing products.

Successful traits of a biochemical engineer include strong verbal and math skills, patience, a vivid imagination, and keen attention to detail.

JOB OUTLOOK

Biochemical engineering is considered a top field for growth within the green industry. The engineering field as a whole is expected to grow at an 11 percent rate from 2008 to 2018, and the area of specialization will impact such growth. Research, development, and consulting services will drive growth. Strong competition between international companies in the development of green technology to meet the rising demand for it will encourage such growth. Engineers in all fields will be needed to increase manufacturing productivity and develop new products and processes. In addition to the growing demand for engineers, the replacement of retiring engineers will also fuel demand. It is essential for engineers, especially those in the biochemistry field, to continually develop their knowledge in emerging trends in the green and scientific communities. This continuing education will help such engineers meet employer expectations. Those who have stayed abreast of new developments will also be able to position themselves strongly within an organization when seeking promotions and deflect layoffs.

EARNINGS

According to the BLS, the hourly wage for an entry level position is US$27.17 per hour (US$56,520 annually). The bottom quarter of wages reaches US$34.11 per hour (US$74,940 annually), while the top quarter reaches US$54.15 per hour (US$112,630 annually). Top earners in this field typically receive US$67.15 per hour (US$139,670 annually).

RELATED OCCUPATIONS

Fields related to biochemical engineering include:

- Biological scientist
- Water treatment plant chemist
- Chemical technician
- Biomedical engineer
- Agricultural scientist
- Chemist
- Chemical engineer
- Ceramic engineer
- Botanist

SOURCES OF ADDITIONAL INFORMATION

American Chemical Society. http://www.acs.org

American Institute of Chemical Engineers. http://www.aiche.org

The American Society for Biochemistry and Molecular Biology. http://www.asbmb.org

FURTHER READING

Bureau of Labor Statistics, U.S. Department of Labor. *Chemical Engineers.* Accessed March 14, 2012. http://www.bls.gov/oes/current/oes172041.htm.

Mendez, Miguel (Mike). "The Role of Chemical Engineering in Green Engineering." *Chemical Engineering,* December 2007. Accessed March 14, 2012. http://www.aspentech.com/publication_files/Chemical_Engineering_Green_Engineering_1207.pdf.

Michigan.gov. *#380 Biochemist.* Michigan Jobs and Career Portal. Accessed March 14, 2012. http://www.michigan.gov/careers/0,1607, 7-170-46398-64793—,00.html.

O*Net OnLine. *Biochemical Engineers.* Accessed March 16, 2012. http://www.onetonline.org/link/summary/17-2199.01.

ROBOTICS ENGINEERS

NATURE OF THE WORK

Robotics engineers are the people behind the manufacture of the huge equipment found in textile factories, car manufacturing plants, or medical and military equipment. A robotics engineer not only creates the machines responsible for building a car and other heavy-scale machinery but also is responsible for maintaining and developing new applications for such technology. Conducting research to advance robotics is also another integral responsibility of a robotics engineer. A major benefit for the production of robots is that it relieves humans from strenuous and often dangerous labor.

Robotics engineering is one of the most interdisciplinary fields of engineering because it takes knowledge from different sectors of engineering to put together a single robot, whether for manufacturing, military, or medical purposes. For instance, the robot's structure is designed and created by a mechanical engineer. This engineer will ensure that all joint areas are working correctly and all bearings flow smoothly. Electronic engineers are called in when the structure is complete, and it goes from being a simple metal structure into a moving robot. These engineers work on its sensors and electrical conditioning. The computing hardware required for the robot is then implemented by computer engineers. In the end, robotics engineers pull all this together to create the finished robot.

The desired skill set for a career in robotics engineering is knowledge of mathematics and science, as well as the ability to work deftly with one's hands. Because of the hands-on nature of the work, robotics engineers are often required to work on-site. For example, robotics engineers who are employed by car manufacturers will often be

> ## AT A GLANCE FACT BOX
>
> **SOC:** 17-2199.08
> **Preferred Education:** As with most engineering careers, a graduate degree is preferred, in this case an advanced degree in electrical or mechanical engineering
> **Average Salary:** Varies
> **Other Information:** This job can be very specialized and often requires multidisciplinary skills, which may lead to on-the-job training

called into the factory to inspect, fix, or upgrade robots. If they are in the medical field, their specialization may call them into a hospital room to inspect how a physician is using the robotic technology and consider possibilities for improvement in the machine.

Areas of specialization within the robotics engineering field include artificial intelligence, computer architecture, operating systems, and networks. However, areas of subspecialization within a specific field are also common. Robotics engineers are often employed in the transportation, aerospace, aeronautics, and automotive industries.

The Green Effect on Robotics Engineering There is a growing interest in investing in green technology because of the effect of changing government regulations on manufacturers, as well as a shift in personal views.

Therefore, the field of green technology and the robotics engineering behind it are growing. Robotics engineering is considered an emerging green career path. Because automotive manufacturing is a major industry for robotics engineers, there is a natural correlation between the expansion and sales of green cars (i.e., hybrid, electric, clean diesel) and the opportunity for growth in robotics engineering. The American Recovery and Reinvestment Act of 2009 included an extension of tax breaks for green automobiles purchased after 2009. This act was intended to promote the growth of green technology in automotive sales and the green robotics engineering occupations behind the manufacture of them.

The growth of solar- and wind-powered energy is another avenue of green robotics engineering. In these fields, robotics engineers are responsible for producing effective and cost-efficient solar panels and wind turbines that speed up production and eliminate the waste involved in the energy conversion process.

WORKING CONDITIONS

The working conditions of robotics engineers vary from project to project as well as in each project stage. Some robotics engineers spend the majority of their time in laboratories creating designs and robotics prototypes. As mentioned earlier, some robotics engineers need to venture on-site to collaborate with other professionals to assess the effectiveness of the robotics involved, create solutions to problems, and upgrade current technology in different settings and industries. Robotics engineers often work a standard 40-hour workweek. However, overtime is sometimes required when project deadlines loom. Depending on the industry and company in question, stress levels will vary.

Although there is some interpersonal communication in this field (depending on stage and scope of project), robotics engineers also spend a lot of time alone analyzing data. They can at times be placed in situations where there are conflicting opinions, and they have to negotiate these situations. They also may be responsible for the safety of others when on-site. The physical work conditions robotics engineers are exposed to may include loud, uncomfortable sounds and areas that house heavy machinery. They may be required to wear safety gear depending on the equipment being used in their surroundings.

EMPLOYMENT

An estimated 234,400 individuals across the United States are employed as robotics engineers (under the heading of mechanical engineers) according to the U.S. Department of Labor's Bureau of Labor Statistics (BLS). The salary range varies, depending on the size of the employer and the experience of the robotics engineer. The states with the most employment opportunities in this field include Michigan (the principal car manufacturing state), California, Texas, Ohio, and Pennsylvania.

Private companies and consulting firms are major employers of robotics engineers, as well as biotechnology companies geared toward creating materials for research groups, hospitals, and universities. Military and space programs are also an avenue for such engineers.

TRAINING, OTHER QUALIFICATIONS, AND ADVANCEMENT

Robotics engineers need to have at minimum an undergraduate degree in electrical, computer, or mechanical engineering. However, as in other engineering fields, a graduate degree is preferred and often required for career advancement. A robotics engineer should have excellent knowledge of engineering and technology, that is, how things are built, and also a working knowledge of many construction tools to create models on their own. Mathematics and science are both instrumental in this field, and a strong grasp of both is essential for success. Additional courses in technology and communications are helpful. With an advanced degree, robotics engineers may move into a leadership role. Individuals with business skills may also start their own robotics consulting firms or companies.

To be successful as a robotics engineer strong critical thinking skills are essential. The ability to find innovative solutions to complex problems is another skill that will help promote success in this field. Strong analytical skills are also required because such engineers spend a lot of time interacting with data. The ability to visualize strongly is essential, especially when in occupations that help develop new technologies for growing industries such as the green sector.

JOB OUTLOOK

The industry growth for robotics engineers will depend partly on the growth of the green sector. This is especially true for the research and manufacturing arenas. Robotics engineers will be called on to create more effective production processes and the mechanics to facilitate these processes. Between the years of 2009 and 2019 the industry is expected to grow at a rate of 6.6 percent.

EARNINGS

According to the BLS, national wages for an entry-level robotics engineer are US$24.30 per hour (US$55,500 annually). The median wage for this occupation is US$37.58 per hour (US$78,160 annually). Top earners receive US$57.44 per hour (US$119,480 annually). Again, wages vary depending on the institution employing the engineer and the engineer's experience in the field.

RELATED OCCUPATIONS

Mechanical and biochemical engineering are fields related to robotics engineering. These fields require similar skill sets, qualifications, and educational requirements for employment and advancement.

SOURCES OF ADDITIONAL INFORMATION

American Society of Mechanical Engineers. http://www
.asme.org/kb/topics/robotics
Carnegie Mellon Robotics Institute. http://www
.ri.cmu.edu
Robotics and Automation Society. http://www.ieee-ras.org
Robotics Industries Association. http://www
.robotics.org

FURTHER READING

American Society of Mechanical Engineers. *Robotics*.
Accessed February 3, 2012. http://www.asme.org/
kb/topics/robotics.
Bureau of Labor Statistics, U.S. Department of Labor.
"Engineers." In *Occupational Outlook Handbook,*
2010–11 Edition. Accessed February 3, 2012.
http://www.bls.gov/oco/ocos027.htm.
hybridCARS. *JD Power Sees 4x Growth in Green Car*
Market by 2016. Accessed February 3, 2012. http://
www.hybridcars.com/news/jd-power-sees-4x-growth-
green-car-market-2016-29806.html.
iSeek Careers. *Robotics Engineers*. Accessed February 3,
2012. http://www.iseek.org/careers/careerDetail?id=
1&oc=100535.
O*NET OnLine. *Green Occupations: 17-2199.08—*
Robotics Engineers. Accessed February 3, 2012.
http://www.onetonline.org/help/green/17-2199.08.
Payment, Simone. *Robotics Careers: Preparing for the*
Future. New York: Rosen Publishing Group, 2011,
pp. 23–25.
The Princeton Review. *Career: Robotics Engineer*. Accessed
February 3, 2012. http://www.princetonreview.com/
careers.aspx?cid=139.
unbiased.co.uk. *Growing Interest in Green and Ethical*
Investment. Accessed February 3, 2012. http://www
.unbiased.co.uk/growing-interest-green-and-ethical-
investment.

CHEMISTS

NATURE OF THE WORK

Chemists are scientists who carefully study substances, that is, the existence of matter (solids, liquids, and gases), how matter changes, and what causes such change. The work a chemist does can be divided into two categories: macroscopic and microscopic. In the microscopic division chemists are often working hands-on with different substances in a laboratory. During this stage they experiment with how various substances work together and the factors that cause change. In the macroscopic capacity, chemists work in theory. They create diagrams and notes on how their microscopic experiments translate into theory and vice versa.

As a chemist, one can expect to spend a lot of time analyzing substances. Chemists try to find out what makes up a particular substance in an attempt to find the active ingredients and other information. One use of such experiments is to create synthetic versions of natural substances or to try to create an entirely new substance.

The daily activity of chemists depends on their job title. For instance, a *quality control chemist* inspects raw materials as well as intermediate and final products to ensure they meet the set standards for such products. This type of chemist is often involved in a manufacturing setting. By contrast, an *industrial research chemist* often performs both physical and chemical tests on different materials. They can help improve existing products and create new ones. An industrial research chemist may be called on to provide customers with technical support, as well as create products formulated specifically to a client's needs.

Chemists may also work in the field of sales. A sales representative with a background in chemistry often

works with a pharmaceutical or chemical company. In addition to helping customers solve specific problems with particular products, they are responsible for the sale of new products to clients.

Forensic chemists are often employed by a government agency. They analyze substances found at a crime scene. As part of their responsibilities, forensic chemists may be called into court as an expert witness to testify on their findings.

Environmental chemists will often work for agencies eager to develop processes that help with purification systems such as those used by the U.S. Department of Energy, the U.S. Environmental Protection Agency, and other such entities.

Depending on the level of education received, chemists may work in education. The level that is taught depends highly on the degree held; college-level

---

AT A GLANCE FACT BOX

SOC: 19-2031.00
Preferred Education: Bachelor's of science in chemistry for entry level positions; research positions require a master's or doctoral degree in chemistry or a related field
Average Salary: US$68,320 annually
Other Information: Chemists should possess excellent knowledge of chemistry and other fields of science and must also have strong communication skills

---

chemistry, for example, requires a master's degree at minimum. Chemists are also found in the preservation field, preserving and restoring historical documents. The list of opportunities available for chemists continues to grow and may include career options in medicine, law, writing, and consulting.

Green Chemistry Green chemistry is a relatively new area that began in 1991. At that time widespread concern was emerging over human health and the effects of waste, pollution, and the by-products of industrial chemicals on the human body. Green chemistry found its basis with advancements made with catalysis, atom-economical synthesis, degradable materials, and alternative solvents, among others. These advancements gave green chemistry its foundation to address growing concerns. Since then, chemists in the green chemistry field have produced thousands of documents such as research papers and new scientific journals. One example is the *Green Chemistry Journal* established by the Royal Society of Chemistry. Breakthroughs in this field include green solvents (which reduce solvent waste), biobased transformations and materials (used as alternatives to fossil fuels), alternative energy science, next-generation catalyst design, and molecular design, which creates chemicals that reduce hazardous waste.

WORKING CONDITIONS

Generally, chemists work in well-lit, well-equipped laboratories. They may also work in classrooms or offices. They usually have regular schedules and work approximately 40 hours a week. The nature of their research may take them outdoors or inside chemical plants. Chemists may work with hazardous materials, which require special protective gear. Depending on their specialization, stress levels and time commitments vary.

EMPLOYMENT

According to the U.S. Department of Labor's Bureau of Labor Statistics (BLS), in May 2010, there were an estimated 80,180 chemists employed throughout the United States. As of 2011 manufacturers employed 60 percent of chemists in the workforce, mainly within the chemical manufacturing field. The industries inside the manufacturing sector that are popular for chemists include plastics, food, and electronics manufacturing; biotechnology; and pharmaceutical manufacturers. Manufacturers producing paints, detergents, and cosmetics also need chemists to continually improve current products and create new items.

Beyond these industries, the second largest employer of chemists is in academic institutions. Chemists with a bachelor's degree are often found in a secondary teaching

setting. However, if a chemist is employed by a university, strong emphasis is placed on research and those with graduate-level degrees are preferred. The scope of career opportunities for an individual with a chemistry background is extensive, depending on specialization. Extended opportunities include marketing, sales, public relations, technical writing, patent law, and quality control as well as analyses and testing.

According to the BLS, there are several top-paying industries for chemists. These include oil and gas extraction, the U.S. federal government, aerospace products and parts manufacturing, and other fabricated metal product manufacturing, as well as scientific research and development services. The states with the highest levels of employment for this field are California, New Jersey, Texas, Pennsylvania, and New York. The highest paying states are Maryland, New Mexico, Delaware, and Massachusetts, along with Washington, DC.

TRAINING, OTHER QUALIFICATIONS, AND ADVANCEMENT

During the course of an undergraduate degree in chemistry, students take a series of chemistry, physics, and mathematics classes, along with elective classes. If American Chemical Society certification is to be acquired upon graduation, advanced chemistry is required of the student. Entry-level chemists with a bachelor of science in chemistry often work under the close scrutiny of seasoned chemists, usually those with advanced degrees such as a master's or doctoral degree. Quality control and research assistant positions are other entry-level positions. Many companies have programs that offer help in funding graduate study for their employees because this is seen as an investment in the company as well.

Acquiring a doctoral degree in the field of chemistry usually takes five years. Graduate students pursuing a doctoral degree in chemistry are expected to spend anywhere between 40 and 60 hours per week conducting research. The pressures of pursuing such a degree are often immense, with limited vacation time (compared with the undergraduate course of study).

Successful individuals in this field are able to apply scientific rules and theories to solve problems. They are able to comprehend written material, stay current on scientific developments, and pay strong attention to detail. Computer skills are also essential because employers prefer candidates who are computer literate.

Advancement in this field often comes with increased independence and flexibility in research and may depend on research funding. Many chemists move into managerial positions, open their own consulting firms, or spend an increasing amount of time setting research policy.

JOB OUTLOOK

The expected growth of this field, according to the BLS, at 3 percent between 2008 and 2018 is slower than the average for other fields. A number of factors influence this rate, including increased competition from several sources. Those with advanced degrees have better entry and growth opportunities. The growth that is occurring is related to the green technology sector and the need for expanding technologies related to scientific advances within this field.

EARNINGS

Earnings at the entry level begin at US$18.87 per hour (US$39,250 annually). The median wage for several years of experience is US$32.85 per hour (US$69,320 annually). Top earners in the field receive US$55.83 per hour (US$116,130 annually).

RELATED OCCUPATIONS

Occupations related to the chemistry field include the following:

- Biologist
- Chemical engineer
- Environmental engineer
- Materials scientist
- Medical technologist
- Pharmacist
- Pharmacologist

SOURCES OF ADDITIONAL INFORMATION

American Chemical Society. http://www.acs.org
American Institute of Chemists. http://www.theaic.org
Chemical Heritage Foundation, http://www.chemheritage.org

FURTHER READING

Anastas, Paul. "Twenty Years of Green Chemistry." *Chemical & Engineering News,* June 27, 2011. Accessed February 6, 2012. http://pubs.acs.org/cen/coverstory/89/8926cover6.html?utm_source=feedburner&utm_medium=feed&utm_campaign=Feed%3A+EnvironmentalScienceTechnologyOnline News+(ES%26T+Online+News)&utm_content=My+Yahoo.

Bureau of Labor Statistics, U.S. Department of Labor. "19-2031 Chemists." In *Occupational Employment Statistics: Occupational Employment and Wages, May 2010.* Accessed February 7, 2012. http://www.bls.gov/oes/current/oes192031.htm.

———. "Chemists and Materials Scientists." In *Occupational Outlook Handbook 2010–11 Edition.* Accessed February 7, 2012. http://www.bls.gov/oco/ocos049.htm.

Chemistry Explained. *Careers in Chemistry.* Accessed February 7, 2012. http://www.chemistryexplained.com/Bo-Ce/Careers-in-Chemistry.html.

Employment Development Department. *Labor Market Information.* Accessed February 7, 2012. http://www.calmis.ca.gov/file/occguide/chemist.htm.

Georgia State University. *B.S. in Chemistry.* Accessed February 7, 2012. http://www.gsu.edu/bs_chemistry_pa.html.

O*NET OnLine. *Green Occupation: 19-2031—Chemists.* Accessed February 7, 2012. http://www.onetonline.org/help/green/19-2031.00.

COMMERCIAL AND INDUSTRIAL DESIGNERS

NATURE OF THE WORK

Automobiles, appliances, children's toys, and other manufactured products used on a daily basis are all the creations of commercial and industrial designers. Almost anything for sale today, from electronic devices and pens to table lamps and toys, is conceived and engineered by commercial and industrial designers. This type of engineering differs from other engineering fields because it deals with the business aspect of selling a product in addition to its actual creation. Commercial and industrial designers begin by creating a blueprint for a product. This process begins with either hand-drawn sketches or computer-based designs.

When creating these blueprints, a commercial and industrial designer must keep in mind the needs of the manufacturer of the product, the needs of the consumer once the product is made, and how marketable the product will be. Once a concept is agreed upon by a team of engineers, a model is usually created. The initial model is often tweaked several times to meet customer expectations or to adjust faults within the model. When the model is considered ready, it is the responsibility of a commercial and industrial designer to present it to investors and groups of consumers. Such presentations may introduce further tweaks to the model before production.

These designers are not only responsible for designing the products, but they must also consider the cost of production and the most efficient ways of distribution and sustainability in their design and chosen production process. They also have to consider the pros and cons of creating new products versus updating older ones. The 21st century has brought with it an appeal for upgrades. Technology is continually being upgraded to provide the

AT A GLANCE FACT BOX

SOC: 27-1021.00
Preferred Education: Bachelor's degree
Preferred Specialty: Industrial design, engineering, or architecture
Average Salary: US$58,230 annually
Other Information: Business skills as well as strong creativity, self-discipline, and organizational skills are essential for success in this field

consumer market with better, faster, and more viable products.

This field is highly dependent on technology. The tools used on a daily basis include computers, digital cameras, and design software. The design software is used frequently to bring manual sketches to life and to easily alter designs during the production process. Business skills are also needed to help sell the product to investors and to make it appealing to consumers. This field, therefore, entwines engineering principles, art, and business skills.

Green Sustainability in Commercial and Industrial Design Principles of green sustainability have found their way into the commercial and industrial design field. Rather than creating a product that uses materials without consideration of the effect the materials could have on the planet, green sustainability and the "Cradle-to-Cradle" perspective (defined by William McDonough) infuse this science with social responsibility. According to the article "Cradle-to-Cradle Design and the Principles of Green Design," the goal of this framework is to create "the design of a commercially productive, socially beneficial and ecologically intelligent industrial system." This framework is based on 12 strategic theories of green engineering that are used to enhance sustainability in the production engineering fields. The foundation for these 12 theories can be distilled into three basic principles: "waste equals food" (or the natural system in which one organism's waste is another organism's food), the use of "solar income" (or the amount of sunlight that falls on Earth), and the ability to celebrate diversity.

The Basis of the Cradle-to-Cradle Framework The designs created within this framework aim to solve rather than temporarily relieve man-made environmental hazards. The principles of the Cradle-to-Cradle design work by assuming that the natural world should serve as the ultimate example for creating new design for practical use. For instance, using the concept of "waste equals food," designers infuse the regenerative system found in nature into the designs of new products. This philosophy encourages design engineers to use high-tech synthetics and the like to create a production system that incorporates production, use, recovery, and remanufacture.

Using "solar income" is another basis for this framework. Living things thrive on the sun's energy. The Cradle-to-Cradle framework urges designers to tap into the sun's energy by using direct or passive solar energy such as the growing daylighting trend. *Daylighting* maximizes natural lighting to illuminate building space instead of using electricity alone.

The final basis for this framework is to celebrate diversity. The conscientious engineer creates sustainable products that fit into the local ecological system. For instance, when a product is being developed the focus is not solely on the product itself but also on its surroundings. The engineer must ask where and how the product will fit to enhance its intended environment. This becomes the responsibility of the commercial and industrial designer and is the foundation for the 12 principles of green engineering.

The 12 Principles of Green Engineering The 12 principles of green engineering are as follows:

1. Create products that are as non-hazardous as possible.
2. Prevent waste rather than find solutions to waste.
3. Minimize energy and materials consumption throughout production.
4. Aim to maximize space, energy, mass, and time efficiency.
5. Focus on end results and the impact of products on the environment rather than solely concentrating on the immediate product itself.
6. Choose designs that take into account reuse, recycling, and suitable disposal of products.
7. Make design durability the intended goal for products rather than product immortality.
8. Design products that meet specific needs. Generic creations, which are considered flawed, should be avoided.
9. Minimize material variety in production, allowing for easier disassembly.
10. Design products to integrate and connect with the available energy and materials used in production. Interconnect energy and material flows.
11. Create products geared toward a commercial afterlife, where parts can be reused after the initial purpose of the product has been dissolved.
12. Renew and do not deplete. All materials used during production should be renewable.

WORKING CONDITIONS

Commercial and industrial designers who are employed by large manufacturing firms often work in well-lit spaces with the latest technology in hardware and software at their disposal. When additional research on a product is needed, a designer may travel to testing facilities, design centers, or clients' homes. Those employed in large manufacturing firms often have regular schedules, working around 40 hours per week. Commercial and industrial designers who are employed with smaller manufacturing firms or who have their own consulting firms may work longer hours and travel more frequently to meet deadlines and expectations.

EMPLOYMENT

There are about 28,670 commercial and industrial design engineers employed throughout the United States. The fields that offer the highest levels of employment in this area, according to the U.S. Department of Labor's Bureau of Labor Statistics (BLS), are architecture, engineering, and related services; specialized design services; miscellaneous manufacturing; plastics product manufacturing; and motor vehicle parts manufacturing. The highest-paying industries are motor vehicle manufacturing, business schools and computer and management training, navigational controls manufacturing, architectural engineering and related services, and motor vehicle parts wholesalers. The U.S. states with the highest levels of employment for this field are Michigan, California, New York, Pennsylvania, and Illinois. The U.S. states with the highest salaries are Kansas, Oregon, Mississippi, Michigan, and Massachusetts.

TRAINING, OTHER QUALIFICATIONS, AND ADVANCEMENT

A bachelor's degree in industrial design, architecture, or engineering is necessary for an entry-level position in this field. An undergraduate wishing to find a career after graduation as a commercial and industrial designer should consider taking courses in design, sketching, computer design, and manufacturing methods, as well as other engineering courses such as mathematics and physics. Because business marketing concepts are an integral part of this field, many candidates pursue graduate degrees in business management to advance their careers.

An aesthetic awareness is needed for success as a commercial and industrial designer, which means a good sense of proportion, color, and creativity. In addition to making their products useful and artistic, commercial and industrial designers must be able to communicate their ideas effectively both verbally and nonverbally. Self-discipline is also important because many commercial and industrial designers have flexible schedules, and if they are not sufficiently self-disciplined, deadlines may be missed.

To advance as a commercial and industrial designer, continuing education, often in the form of on-the-job training provided by many manufacturers, is needed. Several years of experience are also necessary. When these qualifications have been met, commercial and industrial designers can advance to supervisory roles, such as chief designer or design department head. Teaching at the university level is also a popular option for many such designers. Experienced commercial and industrial designers may also use their business skills and creative talent to open small consulting firms.

JOB OUTLOOK

The prospective job outlook for this industry is 9 percent growth between 2008 and 2018. This increase is due in part to consumer demand for renewed products. A growing emphasis on safety, quality, and ecologically sound products as well as a consistent need to upgrade products in the 21st century will also fuel this growth. Although 9 percent is positive growth, the industry will not grow at maximum capacity in the United States because of manufacturers sending such positions to locations closer to their product suppliers. Competition in this field is strong; highly skilled individuals compete for similar positions. A designer who specializes in a particular area of design can help increase the chance of employment in a firm that also specializes in that area.

EARNINGS

According to the BLS, the lowest 10 percent of commercial and industrial designers earn US$15.96 per hour (US$33,190 annually). Twenty-five percent of engineers in this field earned US$20.73 per hour (US$43,120 annually). The median wage for this field is US$27.99 per hour (US$58,230 annually). The top earners at 90 percent earn US$45.32 per hour (US$94,270 annually).

RELATED OCCUPATIONS

Individuals with similar interests to commercial and industrial designers may find the following fields beneficial:

- Architectural designers
- Floral designers
- Graphic designers
- Drafters
- Computer software engineers

SOURCES OF ADDITIONAL INFORMATION

The Industrial Designers Society of America (IDSA). http://www.idsa.org
International Council of Societies of Industrial Design (ICSID). http://www.icsid.org
National Association of Schools of Art and Design. http://nasad.arts-accredit.org

FURTHER READING

Anastas, Paul T., and Julie Zimmerman. "Design Through the 12 Principles of Green Engineering." *Environmental Science and Technology,* 37 (5), 2003: 94A–101A. DOI: 10.1021/es032373g. Accessed February 29, 2012. http://pubs.acs.org/doi/abs/10.1021/es032373g.

Bureau of Labor Statistics, U.S. Department of Labor. "Commercial and Industrial Designers." In *Occupational Outlook Handbook, 2010–11 Edition.* Accessed February 10, 2012. http://www.bls.gov/oco/ocos290.htm.

McDonough, William, Michael Braungart, Paul Anastas, and Julie Zimmerman. "Cradle-to-Cradle Design and the Principles of Green Design." Originally published in *Environmental Science and Technology,* December 1, 2003. Accessed February 10, 2012. http://www.mcdonough.com/writings/c2c_design.htm.

New Jersey Institute of Technology. "Industrial Engineering." *University Catalog NJIY.* Accessed February 10, 2012. http://catalog.njit.edu/graduate/programs/industrialengineering.php.

O*NET OnLine. *Summary Report for: 27-1021.00—Commercial and Industrial Designers.* Accessed February 10, 2012. http://www.onetonline.org/link/summary/27-1021.00.

SECTOR OVERVIEW: RECYCLING AND WASTE REDUCTION

In its 2009 report titled "Greening of the World of Work: Implications for O*NET-SOC and New and Emerging Occupations," O*NET included recycling and waste reduction in its list of 12 major green economy sectors. O*NET identified these sectors as key to the green economy after extensive research on extant information. It concluded that economic activity within the recycling sector is critical to the definition of a green economy. This includes both solid and liquid waste recycling materials and a reduction in the use of fossil fuels.

Recycling transforms materials that would otherwise become waste into valuable resources. As a result, many proponents of recycling argue that not only does it help conserve natural resources, such as fossil fuels used in manufacturing, but it also reduces factory emissions, and, by transforming waste into usable products, recycling mitigates the need for landfills. These benefits are instrumental to the success of a green economy.

Information from Ohio State University's College of Food, Agricultural, and Environmental Sciences suggests that the importance of recycling in reducing the use of fossil fuels and decreasing pollution and greenhouse gas emissions cannot be overstated. Recycling aluminum, for example, requires 95 percent less energy than producing aluminum from raw material. Recycling paper uses two-thirds (64 percent) less energy than starting from wood pulp, and recycling plastic saves up to 60 percent of the energy required to start from raw materials. Further evidence of the importance of recycling to a green economy comes from Earth911, a for-profit, environmental services company based in Scottsdale, Arizona. On its website, Earth911 reports the following progression of job creation in processing solid waste. Incinerating

10,000 tons of waste creates one job. Landfilling the same amount of waste creates six jobs, whereas recycling 10,000 tons of waste creates 36 jobs.

Clearly, efforts by governmental, educational, and private entities have established the argument for the critical role of the recycling and waste reduction sector in a green economy. Further, the sector's importance will only become stronger. Not only does the world's population continue to increase but so too does the amount of waste generated per person. The U.S. Environmental Protection Agency (EPA), which has collected and reported data on the generation and disposal of waste in the United States for more than 30 years, reports that municipal solid waste per person per day increased from 2.7 pounds in 1960 to 4.3 pounds in 2009, an increase of 62 percent. It follows, then, that as the need for and the prevalence of recycling continue to grow, so will the need for more workers across a broad range of skill levels to collect, sort, and process recyclables.

Several steps are necessary for unwanted by-products to become a usable resource. Workers with specific skill levels are needed at each step: drivers, sorters, technicians, mechanics, and coordinators, as well as skilled employees in support roles, such as management, sales, logistics, and human resources. These workers are classified into specific industries, including construction and extraction occupations, production occupations, and transportation and material moving occupations.

O*NET has determined that these industries within the recycling and waste reduction sector include green jobs with two broad definitions. Green Enhanced Skills occupations exist already in the standard occupational classification system. The essential purpose of these jobs has not changed; however, there is significant revision to the skills, responsibilities, and core functions of the workers in these jobs. Green New and Emerging occupations require uniquely different work and employee requirements that are now necessary owing to the growth of a green economy. Because many of these jobs require no formal education beyond high school, regardless of which definition or industry they fall into, the recycling and waste reduction sector is considered an area of opportunity for workers without the education or other credentials to compete in occupations with greater requirements.

The recycling process always begins with the consumer, whether households, businesses, institutions, or construction sites. Waste materials, the unwanted by-products of consumption, are gathered by refuse and recyclable materials collectors, who deliver the solid waste material to a materials recovery facility (MRF), where they are sorted by type. In the case of hazardous waste, such as asbestos, lead-based paint, or contaminated soil, to name a few, only workers who are specially trained in the collection, shipment, or processing of such materials can be involved in the process.

Depending on the MRF, sorting recyclables can be a labor-intensive endeavor. In some facilities workers standing alongside conveyor belts sort the materials by hand. In other MRFs, technology, such as high-power magnets or strong fans, is used to automatically separate materials into type. Once sorted, the waste is then processed into raw materials and packaged for ease of shipping to manufacturers, who use the materials previously considered waste as resources for new products.

Significant investments in recycling by national, state, and local governments as well as private companies have led to increased demand for employment in this sector. The U.S. Department of Labor's Bureau of Labor Statistics (BLS) forecasts an increase of 14 percent from 2006 to 2016 for occupations related to waste management. Rather than being equally distributed, some regions of the United States and other parts of the world will experience a greater increase in employment demand than others. For example, recycling is more prevalent on the west coast and northeast of the United States.

Several trends are improving the efficiency of recycling efforts and, therefore, the availability of recycled materials. Two such trends are the growth of curbside recycling and single-stream recycling. As the name implies, curbside recycling means that consumers simply place their recyclables at the end of their driveways on specified days, and the materials are picked up just like the household's trash is retrieved. According to the EPA, local governments today provide curbside recycling services to more than half of U.S. households, and the number is growing. Furthermore, the EPA has discovered that, when

executed well with a strong recycling ethic and enforcement of process requirements, curbside recycling programs are actually less costly than waste retrieval and disposal in landfills.

Increasingly, recycling is becoming single-stream, which means that all recyclables are collected together and sorted later. Consumers prefer single-stream recycling because they do not have to sort waste materials and maintain separate bins for each type, thereby making recycling almost as easy as discarding trash. Material-moving companies prefer single-stream recycling because it requires fewer trucks and pick-ups. Furthermore, according to Earth911, evidence suggests that single-stream recycling increases the quantity of household recyclables, probably because of the reduced time and effort by consumers.

Another trend that is affecting the recycling and waste reduction sector is the prevalence of electronic waste, such as computers, televisions, and cell phones. The Institute of Recycling Industries reports that the global e-cycling industry was worth US$5.4 billion in 2009 and is expected to reach US$14.7 billion by the end of 2014, an increase of more than two and a half times. With one or more components classified as hazardous, the disposal and recycling of electronic waste, *e-cycling,* is increasingly being regulated by governments. The EPA says that about half of the states in the United States currently have laws on disposal and recycling of electronics with several others considering similar laws.

With such trends improving the use and efficacy of recycling efforts, combined with a growing need for reductions in the use of fossil fuels and the amount of waste generated by the world's population, the recycling and waste reduction sector will remain a critical part of any green economy. Continued investment in recycling infrastructure and technology by both the public and private sectors reinforces the importance of this growing sector.

FURTHER READING

Dierdorff, Erich C., Jennifer J. Norton, Donald W. Drewes, and Christina M. Kroustalis. "Greening of the World of Work: Implications for O*NET-SOC and New and Emerging Occupations." *O*NET,* February 12, 2009. Accessed March 19, 2012. http://www.onetcenter.org/dl_files/Green.pdf.

Earth911. *Curbside Recycling.* Accessed December 29, 2011. http://earth911.com/recycling/curbsiderecycling.

Heimlich, Joe E. "Recycling." *Ohio State University Fact Sheet.* Accessed December 29, 2011. http://ohioline.osu.edu/cd-fact/0108.html.

Liming, Drew. "Careers in Recycling." *Bureau of Labor Statistics* U.S. Department of Labor, September 2011. Accessed March 19, 2012. http://www.bls.gov/green/recycling/.

U.S. Environmental Protection Agency. "Municipal Solid Waste Generation, Recycling, and Disposal in the United States: Facts and Figures for 2010." EPA-530-F-11-005, November 2011. Accessed March 19, 2012. http://www.epa.gov/wastes/nonhaz/municipal/pubs/msw_2010_factsheet.pdf.

———. "Recycling." Accessed December 29, 2011. http://www.epa.gov/epawaste/conserve/rrr/recycle.htm#steps.

HAZARDOUS MATERIALS REMOVAL WORKERS

NATURE OF THE WORK

Hazardous materials (HAZMAT) removal workers are classified in several different green economy sectors, including environment protection, green construction, and recycling and waste reduction. This essay presents characteristics of HAZMAT removal workers in the latter sector, in which the workers are responsible for identifying, removing, and disposing of materials that are unwanted by-products of other industries such as construction, manufacturing, or scientific research.

Hazardous materials are defined and regulated in the United States by laws and regulations administered primarily by the U.S. Environmental Protection Agency (EPA), U.S. Occupational Safety and Health Administration (OSHA), U.S. Department of Transportation, and the U.S. Nuclear Regulatory Commission. A hazardous material is defined as any item or substance that is harmful or toxic to people, animals, or the environment. Hazardous materials include asbestos, lead-based paint, radioactive waste, contaminated soil, spent fuel, and, increasingly, electronic waste. Although not typically considered hazardous, mold, when present in large quantities, is often removed by HAZMAT specialists because of the harsh allergic reactions it can cause.

O*NET categorizes hazardous materials removal workers as a Green Enhanced occupation, meaning activities and technologies in the green economy will significantly change work performed by employees in this occupation. For example, hazardous materials removal workers have always been responsible for surveying and monitoring worksites using handheld tools, but with

AT A GLANCE FACT BOX

SOC: 47-4041.00
Preferred Education: High school diploma or equivalent
Average Salary: US$30,630 to US$46,300 annually
Other Information: Employment opportunities are expected to grow 15 percent from 2008 to 2018, faster than the national average. Federal, state, and local governments regulate training, certification, and licensing to work with specific materials or situations.

advances in technology the work is increasingly being done remotely to improve safety.

Typically, work with hazardous materials can be predicted and is therefore planned months, and sometimes years, in advance. This is the case in construction or demolition endeavors. At other times, emergencies in which harmful substances have been unexpectedly compromised, such as oil spills, trucking accidents, or train derailments, require an immediate, spontaneous response. Regardless of the circumstance, hazardous materials removal workers must be knowledgeable about federal and state laws and other governmental safety regulations and procedures as they go about their daily responsibilities.

The responsibilities of HAZMAT employees vary depending on the job and material with which they are working. Workers first sort materials into those which can be recycled and those which require treatment. Because of the potential danger, HAZMAT employees often work in teams. They must follow laws, strict rules, and detailed procedures at all times. Hazardous materials removal employees are responsible for their own health and safety as well as that of their coworkers and the general public.

Employees who work with hazardous materials use a wide variety of tools to assess situations, determine appropriate responses, and then *remediate*, or remove, potentially dangerous substances. Monitoring, sampling, and measuring tools determine levels of radioactive waste or other contamination in air, soil, and water. After the site has been evaluated, tools used to decontaminate work sites range from the commonplace, such as brooms or mops, to power tools, such as sandblasting equipment, to highly sophisticated technology, such as remote robots. Because hazardous materials are rarely stored where they were created, some HAZMAT workers are experienced in using heavy equipment, including cranes, forklifts, earthmoving machines, and large trucks. They organize and label materials at containment sites and may build scaffolding or air- and water-tight vessels to store hazardous waste.

Because of the potential danger, the hazardous materials removal field is full of specializations, certification, and licensure regulated by federal organizations, which recognize various levels of training depending on the type of work HAZMAT employees do and the materials with which they work. Topics covered in training must comply with federal guidelines and requirements.

WORKING CONDITIONS

As the name of the occupation implies, working conditions can be dangerous for hazardous materials removal workers. As a result, they often work in highly structured, highly supervised situations. HAZMAT employees typically follow strict procedures in processing and remediating dangerous substances. Depending on the situation, government regulations can require one supervisor for as few as 10 HAZMAT employees.

Employees in hazardous materials removal situations must wear extensive protective clothing to prevent injuries caused by contact with the hazardous materials. Such protection may include fully encapsulated suits, jumpsuits, liquid splash or vapor protective clothing, gloves, shoe covers, and eye shields. This protective clothing is often hot and uncomfortable, particularly in enclosed or confined work spaces. Depending on the circumstances, HAZMAT employees are sometimes required to work while wearing respirators to protect them from toxic gases or other contaminated airborne particles.

Hazardous materials removal workers have a varying workweek depending on the circumstances. When work is anticipated and planned in advance, a typical 40-hour workweek is standard, although overtime and shift work can be expected as necessary. HAZMAT workers removing materials from sites that are in use but are being renovated may be required to work evenings and weekends while other people are not present to complete the project in the allotted timeframe. Of course, in emergency situations such as accidental contamination HAZMAT workers can be called upon at all hours of the day and on weekends.

EMPLOYMENT

The U.S. Department of Labor's Bureau of Labor Statistics (BLS) estimates nearly 42,000 hazardous materials removal workers in the United States in 2008, predominantly in the remediation and waste management services industry. Other employers include waste collection, treatment, and disposal companies, as well as management, scientific, or technical consulting firms. The power generation and distribution industry also has a relatively high concentration of hazardous materials removal workers. Although far smaller in scope, the top-paying industries for this occupation include education, government, scientific research, and aerospace product and parts manufacturing.

U.S. states with the highest levels of employment for hazardous materials removal workers are California, New York, Texas, Washington, and Ohio. U.S. states with the highest concentration (per capita) of HAZMAT workers are in the northwest: Alaska, Idaho, and Washington.

TRAINING, OTHER QUALIFICATIONS, AND ADVANCEMENT

Formal education beyond high school is not required. However, on-the-job training for up to one year is common. Federal, state, and even local government standards make additional training necessary for areas of specialization within HAZMAT occupations. One to three months of training and licensing are typically required for each additional material to be handled.

OSHA recognizes five different levels of training according to the Hazardous Waste Operations and Emergency Response Standard (HAZWOPER). The level of training for individual employees depends on the materials and hazards they face on the job. Each subsequent level requires additional subjects and training times. There are many sources for OSHA-compliant training, including colleges or universities, labor unions, employers, and industry associations. Employers are responsible for ensuring that workers undergo the requisite formal training and that the training complies with OSHA standards. Required subjects include personal protective equipment, site safety, recognition of hazards, decontamination procedures, and health implications.

General construction site workers are required to undergo 40 hours of instruction with additional hands-on instruction. Workers at treatment, storage, or disposal facilities also need annual refresher training. Specialized training is mandated for all emergency and disaster response workers. HAZMAT employees who treat and handle asbestos, lead, or radioactive waste are required to undergo extensive specialized training, certification, and licensure in their areas of concentration.

Mechanical skills are important, including knowledge of the use, maintenance, and repair of machines and tools. Because of the use of extensive protective clothing and gear, sometimes in confined spaces, employers prefer workers with physical strength and manual dexterity. Knowledge of chemical compositions and properties is helpful, as is knowledge of basic mathematical calculations, particularly in bioremediation situations in which naturally occurring organisms are used to decompose hazardous waste into harmless or even usable substances.

HAZMAT employees are often confronted with situations that require quick evaluation and competent handling according to OSHA or EPA standards and state or local government regulations. As a result, advanced communication skills with supervisors and peers will be helpful along with a detail-oriented mindset and critical thinking and decision-making abilities.

JOB OUTLOOK

According to O*NET, government economists expect employment opportunities for HAZMAT workers to grow 14 to 19 percent between 2008 and 2018, faster than the national occupational average. Growth is expected to be strongest in administration and support of waste management remediation services. Employment for hazardous materials removal workers is not typically affected by economic downturns.

Increased consciousness regarding the environment and pressure for cleaner, more environmentally friendly facilities are expected to fuel job growth in HAZMAT occupations. According to the BLS, a renewed interest in nuclear power production versus the continued use of fossil fuels may lead to the reactivation of nuclear facilities and would result in the need for additional remediation employees. Conversely, demand for asbestos and lead abatement workers will decline somewhat because these hazardous materials have not been used in construction since the 1970s.

EARNINGS

The salary for HAZMAT removal employees varies by the type of job and required training. According to the BLS, annual income for hazardous materials removal workers ranges from a low of US$30,000 to a high of US$46,000, with an average salary in 2009 of US$40,270. Workers with specific areas of expertise, including treatment, storage and disposal, or decontamination, receive higher salaries.

RELATED OCCUPATIONS

Occupations that have similar functions or educational requirements as a hazardous materials removal workers include the following:

- Asbestos abatement workers
- Decommissioning workers
- Emergency or disaster response workers
- Lead abatement workers
- Maintenance workers, machinery
- Radiation safety technicians
- Remediation or decontamination specialists
- Treatment, storage, and disposal workers
- Water and liquid waste treatment plant and system operators

SOURCES OF ADDITIONAL INFORMATION

Dangerous Goods Advisory Council. http://www.dgac.org
Pipeline and Hazardous Materials Safety Administration. http://phmsa.dot.gov

FURTHER READING

Bureau of Labor Statistics, U.S. Department of Labor. "47-4041 Hazardous Materials Removal Workers." In *Occupational Employment Statistics: Occupational Employment and Wages, May 2010.* Accessed December 23, 2011. http://www.bls.gov/oes/current/oes474041.htm.

———. "Hazardous Materials Removal Workers." In *Occupational Outlook Handbook, 2010–11 Edition.* Accessed December 23, 2011. http://www.bls.gov/oco/ocos256.htm.

Career One Stop: Pathways to Career Success. *562211 Hazardous Waste Treatment and Disposal.* Accessed March 22, 2012. www.careerinfonet.org.

———. *Explore Green Careers: Recycling and Waste Reduction.* Accessed December 23, 2011. http://www.careeronestop.org/GreenCareers/ExploreGreenCareersRecyclingandWasteReduction.aspx.

Center for Public Environmental Oversight. *Enhanced Bioremediation.* Accessed February 1, 2012. http://www.cpeo.org/techtree/ttdescript/ensolmx.htm.

College Board. *Career: Hazardous Materials Removal Workers.* Accessed December 23, 2011. http://www.collegeboard.com/csearch/majors_careers/profiles/careers/101614.html.

Earth 911.com. *Hazardous.* Accessed February 1, 2012. http://earth911.com/recycling/hazardous/.

Institute of Hazardous Materials Management. *What Are Hazardous Materials.* Accessed February 1, 2011. http://www.ihmm.org/index.php?option=com_content&view=article&id=61&Itemid=161.

iseek Careers. *Hazardous Material Workers.* Accessed December 23, 2011. http://www.iseek.org/careers/careerDetail?id=0&oc=100338.

O*NET OnLine. *Hazardous Materials Removal Workers.* Accessed December 23, 2011. http://www.occupationalinfo.org/onet/79999d.html.

———. *Summary Report for: 47-4041.00—Hazardous Materials Removal Workers.* Accessed December 23, 2011. http://www.onetonline.org/link/summary/47-4041.00.

U.S. Environmental Protection Agency. *Wastes—Hazardous Wastes.* Accessed February 1, 2012. http://www.epa.gov/epawaste/hazard/index.htm.

———. *Hazardous Wastes in Your Community.* Accessed February 1, 2012. http://www.epa.gov/epawaste/wycd/manag-hw/e00-001a.pdf.

REFUSE AND RECYCLABLE MATERIAL COLLECTORS

NATURE OF THE WORK

The job of a refuse and recyclable material collector is to gather recyclables from consumers, whether households, businesses, or construction sites, and transport them to a materials recovery facility (MRF). The trucks used to collect refuse and recyclables are large commercial vehicles with multiple ton capacities. These vehicles require skill and on-the-job experience to operate. As a result, drivers have to follow detailed safety procedures that in some instances may be mandated by the national, state, or local government.

Making the job even more challenging, municipal refuse and recyclable material collectors drive through residential areas, sometimes with heavy traffic, narrow streets, one-way streets, and alleyways. Workers also operate the truck's mechanical equipment, such as hydraulic lifts and compactor bodies that compress the collected waste.

Refuse and recyclable material collectors are also responsible for inspecting their trucks both at the beginning and at the end of their shifts. Some items of inspection include tire pressure, fluid levels, and functioning of safety equipment. Depending on the employer, these workers may be responsible for all or some of the maintenance as well, such as putting air in the tires, adding fluids, and cleaning the interior and exterior of the vehicles.

The U.S. Department of Labor's Bureau of Labor Statistics (BLS) classifies refuse and recyclable material collectors as a *green enhanced skills occupation*, which means activities and technologies in the green economy will significantly change work performed by employees in this occupation. The work accomplished will remain the same; however, the tools, methods, or processes followed

---

AT A GLANCE FACT BOX

SOC: 53-7081.00
Preferred Education: High school diploma or equivalent preferred, although not necessarily required
Average Salary: Varies; median income is US$34,310
Other Information: Class A or B commercial driver's license required

---

will evolve. To meet the demands of the green market, refuse and recyclable material collectors must be able to identify and know how to process recyclable materials while following local, state, and federal standards. This includes materials such as electronic waste that carry their own legislation for disposal in some states.

WORKING CONDITIONS

Refuse and recyclable material collectors have to be relatively healthy and physically fit because the job is physically demanding. They must be able to hoist, push, and pull heavy loads repeatedly throughout the day. Some employers actually require their workers to pass physical exams because the work can be so physically challenging.

Due to the nature of the job, refuse and recyclable material collectors work outside in all seasons and all weather conditions, be it extremely hot or uncomfortably cold. The occupation calls for shift work that typically lasts eight hours, if not more. The length of the route, the number of stops, and the distance between the stops may determine the shift length, with some shifts starting as early as 5 a.m. to accommodate days with longer routes.

Collectors often work in teams of two or more with one worker to drive the truck and the others to exit the vehicle, lift the recycling bins, and transfer the material into the truck. In more rural settings, one worker alone may be responsible for driving the truck and for collecting and dumping the waste. This requires the collector to exit and reenter the vehicle at each stop. Larger or better-funded municipalities and private companies may own higher-end truck models equipped with hydraulic lifting mechanisms that automatically lift and empty recycling bins.

Refuse and recyclable material collectors drive designated routes that are usually planned in great detail. These drivers are allotted a specific amount of time to complete their routes. Good communication skills with supervisors and peers are helpful because routes and schedules will often be affected by weather, accidents, or equipment breakdowns. A strong ability to manage time and a keen knowledge of cardinal directions (north, east, south, and west) are beneficial.

As part of the transportation and materials moving industry, this occupation can be dangerous, particularly when working along highways. A 2009 article in *Forbes* magazine says that transportation accidents are the most common cause of on-the-job fatalities. Of the more than 5,000 job-related fatalities in the United States in 2008, transportation accidents accounted for more than one-third, or 40.5 percent.

EMPLOYMENT

Drivers may be employed in the public or private sector. Some work for their local municipal government while others work for private waste collectors that are contracted by local governments. The waste collection, waste treatment and disposal, and remediation industries employ more than half of refuse and recyclable material collectors, with governmental bodies employing most of the remainder.

States with the greatest number of refuse and recyclable material collectors are larger states with large populations, including: California, New York, Texas, Pennsylvania, and Ohio. Large populations mean more consumers with greater amounts of recyclables needing to be collected.

TRAINING, OTHER QUALIFICATIONS, AND ADVANCEMENT

Little work experience or training is required for most workers in this occupation. Prospective candidates should have a high school diploma or the equivalent, although O*NET

reports that one-third of refuse and recyclable material collectors have less than a high school education. About half of the people employed in this occupation do have a high school diploma. Beyond education, recycling companies prefer drivers with several years' experience with large commercial trucks. Most of the training is on-the-job.

Because they drive heavy commercial vehicles with multiple-ton capacities, drivers in this occupation must have a class A or B commercial driver's license (CDL) with airbrake endorsement. This license requires a separate driving test using the type of truck equipped with the type of machinery the worker will be using on the job. The U.S. Department of Transportation (DOT) maintains specific requirements for commercial vehicle driving tests. Specific skills must be included in the test, such as pre-trip inspection, placing vehicles in operation, using the vehicle's controls and equipment, operating the vehicle in traffic, turning, decelerating, and braking.

Due to DOT regulations, refuse and recyclable material collectors have to pass drug-screening tests and sometimes background checks. In consideration of DOT requirements, it behooves candidates to always maintain a clean driving record.

Other licensing may be required, although it varies by state. For example, refuse drivers in Arkansas may be required to carry a "waste tire transporter license." Indiana drivers may be required to carry a "certified solid waste facility operator" license. Refuse and recyclable material drivers in Illinois may be required to have a "scrap processor" license.

JOB OUTLOOK

According to O*NET, the job outlook for workers in refuse and recyclable material collector occupations should be slightly better than the U.S. national average. Projected job growth for these workers from 2008 to 2018 is from 14 percent to 19 percent.

EARNINGS

Earnings for workers in the trucking industry vary widely depending on level of experience, areas of expertise, and geographical region. Refuse and recyclable material collectors are no different. The range of salaries for these workers is quite large, from US$18,730 for entry-level drivers with no experience to US$53,560 for experienced drivers with advanced certification or licensing. The median salary in 2010 was US$34,310.

The top paying states are New York, Washington, Illinois, California, and Alaska.

Salaries for refuse and recyclable material collectors tend to be higher in metropolitan areas with large populations. Topping the list of locations with greater pay are San

Francisco and Oakland, California; the New York City metropolitan area; Chicago, Illinois, and its surrounding communities.

RELATED OCCUPATIONS

Related occupations include:

- Recycle drivers
- Solid waste collectors
- Recycling center operators
- Material moving workers
- Sanitation laborers
- Garbage collectors

SOURCES OF ADDITIONAL INFORMATION

United States Environmental Protection Agency. www .epa.gov

Waste Management. www.thinkgreen.com

FURTHER READING

Bureau of Labor Statistics, U.S. Department of Labor. "53-7081 Refuse and Recyclable Material Collectors." In *Occupational Employment Statistics: Occupational Employment and Wages, May 2010.* Accessed December 30, 2011. http://www.bls.gov/oes/current/oes537081.htm#(3).

———. "Truck Transportation and Warehousing." In *Occupational Outlook Handbook, 2010–11 Edition.* Accessed April 3, 2012. http://www.bls.gov/oco/cg/cgs021.htm.

California Department of Toxic Substances Control. *Electronic Hazardous Waste (E-Waste).* Accessed April 9, 2012. http://www.dtsc.ca.gov/hazardouswaste/ewaste.

CareerOneStop. *Explore Green Careers: Recycling and Waste Reduction.* Accessed December 27, 2011. http://www.careeronestop.org/GreenCareers/ExploreGreenCareersRecyclingandWaste Reduction.aspx.

Employment Development Department, State of California. "Refuse and Recyclable Material Collectors in Ventura County." *California Occupational Guides.* Accessed April 9, 2012. http://www.labormarketinfo.edd.ca.gov/OccGuides/Summary.aspx?Soccode=537081 &Geography=0604000111.

Federal Motor Carrier Safety Administration, U.S. Department of Transportation. *Rules and Regulations for Drivers.* Accessed December 30, 2011. http://www.fmcsa.dot.gov/rules-regulations/administration/fmcsr/fmcsrguide.aspx?section_type=D.

Iowa Green Curriculum Guide. *Comprehensive Human Capital Inventory for the Bridging the Gap Project*, April 2011. Accessed December 30, 2011. http://www.onesourcetrainingiowa.org/Documents/Gap%20Report%20Complete%20April%202011.pdf.

Kneale, Klaus. "America's Deadliest Jobs." *Forbes.com*, August 26, 2009.

Liming, Drew. *Careers in Recycling.* Bureau of Labor Statistics, U.S. Department of Labor, September 2011. Accessed April 18, 2012. http://www.bls.gov/green/recycling/.

MyPlan.com. *Careers, Refuse & Recyclable Material Collectors.* Accessed December 30, 2011. http://www.myplan.com/careers/refuse-and-recyclable-material-collectors/summary-53-7081.00.html.

Occupational Information Network. *Refuse and Recyclable Material Collectors.* Accessed December 30, 2011. http://www.occupationalinfo.org/onet/98705.html.

O*NET OnLine. *Details Report for: 53-7081.00—Refuse and Recyclable Material Collectors.* Accessed December 27, 2011. http://www.onetonline.org/link/details/53-7081.00.

SECTOR OVERVIEW: RENEWABLE
ENERGY GENERATION

Because of the depletion of oil reserves worldwide, the rising price of oil, and ecological concerns regarding environmental protection, few careers are growing faster than those within the renewable energy generation sector. What exactly is renewable energy generation, however?

Renewable or *green* energy generation involves the development, use, and storage of power sources that are not dependent on fossil fuels but that instead use renewable sources such as wind, solar, and ground (geothermal) power; marine power derived from ocean waves, tides, and currents; and bioenergy sources, including energy crops, landfill gas, and biodiesel fuels. The generation of renewable energy will create more jobs, channel energy sources that will last indefinitely or have the ability to be regenerated, help protect the environment, and ultimately reduce the world's dependence on petroleum products.

The renewable energy generation sector includes jobs that are involved with generating or finding ways to produce energy resources that are derived from the earth. According to the U.S. Department of Labor's Bureau of Labor Statistics (BLS), workers in this sector research, develop, maintain, or use technologies and practices to lessen the environmental footprint of the company or industry in which they work. Many of the jobs within this sector involve generating electricity, heat, or fuel from a variety of renewable sources, including wind, biomass, geothermal, solar, and marine power.

WIND

Among the micro-renewable sources, wind is the fastest growing energy source in the United States. Wind-generating capacity in the United States grew 39 percent per year from 2004 to 2009, and the U.S. Department of Energy has predicted that wind power will produce 20 percent of the electricity in the United States by 2030.

Wind turbines harness wind power. A wind farm is a group of wind turbines that are connected to a central utility. Major utility companies that contract with wind energy companies to install and maintain the turbines own most wind farms. According to the American Wind Energy Association, an estimated 85,000 people in the United States were employed in the wind power industry and related fields in 2010. These jobs were previously available in only a few states. However, as of 2010 wind farms operated in almost every state, with concentrations in the midwest, southwest, and northeast regions of the United States. Globally, wind is a major power source for more than 70 countries, including China, the United States, Germany, Spain, India, Italy, France, the United Kingdom, Canada, and Denmark, which made up the top 10 countries in wind power capacity in 2010.

BIOMASS

Biomass, another name for plant material and animal waste, is the oldest source of renewable energy, first used when cavemen discovered fire. Biomass is a valuable renewable resource that, if used to its full potential, will help the world transition to a sustainable energy future. When biomass is produced in a sustainable way, it can last indefinitely, provide an unlimited source of low-carbon energy, and reduce air pollution and net carbon emissions. According to a 2009 Union of Concerned Scientists study, beneficial biomass resources could reduce power plant carbon emissions as much as getting 45 million cars off the road would.

One example of how biomass is produced is photosynthesis. During this process, the chlorophyll in plants uses the sun's energy to convert carbon dioxide and water into carbohydrates. When these carbohydrates are burned, they convert back into carbon dioxide and water and release the energy they captured from the sun.

GEOTHERMAL

Geothermal energy is the power originating from the earth itself. The United States has more geothermal capacity than any other country, with more than 3,000 megawatts in eight states. Eighty percent of this capacity is in California, where more than 40 geothermal plants provide nearly 5 percent of the state's electricity and employ geothermal engineers and other technical workers.

Geothermal energy workers harness the clean and sustainable energy that exists under the earth's surface, which may come from boiling springs in shallow ground, hot rock several miles below the earth's surface, and molten rock adjacent to the earth's center. Workers capture the energy from geothermal sources in a variety of ways, most commonly by drilling holes in the earth's surface to capture steam from heated water that has risen to the surface. This steam is then used to power electric generators.

SOLAR

Because solar energy can be generated anywhere the sun shines, solar power workers are employed around the world. The United States has a great deal of untapped potential in the solar energy industry because nearly every state receives more sunlight per square mile than Germany, which led the world in solar energy production in 2009.

The two types of solar energy technology that are commonly used are photovoltaic and thermal. Photovoltaic energy is created when sunlight photons hit a solar panel, loosen electrons in the material, and create an electrical current. Solar thermal energy harnesses the sun's heat through collectors and uses the energy captured to power electric plants, roof-mounted hot water heaters, and solar pool warmers.

MARINE

Marine energy comes from oceans, which cover 70 percent of the earth's surface. The tides, currents, lunar phases, gravity, and sun's warmth put the oceans in constant motion, and this movement provides an excellent renewable energy source with no negative environmental effects. The energy that the oceans generate includes tidal energy, wave power, ocean current energy, and ocean thermocline energy.

WAVE OF THE FUTURE

Public perception about renewable energy has helped spur the growth of employment in this sector. A 2011 solar energy survey conducted by Applied Materials found that two-thirds of people living in the United States believe that solar energy should play a greater role in helping the country meet its energy needs, and three-quarters feel that decreasing the country's dependence on foreign oil and increasing renewable energy use should be the country's top energy priority. The study also found that 67 percent of those surveyed would be willing to pay higher utility bills if their utility company increased its use of renewable energy. Therefore, energy generated from renewable energy sources should only continue to grow, as should the careers these sources provide.

FURTHER READING

American Wind Energy Association. *U.S. Wind Industry Annual Market Report, Year Ending 2009.* Accessed March 29, 2012. http://www.awea.org/_cs_upload/ membercenter/membersecurity/market_reports/ 7758_2.pdf.

Applied Materials, Inc. *Cost of Solar Panels Lower than Ever, Americans Optimistic about Future of Technology,* June 20, 2011. Accessed March 7, 2012. http://www.appliedmaterials.com/newsroom/news/ cost-solar-panels-lower-ever-americans-optimistic- about-future-technology.

Bureau of Labor Statistics, U.S. Department of Labor. *Measuring Green Jobs.* Accessed March 7, 2012. http://www.bls.gov/green/.

Union of Concerned Scientists. *How Biomass Energy Works.* Accessed March 7, 2012. http://www .ucsusa.org/clean_energy/technology_and_impacts/ energy_technologies/how-biomass-energy-works .html.

U.S. Department of Energy. *20% Wind Energy by 2030.* Accessed March 7, 2012. http://www.20percentwind .org/20p.aspx?page=Report.

BIOMASS PLANT ENGINEERS

NATURE OF THE WORK

Biomass engineers help develop the processes and technology used to provide energy from alternative sources such as biomass to homes and businesses at reasonable prices. The biomass plant engineer's job is to convert biomass, which can be garbage, wood, biological waste, and landfill gases, into a usable form of energy or fuel through scientific thermal, chemical, and biochemical conversion methods.

Combustion is the main way that biomass is converted into energy. Biomass engineers use combustion to burn the biomass, which in turn boils water and produces steam. This steam spins a turbine to produce electricity. The amount of energy produced by the biomass is determined by the method and technology used for the conversion. Biomass engineers are responsible for maintaining and using the current conversion processes.

Some of the tasks completed by biomass engineers include:

- Designing waste, emissions, and turbine components for biomass plants
- Performing process and equipment design using the principles of mass and energy conservation, fluid dynamics, and heat transfer
- Examining test results to determine the differences between predictions and actual measurements
- Obtaining data on fermentation process developments
- Giving presentations on projects and helping write operating procedures and technical brochures
- Ensuring that biomass plants are environmentally compliant
- Providing analysis and expertise for federal, state, and local governments

---

AT A GLANCE FACT BOX

Preferred Education: Bachelor's degree in biochemical, chemical, electrical, mechanical, or systems engineering
Preferred Specialty: Analytical chemistry, biochemistry, biology, microbiology, molecular biology
Average Salary: US$90,270 annually
Other Information: In 2008, there were 183,000 biochemical engineers in the United States. Thirty-two percent were employed in manufacturing, 25 percent worked in professional, scientific, and technical services, 16 percent worked for federal and state governments, and 27 percent worked in other industries, including self-employment and administrative and support services.

The focus for many biomass plant engineers and the plants they help run is to contribute to the production of carbon neutral energy derived from local fuel sources and to confirm that biomass fuel sources are grown locally and fully sustainably. As the world's energy needs continue to grow, the use of local biomass fuels will help reduce the dependence on petroleum products and imported energy sources. For this reason, the opportunities available to biomass plant engineers will continue to grow worldwide.

Tools and Technology Although the tools and technology that biomass engineers use depend somewhat on the project, their employer, and the tasks they need to perform, the software used typically includes:

- Analytical or scientific
- Life-cycle assessment
- Modeling
- Computer-aided design (CAD)
- Spreadsheet
- Word processing

Some of the tools biomass engineers commonly use in the course of their jobs include distributed control systems; mass analyzers and detectors, which take ionized gases, separate them based on charge to mass ratios, and convert them to digital output; gas chromatographs, which separate and analyze compounds that can be vaporized without decomposing; catalytic combustion analyzers; fermenters; furnaces; turbines; and boilers.

WORKING CONDITIONS

Biomass plant engineers are usually employed at plants close to the source of the energy. In some cases, the plants can be set in remote, rural areas; many are placed in developing countries that have large amounts of biomass resources. Biomass engineers enjoy a job with a great deal of variety, and they often split their time between their office at the plant and laboratory and project sites. These professionals work both independently and as part of a team. They should be able to multi-task and be adaptable. Biomass plant engineers must process a great deal of information from a variety of sources to solve complex engineering problems that routinely come up in the biomass industry.

Most biomass plant engineers work a standard 40-hour work week with occasional overtime during busy times. Travel may be necessary to interact with clients or to work at job sites because of a shortage of qualified local engineers. When working both on and off-site, biomass engineers may experience extreme temperatures or strong odors and are often required to use safety equipment and follow standard safety protocols.

EMPLOYMENT

Biomass plant engineers are typically employed at biomass energy-producing power plants throughout the world, including the following, where trained engineers have made numerous contributions:

- Bay Front, Ashland, Wisconsin. Biomass engineers installed a system that allows for the feeding of 100 percent biomass, 100 percent coal, or any combination of the two.
- Shasta, located nine miles northwest of Redding, California. Biomass engineers developed a process that accepts the blending of all fuels into a homogenous mixture that allows the boilers to fire at a consistent

rate and maintain maximum load under all conditions while remaining environmentally compliant.

- Stratton, Stratton, Ohio. This biomass plant is a 49-Mw wood-fired power plant that is one of only three biomass plants in Southern California. It draws fuel from the greater Los Angeles basin area.
- Ridge Generating Station, Auburndale, Florida. This is an urban waste power plant located next to a landfill.
- Lahti Energy, Lahti, Finland. This plant produces power and heat for the city of Lahti.
- Colmac Energy, Mecca, California. It is the largest biomass-fueled power plant in California and has operated for more than 18 years.
- Greenidge, Torrey, New York. Biomass engineers use this plant to demonstrate that a separate fuel feed system can have economically favorable results.
- Williams Lake, British Columbia. This is the largest biomass power plant in North America. It has the largest single boiler and the lowest heat rate of any 100 percent biomass-fired power plant.
- Tilbury, England. In January 2012, it was announced that the world's largest biomass plant would begin production in Tilbury, England. According to a report by Reuters, the new power station will burn wood pellets to produce electricity and is located on the site of the Tilbury coal-fired plant, which reportedly will be closed by the end of 2015.

TRAINING, OTHER QUALIFICATIONS, AND ADVANCEMENT

Biomass engineers commonly possess a wide variety of academic backgrounds, but the minimum educational requirement is a bachelor's degree in engineering or a related field of study. Some biomass plant engineers have earned master's or doctoral degrees in a biomass-related specialty. Most biomass engineers have a background in analytical chemistry, biochemistry, biology, microbiology, molecular biology, or one of the following engineering specialties:

- Biochemical
- Chemical
- Electrical
- Mechanical
- Systems engineering

Biomass engineering is a competitive field, and employers generally require job candidates to have two to seven years of work experience to be considered for a biomass plant engineer position. Experience in energy, resource recovery systems, vehicle integration, and sanitary and environmental consulting may help to secure employment.

A Professional Engineer's (PE) license is not required for most biomass engineers, but a licensed professional will usually have an edge when competing for higher-level positions. Engineers who want to obtain a PE license will need to pass the Engineer-in-Training or Fundamentals of Engineering examination. To sit for the exam, an engineer must have completed a minimum of three years of coursework from a college or university engineering program that has been accredited by the Accreditation Board for Engineering and Technology (ABET) or must have three years of engineering-related experience. The candidate must then pass the professional examination, which requires a bachelor's degree in engineering from an ABET-accredited school and two years of eligible engineering experience; engineers without a bachelor's degree in engineering must have six years of eligible experience. The PE license must be renewed every two years.

Experienced biomass plant engineers may join consulting firms or become self-employed. Seasoned engineers may also be asked to take on additional responsibilities and work on more complex projects. Some enter academic fields where they conduct research, teach, and publish scientific works.

JOB OUTLOOK

Because this was an emerging position in 2011, data regarding the number of biomass plant engineers employed in the United States was not readily available, but the world's growing interest in sustainability, protection of the environment, and the development of alternative energy sources indicate that future employment opportunities should increase.

EARNINGS

As of 2011, biomass engineers earned between US$80,000 and US$110,000 annually, although the job is emerging and a formal salary survey was not yet available. As with many industries, actual salaries depend on the pay structure that is followed by each employer, which is based on work performed, experience, the type of project, and the level of skill required.

Biomass plant engineers commonly receive generous benefit packages that usually include medical, dental, vision, and life insurance as well as sick leave, annual leave, paid holidays, and retirement plans. Some plants may also provide bonuses for employees.

RELATED OCCUPATIONS

The duties of biomass plant engineers are similar to those of the following occupations:

- Chemical plant engineer
- Food processing plant engineer
- Metals manufacturing engineer
- Biomass engineer
- Biofuel chemist
- Geotechnical design engineer

SOURCES OF ADDITIONAL INFORMATION

Biomass Power Association. http://www.usabiomass.org
Natural Renewable Energy Laboratory. http://www.nrel.gov
Natural Science Foundation. http://www.nsf.gov

FURTHER READING

California Occupational Guides. *Biomass Engineers in California*. Accessed February 12, 2012. http://www.calmis.ca.gov/file/occguide/Biomass-Engineers-Green.pdf.

Renewable Energy Sector Compass. *Biomass Engineer*. Accessed February 13, 2012. http://www.rescompass.org/english,1/job-profiles,14/technical-design-consultants,38/biomass-engineer,262.html.

Schaps, Karolin. "RWE to Open UK's Biggest Biomass Plant This Month." *Reuters*, January 5, 2012. Accessed February 29, 2012. http://www.reuters.com/article/2012/01/05/us-britain-rwe-tilbury-idUSTRE8040O320120105.

Wiltsee, G. *Lessons Learned from Existing Biomass Power Plants*. Golden, Colorado: National Renewable Energy Laboratory, 2000. Accessed February 12, 2012. http://www.nrel.gov/docs/fy00osti/26946.pdf.

SOLAR POWER PLANT TECHNICIANS

NATURE OF THE WORK

Electricity is one of the world's most important resources. It can be generated by various energy sources, one of them solar power. Large-scale solar power is generated at solar power plants, and solar power plant technicians, also known as operators, control the machinery that generates electricity.

Solar power plant technicians are competent in a variety of areas of a solar power plant. These technicians operate, maintain, and repair the equipment, controls, and electrical systems at the plant. The technicians are responsible for starting, stopping, monitoring, and adjusting all equipment and must also document the status of the system and communicate their findings to team members and supervisors.

Solar power plant technicians monitor solar displays and generators and regulate output from the generators. They do this via computer from the control room and by making regular rounds through the plant, checking that all equipment is operating properly. They use computers to report unusual incidents or equipment that is malfunctioning and to record the maintenance performed during their shift.

Solar power plant technicians spend much of their time maintaining solar power plants. They perform routine as well as mid-level maintenance on their own, and also assist with advanced and sometimes complex maintenance activities that require the expertise of more specialized technicians. Solar power plant technicians also perform routine operational testing and make necessary adjustments to facility equipment. Technicians also update the equipment operating logs, troubleshoot and repair

machinery, order parts and supplies, and clean assigned areas of the plant.

Some concentrating solar power (CSP) plants, which feature large mirrors that are arranged to catch and focus sunlight for power generation, have a secondary source of power generation, often natural gas-powered turbines that generate power at night when sunlight is not available. Solar power plant technicians who work in CSP plants are also responsible for monitoring this secondary equipment and determining when to switch from solar power to natural gas.

AT A GLANCE FACT BOX

Preferred Education: High school diploma or GED, completion of a certificate or two-year degree program, and on-the-job training

Preferred Specialty: Photovoltaics, solar-thermal systems, and solar architecture. Those with a mechanical, technical, and strong computer background generally have preference.

Average Salary: US$64,270 annually

Other Information: Between 2008 and 2018, the overall employment of solar power plant technicians is predicted to experience little or no change, but job opportunities should be excellent because of a large number of retiring workers, an increasing demand for solar power, and U.S. federal legislation that offers incentives for new plants

---

Recruiters in the solar power industry look for certain traits in technicians, including:

- Strong math and science backgrounds, especially in algebra and trigonometry
- Proficiency in working with tools
- Problem-solving and mechanical abilities

WORKING CONDITIONS

Solar power plant technicians spend time in control rooms, sitting or standing at a control station. Although their work may not be physically strenuous, it can be mentally taxing because it requires constant attention. When technicians make rounds at the plant or perform work outside the control room, they may be exposed to hazards such as electric shocks, falls, and burns.

Because electricity is provided around the clock, solar power plant technicians typically work one of three eight-hour shifts or one of two 12-hour shifts on a rotating basis, with all technicians alternating the various shifts periodically. Working on rotating shifts is taxing to the body because of the constant change in work and sleep patterns. Solar power plant technicians must sometimes be on call for emergencies because customers need reliable electrical power 24 hours a day, seven days a week. In the event of power failures, technicians must be prepared to work quickly, efficiently, and sometimes during inclement weather.

EMPLOYMENT

Power plant technicians, distributors, and dispatchers held about 50,400 jobs throughout the United States in 2008, and 35,400 of these jobs were power plant technician positions.

In 2008, there were more than 30 utility-scale solar power plants of one megawatt or larger, operating or under development in the United States. With a few exceptions, these plants are clustered mostly in the southern part of the country in the following states: New Mexico, California, Florida, Arizona, North Carolina, New Jersey, and Nevada.

TRAINING, OTHER QUALIFICATIONS, AND ADVANCEMENT

Many solar power plant technicians are required to have a technical or associate degree, although some move into the technician position through related electrical and computer experience in another field. Because many power plant monitoring systems are computerized, technicians must have extensive computer operation and troubleshooting skills in addition to the mechanical and technical skills necessary to operate a power plant. Some technicians complete a formal apprenticeship or are trained in the military, whereas others get on-the-job training, spending up to a year in a classroom setting before starting to train at the plant. Employers may administer written and oral tests throughout the training, and it can take up to three years to transition from a new hire to a journeyman-level solar power plant technician. Once trained, technicians also receive continuing education that might involve testing on power plant simulators that replicate issues they might encounter while on the job.

To ensure that technicians have the proper knowledge, companies sometimes require workers to take the Power Plant Maintenance (MASS), and Plant Operator (POSS) exams administered by the Edison Electrical Institute. These tests measure reading comprehension, understanding of mechanical concepts, and spatial and mathematical ability.

Certification by the North American Energy Reliability Corporation (NERC) is necessary for certain positions. The three types of certification offered by the NERC include:

- Reliability coordinator
- Transmission operator
- Balancing authority

Many companies also require a strong background in mathematics and science, and plant technicians often obtain additional skills through specialized training courses. Because there are security concerns surrounding power plants, technicians are often subject to background checks, must have a clean criminal record, and must be willing to submit to random drug tests.

Most entry level technicians start out as helpers or laborers and advance to positions with more responsibility, with workers generally being classified into three to five levels based upon experience. Each level requires more training, mandatory waiting times, and completion of exams. With training and experience, solar power plant technicians can advance to supervisory, trainer, or consulting positions.

JOB OUTLOOK

Job opportunities for solar power plant technicians are strongest in the southwestern region of the United States and also in remote rural areas. Job opportunities for well-qualified workers are expected to be excellent for several reasons:

1. Because of cost-cutting measures that led to layoffs of younger workers in the 1990s, large numbers of workers in the electrical power industry will reach retirement age between 2008 and 2018.
2. Utilities have set up numerous education programs at community colleges and high schools across the United States.
3. Solar power plant technician positions are relatively high paying.

4. The expansion of solar technology and the creation of new jobs within that industry depend upon the amount of government incentives given to the development of solar energy, and also the price of oil and other fuels, both of which have been increasing.

In this expanding job market, workers with strong technical and mechanical skills will fare the best.

EARNINGS

The salaries of solar power plant technicians can vary widely, but most earn between US$18,000 and US$64,270 per year, depending upon the employer's pay structure, the geographical location, the type of position, and the skills required. Technicians who are employed by large solar power plants often enjoy benefits including sick leave, annual leave, paid holidays, health insurance coverage, and retirement plans.

RELATED OCCUPATIONS

- Site assessors
- Electricians
- Plumbers
- Roofers

SOURCES OF ADDITIONAL INFORMATION

Solar Energy Industries Association. http://www.seia.org

National Renewable Energy Laboratory. http://www.nrel.gov

American Public Power Association. http://www.publicpower.org

Solar Living Institute. http://www.solarliving.org

American Solar Energy Society. http://www.ases.org

FURTHER READING

Bureau of Labor Statistics, U.S. Department of Labor. *Careers in Solar Power.* Accessed February 14, 2012. http://www.bls.gov/green/solar_power/#operation.

———. *On the Grid: Careers in Energy.* Accessed February 14, 2012. http://www.bls.gov/ooq/2008/fall/art02.pdf.

———. "Power Plant Operators, Distributors, and Dispatchers." In *Occupational Outlook Handbook, 2010–11 Edition.* Accessed February 14, 2012. http://www.bls.gov/oco/ocos227.htm.

SUSTAINABLE DESIGN SPECIALISTS

NATURE OF THE WORK

Although sustainable design in the New World dates back to 1200 BCE to CE 1300 when the Anasazi Indians of Arizona, Colorado, New Mexico, and Utah built entire villages so that all the homes in them could be heated with solar energy, the contemporary green building effort was spurred by the environmental movement of the 1960s and the rising price of oil in the 1970s. Sustainable design supports an increased commitment to environmental stewardship and conservation and attempts to balance costs with environmental, societal, and human benefits while meeting the intended mission and function of the building.

The main goal of sustainable design specialists is to create a building that will have minimal negative impacts on the environment, protect the health of its occupants, and improve building performance by reducing the consumption of non-renewable resources. This can often be accomplished by making use of sustainable forms of energy, such as solar power minimizing waste in building materials, and creating healthy and productive building environments that are affordable. Sustainable design specialists have the ability to:

- Enhance the building's potential
- Find alternatives to non-renewable energy sources
- Make use of building materials and products that are environmentally friendly
- Reuse and recycle construction and demolition materials
- Find ways to protect and conservatively use water sources
- Landscape with plants that have low water and pesticide needs
- Use recycled materials for paving, furnishing, composting, and mulching
- Optimize space through environmentally friendly products

AT A GLANCE FACT BOX

Preferred Education: Bachelor's degree; many jobs require a master's or professional degree and/or the LEED Accredited Professional (AP) credential

Preferred Specialty: Architecture, urban planning, or engineering (civil, electrical, landscape, and mechanical), with emphasis in mathematics, science, and art

Average Salary: As of 2011, the U.S. Department of Labor's Bureau of Labor Statistics (BLS) had not compiled wage data specific to the green construction industry and sustainable design specialists; however, the average wage for those in comparable positions is as follows: architect: US$77,210 annually; electrical engineer: US$84,350 annually; and urban and regional planner: US$63,040 annually

Other Information: In 2008, architects held about 141,200 jobs in the United States, most working in architectural firms, although about 20 percent were self-employed. During this same time period, there were about 301,500 electrical and electronics engineers in the United States. In 2010, approximately 40,300 urban and regional planners worked in the United States, two-thirds employed in local government, with the remainder working in professional, scientific, and technical services.

- Design operational and maintenance practices that emphasize sustainability
- Use the simplest technology appropriate to the functional need
- Incorporate passive energy-conserving strategies that are responsive to the local climate
- Adhere to the "smaller is better" theory by making full use of space through flexibility
- Combine a properly-sized and energy-efficient heating and cooling system with a thermally efficient building shell
- Avoid energy-intensive, environmentally damaging, waste producing, and hazardous materials
- Respect the natural and cultural resources of a building site and minimize the impacts of development on the site

Why is sustainable design important? A sustainable building, also known as a green building, is designed, built, renovated, operated, or repurposed in an ecologically efficient manner. Some of the economic benefits of sustainably designed buildings include:

- Lower operating costs over the life of the building, although upfront costs may be higher
- Improved health, comfort, and productivity of the building's occupants
- Promotion of a more efficient use of energy, water, and other raw materials for less depletion of natural resources
- Reduction of pollution and landfill wastes associated with the creation and operation of the building

Sustainable building design strives to balance human needs (although not necessarily their wants) with their impact on the environment. Sustainable design specialists use their expertise in architecture, engineering, and sustainability to take an integrated, holistic approach to their designs that will integrate cost, environmental benefits, and the mission and purpose of the facility seamlessly into the construction process. In general, sustainable design specialists take the following factors into consideration when designing a building:

- Climate
- Temperature
- Sunlight
- Wind speeds and direction
- Moisture
- Vegetation
- Weather considerations, such as rainfall and storms
- Topography
- Water bodies
- Hydrology
- Geology/soil
- Seismic activity

- Proximity to mass transit
- Pests
- Wildlife
- Human factors
- Cultural resources

WORKING CONDITIONS

Sustainable design specialists work in offices, typically on design teams with other professional architects and engineers. They conduct research, develop ideas, and integrate them into sustainable building plans. These workers must be extremely skilled on computers and use computer-aided design (CAD) software extensively. They must also be knowledgeable in other software such as Microsoft Word, Excel, PowerPoint, Access, Acrobat, and PageMaker.

The process of designing sustainable buildings begins with the selection of the site and design specialists spend considerable time outdoors touring sites and evaluating nearby weather conditions, local infrastructure, vegetation, water sources, access roads, parking, and many other considerations.

EMPLOYMENT

Sustainable design specialists work in a variety of settings, including architecture firms, design firms, construction companies, city and urban planning offices, and government agencies. Professionals of this type are employed throughout the United States, particularly in urban areas.

According to the Environmental and Energy Management News website, some of the sustainable building trends that affected the employment of sustainable design specialists in 2011 and 2012 included:

- The economy: With the real estate industry and new construction still stagnant, the focus of sustainable building has shifted to the "greening" of existing buildings.
- Water issues: Extreme weather events in the past several years have increased public awareness of flooding and storm water control, which can be addressed by green roofs and rainwater recovery systems.
- Saving money: Natural gas prices were consistently lower than fuel oil or coal across the United States, and more buildings were beginning to make the switch to natural gas.
- Looking beyond conventional energy sources: Building owners now consider alternative energy sources such as wind, solar, geothermal, and aquifer air temperature control systems.
- Evaluating performance as well as design: Building owners have shown a greater interest in commissioning testing to determine whether green technologies actually performed as predicted.

• Growing government work: A number of government buildings are making an effort to build or refurbish to LEED standards.

TRAINING, OTHER QUALIFICATIONS, AND ADVANCEMENT

Although the field is emerging, sustainable design specialists typically have a minimum of a bachelor's degree in a field such as architecture, engineering, or urban planning. Architects are required to be licensed to work in the United States, and engineers are typically required to be licensed and complete a specific amount of continuing education hours each year. Many sustainable design jobs require advanced degrees and a handful of U.S. universities, among them the Catholic University of America, now offer a master's of science in sustainable design.

A growing number of employers require that employees such as sustainable design specialists also obtain the LEED credential. A large advocate for sustainable construction is the United States Green Building Council (USGBC). The USGBC created standards to rate buildings by their level of sustainability and maintains those standards under the building rating system known as Leadership in Energy and Environmental Design, or LEED. The sister organization of USGBC, the Green Building Certification Institute (GBCI), uses the USGBC standards to rate buildings using a LEED certification. Depending upon how a building is scored, it will receive a LEED certified silver, gold, or platinum rating. Some jurisdictions have incorporated the LEED designation into their building codes.

Besides LEED, there are other green building certifications in the United States, among them the Green Building Initiative, which certifies buildings as well as professionals in the green building industry, and the National Center for Construction Education and Research (NCCER), an organization that has developed a certification for construction supervisors.

JOB OUTLOOK

According to the BLS's "Careers in Green Construction," published in June 2011, interest in green construction has grown dramatically in the last few years, and McGraw-Hill has estimated that the green building industry in the United States went from a value of US$3 billion in 2005 to a value between US$43 and US$54 billion in 2010, more than 14 times the value in spite of a national recession from 2007 to 2009. By 2015, McGraw-Hill estimates that the value of this sector will have grown to between US$120 and US$145 billion. As the size of the industry grows, its workforce will as well. Therefore, the job outlook for sustainable design specialists is very good.

EARNINGS

Sustainable design specialists are generally well-paid professionals, earning in the range of US$63,000 to more than US$84,000 per year. Salaries are dependent upon the employer, the geographic area, the education and credentials of the designer, and the skills required for the job. Most sustainable design specialists are also eligible for a variety of benefits, including health and life insurance, sick leave, annual leave, paid personal leave, and retirement plans.

RELATED OCCUPATIONS

The duties of sustainable design specialists are similar to those of the following occupations:

• Architect
• Engineer
• Urban planner
• Products specialist
• Design specialist
• Urban design specialist

SOURCES OF ADDITIONAL INFORMATION

American Society of Interior Designers. www.asid.org
National Association of Home Builders. www.nahb.org
United States Green Building Council. www.usgbc.org

FURTHER READING

Karell, Mark. "Recent Trends in Sustainable Building." *Environmental Leader*, February 22, 2012. Accessed February 23, 2012. http://www.environmentalleader.com/2012/02/22/recent-trends-in-sustainable-building.

Life at HOK. *Q+A: Burning Calories with HOK Washington, D.C., Sustainable Design Specialist Sean Quinn.* Accessed February 16, 2012. http://hoklife.com/2011/06/02/qa-burning-calories-with-hok-washington-dc-sustainable-design-specialist-sean-quinn.

Liming, Drew. *Careers in Green Construction.* Bureau of Labor Statistics, U.S. Department of Labor, 2011. Accessed February 15, 2012. http://www.bls.gov/green/construction/construction.pdf.

U.S. Department of the Interior. *Guiding Principles of Sustainable Design.* National Park Service: Denver Service Center, 1993.

U.S. General Services Administration. *Sustainable Design Program.* Accessed February 15, 2012. http://www.gsa.gov/portal/content/104462.

WIND ENERGY ENGINEERS

NATURE OF THE WORK

Engineers in the wind power industry are involved in all phases of harnessing wind energy. They design and develop wind turbines, supervise production in factories, test manufactured products to maintain quality, and troubleshoot design or component issues. Wind energy engineers estimate the time and cost required to complete projects and look for ways to make production processes more efficient. In a supervisory role, engineers are responsible for major components or entire projects and may lead a team of engineers and technicians.

Wind energy engineers design both underground and overhead wind farm systems. They create models to enhance the layout of wind farms, monitor construction to ensure compliance with regulatory standards and environmental requirements, and analyze the operation of wind farms to determine reliability, efficiency, and performance. They also analyze component failures to determine the cause and provide technical support to designers of prototype wind turbines.

A wind energy engineer's job continues beyond the installation and start-up of the wind farm. Engineering professionals must constantly monitor the operation of wind farms by obtaining and analyzing data regarding the performance, efficiency, and operational costs related to the farms. They use these data to develop programs to improve the performance of wind turbines.

Because of the complexity of wind turbines, several types of engineers are used in the industry. Some of the

> ### AT A GLANCE FACT BOX
>
> **SOC:** 17-2199.10
> **Preferred Education:** Bachelor's degree
> **Preferred Specialty:** Electrical engineering, mechanical engineering
> **Average Salary:** US$90,270 annually
> **Other Information:** In 2008, 32 percent of the wind energy engineers in the United States were employed in manufacturing, 25 percent worked in professional, scientific, and technical services, 16 percent worked for federal and state governments, and 27 percent worked in other industries, including self-employment and administrative and support services.

engineers employed in the wind power industry and their roles include the following:

- Aerospace engineers, who supervise the manufacture of wind turbine blades and help meteorologists determine wind farm sites
- Civil engineers, who design and supervise the construction of wind farms and specialize in structural, transportation, construction, and geotechnical engineering

- Electrical engineers, who design, develop, test, and supervise the manufacture of electric motors, machinery controls, lighting and wiring of turbines, generators, communication systems, and transmission systems
- Environmental engineers, who consider the potential impact that wind turbines have on the environment, such as noise, visual appearance, interference with telecommunications, and effects on local species
- Health and safety engineers, who study the potential hazards of wind turbines and implement safety and loss prevention procedures
- Industrial engineers, who focus on increasing productivity and minimizing the costs of operating wind turbines
- Materials engineers, who work with various materials used in the construction of wind turbines, including metals, plastics, ceramics, semiconductors, and composites
- Mechanical engineers, who help develop tools and mechanical devices used in wind turbines, including components, wind turbine systems, and the machinery used to manufacture and test wind turbines

Some of the tools that wind energy engineers use regularly in their jobs include anemometers, which measure the velocity and pressure of wind; barometers; radar-based surveillance systems; portable meteorological stations; and sonic detection equipment.

Engineers use computers extensively to produce and analyze designs, generate specifications for parts, monitor product quality, and simulate and test how a turbine or other component operates. Some of the software used by wind energy engineers includes analytical or scientific software, computer-aided design software, and map creation software such as Google Earth Pro.

WORKING CONDITIONS

Wind energy engineers typically work in offices, laboratories, and industrial settings. Some do a significant amount of travel to plants or worksites in the United States as well as overseas. Engineers who monitor wind turbines must be physically capable of climbing towers that may exceed 100 yards in height.

Jobs in wind energy engineering typically offer above-average pay and benefits, flexible schedules, and a high degree of job satisfaction. Wind energy engineers often enjoy a work atmosphere filled with educated colleagues, challenging work, and many exciting opportunities.

EMPLOYMENT

Federal and state government laboratories, universities, wind farms, and private corporations employ wind energy

engineers who play key roles in wind turbine research and development. The majority of the jobs are in the manufacturing sector, and hundreds of companies are involved in manufacturing turbines and turbine components.

Wind turbines are large, complicated pieces of machinery designed and built by companies known as original equipment manufacturers (OEMs). Because of the fierce competition in the industry, each firm must find innovative ways to make turbines more powerful, efficient, and reliable while also keeping costs down. Talented wind energy engineers who design, develop, and build better wind turbine systems are in great demand. The blades, tower, and nacelle of wind turbines may be manufactured by the OEMs themselves or may be contracted out to suppliers, many of which are located around industrial areas in the Midwest and along the Great Lakes coastline in the United States.

Some companies that offer wind energy engineers worldwide opportunities include GE Energy (GE), Nordic Windpower, Sandia National Laboratories, and Siemens Wind Power. Wind engineers employed by GE work all over the world, including Australia, Germany, India, China, Thailand, and the United States. Nordic Windpower is based in the United States with an engineering design office in the United Kingdom. Sandia National Laboratories is a government-owned, contractor-operated facility managed by Lockheed Martin Corporation for the U.S. Department of Energy National Nuclear Security Administration. Siemens Wind Power is a leading supplier of wind turbines as well as a global leader in the offshore wind power market, with locations throughout Europe, Asia, and the United States.

TRAINING, OTHER QUALIFICATIONS, AND ADVANCEMENT

Wind energy engineers are typically required to have a bachelor's degree in an engineering specialty. Many jobs involving research at a laboratory, a university, or a private corporation may require a master's or doctoral degree. In addition, engineers are typically licensed and are expected to complete continuing education to keep current with changes in their specialty and in wind energy technology.

Wind turbine manufacturers prefer to hire engineers with a minimum of three to five years of experience in their respective field. These employers also look for engineers who possess a working knowledge of commonly used systems and processes. Newly hired engineers are typically given additional training lasting several weeks or months before an assignment and undergo extensive on-the-job training as well.

Entry-level wind energy engineers may also be hired as interns or junior team members and learn by working under the supervision of senior engineers. As they gain experience and knowledge, they are assigned more difficult tasks and given greater independence. Some wind energy engineers become managers or enter sales jobs in which their engineering background enables them to discuss the technical aspects of a product and give assistance in product planning and installation.

Certifications are usually required depending on the systems used by a particular manufacturer. Wind energy engineers can also obtain a Certified Renewable Energy Professional certification from the Association of Energy Engineers. Licensure as a professional engineer is recommended but may not be required by many wind turbine manufacturers.

JOB OUTLOOK

According to the U.S. Department of Labor's Bureau of Labor Statistics (BLS), wind energy was the fastest growing energy source in 2010 and could contribute as much as 20 percent of the nation's electricity by 2030. Employment opportunities for wind energy engineers are expected to vary in growth by specialty. The employment outlook for aerospace, electrical, mechanical, and civil engineers is especially favorable because they play a particularly important role in wind power.

Overall, the job outlook for wind energy engineers is strong, with the projected growth from 2008 to 2018 expected to be an average of 7 to 13 percent. Job openings in the United States during that same time period are anticipated to be more than 50,000.

EARNINGS

Starting salaries for wind energy engineers are among the highest salaries for all college graduates. Salaries vary widely according to geographic location, with wind energy engineers in Nebraska averaging slightly less than US$50,000 per year in 2009, whereas those with similar positions in Washington, DC, made more than US$120,000 annually. The highest paying locations for wind energy engineers in 2009 included the following:

- Atlantic City, New Jersey: US$121,420
- Washington, DC: US$118,970
- St. Mary's County, Maryland: US$116,680
- Bethesda, Maryland: US$115,620
- Los Alamos County, New Mexico: US$115,570

- Amarillo, Texas: US$115,510
- Burlington, Vermont: US$114,880
- Newark, New Jersey: US$114,440
- Boulder, Colorado: US$114,250

RELATED OCCUPATIONS

The duties of wind turbine service technicians are similar to those of the following occupations:

- Aerospace engineers
- Civil engineers
- Electrical engineers
- Electronics engineers
- Environmental engineers
- Health and safety engineers
- Industrial engineers
- Materials engineers
- Mechanical engineers
- Engineering technicians

SOURCES OF ADDITIONAL INFORMATION

American Association for Wind Engineering. http://www.aawe.org
American Wind Energy Association. http://www.awea.org
Association of Energy Engineers. http://www.aeecenter.org
National Society of Professional Engineers. http://www.nspe.org

FURTHER READING

Bureau of Labor Statistics, U.S. Department of Labor. *Careers in Wind Energy*. Accessed January 14, 2012. http://www.bls.gov/green/wind_energy/.
O*NET OnLine. *Summary Report for: 17-2199.10— Wind Energy Engineers*. Accessed January 14, 2012. http://www.onetonline.org/link/summary/17-2199.10.
Science Buddies. *Science Careers: Wind Energy Engineer*. Accessed January 15, 2012. http://www.sciencebuddies.org/science-fair-projects/science-engineering-careers/Energy_windenergyengineer_c001.shtml.
WindEnergyJobsInfo. *Wind Energy Jobs Are Booming*. Accessed January 15, 2012. http://www.windenergyjobsinfo.com/.

SOLAR ENERGY SYSTEMS ENGINEERS

NATURE OF THE WORK

Sunlight is the most abundant source of energy on the planet. Solar energy systems engineers take on the task of harnessing its power, which could easily exceed current and future electricity demand. Solar energy systems engineers use the principles of science and mathematics to apply scientific research to commercial functions. They are responsible for designing solar energy systems that help make residential, commercial, and industrial buildings more energy efficient, reduce emissions from electricity generation, and reduce overall energy costs.

When solar engineers work on a design for a client, they typically analyze the site, evaluate the existing energy system, perform a variety of engineering calculations, conduct detailed research to determine the best technology to meet the client's needs, and experiment with various system layouts before determining the best one. Some of the tasks performed by solar energy systems engineers in the course of their jobs include the following:

- Creating plans, checklists, diagrams, and schedules for solar energy system development
- Designing photovoltaic (PV) or solar thermal systems for private homes and commercial buildings
- Developing standard operating procedures and quality and safety standards for workers who install solar energy components
- Providing technical direction and support to solar installation teams
- Reviewing plans and recommending engineering changes to achieve solar energy productivity objectives

One common solar energy system designed by solar engineers is the solar hot water system. Solar hot water

AT A GLANCE FACT BOX

SOC: 17-2199.11
Preferred Education: Bachelor's degree
Preferred Specialty: Electrical and mechanical engineering
Average Salary: US$43.40 per hour, or US$90,270 annually
Other Information: In 2008 there were 183,000 solar energy systems engineers in the United States. Thirty-two percent of them were employed in manufacturing, 25 percent worked in professional, scientific, and technical services, 16 percent worked for federal and state governments, and 27 percent worked in other industries, including self-employment and administrative and support services.

heating systems follow the basic premise that the shallower water of a lake is usually warmer than the deep water below due to the radiant sunlight the shallow water receives. Solar hot water heating systems designed by engineers have two main parts: a solar collector and a storage tank. The collector is usually a thin, flat, rectangular box with a transparent cover that faces the sun and is mounted on a roof. Small tubes run through the box and carry fluid to be heated. These tubes are attached to an absorber plate that is painted black to absorb the heat. As the heat builds up in the collector, it heats the fluid that is running through the tubes, which is then routed into a storage tank.

Solar engineers design both active and passive solar heating systems, but active systems are most common. Active solar systems use pumps to move the hot liquid between the collector and the storage tank, whereas passive systems rely on gravity and the natural tendency of water to circulate as it is heated. Swimming pools can also be heated this way, with the pool serving as the storage tank.

The sun's energy can be harnessed as either light or heat. Solar energy systems engineers use the process of converting light, or *photons*, to electricity, or *voltage*. This process is called the PV effect. Because only sunlight of certain energies will work efficiently to generate electricity and PV applications are most effective in areas with a proportionately large amount of daily sunlight, solar engineers focus their energy and expertise on improving solar cell efficiencies while holding down the cost per cell.

Tools and Technology Solar energy engineers use a variety of tools in their jobs, including ageing ovens, which simulate the effects of long-term exposure to heat on rubber and plastics; calorimeters, which measure the heat of chemical reactions or other physical changes; thermogravimetric analyzers, which determine the change in weight of an object when the temperature changes; coulometers, which measure the magnitude of an electrical charge; laboratory evaporators, potentiometers, or voltage dividers; scanning electron microscopes; and spectrometers, which measure light properties over a portion of the electromagnetic spectrum.

Solar energy systems engineering positions require a high level of computer skills and capabilities. These professionals must successfully complete college coursework in computer science and computer-aided design software and be familiar with other specific types of software, including analytical or scientific software, development environment software, and Microsoft Office software including Access, Outlook, PowerPoint, Excel, and Word.

WORKING CONDITIONS

Solar energy systems engineers have much variety in their working environment. They sometimes speak directly with clients to collect data regarding their energy needs. A certain amount of their workday may also be spent outdoors, where they may be working on a building site in the United States or abroad doing tests, calculations, and research. Solar energy engineers also spend a significant amount of time in their offices on their computers.

These engineers are team players. They often work in collaboration with other multidisciplinary professionals in reviewing structural energy requirements, local climates, solar technology, and thermodynamics to develop creative solar energy solutions for clients.

EMPLOYMENT

Most solar energy systems engineers work in offices, laboratories, or industrial plants. They usually work for manufacturers of solar equipment, and their jobs frequently require travel to different work sites in the United States, Europe, and Asia.

Solar equipment manufacturers and other employers in the solar energy industry are seeking out employees with a suitable background for solar energy engineering. The Solar Foundation reported in 2010 that 53 percent of solar manufacturing firms had expressed difficulty in locating and hiring qualified engineers during that year.

TRAINING, OTHER QUALIFICATIONS, AND ADVANCEMENT

Solar energy systems engineers usually need a bachelor's degree in an engineering specialty such as electrical or mechanical engineering, although not all solar energy systems engineers possess these backgrounds. Some have degrees in natural science or math, electrical or mechanical drafting, or engineering technology or have backgrounds in heating, ventilation, and air conditioning. Some of the various backgrounds of engineers who work in the solar power industry include the following:

- Materials engineers, who develop, process, and test the materials used for products in the solar industry
- Chemical engineers, who design equipment and processes for the manufacturing of solar cells
- Electrical engineers, who design, develop, test, and supervise the manufacture of the electrical components used in the solar industry
- Industrial engineers, who maximize the efficiency of solar energy production
- Mechanical engineers, who work on machines used in the manufacturing of solar panels

Engineers who work directly with the public must have a professional engineer license. To keep current with the rapidly changing face of solar energy technology, most take advantage of the continuing education opportunities that are available. Some engineering positions in solar energy require a graduate degree in engineering.

Solar energy systems engineers must have the ability to recognize and solve problems and be able to apply general engineering principles to specific challenges in the solar energy industry. They must have the ability to express themselves well both orally and in writing. Frequently they are asked to communicate with customers regarding their energy needs and write reports on the solar system projects on which they are working. Computer skills are extremely important, as is attention to detail, the ability to analyze situations and problems, and the persistence necessary to design the most efficient and cost-effective solar systems possible.

Many experienced solar energy systems engineers are called on to supervise or train project team members as necessary and to head up entire teams of engineers and other professionals involved in the design of solar energy systems. They may oversee all phases of solar energy systems including design, budget, construction, installation, maintenance, support, data compilation, and report writing.

JOB OUTLOOK

The projected job growth for solar energy systems engineers between 2006 and 2016 is 7 to 13 percent, meaning that this professional is and will continue to be in demand.

The solar power market increased from 427 megawatts in 2002 to 1,744 megawatts in 2006, with solar power revenues growing in the United States from approximately US$10.6 billion in 2006 to US$31.5 billion in 2011. Governments, businesses, and consumers are increasingly supporting the development of solar energy sources, which creates engineering jobs in that sector.

EARNINGS

Solar energy systems engineers are in demand and are usually well paid for their work. In the United States, they earn an average of US$90,270 annually, although salaries can vary greatly depending on the company, location, industry, benefits, and the engineer's experience.

RELATED OCCUPATIONS

The duties of solar energy systems engineers are similar to those of the following occupations:

- Materials engineers
- Chemical engineers
- Electrical engineers
- Industrial engineers
- Mechanical engineers
- Computer software developers
- Engineering technicians

SOURCES OF ADDITIONAL INFORMATION

American Solar Energy Society. http://www.ases.org

Association of Energy Engineers. http://www.aeecenter.org

Solar Energy Industries Association. http://www.seia.org

FURTHER READING

Bureau of Labor Statistics, U.S. Department of Labor. "Careers in Solar Power." *Green Jobs.* Accessed January 16, 2012. http://www.bls.gov/green/solar_power/.

CollegeToolKit.com. *Solar Energy Systems Engineers.* Accessed January 16, 2012. https://www.collegetoolkit.com/careers/solar_energy_systems_engineers/overview/17-2199.11.aspx.

Engineering.com. *Passive Solar Systems & Solar Hot Water.* Accessed January 16, 2012. http://www.engineering.com/SustainableEngineering/RenewableEnergyEngineering/SolarEnergyEngineering/PassiveSolarSystemsSolarHotWater/tabid/3892/Default.aspx.

Green LMI Consulting. *National Solar Jobs Census 2010.* The Solar Foundation: Washington, DC, 2010. Accessed March 8, 2012. http://www.thesolarfoundation.org/sites/thesolarfoundation.org/files/Final%20TSF%20National%20Solar%20Jobs%20Census%202010%20Web%20Version.pdf.

MyMajors. *Career: Solar Engineer.* Accessed January 16, 2012. http://www.mymajors.com/careers-and-jobs/Solar-Engineer.

O*Net OnLine. *Summary Report for: 17-2199.11—Solar Energy Systems Engineers.* Accessed January 16, 2012. http://www.onetonline.org/link/summary/17-2199.11.

Science Buddies. *Science Careers: Solar Energy Systems Engineer.* Accessed January 16, 2012. http://www.sciencebuddies.org/science-fair-projects/science-engineering-careers/Energy_solarenergysystemsengineer_c001.shtml.

SOLAR SALES REPRESENTATIVES AND ASSESSORS

NATURE OF THE WORK

Solar sales representatives and assessors sell equipment that will help their customers reap the benefits of solar energy. These professionals determine the energy needs of new and existing customers, suggest specific solar systems or equipment, and provide proposals and price quotes. They sell all types of solar systems, components, and raw materials to consumers and businesses.

Assessors determine how much solar energy can be harvested at a particular location and then make recommendations based on that assessment. Site assessors help sales representatives determine the best type, size, and layout of solar panels and help draw up plans for installation crews. They may take readings of sunlight at a proposed location, review weather patterns, and calculate potential costs and savings. Site assessors are typically retained by companies for commercial projects for which substantial investment is involved, although site assessors may also consult with homeowners or solar installation companies on residential projects.

Successful solar sales representatives and assessors have the scientific background to provide customers with technical information about solar power, solar systems, equipment, and required services. Using this knowledge enables them to create customized solar energy management packages and demonstrate the use of solar equipment to customers and dealers. When giving an assessment, solar sales representatives and assessors provide site-specific information to help customers satisfy their energy needs. These assessments can cost between US$200 and US$1,000 depending on the complexity of the site and the technology required.

AT A GLANCE FACT BOX

SOC: 41-4011.07
Preferred Education: Bachelor's degree
Average Salary: US$35.44 per hour or US$73,710 annually
Other Information: In 2008 there were 433,000 solar sales representatives and assessors employed in the United States. Fifty-eight percent were employed in wholesale trade, 11 percent worked in manufacturing, 10 percent worked in professional, scientific, and technical services, and 21 percent worked in other industries including information services.

Some of the tools used by solar sales representatives and assessors include the following:

• Computers
• Digital cameras
• On-site equipment such as ladders, measuring tapes, and solarimeters (devices that measure direct and diffuse solar radiation)
• Computerized data collectors

Those who sell solar equipment use technology to make doing their job easier and more efficient. Some of the specialized software that these professionals should be familiar with includes solar analysis software; Autodesk

AutoCAD software; Google SketchUp; customer relationship management software such as Salesforce.com; Microsoft software including Outlook, Office, PowerPoint, Project, Excel, and Word; and Internet browser software.

WORKING CONDITIONS

Solar sales representatives and assessors spend a great deal of time on the road, traveling to sites to speak with current and prospective clients. Many of these individuals have large territories to cover, sometimes encompassing several states. They may be away from home for weeks at a time, traveling by automobile or by plane. Other solar sales representatives may have smaller territories to cover and spend only an occasional few nights away from home.

Some solar sales representatives and assessors may work a standard 40-hour work week, but many work more than 50 hours per week. A typical work schedule involves making sales calls during the regular workday and performing the planning and paperwork responsibilities associated with the job during evenings and weekends. Despite a somewhat irregular work routine, many solar sales representatives enjoy the freedom of determining their own schedules.

EMPLOYMENT

Manufacturers and wholesalers of solar equipment employ many sales representatives and assessors in the solar energy industry, although a growing number of manufacturers choose to outsource sales activities to independent companies. Other sales representatives and assessors work in retail organizations and professional, technical, and scientific firms, and some are self-employed.

Growth in this profession between 2008 and 2018 is projected to be the greatest in independent sales companies because more solar manufacturers are expected to outsource sales. Because of the variety of solar equipment and services that may be sold, opportunities will be available throughout all areas of the United States as well as around the world.

TRAINING, OTHER QUALIFICATIONS, AND ADVANCEMENT

Although there is typically no educational requirement for those engaged in sales, many positions dealing with scientific and technical products, such as those in solar energy, may require a bachelor's degree. Previous sales experience is also helpful. Most of all, solar sales representatives and assessors should know the ins and outs of solar power, including:

- What net metering involves
- Energy usage as it relates to system sizing
- The importance of shading considerations
- The purpose of an invertor
- Prevention of roof leakage

All solar sales representatives and assessors, whether they are new to the industry or have many years of experience, need to attend conferences, read trade publications and blogs, participate in networking sessions, and take classes to stay abreast of the many changes taking place in solar energy.

Solar sales representatives and assessors must have excellent communication skills and the desire to sell. They must be goal oriented and persuasive, have the ability to work with minimal supervision, and be cooperative team players. Because a sale can take weeks or even months to finalize, this job also requires patience and perseverance.

Certifications that recognize the skills of successful sales representatives are available. Many solar sales representatives and assessors have either the Certified Professional Manufacturers Representative (CPMR) or the Certified Sales Professional (CSP) certification, both of which are offered by the Manufacturers Representatives Education Research Foundation. The Midwest Renewable Energy Association also offers a Site Assessment Certificate for professionals who involve customers in the development of solar energy systems for their homes and businesses. The site assessment certificate is a credential that establishes an entry-level competency in the renewable energy field, which includes solar energy. Those who wish to become certified typically must complete some type of formal training and successfully pass an examination.

Sales representatives who are positioned for advancement will often assume a larger account or sales territory for which commissions may be larger. Work hours, however, may be longer, and work may be more rigorous for those who are looking to advance. Sales representatives with proven sales ability as well as solid leadership skills may be promoted to higher-level sales positions within their company such as supervisor, district manager, or vice president.

The opportunity for advancement often depends on whether an individual is working for a manufacturer, a wholesaler, or an independent company. Sales representatives who work for manufacturers or wholesalers sometimes have the ability to advance into sales trainer positions where they are responsible for educating new employees.

JOB OUTLOOK

According to the U.S. Department of Labor's Bureau of Labor Statistics (BLS), solar sales representatives and assessor jobs will grow 7 percent, or "about as fast as average" between 2008 and 2018. Because of the large scope of this occupation, this growth may account for approximately 143,200 new jobs. Job prospects are expected to be best for those with a college degree, knowledge of the solar energy industry, and the communication skills necessary to be a successful salesperson. Employment growth in this industry is expected to be the greatest among independent sales companies as the trend among manufacturers will continue to be to outsource sales opportunities to independent agents rather than employ their own in-house sales staff. By outsourcing sales responsibilities to contractors, manufacturers attempt to keep overhead costs down and keep solar equipment affordable for consumers.

According to the Solar Foundation's National Solar Jobs Census 2011, solar sales and distribution is the fastest growing sector within the solar energy industry, growing by 13.8 percent from 2010 to 2011. Solar sales and distribution firms expect to add 35 percent more sales workers through July 2012, according to the census. Employers sometimes experience difficulty in finding quality sales workers.

Ontility, a full-service solar sales, distribution, and development firm in Houston, Texas, is one solar firm that is experiencing phenomenal growth. This growth required the company to hire additional sales staff and from 2010 to 2011, the company went from 35 employees to 77. One of the company's challenges has been gauging how and when to fill positions and best manage this growth.

EARNINGS

Solar sales representatives and assessors are usually paid a combination of salary and commissions or a salary plus a bonus that is tied to sales performance. The bonus is usually reflective of a percentage of individual sales, individual performance, performance of the salesmen in a group or district, the sales of an entire company, or a combination of several of these.

Sales representatives who work directly for solar equipment manufacturers or wholesalers are typically reimbursed for their expenses, including the cost of meals, transportation, lodging, and entertaining clients, but independent sales representatives usually are not. Likewise, solar sales representatives and assessors who work directly for manufacturers and wholesalers may also receive other benefits, such as use of a company car and airline frequent flyer mileage, whereas independent sales representatives are not usually afforded these perks. Conversely, independent sales representatives may earn higher salaries and commissions to make up for the lack of these benefits.

Although average earnings in this occupation are relatively high, solar sales representatives and assessors often work more than 40 hours per week and sometimes feel pressure and stress because their income as well as job security depends entirely on their ability to sell. Their employers often set quotas that they are expected to meet, adding to the stress. They also work almost exclusively with people, which can be rewarding but is also quite demanding.

RELATED OCCUPATIONS

The duties of solar sales representatives and assessors are similar to those of the following occupations:

• Advertising sales agents
• Purchasing managers, buyers, and purchasing agents
• Sales engineers
• Sales worker supervisors
• Retail salespersons

SOURCES OF ADDITIONAL INFORMATION

American Solar Energy Society. http://www.ases.org
Professional Sales Representative Organization. http://www.avreps.org
Solar Energy Industries Association. http://www.seia.org

FURTHER READING

Bureau of Labor Statistics, U.S. Department of Labor. "Sales Representatives, Wholesale and Manufacturing." In *Occupational Outlook Handbook, 2010–11 Edition.* Accessed January 21, 2012. http://www.bls.gov/oco/ocos119.htm.
O*Net OnLine. *Details Report for: 41-4011.07—Solar Sales Representatives and Assessors.* Accessed January 21, 2012. http://www.onetonline.org/link/details/41-4011.07.
The Solar Foundation. *National Solar Jobs Census 2011: A Review of the U.S. Solar Workforce, October 2011.* Accessed March 8, 2012. http://thesolarfoundation.org/sites/thesolarfoundation.org/files/TSF_JobsCensus2011_Final_Compressed.pdf.
Solar Power Rocks.com. *How Do I Get Started in the Solar Industry?* Accessed January 21, 2012. http://solarpowerrocks.com/solar-employment/how-do-i-get-started-in-the-solar-industry/.

SOLAR ENERGY INSTALLATION MANAGERS

NATURE OF THE WORK

The main responsibility of solar energy installation managers is to direct work crews in the installation of residential or commercial solar photovoltaic or thermal solar energy systems.

Solar energy installation managers must have a deep understanding of how solar energy works. Photovoltaic power uses solar cells that convert the sunlight's energy into electricity. This conversion is achieved through a process that involves sunlight hitting a solar panel and being absorbed by a semiconducting material. Electricity is produced when the photons in the sunlight knock electrons loose from their atoms and allow them to flow through the material, producing direct current (DC) electricity. A converter is used to convert the DC electricity to alternating current (AC) for household use.

Individual solar cells are arranged onto a solar panel, which is placed on a thin strip of aluminum backing and covered with a plastic film. Several of the panels are usually organized into an array, which is designed to produce enough capacity to generate the desired amount of energy. Solar systems can be installed on the ground, on poles, or on the roof or sides of buildings. A single cell will produce enough energy to power a small device, but a larger array is required to power a residential or commercial building. It is the responsibility of the solar energy installation manager to work with other professionals involved in the project to design a solar energy system that will meet the customer's needs.

A solar energy installation manager's job requires scientific knowledge of solar energy, critical thinking abilities, communication skills, and an extensive working knowledge of solar energy systems. Solar energy installation managers

may perform a variety of functions during the installation of a solar energy system, including creating the initial design according to a customer's needs, travelling to a job site to evaluate layout of the system, examining product and installation costs, and presenting a proposal or estimate to a customer.

Solar energy installation managers are responsible for estimating the materials, equipment, and staffing needed for installation projects. They may also be in charge of all installation-related paperwork, including applying for and processing permits, tax credits, and any required coordination with power companies. When it is time to install a solar energy system, managers are on the job site with their crew, supervising the installation, checking supplies, ensuring a safe working environment, and helping keep the job running on schedule and within budget.

Some of the tools that solar energy installation managers use on a regular basis include:

- Calculators
- Front-end loaders
- Digital refractometers (devices that measure how light travels through a material)
- Extension ladders
- Hand tools such as locking pliers, pipe wrenches, jigsaws, and screwdrivers

Solar energy installation managers also use a high degree of technology in their jobs. Familiarity with software programs including computer-aided design (CAD) software, customer relationship management (CRM) software, electronic mail software, mapping software, and Microsoft software packages, including Outlook, Office, Office SharePoint Server (MOSS), PowerPoint, Project, Excel, and Word, is standard.

WORKING CONDITIONS

The work schedules of solar energy installation managers depend upon the sun, quite literally. Their hours are similar to that of construction workers, with long hours some days followed by days of lighter workloads. Managers spend the majority of their workdays at sites, either speaking with clients or directing installations, and many start early in the morning to beat the heat in warmer climates. If it is raining, they may not be able to work onsite at all because wet weather can make installation dangerous for them and their crew. Solar energy installation workers and managers cannot be afraid of heights. Although most commercial installations take place on flat roofs, many residential installations are on pitched roofs with steep slopes.

Because no two solar installation jobs are likely to be the same, every day for a solar energy installation manager may be filled with unique challenges. A typical installation on a home takes approximately three days to complete whereas large commercial installations may take several months. Managers often have additional duties, such as arranging work permits and inspections, altering a design around the structure of a building, or troubleshooting existing solar systems that are not working properly.

EMPLOYMENT

Solar energy installation managers typically work for specialty trade contractors including electrical, plumbing, and heating and cooling, as well as outdoor swimming pool contractors. About half of all solar photovoltaic installers and managers in the United States, some 698,000 workers

in 2008, were employed in California, a state that provides a number of incentives for use of solar power. Because solar power often requires a large upfront investment, tax credits and other incentives provided by governments help make solar power a more affordable energy alternative for individual consumers and businesses, and states without these incentives may have fewer job opportunities.

TRAINING, OTHER QUALIFICATIONS, AND ADVANCEMENT

Solar energy installation managers may work alongside roofers, electricians, and plumbers while completing an installation. Many managers enter the field with previous experience in one or more of these fields. They may also start out as a solar panel installer and work their way up to a management position.

Although there is no formal training standard for solar energy installation workers, most have a background in construction or as an electrician. Training courses vary widely and are offered by trade schools, apprenticeship programs, or photovoltaic module manufacturers. Solar energy installation managers typically have significant work experience in solar energy installation along with a management background gained through experience or by completing a certificate or associate degree program.

Because of the high skill level required, clients sometimes ask that both the installation manager and the installers who work independently obtain a general contractor's license. Certification is not necessary but can improve the job and advancement prospects of solar energy installation managers and many larger projects require such credentials.

Many solar installation managers are licensed general contractors and may have also earned licensure through the North American Board of Certified Energy Practitioners (NABCEP). According to NABCEP, to be eligible to sit for the NABCEP solar heating installer certification candidates must meet basic requirements, including:

- Be a minimum of 18 years of age
- Meet prerequisites of related experience and/or education
- Complete an application to take the NABCEP Solar Heating Installer Certification exam
- Sign a code of ethics
- Pay all applicable fees
- Pass the NABCEP Solar Heating Installer Certification exam

The candidate must meet the prerequisites, which require qualifications such as having a certain number of years of experience installing solar systems in addition to completion of cumulative training, being an existing licensed contractor in good standing in solar or a construction-related area, and other specific types of solar energy experience.

JOB OUTLOOK

This job is expected to grow "faster than average" or from 14 to 19 percent between 2008 and 2018, as projected by the U.S. Department of Labor's Bureau of Labor Statistics (BLS). According to the Solar Foundation's National Solar Jobs Census 2011, as of August 2011 solar installation firms expected to add more than 13,000 solar workers over the next 12 months, representing 25 percent growth. The majority of U.S. solar installation companies work on systems of various sizes, with the majority installing energy systems in residential homes and small commercial businesses.

Some firms contract out part of their installation work, resulting in more highly refined occupational areas and fewer workers who are expected to conduct multiple installation activities. As a result, solar energy installation managers may supervise a more specialized crew of installation workers in the future. Photovoltaic installers led all solar job categories in growth between 2010 and 2011, and installation managers also enjoyed 30 percent job growth during that time period.

EARNINGS

According to the BLS, solar energy installation managers earn an average of US$28.21 per hour, or US$58,680 annually, and those who are trained as electricians or are licensed as general contractors are often paid significantly more. Wages and benefits vary by employer and geographic location.

RELATED OCCUPATIONS

Jobs that have a similar skill set to solar energy installation managers are:

- Electrical and electronics engineering technicians
- Electrical and electronics installers and repairers
- Heating, air conditioning, and refrigeration mechanics and installers
- Line installers and repairers

SOURCES OF ADDITIONAL INFORMATION

The American Solar Energy Society. http://www.ases.org
North American Board of Certified Energy Practitioners. http://www.nabcep.org
The Solar Energy Industries Association. http://www.seia.org

FURTHER READING

Bureau of Labor Statistics, U.S. Department of Labor. *Green Jobs: Solar Power, Careers in Solar Power*. Accessed January 22, 2012. http://www.bls.gov/green/solar_power/solar_power.pdf.
North American Board of Certified Energy Practitioners. *The Need for Certification*. Accessed January 22, 2012. http://www.nabcep.org/certification/the-need-for-certification.
O*NET OnLine. *Details Report for: 47-1011.03—Solar Energy Installation Managers*. Accessed January 22, 2012. http://www.onetonline.org/link/details/47-1011.03.
The Solar Foundation. *National Solar Jobs Census 2011, A Review of the U.S. Solar Workforce*, October 2011. Accessed March 11, 2012. http://thesolarfoundation.org/sites/thesolarfoundation.org/files/TSF_Jobs Census2011_Final_Compressed.pdf.

SOLAR PHOTOVOLTAIC INSTALLERS

NATURE OF THE WORK

Solar photovoltaic installers are responsible for assembling, installing, and maintaining solar photovoltaic (PV) systems on roofs or other structures. These systems collect the sun's energy. The term *photovoltaic* refers to the process of converting the sun's energy (or radiant energy) into electrical energy.

In solar PV systems, solar cells are used to convert sunlight into electricity. These cells are connected together to form modules that are mounted by solar photovoltaic installers on the ground, on poles, on the sides of structures, or on the roofs of buildings. The most common type of solar module is the three-by-five-foot flat framed panel that is mounted on a roof by a solar photovoltaic installer. Thanks to recent advances in technology, however, solar modules can also be flexible panels, roof tiles, and shingles and can be combined with building materials such as siding and windows.

When doing an installation, solar photovoltaic installers must determine whether solar panels can fit on the roof of a structure and whether the roof can support the weight of panels. If the roof does not meet the requirements, the installer can make adjustments to modify the solar panel layout or can add extra support framework so that the roof will be able to handle the weight of the system. Once modifications have been made or if the roof needs no modifications, the next step for the solar photovoltaic installer is to attach the racking, or structural framework, to the roof. The solar panels are then attached to the racking and connected to wires that lead to a basement, garage, or outside box and hooked up to an inverter. The inverter turns the direct current (DC) generated by the solar cells into

alternating current (AC) that is used to power homes and businesses.

Tools and Technology Solar photovoltaic installers need solid mechanical skills and must be able to work with various tools to install solar panels and other necessary equipment. Some of the tools that solar photovoltaic installers use in their jobs include:

- Claw hammers
- Sledgehammers
- Power drills

AT A GLANCE FACT BOX

SOC: 47-2231.00
Preferred Education: High school diploma or GED plus a vocational or associate's degree in solar photovoltaic systems
Preferred Specialty: Electrical, roofing, or general construction experience
Average Salary: US$16.59 per hour, or US$34,500 annually
Other Information: Industry developments and research into solar photovoltaic power since 1970 have decreased the costs and increased the production of solar photovoltaic systems. This has enlarged the markets for PV installation globally.

- Screwdrivers
- Wire cutters
- Site evaluation tools such as tape measures, laser-assisted measuring devices, and digital cameras
- Multimeters (devices that allow the installer to measure the voltage, current, and resistance of wires) and amp clamps (a clamp that allows the installer to check the current draw of an electrical system)

Solar photovoltaic installers must be adept at several types of software, including project management software and various Microsoft software packages, including Outlook, Office, Excel, and Word.

WORKING CONDITIONS

A solar photovoltaic installer works mainly outside, and weather often determines the work schedule. Installers may work in extremely hot, humid conditions, but rain makes installation extremely dangerous and as a result, during rainy weather there may be days when installers work very little if at all.

Although most solar PV installers work standard 40-hour weeks, favorable weather conditions during the spring and summer might require long hours of work for several days in a row, such as four 10-hour days plus overtime, especially if they are working on a large commercial project. Most installation jobs take several days to complete, depending on the size of the system and the number of workers assigned to the project.

The job of a solar photovoltaic installer is a physically demanding one, and because many days are spent on the top of a roof, installers cannot be afraid of heights. Possible dangers include steeply sloped roofs, loose shingles, and the risks of a high-voltage electrical installation. For this reason, installers take special safety precautions, which include wearing equipment such as harnesses, hard hats, boots, gloves, and eye protection to avoid injury. Because solar panels typically weigh between 30 and 40 pounds, heavy lifting is also a regular part of the job.

Although the steps involved in installing solar photovoltaic systems are similar, each installation is unique, which keeps the job interesting. Solar photovoltaic installers also have the satisfaction of installing a system that will provide clean, sustainable energy for many years to come.

EMPLOYMENT

Most solar photovoltaic installers work in the specialty trade contractors industry, which includes electrical and plumbing, heating, utilities, and air conditioning contractors. Installers may find employment opportunities through college placement offices and training facilities, professional associations, classified ads, and Internet job boards.

Some employers that hire solar photovoltaic installers include:

- Akeena Solar, a major installer of both residential and commercial Andalay Solar Power Systems in the state of California
- Eagle Point Solar, installers of grid-tied power systems, which provide the opportunity to buy and sell electricity
- SolarCity, a company that provides solar power for homes and businesses in Arizona; California; Colorado; Connecticut; Delaware; Hawaii; Maryland; Massachusetts; New Jersey; New York; Oregon; Pennsylvania; Texas; Washington, DC; and Washington State

TRAINING, OTHER QUALIFICATIONS, AND ADVANCEMENT

In general, solar photovoltaic installers must have a high school diploma or a GED. Although some employers are willing to provide solar photovoltaic installation training, many look for workers who have prior experience as an electrician or a roofer or who have worked in the general construction industry.

More community colleges are offering training in solar photovoltaic installation, and the distributors and manufacturers of PV panels often provide training in the use of their equipment, although these courses are sometimes offered only to contractors and not to the general public. There are also online solar training workshops available that provide a range of information from the fundamentals of solar photovoltaic installation to intensive training that includes hands-on undertakings.

Solar photovoltaic installers who want to go into business for themselves in California must be licensed through the California Contractors State License Board (CSLB). Some employers also require that PV installers have an electrician's license if they are going to perform electrical work.

In California, the solar PV installer was recognized as an occupation for apprenticeship in 2011, and some training facilities have begun to offer continuing education courses in solar photovoltaic installation to journeyman electricians. Most apprenticeship programs require that applicants be at least 18 years of age, have a high school diploma or a GED, possess a valid driver's license, and pass an entrance exam.

Although the job duties of entry-level installers may include lifting, carrying, staging, mounting, and helping the rest of the installation crew, more experienced solar PV installers may have the responsibility for measuring, cutting, drilling, and fastening structural support framework and mounting solar modules. Solar photovoltaic installers with electrical experience may help wire the inverter to the grid and perform electrical measurements, such as checking the AC/DC current and voltage.

The most experienced workers, who are often certified through the North American Board of Certified Energy Practitioners (NABCEP) or are licensed as electricians, may be promoted to supervisor or senior installer and provide leadership and training for a solar PV installation crew. They sometimes also go into sales of solar energy systems, become systems designers, advance to executive management positions, or start their own businesses.

JOB OUTLOOK

Industry experts estimated that there were approximately 7,000 solar photovoltaic installers working in the United States in 2009. Half of these jobs were located in California. The job outlook for solar photovoltaic installers is good, and the job is projected to grow an average of 7 to 13 percent between 2008 and 2018, with around 26,600 new jobs being added in the United States during that time.

EARNINGS

Solar photovoltaic installers earned an average of US$16.59 hourly, or US$34,500 per year in 2008. Salaries usually depend upon the pay structure of the employer and are based upon the work performed, the nature of the project, and the skill and experience of the installer. Solar photovoltaic installers who have passed the NABCEP entry-level exam may start at a higher salary than those who do not have this certification.

Although smaller companies may not offer benefits to workers such as solar photovoltaic installers, larger companies often provide medical, dental, life, and vision coverage to installers, along with vacation, paid sick leave, and retirement plans. Self-employed installers must provide these benefits for themselves.

RELATED OCCUPATIONS

- Carpenters
- Electricians
- Heating, air conditioning, and refrigeration mechanics and installers
- Roofers

SOURCES OF ADDITIONAL INFORMATION

American Solar Energy Society. http://www.ases.org
California Solar Energy Industries Association. http://calseia.org
North American Board of Certified Energy Practitioners. http://www.nabcep.org
Solar Energy Industries Association. http://www.seia.org

FURTHER READING

Bureau of Labor Statistics, U.S. Department of Labor. *You're a* What? *Solar Photovoltaic Installer.* Accessed February 8, 2012. http://www.bls.gov/opub/ooq/2009/fall/yawhat.pdf.
Employment Development Department, State of California. "Solar Photovoltaic Installers in California." *California Occupational Guides.* Accessed February 8, 2012. http://www.calmis.ca.gov/file/OccGuide/Solar-PV-Installers-Green.pdf.
O*NET OnLine. *Summary Report for: 47-2231.00— Solar Photovoltaic Installers.* Accessed February 8, 2012. http://www.onetonline.org/link/summary/47-2231.00.

SOLAR THERMAL INSTALLERS
AND TECHNICIANS

—■—

NATURE OF THE WORK

Although the United States reached peak oil production in 1970 and no one knows when global oil production will peak, there will come a time when the world's supply is exhausted. The sun, however, produces 4×10^{26} watts of energy every second and experts believe this will continue for another five billion years. The sun is the world's most reliable and ample source of energy.

There is a difference between photovoltaic (PV) energy conversion and solar thermal technology. Photovoltaic energy conversion is a direct transformation of the sun's energy into electricity and it is generally effective only during daylight hours because storing electricity is not an efficient process. Solar thermal electric energy generation, in contrast, uses the sun's energy to create heat, which in turn heats up a liquid or gas that is used to power a generator to make electricity. The heat that is created is stored easily and efficiently, greatly improving the price and availability of solar electricity in all conditions.

The United States Energy Information Administration categorizes solar thermal collectors as low-, medium-, or high-temperature collectors. Low-temperature collectors are flat plates typically used to heat swimming pools. Medium-temperature collectors are flat plates used to heat water or air for residential or commercial use. High-temperature collectors use mirrors or lenses to collect sunlight for electrical power production.

There are two methods of solar thermal energy collection: line focus collection and point focus collection. Line focus collection involves rotating a curved, mirrored trough all day, tracking the sun. Point focus collection requires a series of mirrors that surround a single tower,

known as a power tower. The mirrors focus the sun's rays toward a point on the tower, which then transfers the heat created into a more usable energy form.

Line focus collection is less expensive and less difficult to operate, but it is not as efficient as point focus. The higher efficiency of the point focus collection, however, brings down the costs necessary to operate a solar thermal energy system. Solar thermal installers and technicians analyze the pros and cons of both methods and determine which is best for each situation.

AT A GLANCE FACT BOX

SOC: 47-4099.02

Preferred Education: High school diploma plus basic construction skills training and some construction experience. A course outlining solar hot water installation techniques is also helpful.

Average Salary: US$16.59 per hour, or US$34,500 annually

Other Information: In 2008, there were 60,000 solar thermal installers and technicians employed in the United States. Thirty-eight percent were employed in the construction industry, 17 percent in administrative and support services, 15 percent in state and local government, and the remaining 30 percent in other industries, including self-employment and manufacturing.

Solar thermal installers and technicians install or repair solar energy systems that are made to collect, store, and circulate solar-heated water for use in homes, businesses, and industries. One of their main responsibilities is to help in the installation and construction of solar power systems in which concentrators, fans, collectors, and pumps are needed. These workers also design the apparatus that collects heat from the sun.

Although they typically have skills closely related to those in traditional plumbing, heating, air conditioning, or refrigeration installation, solar thermal installers and technicians have specific knowledge about solar energy systems and the use of green materials, which separates them from the standard plumber or heating, ventilation, and air conditioning (HVAC) technician. Some of the duties routinely performed by solar thermal installers and technicians include:

- Designing solar thermal systems, including active or indirect, passive direct or indirect, or pool systems
- Ensuring that solar thermal systems operate efficiently by performing routine maintenance or repairs
- Installing pumps and plumbing
- Checking the structural integrity of mounting surfaces
- Choosing the best tilt for solar collectors
- Connecting water heaters and storage tanks to power sources
- Identifying potential safety hazards when installing solar thermal systems
- Determining locations for all the components of the system
- Filling and checking tanks, pipes, and fittings for leaks
- Training solar thermal system owners in various aspects of solar thermal systems, including start-up, shut-down, maintenance, troubleshooting, and safety procedures

Tools and Technology Solar thermal installers and technicians must be skilled at using hand tools in their work. Some of these tools include:

- Calculators
- Power drills and drill bits
- Digital refractometers
- Extension ladders
- Locking pliers
- Digital multimeters, which measure the resistance, voltage, and current of electrical systems
- Pipe wrenches
- Jig saws
- Soldering equipment, including guns or irons
- Stud locators

- Extruders
- Propane torches
- Measuring tapes
- Wire cutters

Technology is also a part of the daily duties of solar thermal installers and technicians; thus they must be familiar with various software programs, including scheduling software, cost estimating software, and various Microsoft programs, including Outlook, Office, Excel, and Word.

Solar thermal installers and technicians commonly possess the following skills and characteristics:

- Experience and skill using hand tools
- Familiarity with plumbing and electrical connections
- Ability to lift weight in excess of 80 pounds
- Willingness to work in hot conditions
- Great attention to detail
- Awareness of safety precautions
- No fear of heights

WORKING CONDITIONS

Solar thermal installers and technicians work mostly outdoors in all types of weather. The demands of the job, which include lifting heavy tools and equipment, navigating steep rooftops, and working in cramped quarters, make it necessary for installers and technicians to be physically fit and active.

Most solar thermal installers and technicians work 40 hours per week, although they often work extended hours in the spring and summer months. Rainy, wet weather conditions may interfere with and delay work schedules.

EMPLOYMENT

Solar thermal installers and technicians commonly work for specialty trade contractors in the electrical, plumbing, and heating and cooling industries as well as for outdoor swimming pool contractors. Individuals typically work under the license of their employer.

Solar thermal plants that employ solar thermal installers and technicians are being built around the world, making solar thermal installers and technicians an emerging occupation. Solar thermal technologies are being developed and advanced by companies including:

- eSolar, based in California
- Brightsource, based in California
- Abengoa, based in Spain and Algeria
- Acciona, based in Spain
- Ausra, based in California
- Schott Solar, based in Germany

In California, those wishing for self-employment as a solar installation contractor must typically pass a written exam and a background check to obtain a specialty solar contractor's license through the California Department of Consumer Affairs, Contractors State License Board.

TRAINING, OTHER QUALIFICATIONS, AND ADVANCEMENT

Solar thermal installers and technicians made up a relatively small group of employees in 2008, but the profession is growing, and according to experts, solar thermal heating is the fastest growing industry in the world. A basic construction skills course along with an introduction to solar hot water installation course, which covers the basics of solar water heating systems, including how to install, maintain, and service solar thermal systems, is usually sufficient to obtain an entry-level job as a solar thermal installer and technician. Some employers will provide formal on-the-job training opportunities and others may offer apprenticeship programs.

The North American Board of Certified Energy Practitioners (NABCEP) is the national certification organization for professional installers in the field of renewable energy. NABCEP offers voluntary certification to provide national standards for solar heating installers that not only distinguishes certified workers from their competition, but also protects the public by giving them a credential by which to judge the competency of solar thermal installers.

Experienced installers and technicians may advance into positions such as building superintendents, cost estimators, salespeople, or marketers, or they may choose to become self-employed and operate their own solar thermal installation business.

JOB OUTLOOK

As more consumers turn to solar power to meet their energy needs, solar thermal installers and technicians will enjoy growing job opportunities.

According to Ausra, Inc., a solar power company, solar thermal power plants create two times the skilled, high-paying jobs of conventional power plants that use fossil fuels. Jobs for solar thermal installers and technicians are projected to be favorable between 2008 and 2018, and experts predict approximately 7 to 13 percent growth in the industry, resulting in approximately 26,600 job openings.

EARNINGS

Solar thermal installers earn an average of US$13 to US$19 per hour. Salaries depend upon the pay structure of the employer, the nature of the project, and the skills of the installer and technician. Workers in large cities may earn larger salaries than those in smaller towns, although this is not always the case.

RELATED OCCUPATIONS

- Heating, air conditioning, and refrigeration mechanics and installers
- Helpers of pipelayers, plumbers, pipefitters, and steamfitters
- Plumbers, pipefitters, and steamfitters
- Sheet metal workers
- Solar energy installation managers
- Solar energy systems engineers
- Solar photovoltaic installers

SOURCES OF ADDITIONAL INFORMATION

Midwest Renewable Energy Association. www .midwestrenew.org
North American Board of Certified Energy Practitioners. www.nabcep.org.
Solar Energy International. www.solarenergy.org.

FURTHER READING

Ausra, Inc. *An Introduction to Solar Thermal Electric Power.* Accessed March 31, 2012. http://www.ausra .com/pdfs/SolarThermal101_final.pdf.

California Occupational Guides. *Solar Thermal Installers and Technicians in California.* Accessed February 11, 2012. http://www.calmis.ca.gov/file/occguide/ solar-thermal-installers-green.pdf.

Green Careers Guide. *Solar Thermal Is the Fastest Growing Industry in the World.* Accessed February 11, 2012. http://www.greencareersguide.com/Solar-Thermal-Is-the-Fastest-Growing-Industry-in-the-World.html.

O*NET OnLine. *Summary Report for: 47-4099.02— Solar Thermal Installers and Technicians.* Accessed February 11, 2012. http://www.onetonline.org/link/ summary/47-4099.02.

Solar Developments. *Solar Energy Fact Sheets.* Accessed March 29, 2012. http://www.solardev.com/ SEIA-makingelec.php.

Solar-Thermal.com. *Solar Thermal Energy, an Industry Report: The Sun Is Our Source.* Accessed February 11, 2012. http://www.solar-thermal.com/solar-thermal .pdf.

GEOTHERMAL TECHNICIANS

■

NATURE OF THE WORK

Geothermal technicians work with the energy that is derived from the earth itself. The word *geothermal* comes from the Greek term *geo*, which means *earth*, and *thermal*, which means *heat*. One example of geothermal energy is the geysers naturally present throughout Yellowstone National Park. Geothermal technicians tame the clean and sustainable energy that exists in various levels under the earth's crust. This energy can come from:

- Hot springs that occur in shallow ground
- Hot rock located several miles beneath the earth's surface
- Molten rock or magma found near the center of the earth, where the temperature may measure 11,000 degrees Fahrenheit

Geothermal technicians install and repair geothermal heating and cooling systems. Their work includes identifying and repairing problems with geothermal equipment and electrical systems, monitoring the operations of geothermal plant equipment or systems, maintaining and repairing the system as needed, and adjusting production systems to meet demand for geothermal power.

Geothermal technicians install residential geothermal heating systems, also known as ground source heat pumps. These systems typically have three main components:

- A loop installed underground near the home
- A pump that heats water by circulating it through the loop
- A distribution system that delivers the heat to the rest of the house

---

AT A GLANCE FACT BOX

SOC: 49-9099.01
Preferred Education: High school diploma and completion of a vocational training program in heating, ventilation, and air conditioning (HVAC)
Average Salary: US$17.51 per hour or US$36,420 annually
Other Information: In 2010, there were 144,000 geothermal technicians employed in the United States. Fifteen percent of them were self-employed, 13 percent worked in state and local government, 12 percent were employed in wholesale trade, 11 percent worked in retail trade, and the remaining 39 percent were employed in other industries, including construction and manufacturing.

Before installing geothermal systems, technicians might inspect and test specific sites to determine the amount of heat available below the earth's surface. They also check the water for flow strength and for the presence of toxic materials, and they decide on the best system to provide heating and cooling in each situation.

Geothermal technicians are often the workers who dig trenches and install pipes to channel geothermal energy in the form of hot and cool air. Once the pipes are installed, the technicians weld them to pumps and compressors and prepare the system by filling it with water and then quickly draining it. They also check to make sure that electrical switches, transmitters, gauges, and other equipment are linked properly. Geothermal technicians evaluate the flow and temperature of the air coming from the pumps to see if their initial tests were correct, and they make adjustments when necessary. Once a geothermal system has been installed, the technicians continue to check the instruments to ensure proper operations. They may keep logs of maintenance and repair, make necessary equipment adjustments, and collect data regarding trends in the heat collected to help maintain consistent energy production.

Because geothermal energy is a relatively new form of energy, geothermal technicians are also responsible for educating their customers regarding the environmental and economic benefits of this type of power. They may explain that geothermal systems burn no fossil fuels and create no pollution, and although they may be somewhat expensive to purchase and install, geothermal systems potentially produce long-term savings by keeping utility bills low. Geothermal heating is one of the most efficient systems available, with heating efficiencies that measure 50 to 70 percent higher than other systems. This efficiency translates into lower heating costs.

Tools and Technology Some of the tools that geothermal technicians use in their job include:

- Coil tubing units
- Trench compacters
- Claw hammers
- Well drilling rigs
- Depth meters
- Pipe cutters
- Alignment clamps
- Grout mixers
- Air wrenches
- Ratchets
- Respirators
- Screwdrivers
- Wire strippers
- Welding tools

Geothermal technicians must be adept at various types of software, including ClimateMaster GeoDesigner, Thermal Dynamics Group Loop Design (GLD), and WaterFurnace International Ground Loop Design PREMIER; industrial control software (DCS systems); and specific Microsoft software programs such as Excel and Word.

WORKING CONDITIONS

Although geothermal technicians work both indoors and outdoors, they may spend much of their workday out in the elements digging trenches and installing pipes. They are often exposed to hot and cold temperatures, depending upon weather conditions and the location where they are working, and they are sometimes exposed to contaminants as well as hazardous conditions, settings, and equipment. They sometimes climb to high places to do their jobs, and they are often exposed to loud and distracting noises.

They almost always wear protective or safety gear, including hardhats, safety goggles, and other specialized equipment. Although they commonly work a standard day, evening, or night shift in geothermal plants, geothermal technicians are sometimes required to work overtime to meet deadlines. When installing heating and cooling systems, they may have to travel back and forth to construction sites.

EMPLOYMENT

The most active geothermal resources are usually found where earthquakes and volcanoes are located. Most of the geothermal activity in the world occurs in an area called the Ring of Fire that encircles the Pacific Ocean. Twenty countries, including the United States, had geothermal power plants in 2008 and generated approximately 60.4 billion kilowatt hours (kWh). The United States was the number one producer, followed by the Philippines, El Salvador, and Iceland.

The United States leads the world in geothermal energy production. In 2010, five states had geothermal plants: California, Nevada, Utah, Idaho, and Hawaii. California generates the most electricity from geothermal sources, and the Geysers' dry steam reservoir located in northern California is the largest known dry steam field in the world. It has been producing electricity since 1960.

Most geothermal technicians work for geothermal power plants, utility companies, and at local, state, and federal government-sponsored power plants. There are three basic types of geothermal plants that employ technicians:

- Dry steam plants, which use steam piped directly from a geothermal reservoir to turn the generator turbines
- Flash steam plants, which take high-pressure hot water from deep beneath the surface of the earth and convert it to steam to drive the turbines
- Binary cycle power plants, which transfer geothermal heat from hot water to another liquid that turns to steam to power the turbines

The United States has more geothermal capacity than any other country, with more than 3,000 megawatts in eight states. Eighty percent of this capacity is in California, where more than 40 geothermal plants provide nearly

5 percent of the state's electricity and employ numerous geothermal technicians.

TRAINING, OTHER QUALIFICATIONS, AND ADVANCEMENT

Geothermal technicians must have a high school diploma or have successfully passed a General Educational Development test, and most must also complete a formal training program in heating, ventilation, and air conditioning (HVAC). Vocational technical schools and two-year colleges commonly offer HVAC training programs, and as this profession grows, experts say that programs focusing specifically on geothermal energy will be more commonly offered.

In May 2011, UtilitiesJobs.com reported that a "looming shortage in qualified staff for the U.S. geothermal industry sector has spurred the rise of a number of educational programs." These programs include an entry-level geothermal program sponsored by the Churchill County Social Services Strategic Training Employment Program and offered by Western Nevada College, Fallon. More geothermal courses are offered at Gateway Technical College in locations throughout Wisconsin as part of a two-year associate degree in Geothermal Technician and a one-year diploma in Geothermal Installer Technician.

After an HVAC or geothermal training program is completed, most geothermal technicians spend several years learning the practical skills on the job from more experienced workers. These practical skills may include learning to use equipment and tools, repairing heating and cooling systems, and providing customer service. Some geothermal technicians may complete apprenticeships to learn the trade.

Geothermal technicians must have experience measuring and verifying energy systems, should possess a sound understanding of HVAC systems, and have good communication skills, both verbal and written.

JOB OUTLOOK

Because of a continued interest in sustainable energy and a cleaner environment, more and more geothermal energy systems will be installed in the coming years, and technicians will continue to be in demand. From 2009 to 2019 the profession is expected to grow about 9.2 percent in the United States, and approximately 15,640 new technician jobs will be added. Highly skilled technicians will have the best employment prospects.

EARNINGS

Geothermal technicians earn US$17.51 per hour, or US$36,420 annually. They usually work full time and receive benefits including sick leave, paid vacation, health insurance, and some type of retirement plan.

RELATED OCCUPATIONS

- Electronics engineering technologists
- Engineering technicians
- Geothermal production managers
- Heating and cooling system mechanics

SOURCES OF ADDITIONAL INFORMATION

Eastern Heating & Cooling Council. http://www.eh-cc.org
International Ground Source Heat Pump Association (IGSHPA). http://www.igshpa.okstate.edu
U.S. Energy Information Administration. http://www.eia.gov

FURTHER READING

Energy Kids. "Geothermal Basics: What Is Geothermal Energy?" *U.S. Energy Information Administration.* Accessed February 6, 2012. http://www.eia.gov/kids/energy.cfm?page=geothermal_home.

Hawai'i Green Jobs Initiative. *Geothermal Technicians.* Department of Labor & Industrial Relations. Accessed April 3, 2012. https://greenjobshawaii.hirenethawaii.com/default.asp?pg=C-GEOTHERMALTECHS#Reloccs.

iSeek Careers. *Geothermal Technicians, Education and Training.* Accessed February 6, 2012. http://www.iseek.org/careers/careerDetail?id=3&oc=100548.

O*NET OnLine. *Custom Report for: 49-9099.01—Geothermal Technicians.* Accessed February 6, 2012. http://www.onetonline.org/link/custom/49-9099.01.

UtilitiesJobs.com. *New Geothermal Education Programs to Address Worker Shortage.* May 6, 2011. Accessed February 6, 2012. http://www.utilitiesjobsblog.com/2011/05/new-geothermal-education-programs-to.html.

WIND TURBINE SERVICE TECHNICIANS

NATURE OF THE WORK

The wind turbine service technician position may appeal to individuals who enjoy working outdoors at extreme heights or in extreme conditions, those who enjoy solving problems using a hands-on approach, and those who are attentive to detail and able to work with minimal supervision.

Wind turbine service technicians perform a variety of tasks associated with wind turbines. These include inspecting or repairing turbine blades and other components, diagnosing problems with generators and control systems, making adjustments for proper turbine operation, and conducting tests on the equipment, structures, and components of wind systems.

Technicians may help train installers, distributors, end-users, and other service technicians in the procedures involved with wind turbine operation. They may work independently or in conjunction with engineers and other technicians and are usually responsible for the administration of the site, which may contain one turbine or hundreds of them, depending on the size of the wind farm. Wind technicians may also collect turbine data for testing or for use in research or analysis projects.

Wind technicians are required to know the basic parts of a wind turbine, which include the tower, blades, and nacelle. The nacelle is a compact, rectangular box resting on top of the tower that contains the turbine's gears, drive shaft, generator, and other mechanical and electrical components. Wind technicians service the blades or nacelle by entering the turbine through the base of the tower and climbing a ladder or taking an elevator up through the tower shaft. While in the nacelle, technicians clean and lubricate the machinery and look for any

problems in the generator. They also take inventory and order parts for the turbines.

Wind turbine service technicians must be familiar with certain tools and technology to successfully perform their jobs. Some of the tools of the trade are claw hammers, sledgehammers, hotsticks, lubricant oil sampling kits, wire strippers, hydraulic torque machines, manual torque wrenches, voltage testers, conventional and electric watt meters, and electric winches. Wind technicians not only must be able to use these tools but also must maintain them and take inventory of them. Wind technicians typically also use technology including computerized diagnostic software; Microsoft programs including Outlook,

PowerPoint, Project, Excel, and Word; computerized maintenance management software; and industrial control systems software.

WORKING CONDITIONS

No two days are usually alike for wind turbine service technicians, although an average workday is often spent climbing into turbines and performing inspections. There is much variety in the work wind technicians do, ranging from climbing up wind turbine towers to inspect, maintain, or repair equipment, to fixing a circuit board, to changing a light bulb. Technicians also frequently work in cramped spaces. Although nacelles are about the size of a bus, they contain massive pieces of machinery and do not have a lot of room in which to maneuver. Sometimes wind technicians work outside while being suspended hundreds of feet in the air on top of the nacelle and, for safety, wear harnesses attached to rings on the nacelle.

Although wind technicians usually work a standard 40-hour workweek or a rotation shift schedule, many of them are employed on an on-call basis, meaning that they must be available to work at all times to keep the turbines running. Because wind turbines are often in remote locations, many wind turbine service technicians live in sparsely populated areas for extended periods of time. However, some leave the site and travel, especially if they work at multiple sites, and stay in one place for only a short time. They work in a variety of settings, including desert and mountainous regions and are often outdoors in all types of weather conditions.

Because of the physical nature of the job, wind technicians must be physically fit and extremely safety conscious. In the course of a typical workday, they may be asked to climb several turbine towers, often carrying load-bearing harnesses. There are safety risks involved in being a wind turbine service technician. The job typically includes safety briefings where technicians talk about potential hazards so that they will be able to take the necessary precautions, such as wearing the right gear and using the buddy system, which requires that two technicians always work together.

EMPLOYMENT

Energy providers, manufacturers, and project developers, both in the public and private sector, employ wind technicians. They typically work at wind farms, and most wind farms in the United States are located in the Midwest and in Texas and California. As of 2008, 170,000 people were employed as wind turbine service technicians in the United States. Globally, Europe was the leader in offshore wind energy as of 2010, with operations located in Denmark, Belgium, Finland, Germany, Ireland, the Netherlands, Sweden, Norway, and the United Kingdom.

TRAINING, OTHER QUALIFICATIONS, AND ADVANCEMENT

Because the job is relatively new, there is no definitive way to receive training to become a wind turbine service technician. Many technicians receive their training at trade schools and community colleges where they complete one-year certificate programs or two-year degree programs in wind turbine maintenance. Students in certificate programs take classes in turbine design, diagnostics, basic turbine repair, and control and monitoring systems. Two-year degree programs combine the courses offered in certificate programs with general education courses. Many programs also include hands-on training working on turbines and blades and offer opportunities to tour manufacturing facilities.

As of 2010 there were no standard certifications for wind turbine service technicians, but organizations such as the American Wind Energy Association (AWEA) had begun to develop guidelines for a core curriculum for educational programs and identify the skill sets necessary for success as a wind turbine service technician. In January 2011 AWEA announced the first recipients of the organization's new Seal of Approval for wind turbine service technician training programs. The AWEA Seal of Approval program measures whether educational and training institutions with technician programs are teaching the skills that an entry-level service technician needs, as identified by experts among AWEA's 2,500 company members. The first Seal of Approval recipients included the following:

- Columbia Gorge Community College Renewable Energy Technology nine-month certificate program for wind turbine service technicians, The Dalles, Oregon
- Iowa Lakes Community College Associate of Applied Science Degree in Wind Energy and Turbine Technology program, Estherville, Iowa
- Texas State Technical College Associate of Applied Science Degree in Wind Energy and Turbine Technology program, Sweetwater, Texas

As wind turbine service technicians gain experience and master the skills required for the job, they can take on more management responsibilities and work their way up to become lead technicians. Although managers usually have additional duties, such as completing paperwork and site safety responsibilities, they have the potential to earn a much higher wage, up to US$50 an hour.

JOB OUTLOOK

The amount of energy provided by wind turbines in the United States grew by 39 percent per year from 2004 to 2009. As new wind farms spring up, job opportunities for wind turbine service technicians are projected to increase as well.

In the United States, wind turbine service technician jobs are expected to grow an average of 7 to 13 percent from 2008 to 2018, and approximately 41,800 job openings are anticipated during that time period. In 2008, the number of wind technicians who were self-employed or worked in the construction industry grew the most.

EARNINGS

As of 2010, entry-level wind service technicians could expect to start out at approximately US$15 per hour, earning a yearly salary of US$35,000 to US$40,000 per year in the United States, although wages and benefits typically varied according to employer and location. Industry sources reported a shortage of qualified wind power service technicians in 2010, and competition among employers for the most experienced employees drove salaries up in some companies.

RELATED OCCUPATIONS

- Energy efficiency engineer
- Environmental engineer
- Environmental engineering technician
- Wind energy engineer
- Wind energy operations manager
- Wind energy project manager

SOURCES OF ADDITIONAL INFORMATION

American Wind Energy Association. http://www.awea.org

European Wind Energy Association. http://www.ewea.org

The National Center for Construction Education and Research. http://www.nccer.org

The U.S. Department of Energy. http://www.energy.gov

FURTHER READING

Bureau of Labor Statistics, U.S. Department of Labor. *Careers in Wind Energy.* Accessed January 14, 2012. http://www.bls.gov/opub/ooq/2010/winter/art02.pdf.

Hamilton, James, and Drew Liming. *Careers in Wind Energy*, September 2010. Accessed January 14, 2012. http://www.bls.gov/green/wind_energy/wind_energy.pdf.

Liming, Drew. *You're a What? Wind Turbine Service Technician.* Accessed January 14, 2012. http://www.bls.gov/opub/ooq/2010/fall/yawhat.pdf.

O*NET OnLine. *Summary Report for: 49-9081.00—Wind Turbine Service Technicians.* Accessed January 14, 2012. http://www.onetonline.org/link/summary/49-9081.00?redir=49-9099.02.

MACHINISTS

■

NATURE OF THE WORK

Virtually nothing can be manufactured without the proper tools, and it is a machinist who fashions the tools used to make everything from solar panels and wind turbines to automobiles and airplanes.

Although the job of a machinist may not necessarily be a green job itself, the required skill set can often be applied to sustainable industry. For example, manufacturing green products often demands the expertise of machinists. Some machinists may possess a specific set of skills geared to a certain sustainable energy industry such as geothermal heat pump machinists and machinists who make parts for solar panels. Machinists employed in the automotive industry may be considered green if the auto plant produces energy-efficient vehicles.

Machinists use tools such as lathes, milling machines, and grinders to produce precision metal parts exactly to the specifications they are given via mechanical drawings. They are responsible for setting up and operating various special machine tools that are used to produce precision parts and instruments. They must have knowledge of the properties of the metals they work with and great skill with machine tools to successfully produce products, from bolts to automobile pistons, that will meet precise specifications, or *tolerances*, determined by engineers.

Machinists who have been trained in green technology skills are often employed in sustainable building construction, solar panel and solar thermal systems installation, building of wind turbines, and other infrastructure projects. Green building opportunities may be one of the easiest ways for a machinist to transition to something new because creating parts for green technologies involves

---

AT A GLANCE FACT BOX

SOC: 51-4041.00

Preferred Education: Vocational school training, a two-year associate's degree, or a bachelor's degree. Some machinists gain skills from long-term apprenticeship programs or on-the-job training.

Preferred Specialty: Mathematics, specifically trigonometry, geometry, metalworking, drafting, calculus, and physics

Average Salary: US$18.52 per hour, or US$38,520 annually

Other Information: In 2008, there were 422,000 machinists employed in the United States. Seventy-eight percent were employed in the manufacturing industry and the remaining 22 percent were employed in other industries, including administrative and support services and wholesale trade.

---

working with new materials while performing many existing duties.

For example, the job description of a wind turbine machinist is similar to that of any other production machinist, except that wind turbine machinists specialize in the production of metal and plastic parts for wind turbines. Like machinists in other industries, wind turbine machinists review blueprints for the specific part to be made, select the tools and equipment necessary to shape the piece, and decide where to drill the materials they are working with.

Tools and Technology The technology of machinery changes rapidly, and machinists must learn to operate a wide variety of specialized tools in their jobs, among them:

- Gauges
- Inspection fixtures
- Hammers
- Adjustable parallels and plain calipers
- Rules, scales, and vernier calipers
- Lasers
- Water jets
- Face mills and end mills
- Electrified wires
- Lathes
- Grinding machines
- Micrometer tools
- Milling cutters
- Drilling machines
- Milling machines
- Turning machines

Machinists must also be comfortable with technology, including software programs such as:

- Analytical or scientific software such as Armchair Machinist, CNC Consulting Machinists' Calculator, and EditCNC
- Computer-aided design (CAD) software
- Computer-aided manufacturing (CAM) software
- Project management software such as Kentech Kipware PLN and Kentech Kipware TRK
- Spreadsheet software such as Microsoft Excel

When fashioning, or "machining" a part, machinists must first check the electronic or printed blueprints or the requirements made by engineers for a particular job. Based on this initial review, they determine where to cut or bore into a piece of material such as steel, aluminum, brass, copper, vanadium, zinc, lead, titanium, silicon, rubber, glass, or plastic (known as a *workpiece*) that is being shaped into a machine part. The cutters used by machinists must be harder and tougher than the materials that are being cut and are commonly made of high-speed steel, tungsten carbide, ceramics, Borazon (a form of cubic boron nitride that is one of the hardest materials known), and diamond.

Machinists must decide how fast to feed the workpiece into the cutter and how much of the material to remove. They work with very small tolerances, usually within 0.010 inch or 0.25 mm. They also select the tools and materials for the job, plan out the sequence of operations required to produce the part, and mark where the cuts are to be made on the workpiece. After the

preliminary work is completed, machinists perform the following operations while constantly monitoring the feed rate and speed of the machine:

- Position the workpiece on the drill press, lathe, milling machine, or other type of machine
- Set the controls on the machine
- Make the proper cuts

Machinists must also ensure that the workpiece is properly lubricated and cooled. This is important because machining creates a substantial amount of heat. Because most metals expand when heated, machinists must adjust their cuts relative to the temperature of the workpiece.

While cutting, machinists must pay attention to sounds that may indicate problems, such as the noise a dull cutting tool makes. If the machinist hears the sound of excessive vibration, the cutting speed must be adjusted to compensate for the vibration, which may reduce the accuracy of the cuts. After the part is cut, machinists use measuring tools to check the accuracy of their work against the blueprints.

Many modern machine tools are computer numerically controlled (CNC), and CNC machines follow a computer program that controls the cutting speed, changes dull tools, and performs all the necessary cuts. Most machinists train in CNC programming and can write basic programs themselves and modify programs as needed in response to problems that may have occurred during test runs. These modifications, which are called *offsets*, fix problems and improve the efficiency of the operation. This is especially true for machinists in sustainable industries, and many wind turbine machinists are required to operate, maintain, and even program CNC tools to create new parts for turbines.

WORKING CONDITIONS

Most machinists work in clean, well-lit, and well-ventilated surroundings. Because computer-controlled machines are usually at least partially enclosed, a machinist's exposure to noise, debris, and the chemicals used to cool workpieces is somewhat reduced. However, working around machinery presents certain dangers, and machinists must be aware of and follow safety precautions and wear protective equipment such as safety glasses and earplugs. Caution must be taken when handling the hazardous coolants and lubricants used on workpieces.

Machinists stand on their feet most of the workday and sometimes have to lift heavy workpieces. They typically work a 40-hour workweek, although companies are extending hours of operation to make better use of expensive equipment, so some machinists are required to work evening and weekend shifts. Overtime work can be common during peak production periods.

EMPLOYMENT

In 2008, more than 90 percent of the workers in this industry were employed by manufacturing industries. Machinists held about 421,500 positions in the United States, 78 percent of them in manufacturing industries such as machine shops and transportation manufacturing.

TRAINING, OTHER QUALIFICATIONS, AND ADVANCEMENT

Machinists receive their training in many ways, including vocational high schools, vocational programs in community or technical colleges, apprenticeship programs, and on-the-job training. Some employees who previously worked as machine setters, operators, or tenders sometimes move into machinist positions. While in high school, those who aspire to be machinists should take math courses such as trigonometry and geometry, as well as blueprint reading, metalworking, and drafting, if available.

Machinists who learn their trade through apprenticeship and on-the-job training programs are required to complete more than 12 months of on-the-job training or combined work experience and formal classroom instruction to develop the skills needed for adequate job performance. This includes formal and informal apprenticeships that may last up to four years and short-term intensive employer-sponsored training workers must successfully complete to remain eligible for employment. During their apprenticeship, machinists work under the supervision of experienced machinists.

One of the best ways to learn the machinist trade may be a formal apprenticeship program sponsored by a union or a manufacturer, but these programs are sometimes hard to get into. Apprentices must have a high school diploma or GED and usually have taken courses in algebra and trigonometry.

To standardize the skill level of machinists, a number of training facilities, state apprenticeship boards, and colleges may offer certification programs. Certified machinists may enjoy enhanced career opportunities, and their employers are better able to judge their abilities. Journey worker certification can also be obtained from state apprenticeship boards after a machinist has completed an apprenticeship.

In June 2011, Jobs for the Future, a nonprofit education and workforce development organization, announced that it would contribute more than US$6 million toward local green training job programs in seven U.S. cities, including Boston, Massachusetts; Detroit, Michigan; Milwaukee, Wisconsin; Philadelphia, Pennsylvania; Seattle, Washington; and Washington, DC, according to the company's website. The project, the GreenWays Initiative, focused on four industry sectors that employ machinists directly and indirectly: green construction, auto technology, manufacturing, and utilities. The initiative was funded by a grant awarded by the U.S. Department of Labor.

In Chicago, the funding was in response to an identified need for CNC machinists in small and large fabricated metal manufacturing employers, including Ford Motor Company. Some of the targeted occupations included CNC machine operators, machinists, and programmers. These occupations are continuing to grow and are expected to add more than 4,000 new and replacement jobs from 2011 through 2016. The grant money distributed to Washington, DC, was earmarked for the green construction industry, including the solar panel installation industry, in which trained machinists are also in demand.

Machinists can advance in several ways. Experienced machinists may become CNC programmers, tool and die makers, or mold makers. Machinists may also be promoted into supervisory or administrative positions, and some open their own machine shops.

JOB OUTLOOK

Although the U.S. Department of Labor's Bureau of Labor Statistics (BLS) predicted in 2010 to 2011 that employment for machinists would slowly decline, job opportunities were still expected to be favorable because of retirements of older workers and a shift in education away from production-oriented occupations. As a result, the number of workers training to be machinists is expected to be less than the number of available positions.

According to a 2009 report, the National Association of Manufacturers found that 90 percent of manufacturers surveyed indicated a moderate to severe shortage of qualified skilled manufacturing and production employees such as machinists. Similarly, the Center for Labor and Community Research published a 2001 report titled "Creating a Manufacturing Career Path System in Cook County" indicating that Chicago manufacturers were facing an acute shortage of machinists in green industries, calling such positions "pillars of a manufacturing business."

EARNINGS

The average hourly wage of machinists in 2008 was US$17.41 per hour, with machinists employed in the aerospace product and parts manufacturing industry earning as much as US$19.49 per hour. Those working in metalworking machinery manufacturing averaged US$17.90 per hour, whereas machinists who worked in motor vehicle parts manufacturing earned about US$17.06 per hour. Those employed in machine shops were paid an average of US$16.93 per hour, and machinists in the employment services industry earned US$12.94 per hour.

Generally, apprentices earned much less than experienced machinists, but their earnings typically rise quickly as their skills improve. Also, most employers are willing to pay for an apprentice's training classes, an added benefit.

RELATED OCCUPATIONS

The duties of machinists are similar to those of the following manufacturing occupations:

- Computer control programmers and operators
- Industrial machinery mechanics and millwrights
- Machine setters, operators, and tenders—metal and plastic
- Tool and die makers

SOURCES OF ADDITIONAL INFORMATION

Fabricators and Manufacturers Association. http://www.fmanet.org

International Association of Machinists and Aerospace Workers. http://www.goiam.org

The United States Department of Labor. http://www.doleta.gov

FURTHER READING

Bureau of Labor Statistics, U.S. Department of Labor. "Machinists." In *Occupational Outlook Handbook, 2010–11 Edition.* Accessed February 19, 2012. http://www.bls.gov/oco/ocos223.htm.

Chicago Manufacturing Renaissance Council. *Making Chicago a Leader in Manufacturing for Renewable Energy: Workforce and Supply Chain Challenges, A Report to the Chicago Climate Action Plan and its Renewable Energy Task Force.* Accessed March 9, 2012. http://clcr.org/clcr/publications/green_manufacturing.pdf.

Green Careers Guide. *Wind Turbine Machinist Job.* Accessed March 9, 2012. http://www.greencareersguide.com/Wind-Turbine-Machinist.html.

O*NET OnLine. *Details Report for: 51-4041.00—Machinists.* Accessed February 19, 2012. http://www.onetonline.org/link/details/51-4041.00.

Texas CARES. *51-4041.00 Machinists.* Accessed February 19, 2012. http://www.texascaresonline.com/profile/occdata.asp?onetcode=51-4041.00.

The Urban Institute. "Low-Skill Workers' Access to Quality Green Jobs," Brief 13, May 2010. Accessed March 9, 2012. http://www.urban.org/uploadedpdf/412096-low-skilled-worker.pdf.

BIOMASS PLANT TECHNICIANS

NATURE OF THE WORK

Biomass plant technicians monitor the activities of biomass plants and also perform needed plant maintenance. Biomass plants are like fireplaces: when wood is burned to heat a room, it is the equivalent of a small-scale biomass plant creating energy from a plant source (wood). Biomass plants turn the by-products from people, plant sources, and alcohol into energy in the form of electricity and heat. The biomass plant technician's job is to keep this process going.

It is not difficult to extract energy from biomass. In fact, people have been doing it for thousands of years. For example, sitting around a campfire is taking advantage of the heat created by burning biomass. When it is burned on a larger scale, biomass can be used to create electricity.

When waste comes to the plant in the form of dead trees, branches and stumps, manure, grasses, or other plant refuse such as yard clippings, biomass plant technicians evaluate its quality and volume before it is burned to release energy. The technician loads the waste and then operates the mechanisms of the plant to keep the waste moving through the system, where it is converted into energy. The technicians keep detailed reports of the amount of energy made and the amount of waste burned, and submit the data to their supervisors. Biomass plant technicians also do frequent maintenance checks and repairs on the plant machinery and keep a detailed supplies inventory.

Biomass is an alternative energy source that can come from five distinct sources:

1. Garbage
2. Wood

3. Waste
4. Landfill gases
5. Alcohol fuels

There are three types of biomass that are used for energy production: biofuels, which are made by converting biomass into liquid fuels; biopower, which burns biomass directly to convert it into electricity; and bioproducts, which are made by converting biomass into products that are typically manufactured with petroleum products.

According to O*NET, some of the work duties of biomass plant technicians include:

- Calculating biomass feedstock for the generation of power
- Assessing the quality of the biomass feedstock
- Keeping inventory of parts and supplies of biomass plants
- Calibrating devices on fuel, chemical, and water meters
- Operating the equipment required to heat biomass and regulate biomass-fueled generators
- Inspecting biomass power plants or equipment
- Reading and interpreting instruction manuals and technical drawings
- Reading technical drawings related to biomass power or biofuels production equipment or processes
- Preparing and managing budgets for the plant
- Ensuring that plant facilities are in compliance with safety regulations

Biomass plant technicians should be observant and detail oriented to have analytical reasoning skills, to manage their time efficiently, and to function as part of a team as well as independently. They should have a general understanding of the principles behind biomass, including safety principles, knowledge of the current equipment and technology used to operate a biomass plant, and the ability to communicate effectively, both verbally and in the writing of reports.

Tools and Technology Biomass plant technicians must be familiar with numerous tools used in their work, including:

- Biomass dryers
- Reclaim feeders
- Fuel metering conveyors
- Radial stackers
- Front end loaders
- Biomass screeners
- Steam turbines, generators, and boilers
- Belt conveyor systems

Biomass plant technicians use technology and computers to conduct much of their work at the plant and must be familiar with analytical or scientific software, industrial control software, inventory control software, and Microsoft programs such as Excel and Word.

WORKING CONDITIONS

Plant technicians who work in the bioenergy industry usually work close to the source of the biomass, often in rural areas, agricultural regions, and forests. Many work in the state of California, where almost half of the biomass plants in the United States are located.

EMPLOYMENT

According to the Worldwatch Institute, four countries, Brazil, the United States, China, and Germany, led the world in biomass development in 2011. Brazil's ethanol industry is estimated to employ about 300,000 workers. Indonesia and Malaysia had a small but growing share of biofuels production. In the United States, biomass resources are available in every region. In 2004, the ethanol industry created 147,000 jobs, and as of 2011 biomass accounted for approximately 4 percent of the nation's total energy consumption.

In the state of California, where 45 percent of the biomass plants in the United States are located, experts estimate that approximately 350 companies employ bioenergy workers such as biomass plant technicians. Most of these employers were in the utilities sector, followed by professional, scientific, and technical services; public administration; manufacturing; and agriculture, forestry, fishing, and hunting. Approximately half of these employers provide services in the biomass sector.

In California, biomass plants are clustered in about 22 counties, with the majority of the facilities located in the central valley and far north regions. These plants produce about 60 million bone dry tons of biomass each year, five million tons of which are burned to make electricity.

TRAINING, OTHER QUALIFICATIONS, AND ADVANCEMENT

Although some biomass plant technicians come into the industry with formal training, many gain experience through on-the-job training and extensive training programs available through their employers. In 2008, the U.S. Department of Labor's Bureau of Labor Statistics (BLS) estimated that 52 percent of employed biomass technicians had a high school degree or less, whereas 41 percent had earned some college credit. Technical and community colleges offer associate degree programs in bioenergy and in the specific technologies associated with biomass energy, such as process technology or other science-related fields, although specific training programs had not been developed as of 2011.

Entry-level biomass plant technicians often work under the supervision of more experienced team members and, with experience, may become supervisors themselves. Higher-level positions in the biomass industry usually require a minimum of a bachelor's degree.

JOB OUTLOOK

The job opportunities for biomass plant technicians are projected to decline 3 to 9 percent between 2008 and 2018. Around 2,900 job openings are projected during that time period.

EARNINGS

The average annual income for biomass plant technicians in 2009 was US$51,980, and half of those earned between US$38,290 and US$60,240. The lowest earners made approximately US$29,060. Those paid the best earned more than US$69,440. Technician jobs in the oil and gas industry, scientific research, and developmental services generally paid the most. Pay is generally hourly, and work is usually done in shifts.

RELATED OCCUPATIONS

- Nuclear power reactor operators
- Power distributors and dispatchers
- Power plant operators
- Stationary engineers and boiler operators
- Water and wastewater treatment plant and system operators

SOURCES OF ADDITIONAL INFORMATION

Advanced Biofuels Association. http://www .advancedbiofuelsassociation.com

Biomass Power Association. http://www.biomass.org

Renewable Fuels Association. http://www.ethanolrfa .org

FURTHER READING

"The Biomass Economy." *NREL,* July 2002. Accessed February 12, 2012. http://www.afdc.energy.gov/ afdc/pdfs/6748.pdf.

Inside Jobs. *Biomass Plant Technician.* Accessed February 12, 2012. http://www.insidejobs.com/jobs/ biomass-plant-technician.

my Footpath. *Biomass Plant Technician Careers Information.* Accessed February 12, 2012. http://myfootpath.com/ careers/science-careers/biomass-plant-technician-careers/.

National Renewable Energy Laboratory. *Learning About Renewable Energy.* Accessed February 12, 2012. http://www.nrel.gov/learning/re_biomass.html.

O*NET OnLine. *Details Report for: 51-8099.03— Biomass Plant Technicians.* Accessed February 12, 2012. http://www.onetonline.org/link/details/ 51-8099.03#WagesEmployment.

Worldwatch Institute. *Jobs in Renewable Energy Expanding.* Accessed March 20, 2012. http://www .worldwatch.org/node/5821.

SECTOR OVERVIEW: RESEARCH, DESIGN, AND CONSULTING SERVICES

Although the green economy is creating new positions in fields such as renewable energy, it is also changing occupations that are indirectly related to the sustainability movement. Occupations in business, marketing, health care, and engineering have been redefined to include tasks that make a company's production processes more environmentally friendly or that lead to the development of products that will benefit the environment or conserve natural resources.

The development of alternative energy sources has driven the expansion of many technical fields such as engineering. The demand for biochemical engineers, who develop processes to convert biomass to fuels; electrical engineers, who develop alternate energy sources; and fuel cell engineers, who design fuel cell systems for vehicles, is expected to grow between 2008 and 2018, according to the Occupational Information Network (O*NET), a U.S. job database produced by the U.S. Department of Labor/ Employment and Training Administration.

Industrial manufacturing of green technology will also create the need for employees in ancillary positions. New and emerging occupations in this sector include logistics managers, who work toward improving the supply chain efficiency and conservation of energy in manufacturing processes, and manufacturing engineers, who develop technologies to reduce greenhouse gas emissions and the use of toxic and nonrenewable materials. Moreover, as state and federal governments in the United States enact laws to monitor and reduce greenhouse gas emissions, new jobs have been created to help the industry comply with these regulations. These new positions include greenhouse gas emissions permitting consultants, sustainable design specialists, and methane capturing system engineers.

The green movement has also dramatically changed the retail sector because demand for sustainable products has grown. A survey of more than 1,000 consumers found that in 2008 alone, U.S. citizens doubled their spending on green products and services to US$500 billion, according to a study by Penn Schoen and Berland Associates, a market research firm that studies the green economy. Green products are made from natural materials, with the goal of being 100 percent reusable, recyclable, or biodegradable so that they are never deposited in a landfill. These new sustainable products include clothing, carpeting, furniture, shampoo, and household cleaners that are made from recycled materials. Switching to reusable materials attracts customers and saves millions of dollars because companies can resell materials such as cardboard to recyclers.

As a result of these new sustainable products, new occupations such as green marketers, who develop branding and sales initiatives for sustainable products, have emerged. Green marketers also conduct research on consumer opinions and buying habits to identify target audiences for green products and write market content for green product websites and brochures. Existing occupations in the business sector are also being modified to incorporate sustainable products and services. Wholesale and retail buyers, for example, must now analyze environmental aspects of merchandise and identify green commodities such as alternative energy or carbon-neutral products when making purchasing decisions.

The financial operations sector has also changed as customers seek out securities and commodities traders who will invest in companies that have incorporated sustainable practices into their operations. Besides making recommendations for environmentally responsible investments, personal financial advisors inform clients about the tax benefits, government rebates, and other financial benefits of energy-efficient home improvements or alternative fuel car purchases.

TRAINING FOR JOBS IN RESEARCH, DESIGN, AND CONSULTING

Obtaining a position in this sector will require specialized skills in areas such as engineering, business consulting, and sales and marketing. Most of these positions require a bachelor's degree, but some do not. Computer skills are essential for the majority of the positions in this sector. Marketing managers, for example, must track purchases using spreadsheets and create websites or newsletters with specialized software. Automotive engineers must be proficient with analytical software, computer-aided design and graphics, and photo-imaging programs.

A small percentage of professionals in this sector hold master's degrees in their fields. According to an O*NET survey, the percentage of engineers with master's degrees ranges from 10 percent for manufacturing engineers to 36 percent for nuclear engineers. Among other occupations, 16 percent of financial analysts and 23 percent of software developers hold master's degrees, the survey showed.

Besides college degrees, several years of work-related experience are also needed for many occupations in research, design, and consulting. In addition, several occupations require skills in using specialized tools: photonics engineers, who design technologies using light energy; hydrologists, who conduct research on underground and surface waters; and remote sensing technicians, who apply remote sensing technologies to help scientists in areas such as natural resources or homeland security.

JOB OUTLOOK FOR POSITIONS IN RESEARCH, DESIGN, AND CONSULTING

Occupations in research, design, and consulting account for a substantial portion of employment growth in the green economy, although they are not directly tied to green technology. It is estimated that these indirect positions have grown faster than direct green jobs, increasing by 52 percent since 1990, whereas direct jobs expanded by 38 percent according to a 2008 report prepared for the United States Conference of Mayors. In the future, the report projects that these occupations will continue to expand but at a slower rate, with one single indirect job added for every two direct jobs.

The demand for indirect green jobs varies by profession. Personal financial advisors are in high demand, and the projected growth for this occupation between 2008 and 2018 is 30 percent, a much faster rate than average, with 85,300 new job openings expected during that period according to O*NET. Other high-demand occupations are software developers, with a growth rate of at least 20 percent and 153,400 new jobs created, and public relations specialists, with the same growth rate and 131,300 new jobs projected.

Occupations that are projected to have slower than average growth are automotive engineers, with an increase of 3 to 6 percent and 75,700 jobs created; wholesale and retail buyers, with little or no change in growth and 37,000 jobs created; and chemists, which will also have little or no change in growth and 30,000 new job openings.

FURTHER READING

Bhanoo, Sindya. "Products That Are Earth-and-Profit Friendly." *The New York Times,* June 11, 2010. Accessed January 6, 2012. http://www.nytimes.com/2010/06/12/business/energy-environment/12sustain.html?scp+1&s.

Global Insight. *U.S. Metro Economies: Current and Potential Green Jobs in the U.S. Economy,* October 2008. Accessed January 11, 2012. http://www.usmayors.org/pressreleases/uploads/greenjobsreport.pdf.

O*NET OnLine. *Details Report for: 17-2199.01—Biochemical Engineers.* Accessed April 9, 2012. http://www.onetonline.org/link/details/17-2199.01.

———. *Details Report for: 17-2071.00—Electrical Engineers.* Accessed April 9, 2012. http://www.onetonline.org/link/details/17-2071.00.

———. *Details Report for: 17-2141.01—Fuel Cell Engineers.* Accessed April 9, 2012. http://www.onetonline.org/link/details/17-2141.01.

MARKETING MANAGERS

—■—

NATURE OF THE WORK

After green brands such as Whole Foods, a retailer of natural and organic foods, and Seventh Generation, a brand of green cleaning products, were introduced to the public in the early 1980s, a new group of consumers emerged who were interested in buying products that were healthier, more environmentally friendly, and made from natural resources. By the latter half of the 1980s, this growing consumer group became an influential force in marketing and manufacturing. At the same time, the term "green marketing" was coined.

Since the 1980s, the number of green products available to purchase exploded as consumers became concerned with people, planet, and profits, known as the triple bottom line. This growing interest in sustainability spawned thousands of new products such as SunChips, a brand of multigrain chips sold in bags made with solar energy; the Toyota Prius, the leading hybrid car in America; and BPA-free water bottles. Iconic brands such as Clorox and Windex began product lines that were considered sustainable, although sales of these products fell as the recession from 2007 to 2009 lingered.

Marketing managers direct and coordinate activities to promote products and services in conjunction with advertising and promotion managers. One of their core responsibilities is to identify, develop, and evaluate marketing strategies based on the objectives of the company or client, the market characteristics, and cost factors. Marketing managers help develop new products by evaluating such factors as budget expenditures, research and development appropriations, and return-on-investment and profit-loss projections. To ensure the sale and profitability of products, lines, or services, they

AT A GLANCE FACT BOX
SOC: 11-2021.00
Preferred Education: Bachelor's degree
Average Salary: US$122,720 annually
Other Information: Many marketing manager positions are filled through promotions of experienced staff or related professionals, such as advertising specialists

use sales forecasting or strategic planning, they analyze business developments, and they monitor market trends.

Because consumer demand for environmentally friendly products has risen, marketing managers have to consider a product's green value when formulating a marketing campaign. When developing new products, they must consult with buying personnel to determine strategies for sustainable products. They must develop business cases for creating environmental marketing strategies and integrate sustainable information into the promotion and advertising of the product. Another key responsibility is to recommend modifications to products, their packaging, or their production processes to improve their sustainability.

Marketing managers need to incorporate green marketing into their strategies because the consumer group interested in sustainable products is substantial. About 12 percent of the U.S. population can be classified as

"True Greens," or consumers who look for and regularly purchase sustainable products, according to the market research company Mintel. About 68 percent of consumers can be labeled as "Light Greens," or consumers who sometimes buy green products.

One problem that has arisen in the green product market is the practice known as "greenwashing," which refers to industries that make a false or exaggerated claim that they have adopted green practices. Companies that purport to be reducing their carbon footprints may, in fact, be making only a minimal commitment to sustainability and may be more concerned with increasing profits. Despite the confusion about green labels in the marketplace, many marketers believe that companies that cannot legitimately claim to be green will be left behind by consumers who seek greener alternatives.

WORKING CONDITIONS

Marketing managers often work in office environments. In many cases, they work closely with the company's executive vice president, who directs the overall advertising, marketing, promotions, sales, and public relations policies in a large firm. With constant deadlines, marketing managers often work under pressure, particularly when schedules change or problems emerge. Travel is often required to meet with customers in other locations and to attend association meetings and other industry events and tradeshows. Job transfers between headquarters and regional offices occur frequently. The hours are long and include working on evenings and weekends. A survey in 2008 by the U.S. Department of Labor's Bureau of Labor Statistics (BLS) found that more than 80 percent of advertising, marketing, promotions, public relations, and sales managers worked 40 hours or more per week.

EMPLOYMENT

In 2010 there were 164,590 marketing managers in the United States, according to the BLS. Marketing managers work in almost every industry. The top industries employing marketing managers include professional, scientific, and technical services firms as well as financial institutions and insurance providers. These firms employed about 32 percent of marketing managers. Marketing managers also work in small companies where they often outsource some of the responsibilities for creating a marketing plan such as writing copy, developing websites, graphic design, and conducting market research.

TRAINING, OTHER QUALIFICATIONS, AND ADVANCEMENT

Although marketing managers may hold a variety of educational backgrounds, many employers prefer a bachelor's or master's degree in business administration with an emphasis on marketing. Coursework in accounting, finance, mathematics, economics, business law, and management is also preferred. What makes a job candidate stand out in this highly competitive field is experience working in an internship during college.

Marketing manager positions are often filled by experienced staff professionals or personnel working in related fields. Those interested in this career, however, can enter the field from the outside with a combination of work experience and educational credentials. Marketing managers often start their careers as interns or marketing representatives and can advance quickly within a company depending on the firm's size and job growth.

Because many marketing campaigns have migrated online, computer skills are necessary to manage data, create reports, and promote services. Familiarity with the Internet and with social media such as Facebook and Twitter is also an advantage. Fluency in a foreign language, particularly Spanish, is beneficial because many marketing firms target various segments of the population to promote their services.

Marketing managers need to be creative, highly motivated, flexible, and decisive. Because they often work under pressure, they must be able to deal with stress and focus well so that they can complete projects on deadline. Communication skills, both oral and written, are essential because marketing managers must work with other managers, staff, and the public. Marketing managers should have good judgment and tact, and an exceptional ability to build and maintain effective personal relationships with supervisors, staff, and client firms.

In addition to experience, leadership, and ability, marketing professionals may advance their careers by taking management training courses offered by the company, at local colleges and universities, or at professional associations. There are a number of associations serving the marketing field, some of which offer services geared toward specific areas within the industry. The American Marketing Association offers a full range of services, including workshops, publications, resources, training, and events, many of which incorporate information about going green. The Business Marketing Association focuses on business-to-business marketers, and many articles on its website deal with adding sustainability to business-to-business markets. The Direct Marketing Association emphasizes responsible marketing and offers networking opportunities, education, and research. The Web Marketing Association serves professionals who specialize in Internet marketing and web development.

There are also a number of certifications available for professionals working in the marketing field. These certifications, many of which are available online, allow professionals to prove to employers that they have the skills and experience to be considered among the best in the field. The Certified Product Manager and the Certified Product Marketing Manager are among the most common certifications obtained, and they cover topics such as product life cycles, core thinking, theory, and the terminology used in the industry. Internet marketers can earn a Certified eMarketer certification that focuses on basic Internet skills, e-mail marketing, e-commerce, website design, search engines, and ethics.

JOB OUTLOOK

Employment of marketing managers is expected to grow at an average rate of 12 percent between 2008 and 2018, according to the BLS. It is estimated that 21,900 new jobs will be created during this time. The competition for these positions is expected to be strong. The job growth will be driven by new goods and services and the need to promote them in the marketplace. College graduates with exceptional computer skills and an ability to create marketing plans using new tools such as social media will be best qualified for available positions.

The states with the highest employment level for marketing managers in 2010 were California (29,730 jobs), New York (10,370 jobs), Texas (10,150 jobs), Illinois (8,770 jobs), and New Jersey (7,380 jobs).

The metropolitan areas with the highest employment levels for this field in 2010 were New York–White Plains–Wayne, New York, New Jersey (9,480 jobs); Los Angeles–Long Beach–Glendale, California (6,630 jobs); Chicago–Naperville–Joliet, Illinois (6,510 jobs); San Jose–Sunnyvale–Santa Clara, California (6,340 jobs); and Atlanta–Sandy Springs–Marietta, Georgia (5,050 jobs).

EARNINGS

The mean hourly wage for marketing managers in May 2010 was US$59.00. The mean annual salary was US$122,720, according to the BLS.

The states with the highest salaries for marketing managers in 2010 were New York (US$156,420), New Jersey (US$143,340), Delaware (US$139,430), California (US$139,170), and Virginia (US$136,590).

The top-paying metropolitan areas for marketing managers in 2010 were San Francisco–San Mateo–Redwood City, California (US$161,440); New York–White Plains–Wayne, New York, New Jersey (US$160,510); Framingham, Massachusetts (US$159,840); San Jose–Sunnyvale–Santa Clara, California (US$152,560); and Newark–Union, New Jersey (US$149,520).

RELATED OCCUPATIONS

- Advertising and Promotions Managers
- Sales Managers
- Wholesale and Retail Buyers
- Public Relations Specialists
- Demonstrators and Product Promoters

SOURCES OF ADDITIONAL INFORMATION

American Marketing Association. http://www
.marketingpower.com
Business Marketing Association. http://www
.marketing.org
Direct Marketing Association. http://www.the-dma
.org
Web Marketing Association. http://www
.webmarketingassociation.org

FURTHER READING

Bhanoo, Sindya. "Products That Are Earth-and-Profit Friendly." *New York Times on the Web*, June 11, 2010. Accessed March 12, 2012. http://www
.nytimes.com/2010/06/12/business/energy-environment/12sustain.html?scp+1&s.

Bureau of Labor Statistics, U.S. Department of Labor. "Advertising, Marketing, Promotions, Public Relations, and Sales Managers." In *Occupational Outlook Handbook, 2010–11 Edition*. Accessed January 11, 2012. http://www.bls.gov/oco/ocos020.htm.

———. "11-2021 Marketing Managers." In *Occupational Employment Statistics: Occupational Employment and Wages, May 2010*. Accessed January 16, 2012. http://www.bls.gov/oes/2010/may/oes112021.htm.

Gronewold, Nathanial. "Corporate 'Sustainability' Push Flowers in Sluggish Economy." *New York Times on the Web*, November 17, 2010. Accessed March 11, 2012. http://www.nytimes.com/gwire/2010/11/17/17greenwire-corporate-sustainability-push-flowers.

JobDescriptions.net. *Marketing Manager Job Description & Career Opportunities*. Accessed January 16, 2012. http://www.jobdescriptions.net/business/marketing/.

Meyer, Russ. "A History of Green Brands 1960s and 1970s—Doing the Groundwork." *Fast Company*. Accessed January 12, 2012. http://www.fastcompany.com/1568686/keen-to-be-green-50-years-of-people-planet-and-profits.

MyPursuit.com. *Marketing Manager*. Accessed January 12, 2012. http://www.mypursuit.com/careers-11-2021.00/Marketing_Manager.html.

O*NET OnLine. *Details Report for: 11-2021.00-Marketing Managers*. U.S. Department of Labor, Employment and Training Administration. Accessed January 11, 2012. http://www.onetonline.org/link/details/11-2021.00.

U.S. News University Directory. "Marketing Manager Job Description, Salary Information and Career Overview." *U.S. News & World Report.* Accessed January 12, 2012. http://www.usnewsuniversitydirectory.com/careers/marketing-managers_10685.aspx.

USMayors.org. *Current and Potential Green Jobs in the U.S. Economy*, Oct. 2008. United States Conference of Mayors. January 11, 2012. Accessed March 11, 2012. http://www.usmayors.org/pressreleases/uploads/greenjobsreport.pdf.

PERSONAL FINANCIAL ADVISORS

NATURE OF THE WORK

In the late 1990s, consumers began using their investment dollars to fight climate change. Reacting to the threat of global warming, they began focusing their investments in companies that did the least environmental damage and that were trying to limit their greenhouse gas emissions. Investors began to turn away from companies considered environmentally detrimental and to pressure management through shareholder resolutions to reduce practices that are harmful to the environment.

Green consulting became a service in high demand as consumers showed increasing interest in socially responsible investing. Professionally managed assets following socially responsive practices in the United States reached US$3.07 trillion in 2010, a 34 percent increase since 2005 according to the Social Investment Forum Foundation's "Report on Socially Responsible Investing Trends in the United States." The report estimates that nearly one out of every eight dollars under professional management in the United States, amounting to 12.2 percent, is involved in socially responsible investing.

With the growing interest in companies that are fighting climate change, personal financial advisors now play a key role in directing their clients to environmentally responsible investments. Personal financial advisors evaluate the financial needs of individuals and help them make decisions in investments, insurance, and tax law planning. They assist individuals in creating a comprehensive financial plan that incorporates retirement, education expenses, and investment strategies. The types of investments they evaluate include stocks, bonds, mutual funds, real estate, and business investments.

AT A GLANCE FACT BOX

SOC: 13-2052.00
Preferred Education: Bachelor's degree
Average Salary: US$91,220 annually
Other Information: About 29 percent of personal financial advisors are self-employed and own small investment advisory firms

---

Because many personal financial advisors are licensed to buy and sell stocks, bonds, derivatives, annuities, and insurance products, they can specialize in recommending socially responsible investments to their clients. There are three approaches that are typically used in socially responsible investing, according to the Forum for Sustainable and Responsible Investment. These approaches are:

1. Screening. This strategy, which involves both positive and negative screens, evaluates investment portfolios or mutual funds based on social, environmental, and positive governance factors. With positive screening, investors are encouraged to choose companies that practice strong corporate social responsibility (CSR), including using sustainable environmental operations and adopting clean technologies. Negative screens involve avoiding investing in companies whose products and business practices are harmful to individuals, communities, or the environment.

2. Shareholder Advocacy. Investors who want to change a company's policies on environmental or other issues can engage in dialogue with companies on how they can modify their policies. This strategy often involves filing shareholder resolutions on topics such as climate change, which generate pressure on the company's management, attract media attention, and educate the public on environmental and other issues.

3. Community Investing. This approach directs capital from investors and lenders to communities that lack traditional financial services institutions. Providing access to credit, equity, capital, and basic banking products in these communities allows for the establishment of new businesses and the development of vital community services, such as affordable housing, child care, and healthcare.

Another method of evaluating corporate social responsibility was developed by Ceres, a non-profit network of investors, environmental organizations, and other public interest groups. In 1989 Ceres created a 10-point code of corporate environmental conduct to be endorsed by companies. More than 50 companies have since endorsed the Ceres Principles, which include protection of the biosphere, sustainable use of natural resources, and energy conservation.

Besides offering advice about environmentally responsible investments, personal financial advisors inform clients about tax benefits, government rebates, or other financial benefits of purchasing an alternative fuel vehicle, constructing an energy efficient home, or remodeling an existing residence.

Personal financial advisors typically work with many clients and spend part of their time marketing their services to attract new customers. They often meet potential clients by giving seminars or attending social or business networking events. When a new client signs on, the advisor typically schedules a consultation to analyze the customer's financial needs. With today's technology, this consultation can be done in person or through video conferencing services over the Internet. Financial advisors usually meet with established clients on an annual basis to suggest new investments or to modify their financial plan based on any life changes such as marriage, disability, or retirement.

WORKING CONDITIONS

Personal financial advisors work out of their homes or in offices, and usually work standard business hours. In addition to meeting with clients, personal financial advisors often travel to attend conferences, training sessions, or out-of-town client consultations. Many financial advisors also teach classes or hold seminars at nights or on weekends.

EMPLOYMENT

In 2008 there were 208,400 personal financial advisors in the United States according to the U.S. Department of Labor's Bureau of Labor Statistics (BLS). About 29 percent of personal financial advisors are self-employed. Others work for established financial investment companies, brokerage firms, or one of the many new green investment companies that have emerged in this rapidly growing field.

The states with the highest employment levels for personal financial advisors in 2010 were New York (23,500 jobs), California (21,890 jobs), Texas (12,180 jobs), Florida (11,430 jobs), and Illinois (6,860 jobs). The metropolitan areas with the most jobs in this field were: New York–White Plains–Wayne, New York, New Jersey (19,810 jobs); Los Angeles–Long Beach–Glendale, California (5,900 jobs); Chicago–Naperville–Joliet, Illinois (5,670 jobs); Boston–Cambridge–Quincy, Massachusetts (4,700 jobs); and San Francisco–San Mateo–Redwood City, California (4,050 jobs).

TRAINING, OTHER QUALIFICATIONS, AND ADVANCEMENT

Personal financial advisors need a minimum of a bachelor's degree to work in the field. Many investment companies, however, require candidates to have a master's degree in business administration, business finance, statistics, or accounting. Other requirements are a strong mathematical background as well as communications and problem solving skills. Financial advisors must also be able to work independently and must be self-motivated, detail-oriented, and familiar with money markets, foreign markets, and tax laws.

Licensure is another key requirement to work as a personal financial advisor. Most companies require personal financial advisors to be licensed through the Financial Industry Regulatory Authority (FINRA), which offers a variety of licenses. Newly hired financial advisors are often required to obtain licensure within a specific timeframe after accepting a position.

Another organization that offers certification is the CFA Institute, which offers the Chartered Financial Analyst (CFA) certification. This organization requires candidates to pass a series of exams that cover economics, portfolio management, financial markets, securities analysis, and other topics related to the financial analyst industry. Financial analysts must have a bachelor's degree and four years of experience in the field to qualify for this certification. Often this certification is viewed as an alternative to pursuing a master's degree.

Personal financial advisors may also benefit from joining the Commercial Finance Association (CFA), the largest association for investment professionals in the world. CFA offers a full range of educational and career resources as well as certifications for professionals in the field.

Another professional organization is the Forum for Sustainable and Responsible Investment, an association for professionals engaged in socially responsible and sustainable investing. The forum offers conferences, educational resources, and job listings in the socially responsible investment field.

JOB OUTLOOK

Employment of personal financial advisors is expected to increase by 30 percent between 2008 and 2018, a rate that is much faster than the average for all occupations according to the BLS. This growth will be driven by the millions of people expected to retire within this period. With more baby boomers reaching retirement age, the projected surge in their investments will require the help of experts to manage their portfolios.

As the field of personal financial advising becomes increasingly attractive, there will be increasing competition for positions. Many will enter the field by working for a bank or a brokerage firm. Candidates with strong selling skills will be the most successful, and a college degree and certification will be an advantage.

EARNINGS

The median annual wage of personal financial advisors was US$91,220 in 2010 according to the BLS. Personal financial advisors employed by financial services firms are typically paid a salary plus bonus. Financial advisors who are self-employed earn money by charging a percentage of the client's assets being managed as well as hourly fees for their services and fees on stock and insurance purchases. Advisors also receive commissions for any financial products they sell.

The states with the highest salaries for personal financial advisors in 2010 were New York (US$136,310), Connecticut (US$119,770), Massachusetts (US$118,400), New Jersey (US$99,560), and Pennsylvania (US$98,800), according to the BLS. The top-paying metropolitan areas for the field were San Francisco–San Mateo–Redwood City, California (US$151,470); New York–White Plains–Wayne, New York, New Jersey (US$142,000); Utica–Rome, New York (US$140,180); Worcester, Massachusetts (US$136,860); and Lancaster, Pennsylvania (US$134,230).

RELATED OCCUPATIONS

- Purchasing agents, except wholesale, retail, and farm products
- Insurance adjusters, examiners, and investigators
- Cost estimators
- Assessors
- Credit analysts
- Financial analysts
- Tax preparers
- Bill and account collectors

SOURCES OF ADDITIONAL INFORMATION

Ceres. http://www.ceres.org
Commercial Finance Association. http://www.cfa.com
Forum for Sustainable and Responsible Investment. http://ussif.org

FURTHER READING

Bureau of Labor Statistics, U.S. Department of Labor. "13-2052 Personal Financial Advisors." In *Occupational Employment Statistics: Occupational Employment and Wages, May 2010.* Accessed January 17, 2012. http://www.bls.gov/oes/current/oes132052.htm.

———. "Personal Financial Advisors." In *Occupational Outlook Handbook, 2010–11 Edition.* Accessed January 16, 2012. http://bls.gov/oco/ocos302htm.

JobDescriptions.net. "Financial Analysts and Personal Financial Advisors Job Description and Career Opportunities." 2011. Accessed January 17, 2012. http://www.jobdescriptions.net/business/financial-analysts/.

O*NET OnLine. *Details Report for: 13-2052.00— Personal Financial Advisors.* Accessed January 16, 2012. http://www.onetonline.org/link/details/13-2052.00.

Rosenthal, Elisabeth. "Investment Funds Push an Environmental Agenda." *The New York Times,* November 28, 2008. Accessed January 17, 2012. http://www.nytimes.com/2008/11/28/business/28green.html?sq=environmentally.

Social Investment Forum Foundation. "Report on Socially Responsible Investing Trends in the United States." 2010. Accessed January 16, 2012. http://ussif.org/resources/research/documents/2010TrendsES.pdf.

Wikinvest. "Environmentally Responsible Investing." 2010. Accessed January 17, 2012. http://www.wikinvest.com/wiki/Environmentally_Responsible_Investing.

INDUSTRIAL ENGINEERS

NATURE OF THE WORK

In the early 1970s, a new standard in engineering was developed that focused on reducing excessive consumption and waste of products in U.S. industry. As consumers became more environmentally conscious, their concerns began to affect the companies making the products they purchased. Green engineering became a systems-level approach to the design of product and process that treated environmental concerns as primary objectives rather than optional constraints. Reducing a company's carbon footprint (or total amount of greenhouse gas emissions by a company, organization, or person) was viewed as a goal that was consistent with manufacturing a high quality product while reducing wasteful practices. Companies that went green not only reduced operating costs but also added value for their customers.

Industrial engineers are involved in developing the most effective ways to utilize the basic factors of production (people, machines, material, information, and energy) to make a product or provide a service. Industrial engineers focus on increasing productivity through the management of people, methods of business organization, and best use of technology. To reach optimal efficiency, industrial engineers study product requirements and then create manufacturing and information systems to make those products. They work on developing management control systems to help in financial planning and cost analysis and create production planning and control systems to ensure product quality. They also design improvements in systems for distributing goods and services and determine the most efficient plant locations.

Green engineering works in conjunction with lean manufacturing, a business strategy that attempts to

eliminate waste while efficiently delivering quality products at the lowest cost. Because there is an environmental impact for all manufacturing processes, industrial engineers can have a significant impact in designing processes that minimize this impact. Writing in the *Industrial Engineer,* Kyle Bedal, Matthew Franchetti, Selena Grodek, and Jenny Ulloa identified the six goals of green engineering:

- Selecting low environmental impact materials
- Avoiding toxic or hazardous materials
- Choosing cleaner production processes
- Maximizing energy and water efficiencies
- Designing for waste minimization
- Designing for recyclability and reuse of material

With these goals in mind, industrial engineers can set the stage for developing environmentally-conscious manufacturing by preventing problems that will damage the environment, by improving productivity, and by eliminating waste. Creating an environmentally renewable product that yields zero waste to the landfills is a key goal for industrial engineers. They also aim to design and install system improvements that are sustainable in the long-term rather than develop changes that may only produce short-term gains. In this way, industrial engineers can become potential leaders in green systems implementation while achieving standards outlined in lean engineering.

In a brief history of industrial engineering, J.T. Black and Don T. Phillips, both professors of industrial and systems engineering, wrote in *Industrial Engineer* that "...engineers make things; industrial engineers make things better; lean engineers make things better, faster, cheaper in a flexible way. And lean, green industrial engineers pave the way for the future."

WORKING CONDITIONS

Industrial engineers typically work in manufacturing industries, but they are also employed by consulting firms, healthcare services, and the communications industry. As part of their responsibilities, industrial engineers work with a wide array of software used for analytical computer-aided design, development environment, industrial control, and project management. Industrial engineers often investigate industrial accidents and must apply their knowledge of current policies, regulations, and industrial processes to write a report to management on the incident.

Industrial engineers typically work a standard 40-hour workweek, although if a deadline approaches they may need to work overtime to complete it. Depending on the place of employment, some travel might be necessary. The environment in which an industrial engineer works also depends on his or her place of employment. Some engineers work in clean, well-lit, climate-controlled offices, whereas others work in production or factory areas and may be exposed to fumes, noise, and changing weather conditions. They may work as part of a team or may supervise other engineers or technicians.

EMPLOYMENT

In 2010, there were 202,990 industrial engineers working in the United States, according to the U.S. Department of Labor, Bureau of Labor Statistics. Industrial engineers work in manufacturing industries, consulting firms, healthcare services, and the communications sector. The industry with the highest level of employment of industrial engineers in 2010 was the aerospace product and parts manufacturing sector, which had 16,090 industrial engineering jobs. The next highest level of employment of industrial engineers was in architectural, engineering, and related services, followed by navigational, measuring, electromedical, and control instruments manufacturing.

The states with the highest level of employment of industrial engineers in 2010 were Michigan (19,680 jobs), California (18,310 jobs), Texas (14,680 jobs), Pennsylvania (10,940 jobs), and Ohio (10,840 jobs).

The metropolitan areas with the highest employment level of industrial engineers in 2010 were Warren–Troy–Farmington Hills, Michigan (7,100 jobs); Los Angeles–Long Beach–Glendale, California (5,530 jobs); Minneapolis–St. Paul-Bloomington, Minnesota, Wisconsin (5,210 jobs); Detroit–Livonia–Dearborn, Michigan (4,710 jobs); and Chicago–Naperville–Joliet, Illinois (4,450 jobs).

TRAINING, OTHER QUALIFICATIONS, AND ADVANCEMENT

Nearly all entry-level engineering jobs require candidates to have a bachelor's degree in engineering. A degree in natural science or mathematics may qualify college graduates for some engineering jobs. Engineers trained in one specialty of engineering may also qualify for jobs in another area in which engineers are in high demand.

Students in industrial engineering programs take courses such as engineering economic analysis, computer integrated manufacturing, facilities design, engineering graphics, manufacturing engineering processes, quality control, process modeling and simulation, forecasting, and testing.

Industrial engineers often move into management because their work is closely aligned with the work of their managers. To maximize resources, industrial engineers collect, analyze, and arrange factual information to help meet management's objectives.

With the growing use of automation, robotics, sensors, and faster computers that have revolutionized U.S. industry, systems engineering is emerging as a discipline that prepares students for working with large, complex systems as an integrated process. Another discipline, operations research, also supports the techniques used in industrial engineering.

In the United States, licensure is required for engineers who offer their services to the public in all 50 states and the District of Columbia. The requirements to become licensed, or a professional engineer, include a degree from an engineering program, recognized by the Accreditation Board for Engineering and Technology (ABET), four years of relevant work experience, and completion of a state exam. After graduation, engineers can take the first of two stages in the examination, called the Fundamentals of Engineering exam. The second examination, called the Professional of Engineering exam, can be taken after engineers acquire suitable work experience.

To advance their careers, engineers should be inquisitive, creative, analytical, and detail-oriented. They should have excellent oral and written communications skills and an ability to work as part of a team. Engineers who advance their skills by taking professional certifications will be more successful in gaining promotions.

Engineering graduates are typically assigned to work under the supervision of experienced engineers and may receive more formal training in seminars or classes if they work for a large company. Newly hired engineers are assigned more difficult projects with the independence to develop designs, solve problems, and make decisions once they gain knowledge and experience. Industrial engineers may advance to become engineering managers or enter other sales or managerial positions.

JOB OUTLOOK

Employment of industrial engineers will grow by 14 percent between 2008 and 2018, faster than the average for all occupations. The growth will be driven by companies looking for ways to reduce costs and raise productivity; such companies will hire industrial engineers to develop more efficient processes. This increase in demand for industrial engineers will occur despite the declining employment in the manufacturing sector. Because their work is similar to the responsibilities of management, industrial engineers sometimes leave the profession to enter management positions. This turnover of industrial engineers to new positions or to other occupations will create job openings for new hires in the field.

EARNINGS

In 2010, industrial engineers earned an average of US$78,450, according to the U.S. Department of Labor's Bureau of Labor Statistics. The average hourly wage for industrial engineers in 2010 was US$37.72.

The top-paying states for industrial engineers in 2010 were Alaska (US$103,330), New Mexico (US$96,130), Wyoming (US$92,940), Arizona (US$92,940), and Maryland (US$89,990).

The metropolitan areas with the highest income for industrial engineers in 2010 were Warren–Troy–Farmington Hills, Michigan (US$86,150); Los Angeles–Long Beach–Glendale, California (US$88,740); Minneapolis–St. Paul–Bloomington, Minnesota, Wisconsin (US$81,080); Detroit–Livonia–Dearborn, Michigan (US$83,560); and Chicago–Naperville–Joliet, Illinois (US$71,510).

RELATED OCCUPATIONS
- Aerospace engineering and operations technicians
- Aerospace engineers
- Biomedical engineers
- Computer hardware engineers
- Drafters
- Mining and geological engineers
- Surveying and mapping technicians

SOURCES OF ADDITIONAL INFORMATION
Association of Energy Engineers. http://www.aeecenter.org
Institute of Industrial Engineers. http://www.iienet2.org
United States Environmental Protection Agency. http://www.epa.gov

FURTHER READING
Association of Energy Engineers. *Green Jobs: Survey of the Energy Industry.* Accessed January 26, 2012. http://www.aeecenter.org/files/reports/SurveyofTheGreenEnergyIndustry2011.pdf.
Bureau of Labor Statistics, U.S. Department of Labor. "17-2112 Industrial Engineers." In *Occupational Employment Statistics: Occupational Employment and Wages, May 2010.* Accessed January 25, 2012. http://www.bls.gov/oes/current/oes172112.htm.
———. "Engineers." In *Occupational Outlook Handbook, 2010–11 Edition.* Accessed January 25, 2012. http://www.bls.gov/oco/ocos027.htm.
Franchetti, Matthew, Kyle Bedal, Jenny Ulloa, Selena Grodek. "Lean and Green: Industrial Engineering Methods Are Natural Stepping Stones to Green Engineering." *Industrial Engineer* September, 2009.
JobDescriptions.net. "Industrial, Health, and Safety Engineer Job Description & Career Opportunities." Accessed January 25, 2012. http://www.jobdescriptions.net/engineering/industrial-health-and-safety-engineer/.
McManus, Kevin. "Are You a Green IE?" *Industrial Engineer* 2010.
Michigan Jobs and Career Portal. *#146—Industrial Engineers.* Accessed April 3, 2012. http://www.michigan.gov/careers/0,1607,7-170-46398-64585—,00.html#Work.
O*NET OnLine. *Summary Report for: 17-2112.00–Industrial Engineers.* Accessed January 25, 2012. http://www.onetonline.org/link/summary/17-2112.00.
Phillips, Don T., J.T. Black. "The Lean to Green Evolution: a Brief History of Industrial Engineering and What It Means for the Future." *Industrial Engineer* 2010.
United States Environmental Protection Agency. *What Is Green Engineering?* Accessed January 26, 2012. http://www.epa.gov/oppt/greenengineering/pubs/whats_ge.html.

SALES REPRESENTATIVES, WHOLESALE AND MANUFACTURING, TECHNICAL AND SCIENTIFIC PRODUCTS

NATURE OF THE WORK

As many homeowners retrofit their residences to make them more energy efficient, they are purchasing energy-efficient appliances, solar panels for their rooftops, and geothermal wells that can heat and cool their houses. The popularity of these products is rising as a growing number of states offer tax credits for energy-saving devices installed in homes. Because energy-producing systems such as geothermal heat pumps can decrease the demand for electricity, many utility companies are also offering rebates to consumers.

This surge in energy-saving technology has created a need for sales representatives who specialize in green products for homes, schools, and businesses. Sales representatives can also play a role in promoting green materials used in manufacturing processes. One area that green sales representatives can focus on is the development of the raw materials used in manufacturing. Green chemicals, for example, use and produce fewer or no polluting or hazardous materials. Companies that use green chemicals produce safer products for users, improve efficiency, and reduce waste.

Computer manufacturers have also embraced the sustainability movement and are focusing on three strategies: reducing, reusing, and recycling. Several computer companies are following an initiative launched by the European Union in 2003 that restricts the use of six hazardous materials in manufacturing processes. Fujitsu, for example, uses mercury-free backlight LED technology for

AT A GLANCE FACT BOX

SOC: 41-4011.00
Preferred Education: No degree required
Average Salary: US$84,360 annually
Other Information: Earnings for sales representatives are usually based on a combination of salary and commission.

power-saving screen brightness and has restricted toxic flame retardants from its products. Apple Inc. conducted an analysis of its environmental footprint and concluded that 98 percent of its greenhouse gas emissions are directly related to its products and the remaining 2 percent are related to its facilities. To make its products more environmentally friendly, Apple has designed its computers so that they are produced with less material, shipped in smaller packaging, and free of toxic substances.

Sales representatives who specialize in technical or scientific products may present information to their customers about any changes a company has made to make their products greener. They may also inform their customers about sustainable practices that can be used in manufacturing, such as the responsible use and disposal of products, waste reduction, or product or byproduct recycling. They can also educate their customers about the energy efficiency or environmental impact of their products and about the tax benefits or governmental rebates associated with energy-efficient scientific or technical products such as solar panels.

No matter what type of product they sell, the primary duty of sales representatives is to generate interest in their products and arrange for their products to be sold to wholesalers or manufacturers. Sales representatives, often called manufacturer's representatives or manufacturer's agents, typically work for manufacturers, wholesalers, or technical companies. They may work for a single company or represent several companies and sell a variety of products.

Rather than selling directly to customers, sales representatives deal with businesses, government agencies, and other organizations. The process of promoting and selling their products, which can take several months, can take place in person or on the phone. Their volume of sales depends on how effective they are in describing their product, explaining its benefits, conducting demonstrations, and answering customer questions.

Sales representatives monitor the development of new products and the changing needs of their customers in several ways. They attend trade shows at which new products and technologies are displayed and they attend conferences and conventions to meet other sales representatives or to develop clients. Sales representatives often team up with a technical expert or a sales engineer to sell a product. Although the technical expert explains the product and answers questions from the customers, the sales representative sets up the meeting, introduces the product, and closes the sale.

WORKING CONDITIONS

Sales representatives travel frequently because they often have large territories to cover. If their region includes several states, they may be away from home for several days or several weeks at a time, traveling from city to city by airplane. When assigned to a smaller territory, they may travel by car, spending several nights on the road.

This occupation can be stressful because sales representatives are often expected to meet goals or quotas set by their companies. Their income and job are directly impacted by the volume of merchandise they sell. The hours for sales representatives can be long. A 2008 survey showed that about 48 percent of sales representatives worked an average of 40 hours per week, and 24 percent worked more than 50 hours per week. Sales representatives typically make calls to prospective clients during the day, so their planning and paperwork may be completed at night or on weekends. They often work from their home and have the freedom to set their own schedules.

EMPLOYMENT

In 2010, there were 381,080 sales representatives working in wholesale and manufacturing industries and specializing in technical and scientific products in the United States according to the U.S. Department of Labor's Bureau of Labor Statistics (BLS). These professionals work most often in the following industries: wholesale electronic markets, professional and commercial equipment and supplies wholesalers, drugs wholesalers, computer systems design, and electrical and electronic goods wholesalers.

The states with the highest level of employment in this occupation in 2010 were California (45,060), Texas (31,790), Florida (31,390), Ohio (21,040), and Illinois (18,090).

The metropolitan areas with the highest level of employment in this occupation in 2010 were Chicago–Naperville–Joliet, Illinois (12,750); Atlanta–Sandy Springs–Marietta, Georgia (10,450); Dallas–Plano–Irving, Texas (9,550); Los Angeles–Long Beach–Glendale, California (9,510); and Boston–Cambridge–Quincy, Massachusetts (9,130).

TRAINING, OTHER QUALIFICATIONS, AND ADVANCEMENT

Sales representatives can qualify for positions with a high school diploma or its equivalent although some jobs that deal with scientific or technical products may require a bachelor's degree. Companies often require new hires to take formal training programs that may last as long as two years. Beginning sales representatives are typically trained by accompanying experienced professionals on their sales calls. As they learn about the company's products and clients, new hires are given their own territories to cover.

Excellent communication skills and the desire to sell are the most important skills sales representatives need to enter the profession. Sales representatives should be goal-oriented, persuasive, patient, and perseverant. They should have a pleasant personality and appearance and have the ability to work well independently and as part of a team.

Many sales representatives obtain certifications that provide formal recognition of their skills. The most common are the Certified Professional Manufacturers Representative (CPMR) or the Certified Sales Professional (CSP) certifications offered by the Manufacturers Representatives Education Research Foundation.

Promotions of sales representatives often involve assignments to larger accounts or territories that may offer larger commissions. Sales representatives with good sales records and leadership skills may also advance to higher-level positions such as sales supervisor, district manager, or vice president of sales.

JOB OUTLOOK

Employment of sales representatives for wholesale and manufacturing industries specializing in technical and scientific products is expected to grow by 10 percent between 2008 and 2018, a rate faster than average for all occupations. The number of new jobs that will be created during that period for this occupation will be 42,000 according to the BLS. The job prospects will be best for those with a college degree, the appropriate technical expertise, and the personal skills necessary for a successful sales career. As the growth in technological advances continues, sales representatives will be needed to ensure that retailers offer the newest products to their customers and that companies acquire the tools to increase their operation's efficiency and sustainability.

EARNINGS

In 2010, sales representatives for wholesale and manufacturing industries specializing in technical and scientific products earned an average of US$84,360. The average hourly wage for this occupation in 2010 was US$40.56.

The top-paying states for this occupation in 2010 were Idaho (US$128,970), New Jersey (US$102,950), Nevada (US$99,600), Wyoming (US$98,510), and New Hampshire (US$97,800).

The metropolitan areas with the highest incomes for this occupation in 2010 were Rapid City, South Dakota (US$133,110); Cape Coral–Fort Myers, Florida (US$121,980); Longview, Washington (US$120,840); Auburn–Opelika, Alaska (US$118,150); and Des Moines–West Des Moines, Iowa (US$115,830).

RELATED OCCUPATIONS

Sales ability and product knowledge are also key skills for these other fields:

- Advertising sales agents
- Insurance sales agents
- Purchasing managers, buyers, and purchasing agents
- Real estate brokers and sales agents
- Sales engineers
- Sales worker supervisors
- Securities, commodities, and financial services sales agents

SOURCES OF ADDITIONAL INFORMATION

Manufacturers' Representatives Educational Research Foundation. http://www.mrerf.org

FURTHER READING

Apple.com. *The Story Behind Apple's Environmental Footprint*. Accessed February 15, 2012. http://www.apple.com/environment/.

Bedal, Kyle, Matthew Franchetti, Selena Grodek, and Jenny Ulloa. "Lean and Green: Industrial Engineering Methods are Natural Stepping Stones to Green Engineering." *Industrial Engineer,* September 1, 2009. Accessed January 25, 2012. http://www.iienet2.org/landing.aspx?id=973.

Bureau of Labor Statistics, U.S. Department of Labor. "41-4011 Sales Representatives, Wholesale and Manufacturing, Technical and Scientific Products." In *Occupational Employment Statistics: Occupational Employment and Wages, May 2010.* Accessed February 15, 2012. http://www.bls.gov/oes/current/oes414011.htm.

———. "Sales Representatives, Wholesale and Manufacturing." In *Occupational Outlook Handbook, 2010–11 Edition.* Accessed February 6, 2012. http://www.bls.gov/oco/ocos119.htm.

Business Link. *Efficient Design and Resource Use in Chemical Manufacturing.* Accessed February 15, 2012. http://www.businesslink.gov.uk/bdotg/action/detail?itemId=1083098935&type=RESOURCES.

Fujitsu PC Asia Pacific. *PC Manufacturing Goes Green.* Accessed March 2, 2012. http://www.fujitsu.com/my/services/computing/pc/resources/articles/green.html.

JobDescriptions.net. *Sales Representative Job Description & Career Opportunities.* Accessed February 10, 2012. http://www.jobdescriptions.net/business/sales-representative/.

Kreahling, Lorraine. "Digging Up Energy Savings Right in Your Backyard." *The New York Times,* March 7, 2011. Accessed February 16, 2012. http://www.nytimes.com/2011/03/08/science/08geothermal.html?scp=1&sq=geothermal%20energy%20for%20homes&st=cse.

Matzen, Evan. "Green Your Sales Team: Q&A with a Regional Sales Director." *GreenBlogic.com,* November 4, 2011. Accessed February 10, 2012. http://greenblogic.com/wwwgreenblogiccom/bid/48029/Green-Your-Sales-Team-Q-A-with-a-Regional-Sales-Director.

O*NET OnLine. *Details Report for: 41-4011.00—Sales Representatives, Wholesale and Manufacturing, Technical and Scientific Products.* Accessed February 15, 2012. http://www.onetonline.org/link/details/41-4011.00.

Wisconsin Manufacturing Extension Partnership. *Profitable Sustainability Initiative Helps Quality Packaging Grow Sales and Jobs.* Accessed February 10, 2012. http://www.wmep.org/customer-successes/profitable-sustainability-initiative-helps-quality-packaging-grow-sales-and-jobs.

SECTOR OVERVIEW: TRANSPORTATION

Environmental concerns are increasingly influencing economic decisions around the world and across many industries, but few sectors are as directly impacted as the transportation sector. Transportation jobs of all types have a direct and measurable impact on the environment and the green economy. Vehicles and other technologies that consume fossil fuels and emit pollution and carbon emissions are the center of global environmental concern. The workers in this sector directly influence both of these factors through their own concerns and through their application of developing technology.

Workers in the transportation industry deal with every aspect of transport. They maintain and repair the engines and vehicles that move people and materials from one place to another, they calculate and manage the loading process, they plan the routes these vehicles follow, and they design, test, and build the next generation of engines and technologies. In doing so, these workers have a great impact on the environment. Transportation professionals calibrate engines and exhaust systems, design more efficient fuel cells, devise more intelligent ways of loading and unloading passengers and freight, and operate the vehicles themselves in the most efficient manner possible.

Aiding transportation workers in this endeavor are continuing improvements in technologies such as solid fuel-cell engines, hybrid engines, and increasingly sophisticated tracking and routing software. Building on the work of previous generations, workers in the transportation sector are actively creating the future. A new idea to improve the efficiency of freight loading soon becomes standard practice, resulting in a less costly process that benefits not only the industry but the entire world.

Because of this transformation to a greener economy, new careers in the transportation industry are being created. Jobs such as fuel cell technicians and fuel cell engineers did not exist 10 years ago. Careers such as supply chain managers and freight forwarders have taken on new importance and scope because their work is increasingly seen as a simple and cost-effective way of improving the environmental impact of an organization. In fact, any career involving logistics has become more important as shipping and transportation becomes simultaneously more global and more local. Corporations and other organizations need to ship people and goods around the world quickly, requiring local warehouses and local transportation infrastructure.

Logistics is quickly becoming one of the most important aspects of the green economy. It represents practical, in-the-field strategies that reduce waste and increase performance, often without expensive technology. At the same time, the concept of reverse logistics is becoming more important and is just as highly emphasized in many organizations. Reverse logistics represents a new way of extending a green economic model. It involves environmentally aware manufacturing and shipping, working beyond the design, manufacturing, and sale of a product to consider the eventual fate of that product. This ensures that any materials that can be re-used or re-purposed are used. Reverse logistics has the potential to be the most important aspect of any organization's planning.

The transportation industry's potential as both a job market and green economic spearhead is unparalleled. No matter how other industries or lifestyles change, resources, products, and people must be moved from one place to another. The way this is accomplished has perhaps the greatest impact on environmental concerns possible because it is not only the design, manufacturing, and logistics that have impact but also the people who operate the vehicles and machinery themselves. Drivers, technicians, maintenance workers, and shipping clerks simultaneously perform vital work for their companies, governments, or organizations and have tremendous environmental influence. This environmental impact comes from maintaining their vehicles for maximum efficiency, studying and adjusting routes to improve fuel economy, carefully calibrating on-board computer systems to ensure the most accurate readings and efficiency, and refining warehouse usage over time to reduce wasted energy and space. Although new technologies and overhauls of company policies can have an immediate impact on environmental issues, these "long-tail" decisions made by thousands of individuals across the United States and around the world have just as much impact, if not more so, under the right circumstances.

Technology, however, remains the main focus of the transportation industry in its quest to reduce pollution and increase cost-effective environmental policies, and as a result job opportunities are created. For each automotive engineer or fuel cell engineer working to produce the next generation of transportation technology, automotive engineering technicians and fuel cell technicians are on hand to assist with the design and implementation of these new technologies. The increasing complexity of cutting-edge car technology has increased demand for engineers and technicians throughout every aspect of the automotive industry, but the educational barriers of many of these jobs remain relatively low, resulting in great opportunities for career change and advancement.

The transportation industry remains insulated from many economic and technological shifts as well, because no matter the changing economic or technological environment, transport remains essential. Rather than moving to another industry, however, business tends to shift from one sector to another within the industry. Transportation of goods via trucks, for example, has been in slight decline because of the costs of fossil fuels and concern over the environmental impact of pollution-creating engines on the roads. Much of this business, however, has simply shifted to alternative shipping methods such as train freight, which is more environmentally friendly. This has also

sparked energetic competition between sectors; for example, rail companies in the United States have aggressively pursued the freight normally hauled by the trucking industry, citing their higher efficiency and lower fuel costs. This kind of competition also drives job opportunities, as companies scale up their manpower. Skilled workers such as bus and truck mechanics or rail-track maintenance workers are in demand as their skills are needed to help their companies compete with other modes of transport. The competition to be the most efficient and environmentally friendly mode of transportation results in increased better-paying jobs. Transportation industries will continue to proactively comply with increasingly stringent environmental regulations around the globe and an increasingly aware public that seeks to do business with companies that take their environmental responsibilities seriously, and the jobs in this sector will show that green focus.

FURTHER READING

Andrews, John, and Bahman Shabani. "Re-envisioning the role of hydrogen in a sustainable energy economy." *International Journal of Hydrogen Energy* 37.2 (2012): 1184+. *Academic OneFile.*

Bourgeois, Matt, et al. "Tax incentives of going green." *The CPA Journal* 80.11 (2010): 18+. *Academic OneFile.*

ClimateBiz Staff. "Report Identifies 'Carbon Efficiency' as Key to Growing Market Share." *GreenBiz.com*, August 20, 2009. Accessed March 16, 2012. http://www.greenbiz.com/news/2009/08/20/report-identifies-carbon-efficiency-key-growing-market-share.

Harps, Leslie Hansen. "From Factory to Foxhole: The Battle for Logistics Efficiency." *Inbound Logistics*, July 2005. Accessed March 16, 2012. http://www.inboundlogistics.com/cms/article/from-factory-to-foxhole-the-battle-for-logistics-efficiency/.

Lockridge, Deborah. "The Changing Face of Trucking Part 2: Riding the Rails." *Trucking Info*, June 16, 2010. Accessed March 16, 2012. http://www.truckinginfo.com/news/news-detail.asp?news_id=70724.

"Recover and produce: Ways to Reap Value After a Product's Life Cycle Ends." *Industrial Engineer* 43.3 (2011): 14. *Academic OneFile.*

"Skyrocketing oil prices." *U.S. Rail News* 23 Mar. 2005: 46. *Academic OneFile.*

TRANSPORTATION MANAGERS

NATURE OF THE WORK

Transportation management is largely an office-bound job, requiring extremely high communication skills. It is also very detail-oriented, in that a transportation manager needs to have familiarity with all methods of transport and shipping (air, sea, rail, or road) and these methods' relative costs and benefits (although a concentration in a specific type of transport is necessary if the position requires it, for example, a specific concentration on rail transport if working for a railroad or rail freight company). Transportation managers also must have knowledge of local and national regulations, tolls, and laws. As a result, it is a position usually awarded to someone who already has deep experience within the transportation or logistics field.

In addition to managing day-to-day operations, transportation managers also analyze existing resources, procedures, and other factors to improve efficiencies or adjust policies to improve overall performance and service. Transportation managers are responsible for managing costs as well as physical fleets of vehicles and the staff that operate them. This includes both the purchase of raw materials (fuel) and maintenance services.

As such, the transportation manager is generally responsible for emissions standards of vehicle fleets and thus has a very large impact on the environmental standards of the organization. Increasingly, transportation managers are expected to take more than simple cost into account when purchasing or leasing vehicles for transportation and shipping. Fuel-efficient and alternative-fuel vehicles must be considered, along with the differing energy and maintenance requirements of such new technologies.

A transportation manager is also a supervisory position. Transportation managers are often responsible for hiring, training, and supervising employees as well as bargaining with staff (unionized and otherwise) and making efficient use of the available resources. Usually an intimate knowledge of local terrain, suppliers, and traffic conditions is vital. A firm understanding of maps and navigational aids is also essential.

WORKING CONDITIONS

As a largely office job, the hours of a transportation manager are relatively steady and follow predictable day and night shifts, usually eight hours each. There is little physical stress or danger of injury but a great deal of mental stress because there are large amounts of data to collate and manage. It is also a largely sedentary job with all the associated health dangers of a sedentary lifestyle.

Most transportation managers work with complex computer systems that track the large fleets of vehicles under their care, as well as a variety of communication technologies including phones, email, and radio.

Stress is often cited as a major concern for transportation managers. The complexity of the job responsibilities coupled with unexpected obstacles such as vehicle breakdowns, changing weather conditions, and the variable performance of third-party vendors or suppliers can make every day a different challenge than the last. Transportation managers are also expected to seek and exploit opportunities to save money, time, and resources at all stages of the job, meaning they must remain highly focused and detail-oriented at all times.

EMPLOYMENT

Transportation manager positions are available in both the private sector and in government agencies; any organization that has a large fleet of vehicles to manage. Careers are available in shipping docks, railroads, airports, and municipalities and state governments, as well as large companies such as FedEx or UPS.

Overall, the trend for transportation manager positions in the United States is downward. In 2008 there were 99,700 such jobs according to the U.S. Department of Labor's Bureau of Labor Statistics (BLS). By 2018 this is predicted to shrink by almost 5 percent.

TRAINING, OTHER QUALIFICATIONS, AND ADVANCEMENT

Most transportation manager positions require a bachelor's degree at a minimum; however, on-the-job experience is extremely important and candidates with strong experience are often selected despite lacking a college degree. The most common degree specialty is logistics, which is a discipline that informs almost all aspects of transportation management. A degree, however, is usually only important when breaking into the profession at entry level. Advancement is due to experience and training on the job.

One main certification is sometimes, although not always, required by employers: Certification in Transportation and Logistics (CTL), offered by the American Society of Transportation and Logistics. The North American Transportation Management Institute also offers several certification programs that can be attractive to employers, if not usually required.

Transportation managers are usually culled from within the existing workforce to ensure candidates have the local experience and knowledge necessary. Advancement can be slow in this sector as a result.

Transportation managers must have excellent written and verbal communication skills regardless of education level. They must also have excellent interpersonal relation skills and manage their time well because the logistics of large transportation systems can be complex and volatile. They must be able to process large amounts of information quickly and must be decisive.

Computers play a large and increasing role in this work, and familiarity with various software suites is a necessity. It is common for large-scale organizations and corporations to use custom software that is specific to their business model and transportation needs. Such in-house software suites will need to be learned, and experience with it will most likely be a requirement for the transportation manager position. However, there are some standard software packages used "off the shelf." Some examples of applications used by transportation managers on a daily basis are:

- **ABECAS Insight Freight Management System.** This software is used for incorporating order entry, dispatching, resource (truck, trailer, and driver) tracking, messaging, trip building and control, freight billing, and settlements processing for drivers/contractors/outside carriers
- **Eaton Fleet Advisor.** This program is an integrated information technology system that enables trucking companies to manage shipments "on the fly" using on-board computers and satellite communications
- **Airline Global Distribution System (GDS) software.** This system helps manage reservations in real time
- **Cadre Technologies Cadence Transportation Management System.** This software is used to fill, track, and confirm freight deliveries
- **ALK Technologies FleetSuite.** This program has routing, mileage, and mapping software

As managers, transportation managers must also deal with staff, scheduling time off, preparing and discussing performance reviews, and ensuring that staff is properly trained and, if necessary, certified. The transportation manager must not only master technological advances as they are incorporated into their fleets and other aspects of their work but also ensure that the training of their staff remains current. This includes training staff to use fuel-efficient driving and maintenance techniques, keeping drivers trained to operate electric and solid-fuel-cell vehicles, seeking more fuel-efficient routes for vehicles, and ensuring that all environmental regulations are understood and followed.

Although most transportation managers do not belong to unions, the staff that they supervise and delegate to are usually members of unions. Experience in negotiating with union representatives and knowledge of and adherence to union rules is a necessity.

JOB OUTLOOK

As of 2008, the BLS counted 99,700 transportation manager positions in the United States. The number of jobs is predicted to shrink slowly over the next decade, but the rate of predicted contraction (approximately 5 percent) is not large, resulting in a prediction of 94,400 jobs in 2018.

The reasons behind this shrinking job market include the ongoing efforts by organizations of all types to find more efficient ways to ship their materials and goods and provide transportation to the public. A more modern approach to storage, which sees more efficient warehouse space located closer to population centers so that items can be shipped out to customers more quickly, and the use of complex logistics and computer models to find more efficient supply-chain procedures has resulted in reductions in fleet sizes. Fewer trucks, planes, and train cars are delivering the same amount or even more goods as before. Smaller transportation fleets naturally need fewer managers.

However, considering the internal nature of most of the candidate selections and the fact that this job is almost never attained via an outside interview, the number of available positions is relatively small. The best way to attain a transportation manager position is to work upward from within an organization. In some organizations (municipal transit systems, for example) it is possible to begin working as a driver or train operator and attain the experience and knowledge necessary to qualify for a transportation management position over time.

EARNINGS

Wages for transportation managers vary from industry to industry; positions in the warehousing, general freight, and local government sectors have the most positions available but pay on the lower end of the scale, whereas positions within the energy industry are much less prevalent but pay significantly better.

Transportation managers in the warehousing and storage sector, for example, have an annual mean salary of US$79,370, whereas transportation manager jobs in the oil and gas extraction sector have an annual mean salary of US$134,560. The average entry-level salary is US$45,320. Experienced transportation managers can earn in excess of $130,000 per year.

As with many other careers, the areas of the country that offer the most employment opportunities are the population centers: California (10,770 positions), Texas (8,000 positions), and New Jersey (4,590 positions). However, the best-paying areas of the country are smaller and offer significantly fewer jobs. Whereas California's annual mean salary is US$90,360, Washington, DC, with just 360 positions recorded, offers an annual mean wage of US$120,900 for transportation managers. Likewise, Delaware offers just 340 positions but a mean annual salary of US$119,660.

New Jersey offers the best combined situation, being in the top three states of positions available and offering an annual mean salary of US$105,210.

RELATED OCCUPATIONS

- Buyers and purchasing agents, farm products
- Captains, mates, and pilots of water vessels
- Industrial production managers
- Purchasing managers
- Railroad conductors and yardmasters
- Transportation inspectors
- Travel guides

SOURCES OF ADDITIONAL INFORMATION

American Association of Railroad Superintendents. www .railroadsuperintendents.org
American Society of Transportation and Logistics. www .astl.org
Institute of Transportation Engineers. www.ite.org
North American Transportation Management Institute. www.natmi.org
Transportation and Logistics Council, Inc. www .tlcouncil.org

FURTHER READING

Bureau of Labor Statistics, U.S. Department of Labor. *11-3071 Transportation, Storage, and Distribution Managers.* Accessed March 2, 2012. http://www.bls .gov/oes/current/oes113071.htm.
Edwards, John. "A Day in the Life of a Transportation Manager." *Inbound Logistics,* January 2009. Accessed April 10, 2012. http://www. inboundlogistics.com/cms/article/a-day-in-the-life-of-a-transportation-manager.
O*NET OnLine. *Summary Report for: 11-3071.01— Transportation Managers.* Accessed March 2, 2012. http://www.onetonline.org/link/summary/ 11-3071.01.
wiseGEEK.com. *What Does a Transportation Manager Do?* Accessed March 2, 2012. http://www .wisegeek.com/what-does-a-transportation-manager-do.

SUPPLY CHAIN MANAGERS

NATURE OF THE WORK

Supply chain managers are an increasingly essential component to any business that requires materials and resources to operate. Technological advancement means that new and often rare materials (e.g., rare-earth minerals) are required for new products, and supply chain managers are in charge of locating suppliers and ensuring economical and uninterrupted access to these resources on a daily or even hourly basis. This involves not only identifying and negotiating with suppliers but also coordinating the purchasing, transporting, warehousing, and distributing of these materials.

Additionally, supply chain managers must continually forecast the prices of supplies and the cost of shipping and storing them, adjusting in real-time for global market fluctuations and transport obstacles. They must also enforce strong inventory management to ensure resources are not overstocked or allowed to dwindle at key times. Supply chain managers endeavor to follow market trends to know when to purchase materials at the most advantageous prices. They must be aware of the weather in the areas they draw supplies from, adjusting for climate effects that could have a disastrous effect on a supply chain. Supply chain managers need to be well-versed in the details of the materials they purchase, inspecting for quality and other factors, and able to identify and switch to alternative vendors as necessary.

The supply chain is increasingly seen as one of the key ways an organization can meet or exceed environmental regulations and goals because the supply chain usually contributes the most to carbon footprints. Two important trends are reverse logistics and transparent environmental impact data.

AT A GLANCE FACT BOX

SOC: 11-9199.04
Preferred Education: Bachelor's degree
Preferred Specialty: Logistics
Average Salary: US$96,450 annually
Other Information: Although not required, more than one quarter of all purchasing professionals hold a Certified Purchasing Manager (CPM) certification. There is no single job title associated with this career; some alternative titles are procurement manager, sourcing manager, and operations manager. Job descriptions must be read carefully to determine their appropriateness.

Reverse, or aftermarket logistics, focuses on what happens *after* the point of sale. Issues include streamlining customer service and examining the environmental impact of packaging both at its point of creation and its point of disposal. Packaging concerns have been marked by a movement to lighter, less wasteful packaging and a switch to recycled or alternative materials rather than traditional plastic and paper packaging. Additional issues include more aggressive and efficient service policies that extend the useful lifetime of products, and comprehensive recycling programs ensuring proper disposal or reuse of materials after a product's useful lifetime. It is estimated that almost a trillion U.S. dollars is spent annually on what can collectively be referred to as reverse logistics, making it one of the most important aspects of a logistics engineer's or supply chain manager's job today.

Supply chain managers are increasingly expected to gather data about their supply/distribution chains beyond simple costs and transport, collecting information about the environmental policies of their suppliers and the environmental impact of the materials supplied. Companies are expected to make these data sets transparent and available to demonstrate that they are seeking the most efficient and environmentally friendly paths for their supply chains. Wal-Mart Stores, Inc., for example, has engaged in an ongoing effort to collect sustainability information regarding every product it sells. Many supply chain managers work with the Sustainability Consortium (an organization with diverse worldwide members who drive standards and research to help its members make informed decisions about the environmental impacts of their products) in order to define and work toward these goals.

This requires strong interpersonal communication skills because conferring with suppliers, transportation managers, customs officials, and co-workers in a diplomatic and flexible manner is essential.

In past years supply chain management was considered a middle-management position. In recent years, however, large organizations such as Wal-Mart have begun elevating the role of supply chain manager to a more strategic level, calling on the expertise and knowledge of the supply chain manager to help predict and shape the company's future growth. This elevated role is becoming more common and salaries are rising commensurately.

WORKING CONDITIONS

Supply chain manager is generally an office-based position, sedentary and communications-based. Travel is often required, however, because supply chain managers often meet with vendors and suppliers in person, inspect facilities to determine their suitability, or travel to other corporate offices to coordinate with other departments of the company to ensure an efficient and unbroken supply chain.

Much of the work of a supply chain manager is done over the phone, over the Internet via e-mail or Skype, and other such direct communications. Supply chain managers work on computer systems to track prices, warehousing, and transportation aspects of the chain. The job is not physically strenuous but it can be considered high stress.

With the increased focus on the environmental impact of supply and distribution chains, many new technologies have been introduced into the supply chain manager's sphere. In an effort to analyze the complete life cycle of a product from raw materials to the customer, radio-frequency identification (RFID) technology is often implemented, allowing the supply chain manager to

collect data on materials and products at every step of the supply chain. The supply chain manager must also be aware of and knowledgeable about technologies that traditionally were not part of their concern. For example, renewable energy sources can be implemented throughout the supply chain, not only in the vehicle fleets. Low-energy or solar lighting can be used in warehouses. As a result, supply chain managers must remain educated and up-to-date on any technologies that might beneficially impact the supply chain.

Although office-based, supply chain managers should expect to be in contact with warehouse, dock, or garage environments on a regular basis. They will also need to interact with a wide variety of people from different career backgrounds and other countries and cultures, some of whom may not speak English as a native language. Flexibility in interpersonal interactions and a good knowledge of international customs and regulations is a necessity.

EMPLOYMENT

Supply chain managers are employed in almost every industry, including local and federal governments. Almost every company, from manufacturers to restaurants to bus lines to fashion houses, has some need of supply chain management. As a result, supply chain manager jobs are generally available in all regions of the United States (and globally), so workers are often able to choose where they wish to live and work.

The Internet has also transformed the supply chain career to a great extent; companies such as Amazon.com and Dell Computers must now be able to track the supply chain not only from vendors and suppliers but all the way to delivery to a customer in real-time. The shift from purchasing products in local brick-and-mortar stores to purchasing from Internet stores that can maintain warehouses wherever it is most cost-efficient has enlarged the role of the supply chain manager even further, and this trend promises to continue in the future. Shipping giants such as UPS have also benefitted from this shift, as Internet retailers must ship their products to customers. Transport companies such as UPS also employ supply chain managers.

This shift from traditional store shopping allows the supply chain to be much more efficient because products can be shipped in larger bulk to local warehouses, reducing the need for large fleets of pollution-emitting trucks and other vehicles and increasing the efficiencies of scale in larger, more modern warehouse facilities.

TRAINING, OTHER QUALIFICATIONS, AND ADVANCEMENT

Most supply chain manager positions require a bachelor's degree at a minimum, usually with a concentration in logistics. Employers are not looking for generalists who can be trained; for the most part they are seeking candidates who have received specific training in college programs or who have extensive work experience in the supply chain field. Sometimes a general bachelor's of science or business administration is acceptable. As with other jobs in supply/transportation, sometimes work experience trumps education and certifications and some supply chain managers are promoted from within an organization.

The most common post-college certifications supply chain managers can attain are the APICS Certified Supply Chain Professional (CSCP) and Certified in Production and Inventory Management (CPIM) programs administered by the Association for Operations Management, and the Certified Purchasing Manager (CPM) administered by the Institute for Supply Management. Although rarely required, these certifications can sometimes substitute for on-the-job experience when seeking a supply chain manager position.

Supply chain managers are usually recruited from within organizations from people already familiar with the business and the supply side. When not recruited internally, they are usually recruited from universities that offer well-established supply chain management programs (such as Arizona State, the University of Tennessee, Michigan State University, and the University of Wisconsin at Madison). A third way to enter this career is to participate in an internship program, which will offer experience and insight that can substitute for direct work experience.

Supply chain management is a career requiring excellent verbal and written communication skills. It requires a personality that is detail-oriented and logical, a person who can recognize patterns easily and interpret data quickly. A successful supply chain manager has an excellent attention span and can focus on details even when the work environment is chaotic or in flux. Strong math skills are often essential. Above all, they must be expert problem-solvers, able to identify the true source of a problem and quickly devise a solution.

The level of education and experience are the key factors for salary and advancement of supply chain managers. Supply chain managers with a high school degree earn an average of 10 to 20 percent less than those with college degrees. Salaries also rise with the number of years of experience.

JOB OUTLOOK

The job outlook for supply chain managers is excellent. The U.S. Department of Labor's Bureau of Labor Statistics (BLS) predicts approximately 7 percent growth in the number of supply chain management jobs from 2008 to 2018. Additionally, because the position requires a specific educational or work-experience background or both, this limits the number of qualified candidates for supply chain managers, making it easier for those with the proper background to find employment.

This career has global significance and as a result has been affected by economic troubles experienced worldwide, mainly in the shipping sector. As this is just one aspect of the supply chain manager's role, this has not affected the overall job outlook much. The number of available positions is expected to continue to rise at a steady rate. Emerging green technologies have served to expand the role and importance of the supply chain manager. Reduction of carbon footprints and consumer perception as being environmentally friendly have been recognized as some of the most important factors in the future growth of a company in the modern world, and the supply chain is the single most important factor in these issues. As a result, supply chain managers continue to be in great demand despite economic downturns.

One final factor to consider is that supply chain careers have been increasingly identified as "up-and-coming" careers, and more people are entering supply chain-oriented degree programs, meaning that even as job opportunities rise, more candidates will exist vying for them in the coming years.

EARNINGS

Earnings for supply chain managers have risen steadily in recent years, from a median of US$80,000 in 2006 to a median of US$88,000 in 2010.

Average salaries vary by region: The northeast United States supports the highest average salaries (on average US$114,113 annually) with the west and southwestern United States not far behind. Lowest salaries are found in the southeast United States, but this is slowly changing as manufacturing jobs, and thus supply chain management positions, continue to shift into the southeastern United States. Currently the average salary for supply chain managers in the southeast is US$85,144.

The highest-paying industries for supply chain managers are the chemicals industry (average annual salary of US$133,077), pharmaceuticals and healthcare (US$117,742), petroleum and coal (US$115,740), and computer equipment (US$107,510).

RELATED OCCUPATIONS

Supply chain managers have similar career goals with any profession that involves logistics, such as:

- Procurement clerks
- Transportation managers
- Food service managers
- Lodging managers

- Sales engineers
- Sales representatives, wholesale and manufacturing

SOURCES OF ADDITIONAL INFORMATION

The Association for Operations Management. http://www.apics.org

Institute for Supply Management. http://www.ism.ws

Logistics Management Magazine. http://www.logisticsmgmt.com

The Sustainability Consortium. http://www.sustainabilityconsortium.org

FURTHER READING

Bossers, Lauren. "The Supply Chain Manager as Superhero." *The 21st Century Supply Chain*, January 12, 2011. Accessed March 19, 2012. http://blog.kinaxis.com/2011/01/the-supply-chain-manager-as-superhero/.

Burnson, Patrick, executive editor. "Logistics Management 27th Annual Salary Survey: Ready to Move Up."

Logistics Management, April 7, 2011. Accessed March 19, 2012. http://www.logisticsmgmt.com/article/27th_annual_salary_survey_ready_to_move_up/.

Fisher, Anne. "2011's Hottest Job You Never Thought Of." *CNNMoney*, December 27, 2010. Accessed March 19, 2012. http://management.fortune.cnn.com/2010/12/27/2011%E2%80%99s-hottest-job-you-never-thought-of/.

Gunther, Marc. "Just How Sustainable is Walmart?" *GreenBiz.com*, December 5, 2011. Accessed March 19, 2012. http://www.greenbiz.com/blog/2011/12/05/just-how-sustainable-walmart.

Leybovich, Ilya. "2010 Supply Chain Salaries." *ThomasNet News*, June 22, 2010. Accessed March 19, 2012. http://news.thomasnet.com/IMT/archives/2010/06/2010-supply-chain-salaries.html.

WetFeet. *Supply Chain Management*. Accessed March 19, 2012. http://www.wetfeet.com/careers-industries/careers/supply-chain-management.

LOGISTICS MANAGERS

NATURE OF THE WORK

A logistics manager oversees and coordinates several different aspects of a company's functions, ensuring that schedules are maintained, warehouse stock is accurate and appropriate, and the workforce is proportional and efficiently organized. This combines a firm knowledge of the company's transportation, storage, and personnel capacities with a managerial outlook and requires the ability to collate, digest, and comprehend large amounts of data. Logistics managers work to ensure that no delays occur in order processing, fulfillment, or shipping by adjusting transportation schedules, warehouse capacities and locations, and workforce size and configuration on a constant, real time basis.

Logistics managers must also be versed in all local, state, national, and international laws and regulations that may affect their supply or distribution chains. These laws and regulations increasingly include rules regarding the environmental impact of all aspects of the supply/distribution chain, from the acquisition of raw materials to the storage or disposal of waste materials to the efficiency of shipping methods and the packaging of final products. All of these aspects are in the realm of the logistics manager.

WORKING CONDITIONS

Logistics managers mainly work in an office environment, sometimes with fixed hours and a normal workweek. However, the constantly shifting nature of logistics often requires irregular hours, some overtime, and travel. Logistics managers are expected to visit warehouse and garage sites to physically interact with and inspect the

AT A GLANCE FACT BOX

SOC: 11-3071.03
Preferred Education: Bachelor's degree
Preferred Specialty: Logistics management
Average Salary: US$80,210 annually
Other Information: As a coherent individual role, logistics manager originated in military operations as armies and equipment became larger and more complex. The military remains one of the largest employers of logistics management professionals.

goods they are overseeing and the workforce/fleet they are using to accomplish the tasks.

They rely heavily on computers, especially spreadsheets and custom-built computer systems for tracking of inventory and vehicle fleets, much like transportation managers, with whom they work closely. They also rely heavily on communication technologies including phone, email, and potentially instant-on communications such as radio connection with warehouses or drivers, GPS devices, and radio frequency identification (RFID) technologies.

In some industries logistics managers are expected to work more in the field. The oil and gas industries and the military are two such organizations. Logistics managers in these areas are expected to spend much of their time outside an office environment, thus they must be comfortable using mobile technologies to communicate with and keep track of their supply and distribution forces.

Stress can be a major concern in this career as many factors that affect the work of logistics managers are beyond their control: weather, international relations, political upheavals, and relationships with organized labor are just a few aspects of the supply/distribution chain that can adversely affect logistics managers' ability to perform their job. For example, China has recently sought to restrict foreign access to many of the rare earth minerals mined within its borders that are routinely used in any number of electronics devices, forcing logistics professionals in many industries to seek alternative suppliers of these minerals.

EMPLOYMENT

Logistics managers are needed in a wide variety of businesses, not just in areas with a concentration on shipping. Any business that has a supply chain and/or distribution channels to be managed is in need of logistics management on some scale. As markets become increasingly global and as manufacturing and shipping become increasingly concerned with green energy policies, the role of the logistics manager becomes more important as it adds new concerns to the traditional data points of cost, space, manpower, and technology. In addition to those classic considerations, companies must consider energy efficiency, geographical appropriateness in terms of warehouse space, fuel costs in relation to the age and condition of a vehicle fleet, and environmental impact of manufacturing, warehousing, and transportation of their goods.

With the introduction of the carbon tax concept, companies and organizations worldwide are considering the amount of carbon dioxide, methane, or nitrous oxides (greenhouse gases) emitted by their supply chains, also known as their carbon footprint (the total amount of greenhouse gases emitted by a company or organization), and logistics managers are at the forefront of these initiatives. This concept also affects organizations other than businesses. For example, charities, government agencies, and ports and airports all need the services of logistics managers who are familiar with and are capable of working within the increasing green scrutiny of governments and environmentally aware populations.

One of the major employers of logistics managers is the U.S. military, a large, complex organization with unique supply chain requirements. The U.S. military does hire civilian workers in this role, so enlistment in the military is not a requirement. As the military works to adapt to a focus on smaller, more targeted deployments as opposed to the traditional standing forces, logistics becomes more and more important, especially as traditional

port-to-port approaches to supply have become outdated. In addition, there is a new concentration on a green approach to weapons; the Strategic Environmental Research and Development Program (SERDP) has as its explicit goal the reduction of environmental impact and increased sustainability of mission capabilities. This focus on environmental issues from the U.S. Department of Defense increases the importance of logistics managers in this field as well.

TRAINING, OTHER QUALIFICATIONS, AND ADVANCEMENT

Although on-the-job experience and skills acquired from in-the-field work are highly valued in the industry and can be sufficient qualification for a logistics manager position, an associate degree or (preferably) a bachelor's degree is increasingly considered the minimum requirement for this position. A concentration in Logistics or Business Management is preferred.

Some of the most prominent university programs for logistics according to the *U.S. News and World Report* rankings are Michigan State University, Massachusetts Institute of Technology (MIT), Pennsylvania State University, and Arizona State University.

The International Society of Logistics (SOLE) offers several certification programs that can be valuable for career advancement and further education (listed from basic to advanced):

- Demonstrated Logistician (DL)
- Demonstrated Senior Logistician (DSL)
- Demonstrated Master Logistician (DML)
- Certified Master Logistician (CML)

In addition, the American Society of Transportation and Logistics manages the Certification in Transportation and Logistics (CTL) program, which is targeted to logistics managers with minimum educational or work experience qualifications.

General comfort with computer systems is essential, specifically with database and tracking software. Familiarity with specific software applications can be immensely useful to candidates for logistics manager positions:

- Materials requirements planning logistics and supply chain software such as Four Soft 4S VisiLog or Oracle E-Business Suite Logistics
- Enterprise resource planning (ERP) software such as SAP ERP Operations and Transtek Compass ERP
- Database user interface and query software such as Microsoft Access and Microsoft SQL Server

Logistics manager is an executive-level position that is usually attained after some years of experience working with supply and distribution in the chosen industry.

Increasingly, college-level degrees and even postgraduate degrees are becoming a requirement, although it is still possible to begin a career in logistics management with a high school degree and by working up to the position based entirely on experience in the industry. Degrees and certifications substitute for these years of experience, however.

Generally, logistics managers need to possess basic managerial skills because they supervise employees as part of their daily duties. They need to be detail-oriented and have the ability to parse large and rapidly changing streams of data to make on-the-fly adjustments. They must be able to work well with other people in a spirit of cooperation and mutual goals and must be comfortable acting on their own initiative and judgment. The logistics manager is sometimes an individual position and sometimes part of a team.

JOB OUTLOOK

The job outlook for logistics managers is very good, with a predicted growth of available positions over the coming decade of between 7 and 13 percent according to the U.S. Department of Labor. As of 2008 there were a reported 898,000 logistics manager jobs in the United States, with almost 300,000 job openings predicted over the next few years.

Job security is very good. In the past logistics managers were often employees with a great deal of in-house work experience at a company, who were very familiar with the company's processes and supply/distribution chains. However, as these aspects of doing business globally become more complicated with new technologies and the increasing awareness of carbon footprints and other environmental issues associated with supply/distribution chains, a college degree is increasingly seen as a necessary minimum requirement.

EARNINGS

The median salary for logistics managers in the United States is US$84,520, with a range from entry-level (US$45,320) to the top 10 percent of earners (US$130,000). The best-paying areas of the country for logistics managers are Washington, DC (average yearly salary of US$117,390), Delaware (US$116,290), New Jersey (US$101,870), New York (US$101,590), and Florida (US$100,680).

One of the best-paying industries for logistics managers is energy, specifically the oil industry. Green initiatives have affected this industry powerfully in recent years, making the already complex business of extracting, refining,

and transporting raw materials even more in need of logistical management.

RELATED OCCUPATIONS

In addition to working closely with transportation managers and supply chain managers, logistics managers share a great many aspects of their working life with these careers.

SOURCES OF ADDITIONAL INFORMATION

American Society of Transportation and Logistics. http://www.astl.org

Council of Supply Chain Management Professionals. http://www.cscmp.org

International Society of Logistics. http://www.sole.org

Strategic Environmental Research and Development Program. http://www.serdp.org

FURTHER READING

Carlson, Rob, and Daniel Grushkin. "The Military's Push To Green Explosives Using Synthetic Biology." *Climate Connections.* Accessed March 28, 2012. http://climate-connections.org/2012/01/20/the-militarys-push-to-green-our-explosives-using-synthetic-biology.

Council of Supply Chain Management Professionals. *Careers in Supply Chain Management.* Accessed March 28, 2012. http://www.careersinsupplychain.org.

Eye for Transport. *Green Transportation & Logistics European Report 2008–09.* Accessed March 28, 2012. http://www.greenlogisticsforum.com/europe/free_report.shtml.

Harps, Leslie Hansen. "From Factory to Foxhole: The Battle for Logistics Efficiency." *Inbound Logistics.* Accessed March 28, 2012. http://www.inboundlogistics.com/cms/article/from-factory-to-foxhole-the-battle-for-logistics-efficiency.

Logistics Manager.com. Accessed March 28, 2012. http://www.logisticsmanager.com.

O*Net OnLine. *Summary Report for: 11-3071.03—Logistics Managers.* Accessed April 3, 2012. http://www.onetonline.org/link/summary/11-3071.03?redir=11-9199.06.

State University.com. *Logistics Manager.* Accessed March 28, 2012. http://careers.stateuniversity.com/pages/cwzulypmy8/Logistics-Manager.html.

"Supply Chain Management/Logistics Rankings." *U.S. News & World Report.* Accessed March 28, 2012. http://colleges.usnews.rankingsandreviews.com/best-colleges/rankings/business-supply-chain-management-logistics.

LOGISTICS ANALYSTS

NATURE OF THE WORK

As implied by the job title, a logistics analyst examines processes within a supply/distribution chain to solve immediate problems, identify potential problems, increase efficiency and cost-effectiveness, or decrease environmental impact. The specific aspects analyzed vary from billing streams and inventory tracking to transport and route analysis or even manpower and staffing. Any aspect of the supply chain falls within the scope of the logistics analyst's purview.

As part of their job, logistics analysts maintain large databases of information about the supply chain to have sufficient data to interpret. This means collecting and sorting information on all aspects of the supply chain, such as raw materials acquisition and shipping, third-party vendors, warehousing, manufacturing techniques and workforces, order fulfillment, shipping, and customer service.

One of the major roles of the logistics analyst in the modern job market is to seek ways an organization can reduce its carbon footprint and otherwise improve its environmental record. This begins with being completely knowledgeable of and informed about local and international environmental standards and regulations, and then taking this information into account when collecting data and analyzing them. This also increases the amount of data that must be collected and reviewed. New technologies such as vehicle GPS tracking systems and warehouse environment monitoring systems give the logistics analyst the data required to make recommendations for improving environmental performance by showing where energy is being lost or where less can be used, streamlining the process.

WORKING CONDITIONS

Logistics analysts work mainly in offices for workweeks of about 35 to 40 hours. They typically enjoy industry-standard benefits, such as health insurance and paid vacation. It is a largely sedentary job, performed using computer systems and communications technology such as cell phones and e-mail. Communications are an essential part of the job and logistics analysts are expected to be in constant touch with all departments and aspects involved with the supply chain.

A logistics analyst is usually a team-oriented job at the entry and middle levels, with several analysts sharing responsibility for all or part of a supply/distribution chain or other aspect of an organization. Data, interpretations, and forecasts are shared liberally and examined by other members of the team, verifying results and generating alternative ideas or forecasts.

The work done by logistics analysts can be stressful because the typical supply/distribution chain is volatile and dynamic. Logistics analysts may be called into the office at any time to deal with emergencies caused by weather, world events, or physical breakdowns, so although they generally work an average workweek, overtime is not uncommon.

EMPLOYMENT

As with other logistics professionals, logistics analysts are employed evenly across the country and internationally in a large variety of industries. Any organization or company with a supply or distribution channel or transport fleet to manage has need of logistics professionals to design, maintain, and review their supply chain systems and procedures.

As of 2008 there were approximately 100,000 logistics analyst jobs in the United States according to the U.S. Department of Labor's Bureau of Labor Statistics (BLS), with extremely high growth predicted for the decade between 2008 and 2018 (20 percent). The U.S. federal government (not including the U.S. Postal Service) is the largest employer of logistics analysts in the country (25 percent of all positions), followed by the manufacturing industries (23.6 percent) and professional, scientific, and technical services (15.4 percent). However, it should be noted that any corporation or organization that has a supply and distribution chain of any kind will have logistics professionals employed to aid in the design, maintenance, and supervision of their internal systems. Logistics analysts can be found in almost every sector of the workplace. According to the BLS, Michigan has the highest concentration of logistics analyst jobs in the United States.

One reason for this increase in job opportunities for logistics analysts is the rising focus on the environmental impact of an organization and the recognition that logistics can address many of these concerns. Most notably, these concerns can be addressed in the supply chain, which is generally acknowledged to generate the most carbon dioxide emissions and have the greatest environmental impact of any aspect of a business. The augmented need to analyze all aspects of an organization and streamline procedures and protocols to make energy use as efficient as possible and waste disposal as green as possible has increased the importance of and demand for logistics analysts.

Another key environmental development fueling the demand for logistics analysts is the rising concern with reverse logistics, which seeks to extend efficient resource and waste management beyond the point of sale. This is essentially a second field of operations, often requiring its own team of logistics analysts to oversee.

TRAINING, OTHER QUALIFICATIONS, AND ADVANCEMENT

Almost all logistics analysts have a bachelor's degree at minimum, usually in engineering or logistics. An increasing number of logistics analyst jobs require a master's degree as well. Some of the top schools offering degrees in logistics management or similar fields are the Massachusetts Institute of Technology (MIT), Ohio State University, and Arizona State University.

It is common for logistics analysts to seek a Six Sigma certification. Six Sigma is a training program developed by Motorola that focuses on identifying and solving supply chain problems. There is no standard certification body; instead, many organizations conduct internal training and certifications, and organizations such as the American Society for Quality offer external training and certification exams.

As with other logistics-based positions, a logistics analyst can expect to be part of a team at the entry level, working on a small portion of a larger supply/distribution chain. Advancement is usually gradual, with the logistics analyst taking on larger pieces of the supply chain until they are overseeing most if not all of the organization's logistics. Advancement often means supervising employees as the scope of the job expands.

Logistics analysts need to be detail-oriented and focused and must be able to review and comprehend a very large data field very quickly. They must be adept at perceiving patterns and modeling predictions using existing data to forecast future events. They must possess excellent interpersonal communication skills and be able to adjust to changing conditions in the supply chain.

A comfort with math and science is necessary, as is comfort with computer systems. Some of the most commonly encountered computer software applications in a logistics analyst's job are:

- Four Soft 4S VisiLog (materials requirements planning logistics and supply chain software)
- Oracle E-Business Suite Logistics (materials requirements planning logistics and supply chain software)
- Minitab software (analytical or scientific software)
- Microsoft Excel (spreadsheet software)

JOB OUTLOOK

The logistics analyst career is expected to grow at a very aggressive rate in the next few years, with the BLS predicting more than 20 percent job growth in this field by 2018. This explosion is due to the enhanced position of logistics in all manner of industries, spurred by the cost-savings that efficient logistics management can achieve as well as the renewed emphasis on environmental impact. Increasingly, companies are seeing reduction of environmental impact at the supply chain level as a key component of future growth, and this has made the hiring of competent logistics analysts necessary in almost all fields.

However, an increasing number of candidates for the logistics analyst position are emerging from college programs because logistics is seen as a growing field and many students are encouraged to pursue it as a career. The environmental importance of the discipline is also serving to make the position more attractive to younger candidates. As a result, despite the quickly growing field of job opportunities, competition for jobs remains very high.

EARNINGS

The average entry-level salary for a logistics analyst was US$43,600 in 2008; the average senior logistics analyst's salary was US$75,900. The highest-paying industry for logistics analysts is in the computer systems/IT industry, followed by scientific and technical consulting services, and the U.S. federal government. Benefits are in line with industries standards.

Regionally, the highest-paying areas of the United States for logistics analysts match up with the population centers of the country according to the BLS, with Massachusetts paying the highest annual mean wage (US$100,660), followed by New York (US$100,350), Georgia (US$98,780), Virginia (US$95,970), and New Hampshire (US$93,380).

Although demand for logistics analysts is expected to be high in the coming decade, salaries are not expected to rise significantly because of the high number of potential candidates expected to be available.

RELATED OCCUPATIONS

Jobs with similar skills include:

- Supply chain manager
- Transportation manager
- Logistics manager
- Logistics engineer

SOURCES OF ADDITIONAL INFORMATION

The American Society for Quality. http://www .asq.org

The Institute of Industrial Engineers. http://www .iienet2.org

Journal of Transportation Management. http://business .wayne.edu/faculty/trans-management.php

Logistics Management. http://www.logisticsmgmt .com

FURTHER READING

Becomeopedia.com. *How to Become a Logistics Analyst.* Accessed March 19, 2012. http://www .becomeopedia.com/how-to/become-a-logistics-analyst.php.

Bureau of Labor Statistics, U.S. Department of Labor. "13-1111 Management Analysts." In *Occupational Employment Statistics: Occupational Employment and Wages, May 2010.* Accessed March 19, 2012. http://www.bls.gov/oes/current/oes131111 .htm.

O*NET OnLine. *Summary Report for: 13-1081.02— Logistics Analysts.* Accessed March 19, 2012. http://www.onetonline.org/link/summary/ 13-1081.02.

Six Sigma Training. *Six Sigma Training & Certification.* Accessed March 19, 2012. http://www .sixsigmatrainingguide.com/.

"What Is a Logistics Analyst? A Perspective from One British University on Increasing Student Awareness and Knowledge of Logistics Education and Career Opportunities (Report)." *Journal of Transportation Management* Fall 1997: 9(7).

"Work Perfect: The Day We Strive For." *Industrial Engineer* 42.4 (April 2010): 66(1).

AEROSPACE ENGINEERS

NATURE OF THE WORK

Aerospace engineers design, construct, and test aircraft, spacecraft, missiles, and other technologies. This work includes body and chassis design, engine and other systems design, materials research, environmental impact studies, and manufacturing techniques development. An aerospace engineer designs system components or entire crafts, then assists in the acquisition or fabrication and testing of materials, the building and testing of prototypes, and the design and implementation of manufacturing of the finished product.

The work is usually done as part of a team, with engineers assigned to different portions of a design, although senior aerospace engineers will work on single projects of their own design from beginning to end. There is usually a great deal of interaction with customers, both internal and external, as aerospace engineers are expected to deliver highly specific designs and end products. This also includes involvement with customers or other divisions within an organization in regard to resolving bugs or systems failures after manufacturing, essentially providing customer support.

In addition to designing and constructing new craft, an aerospace engineer is expected to review existing designs, including designs of craft already in service, and offer pathways to retrofit, update, or revise the existing design to meet new requirements. These new requirements can be new military technology added to existing aircraft or missile stock, retrofitting aircraft to meet new safety regulations, or improving fuel efficiency and pollution standards of existing designs to comply with changing environmental regulations worldwide. Both civilian and military air fleets are subject to increasingly strict air pollution standards, and aerospace engineers are integral

to this initiative through the design of more efficient aircraft for future service and the revision of existing aircraft to economically improve environmental impact.

WORKING CONDITIONS

Aerospace engineers typically work in office settings, although they may also need to be familiar and comfortable with laboratory and factory settings because they may be expected to review testing and manufacturing procedures. Teamwork is an important aspect of the job because complex projects require a large number of engineers working together and with supply chain, manufacturing, and fabrication teams and customers. Although working in team situations is common, an aerospace engineer is expected to work independently in service to the team's goals.

Although most aerospace engineering positions have fixed hours in a standard 40-hour work week, overtime and longer-than-usual hours are common, especially when deadlines for delivery of designs or prototypes are looming. Despite testing and rigorous research, systems often behave unpredictably when first deployed, and aerospace engineers must be available to react to problems and unexpected events, designing solutions and work-arounds quickly and efficiently.

In a corporate environment, which is very common for aerospace engineers, there is usually a typical corporate culture that involves meetings and desk-based work. However, the research and development aspects of the career often require more hands-on work. Many aerospace engineers pursue the career out of a passion for science, flight, or space exploration, and many often express dismay at the "office politics" they encounter.

EMPLOYMENT

According to the U.S. Department of Labor's Bureau of Labor Statistics (BLS), there were 78,450 aerospace engineer jobs in the United States as of May 2010. This number is expected to increase by about 10 percent by 2022. The increase in job opportunities can be ascribed to the aging of fleets in the airline industry, requiring new aircraft that are more fuel-efficient and environmentally friendly as the airline industry attempts to stay profitable in the face of economic and environmental challenges, and the overall push for more fuel-efficient, lower-pollution transport. Aircraft pollution is a major concern and concentration of environmental efforts, and this has burnished the status of and need for aerospace engineers to address the needs of changing industries.

The largest employer of aerospace engineers is the aerospace industry itself, with about 28,710 jobs as of May 2010. The other top employers of aerospace engineers are architectural, engineering, and related services, with 12,150 jobs; scientific research and development services, with 10,820 jobs; and the federal government, with 9,220 jobs.

TRAINING, OTHER QUALIFICATIONS, AND ADVANCEMENT

At a minimum, an aerospace engineer will need a bachelor's degree in aerospace, aeronautical, and astronautical/space engineering or a related field such as electrical and electronics engineering or mechanical engineering. Master's degrees are also common, and most aerospace engineers who start out with a bachelor's degree will acquire a master's degree at some point in their careers.

Aerospace is a combined discipline until partway through a degree program, typically the third year of a four-year program. At this point, there is often an "aero" track and a "space" track that students can pursue if they have a specific career target in mind.

No licensing or certification is required for aerospace engineers, although some do acquire a professional engineer (PE) license, which can be useful. The PE license is administered by the National Society of Professional Engineers and is composed of a written examination.

At the entry level, aerospace engineers may be assigned a small part of a larger project, usually under the direct supervision of a senior engineer. The ability to communicate ideas and suggestions is critical to advancement. Aerospace engineering is not regarded as a draftsmen-type job, merely rendering professional-level schematics, but as a creative position. Problem solving and innovative ideas are expected from an aerospace engineer, and a lack of perceived contribution can hold back a career.

A strong affinity for and understanding of science, engineering, and mathematical concepts are essential to a career as an aerospace engineer. Additionally, attention to detail, creative thinking, and innovation are important traits any successful aerospace engineer must have. Writing is an essential skill for an aerospace engineer: The quality of ideas is lost if they cannot be communicated in writing in a clear, easily understood manner. Familiarity and comfort with specific tools, such as flow meter cluster or parallel computer systems, lasers, milling cutters, and centerless or surface grinders, is extremely important.

Software is also important as it is involved in almost every aspect of the job, including the manufacturing portion. Examples of common software packages that aerospace engineers use are:

- ANSYS software, Alstom ESARAD, Alstom ESATAN, Altera Quartus II, Analytical Graphics STK Expert Edition
- Autodesk AutoCAD software, computer-aided design (CAD) software, Dassault Systemes CATIA software, Dassault Systemes SolidWorks software, Mathsoft Mathcad
- Computer-aided manufacturing (CAM) software, PTC Pro/ENGINEER software
- Ada, C, Digital Equipment Corporation DIGITAL Fortran 90, IBM Rational ClearQuest, Microsoft Visual Basic
- Microsoft Visual C++, practical extraction and reporting language (Perl), Sun Microsystems Java

JOB OUTLOOK

Aerospace engineering is a fast-growing employment field and is expected to grow by approximately 10 percent by 2022. Job security is very high, and compensation is rising. Despite economic turmoil worldwide, the need for new technologies and new designs in commercial and military aircraft is expected to drive the need for aerospace engineers to fill vacant as well as newly created positions.

The number of graduates seeking jobs in aerospace engineering has gone up slightly in the last few years, but this has been outpaced by the number of available jobs; thus employment chances remain high.

Environmental concerns have also spurred employment in the aerospace engineering field. New requirements for fuel efficiency, pollution reduction, and economy have driven a need for more efficient aircraft made from lighter, stronger materials that use less fuel and create less waste. The large number of existing aircraft fleets, however, means that older designs cannot simply be discarded. Instead, they must be retrofitted to conform to new regulations and laws. This combination has increased demand for aerospace engineers in the commercial and military fields.

EARNINGS

According to a survey conducted by the National Association of Colleges and Employers, the average entry-level aerospace engineering job for applicants with bachelor's degrees was US$48,028 per year. Those with master's degrees were offered US$61,162 on average.

The best-paying industries for aerospace engineers are machinery, equipment, and supplies merchant wholesalers at an annual mean wage of US$118,420, followed by the air transportation industry at US$114,300.

The best areas of the United States for aerospace engineering jobs are California, with 19,460 jobs; Texas, with 8,750 jobs; and Washington state, with 6,460 jobs. California only ranks as the fifth best-paying area of the country, however, with Maryland at a mean annual wage of US$117,160; Virginia at US$116,280; Washington, DC, at US$115,180; and Alabama at US$113,630.

RELATED OCCUPATIONS

- Architectural and engineering managers
- Civil engineers
- Electrical engineers
- Industrial engineering technicians
- Industrial engineers
- Marine engineers and naval architects
- Mining and geological engineers, including mining safety engineers
- Petroleum engineers

SOURCES OF ADDITIONAL INFORMATION

American Institute of Aeronautics and Astronautics. http://www.aiaa.org
American Society for Engineering Education. http://www.asee.org
Federal Aviation Administration. http://www.faa.gov
National Society of Professional Engineers. http://www.nspe.org

FURTHER READING

Aerospaceweb.org. *Aerospace Engineering 7*. Accessed March 2, 2012. http://www.aerospaceweb.org/question/careers/q0273.shtml.

Holzman, David. "Plane Pollution." *Environmental Health Perspectives* 105: 1300–1305. Accessed March 2, 2012. http://dx.doi.org/10.1289/ehp.971051300.

NACE. *NACE Salary Survey: Starting Salaries for New College Graduates*. Accessed March 2, 2012. http://www.naceweb.org/uploadedFiles/NACEWeb/Research/Salary_Survey/Reports/SS_January_exsummary_4web.pdf.

Norris, Guy. "Surprising Designs for Eco-Friendly Airliner." *Aviation Week*. Accessed March 2, 2012. http://www.aviationweek.com/aw/generic/story.jsp?id=news/awst/2012/01/16/AW_01_16_2012_p21-413463.xml&channel=comm.

Princeton Review. *Career: Aerospace Engineer*. Accessed March 2, 2012. http://www.princetonreview.com/careers.aspx?cid=5.

TRANSPORTATION ENGINEERS

NATURE OF THE WORK

A transportation engineer works to develop new transportation projects for surface transportation and to analyze existing traffic patterns and propose new projects to solve problems or to increase efficiency. This involves studying existing transport systems (including roads, airports, and commuter rail systems), identifying solutions to current issues or developing improvements, then designing and planning new projects while working within whatever local, state, or federal regulations apply to the scope of the project (whether a modification to an extant system or new construction). One of the most important facets of this job is the ability to analyze environmental impact reports, which are almost always required for any large-scale transportation project in the United States (and often internationally as well).

The transportation engineer is responsible for preparing all specifications and plans for such projects and must be able to check construction plans, blueprints, and cost estimates to ensure that they comply with all applicable codes and that efficient construction techniques are followed. This includes reviewing bids, and therefore knowledge of market values and resource availability is essential. Much of this knowledge comes from on-the-job experience.

Although primarily focused on transportation systems, a transportation engineer's scope also includes subsidiary systems such as channels, dams, irrigation projects, pipelines, power plants, and water and sewage systems. Any system or structure that affects the transportation system in question falls under the scope of the transportation engineer, so a wide array of knowledge is necessary for the job.

AT A GLANCE FACT BOX

SOC: 17-2051.01
Preferred Education: Bachelor's degree
Preferred Specialty: Civil engineering
Average Salary: US$77,560 annually
Other Information: Nearly half of all transportation engineers today have master's or doctoral degrees. Although usually not necessary for employment, these advanced degrees can be required for teaching or research positions.

One of the emerging focuses for transportation engineers is the positive impact that more fuel-efficient and less fossil fuel-dependent transportation systems can have on the environment. Increasingly, these aspects of transportation design and planning are taking precedence, as well-designed transportation systems can significantly reduce carbon emissions and other forms of pollution. Additionally, transportation engineers are increasingly required to review existing systems and seek ways to reduce environmental impact with refinements, alterations, or replacement projects.

Some transportation engineers choose to specialize, working exclusively in surface roads, rail systems, or airport design and administration. More commonly, transportation engineers work on all aspects of a new or existing transportation system.

WORKING CONDITIONS

Transportation engineers work primarily out of offices, performing the bulk of their work on computers and through communication technologies such as phones, e-mail, text messaging, and video conference. Occasionally on-site visits and inspections are required to judge the stability of existing systems or the quality of in-progress construction.

Transportation engineers use computers to analyze data gathered either from on-site visit or from available databases. There is a great deal of virtualization, so the ability to visualize physical properties from data sets and deal with abstracts is essential.

As transportation engineers advance in their careers, they will take on increasingly larger scale and more complex projects, which will eventually involve supervising lower-level engineers and other employees. Although the specific work of a transportation engineer is generally individual and solitary, working as a member of a team and eventually overseeing others is an aspect of the job and requires managerial skills.

EMPLOYMENT

According to the U.S. Department of Labor's Bureau of Labor Statistics (BLS), there were 278,000 civil engineering jobs in the United States in 2010, of which about 25,000 were transportation engineering positions. The industries employing the most transportation engineers are manufacturing, technical and scientific consultants, and federal, state, and local governments. Manufacturers of transport-related materials and products often employ transportation engineers to develop and refine the materials (road surfaces, de-icing agents, and so on) and technologies used in transportation systems.

More commonly, transportation engineers are employed by governmental agencies charged with planning, improving, and constructing these systems. The transportation infrastructure in the United States is aging, and systems such as subways, bridges, and even the basic roads within cities and the highways that link them increasingly need repair and reevaluation from a green perspective. As a result governmental agencies remain the main employer for transportation engineers.

TRAINING, OTHER QUALIFICATIONS, AND ADVANCEMENT

Transportation engineers usually attain a bachelor's degree in a specialty such as civil engineering; such a degree is virtually required for any position. Increasing numbers of transportation engineers have advanced degrees as well, but this is not currently a requirement for most positions.

There are no required certifications for transportation engineers, but certifications are often looked upon favorably by potential employers and for career advancement. The Transportation Professional Certification Board (TPCB), in conjunction with the Institute of Transportation Engineers, offers two certifications: Professional Traffic Operations Engineer (PTOE) and Professional Transportation Planner (PTP). Both are attained via a written examination administered by the TPCB.

Entry-level transportation jobs are often described as "trainee" jobs; they are designed to let the individual learn the specifics of the transportation systems they will be working on. This usually involves working under more experienced engineers and taking assignments from their superiors to complete specific tasks. As their familiarity with the systems grows, there are usually intermediate and then advanced jobs that bring more autonomy and responsibility. Advancement for transportation engineers is usually very systematic, with career paths clearly defined within an organization (for example, frequent job titles are transportation engineer I, transportation engineer II, or intermediate transportation engineer or similar).

Transportation engineers need to have strong math and science skills and knowledge, as well as excellent attention to detail and logic. They will need to work well in cooperation with other individuals and groups because large-scale transportation projects can involve huge numbers of agencies, contractors, and individual consultants working together to achieve goals. Although it is a largely sedentary career, transportation engineers do need to visit construction sites and other areas involved in the transportation system (garages, airports, roadways) and thus some physical exertion is usually required.

Advancement within the transportation engineer field will also require increased specialization and supervision of lower-level employees. Anyone seeking to advance to the top of the field will eventually need to lead a team on a project, which will involve typical managerial aspects of a job, such as reviewing work performance, promotion and salary increase recommendations, and ensuring all members of a team are productive.

Familiarity with the following software applications is often required or at least highly desired:

- Bentley GEOPAK Civil Engineering Suite (computer-aided design [CAD] software)
- Bentley Microstation (CAD software)
- McTrans HCS+ (analytical or scientific software)
- Trafficware SynchroGreen (analytical or scientific software)
- Bentley InRoads software (map creation software)
- ESRI ArcGIS software (map creation software)

JOB OUTLOOK

Job growth for transportation engineers is expected to be very good from 2008 to 2018, with a growth rate of more than 20 percent predicted. There are several reasons for this robust job growth. One reason is that urbanization is increasing worldwide. As cities spread, new transportation systems (such as roads or commuter rail) need to be constructed to service newly developed areas and existing transportation systems (roads, rail, highways, airports) must be extended and revised to handle a higher volume. Additionally, larger cities create more pollution, and transportation engineers are increasingly tasked with finding ways to reduce the environmental impact of existing systems by re-routing roads into more efficient patterns or increasing the amount of public transportation available to citizens as well as ensuring that new additions to a city's transport systems are designed with the goals of reduced carbon footprints and lowered pollution in mind.

Existing transportation systems will also need to be increasingly re-evaluated for their environmental impact, and the aging of existing infrastructure will require massive repair projects. This ensures that transportation engineers will be in great demand for the foreseeable future. Huge transportation projects such as New York City's Second Avenue subway often take decades and large teams of engineers to plan, implement, and complete.

EARNINGS

According to the BLS, the average annual salary for a transportation engineer in the United States is US$77,560. Entry-level transportation engineering jobs pay a median annual salary of US$48,836. Senior transportation engineers can earn as much as US$114,000.

The highest-paying areas of the country for transportation engineering positions are California (US$92,100), Louisiana (US$88,000), and Alaska (US$85,100), with the lowest-paying areas being Puerto Rico (US$50,200), Montana (US$62,000), and South Dakota (US$62,600). The higher salaries in this field are located near large population centers where public transportation is essential or in port cities and pipeline areas where shipping and freight concerns require sophisticated and environmentally friendly transport systems.

RELATED OCCUPATIONS
- Aerospace engineers
- Landscape architects
- Marine engineers and naval architects
- Materials engineers
- Transportation managers

SOURCES OF ADDITIONAL INFORMATION

Institute of Transportation Engineers. http://www.ite.org
Transportation Professional Certification Board, Inc. http://www.tpcb.org

FURTHER READING

Bureau of Labor Statistics, U.S. Department of Labor. "Engineers." In *Occupational Outlook Handbook, 2010–11 Edition.* Accessed March 20, 2012. http://www.bls.gov/oco/ocos027.htm.

CNN Money. "51. Transportation Engineer." *Best Jobs in America.* Accessed March 19, 2012. http://money.cnn.com/magazines/moneymag/bestjobs/2010/snapshots/51.html.

Science Buddies.org. *Science Careers: Transportation Engineer.* Accessed March 19, 2012. http://www.sciencebuddies.org/science-fair-projects/science-engineering-careers/CE_transportationengineer_c001.shtml.

State University.com. "Transportation Engineer Job Description, Career as a Transportation Engineer, Salary, Employment—Definition and Nature of the Work, Education, and Training Requirements, Getting the Job." *Job Description and Careers.* Accessed March 19, 2012. http://careers.stateuniversity.com/pages/826/Transportation-Engineer.html.

Trachy, Robert, Jr. "My visit to RE." *Public Management* 76.11 (1994): 23+. *Academic OneFile.*

Yglesias, Matthew. "Train in Vain." *Slate,* January 27, 2012. Accessed March 19, 2012. http://www.slate.com/articles/business/moneybox/2012/01/mass_transit_vs_highways_the_department_of_transportation_rule_that_is_killing_american_cities_.html.

ELECTRONICS ENGINEERS, EXCEPT COMPUTER

NATURE OF THE WORK

Electronics engineers design and develop electronic components for a wide variety of purposes and industries, including industrial, manufacturing, military, or scientific use. These components can be designed for use in telecommunications, guidance systems, analytical equipment, construction equipment, or transportation applications.

An electronics engineer takes requirements from customers or other divisions within an organization, designs electronic components that will satisfy these requirements, and then aids in the construction, testing, and adjustment of these components. This involves using design software and equipment, creating sketches and circuit maps, and overseeing the manufacture, installation, and operation of the components or groups of components they create.

Electronics and digital devices impact every aspect of modern life, and the environment is no exception. Electronics engineers are at the forefront of the search for technological solutions to the problems of reducing carbon footprints, curbing fossil-fuel consumption, and pursuing alternative energy. Electronics engineers design and construct components in many vehicles that monitor and manage the consumption of fuel and design the systems in hybrid vehicles that manage energy usage to achieve the utmost efficiency under any driving condition. They are involved in creating devices to reduce pollution and to detect it, to process it into benign or useful materials, or to eliminate its creation altogether.

In addition, electronics engineers have always been a part of the teams that develop recycling solutions (e.g., water treatment components, plastic and can sorting machines) and alternative energy generation equipment

AT A GLANCE FACT BOX

SOC: 17-2072.00
Preferred Education: Bachelor's degree
Preferred Specialty: Electrical engineering
Average Salary: US$90,170
Other Information: Starting salaries for electronics engineers tend to be among the highest of all college graduates

(e.g., solar cells and wind turbines). These technologies continue to be developed, analyzed, and improved upon by electronics engineers and others.

One of the newer green concepts that electronics engineers are involved in is the "remanufacturing" trend, which proposes that end-of-life products discarded by consumers or companies should be collected and their parts and materials reused in the manufacture of new products. Electronics engineers are at the forefront of designing new products so that they can someday be disassembled easily for this purpose and designing machinery and components to automate the recovery of parts and materials efficiently.

WORKING CONDITIONS

Most electronics engineers work standard 40-hour weeks in an office or laboratory settings and receive industry-standard benefits such as health insurance and paid vacations. There is a high degree of cooperation and teamwork involved; engineers must work with customers or colleagues in other divisions to create requirements as well as other engineers or divisions within an organization to develop a product or component.

Some electronics engineers spend much of their time in industrial settings or on construction sites, supervising the implementation or manufacture of components they have either designed or reviewed and modified. Electronics engineers working in the petroleum or other energy-related industries often work under somewhat unsafe or risky conditions, such as on drilling rigs on the ocean or in isolated areas with few modern conveniences, such as the Antarctic. Electronics engineers can generally choose which type of work they prefer to do.

EMPLOYMENT

According to the U.S. Department of Labor's Bureau of Labor Statistics (BLS), there were approximately 143,700 electronics engineer jobs in the United States in 2008. There is expected to be little or no change in the number of job opportunities for electronics engineers in the near future, with just 3,340 jobs predicted to open up in the next 10 years. Despite robust demand for an increasing number of electronic devices and an increasing use of electronic and digital components, international competition is serving to hold jobs static in the United States.

The number of jobs in electronics engineering coincides closely with the technological centers of the country. According to the BLS, the areas of the country offering the most employment opportunities in this field are California (27,170 jobs), Texas (12,630 jobs), New Jersey (5,110 jobs), Florida (5,080 jobs), and Illinois (5,070 jobs).

The U.S. federal government is the largest single employer of electronics engineers, with 17,790. This is followed by wired telecommunications carriers (16,260 positions); semiconductor and other electronic component manufacturers (14,700 positions); architectural, engineering, and related services (11,480 positions); and navigational, measuring, electromedical, and control instruments manufacturers (10,780 positions).

TRAINING, OTHER QUALIFICATIONS, AND ADVANCEMENT

Electronics engineers need to have a bachelor's degree in electrical engineering or an equivalent discipline for entry-level positions. Although not universally required, there are several certifications that are useful for professional advancement. For example, an electronics engineer can receive certification as an Engineer-In-Training (EIT), or can pass the Fundamentals of Engineering (FE) and the Professional Engineer (PE) exams for certification (all of which are administered by the National Council of Examiners for Engineering and Surveying).

An entry-level electronics engineer will usually have a very specific and narrow piece of a larger project on which to concentrate. As engineers advance within an organization they will take on more varied facets of larger projects, until ultimately they are supervising an entire project on their own. This final stage usually involves supervising employees, fellow engineers, and outside vendors. One of the most crucial keys to advancement for an electronics engineer is staying current in the field. Although there are few required certifications, electronics engineers are expected to continue learning throughout their careers because technology changes very quickly.

Advanced degrees will certainly help electronics engineers gain promotions and salary increases. Engineers who receive master's or doctoral degrees can earn 10 to 30 percent more than electronics engineers who hold only a bachelor's degree.

Excellent math and science skills are very important to a prospective electronics engineer. An excellent attention span and attention to detail, comfort with independent thought and action, and good interpersonal communication skills are also required. The ability to work with a team while still pursuing independent ideas is essential.

There are several commonly encountered software packages that an electronics engineer will need to be familiar with:

- Autodesk AutoCAD software (computer-aided design [CAD] software)
- Mentor Graphics PADS (computer-aided design [CAD] software)
- Assembler (programming language)
- C (programming language)
- Ansoft Simplorer (analytical or scientific software)
- The MathWorks Simulink (analytical or scientific software)

JOB OUTLOOK

Despite the increasing demand for electronic devices and components, the job outlook for electronics engineers in the United States is expected to hold steady, with little or no job growth predicted for the future. This is due to international competition because emerging economies around the world have begun to produce numerous qualified electronics engineers, thus shifting jobs traditionally found in the United States elsewhere.

At the same time, the steadily increasing demand for both consumer electronics and electronic components embedded in existing technologies such as cars, phones, and televisions means that job security is very good. Once a career is secured, an electronics engineer can generally expect to remain employed, with regular promotion and good compensation.

The emerging green initiatives in almost all aspects of manufacturing and consumer goods promise to brighten the employment outlook for electronics engineers considerably in the coming years. More cars will come equipped with embedded electronics to improve energy consumption and pollution generation, more devices will become "smart" with the inclusion of digital components to actively manage user experience, and the replacement and upgrading of infrastructure throughout the country will eventually spur the need for more electronics engineers.

EARNINGS

The average yearly salary for electronics engineers in the United States is US$90,170. Entry-level electronics engineering jobs pay an average of US$55,530, whereas senior-level electronics engineering jobs pay an average of US$129,920.

According to the BLS, New Jersey offers the highest salary for electronics engineers with an annual mean salary of US$109,740. Rhode Island (US$109,050), Washington, DC (US$105,970), California (US$102,910), and Massachusetts (US$101,750) offer the next-highest salaries. The lowest wages are found in South Dakota (US$62,500), West Virginia (US$66,300), Montana (US$67,200), Arkansas (US$67,500), and Idaho (US$69,700).

Surprisingly, the best-paying industries for electronics engineers do not coincide with the industries offering the most jobs. Business schools and computer and management training lead the field with an annual mean salary of US$110,680, followed by petroleum and coal products manufacturing (US$104,410), aerospace product and parts manufacturing (US$103,710), electronic shopping and mail-order houses (US$103,640), and satellite telecommunications (US$103,270).

RELATED OCCUPATIONS

- Aerospace engineers
- Avionics technicians
- Electrical engineers
- Electrical and electronics drafters
- Electrical and electronics repairers, commercial and industrial equipment
- Industrial engineering technicians
- Inspectors, testers, sorters, samplers, and weighers
- Mechanical engineers
- Model makers, metal and plastic

SOURCES OF ADDITIONAL INFORMATION

Institute of Electrical and Electronics Engineers. http://www.ieee.org

The National Council of Examiners for Engineering and Surveying. http://www.ncees.org

The National Society of Professional Engineers. http://www.nspe.org

FURTHER READING

Bureau of Labor Statistics, U.S. Department of Labor. "*17-2072 Electronics Engineers, Except Computer*." In *Occupational Employment and Wages, May 2010*. Accessed February 20, 2012. http://www.bls.gov/oes/current/oes172072.htm.

Engineers Guide USA. *Electrical and Electronics Engineer Job Outlook*. Accessed February 20, 2012. http://www.engineersguideusa.com/Careers/Electrical_and_Electronics_Engineer_job_outlook.htm.

Institute of Industrial Engineers. "Recover and Produce: Ways to Reap Value after a Product's Life Cycle Ends." *Industrial Engineer* 43 (3):14.

Nature Publishing Group. "Across China's Frontier." *Nature* 439 (February 16, 2006):781.

Sloan Career Cornerstone Center. *Electrical Engineering*. Accessed February 20, 2012. http://www.careercornerstone.org/eleceng/eleceng.htm.

FUEL CELL ENGINEERS

NATURE OF THE WORK

Fuel cell engineers are primarily designers, creating specifications and evaluating fuel cell components for a variety of applications, including vehicles, portable energy devices, and products such as cell phones and portable computers. Analyzing test data or data collected from in-use cells, fuel cell engineers use software to calculate efficiency statistics to identify ways to improve on an existing design or to create a superior design using different materials or configurations. They also assist in the manufacture of prototypes, assess and analyze tests of new cells, and review vehicle and component designs and requirements to predict and solve problems and improve fuel cell performance and efficiency.

Fuel cells are seen as a viable alternative to traditional fossil fuel energy sources, especially for personal vehicles. The demand for more efficient fuel cells is growing. Although fuel cells can eliminate much of the traditional carbon-based pollution from a gas-burning engine (they emit water vapor or other similarly harmless materials), the cells themselves are created from highly toxic materials and safe disposal of depleted cells is problematic.

The job of a fuel cell engineer is viewed as an important green career, with demand for jobs increasing as automotive and other industries replace traditional fossil-fuel–based vehicles with more environmentally friendly fuel-cell models using hydrogen fuels, which emit water vapor as their only byproduct. Despite a relatively modest job growth predicted for the immediate future, job opportunities for fuel cell engineers are expected to grow aggressively as a career.

> ## AT A GLANCE FACT BOX
>
> **SOC:** 17-2141.01
> **Preferred Education:** Bachelor's degree
> **Preferred Specialty:** Chemical engineering
> **Average Salary:** US$78,160 annually
> **Other Information:** According to the U.S. Department of Labor's Bureau of Labor Statistics (BLS), 78 percent of all fuel cell engineers have a bachelor's degree or higher

The automotive industry is the major driving force behind fuel cell technology because their products will use and promote fuel cell technology to the greatest degree in the United States. Major automotive manufacturers such as Daimler, Honda, Hyundai, and Toyota all expect to roll out their first hydrogen-based fuel cell automobiles in 2015. This will undoubtedly set off a rapid expansion of the industry overall, with demand for fuel cell engineers following suit.

WORKING CONDITIONS

Most fuel cell engineers work in office or laboratory environments, usually working a standard 40-hour workweek and earning industry standard benefits. The work is often computer-centric, using software to model designs and predict reactions. Stress is sometimes cited as a job concern because deadlines sometimes require fuel cell engineers to work longer hours.

Although largely a sedentary position, occasionally fuel cell engineers will visit manufacturing sites such as factories or testing facilities where the fuel cells they design are evaluated. These situations can expose fuel cell engineers to dangerous conditions and physically stressful environments.

EMPLOYMENT

The BLS includes fuel cell engineers in a category with all other mechanical engineers. As the importance of fuel cell technology increases the position will become more distinct. According to the BLS there were 239,000 mechanical engineer jobs in the United States in 2008, with job growth predicted to be slower than average (3 to 6 percent) over the next 10 years. However, the increasing importance of fuel cell engineering jobs means that job growth may accelerate as fuel cell technology becomes more essential to a variety of manufacturing sectors.

The main industry employing fuel cell engineers is the manufacturing industry, including the automotive industry, followed by the professional, scientific, and technical service industries. Another important industry for fuel cell engineers is the aerospace industry, in particular the National Aeronautics and Space Administration's (NASA) space program, which relies heavily on fuel cell technology for all of its missions.

Michigan, home of the domestic automotive manufacturing industry, employs the most fuel cell engineers and mechanical engineers overall as of 2010 (30,260), followed by other manufacturing-heavy regions such as California (22,000), Texas (16,170), and Pennsylvania (10,860).

TRAINING, OTHER QUALIFICATIONS, AND ADVANCEMENT

A bachelor's degree is considered the minimum educational requirement for fuel cell engineers, with a concentration in chemical or mechanical engineering preferred. Most fuel cell engineers also attain higher degrees such as a master's or doctoral degree as they advance in their career. Although not required, such degrees are often very advantageous for promotion in the field.

A standard certification as a Professional Engineer (PE) is often required in fuel cell engineer positions with local, state, or federal government agencies, or that serve the public directly in some capacity. This certification is administered by the National Council of Examiners for Engineering and Surveying (NCEES).

As with other engineering jobs, entry-level fuel cell engineers usually work on teams and are assigned a narrow portion of a larger project to work on. As they advance, fuel cell engineers take on larger portions of projects and often work on their own ideas independently of other workers.

Ultimately, managerial experience and skills become required for advancement to the highest levels. Although not necessarily required, advanced degrees, certifications, and continuing education often speed advancement within an organization.

In addition to strong math and science skills, fuel cell engineers need to have excellent attention to detail and a high comfort level with large amounts of information that must be collated and organized. An understanding and comfort with computer systems is also essential. Because of the team-oriented nature of the work, excellent communication skills are an advantage.

Specific computer applications often encountered by fuel cell engineers include:

- FactSage (analytical or scientific software)
- Gaussian GaussView (analytical or scientific software)
- C (programming language)
- Wind River Systems C/C++ Compiler Suite (development environment software)
- Spreadsheet software

JOB OUTLOOK

Currently the job outlook for fuel cell engineers is moderate. The number of available positions is predicted to increase, but at a slower-than-average rate. However, increasing focus on environmental issues in both manufacturing and vehicle pollution across all sectors means an increased demand for fuel cell engineers is expected in the near future.

The bright future predicted for fuel cell engineers is tied to the budding infrastructure for fuel-cell technologies. Currently, there is little to no infrastructure in place in the United States for electric and other alternative fuel solutions for passenger cars and freight vehicles. There are several initiatives at the state and federal level, however, to expand this new infrastructure aggressively over the next decade. For example, the American Recovery and Reinvestment Act passed in February 2009 included significant renewable energy provisions. This increase in infrastructure spending and construction is often compared with similar initiatives and building programs that established the gasoline infrastructure that exists today, which did not exist at all a century ago.

The emerging need for this basic infrastructure to be in place for the fuel cell market to grow is, in fact, one of the factors expected to drive demand for fuel cell engineers in the future because they will need to be involved in the specification and implementation of any such infrastructure designed to power hybrid or electric vehicles using fuel cell technology or the delivery and maintenance of hydrogen-based fuel cells. Currently this infrastructure is prohibitively expensive (hydrogen fueling stations are estimated to cost approximately US$1 million each to build), which will lead to increased demand for fuel cell engineers to devise more cost-efficient construction and design techniques for these stations.

According to the U.S. Department of Energy, vehicle applications of fuel cell technology may open up to 675,000 new jobs by 2050, although this includes all fuel-cell related jobs, not just fuel cell engineers.

Another industry that has growing demand for fuel cell engineers in the future is the cell phone and tablet industry. Cell phone and tablet computers such as the iPad are increasing in popularity, and one major factor in their design is battery life. Fuel cell engineers design and test these batteries, and are called upon to create more efficient batteries that can sustain the video, audio, and computing needs of these increasingly large, increasingly powerful devices. At the same time, fuel cell engineers are expected to make future fuel cell designs for these devices more readily recyclable, using reclaimable materials that can be collected after the useful life of a device and re-used in new offerings.

EARNINGS

The average annual salary for fuel cell engineers is US$78,160. The average entry-level annual salary for a fuel cell engineer is US$40,000.

The highest-paying areas of the country for mechanical engineers overall are Alaska (US$99,400 mean annual wage), Washington, DC (US$96,310), Virginia (US$94,530), Colorado (US$92,010), and California (US$90,860). Michigan, which employs the most mechanical engineers overall and the most fuel cell engineers specifically, offers an annual mean wage of US$85,360.

The top-paying industries for mechanical engineers overall are commercial and industrial machinery and equipment rental and leasing (US$107,580) and oil and gas extraction (US$101,930).

RELATED OCCUPATIONS

- Chemical engineer
- Mechanical engineer
- Materials scientist and engineer
- Energy efficiency engineer
- Environmental engineer
- Environmental engineering technician

SOURCES OF ADDITIONAL INFORMATION

The American Recovery and Reinvestment Act. http://www.recovery.gov

The National Council of Examiners for Engineering and Surveying. http://www.ncees.org

The U.S. Department of Energy. http://eere.energy.gov

FURTHER READING

Bourgeois, Matt, et al. "Tax Incentives of Going Green." *The CPA Journal* 80.11 (2010): 18+. *Academic OneFile.*

Friedemann, Alice. "The Hydrogen Economy: Savior of Humanity or an Economic Black Hole?" *Skeptic* [Altadena, CA] 14.1 (2008): 48+. *Academic OneFile.*

Manjoo, Farhad. "The Rise of the Enormo-Phone." *Slate.* Accessed March 19, 2012. http://www.slate.com/articles/technology/technology/2012/02/samsung_galaxy_note_the_disturbing_new_trend_toward_enormous_smartphones_.html.

Motavalli, Jim. "The Hydrogen Highway: Lots of Fuel-Cell Cars, But in Pockets of America," *Car Talk.* Accessed March 19, 2012. http://www.cartalk.com/content/hydrogen-highway-lots-fuel-cell-cars-pockets-america.

Nuvera.com. "10 Questions with a Fuel Cell Engineer." *Nuvera Blog.* Accessed March 19, 2012. http://www.nuvera.com/blog/?p=1213.

U.S. Department of Energy. *Fuel Cell Technologies Program.* Accessed March 19, 2012. http://www1.eere.energy.gov/hydrogenandfuelcells/.

———. "Jobs in Fuel Cell Technologies." *Fuel Cell Technologies Program.* Accessed March 19, 2012. http://www1.eere.energy.gov/library/pdfs/fuel_cell_green_jobs_fs_9-13.pdf.

AUTOMOTIVE ENGINEERS

NATURE OF THE WORK

Automotive engineers create new vehicle designs or review and improve existing ones. This can include exterior and chassis design as well as internal components ranging from the engine design and exhaust systems to suspension and on-board computer systems designed to increase fuel efficiency or driver experience.

Automotive engineers have a great deal of creative influence on the future look and driving experience of automobiles. Automotive engineers design the aesthetics of exterior shells and are called upon to consider and improve on the aerodynamics of an exterior design, incorporate new fuel efficiency technologies into existing internal combustion engine specifications, and consider the ergonomics of driver controls and the comfort and safety of passengers. They are also involved in other design aspects of the operation of an automobile, from brakes and steering to diagnostic equipment.

Automotive engineers are also key players in the green economy. Automobiles remain an important consumer item around the world, and they account for a significant percentage of the pollution emitted into the atmosphere. Tougher fuel economy and emissions standards are being enacted, and it is the automotive engineer who must find ways to ensure that new vehicles comply with these regulations while retaining performance and comfort standards. Automotive engineers not only take new engine designs using alternative fuels such as hybrid or solid fuel-cell designs and implement them in new vehicle models, but they must also consider existing fuel technologies and find ways to increase efficiency and performance in older cars.

Although automotive engineers have a great impact on automobile-related environmental concerns, they must

AT A GLANCE FACT BOX

SOC: 17-2141.02
Preferred Education: Bachelor's degree
Preferred Specialty: Mechanical engineering or automotive engineering
Average Salary: US$62,880 annually
Other Information: Long-distance and stock car racing organizations hire automotive engineers to get the most speed and driver safety from automobiles by designing the cars differently. This can be an exciting alternative career to corporate automotive manufacturers.

also take into consideration the end users of their products. Their designs and actions directly affect consumers' safety and health. An automotive engineer must include safety considerations above and beyond the minimum requirements of domestic and foreign governments, keeping the well-being of drivers, passengers, and pedestrians in mind through every phase of the design and testing of a new vehicle.

Because of the size and penetration of the automotive market, automotive engineers can have an incredible impact on the future of energy use and environmental impact not only in the United States but also around the world. Cars built in the United States are sold internationally (Buick, a General Motors brand, is the most popular car in China, for example), so improvements in fuel efficiency or emissions put into production in the United States affect the environment worldwide.

Most automotive engineers start by working in team situations on a variety of systems involved with vehicle design and manufacture, but will specialize as they advance in their careers, focusing on one system or aspect of vehicle design.

WORKING CONDITIONS

Automotive engineers work in a variety of environments from offices and simulation labs where they use computers and other technologies to simulate designs to factory floors where their designs are prototyped and built. They may also interact with salespeople and managers at car dealerships to ascertain the needs of the market.

The average work week for an automotive engineer ranges from 40 to 55 hours depending on deadlines for designs and problem solving emergencies when approved designs do not function as expected.

Automotive engineers are also expected to work with professionals from other fields, such as lawyers and government regulators, to ensure their designs meet or exceed legally required minimums for safety and pollution standards. Sometimes they are required or invited to test-drive their own creations to better understand the impact of new technologies or refinements in existing technologies or to work with climate-controlled test chambers that simulate weather conditions. An automotive engineer must be equally comfortable working with advanced computer systems simulating designs and conditions and working hands-on with engines and other car systems, assembling and dismantling as needed. As a result of the need to inspect manufacturing plants or testing facilities, automotive engineers should be prepared for some travel as part of their job.

EMPLOYMENT

The number one employer of automotive engineers is the auto manufacturing industry, but automotive engineers are also employed by engineering consulting firms and often work freelance, opening their own consulting companies.

Although the majority of automotive engineering jobs can still be found in Michigan, which hosts 30,260 mechanical engineering jobs as of 2010, most of the major car manufacturers have moved their research and development units to California, which now almost rivals Michigan in the number of automotive engineering jobs available, with 22,000 positions as of 2010. Texas follows with 16,170 mechanical engineering positions.

TRAINING, OTHER QUALIFICATIONS, AND ADVANCEMENT

A bachelor's degree in mechanical engineering, automotive engineering, or a similar field is required for almost all automotive engineer positions. Master's degrees in a more specific field can be advantageous, especially for advancement, but are not always required.

Certification as a professional automotive engineer or professional mechanical engineer may be required for some positions. These certifications are managed by the Society of Automobile Engineers or the American Society of Mechanical Engineers and typically involve written examinations.

As with other design engineering positions, automotive engineers usually begin by working in teams with other engineers or other professionals, often working on different systems or components of a single design. As they advance, most automotive engineers specialize in certain systems and may work more on their own. Advancement usually requires the management of other engineers. Some senior automotive engineers opt to leave a corporate environment and start their own consulting firms, which work with automotive manufacturers and government agencies to sculpt standards and regulations related to the automotive industry. Automotive engineers with advanced degrees may choose to move into teaching positions at the university or college level.

Automotive engineers must be comfortable and skilled with mechanics and electronics and have strong math skills. Automotive engineers should be organized, have very good attention to detail, and be able to deal with large amounts of data in an efficient and coherent way. They are creative but precise, always balancing inspiration with the need to ensure designs are legal and practical and will attain basic standards of safety and fuel efficiency. Because of the team nature of much automotive design, automotive engineers must also have excellent verbal and written communication skills so they can communicate their ideas in both verbal communication and the preparation of formal design specs and proposals.

Automotive engineers must be comfortable with advanced, complex computer systems. Software applications they may encounter include:

- Gamma Technologies GT-SUITE (analytical or scientific software)
- SoMat eDAQ (analytical or scientific software)
- Autodesk AutoCAD software (computer-aided design)
- Dassault Systemes SolidWorks software (computer-aided design)

- Adobe Systems Adobe Photoshop software (graphics or photo imaging software)
- Ambient Design ArtRage (graphics or photo imaging software)

JOB OUTLOOK

Automotive engineers are grouped by the U.S. Department of Labor's Bureau of Labor Statistics (BLS) as a subset of mechanical engineers, and as such the job outlook is considered lower than average. There were an estimated 239,000 mechanical engineering jobs in the United States as of 2008, and the predicted growth from 2008 to 2018 is expected to be only 3 to 6 percent.

The automotive industry in particular has been difficult to predict. In 2009 many of the largest U.S. car manufacturers such as General Motors, which is based in Detroit, Michigan, were in danger of bankruptcy or default and took on a program of government loans and restructuring to return to profitability, selling or discontinuing several car brands such as Pontiac and Hummer. However, demand for personal automobiles remains high and the industry as a whole is in recovery as of 2012, which should mean increased demand for automotive engineers in the future.

Another consideration is the focus worldwide by governments on the environmental impact of automobiles. Designs no longer remain current and viable for decades at a time. Every year brings new and increasingly stringent environmental regulations for manufacturers in general and automobile manufacturers specifically, so new designs must be produced that result in cleaner, safer, better-performing cars. As a result, automotive engineers enjoy very good job security and should continue to do so for the foreseeable future.

EARNINGS

The BLS estimates mechanical engineers of all kinds receive an average annual salary of US$78,160. Automotive engineers tend to earn slightly less than that with an average annual salary of US$62,880. The average entry-level salary for automotive engineers is US$41,490.

Although it offers the most jobs, Michigan does not offer the best pay for automotive engineers because of the saturation of the job market. Alaska offers the highest salaries to mechanical engineers in general, topping out at US$99,400 annually, followed by Washington,

DC (US$96,310), Virginia (US$94,530), Colorado (US$92,010), and California (US$90,860).

RELATED OCCUPATIONS

- Mechanical engineer
- Electrical and electronics engineer
- Automotive technician
- Chemical engineer
- CAD technician
- Automotive designer

SOURCES OF ADDITIONAL INFORMATION

American Society of Mechanical Engineers. http://www .asme.org
Automotive Engineer Magazine. http://www.ae-plus.com
Global Automakers. http://www.globalautomakers.org
Society of Automobile Engineers. http://www.sae.org

FURTHER READING

Csere, Csaba. "Reviewing the 2012 Honda CR-V." *The New York Times,* January 27, 2012. Accessed March 1, 2012. http://wheels.blogs.nytimes.com/2012/01/27/reviewing-the-2012-honda-cr-v/.

Dron, Will. "Sparks Fly at Chevy Volt Fire Safety Hearing." *TheChargingPoint.com,* January 26, 2012. Accessed March 1, 2012. http://www .thechargingpoint.com/news/Sparks-fly-at-Chevy-Volt-fire-safety-hearing.html.

PR Newswire. "Leaders from Nissan, GE, Google and NHTSA Highlight List of Speakers at SAE 2012 World Congress." *The Wall Street Journal,* January 31, 2012. Accessed March 1, 2012. http://www.market watch.com/story/leaders-from-nissan-ge-google-and-nhtsa-highlight-list-of-speakers-at-sae-2012-world-congress-2012-01-31.

Schools in the USA.com. *Automotive Engineer.* Accessed March 1, 2012. http://www.schoolsintheusa.com/careerprofiles_details.cfm?carid=108.

Science Buddies. *Science Careers: Automotive Engineer.* Accessed March 1, 2012. http://www.sciencebuddies .org/science-fair-projects/science-engineering-careers/ApMech_automotiveengineer_c001.shtml.

Scoltock, James. "Racing on a Budget." *Automotive Engineer,* July 13, 2011. Accessed March 1, 2012. http://ae-plus.com/features/racing-on-a-budget.

AUTOMOTIVE ENGINEERING TECHNICIANS

NATURE OF THE WORK

Automotive engineering technicians assist automotive engineers in designing new systems and components for automobiles and testing completed designs to determine if they meet specified goals and standards. This involves both reviewing the specifications and designs created by the engineer and physically testing the completed prototypes and components, which can include testing separate discrete systems to testing entire automobiles. Automotive engineering technicians also assist in the fabrication of testing equipment or automotive components. In addition to analyzing designs and prototypes, automotive engineering technicians review and analyze test data to determine if expected improvements have been attained. They are also often responsible for determining that test equipment is calibrated properly.

Automotive engineering technicians have a large role in reducing the environmental impact of automobiles. Together with automotive engineers, they work to ensure automobiles meet or exceed safety and emissions standards and they help to identify and use alternative fuels and materials for the construction and operation of new vehicles. They conduct rigorous testing of these improvements in performance, fuel efficiency, and pollution levels to confirm they meet the standards predicted by the design manifest in practice.

Automotive engineering technicians also have an environmental impact on designs they did not assist in creating because they have the largest role in acquiring materials and creating fabrication guidelines for prototypes and production models. As a result, even in situations in which a new vehicle design has not addressed environmental concerns, automotive engineering technicians can bring a

green influence to the design in their choices of materials, vendors, and construction techniques.

WORKING CONDITIONS

Automotive engineering technicians usually work a standard 40-hour work week and enjoy industry-standard benefits, such as paid time off and health benefits. The U.S. Department of Labor's Bureau of Labor Statistics (BLS) reported that in 2008, 24 percent of automotive engineering technicians worked longer than a 40-hour work week on a regular basis. There is usually little travel involved in this career. Although some of an automotive engineering technician's time is typically spent in office environments working with computer equipment to create and review specifications and designs, they also spend

---

---

a significant amount of time in testing facilities where they observe and review prototype and component tests and often calibrate and check the testing equipment for defects.

Automotive engineering technicians may also be required to enter factory environments to assist in the fabrication of components or entire vehicles. They should be comfortable around large-scale equipment such as welding equipment and engine block cranes. As a result, prospective automotive engineering technicians should be ready to work in a variety of conditions, including spaces with no climate control, among loud and potentially dangerous machinery, and in outdoor areas exposed to the elements.

An automotive engineering technician is a team-focused job that requires a great deal of interaction and consultation with other technicians, engineers, and other workers such as third-party vendors, factory workers, and sales staff. Although much of the work is done individually at computer stations or in a laboratory setting, collaboration is a necessity.

EMPLOYMENT

According to the BLS, automotive engineering technicians are considered a part of the mechanical engineering technician group. In 2008, there were 46,100 mechanical engineering technician jobs in the United States. Over the next decade, a slight decline in available jobs is expected, with just 45,500 jobs predicted to be available by 2018.

The main employer of automotive engineering technicians in the United States is the automotive industry, which is based in Michigan but has increasing research and development facilities in California. As of May 2010, Michigan offers the most job opportunities in this field, with 4,660 jobs. Also offering job opportunities in this field are Texas (4,230 jobs), California (3,320 jobs), Ohio (2,490 jobs), and New York (1,930 jobs).

The second largest employer of automotive engineering technicians are car dealerships, which employ these skilled workers to test new models and assist mechanics in learning new technologies and designs so that cars can be serviced onsite.

TRAINING, OTHER QUALIFICATIONS, AND ADVANCEMENT

Many automotive engineering technicians do not have a formal degree and most positions do not require one. An associate's degree in automotive engineering technology is often helpful both for finding a job and advancing within an organization.

There is no required certification or licensing for automotive engineering technicians; however, the National Institute for Automotive Service Excellence offers certification for automotive technicians. Although aimed at the maintenance and repair sector, this certification can be helpful in finding a job as an automotive engineering technician and advancing within that career. Although there is no formal certification, ongoing education and staying informed about and familiar with new technologies is essential because the automobile industry has transformed itself into a cutting-edge technological industry that incorporates the latest computer technologies and the most advanced environmental technologies at its disposal into car designs.

Automotive engineering technicians typically begin at the entry level working directly under a more experienced technician in an apprentice-style arrangement. Both technicians are under the direct supervision of an automotive engineer. This allows the new technician to learn the specific systems and organizational dynamics of the company. Advancement includes working more independently and eventually supervising technicians of less experience as well. However, collaboration with other technicians, engineers, and other partners is always a part of the automotive engineering technician's job, even at the highest levels.

Employers routinely send automotive engineering technicians to manufacturer training centers to gain firsthand and before-market knowledge of new components or systems in new model automobiles, thus there may be some minimal travel involved.

Automotive engineering technicians must be comfortable with computer systems and mechanical duties in general, and specifically working with car and engine parts. They must have strong mathematics and design skills. Creativity is a key asset to any automotive engineering technician because designing new vehicles and solving problems for future vehicles are important parts of the job.

Some of the software typically encountered by automotive engineering technicians includes:

- Autodesk AutoCAD Mechanical (computer-aided design software)
- Autodesk Inventor (computer-aided design software)
- Analytical or scientific software
- Data acquisition software
- Road simulators
- Spreadsheet software

JOB OUTLOOK

The BLS considers automotive engineering technicians to be a subset of mechanical engineering technicians, which affects the predicted job growth for this position. Although job growth is predicted to be flat until 2022 for mechanical engineering technicians, job growth for automotive engineering technicians is likely to increase because of the growing need for new and updated car designs and components. Because of consumer desire for cars that run on alternative fuels, the governmental requirement for cars that produce lower emissions, and the United States' need to compete on an international level with the automobile industries of Japan, Germany, and other countries, the demand for qualified and creative automotive engineering technicians is likely to grow steadily. The economic outlook for the U.S. automobile industry has changed dramatically since 2008, when the last BLS survey was conducted. With major U.S. companies such as Chrysler Group and Ford Motor Co. reporting profits and recovery from near-bankruptcy, there is every reason to expect job opportunities for automotive engineering technicians to defy predictions.

In fact, the coming wave of alternative-fuel vehicles will require a wholesale revision of most existing car designs to either include hybrid options or to do away with fossil-fuel–based engine technologies altogether. This will mean more money put into automotive research, a trend that has already begun, and thus more jobs for automotive engineering technicians. According to some analysts, this recovery is in part being energized by a renewed focus on passenger cars, as opposed to trucks, and car design, areas which had languished while U.S. automakers focused on the previously more profitable truck-based product lines. These products were largely exempted from emissions and fuel-economy regulations and faced little foreign competition. This renewed focus on car design and technology represents a huge opportunity for automotive engineering technicians.

EARNINGS

The average annual salary of an automotive engineering technician is US$50,100. Alaska is the top-paying state with a mean annual salary of US$63,950, followed by Nevada (US$59,250), Louisiana (US$58,920), Washington (US$57,570), and Missouri (US$56,200). Entry-level automotive engineering technician jobs pay from US$38,000 to US$44,000 on average.

According to the BLS, the best-paying industries for mechanical engineering technicians (of which automotive engineering technicians are a subset) are the petroleum and coal products manufacturing industry (US$70,970 mean annual salary); oil and gas extraction industry (US$68,540); pipeline transportation of crude oil (US$65,290); professional, scientific, and technical services (US$63,740); and alumina and aluminum production and processing (US$62,680).

RELATED OCCUPATIONS

- Automotive engineers
- Mechanical engineering technicians
- Broadcast and sound engineering technicians and radio operators
- Drafters
- Science technicians

SOURCES OF ADDITIONAL INFORMATION

Bureau of Labor Statistics. http://www.bls.gov
The National Institute for Automotive Service Excellence. http://www.ase.com
Society of Automotive Engineers. http://www.sae.org

FURTHER READING

Associate Engine. *An Associate's Degree Can Prepare You for a Qualified Job in the Automotive Industry.* Accessed February 29, 2012. http://www.amahoro-onlus.org/105-an-associates-degree-can-prepare-you-for-a-qualified-job-in-the-automotive-industry.html.

Associated Press. "Automotive Industry Crisis." *The New York Times,* May 25, 2011. Accessed February 29, 2012. http://topics.nytimes.com/top/reference/timestopics/subjects/c/credit_crisis/auto_industry/index.html.

Inside Jobs. *Automotive Engineering Technician Career.* Accessed February 29, 2012. http://www.insidejobs.com/jobs/automotive-engineering-technician.

Texas Cares. *17-3027.01 Automotive Engineering Technicians.* Accessed February 29, 2012. http://www.texascaresonline.com/profile/occdata.asp?onetcode=17-3027.01.

FUEL CELL TECHNICIANS

NATURE OF THE WORK

A fuel cell technician generally works under the supervision of a fuel cell engineer. Fuel cell technicians help to design, assemble, test, and fabricate fuel cells for use in a variety of applications, including digital devices and automobiles. This involves reviewing schematics and specifications, researching materials, supervising construction of prototype cells, testing those prototypes, and comparing/interpreting test results to ensure that the expected power output and efficiency is attained.

Although fuel cell technicians do not generally create designs or schematics for fuel cells, they are expected to be able to easily read, comprehend, and implement fuel cell designs. Fuel cell technicians usually work in teams, interacting with supervising engineers as well as other technicians, workers, and vendors. They are expected to source materials for new designs and interact with laboratory and factory staff to create and test prototype cells. This also involves ensuring that accepted designs for fuel cells can be efficiently and cost-effectively manufactured.

Fuel cell technicians are at the forefront of the green economy in many ways. Fuel cell technology is one of the main ways the automobile industry, which is the largest source of carbon dioxide pollution in the world, is reducing its environmental impact. As fuel cells become more efficient and less resource-intensive, pollution is reduced, and fuel cell technicians, together with fuel cell engineers, are the driving force behind this initiative.

Additionally, fuel cell technology is increasingly being used by large institutions in place of traditional generator systems. Hospitals, schools, and other environments that

AT A GLANCE FACT BOX

SOC: 17-3029.10
Preferred Education: Associate's degree
Preferred Specialty: Fuel cell technology
Average Salary: US$58,020 annually
Other Information: According to Clean Edge Trends (a research and advisory firm devoted to the clean-technology sector), the alternative energy industry, of which fuel cell technicians are a part, generated global revenues of US$144.5 billion in 2009

need to have their own dedicated power systems in case of emergencies or to ensure continuous operating power independent of the grid are increasingly turning to fuel cell installations for these systems. This increases the potential impact fuel cell technicians can have on the environment because these solutions create less pollution and are more efficient than traditional fossil-fuel–based generator solutions.

Fuel cell technicians also work to ensure that newer fuel cells are recyclable because they were made with reclaimable materials or through direct repurposing of spent cells. As fuel cell technology approaches maximum efficiency, the "aftermarket" repurposing of fuel cells or their component materials becomes increasingly essential to a green agenda.

WORKING CONDITIONS

Most fuel cell technicians work in office or laboratory environments. They generally work standard work weeks and receive industry-standard benefits, such as health insurance and paid vacation. Much of the work is performed using computer systems in office environments. However, fuel cell technicians should expect to spend some time in laboratories and on factory floors to perform tests and supervise fabrication of materials.

Although fuel cell technicians generally work a standard week, overtime may be necessary to meet deadlines or solve problems. Stress is sometimes cited as a concern in this career, especially when tested outcomes for new design efficiency and power output do not match predictions made during the design stages. When this happens it is often up to the fuel cell technician to investigate the cause of the failure and offer suggestions to improve the efficiency and performance.

Fuel cell technicians are very team-oriented. Fuel cell technicians interact with a large number of other professionals in the course of their work, ranging from third-party vendors for the acquisition of raw materials (which often requires negotiation skills and diplomacy) to technicians in a factory setting who must be assisted and supervised in the creation of prototype cells.

EMPLOYMENT

The U.S. Department of Labor's Bureau of Labor Statistics (BLS) considers fuel cell technicians to be part of the larger grouping of engineering technicians. Out of 497,300 total jobs under the engineering technicians category, the BLS includes 76,600 positions for fuel cell technicians.

Fuel cell technicians are overwhelmingly employed by the manufacturing industry, led by automobile manufacturers and electronics manufacturers. The former seeks to replace fossil-fuel–powered cars with cars powered by alternative fuels and the latter struggles to meet consumer demand for electronic devices that run off fuel cell battery technology such as cellular phones, laptop and tablet computers, personal stereos, and GPS devices.

Despite the strong demand for these consumer items, job growth is predicted to be slow for fuel cell technicians. This is largely due to the global economic downturn, which saw many large manufacturing companies suffer losses in previous years. However, recent economic recoveries by industries in the United States, most notably the automobile industry, give hope that job growth for fuel cell engineers will not be as slow as predicted.

In the automobile industry specifically, the need to comply with increasingly stringent regulations regarding emissions and performance is driving car manufacturers to aggressively fund research and development of hybrid, fuel cell, and electric automobile technologies, which will create more jobs for fuel cell technicians in the coming years.

The areas of the United States with the highest employment for engineering technicians in general as of May 2010 according to the BLS are California (9,580 jobs), Texas (6,460 jobs), Ohio (3,590 jobs), Michigan (3,570 jobs), and Washington (3,300 jobs).

The U.S. federal government is listed as the largest employer of engineering technicians in general, with 18,540 jobs recorded in May 2010, followed by architectural, engineering, and related services (7,670), scientific research and development services (3,580), local governments (2,900), and aerospace product and parts manufacturing (2,850).

TRAINING, OTHER QUALIFICATIONS, AND ADVANCEMENT

Advanced degrees are usually not required for fuel cell technicians, although a science and math related background and some post-high school education are generally required. An associate's degree from a properly accredited school with a concentration in fuel cell technology is generally sufficient for an entry-level job as a fuel cell technician.

There is no formal certification or licensing required for fuel cell technicians. Most organizations seek qualified applicants with minimum educational attainments and rely on on-the-job training and experience to develop their skills and knowledge. Fuel cell technology is cutting-edge and many fuel cell technicians and engineers are literally creating the knowledge base as they work.

Fuel cell technician jobs do not change much as workers advance. At the entry-level the fuel cell technician may have more supervision and work on narrower aspects of projects such as specific components of a single cell design. As they advance they will have less supervision and be in charge of larger aspects of a project or eventually of an entire project on their own.

A fuel cell technician must have excellent attention to detail and the ability to quickly synthesize and comprehend large amounts of data. Good interpersonal skills and communication skills are also essential due to the collaborative nature of the job. A fuel cell technician must have a very strong interest in and comfort with scientific subjects in general, including physics and chemistry, as fuel cells are typically controlled chemical reactions. Strong experience and comfort with a wide variety of computer systems is also necessary.

Computer software typically encountered by fuel cell technicians include:

- Autodesk AutoCAD software (computer-aided design)
- Data acquisition software

- Load simulators
- Spreadsheet software

JOB OUTLOOK

The BLS predicts slower-than-average job growth for fuel cell technicians in the next decade, estimating only 3 to 6 percent job growth in this field. This, however, reflects the economic outlook of 2008 and may no longer be accurate as the U.S. economic situation, specifically the automotive industry, improves. Additionally, fuel cells are beginning to be seen as solutions for larger-scale power needs, such as those of large institutions that have traditionally relied upon fossil-fuel–based generators of supplemental or emergency power. As a result, the field of organizations requiring the services of fuel cell technicians is growing.

Job security for fuel cell technicians is generally very high. There is little standardization in the technology and fuel cell technicians not only acquire specialized experience within an organization but are also often inventing this knowledge as they help create the specifications and procedures used in the design, testing, and fabrication of fuel cells for production.

EARNINGS

The average annual salary of a fuel cell technician is US$58,020. Entry-level fuel cell technicians can expect to earn approximately US$31,260 annually.

The highest-paying area of the United States for fuel cell technicians is the state of Maine, which offers an annual mean salary of US$79,490, followed by Washington, DC (US$77,400), Virginia (US$73,200), Washington (US$70,600), and Maryland (US$66,600).

The lowest-paying areas of the country for fuel cell technicians are Puerto Rico (US$27,600), Alabama (US$39,300), Kentucky (US$40,800), Arizona (US$47,100), and New Hampshire (US$47,200).

The BLS lists the petroleum and coal products industry as the top-paying industry for engineering technicians in general, paying an annual mean salary of US$88,790, followed by oil and gas extraction (US$73,020), aerospace manufacturing (US$71,070), technical and trade schools (US$70,920), and support activities for air transportation (US$69,330).

RELATED OCCUPATIONS

- Fuel cell engineers
- Avionics technicians
- Civil engineering technicians
- Electrical and electronics engineering technicians
- Electricians
- Materials engineers

SOURCES OF ADDITIONAL INFORMATION

Fuel Cell and Hydrogen Energy Association. http://www.fchea.org
The National Alternative Fuels Training Consortium. http://www.naftc.wvu.edu
Society of Automotive Engineers. http://www.sae.org

FURTHER READING

Andrews, John, and Bahman Shabani. "Re-envisioning the Role of Hydrogen in a Sustainable Energy Economy." *International Journal of Hydrogen Energy* 37(2): 1184–1203.

Crosby, Olivia. *New and Emerging Occupations.* Accessed March 8, 2012. http://www.bls.gov/opub/ooq/2002/fall/art02.pdf.

Dixon, Robert K., et al. "Development and Demonstration of Fuel Cell Vehicles and Supporting Infrastructure in China." *Mitigation and Adaptation Strategies for Global Change* 16 (7): 775–89.

Mohan, Vijay, et al. "Design of a Hydrogen Community." *International Journal of Hydrogen Energy* 37 (2): 1214–19.

MyFuture.com. *Fuel Cell Technicians.* Accessed March 8, 2012. http://www.myfuture.com/careers/salary/fuel-cell-technicians_17-3029.10.

Pernick, Ron. *Clean Energy Outlook: Significant Question Marks Dot the Landscape,* April 5, 2010. Accessed April 9, 2012. http://www.cleanedge.com/views/index.php%3Fid%3D6794.

Valdes-Dapena, Peter. "Hydrogen Fuel Cell Vehicles Join the Army." *CNNMoney,* February 23, 2012. Accessed March 8, 2012. http://money.cnn.com/2012/02/23/autos/army_hydrogen_fuel_cell/.

Williamson, Kari. "Fuel Cell Auxiliary Power Proving Efficient for Yorkshire Emergency Response Vehicles." *Fuel Cells Bulletin* 2011(10): 12–4.

FREIGHT FORWARDERS

NATURE OF THE WORK

A freight forwarder is responsible for incoming and outgoing shipments of goods, materials, or products. They choose the method of transport appropriate for the materials being transported, plan the route that the shipment will take, arrange for storage along the way if necessary, and arrange for all tariffs, tolls, and other costs. Freight forwarders are also responsible for submitting any paperwork required for border crossings or due to local regulations.

A freight forwarder must be familiar with all of the goods being shipped to and from their organization to choose the appropriate shipping method and prepare the route for the vehicles carrying it. They must be familiar with the terrain the shipment will travel across and all necessary local regulations. They are responsible for ensuring orders from external customers or internal shipping agents are filled accurately and delivered on schedule in good condition.

Freight forwarders have a key influence on the environmental impact of the shipping their organization or company engages in because they are expected to plot the most efficient routes for maximum fuel efficiency as well as routes that have the least negative environmental impact on the areas they traverse. Freight forwarders have direct control over the mode of transport as well as the loading of materials onto vehicles. They can thus use their intimate knowledge of the manner and route of transport to guarantee the most environmentally friendly shipping possible.

Freight forwarders also impact the environment by ensuring that goods under their control are shipped properly, kept in the correct environments along the route, and prevented from spoilage or breakage. This not only

---

AT A GLANCE FACT BOX

SOC: 43-5011.01
Preferred Education: High school diploma
Average Salary: US$37,150 annually
Other Information: Most freight forwarders transition to this career from other aspects of the shipping or travel industries

---

prevents waste but also avoids double shipments, which use twice the amount of resources no matter how carefully planned.

For example, in 2010 Danish shipping company Maersk implemented a policy known as "Slow Boat Shipping." By decreasing the average speed of their huge shipping vessels in half, they lengthened the time it takes goods to reach their destinations, but cut fuel costs and greenhouse gas emissions produced by these ships by roughly 30 percent. This concept is spreading to other modes of transport as freight forwarders worldwide seek ways to reduce costs and pollution by re-examining the way they run their shipping routes.

WORKING CONDITIONS

Freight forwarders generally work exclusively in office environments, doing most of their work using lines of communication such as phones, e-mail, text messages, and direct face-to-face interaction. The job is communication-focused, as the typical freight forwarder must interact with clients, coworkers, warehouse managers, customs agents, drivers, ship captains, rail line representatives, and so on, both domestically and internationally as needed.

Freight forwarders typically work standard 40-hour workweeks and receive industry-standard benefits. However, shipping materials globally is fraught with the unexpected, and overtime is expected from freight forwarders if their carefully arranged shipments go awry.

EMPLOYMENT

The U.S. Department of Labor's Bureau of Labor Statistics (BLS) states that there were approximately 85,900 freight forwarder jobs in the United States in 2008. Most of these jobs were located in the transportation industry in general, with 52 percent of these jobs found in support firms for the transportation industry, 19 percent in the air transportation industry, 8 percent in courier businesses, and 7 percent in the truck transportation industry.

A significant number of freight forwarders work independently as freelance or third-party vendors, using their experience and contacts to organize shipping for various clients.

The freight transportation arrangement industry is listed by the BLS as employing the most freight forwarders, with 36,470 positions recorded in 2008, followed by scheduled air transportation (11,850 jobs), couriers and express delivery services (7,070 jobs), support activities for air transportation (5,750 jobs), and general freight trucking (5,240 jobs).

California is listed as the U.S. state with the most freight forwarder jobs, with 12,190 jobs recorded in 2008, followed by Texas (9,080 jobs), Florida (8,310 jobs), New York (6,310 jobs), and Illinois (6,280 jobs).

TRAINING, OTHER QUALIFICATIONS, AND ADVANCEMENT

Most freight forwarders do not have advanced degrees. Most entry-level positions require only a high school diploma and basic computer skills.

Freight forwarders are typically licensed by the International Air Transport Association (IATA) to handle airfreight and the Federal Maritime Commission to handle ocean freight. These licenses are typically not required for entry-level positions and can be earned during the course of their career.

Most freight forwarders have some experience within a shipping- or travel-related industry and bring that experience with them in their new position. As a result, entry-level positions for freight forwarders have a lot of responsibility at the start and have very brief training or

probationary periods. Freight forwarders often work as freelancers or self-employed vendors. There is usually little or no supervision of employees.

People seeking careers in freight forwarding should have a firm grasp on logistics and organizational skills, be very comfortable with computer software applications and systems, and have excellent interpersonal communication skills. A potential freight forwarder needs to be highly organized and able to absorb a large amount of information in a short period of time because learning customs and international travel and shipping regulations is a requirement.

Specific software applications used by freight forwarders include:

- IES Ecellerate (compliance software)
- QuestaWeb TradeMaster QW (compliance software)
- AESDirect (user interface and database)
- Oracle JD Edwards EnterpriseOne (enterprise resource planning [ERP] software)
- SAP software (ERP)
- Arcline ArcFreight (materials, requirements, planning, logistics, and supply chain software)
- CEDAS Gateway (materials, requirements, planning, logistics, and supply chain software)
- CargoWise ediEnterprise (materials, requirements, planning, logistics, and supply chain software)
- Kewill Global Trade and Logistics (materials, requirements, planning, logistics, and supply chain software)
- RedBerry Logistics (materials, requirements, planning, logistics, and supply chain software)

JOB OUTLOOK

The BLS considers the outlook for freight forwarders to be very bright, predicting a 24 percent increase in available jobs by 2018, an increase of over 20,000 positions. Freight forwarder jobs are very susceptible to global economic conditions, however, and any significant or long-term economic downturn can result in a lower-than-expected job growth for this career.

The increased focus on efficient and environmentally conscious shipping is driving the growth of freight forwarder jobs. Not only are companies and organizations faced with increasingly stringent regulations on emissions and the carbon footprints of international freight, but they are realizing that logistics can be used to reduce costs and increase profits. Freight forwarders, as the workers with the most influence over the costs and impact of shipping routes and procedures, are in demand to streamline and optimize shipping routes and to develop new approaches that use less fuel and generate less pollution and waste.

The growing influence of the Internet on consumer spending has also affected the growth of the freight forwarder career, as consumers now expect to order any item online and have it shipped to them in a reasonable amount of time. This has put tremendous pressure on companies to reexamine their shipping and warehouse strategies, requiring smaller, more numerous warehouses and storage facilities to enable faster shipping to larger areas, as well as shipping routes that have been expertly reviewed to squeeze every last efficiency from existing resources. This new pressure has created more job opportunities for freight forwarders as companies must expand their shipping operations to remain competitive while maintaining minimum environmental standards.

EARNINGS

The average annual salary for freight forwarders is US$37,150. This ranges from US$22,110 for entry-level to US$58,400 for experienced freight forwarders.

The top-paying industries for freight forwarders are support activities for water transportation (US$56,660); the U.S. federal government (US$52,260); deep sea, coastal, and Great Lakes water transportation (US$50,290); rail transportation (US$48,050); and specialized freight trucking (US$45,650).

The top-paying areas of the United States for freight forwarders are Connecticut (US$54,700), Wyoming (US$49,700), Washington (US$49,150), Massachusetts (US$46,360), and Nebraska (US$44,500).

RELATED OCCUPATIONS

- Postal service clerks
- Postal service mail sorters, processors, and processing machine operators
- Shipping, receiving, and traffic clerks
- Weighers, measurers, checkers, samplers, and recordkeepers

SOURCES OF ADDITIONAL INFORMATION

Federal Maritime Commission. http://www.fmc.gov
International Air Transport Association. http://www.iata.org
International Federation of Freight Forwarders Associations. http://www.fiata.com
National Customs Brokers and Forwarders Association of America, Inc. http://www.ncbfaa.org

FURTHER READING

Azadian, Farshid, Alper E. Murat, and Ratna Babu Chinnam. "Dynamic Routing of Time-Sensitive Air Cargo Using Real-time Information." *Transportation Research Part E: Logistic and Transportation Review* 48.1 (2012): 355–372.

Bureau of Labor Statistics, U.S. Department of Labor. "Cargo and Freight Agents." In *Occupational Outlook Handbook, 2010–2011 Edition.* Accessed March 26, 2012. http://www.bls.gov/oco/ocos281.htm.

Export.gov. *What Is a Freight Forwarder?* Accessed March 9, 2012. http://export.gov/logistics/eg_main_018144.asp.

Inside Careers. *Freight Forwarding.* Accessed March 9, 2012. http://www.insidecareers.co.uk/__802574d80054b660.nsf/id/8dgkyqakim!opendocument.

Krajewska, Marta Anna, and Herbert Kopfer. "Transportation Planning in Freight Forwarding Companies." *European Journal of Operational Research* 197.2 (2009): 741–751.

Rosenthal, Elisabeth. "Slow Trip Across Sea Aids Profit and Environment." *The New York Times,* February 16, 2010. Accessed March 9, 2012. http://www.nytimes.com/2010/02/17/business/energy-environment/17speed.html.

Xue, J., and K.K. Lai. "A Study on Cargo Forwarding Decisions." *Computers & Industrial Engineering* 33.3-4 (1997): 63–66.

DISPATCHERS, EXCEPT POLICE, FIRE, AND AMBULANCE

NATURE OF THE WORK

Dispatchers work to schedule staff, equipment, or vehicles to satisfy repair, installation, or delivery needs. This involves ensuring work crews are fully staffed at appropriate times, equipment orders are filled, and transport is arranged on a timely basis. Dispatchers also must stay in touch with crews and drivers in the field, working continually to ensure that appointments are kept and workers are not idle.

Dispatchers must be experts at coordination and scheduling, able to estimate how long service calls and installations will take so that crews can be kept busy at all times but still have enough time to complete their work. They must ensure that transport and equipment is scheduled appropriately so that workers have the materials and tools needed at each job site. They must also ensure that there are enough resources to compensate for vehicle breakdowns, waste, and equipment malfunction in the field.

Dispatchers also work for shipping companies and coordinate deliveries of purchased goods. This involves coordinating a large fleet of trucks or other vehicles, reviewing orders and organizing packages, planning routes, and staying in touch with drivers to update customers on the progress of their shipments and to update drivers on travel conditions or other situations that may affect their ability to make deliveries.

Dispatchers are also employed to manage rail systems, which are fleets of vehicles that travel on fixed rails. Route organization for these fleets is limited to available lines. This can make the efficient ordering of transport more complex and heightens the possibility of a crash if the dispatcher does not focus closely on what stock is moving along the existing rail lines at a given moment.

AT A GLANCE FACT BOX

SOC: 43-5032.00
Preferred Education: High school diploma
Average Salary: US$34,560 annually
Other Information: Although most dispatchers do not belong to labor unions or other organizations, a significant number do belong to the Service Employees International Union (SEIU)

Because of their control over scheduling and resource management, dispatchers have a large amount of influence over the environmental impact of the organizations for which they work. Dispatchers must ensure that available resources are used as efficiently as possible, loading vehicles with workers and equipment to use the fewest vehicles possible to cover the largest area possible, and to pre-plan service and installation visits to reduce or eliminate waste and redundant visits to the same work site.

WORKING CONDITIONS

Dispatchers work in office settings, almost exclusively using computer and communication technology such as radio and telephones to coordinate with garages, drivers, workers, and customers. They generally work standard 40-hour work weeks and enjoy industry-standard benefits.

Dispatchers almost always work indoors in climate-controlled situations and rarely need to travel or be on-site. Dispatchers often work rotating shifts, however, and may find themselves working during different parts of the day, including late at night or early in the morning.

Dispatchers must gather information constantly, monitoring traffic and weather conditions and staying in touch with both workers and customers to ensure they have the most recent information.

Stress is a natural concern for dispatchers. The more complex an organization is, the more difficult it can be to coordinate large numbers of vehicles, workers, and equipment between multiple job sites. Another cause of stress for dispatchers is the large number of things they have little or no control over, such as traffic patterns, weather, and vehicle or equipment breakdowns. As a result even the most carefully planned work day can have completely unpredictable problems that must be surmounted in real time to keep all appointments while still maintaining a high level of efficiency and environmentally friendly resource management.

Dispatchers work in very sedentary environments, sitting for long periods of time, and suffer typical health-related problems stemming from this lifestyle, including lower back pain, eyestrain, and cardiovascular complications. Care must be taken to exercise and stay in good physical shape despite the requirements of the job.

EMPLOYMENT

The U.S. Department of Labor's Bureau of Labor Statistics (BLS) estimates there were 180,540 dispatcher jobs in the United States as of May 2010. The industry employing the most dispatchers is general freight trucking, with 24,040 jobs, followed by local governments (12,470 jobs), building equipment contractors (10,580 jobs), specialized freight trucking (9,060 jobs), and the taxi and limousine service industry (7,330 jobs).

California is the U.S. state with the largest number of dispatcher jobs (19,710) as of May 2010, followed by Texas (18,920 jobs), New York (13,500 jobs), Florida (9,500 jobs), and Illinois (7,440 jobs).

TRAINING, OTHER QUALIFICATIONS, AND ADVANCEMENT

Dispatchers generally do not need an advanced degree. A high school diploma is generally sufficient for most entry-level jobs. Career advancement involves on-the-job experience and training.

Generally, no certifications or licenses are required for this career. However, dispatchers working in the aviation field will need an aircraft dispatcher certification, administered by the Federal Aviation Administration.

Although entry-level dispatchers may spend some time working under the supervision of an experienced dispatcher, generally dispatchers of any level work on their own. As a dispatcher gains experience and seniority, advancement to a supervisory role in larger organizations that require more than one dispatcher be on duty may be possible. Advancement is difficult for many dispatcher jobs unless the organization is large enough to need several dispatchers on duty at a time or has several different fleets of vehicles or teams of workers to be coordinated.

An organized, detail-oriented mindset is crucial for dispatchers, who must coordinate large amounts of disparate information and make immediate changes to schedules and routes in response. A high tolerance to stress is also necessary because the job can be unpredictable and fast-paced. A comfort with technology, including radio equipment and computer software, is also necessary.

Specific software applications usually encountered by dispatchers include:

- Air-Trak Cloudberry (mobile location based services software)
- Global positioning system (GPS) software (mobile location based services software)
- Bornemann Associates Flight Plan (aviation ground support software)
- Sabre software (aviation ground support software)
- Computer-aided dispatching auto routing software
- Rail Traffic Track Warrant Control System

JOB OUTLOOK

Job opportunities for dispatchers are expected to decline slightly over the coming decade. (The BLS predicts a 3 percent decline by 2018.) This is due in large part to the increasing efficiency of established dispatchers and the technologies available to them. Computerized scheduling and tracking software enables dispatchers to handle larger fleets of vehicles and staff without additional help, and an increased presence of automated dispatching technology allows organizations to hire fewer dispatchers to supervise them.

This transition to computerized, automated dispatching systems, however, does represent opportunity because older workers who are unfamiliar with these new systems retire and need to be replaced. Job-seekers with experience with these systems or an ability to learn computer software applications and other digital systems will find sufficient job opportunities as the older workforce steps down or seeks jobs that do not require these skills.

Although no certifications or ongoing education are required for dispatchers as a rule, the technological base for the job is changing rapidly, and dispatchers must stay abreast of new developments, not only to remain employed but also to attain the high standards for efficiency and environmental impact held by their employers and local governments. Companies and organizations that employ large fleets of vehicles and teams of workers are under ongoing pressure to reduce their emissions and environmental impact while maintaining high levels of customer service and satisfaction. As a result, new technologies that empower dispatchers to have real-time control over their fleets and staff are being adopted constantly. It is incumbent on dispatchers to stay up-to-date on these new technologies as they are adopted.

EARNINGS

According to the BLS, the average annual salary for dispatchers was US$34,560 in 2008. Entry-level salaries for this career average US$21,030 whereas experienced workers can earn as much as US$58,610.

The top-paying industries for dispatchers are scheduled air transportation (US$60,120), rail transportation (US$59,530), scientific research and development services (US$58,380), natural gas distribution (US$56,310), and the U.S. postal service (US$54,880).

The top-paying U.S. states for dispatchers are Delaware (US$43,020), Connecticut (US$42,940), Wyoming (US$42,270), Alaska (US$42,220), and Nebraska (US$41,610).

RELATED OCCUPATIONS

- Licensing examiners and inspectors
- Counter and rental clerks
- Procurement clerks
- Hotel, motel, and resort desk clerks
- Reservation and transportation ticket agents and travel clerks
- Police, fire, and ambulance dispatchers
- Subway and streetcar operators

SOURCES OF ADDITIONAL INFORMATION

American Train Dispatchers Association. http://atdd .homestead.com

Federal Aviation Administration. http://www.faa.gov

Mass Transit Magazine. http://www.masstransitmag.com

World Airline Dispatcher Schools. http://www.fltdisp.com

FURTHER READING

Derby, Ann, and Jan Kijowski. "Real-Time Benefits." *Mass Transit,* April 2, 2011. Accessed March 9, 2012. http://www.masstransitmag.com/article/10248313/ real-time-benefits.

Dreier, Troy. "iTruckIt Boosts Package Delivery Efficiency." *PC Magazine Online,* January 4, 2011. Accessed April 9, 2012. http://appscout.pcmag.com/ apple-ios-iphone-ipad-ipod/268960-itruckit-boosts-package-delivery-efficiency.

Getline, Meryl. "What Exactly Does an Airline Dispatcher Do?" *USA Today,* May 9, 2005. Updated May 10, 2005. Accessed March 9, 2012. http:// www.usatoday.com/travel/columnist/getline/ 2005-05-09-ask-the-captain_x.htm.

Gonnerman, Jennifer. "The Town Car 500: Livery-Cab Drivers Are Racing for a Dwindling Number of Calls, and a Lone Teenage Dispatcher Is Referee of the Road." *New York,* February 22, 2009. Accessed April 9, 2012. http://nymag.com/news/features/54678.

SHIPPING, RECEIVING, AND TRAFFIC CLERKS

NATURE OF THE WORK

A shipping, receiving, and traffic clerk supervises and expedites all shipments arriving or leaving an organization. They receive and review packing orders, assemble shipments, package them, address them, and ensure they have prepared the necessary paperwork including documents such as bills of lading, customs forms, and packing slips. When shipments are received, they examine the address to ensure the shipments have arrived in the correct location, prepare them for internal routing or distribution, and check enclosed documentation to ensure proper procedures were followed. They also inspect received goods to ensure no damage has occurred en route.

Record keeping is also an important role of a shipping, receiving, and traffic clerk's daily work. Data about a shipment's origin or destination, weight, contents, and associated shipping fees must be kept for both accounting and legal requirements, and it is the job of a shipping, receiving, and traffic clerk to ensure that these records are accurate. Shipping, receiving, and traffic clerks are also expected to track shipments and predict arrival times and shipping costs accurately.

Shipping, receiving, and traffic clerks have an influence over the environmental impact of the organizations they work for because they have a direct and lasting influence on the efficiency, fuel economy, and emissions of all shipments going in and out of a facility. Shipping, receiving, and traffic clerks use their organizational skills and the automation equipment at their disposal to load trucks and other vehicles as efficiently as possible, reducing the number of vehicles required to move goods from place to place. They also create and refine loading and

unloading procedures, which can be used to pack more goods into existing vehicles, reducing the numbers of polluting vehicles.

WORKING CONDITIONS

Most shipping, receiving, and traffic clerks work indoors, typically in office or warehouse environments, frequently moving between the two. There is frequently a mailroom or office where records are kept and communication with outside contacts takes place. In smaller organizations, this area often doubles as the shipping and receiving area where packages are prepared and received. In larger organizations there may be a warehouse area where the shipping, receiving, and traffic clerk must also work.

Most shipping, receiving, and traffic clerks work a standard 40-hour work week and receive industry-standard benefits. Some lifting and other physically strenuous activity

---

> ## AT A GLANCE FACT BOX
>
> **SOC:** 43-5071.00
> **Preferred Education:** High school diploma or GED
> **Average Salary:** US$27,660 annually
> **Other Information:** In some larger organizations, the roles of a shipping, receiving, and traffic clerk may be split into three distinct positions: shipping clerk, receiving clerk, and traffic clerk

---

may be expected of the shipping, receiving, and traffic clerk, especially in smaller organizations that may not have dedicated warehouse or mailroom staff. Mechanical assistance is often present to move heavy or large items, but even in these situations some physical exertion is expected.

Shipping, receiving, and traffic clerks may be required to work overtime during periods of heavy shipping activity for the organization or company. During these periods even clerks who are not normally required to perform heavy lifting or transport may find themselves asked to do so.

EMPLOYMENT

According to the U.S. Department of Labor's Bureau of Labor Statistics (BLS), there were approximately 687,850 shipping, receiving, and traffic clerk jobs in May 2010. Of these, the couriers and express delivery services industry employed the most, with approximately 45,670 jobs. This is followed by the warehousing and storage industry (31,760 jobs), the employment services industry (30,940 jobs), department stores (26,370 jobs), and the building material and supplies dealers industry (22,630 jobs).

Although shipping, receiving, and traffic clerk jobs can be found throughout the United States, they tend to be concentrated in heavily populated urban areas where shipping centers such as ports, warehouses, and routing depots are located.

California boasts the most shipping, receiving, and traffic clerk jobs in the United States, with 90,960 jobs recorded in May 2010. Texas follows with 56,470 jobs, then New York (41,370 jobs), Florida (40,540 jobs), and Ohio (32,400 jobs).

TRAINING, OTHER QUALIFICATIONS, AND ADVANCEMENT

Shipping, receiving, and traffic clerks typically do not need advanced degrees. A high school diploma is usually sufficient for an entry-level position as a shipping, receiving, and traffic clerk. On-the-job training and field experience are often all that is necessary for continuing education and advancement.

There are no formal certifications or licenses required for shipping, receiving, and traffic clerks. However, certification as a Certified Logistics Professional (CLP), which is administered by the International Warehouse Logistics Association, can be beneficial for both first-time job seekers and established shipping, receiving, and traffic clerks who wish to advance in their careers.

Shipping, receiving, and traffic clerks do not have clearly defined advancement paths. With experience, shipping, receiving, and traffic clerks in larger organizations may take on supervisory roles, managing staff and multiple facilities. The intimate knowledge of product lines, vendors, and procedures within an organization that shipping, receiving, and traffic clerks develop sometimes enables them to move into different career paths within an organization, such as purchasing managers or other shipping-related careers.

Shipping, receiving, and traffic clerks must be very organized and comfortable with tremendous amounts of data. Every shipment in or out has an associated field of data describing it, and this must be sorted quickly, with all requirements pertaining to the shipment's safe handling and legal processing satisfied efficiently. They must be physically able to lift heavy objects and to move around a chaotic and sometimes dangerous environment such as an active warehouse or factory floor. They must also have good interpersonal communication skills because they spend most of their day interacting with other employees or third-party vendors, customs officials, and internal and external customers. A comfort level with computers and certain computer applications is also necessary.

Specific software applications often encountered by shipping, receiving, and traffic clerks include:

- ADi SmartBOL (materials requirements planning logistics and supply chain software)
- eLading (Bill of Lading software)
- Barcode labeling software (label-making software)
- Endicia Internet Postage (label-making software)
- Exact MAX (enterprise resource planning [ERP] software)
- SAP software (ERP software)

JOB OUTLOOK

Automation is adversely affecting the number of shipping, receiving, and traffic clerk positions expected to exist in the future. The BLS predicts a decline of approximately 7 percent in the available jobs by 2018 as machine-based sorting, labeling, and picking becomes more common and affordable to a larger number of organizations.

However, the job outlook is still considered to be bright because of expected turnover as experienced shipping, receiving, and traffic clerks retire or leave for other occupations.

Also, the prospects for future shipping, receiving, and traffic clerk jobs will be brightened by the increased focus on environmental issues because automated systems cannot be relied upon to plot fuel-efficient shipments or understand the environmental impact of different shipping techniques and different goods shipped. Much of the automation that has reduced the availability of shipping, receiving, and traffic clerk jobs has been focused on replacing human labor in the sorting, labeling, loading, tracking and unloading of goods. As it becomes more essential that shipments be processed with environmental concerns foremost, the supervision and planning of an experienced worker will once again be mandatory and job opportunities will increase.

Another green aspect affecting job growth in this field is the changing manner in which shipments are handled. Companies are moving away from centralized mega-warehouses and are embracing a more modern, Internet-inspired system of smaller, more numerous warehouses in key areas of the world. This system allows goods to be shipped much more quickly because they are sourced from nearby warehouses rather than being transported around the globe. Each of these more efficient shipping centers will require a shipping, receiving, and traffic clerk to monitor and supervise the shipping operations.

EARNINGS

The average annual salary for shipping, receiving, and traffic clerks was estimated at US$27,660 in 2008 by the BLS. It should be noted that salaries as low as US$18,000 per year are not uncommon for entry-level positions.

Top-paying industries for this occupation were led by the U.S. postal service, which averaged US$54,680 annually. The U.S. postal service was followed by the telecommunications industry (US$46,160), the U.S. federal government (US$45,090), motor vehicle manufacturing (US$44,000), and water, sewage, and other systems (US$43,880).

The top-paying area of the United States for shipping, receiving, and traffic clerks is Washington, DC, which offers a US$42,740 mean annual wage. This is followed by Alaska (US$39,880), Washington (US$35,890), Massachusetts (US$33,240), and Minnesota (US$32,570).

RELATED OCCUPATIONS

- Cargo and freight agents
- Material moving occupations
- Postal service clerks
- Production, planning, and expediting clerks
- Stock clerks and order fillers

SOURCES OF ADDITIONAL INFORMATION

International Warehouse Logistics Association. http://www.iwla.com

Warehousing Education and Research Council. http://www.werc.org

FURTHER READING

America's Career InfoNet. *Occupation Profile*. Accessed March 9, 2012. http://www.careerinfonet.org/occ_rep.asp?next=occ_rep&Level=&optstatus=011111111&jobfam=43&id=1&nodeid=2&soccode=435071&stfips=34&x=54&y=5.

Bureau of Labor Statistics, U.S. Department of Labor. "43-5071 Shipping, Receiving, and Traffic Clerks." In *Occupational Employment Statistics: Occupational Employment and Wages, May 2010*. Accessed March 9, 2012. http://www.bls.gov/oes/current/oes435071.htm.

O*NET OnLine. *My Next Move: Shipping, Receiving, and Traffic Clerks*. Accessed March 9, 2012. http://www.mynextmove.org/profile/summary/43-5071.00.

RAIL-TRACK LAYING
AND MAINTENANCE EQUIPMENT
OPERATORS

NATURE OF THE WORK

A rail-track laying and maintenance equipment operator plans, installs, and does repair and maintenance work on standard- and narrow-gauge railroad equipment wherever rail lines are used, including freight and commuter rail lines as well as plat yards, mines, and quarries. This includes choosing appropriate ground for the initial laying of track, preparing the site and installing the track, and subsequently ensuring the track remains in usable condition. Walking the track to spot and repair damage, working to clear tracks of ice and snow during inclement weather, and sometimes manually adjusting switches using appropriate tools are common maintenance duties for a rail-track laying and maintenance equipment operator.

A rail-track laying and maintenance equipment operator directly manipulates rail tracks using a variety of equipment. They will often use portable grinders to effect track repairs in the field, cut rails to necessary lengths using specialized rail saws in a plant environment, shift and raise rail tracks using hydraulic lifts, and drill holes through rail tracks or other materials using powerful metal drills.

Although the day-to-day work of the rail-track laying and maintenance equipment operator has not changed much in light of the recent focus on green technologies and environmentally sound economic practices, the rail-track laying and maintenance equipment operator is a key element in the green economy because rail travel will be increasingly used by green-focused industries seeking low-emissions ways to transport materials and equipment. Many large trucking companies have invested in rail stock to move truck trailers "piggyback"

AT A GLANCE FACT BOX
SOC: 47-4061.00
Preferred Education: High school diploma
Average Salary: US$46,230 annually
Other Information: Unlike trucking, air freight, and shipping companies, railroad companies create and maintain their own infrastructure and are not reliant on governments to invest in new equipment or facilities

on flatbed rail cars rather than hauling them via fossil fuel powered trucks. This can be a more fuel-efficient way to move freight, and reduces emissions dramatically. As more industries seek to cut costs and improve their environmental standing by switching from traditional trucking patterns to rail-based shipping and hauling, the green importance of the rail-track laying and maintenance equipment operator increases.

Additionally, all seven major U.S. freight railroads have voluntarily joined with the U.S. Environmental Protection Agency (EPA) to form the SmartWay Transport Partnership, designed to reduce the greenhouse gas emissions and air pollution generated by rail travel. This guarantees that railroads will be in the forefront of all domestic green initiatives, making the role of the rail-track laying and maintenance equipment operator even more important.

WORKING CONDITIONS

The job of the rail-track laying and maintenance equipment operator is a very active and physical one with large amounts of time spent outdoors in various weather conditions as well as in potentially dangerous garage and plant conditions where heavy equipment must be operated to move and manipulate the heavy rail materials. Rail-track laying and maintenance equipment operators are expected to walk long distances to inspect existing tracks for damage.

Rail-track laying and maintenance equipment operators must be physically capable of handling heavy hand tools and operating large-scale equipment. Large hand-held wrenches are commonly employed for small-scale repairs and adjustments along rail lines.

Work schedules for rail-track laying and maintenance equipment operators tend to be organized into shifts. Although many rail-track laying and maintenance equipment operators will work the same shift for long periods of time, it is common for workers to be switched from one shift to another to accommodate changing priorities and address manpower shortages or to meet specific expertise requirements. As such, a rail-track laying and maintenance equipment operator must be prepared to work at any hour of the day.

EMPLOYMENT

As of May 2010 the U.S. Department of Labor's Bureau of Labor Statistics (BLS) estimated there were 15,520 rail-track laying and maintenance equipment operator jobs in the United States. The industry with the highest levels of employment for rail-track laying and maintenance equipment operators was rail transportation, with 10,740 jobs recorded, followed by the other heavy and civil engineering construction industry (1,470 jobs), the support activities for rail transportation industry (500 jobs), and coal mining (40 jobs).

Because the rail transportation industry dominates employment for this career, rail-track laying and maintenance equipment operator jobs can be found nationwide. The states offering the most rail-track laying and maintenance equipment operator jobs as of May 2010 were Illinois (1,140 jobs), Minnesota (620 jobs), Ohio (550 jobs), Oklahoma (500 jobs), and Pennsylvania (490 jobs).

TRAINING, OTHER QUALIFICATIONS, AND ADVANCEMENT

Typically, no specific educational attainment or training is required to become a rail-track laying and maintenance equipment operator aside from a high school diploma and good physical condition.

No formal certification or licensure is required for rail-track laying and maintenance equipment operators. Most of the training occurs on the job and in the field.

An entry-level rail-track laying and maintenance equipment operator may start work as part of a team under a supervising operator. Over time, as these operators gain experience within an organization and expertise on the specific rail and equipment being used, they may advance to supervisory roles themselves, with a team of operators working under their direction to lay and maintain large rail networks.

The two most important personal traits necessary to be a rail-track laying and maintenance equipment operator are comfort with mechanical work and good physical condition and stamina. It is a very physical, hands-on job that requires an ease with mechanical equipment and the ability to work on your feet and with your hands for long periods of time in all weather conditions. The ability to learn via observation and to absorb large amounts of information specific to the rail network being maintained is also crucial, as a rail-track laying and maintenance equipment operator must be able to identify and solve problems when performing visual inspections of the rail.

Typically, rail-track laying and maintenance equipment operators will encounter the following software applications as part of their job:

- Spreadsheet software
- Time accounting software
- Database user interface and query software

JOB OUTLOOK

The job outlook for rail-track laying and maintenance equipment operators is considered very bright, with job growth expected to be between 14 percent and 19 percent over the next 10 years, with a projected 6,500 new jobs by 2018.

This strong job growth is partially because of the ongoing focus on the green economy and environmental concerns throughout the country. Rail is considered a strong, green alternative to trucking in many industries, providing cheaper and more environmentally friendly transport. On the other hand, despite the calls to reduce reliance on fossil fuels, mining for coal continues to grow as an industry, which also requires new track to be laid and maintained. This will also increase demand for rail-track laying and maintenance equipment operators.

Job security for existing rail-track laying and maintenance equipment operators is very good. The more experience an operator gains, the more vital they become to the operations of their employer. Because there will be such a large growth in this industry, companies and organizations will work hard to retain their operators. Organizations that already employ rail solutions as part of a green initiative will likely increase these investments over time because new regulations regarding emissions and pollution disposal are likely to increase.

EARNINGS

The average annual salary for a rail-track laying and maintenance equipment operator is US$46,230 as of May 2010, according to the BLS. At the entry level, an operator can expect to earn about US$30,200 annually and those with a great deal of experience can expect to earn up to US$62,900 in certain industries.

The top-paying industry for rail-track laying and maintenance equipment operators is the coal mining industry, which offers an annual mean salary of US$47,540. This is followed by the rail transportation industry (US$47,350 mean annual salary), the nonresidential building construction industry (US$38,720 mean annual salary), other heavy and civil engineering construction (US$34,420 mean annual salary), and support activities for rail transportation (US$31,030 mean annual salary).

The top-paying state for rail-track laying and maintenance equipment operators is New Mexico, which offers a mean annual salary of US$54,810. This is followed by Utah (US$49,400 mean annual salary), New Jersey (US$48,960 mean annual salary), Delaware (US$47,820 mean annual salary), and Iowa (US$46,960 mean annual salary).

RELATED OCCUPATIONS

Other jobs that have a similar skill set to rail-track laying and maintenance equipment operators are:

- Logging equipment operators
- Paving, surfacing, and tamping equipment operators
- Pile-driver operators
- Operating engineers and other construction equipment operators
- Highway maintenance workers
- Excavating and loading machine and dragline operators
- Mine shuttle car operators

SOURCES OF ADDITIONAL INFORMATION

Association of American Railroads. http://www.aar.org
The Brotherhood of Maintenance of Way Employees. http://www.bmwed.org
Freight Rail Works. http://www.freightrailworks.org
U.S. Railroad News. http://www.usrailroadnews.com

FURTHER READING

Bureau of Labor Statistics, U.S. Department of Labor. "47-4061 Rail-Track Laying and Maintenance Equipment Operators." In *Occupational Employment and Wages, May 2010.* Accessed March 19, 2012. http://www.bls.gov/oes/current/oes474061.htm.
Lockridge, Deborah. "The Changing Face of Trucking Part 2: Riding the Rails." *Truckinginfo,* June 16, 2010. Accessed March 19, 2012. http://www.truckinginfo.com/news/news-detail.asp?news_id=70724.
"Major U.S. Railroads Partner with EPA." *Business and the Environment,* August 2005: 11.
"Skyrocketing Oil Prices." *U.S. Rail News,* March 23, 2005: 46.
"U.S. Railroads Post Robust Earnings, Despite Weak Economic Conditions." *U.S. Rail News,* April 30, 2008: 3.

AUTOMOTIVE SPECIALTY
TECHNICIANS

NATURE OF THE WORK

Automotive specialty technicians are automotive repair workers who specialize in one component or aspect of car repair, in contrast to a general automotive technician or repair worker, who would be expected to address a wide range of problems across all systems. Automotive specialty technicians may specialize in the suspension, the brakes, or the exhaust systems, or even in one component of the engine. This allows the automotive specialty technician to amass a deep knowledge of their particular specialty and quickly and decisively diagnose and address any problems.

Automotive specialty technicians examine vehicles to determine the probable cause of problems and offer cost estimates for work to customers before performing repairs. They dismantle components and perform cleaning, adjustment, or replacement as necessary. They often use advanced and dedicated computer equipment to interface with on-board computer systems in the vehicle to aid in diagnosing problems and identifying solutions.

Automotive specialty technicians are important to the burgeoning green economy for several reasons. Regular maintenance and repair of any vehicle will keep it running at peak efficiency, thus ensuring the most fuel-efficient performance and the lowest-possible emissions even from standard fossil fuel burning engines. Even non-mechanical maintenance such as proper tire inflation can have a tremendous impact on fuel efficiency and emissions in newer automobiles. Automotive specialty technicians also possess detailed knowledge of specific components of a vehicle, enabling them to make precise calibrations, both mechanical and, in some cases, to the on-board computers, that can result in greatly improved performance in both fuel consumption and emissions levels.

AT A GLANCE FACT BOX

SOC: 49-3023.02
Preferred Education: High school diploma or vocational training
Preferred Specialty: Automotive service technology
Average Salary: US$38,200 annually
Other Information: While most high school-level automotive service programs are not considered sufficient training for an automotive specialty technician, they can be a good foundation for further training

---

Automotive specialty technicians have grown in importance as automobiles have become more complex, with computer-controlled components to most engines and other systems of the car. With the advent of electric, hybrid, and fuel-cell–based automobiles, their importance has grown even more. Alternative-energy automobiles are complex and require specialized knowledge to keep them running at top efficiency.

WORKING CONDITIONS

Automotive specialty technicians work most often in garage or machine-shop settings, usually indoors. These are generally very noisy conditions with dangerous equipment in use at all times and are sometimes not climate-controlled. Automotive specialty technicians spend much of their time standing or working in cramped and dirty conditions.

Automotive specialty technicians routinely work around and with dangerous equipment, including welding equipment, pneumatic wrenches, hydraulic lifts, engine cranes, machine lathes, and grinding tools. They also commonly work with sophisticated computer equipment designed to calibrate and detect damage to the complicated computer-controlled systems in modern vehicles.

Automotive specialty technicians also come in contact with dangerous materials, such as the chemicals contained in solid fuel-cell technology or electric/hybrid vehicles. These materials can be dangerous and require careful handling.

Most automotive specialty technicians work a standard 40-hour work week; however, evening and weekend hours can be needed to comply with customer needs.

EMPLOYMENT

Automotive specialty technicians held about 587,510 jobs in the United States as of May 2010, according to the U.S. Department of Labor's Bureau of Labor Statistics (BLS). The majority of these were located in the auto dealership and auto repair sectors, led by the automotive repair and maintenance industry (220,680 jobs). Automobile dealers (185,670 jobs) follow, along with automotive parts, accessories, and tire stores (57,620 jobs), local government (19,820 jobs), and gasoline stations (19,430 jobs).

Population density is the main factor in the number of automotive specialty technician jobs by region because higher populations naturally have more cars in need of repair and maintenance. It is not surprising, therefore, that California has the highest number of automotive specialty technician jobs in the country, with 54,880 recorded in May 2010 by the BLS, followed by Texas with 43,270 jobs, New York with 35,350 jobs, Florida with 35,150 jobs, and Pennsylvania with 31,740 jobs.

TRAINING, OTHER QUALIFICATIONS, AND ADVANCEMENT

Few automotive specialty technicians have a bachelor's degree, although most have some training beyond high school. This training is usually from a vocational school program that specializes in automotive service technology. High school vocational programs that participate in the Automotive Youth Educational Systems (AYES) program are sometimes counted as acceptable substitutes for a vocational program post-high school.

Some automotive specialty technicians do earn associate's degrees from community college programs or similar institutions. However, this is frequently not necessary to find employment or to advance in an existing job. Two-year community college programs are also sometimes used to gain specific training by taking selective courses without taking the time to earn an associate's degree.

A National Institute for Automotive Service Excellence (ASE) certification is often very helpful in finding employment as an automotive specialty technician or in advancing within an established career. Administered by the National Institute for Automotive Service Excellence, these are hands-on tests designed to fit all levels of experience. As automotive specialty technicians advance in their careers, they commonly return to earn higher certifications in line with their work experience.

At the entry level, automotive specialty technicians commonly work as trainee technicians, technicians' helpers, or lubrication workers under the supervision of experienced technicians. Many businesses include formal training for their automotive specialty technicians as part of on-the-job training, ensuring their technicians are familiar with their product line and service needs. Typically, it takes two to five years of work experience to become a fully qualified automotive specialty technician. Employers increasingly send automotive specialty technicians to manufacturer-sponsored or -owned training centers to be trained in the newest technology.

Automotive specialty technicians must be comfortable working with their hands and with mechanical work in general. They must be in good physical condition, able to lift heavy objects and perform physically taxing work. They must also have good interpersonal communication skills and be comfortable with computer systems.

Software commonly encountered by automotive specialty technicians include:

- Alliance Automotive Shop Controller (facilities management software)
- Mitchell OnDemand5 Manager (facilities management software)
- Amcom AUTOS2000 (facilities management software)
- CC2/CC3 body shop management software (facilities management software)
- Scott Systems MaxxTraxx Pro (facilities management software)
- Genisys Fast Fixes (database reporting software)
- Pathfinder (database reporting software)
- ARSIS Automotive Repair Shop Invoice System software
- Hunter WinAlign (analytical or scientific software)
- Nexiq Tech HDS Suite for Palm (analytical or scientific software)

JOB OUTLOOK

Job growth for automotive specialty technicians is projected to be slower than average between 2008 and 2018, with just 5 percent job growth predicted by the BLS. One reason for this is the focus on continuing training that is traditionally part of the car repair job duties; automobile mechanics have been forced to keep up with the changing technology and new designs of automobiles for decades. This means that older automotive specialty technicians, and car repair workers in general, aggressively seek training in new technology, techniques, and car designs, staying current and thus avoiding being replaced by younger workers with more recent training.

However, steady population growth throughout the United States also indicates more cars being sold and operated, so demand for trained automotive specialty technicians should remain steady. A lack of specially trained technicians means employers have some difficulty finding the appropriate technicians to fill open slots, and this will help the job market in this area as well.

The increasing focus on green technologies, fuel efficiency, and emissions reduction will also drive demand for automotive specialty technicians. Requirements for fuel and emissions standards will continue to make automobiles more complex as new systems, often computer-controlled, are added to existing car designs to increase performance. Automotive specialty technicians will be needed to keep these delicate mechanisms calibrated properly and functioning at top efficiency.

EARNINGS

The average annual salary for automotive specialty technicians is US$38,200. At the entry level, an automotive specialty technician can expect to earn about US$20,200 annually. Experienced automotive specialty technicians can sometimes earn an average annual salary of US$59,590 in the right industry.

The top-paying industries for automotive specialty technicians are computer systems design and related services (US$64,910 mean annual salary), scientific research and development services (US$64,280 mean annual salary), food manufacturing (US$62,700 mean annual salary), motor vehicle manufacturing (US$62,140 mean annual salary), and couriers and express delivery services (US$61,300 mean annual salary).

The top mean annual salaries for automotive specialty technicians in the United States occur in the following geographic areas: Alaska (US$51,870), Washington, DC (US$47,180), Maryland (US$43,320), Connecticut (US$43,230), and Massachusetts (US$43,110).

RELATED OCCUPATIONS

Occupations with similar skills and job descriptions are:

- Automotive body and related repairers
- Diesel service technicians and mechanics
- Heavy vehicle and mobile equipment service technicians and mechanics
- Small engine mechanics

SOURCES OF ADDITIONAL INFORMATION

Automotive Youth Educational Systems (AYES). http://www.ayes.org

The International Union, United Automobile, Aerospace and Agricultural Implement Workers of America (UAW). http://www.uaw.org

National Automotive Technicians Education Foundation. http://www.natef.org

National Institute for Automotive Service Excellence. http://www.ase.com

FURTHER READING

Bureau of Labor Statistics, U.S. Department of Labor. "49-3023 Automotive Service Technicians and Mechanics." In *Occupational Employment Statistics: Occupational Employment and Wages, May 2010.* Accessed March 19, 2012. http://www.bls.gov/oes/current/oes493023.htm.

Sutphin, Everett 'Peanut'. "Following the ASE lead." *The Vocational Education Journal* 69.1 (1994): 26+. *Academic OneFile.*

Yap, Eleanor. "Shifting gears." *Motor Age* 115.11 (1996): 58+. *Academic OneFile.*

BUS AND TRUCK MECHANICS AND DIESEL ENGINE SPECIALISTS

NATURE OF THE WORK

Bus and truck mechanics and diesel engine specialists work to maintain and repair all types of trucks, buses, and other heavy-duty vehicles that typically use diesel rather than gasoline to fuel their engines. Bus and truck mechanics and diesel engine specialists are familiar with all systems involved in large vehicles such as buses and trucks, including brake, suspension, exhaust, and electrical systems and engine components. They inspect, test, troubleshoot, and diagnose engine and other system malfunctions and make adjustments as needed to get the vehicle functioning normally. They also perform preventative maintenance including proactively checking belts, tightening bolts, aligning wheels, changing fluids in the engine, and checking tire pressure.

As the job title implies, bus and truck mechanics and diesel engine specialists focus on diesel engines, which are typically used in larger vehicles such as buses and trucks and which have different designs, efficiency minimums, and components than the gasoline engines used in most smaller automobiles. Because of the larger size of the vehicles maintained by bus and truck mechanics and diesel engine specialists, the equipment used to repair and maintain these vehicles is often larger and more difficult to operate.

Bus and truck mechanics and diesel engine specialists have tremendous value in the developing green economy because of their direct control over the fuel efficiency and emissions levels of the engines they work on. Bus and truck mechanics and diesel engine specialists can make careful adjustments to on-board computer systems that control fuel injection and emissions levels, calibrating each engine they work on to excel in fuel consumption

AT A GLANCE FACT BOX

SOC: 49-3031.00
Preferred Education: High school diploma
Average Salary: US$42,250 annually
Other Information: Good near vision (the ability to see small details at close range) is a vital aspect of the job often not mentioned in job descriptions or training manuals

and exhaust levels, even exceeding local and U.S. federal regulations.

Bus and truck mechanics and diesel engine specialists also serve the green economy by keeping these vehicles operating at a high level of safety and efficiency. Trucks and buses often traverse the width and breadth of the continental United States, ferrying people and goods across the country. The performance of these engines and the emissions levels they generate as they travel has the potential to affect every area of the country. As a result, bus and truck mechanics and diesel engine specialists are considered very important to the urgent environmental concerns around the world.

WORKING CONDITIONS

Bus and truck mechanics and diesel engine specialists typically work indoors in garage and repair-shop environments. However, these environments are not always climate-controlled and can be noisy and dangerous. Bus and truck mechanics and diesel engine specialists may also frequently be required to travel to locations where vehicles have broken down and perform repairs in the open in various weather conditions.

Bus and truck mechanics and diesel engine specialists usually work standard 40-hour work weeks, but they are increasingly expected to accommodate shift-scheduling so that organizations and businesses can offer 24-hour service to their customers or internal fleets of vehicles. As a result, a bus and truck mechanic and diesel engine specialist might be required to work unusual hours, including late-night or early-morning shifts.

Bus and truck mechanics and diesel engine specialists also come in contact with dangerous materials, including battery acids, combustible materials such as diesel, and other hazardous chemicals. In general, protective garments and other safety procedures are adhered to in the workplace, and most bus and truck mechanics and diesel engine specialists report only minor injuries typical for anyone working with their hands.

Bus and truck mechanics and diesel engine specialists must also expect to lift heavy objects and operate heavy machinery, such as large wrenches and other hand tools as well as large power tools, including engine cranes, grinders, and lathes.

EMPLOYMENT

The U.S. Department of Labor's Bureau of Labor Statistics (BLS) estimated there were 222,770 bus and truck mechanics and diesel engine specialist jobs in the United States as of May 2010. The industry employing the most bus and truck mechanics and diesel engine specialists is the general freight trucking industry, which employs approximately 28,580 people. Following this is local governments (21,270 jobs), automotive repair and maintenance (18,440 jobs), motor vehicle and motor vehicle parts and supplies merchant wholesalers (16,890 jobs), and specialized freight trucking (12,180 jobs).

Across the United States, the areas offering the most job opportunities for bus and truck mechanics and diesel engine specialists are typically also the areas where shipping and freight hubs can be found. Texas has the most job opportunities, offering approximately 18,860 jobs in May 2010, according to the BLS. Next are California (16,990 jobs), New York (11,760 jobs), Ohio (10,810 jobs), and Pennsylvania (10,520 jobs).

TRAINING, OTHER QUALIFICATIONS, AND ADVANCEMENT

Most bus and truck mechanics and diesel engine specialists do not have advanced degrees, and a high school diploma is usually sufficient for an entry-level position. Attendance of a high school vocational program in automotive service technology or specifically diesel engine repair and maintenance can be helpful in obtaining employment.

In general, no formal certification or licensure is required for employment as a bus and truck mechanic and diesel engine specialist. However, a National Institute for Automotive Service Excellence (ASE) certification may be helpful in finding employment or advancing in an established career.

At the entry level, bus and truck mechanics and diesel engine specialists may be required to perform simple tasks such as cleaning components, checking fluids, and moving vehicles from one area to another. On-the-job training is typically a large part of any bus and truck mechanic's and diesel engine specialist's job, and advancement comes as experience grows. Generally speaking, it takes three to four years of work experience before someone is considered a fully-trained bus and truck mechanic and diesel engine specialist.

Bus and truck mechanics and diesel engine specialists must have a strong level of comfort with mechanical tasks and mechanical systems. They must be in good physical shape and able to lift heavy objects and operate heavy machinery. They must be comfortable working on their own and able to interpret large amounts of data quickly to formulate a solution to a malfunction. Bus and truck mechanics and diesel engine specialists must be capable of working under all kinds of conditions, from noisy indoor shops to outdoor situations involving inclement weather. Increasingly, computer systems and testing equipment are vital parts of large truck and bus engines, and thus a comfort with computers and computerized equipment is essential.

Software commonly encountered by bus and truck mechanics and diesel engine specialists includes:

- Alliance Automotive Shop Controller (facilities management software)
- Mitchell OnDemand5 Manager (facilities management software)
- Amcom AUTOS2000 (facilities management software)
- CC2/CC3 body shop management software (facilities management software)
- Scott Systems MaxxTraxx Pro (facilities management software)
- Genisys Fast Fixes (database reporting software)
- Pathfinder (database reporting software)
- ARSIS Automotive Repair Shop Invoice System software
- Hunter WinAlign (analytical or scientific software)
- Nexiq Tech HDS Suite for Palm (analytical or scientific software)

JOB OUTLOOK

The BLS predicts 6 percent growth in the job market for bus and truck mechanics and diesel engine specialists between 2008 and 2018. This is slower-than-average growth. Although demand for bus and truck mechanics and diesel engine specialists is expected to remain steady, especially for those who have some formal post-high school education, the durability and efficiency of the diesel engine itself is the main cause for this slow growth. Diesel engines are chosen precisely because they do not require as much maintenance or repair as standard gasoline engines, and new designs for diesel engines have only increased this trend.

Possibly offsetting this trend will be the increased use of diesel engines in cars and light trucks as the fuel efficiency and reliability of the diesel engine becomes increasingly attractive to automakers faced with increasing pressure to make their product lines more fuel efficient and less pollutive. This could result in higher demand for bus and truck mechanics and diesel engine specialists to maintain and repair these vehicles.

Job security for bus and truck mechanics and diesel engine specialists is generally good as even the best-designed diesel vehicle requires maintenance and occasional repair. As a bus and truck mechanic and diesel engine specialist advances in his or her career, the experience and knowledge gained becomes increasingly valuable. As a result, job loss is rare and generally only occurs during severe economic downturns.

EARNINGS

The average annual salary for bus and truck mechanics and diesel engine specialists is US$42,250. An entry-level bus and truck mechanic and diesel engine specialist can expect to earn an average salary of around US$26,550. An experienced and certified bus and truck mechanic and diesel engine specialist might earn as much as US$60,830 annually.

The best paying industries for bus and truck mechanics and diesel engine specialists are the U.S. federal government (US$65,540 annual mean salary); scientific research and development services (US$58,880 annual mean salary); motor vehicle manufacturing (US$58,020 annual mean salary); electric power generation, transmission, and distribution (US$57,970 annual mean salary); and support activities for water transportation (US$55,730 annual mean salary).

The top mean annual salaries in the United States for bus and truck mechanics and diesel engine specialists are earned in the following geographic areas: Alaska (US$56,110), Hawaii (US$54,090), Nevada (US$50,360), Washington, DC (US$49,120), and Wyoming (US$49,100).

RELATED OCCUPATIONS

Jobs with similar skills to bus and truck mechanics and diesel engine specialists include:

- Electric motor, power tool, and related repairers
- Heating, air conditioning, and refrigeration mechanics and installers
- Mobile heavy equipment mechanics, except engines
- Motorboat mechanics and service technicians
- Motorcycle mechanics
- Outdoor power equipment and other small engine mechanics
- Stationary engineers and boiler operators

SOURCES OF ADDITIONAL INFORMATION

Association of Diesel Specialists. http://www.diesel.org
National Automotive Technicians Education Foundation. http://www.natef.org
National Institute for Automotive Service Excellence. http://www.ase.com

FURTHER READING

Bohn, Joseph. "Diesel Engine Suppliers Foresee Sales Shifting to Higher Gear." *Automotive News* 5568 (1994): 46. *Academic OneFile.*

Bureau of Labor Statistics, U.S. Department of Labor. "49-3031 Bus and Truck Mechanics and Diesel Engine Specialists." In *Occupational Employment Statistics: Occupational Employment and Wages, May 2010.* Accessed March 19, 2012. http://www.bls.gov/oes/current/oes493031.htm.

Kung, Pang-Jen. "Diesel Engine." *Gale Encyclopedia of Science.* Thomson Gale, 2001. *Academic OneFile.*

"Maserati to Launch Diesel Sedan in 2013." *Auto Business News* [ABN], February 13, 2012. *Academic OneFile.*

Roberts, Graeme. "JAPAN: Audi Soon to Launch Clean Diesels." *just-auto.com,* March 5, 2012. Accessed April 9, 2012. http://www.just-auto.com/news/audi-soon-to-launch-clean-diesels_id120881.aspx.

BUS DRIVERS, TRANSIT AND INTERCITY

NATURE OF THE WORK

Whether they run on diesel, electricity, or an alternative fuel, buses are seen as an environmentally friendly means of transport. According to the Pennsylvania Department of Transportation, if every U.S. citizen who currently rides public transportation to work drove alone in a car instead, the equivalent traffic would fill a nine-lane highway stretching from Los Angeles, California to Boston, Massachusetts. Public transit systems are also credited with reducing fuel consumption, accidents, and injuries.

Transit and intercity bus drivers are key players in these systems. They drive a range of routes and passenger vehicles—from commuter buses within a city to charter buses that cross state lines. Some buses are small and carry only 15 seated passengers; others are large and unwieldy, with up to 100 passengers onboard. Those who drive school buses are considered a separate group because of the different endorsement requirements for these drivers.

In many ways, a bus driver's job is the same regardless of the type of bus being driven. Even newer fuel options and more efficient buses have little effect on the tasks for drivers as they start their day at the bus garage or terminal. Drivers are usually responsible for cleaning the bus's interior and stocking it with the basic safety gear and tickets. With some companies, they also must ensure the bus has sufficient fuel and is operating well.

Once on the road, however, drivers and passengers alike can see a difference in the ride depending on the fuel source for the bus. Hybrid bus makers and the government agencies purchasing them tout not only the improved energy efficiency but also the greater comfort of their vehicles. For example, the transportation agency of San Francisco,

California is building a fleet of diesel–electric hybrid buses as it works toward creating an emission-free public transportation system by 2020. The agency said these buses are not as noisy as their diesel counterparts and produce a smoother ride. Each bus requires less maintenance and replacement of its brakes and transmission as well.

The hybrid buses have other advantages. Unlike the trolleybuses of San Francisco, California, which draw their energy from overhead wires that can come loose and stall a bus or make it difficult to change routes during inclement weather or emergencies, the hybrid buses use a small diesel engine to power a generator and batteries that supply the bus with its needed electricity. The transportation agency is phasing out older diesel vehicles as they add these hybrid buses, which is said to emit 95 percent less particle matter, 40 percent less nitrogen oxide, and 30 percent less greenhouse gas than their predecessors. The same technology is being used in many other large cities, including New York, New York; Boston, Massachusetts; and Seattle, Washington.

Transit bus drivers who operate such hybrid vehicles may run several routes over the course of their day. They generally have a lot of contact with their passengers, collecting tickets, announcing stops, loading disabled passengers, and answering questions. Intercity drivers also need good interpersonal skills, but they generally run one or two longer routes a day and have few stops. Those who drive motor coaches often have the most contact with passengers, in some cases acting as tour guides and spending days at a time in the company of their customers.

Besides driving, the bus driver's main responsibility is safety. Bus passengers on short, busy routes are often standing, and many buses operate during the busiest parts of the day in heavy traffic. Buses run in all types of weather, and drivers must be alert to conditions to ensure an undisturbed ride for those on board. Keeping on schedule is also important—not just when traffic threatens to make a bus late but also when it is so light that the bus could arrive early to a stop.

WORKING CONDITIONS

It can be stressful to be responsible for moving dozens of people in a large vehicle through dense traffic, particularly when passengers are trying to ask questions while the bus is moving. Sitting for long periods can also put a strain on drivers. Drivers should ideally be in good physical condition so that they can help disabled passengers on board and, on charter buses or long-distance routes, load and unload baggage.

Bus drivers often work a set schedule, although rarely during normal business hours. City buses may operate around the clock, with drivers working early morning, late afternoon, evening, or weekend shifts. In smaller communities, drivers may work part-time during either morning or evening commuting hours or work both shifts with time off between. Long-distance drivers may be on the road for several days during each trip, although federal regulations limit how much of that time can be spent behind the wheel.

Bus driving is not an inherently dangerous job, but it has hazards beyond those related to vehicle operation. Most drivers work alone and are in direct contact with passengers, mostly strangers, who could become violent or aggressive. The public nature of the job also exposes them to respiratory viruses and other illnesses.

EMPLOYMENT

According to the U.S. Department of Labor's Bureau of Labor Statistics (BLS), 179,700 people were driving transit or intercity buses in the United States as of May 2010. Most work for a local government agency. Urban or rural transit and charter companies also employ bus drivers. Those who drive buses for schoolchildren and special clients such as elderly or disabled people, one of the largest occupation categories in local government, are not included in these numbers.

States with large cities and thus extensive public transportation systems, such as California and New York, tend to have the highest employment levels for bus drivers. They also offer some of the highest wages. New York, New York, and its surroundings is by far the metropolitan area with the most bus driver jobs. Chicago, Illinois; Los Angeles, California; and Seattle, Washington, also keep many drivers employed.

TRAINING, OTHER QUALIFICATIONS, AND ADVANCEMENT

For bus drivers, the most important qualification is a commercial driver's license (CDL) with passenger endorsements. A high school diploma may be preferred but is not always required; however, a clean driving record, good vision, and negative drug and alcohol tests are necessary. People may attend a driving school to prepare for the CDL test, which has written and practical driving components. CDLs are regulated by state and federal departments of transportation, and requirements may vary from state to state. In general, however, drivers must be at least 21 years old to operate buses that cross state lines and 18 years old to operate intrastate buses. However, many companies set higher standards than the U.S. federal minimums and may not hire drivers until they are at least 24 years old.

Once a potential driver has attained a CDL, the next step is a passenger endorsement. Again, both a knowledge and a skills test are given. Some drivers prepare for this endorsement through training provided by a transportation company, but other companies require drivers to be endorsed before applying. The company then trains new hires on local regulations, routes, and company policies.

Entry-level drivers often run their first routes with an experienced driver on board. New drivers usually then work part-time, covering for experienced drivers taking holiday, vacation, or sick days. Some work part-time for years before they are given a permanent, full-time route. As they gain experience and seniority in a company, drivers may be able to take their pick of routes, hours, and overtime.

Advancement in this field often means leaving the road behind to work as dispatchers, supervisors, or managers or training new drivers. A few charter bus drivers purchase their own buses or start a company with a fleet of buses and a roster of employees. Some switch to driving other vehicles such as heavy trucks that require a CDL, and others switch to operating other public transportation equipment such as light rail.

Good drivers can concentrate on the road regardless of distractions inside or outside the bus. They remain courteous to passengers even when dealing with anger, complaints, or other issues. They enjoy the independence of their work and are capable of making decisions and addressing problems that arise.

JOB OUTLOOK

Rising populations and an increased emphasis on public transportation in cities give a positive job outlook for bus drivers. As gas prices climb and cities spend more money establishing transportation networks, people are increasingly turning to buses for their daily commute. The U.S. Federal Transit Administration reported that every type of public transit produces fewer greenhouse gas emissions per passenger mile than the average single-occupancy vehicle, sometimes up to 75 percent less. The "per passenger mile" portion is key, indicating these savings will only increase as ridership levels rise.

That said, buses are not the most environmentally friendly public transportation option available. The agency's report indicated that trains produce fewer emissions than buses, and some bus drivers may find opportunities by learning to run subway, light, or commuter rail trains. The flexibility of bus routes, however, makes them integral to any public transportation system, and increasingly efficient buses are ensuring their place in the network.

EARNINGS

Bus drivers generally earn an hourly wage of US$17.82 on average, which is close to the mean annual base wage for all U.S. occupations, according to the Department of Labor. Entry-level wages may start at US$10 or less per hour; senior employees may earn more than US$27 per hour.

Those employed by U.S. state and local government agencies are among the highest-paid bus drivers in the country; only those who drive sports teams to events earn higher wages. In many cases, unions are driving high pay for bus drivers. In Madison, Wisconsin, for example, the union contract in effect in 2009 gave priority to senior bus drivers with high base pay when assigning overtime work. As a result, the highest-paid city employee that year was a Madison Metro bus driver. Nearly 70 percent of his earnings for the year were in overtime and other pay according to a report in the *Wisconsin State Journal.* By June 2011, the Metro Transit system had boosted employment numbers and spread overtime more evenly among employees, and the city was expected to make further

changes with new contract provisions that would limit overtime hours, the paper reported.

RELATED OCCUPATIONS

People who operate other large vehicles, many of which require a CDL, do similar work to bus drivers, including the following:

- Industrial truck and tractor operators
- Operating engineers and other construction equipment operators
- Truck drivers, heavy and tractor trailer

SOURCES OF ADDITIONAL INFORMATION

Amalgamated Transit Union. http://www.atu.org
American Bus Association. http://www.buses.org
American Public Transportation Association. http://www.apta.com
Federal Motor Carrier Safety Administration. http://www.fmcsa.dot.gov
Transport Workers Union of America. http://www.twu.org

FURTHER READING

Bureau of Labor Statistics, U.S. Department of Labor. "53-3021 Bus Drivers, Transit and Intercity." In *Occupational Employment Statistics: Occupational Employment and Wages, May 2010,* last modified May 17, 2011. Accessed March 9, 2012. http://www.bls.gov/oes/current/oes533021.htm.

———. "Bus Drivers." In *Occupational Outlook Handbook, 2010–11 Edition.* Accessed February 21, 2012. http://www.bls.gov/oco/cg/cgs021.htm.

———. "An Overview of U.S. Occupational Employment and Wages in 2009." In *Occupational Employment Statistics (OES) Highlights,* June 2010. Accessed March 9, 2012. http://www.bls.gov/oes/highlight_2009.pdf.

Federal Transit Administration, U.S. Department of Transportation. *Public Transportation's Role in Responding to Climate Change.* January 2009. Accessed March 9, 2012. http://www.fta.dot.gov/documents/PublicTransportationsRoleInRespondingToClimateChange.pdf.

Mosiman, Dean. "Madison Metro Driver Highest Paid City Employee." *Wisconsin State Journal,* February 7, 2010. Accessed March 9, 2012. http://host.madison.com/wsj/news/local/govt_and_politics/article_24af32d4-13f4-11df-86b2-001cc4c002e0.html.

Mosiman, Dean, and Nick Heynen. "City Salaries: Bus Drivers No Longer Top the List of Highest

Earners in Madison Government." *Wisconsin State Journal,* June 6, 2011. Accessed March 9, 2012. http://host.madison.com/wsj/news/local/govt-and-politics/city-salaries-bus-drivers-no-longer-top-the-list-of/article_97f7165c-8d70-11e0-9578-001cc4c03286.html.

Pennsylvania Department of Transportation. *PACommutes: Benefits.* Accessed March 1, 2012. http://www.pacommutes.com/public-transit/benefits/.

San Francisco Municipal Transportation Agency. *Muni Hybrid Buses.* Accessed March 1, 2012. http://www.sfmta.com/cms/mfleet/hybrids.htm.

TRUCK DRIVERS, HEAVY
AND TRACTOR-TRAILER

— ■ —

NATURE OF THE WORK

Little about the truck transportation and warehousing industry seems green. Commercial vehicles leave a large carbon footprint, and their drivers ferry products thousands of miles from producer to consumer. Buying local, the concept of slow food as opposed to fast food, and other such movements, as well as rising diesel fuel prices, however, have turned consumer attention to freight transportation, and technological advances are changing the trucks used to move goods and the skills of the people who drive them.

Truck drivers often work only certain legs of a trip between a product's original source and its destination. Items may travel by truck from the manufacturer to a ship, train, or plane, after which another truck may make the final delivery. The trade publication *Parcel*, however, reports that most U.S. freight moves by truck, and only airfreight generates more emissions per ton-mile among the main freight transportation modes. As pollutant emissions become a growing public concern, trucking companies and the manufacturers and retailers who use their services are seeking ways to reduce their emission levels.

To this end, some of the biggest names in consumer products have been streamlining transportation networks and fleets. For example, Walmart reported that it improved the efficiency of its shipping fleet by 65 percent from 2005 to 2010 by putting more goods into fewer loads and by buying more aerodynamic tractors and skirted trailers. The Hershey Company and competing candy maker Ferrero USA Inc., whose brands include Tic Tacs, announced in October 2011 plans to share warehouse space, transportation, and distribution operations. By

AT A GLANCE FACT BOX

SOC: 53-3032.00
Preferred Education: High school diploma
Average Salary: US$24,700 to US$57,500 annually
Other Information: Transportation accounts for 28 percent of U.S. greenhouse gas emissions, and 21 percent of it is related to driving freight trucks

consolidating logistics and sending more goods per truck trip, the companies expected to see reductions in carbon emissions and energy consumption as early as 2012.

Some of these changes to reduce emissions and energy consumption may seem like they would lessen the job opportunities for truck drivers, but e-commerce and a global distribution market are actually expected to generate job opportunities. Drivers may increasingly find themselves carrying combined loads from different companies, bypassing distribution centers for direct routes from a warehouse to a store, or carrying full loads in both directions. Such loads may not be destined for consumers but rather come from them. Target touted its green credentials in 2010 when it set up public recycling stations in every store, saying the move would reduce not only in-store waste but also its "empty miles" by sending delivery trucks back to distribution centers filled with recycled materials.

The vehicles themselves are changing, switching to more efficient engines, tires, and power systems. Some use fuel cells to cut idle time and heat and cool cabs. Others use satellite links to feed drivers information about weather, traffic, and directions. These links also allow dispatchers to track the vehicle's location, fuel usage, and engine performance and to communicate with the driver about route or schedule changes. New designs and systems are being created that address everything from slipstream to alternative fuels, such as those used by hybrid diesel–electric or natural gas–fueled vehicles.

WORKING CONDITIONS

Those in trucking jobs in the United States tend to work slightly longer than a 40-hour week, the U.S. Department of Labor's Bureau of Labor Statistics (BLS) found. These hours, however, are heavily regulated by the U.S. Department of Transportation, and drivers must follow driving time restrictions and keep logs of their hours. Drivers are subject to other U.S. federal regulations as well, such as regular drug and alcohol testing. Most truck drivers choose to work as much as allowed because they are paid based on miles or hours driven. Much of their time behind the wheel is on weekends or holidays and at night to avoid other traffic.

A truck driver's workday may vary depending on the type of goods in a load. Those hauling construction materials, such as lumber or excavated dirt, may work fairly standard hours and drive back and forth between a lumberyard, mill, or fill dirt site and various construction jobsites. Those who work locally and deliver produce often start early in the morning, picking up a loaded trailer and delivering items to area stores throughout the day. But the significant variation in work is mostly based on distance traveled. Local drivers return their trucks to the local trucking firm and go home at night. Long-distance drivers may spend days on the road. Sometimes they drive alone, and other times they share their trip so that one person can sleep while the other is behind the wheel. They also handle safety checks and some maintenance of their rigs while on the road.

Because they generally work alone and sit in one position for long hours, boredom and fatigue are common issues, particularly for long-distance drivers. They also must deal with a variety of traffic and weather conditions and decide how to circumvent delays as much as possible while remaining on schedule. Pickups and deliveries are usually timed so that the entire transportation process runs smoothly, and significant delays can mean items miss the next leg of the journey. Therefore, concerns about arriving on time can be stressful to drivers. Hazards are usually traffic-related and can be avoided by following safety rules and staying alert while behind the wheel.

EMPLOYMENT

Nearly 1.5 million people work as truck drivers with Class A or B licenses in the United States, according to the BLS, placing it among the 15 largest occupations in the country. Truck drivers and driver/sales workers make up slightly under half of the people working in the truck transportation and warehousing industry. Although employment services were once big sources of jobs for people with commercial driver's licenses (CDLs), freight companies now provide the most jobs: About half of all heavy and tractor-trailer truck drivers in the country work in the freight trucking industry. Others are employed by grocery wholesalers, and some specialize in hauling loads for highway and other road construction projects or delivering gasoline to service stations.

More heavy truck and tractor-trailer drivers are based out of Texas than any other state, closely followed by California. Large numbers are also based in Pennsylvania, Florida, and Ohio. Some work out of cities where they frequently pick up or drop off loads, such as Chicago, Illinois; Los Angeles, California; Houston, Texas; and Atlanta, Georgia.

TRAINING, OTHER QUALIFICATIONS, AND ADVANCEMENT

The biggest training and educational requirement for truck drivers relates to obtaining a CDL. Courses at technical or vocational schools teach students how to handle large rigs in a range of conditions, from gridlocked city streets to highway interchanges with high-speed traffic. Students also learn about regulations related to their rig and its freight and sometimes how to operate specialized vehicles such as dump trucks. Such courses may be required by the state before a potential employee can take a CDL test.

Heavy truck drivers must obtain a Class B license. Tractor-trailer drivers need a Class A license, which allows them to drive larger trucks and pull trailers. Such licenses are not issued to people younger than 18 years, and interstate drivers must be at least 21 years old. A clean driving record, good test scores, and proven safety knowledge are requirements for obtaining a CDL in most states. Additional endorsements may be required for drivers hauling particular types of loads, such as hazardous materials, or whose tractors are attached to multiple or particular types of trailers, such as tankers.

Once drivers have obtained their CDL, they typically undergo brief training with a trucking company before they begin work. They may ride along with experienced drivers before they set out on a solo route. Drivers also may be trained in specialized features of a rig, such as how to use auxiliary power units or get the best performance out of a vehicle running on an alternative fuel.

Drivers may work their way up the seniority and pay scale within their company as they advance in the field, landing better schedules, routes, and loads. Some purchase their own trucks, particularly for long-distance driving, and become owner-operators. Others shift out of the driver's seat and into the realm of logistics, sales, warehouse operations, management, or other work in the truck transportation and warehousing industry. Still others learn more about the rigs they drive and become parts distributors or diesel mechanics.

JOB OUTLOOK

Job growth is expected in the trucking industry, although the rate and pace of growth are greatly affected by the overall economy. Economic recessions involve consumers purchasing fewer goods, which means companies need fewer deliveries. That said, e-businesses have undercut local prices in many areas, and bargain hunters make many online purchases that need to be delivered by truck from a warehouse or other location.

In slow times, some drivers may find more opportunities if they shift to hauling a different type of load. For example, despite increased work moving materials for retrofitting buildings with green technologies and materials, overall employment with concrete product manufacturers and other construction contractors has been declining in recent years, mirroring a decline in residential construction jobs since early 2006. Drivers for those employers have the experience necessary to switch to jobs with general freight or warehouse companies, which have added jobs during the same period. They also may find work driving buses or small passenger vehicles if jobs are scarce.

EARNINGS

Heavy and tractor-trailer truck drivers earn US$18.97 per hour or US$39,450 per year on average, according to the BLS. The hourly wage can range from less than US$11.89 for entry-level positions to more than US$27.64 for drivers who have experience, who haul loads across the country, or who have endorsements for hazardous or oversized loads. Many truck drivers are part of one of the largest labor unions in the world, the International Brotherhood of Teamsters, which negotiates wages and benefits for its members.

Although the majority of jobs in this field are with freight trucking companies, the top-paying employers are focused on delivering packages to homes and businesses. There are limited jobs with the U.S. Postal Service, UPS, FedEx, and other express delivery companies, but the mean wage for truck drivers who land these jobs is close to US$26 per hour. Those who move materials for popular sports teams and clubs or who deliver household appliances and airplane parts are also well paid. High

wages are also more common in certain parts of the United States such as Alaska, Nevada, and some New England states.

RELATED OCCUPATIONS

Other drivers who are required to obtain a CDL or undergo training similar to that needed for truck drivers include the following:

- Bus drivers, transit and intercity
- Operating engineers and other construction equipment operators
- Industrial truck and tractor operators

SOURCES OF ADDITIONAL INFORMATION

American Trucking Associations. http://www.truckline.com
Federal Motor Carrier Safety Administration. http://www.fmcsa.dot.gov
International Brotherhood of Teamsters. http://www.teamster.org
International Refrigerated Transportation Association. http://www.irta.org
Professional Truck Driver Institute. http://www.ptdi.org

FURTHER READING

Bureau of Labor Statistics, U.S. Department of Labor. "53-3032 Heavy and Tractor-Trailer Truck Drivers." In *Occupational Employment Statistics: Occupational Employment and Wages, May 2010,* last modified May 17, 2011. Accessed March 16, 2012. http://www.bls.gov/oes/current/oes533032.htm.

———. "Truck Drivers and Driver/Sales Workers." In *Occupational Outlook Handbook, 2010–11 Edition.* Accessed February 21, 2012. http://www.bls.gov/oco/cg/cgs021.htm.

———. "Using Occupational Employment Statistics (OES) Data in a Job Search." In *Occupational Employment Statistics (OES) Highlights,* April 2011. Accessed March 16, 2012. http://www.bls.gov/oes/highlight_jobs.pdf.

Dorfman, Brad. "Target Puts Recycling Bins in All Its Stores." *Reuters,* April 6, 2010. Accessed March 16, 2012. http://www.reuters.com/article/2010/04/06/target-recycling-idUSN0111346620100406.

Federal Transit Administration, U.S. Department of Transportation. *Public Transportation's Role in Responding to Climate Change.* January 2009. Accessed March 16, 2012. http://www.fta.dot.gov/documents/PublicTransportationsRoleInRespondingToClimateChange.pdf.

The Hershey Company. "Hershey Announces Warehouse and Distribution Alliance." October 5,

2011. Accessed March 16, 2012. http://www
.thehersheycompany.com/newsroom/news-release
.aspx?id=1613887

Whiteman, Ken, and Wolf Liebchen. "Green Shipping."
Parcel, November/December 2011. Accessed
March 16, 2012. http://www.parcelindustry.com/
ME2/dirmod.asp?sid=&nm=&type=Publishing&
mod=Publications%3A%3AArticle&mid=
8F3A7027421841978F18BE895F87F791&tier=
4&id=DED31B5251F6472DB087D3981C3E0230.

Walmart. *2011 Global Responsibility Report: Fleet
Improvements.* Accessed March 1, 2012. http://
walmartstores.com/sites/ResponsibilityReport/2011/
environment_energy_Fleet.aspx.

LOCOMOTIVE ENGINEERS

NATURE OF THE WORK

Put simply, locomotive engineers operate trains. Some of these trains carry passengers and others carry cargo. Some run on diesel fuel, others on electricity, and others by gas turbine engines. Locomotive engineers, however, do more than just drive trains. Before the train leaves the station, the engineer has to check the locomotive's mechanical condition and ensure that adequate supplies of fuel, water, and sand are onboard. (A train's traction can be reduced because of slippery rails, usually caused by oil, rain, or decomposing vegetation. Most locomotives have a container of sand that can be sprayed onto the rails using compressed air, thereby improving traction.) Engineers need to make necessary adjustments to controls and document any mechanical or safety issues they uncover during the inspection.

While they are operating the train, engineers monitor controls such as throttles, airbrakes, and instruments that measure speed, along with those that measure amperage, air pressure, and battery charge in brake lines and fuel reservoirs. Indeed, the ability to stop a train is just as important as the ability to make it go, and the engineer is responsible for ensuring that brake examination tests are carried out at shunting stations. Shunting stations are railroad facilities where train cars are separated and reconnected. Locomotive engineers are aware of the condition and makeup of their train, including matters such as the number of cars, the proportion of empty versus loaded cars, and the amount of slack in the train. Railroad cars are loosely coupled; *slack*, sometimes called *slack action*, refers to the amount of movement in one car before the movement is transferred to the next car. Each of these factors can influence speed, acceleration, and braking.

When an emergency arises, the engineer must be able to respond appropriately in conformance with applicable safety rules and procedures.

Locomotive engineers require complete knowledge of their routes, and they need good vision so that they can observe tracks and spot obstructions. They must be familiar with the track system on which they operate. The system may include grades, turnouts, switches, improperly elevated and poorly maintained track, busy work areas, intersections and crossings, and other features that demand the engineer's attention. The engineer has to be skilled at controlling the train's speed; anticipating braking and acceleration needs; negotiating curves, bad track, and dips; and having a feel for train cars that he or she cannot see. When a train is turning, the engineer has to brake slightly in the rear so that there will be more space between the cars, keeping the train more stable. Locomotive engineers must also exercise these skills in fog, rain, snow, and other adverse weather conditions, often at night.

The field of locomotive engineering is beginning to join the green revolution. Train engines do not operate as efficiently as they could and, particularly in the case of diesel-powered engines, they emit pollutants. Typically, a railroad engine needs about 1,200 to 2,100 horsepower to operate in a yard; on a track, it needs from 4,000 to 6,000 horsepower. Trains are usually powered by a single railroad engine that operates at various speeds, but an engine is fuel efficient in only a narrow range of these speeds. Efforts are under way to eliminate, or at least reduce, the problems of fuel inefficiency and exhaust by powering trains with multiple smaller diesel engines. The locomotive engineer can then run the train using one, two, or three engines to produce the needed horsepower level. When horsepower needs are high, all three engines can be run, but when the horsepower needs are low, a single engine can do the job, reducing fuel usage and emissions. The locomotive engineer will then be responsible for operating the train at the most efficient level possible at all times.

Nevertheless, the National Academy of Railroad Sciences cites data from the U.S. Environmental Protection Agency (EPA) noting that railroads are highly efficient and green relative to other forms of transportation. Railroads account for just 9 percent of total transportation-related gaseous emissions and 4 percent of transportation-related particulate emissions while accounting for 42 percent of the United States' intercity freight ton-miles. Other data suggest that locomotive engineers, as part of the railroad industry, have played a role in ensuring a more sustainable future. For example, 43 percent of intercity freight is moved by rail. Between 1980 and 2007, railroads nearly doubled the amount of freight that could be moved with a gallon of fuel. In 1980 a ton of freight could be moved 235 miles on a gallon of diesel fuel; in 2007, the figure was 436 miles. Additional data suggest that freight railroads have increased fuel efficiency by about 85 percent since the mid-1980s, saving some 48 billion gallons of fuel over the next quarter century and reducing greenhouse gas emissions 20 tons every year. According to EPA estimates, shipping freight by rail rather than truck reduces greenhouse gas emissions by two-thirds for each ton-mile; furthermore, the EPA estimates that trucks emit three times more nitrous oxides and particulates than do the diesel engines that locomotive engineers drive. If these statistics are true, then rail transport in the hands of locomotive engineers contributes to the greening of the nation and will continue to do so as rail transport expands.

WORKING CONDITIONS

Historically, the job of the railroad engineer has been highly romanticized. The reality is more mundane. Rail transportation networks operate 24 hours a day, seven days a week, at night and on weekends and holidays.

Locomotive engineers typically work more than 40 hours per week, although the U.S. federal government mandates rest hours and the Rail Safety Improvement Act of 2008 increased the number of hours that train crews must rest between shifts. Some shifts and routes are more desirable than others. Seniority, along with the provisions of union contracts, usually dictate which engineers will be given the most desirable work shifts and routes.

Working conditions can vary by the type of rail transport. Typically, conditions are more pleasant on passenger trains. The shifts are more reliable and regular and the accommodations on passenger trains, such as their appearance and internal temperatures, are likely to be more comfortable. Freight trains, in contrast, operate entirely based on the demands of customers. Schedules tend to be irregular. Engineers are often assigned jobs on short notice, and working nights and weekends is not unusual. Sometimes locomotive engineers have to be extra vigilant because they are hauling hazardous freight. Because both passenger and freight trains operate between points hundreds of miles distant from one another, the engineer often has to spend nights away from home.

Rail yard functions have become increasingly computerized. One of the benefits of this computerization is that rail and switching yards can operate more efficiently, reducing the consumption of fuel and the emission of exhaust. These efficiencies can also be achieved through other technological tools, including expert system software. Some examples of this software include electronic train management systems (ETMS); route navigation and mapping software; and time accounting and tracking software. These technological tools allow the locomotive engineer and his or her company to achieve operating efficiencies consistent with the green economy by reducing fuel consumption and unnecessary wear and tear on facilities and equipment.

EMPLOYMENT

According to the U.S. Department of Labor's Bureau of Labor Statistics (BLS), about 38,700 railroad engineers were employed in 2010. Nearly all were employed in transportation and warehousing, while a small portion were employed in sightseeing and scenic tourism. States with the highest employment level for locomotive engineers were Illinois, California, Pennsylvania, Missouri, and Virginia. States with the highest concentration of locomotive engineers relative to overall employment in the state were Kansas, North Dakota, New Mexico, Arkansas, and Missouri.

TRAINING, OTHER QUALIFICATIONS, AND ADVANCEMENT

Prospective locomotive engineers who would like to receive training in a classroom environment might be interested in attending one of several schools, primarily community colleges, that offer educational programs and training in railroad operations. The largest of these is the National Academy of Railroad Sciences in Kansas, which offers training courses for locomotive engineers.

To become a locomotive engineer, a person must be a high school graduate or the equivalent. The person must be at least 21 years old and have rail work experience, typically as a brakeman or conductor. Locomotive engineers should be in good physical condition with excellent hearing and vision.

In addition to gaining work experience, a prospective locomotive engineer must complete a formal engineering training program that the U.S. Federal Railroad Administration (FRA) has approved. This program includes classes, simulator practice, and hands-on instruction in operating locomotives. Training is often provided by the aspiring engineer's company, although sometimes companies contract this training to outside vendors. Upon completion of training, the employee is eligible to become a federally certified locomotive engineer.

The FRA has extensive requirements for locomotive engineering certification, many having to do with safety. A prospective locomotive engineer has to demonstrate a good safety record through experience as a motor vehicle operator or railroad employee, comply with substance abuse and alcohol and drug regulations, and meet hearing and vision acuity standards. An important part of the vision test is color discrimination because locomotive engineers are required to recognize signs and signals of particular colors. The individual must also be tested and periodically retested on operating rules and performance skills.

JOB OUTLOOK

The BLS predicts that the number of locomotive engineers is likely to increase to 56,200 by 2018, an increase of about 10 percent over 2008 levels. Demand, therefore, will increase at an average rate relative to the economy as a whole. Increases will be largely the result of expected increases in the demand for both freight and passenger rail transportation, which will likely result from increased fuel costs for trucks and passenger cars, making rail transportation a cheaper alternative. Furthermore, the long-term transportation of freight is likely to increase because of expansion in global trade.

Offsetting these factors, however, are some technological trends that "green" the railroad industry but that are likely to reduce demand for engineers. Ongoing advances in remote-control locomotive technology and electronic train management systems (often called positive train control technology) allow for the electronic monitoring of mechanical difficulties and track problems. In turn, this will allow railroads to consolidate duties and improve productivity, somewhat reducing the demand for employees, including locomotive engineers.

EARNINGS

According to the BLS, the average annual wage for locomotive engineers in 2010 was US$50,870, or US$24.46 per hour. Those in the 90th percentile earned US$74,600; those in the 10th percentile earned US$33,550. The middle 50 percent earned between US$39,210 and US$58,050. The top-paying states for locomotive engineers were New Mexico (US$91,820), Arizona (US$68,560), Mississippi (US$68,180), Wisconsin (US$67,410), and Iowa (US$59,520). Wages for locomotive engineers are relatively high in part since approximately 76 percent are unionized employees, compared with approximately 12 percent of workers for all occupations.

RELATED OCCUPATIONS

Other types of transportation workers include:

- Bus drivers
- Truck drivers
- Ship pilots and ship engineers

SOURCES OF ADDITIONAL INFORMATION

Association of American Railroads. http://www .aar.org
Brotherhood of Locomotive Engineers and Trainmen. http://www.ble-t.org
Federal Railroad Administration. http://www.fra.dot.gov
VIA Rail Canada. http://www.viarail.ca

FURTHER READING

Association of American Railroads. *Environment.* Accessed February 20, 2012. http://www.aar.org/ Environment/Environment.aspx.
Association of American Railroads, Policy and Economics Department. *Railroads Green from the Start,* April 2010. Accessed February 20, 2012. http://www.aar.org/~/media/aar/backgroundpapers/ railroadsgreenfromthestart.ashx.
Bureau of Labor Statistics, U.S. Department of Labor. *Employment Projections.* Accessed February 20, 2012. http://www.bls.gov/emp/ep_table_108.htm.
———. "Rail Transportation Occupations." In *Occupational Outlook Handbook, 2010–11 Edition.* Accessed February 20, 2012. http://www.bls.gov/ oco/ocos244.htm.
College Board. *Career: Locomotive Engineers.* Accessed February 20, 2012. http://www.collegeboard.com/ csearch/majors_careers/profiles/careers/102577.html.

Dodge, John. "Electronic Train Management System in Action." *Design News,* October 21, 2008. Accessed February 20, 2012. http://www.designnews.com/document.asp?doc_id=228052 (video).

O*NET OnLine. *Summary Report for: 53-4011.00— Locomotive Engineers.* Accessed February 20, 2012. http://www.onetonline.org/link/summary/53-4011.00.

Spraggins, H. Barry. "The Impact of Rail Freight Transportation upon Environmental Sustainability." *Journal of Academy of Business and Economics,* July 15, 2011. Accessed February 20, 2012. http://www.freepatentsonline.com/article/Journal-Academy-Business-Economics/261080962.html.

Union Pacific. *Creating a Green Locomotive.* Accessed February 20, 2012. http://www.uprr.com/news info/releases/environment/2007/0522_iden.shtml.

U.S. Office of Personnel Management. *Federal Wage System Job Grading Standard for Locomotive Engineering, 5737.* Accessed February 20, 2012. http://www.opm.gov/fedclass/fws5737.pdf.

VIA Rail Canada. *The Life of a Train Engineer.* Accessed February 20, 2012. http://www.viarail.ca/en/useful-info/related-services/via-adventures-expeditions/life-train-engineer.

Index

AUG 2012

From green industries to
green jobs.